This is the first book to describe German literary history up to the unification of Germany in 1990. It takes a fresh look at the main authors and movements, and also asks what Germans in a given period were actually reading and writing, what they would have seen at the local theatre or found in the local lending library; it includes, for example, discussions of literature in Latin as well as in German, eighteenth-century letters and popular novels, Nazi literature and radio plays, and modern Swiss and Austrian literature. A new prominence is given to writing by women. Contributors, all leading scholars in their field, have re-examined standard judgements in writing a history for our own times. The book is designed for the general reader as well as the advanced student: titles and quotations are translated, and there is a comprehensive bibliography.

The Cambridge History of German Literature

The Cambridge History of German Literature

Edited by

HELEN WATANABE-O'KELLY

Exeter College, Oxford

CAMBRIDGE
UNIVERSITY PRESS

Published by the Press Syndicate of the University of Cambridge
The Pitt Building, Trumpington Street, Cambridge, CB2 1RP
40 West 20th Street, New York, NY 10011–4211, USA
10 Stamford Road, Oakleigh, Melbourne 3166, Australia

First published 1997

Printed in Great Britain at the University Press, Cambridge

Typeset in Monotype Sabon 10.5/12 pt

A catalogue record for this book is available from the British Library

Library of Congress cataloguing in publication data

The Cambridge history of German literature / edited by Helen
Watanabe-O'Kelly.
p.   cm.
Includes bibliographical references and index.
ISBN 0 521 43417 3 (hardback)
1. German literature – History and criticism.   1. Watanabe-O'Kelly, Helen.
PT91.C36   1997
830.9–dc20   95–52412   CIP

ISBN 0 521 43417 3 hardback

Contents

Contributors

HELEN FEHERVARY, Professor of German at Ohio State University, is the author of *Hölderlin and the left: the search for a dialectic of art and life* (1977) and was for many years an editor of *New German Critique*. She has published widely on critical and feminist theory and the literature and theatre of the Weimar Republic and the GDR, especially the work of Brecht, Müller, Thomas Brasch, Anna Seghers and Christa Wolf. She has just completed *Writing in the diaspora: a literary life of Anna Seghers* and an edition of Seghers's stories and novellas in translation.

GAIL FINNEY is Professor of German and Comparative Literature at the University of California at Davis. Among her extensive writings on nineteenth- and twentieth-century German and comparative literature are a comparative study of the nineteenth-century novel, *The counterfeit idyll: the garden ideal and social reality in nineteenth-century fiction* (1984), and *Women in modern drama: Freud, feminism, and European theater at the turn of the century* (1989). She has also edited and written the introduction to *Look who's laughing: gender and comedy*, New York: Gordon and Breach, 1994.

RUTH-ELLEN BOETCHER JOERES, Professor of German and Women's Studies at the University of Minnesota, is the author or co-editor of nine books, including *Louise Otto-Peters: die Anfänge der deutschen Frauenbewegung* (1983), *German women in the eighteenth and nineteenth centuries: a social and literary history* (1986), *Out of Line/'Ausgefallen': the paradox of marginality in the writings of nineteenth-century German women* (1989) and *The politics of the essay: feminist perspectives* (1983). She was editor of *Signs: Journal of Women in Culture and Society* from 1990 to 1995.

MORAY MCGOWAN, Professor of German at the University of Sheffield, is the author of a monograph on Marie-Luise Fleißer (1987) and (with Ricarda Schmidt) of *From high priests to desecrators: aspects of contemporary German literature* (1993). He has also worked extensively on

such post-war authors as Botho Strauß, Franz Xaver Kroetz and Heiner
Müller.

BRIAN MURDOCH, Professor of German at Stirling University, is an
authority on Old and Middle High German literature and on the literature of the early modern period. Among his many books and articles
are *The fall of man in the early Middle High German biblical epic*
(1972), *Old High German literature* (1983) and *The Germanic hero*
(1995). He has also written on the war literature of the twentieth
century.

NIGEL F. PALMER, Professor of German Medieval and Linguistic
Studies at the University of Oxford, is known particularly for his
interest in the links between Latin and German literature and in the
exploitation of palaeography and codicology for literary history. He is
the author of *Visio Tnugdali: The German and Dutch translations and
their circulation in the later Middle Ages* (1982) and *Apokalypse – Ars
moriendi . . . Die lateinisch-deutschen Blockbücher des Berlin-
Breslauer Sammelbandes* (1992).

RITCHIE ROBERTSON is a University Lecturer in German and Fellow of
St John's College, Oxford. He has written many articles on a wide
range of nineteenth- and early twentieth-century literature and is the
author of *Kafka: Judaism, politics, and literature* (1985) and *Heine*
(1988) and is currently working on a study of literary responses to the
problems of assimilation by German and Austrian Jews, mainly in the
period 1880–1930.

NICHOLAS SAUL, Senior Lecturer in German and Fellow of Trinity
College Dublin, has written numerous articles on a range of authors
from Frederick the Great to Hofmannsthal, re-evaluating the relationship of Enlightenment, Romanticism, Classicism and *fin de siècle*. He is
the author of *Poetry and history in Novalis and in the tradition of the
German Enlightenment* (1984) and editor of *Die deutsche literarische
Romantik und die Wissenschaften* (1991). He is currently editing a play
by Brentano and writing a book on parodistic sermons in Romanticism
and Classicism.

HELEN WATANABE-O'KELLY, Faculty Lecturer in German and Fellow
of Exeter College, Oxford, is the author of *Melancholie und die melancholische Landschaft. Ein Beitrag zur Geistesgeschichte des 17.
Jahrhunderts* (1978) and *Triumphall shews. Tournaments at German-
speaking courts in their European context 1560–1730* (1992). She has

written many articles on German literature and court culture of the early modern period, on nineteenth-century fiction and on literary translation and is the co-editor, with Pierre Béhar, of *Spectaculum Europaeum. Theatre and spectacle in Europe 1580–1750 – a handbook* (1997).

Preface

The only word in the title of this book which is uncontentious is the word 'Cambridge'. What, for instance, does 'literature' mean? Does it mean writing which claims to be 'high art' or, at the other end of the spectrum, any connected text, whether written down or not? The authors of this history have defined the term as they saw fit in different periods. Charms and spells are discussed in chapter 1, for instance, polemical pamphlets in chapter 3, letters in chapter 4, sermons in chapter 5 and radio plays in chapter 9 – alongside what have been traditionally conceived of as literary forms, of course.

The adjective 'German' when applied to literature is just as difficult to define. Does it mean literature in the German language? Clearly it does. But educated Germans have always been a polyglot people, moving at will between Latin and German for at least the first thousand years of their literary history, writing in Italian at the great courts during the seventeenth century, in French and English during the eighteenth and nowadays using English as the *lingua franca* of science and technology. In certain periods, therefore, we must discuss what Germans wrote rather than merely what they wrote in German. But how do we define 'the Germans'? One cannot simply say that they are those people living within the boundaries of the German-speaking world, for the latter has always contained French, Italian, Danish, Dutch, Hungarian, Serb, Croat, Polish, Czech and Yiddish speakers living side by side with German speakers. In earlier periods one has to operate with that political entity called 'the Holy Roman Empire' while the late-twentieth-century specialist has to deal with the existence of two 'Germanies' and ask herself whether Austrians and Swiss count as 'Germans' for literary purposes and, if they do not, why not.

But these difficulties are as nothing beside those inherent in the term 'history'. Some of my colleagues have already told me that it is impossible nowadays to write a 'history' at all. The calm certainty of previous generations that one could, with the benefit of hindsight, impose a coherent narrative on the past which laid claim to being 'the truth' is no longer possible. We are aware today that any historical narrative is by definition biased, partial and written to fulfil the ideological needs of the day – of an emerging Prussian Empire, of an embattled Austria, of a National Socialist plan for domination or of a post-war Germany longing for self-respect and moral absolution, for instance. There are those who would go further and say that the writing of 'history' is immoral, in that it entails the construction of an official narrative designed to bolster the standing of those in power and to silence, indeed to write out of existence, those of the 'wrong' social class, religious and political beliefs or gender. If, according to this view, any history is doomed before it even starts, how much more futile it is to name a book '*the* history of German literature' – with the little word 'of' implying a completeness which is certainly unachievable.

In spite of all this, it seems to me that each generation has a duty to write and rewrite history, for only by doing so can it confront the present and hope to avoid the mistakes of the past. In the case of Germany, the duty becomes inescapable. Its very complexity clearly makes the task more difficult but also more exciting. How to tell a story which includes Charlemagne and Luther, Kant and Marx, Rilke and Brecht, Walther von der Vogelweide and Christa Wolf? Of course such a story will be a construct, necessarily conditioned by who is telling it, but it does not mean that there can never be a story.

Writing a literary history also means confronting the vexed question of 'the canon'. Does one piece together a narrative which links that selection of authors and works which a later age has decided constitute the 'literature' of a given country? The problem with the German canon, as manifested in school and university teaching programmes not just in the English-speaking world, is that it traditionally consists of an extraordinarily small selection of authors and works: a brief flowering in the Middle Ages, though many departments no longer teach medieval literature, a handful of eighteenth- and nineteenth-century writers, one woman writer in the seventeenth century and one in the nineteenth, no Bavarian literature, no popular literature at all. The authors of this history have tried to escape from the tyranny of such a narrow canon by asking themselves what Germans in a given period were actually reading and writing, what they would have seen at the local theatre and found in the local lending library, rather than confining the discussion solely to those works which we still know of nowadays. This method, of looking at readers as well as at writers, reveals that writing by Germans has in all periods been far richer than it has often been given credit for.

The individual authors of this history were chosen for their proven willingness to rethink the standard story of their own period and each one has done this in his or her own way. No overall editorial line was imposed on them. They were simply exhorted to be 'stimulating yet authoritative, challenging yet scholarly' and to convey their own excitement at and fascination with the period they were writing on. But we have all had to make selections and always with a heavy heart and have in the end included those works which particularly interest us or which seem particularly interesting today. The study of literature is not an optional luxury but the surest way to understand the people which produced it. And who can say, at the end of the twentieth century, that he or she does not need to understand the Germans?

Note on translations

Each title of a work is succeeded by a translation in parentheses. In a few cases, where a German work has an established title in English, we have used that, for example, Goethe's *Die Wahlverwandtschaften* which is universally known as *Elective affinities*. In all other cases the author concerned has provided as close a translation of the original title as possible, simply for the information of the reader. The same thing applies to quotations. In the few cases where we have used an existing translation, that is credited.

Acknowledgements

Helen Watanabe-O'Kelly would like to acknowledge the help of Dr Jill Bepler of the Herzog August Bibliothek, Wolfenbüttel, who read and commented on chapter 3. Helen Fehervary wishes to thank Professors Gisela E. Bahr, Erika Bourguignon and Jost Hermand 'for their counsel and their perceptivity regarding European developments in our century', the Ohio State University College of Humanities for granting her leave and the Department of Germanic Languages and Literatures for graduate research assistance. Her special thanks are due to Alicia Carter Greer.

The Carolingian period and the early Middle Ages (750–1100)

BRIAN MURDOCH

The dominant language of written literature in Germany in the early Middle Ages is Latin. Only a very small amount of writing in German has survived from the reigns of Charlemagne and his successors (from the middle of the eighth century to the early tenth), of the Ottonian emperors (the tenth century) and even of the Salians (taking us through the eleventh century).[1] Far from making the task of presenting German literature in its earliest stages easier, however, this causes difficulties which do not arise once a vernacular literary tradition has established itself. Not only are the definitions of 'German' and of 'literature' problematic, but the more important question arises of whether German literature at this stage may be defined exclusively as literature in German. Part of the interest in the period lies in the emergence, from the eighth century onwards, of a self-conscious written tradition in German within a Christian-Latin literary and intellectual context, but the fact remains that most of the written literature in Germany in the Carolingian period is Latin, whereas material in German is for the most part not literary at all. With what little there is in German, too, the unconsidered acceptance of the idea of 'text' is impossible. Most of the survivals in German before 1100 exist in unique manuscripts and were affected from the start by the inferior position of the language. One of the most interesting poems of the period, the *Muspilli*, dealing with the destruction of the world, is written in the margins and other spaces of a Latin manuscript, causing problems of sense, structure, ordering and sometimes of decipherment.

It is possible to treat everything written in German in this period as literature, but this places works displaying evidence of literary intent beside

---

[1] Throughout this chapter shorter German texts are listed according to E. v. Steinmeyer, *Die kleineren althochdeutschen Sprachdenkmäler* (Berlin, 1916, repr. 1963) and cited as St. followed by a Roman numeral. Additional references are to K. Müllenhoff and W. Scherer, *Deutsche Poesie und Prosa aus dem VIII-XII Jahrhundert* (Berlin, 3rd edn by E. v. Steinmeyer, 1892, repr. 1964) cited as MSD, W. Braune, *Althochdeutsches Lesebuch*, 16th edn by E. Ebbinghaus, (Tübingen, 1979) cited as Lb. and F. Wilhelm, *Denkmäler deutscher Prosa des 11. und 12. Jahrhunderts* (Munich, 1916, repr. 1960) cited as Wilhelm.

For Carolingian Latin see J. P. Migne's *Patrologia Latina* (Paris, 1844–55) cited as PL, though ascriptions are not always accurate.

functional documents or translations. The problem arises, too, of oral material, for the existence of which there is good evidence. Nor is there anything like a standard language. The Carolingian and Ottonian periods coincide roughly with the earliest written stage of the modern language, known as Old High German, but by this is meant a group of dialects spoken in present-day Germany (south of Aachen), Austria and Switzerland, which share *some* linguistic features, notably the consonant changes differentiating them from Low German (the dialects of northern Germany and the Low Countries, plus Anglo-Saxon). But it would be wrong to exclude literature written in the continental Low German dialects of Old Saxon and Old Low Franconian, the ancestors of modern *Plattdeutsch* and of Dutch, although there is insufficient early material in Old Frisian, and Anglo-Saxon is culturally distinct.

One single work, completed in the later ninth century, *could* serve as a beginning for German literature in the modern sense. Otfri(e)d, a Benedictine at the monastery of Weißenburg (now Wissembourg in French Alsace) wrote in the 860s a large-scale version of the Gospel story in rhymed verse, in a dialect of the Southern Rhineland. He was conscious of being an innovator in style, but even more in using a language which he knew was unusual for a literary undertaking. His work, moreover, was intended not just to survive, but to be disseminated. A whole finely written manuscript was devoted to it, and there are several copies. But Otfrid's *Evangelienbuch* did not spring fully armed from nowhere, and various strands of enquiry lead to and from this Gospel-book: how did written German develop to a stage where a major literary work is thinkable? what were Otfrid's literary and theological sources and influences? and what, finally, was the vernacular secular poetry that Otfrid claimed he wished to supplant?

Throughout our period, the primary context of literature is Latin and its framework that of the Roman Church. Writing in German is for a very long time peripheral, whilst Latin texts in a range of genres bear witness to a well-established literary tradition in Germany. Critics have sometimes used Latin writings on a selective basis for filling gaps in what appeared to be a defective national literary history, but this is little better than the complete dismissal of Latin as somehow quite divorced from German. Latin literature written in German territories, by German-speakers, and often with German themes requires consideration, and indeed, the inclusion in literary histories of the period of every scrap of written *German* is even more distorting. It is hard to justify highlighting some ill-written one-liner whilst ignoring a major work written in Germany because it is in Latin.

Although the validity of the term 'renaissance' has been debated, there was under Charlemagne (768–814) both a florescence of literature and the encouragement of an educational and religious policy. The policies were expressed as a series of occasional, though full, edicts, rather than a system as such; but the influence and implementation of his ideas often continued, although emphases were different, into the reigns of his successors, the emperor Lewis the Pious (814–40) and Lewis the German (843–76), king of the East Franks, the German part of Charlemagne's empire. It was against the background of this Carolingian renaissance that German was written down for the first time.

Carolingian Latin literature

Charlemagne's court provided a cultural and literary centre, and efforts were made towards the standardising of canon law, of the monastic rule of St Benedict, of the liturgy, and of the Bible itself, which still circulated in different versions. Charlemagne strengthened the Christianity disseminated in the wake of the Anglo-Saxon mission of St Boniface over all the German tribes (including after much violence the Saxons, to whom he gave eight bishoprics), and he encouraged priestly and perhaps to an extent lay literacy. In what is known as his palace school, established after 792 at Aachen, he gathered a group of scholar-advisers whose poetry and prose was of importance during and after his reign, but for many of whom Germany was an adopted country. The Anglo-Saxon Alcuin (735–804), Charlemagne's principal teacher, wrote much of his work whilst with Charlemagne, and probably encouraged Charlemagne's ideas of a restoration of Roman imperial dignity by the Franks. Other writers gathered to Aachen by Charlemagne included the Spanish Visigoth Theodulf (750–821) and the Lombards Paulus Diaconus (720–800) and Paulinus of Aquilea (726–802). Men like these produced educational texts associated with the study of the *trivium* (rhetoric, grammar and dialectic), and the *quadrivium* (astronomy, arithmetic, music and geometry), the pedagogical basis for further study of the major text-book of the Middle Ages, the Bible. They also wrote annals, history and biography in prose and verse, saints' lives (sometimes as *opera geminata*, with prose and metrical versions side by side), dogmatic theology and biblical commentary, political and philosophical writings, and verse of all kinds, epistolary, nature, commemorative and panegyric, as well as hymns. None of this was entirely new: the poet Venantius Fortunatus had composed encomia for Charlemagne's predecessors, the Merovingians. But Alcuin wrote to Charlemagne in 799 referring to the establishment of an 'Athena nova . . . in Francia' ('a new Athens in France'), even if it was less a new Athens in the land of the Franks than a new Rome, for which the literary models were Vergil, Ovid, Horace and Christian writers like Avitus, Arator or Juvencus. It was Charlemagne's policy that Latin should be understood and understood well, so classical and post-classical works were preserved, and new writing flourished, as it would throughout the subsequent three centuries. Alcuin, his contemporaries and his successors all wrote prose and verse, and the extent to which Latin outweighs German in quantity and in quality has constantly to be borne in mind.

Most important of all the literary activities was the writing of biblical commentaries. Usually derivative of earlier writings, especially those of Augustine and Gregory the Great, these consisted of a detailed exegesis of every verse of the Bible according to the various senses of Scripture – the literal or historical sense, the allegorical or typological (linking New Testament events with those of the Old), the tropological or general-moralising, and the anagogical (interpreting the verse in the light of the end of the world). Alcuin's widely known commentary on Genesis, for example, takes the form of answers to a series of simple questions directed at a *magister* by an enquiring pupil called Sigewulf. Although strictly speaking neither literary nor original, the Carolingian commentaries have a lasting influence on German-language writing down to the eleventh century and beyond.

The forms of classical Latin verse, based on quantity (that is, on long and short syllables) rather than stress, were largely adhered to by the Carolingian Latin poets, who used both the Vergilian and the Leonine hexameter, the latter rhyming at the caesura and the cadence, as well as the Ovidian elegiac couplet, that is, a hexameter, followed by a pentameter with a strong caesura. But we also find an accentual, stress-based verse, and end-rhyme, too, makes its appearance in Latin poetry (rhyme within *prose* composition was a known rhetorical device). Native German poetry seems to have been primarily rhythmic, however, and it used alliteration (stave-rhyme) to link the two halves of a four-stress long-line divided by a caesura, so that the first stress of the second half-line alliterates with at least one of those in the first.

The poets themselves provide a picture of literary activities at Charlemagne's court. Alcuin's poem *Pro amicis poetae* (*The poet's friends*) describes some of his colleagues, and he celebrated many of them either during their lives in shorter poems and in sometimes satirical poetic epistles, or later in epitaphs. His other verse includes nature poetry (there is a famous debate between winter and spring), but a poem about a scriptorium, where monks are copying the 'holy writings of the Church Fathers', which will enable teachers to interpret the Bible, probably best reflects his primary interests.

Many members of the court wrote panegyrics to Charlemagne, and in one of these Theodulf sounded a theme that will be heard later in German, a stress on the absolute rule of (God's) justice even over men of power. Theodulf also produced rhythmic hymns such as that in the liturgy for Palm Sunday, 'Gloria, laus et honor' (still known in a different context as 'All glory, laud and honour'). Another scholar-poet, a Frank named Angilbert, who died as abbot of St Riquier in the same year as Charlemagne, wrote his own epitaph. It is a single quatrain with each line beginning and ending with the same word ('rex', 'lex', 'lux', 'pax'), and it demonstrates briefly and memorably one of the features of the period: a delight in artifice, with acrostics and pattern-poems both frequent and complex.

Historical events were celebrated in verse, and a victory in 796 of Charlemagne's forces under his son Pepin over the Avar Huns was commemorated by Theodulf and in an anonymous short poem which ends with an insistence on the role of God in the shaping of an historical event, something that will be seen again in German. Amongst the major military achievements in Charlemagne's reign were his defeat of the Bavarian leader Tassilo, and the protracted and violent Christianisation of the Saxons, but an early epic poem on the latter, the *Carmen de conversione Saxonum*, (*Song of the conversion of the Saxons*), describing also Charlemagne's meeting with the exiled Pope Leo at Paderborn in 777, was probably by an Anglo-Saxon, while another, about the victory over Tassilo, was written by an 'exiled Irishman' (*Hibernicus Exul*). The Paderborn meeting was described again in an anonymous and fragmentary panegyric from the first decades of the ninth century called simply *Karolus Magnus et Leo Papa* (*Charlemagne and Pope Leo*). The intended audience of all these poems is not always clear; some of the writings of the Aachen school were clearly intended for the immediate circle, but a poem like that on the Avar victory was presumably meant for a wider audience, perhaps of lay nobles.

The compilation of prose annals is of considerable antiquity. In the Carolingian period the major work is the *Annales Regni Francorum*, known as the *Royal annals*, while early ninth-century annals include those of Metz, of Fulda and of St Bertin. They constitute major, if occasionally biased, historical sources, and in these and other historical writings an image gradually develops of Charlemagne and his 'renovatio imperii Romani' ('renewal of the Roman Empire'), until with writers like Regino of Prüm, whose *Chronicon* was written in Trier at the start of the tenth century, Charlemagne's empire is seen as the last of the four great empires of world history. The process begins, perhaps, with a prose biography of Charlemagne in thirty-three chapters (partly modelled on Suetonius), written not long after his death. Einhard, a Frank from the Maingau, educated at Fulda, tells us not only of the emperor's interests in education, but that he ordered the compilation of a collection of old and barbaric songs in German, as well as a grammar of Frankish. We do not have these, but Einhard's *Vita* lists Old High German names for the months and the eight winds supposedly offered by Charlemagne. Einhard's work, edited after his death and provided with an introduction by Walahfrid Strabo (and translated into German in the twelfth century), was much used by later writers. An unnamed late ninth-century 'Poeta Saxo', perhaps from Corvey, used it in the five books of his verse *Annales de gestis Caroli Magni* (*Annals of the deeds of Charlemagne*), stressing how Charlemagne had 'rightly held the sceptre of the Roman Empire', and had brought 'glory, prosperity, rule, peace, life and triumph' to the Franks. The Saxon also mentions Charlemagne's interest in German songs.

The best known of Alcuin's pupils was Hrabanus Maurus (784–856), dubbed 'praeceptor Germaniae', who probably influenced the educational policies of Lewis the Pious, which, while not anti-German, were more strictly theological than his father's. Hrabanus left the abbacy of the important monastery of Fulda for political reasons after the death of Lewis, but, having established relations with Lewis the German, was elevated to the archbishopric of Mainz, in which office he died. Possibly the author of the hymn 'Veni creator spiritus' ('Come Holy Ghost'), a good example of iambic rhythmic short lines with more or less fortuitous rhyme, he is best known for his biblical commentaries and the encyclopaedic *De naturis rerum*, based on the much-read *Etymologies* of Isidore of Seville. His complex work *De laudibus sanctae crucis* (*In praise of the Holy Cross*) is notable, finally, for its use of deliberate artistry, acrostics, number-games and shape-poems, accompanied by prose versions side-by-side with the poems.

Far better as a poet is the unfortunate Gottschalk of Orbais (*c.* 805–869), a Saxon placed as a child in the monastery at Fulda, who tried to leave but was sent instead to another monastery, became embroiled in theological dispute on the subject of predestination, and suffered exile and imprisonment for heresy. One long prayer-poem demonstrates *Tiradenreim*, with one of the rhymes repeated up to sixty times, but he is properly best known for his poem 'Ut quid iubes' ('That which you demand of me') in ten six-line accented strophes, written in about 840 in response to a supposed request from a boy 'for a cheerful song'. It first echoes the Israelites' refusal to sing songs in exile, a link with his own banishment, but then becomes a rhythmic hymn of praise. Diminutives like 'pusiole' ('lad') or even 'diuscule' ('for a little bit of a long time') characterise the whole work, but the elegiac tone is striking, and the theme of exile, real or allegorical, recurs in Latin and German.

Another scholar at Fulda whose role in German literature is unusual, since he achieved fame as the abbot of a French monastery, was Servatus Lupus (or in German, 'Wolf', *c.* 805–62). He had a Bavarian father, and we know from his letters that he liked to read German and perhaps even wrote it, although he is now better known for his preservation of the classics, most notably of Cicero. From his school at Ferrières, however, he sent monks to Prüm, which had links with Fulda, 'in order to obtain knowledge of the German language'. Lupus was friendly with Gottschalk, as was a further Fulda pupil, Walahfrid Strabo (c. 808–49), later abbot of the Reichenau. Walahfrid's best-known poem is an allegory on the plants in his garden, but he wrote among other pieces a hagiographic description of the *Vision of Wetti*. Both Walahfrid and Lupus were at the court of Lewis the Pious, as was the poet-historian Ermoldus Nigellus, whose extensive work in four books, *In honorem Hludowici Christianissimi Caesaris Augusti (In honour of the Most Christian Emperor Lewis)* was designed to help him regain his lost favour with that emperor. The work is in Ovidian elegiac couplets, with much echoing of Vergil, although in the opening verses he cites a range of classical and Christian writers.

There is an Old High German parallel, though not a literary one, to a Latin poem by another Angilbert on the Battle of Fontenoy in 841, where, following the death of Lewis the Pious, his oldest son Lothar fought and was defeated by the two younger brothers Charles the Bald, king of what would become France, and Lewis the German, king of the German territories, after which the *Strasbourg oaths* (St. xv) of mutual non-aggression were sworn by the victors. The eye-witness poem is in triplets, each beginning with a successive letter of the alphabet, and is a moving elegy for the fallen at a battle of considerable European importance. A prose history of the period 814–43 by Nithart, Charlemagne's grandson, cites the Old French and Old High German oaths sworn in 842 by Lewis and Charles respectively (so that the other king's followers would understand), promising not to make common cause with Lothar. Their men swore a similar oath in their own language; French and German are established regional vernaculars, but the context of report is Latin.

There are two Latin prose lives of Lewis the Pious, one written during his lifetime, the other after his death. Thegan(bert), author of the first, was a cleric from Trier, while the second is known only as the Astronomer, from the knowledge displayed in the work. The latter describes not only Lewis's church reforms, but also how he bellowed defiance (in German) at an evil spirit on his deathbed. Thegan makes a literary point, however, describing how well-versed Lewis was in the interpretation of the Scriptures, but how, unlike Charlemagne, he would neither hear, read nor have taught non-Christian poetry. The dominant aesthetic of our period was expressed at the end of the eighth century by Alcuin (and was by no means new even then) when he asked 'what has Ingeld [a Germanic heroic figure] to do with Christ?'

Whilst German writing still occupied a very inferior position, Latin literature flourished throughout the ninth century in the context of the church. Notker Balbulus of St Gallen (c. 840–912), the first of several monks of that name and distinguished by his epithet 'the stammerer', may be the author of the prose *De Carolo Magno*, a later life of Charlemagne, but he is associated in particular with a poetic form which he raised to a high level. The sequence, sung originally as part of the liturgy, is made up of double strophes which match rhythmically syllable for syllable, with separate introductory and concluding strophes. Notker produced the music and words to a cycle based on the liturgical year, and his Christmas sequence illustrates their poetic conciseness: 'Gemit capta / pestis antiqua / coluber lividus perdit spolia. Homo lapsus / ovis abducta / revocatur ad aeterna gaudia.' ('Captive, sighs / the demon of old / the serpent of malice loses its prey. / Fallen man / the sheep led astray / is now called back into eternal joy'). The juxtaposition of fall and redemption becomes a theme in German, but such compactness will not be matched for some time.

Early German functional writing

German was committed to writing in the monasteries, using the Latin alphabet, and Charlemagne's own reforms had provided a unified, neat and legible book-hand based on classical models and known as Carolingian minuscule. There are, it is true, a few pre-eighth-century runic inscriptions, often on *fibulae*, and mostly of names. With questionable exceptions (one might *just* be a prayer against the devil) they are not literature, although a mnemonic poem for the 'Norsemen's alphabet', the *Abecedarium Normannicum* (MSD v) is preserved in a Latin manuscript from St Gallen in a mixture of Germanic languages. Otherwise all written Old High and Old Low German depends entirely upon the church, and almost all of it had a specific and pragmatic purpose: the teaching and understanding of Christian-Latin texts. While Charlemagne's educational reforms must not be exaggerated, his capitularies and admonitions did insist upon the education of priests and monks, and upon (in the *Admonitio generalis* of 23 March, 789) the dissemination of the Creed, the Paternoster and the professions of faith. A ninth-century Bavarian translation of a Latin baptismal sermon, the *Exhortatio ad plebem Christianum* (*Exhortation to Christian people*, St. IX) also calls for the teaching of the 'uuort thera galaupa . . . ia auh thei uuort thes frono gapetes' ('the words of the Creed . . . and also of the Lord's Prayer'). Official pronouncements required sermons, too, to be read in German, by which is implied 'translated from Latin'. We are told in Walahfrid's *Life of St Gall* of a Latin sermon being translated on the spot during the earliest missions. For much of our period, the sermon was the responsibility of the bishop, but although we have numerous Latin homilies by bishops including Hrabanus himself, German evidence beside the *Exhortatio* is slight.

The notion of a standard language is centuries away, and the view that there was a German 'Hofsprache' or court language is no longer held: the court language was Latin. At best there may have been some attempt at standardisation in the important monastery school at Fulda, but wide variations in orthography, vocabulary and syntax are to be expected with monks working in different centres without easy communication. Many of the earlier monasteries of the south were Irish foundations which were gradually regularised under the Benedictine Rule. St Gallen, for example, was brought under the See of Constance and became a royal monastery of some importance under Lewis the Pious and Lewis the German; the imperial foundation at the Reichenau on Lake Constance was similar, as was Murbach in Alsace. Bavarian monasteries included Freising, Wessobrunn, and St Emmeram and Prül at Regensburg. In central Germany other early foundations were at Trier, Prüm in the Eifel, and Echternach, whilst Weißenburg is not far away. Later, Low German monasteries such as those at Werden or Corvey became literary centres. Most of these monasteries had scriptoria and libraries containing the works of the Church Fathers, Isidore, Boethius, Bede, Alcuin, Hraban and usually some Christian-Latin poetry.

Writing down German at all, however, was no simple task. For this hitherto unwritten language there were problems of phonology – how were un-Latin sounds to be represented? – and of translation – how were words like 'trinity', or 'soul' to be translated without an established Christian context? Simple adaptation of the Latin word, literalism, or the use of an equivalent which might have secular or Germanic-religious overtones are all problematic in their own ways. To cite a single example, to render 'dominus', 'lord', as applied to the prince of peace with the Old High German word 'truhtin', '(war-) lord' could not but invite confusion.

The earliest German is in the form of individual words found in the legal codes of the Germanic tribes (which Charlemagne intended to harmonise with codified Roman law), preserved in Latin between the sixth and the eighth centuries. The *Lex Salica*, the laws of the Salian Franks, first written down under the Merovingians, contains legal terms in German signalled by the addition of the word 'malb.', standing for 'malloberg', 'hill of judgement'. The words are archaic, and a later Old High German translation updated the terminology. Influence on literature is small in this case, but with the spread of Christianity a practice developed which continues throughout the period and well beyond it: German glossing. A glossed text is one in which words have been added either by way of explanation or to translate individual Latin words into German. Sometimes only a few words have been glossed, at others all or nearly all, to provide a word-for-word version which is *not*, however, a translation. Sometimes the glosses are interlinear, sometimes marginal; sometimes a word has been glossed more than once, and sometimes the gloss has been scratched rather than inked, or is in a crude code. Sometimes, finally, a manuscript with interlinear or other glosses has been re-copied and the glosses incorporated into the body of the text. The aim is always to help the German-speaker to understand, but a German vocabulary is also being developed. Biblical texts were glossed; a group from the Reichenau include the Psalms and Luke's Gospel, and there are Alemannic, Rhenish and Low Franconian interlinear glosses of the Psalter and of Old Testament canticles. The interlinear glossing of the *Benedictine rule*, and especially of a group of Latin rhythmic poems known as the *Murbach hymns* was so complete that earlier editors succumbed to the temptation of printing the German as if it were continuous text, and they did so too with the *Carmen ad Deum* (*Hymn to the Lord*, St. xxxvii), where the Latin original was probably composed in England or Ireland, and the German glossing certainly does not constitute a 'text'. The 'translation' of a decree passed in 818 known as the *Trierer Capitulare* (St xl), made in the early tenth century, is also a complete interlinear gloss, although it contains interesting legal terminology concerned with wills and gifts.

Reference works as such were also glossed. The Greek title of the *German Hermeneumata* ('explanations') reminds us that it comes from a long tradition of bilingual (originally Greek–Latin) handbooks, and in the eighth century the thematically arranged Latin headwords were provided with German equivalents. From the same period comes a Latin thesaurus, with headwords arranged alphabetically and Latin synonyms added, and known from its first word as *Abrogans*. The Latin words have all been been translated into German, apparently not always with full awareness of the context. Close to glossaries of this kind, too, is the phrase book, of which we have two different examples in Old High German. The first, in a manuscript now in Kassel but written by a Bavarian, belongs to the *Hermeneumata* tradition, but contains also some phrases and indeed what appears to be a (proverbial) comment about the cunning of the Bavarians as opposed to the guilelessness of the Italians. Of greater interest is a later work called (from its current provenance), the *Paris conversation-book*, which preserves what looks like a dialogue. The German comes first, with Latin following and for once not the primary language, even though it is the medium for comprehension. Place-names in the manuscript suggest that these are the notes of someone (one of Lupus's exchange students?) travelling from France to central Germany, and the German is written in a manner which betrays French influence. Many phrases seem to be from a master to an inferior, while some are vulgar, abusive, or curiously personal; occasionally they sound like exercises for the confessional.

Actual translations take us a step further in the evolution of a literary language. Most are again strictly practical and include the Creed and the Lord's Prayer, confessions and baptismal vows (the last two categories being especially well-represented), and even a priest's vow (St. XIII, XLI–LXI). Several of the professions of faith include renunciations of the devil and sometimes of Germanic gods. Even the Paternoster is translated in a variety of ways, however, and an early version, from St Gallen, contains some errors. One prose prayer does seem actually to have been composed in German, however, though it is based on liturgical formulas. The early *Franconian prayer* (St. XI) is a Bavarian transcript of a text originally in Rhenish Franconian, and here a Latin version has been made of the German text and added to it. Slightly later is the *Klosterneuburg prayer* (St. XXXIV), an unpretentious prose request for the forgiveness of sins, and similar compositions are found down to the eleventh and twelfth centuries (Wilhelm XXVIII–XXXI), when amongst the so-called *Rheinau prayers* we find a repeated anaphoric invocation of the Lord, 'herro', well over thirty times.

Of greater literary importance is the *Wessobrunn prayer* (St. II), dating from the beginning of the ninth century, and found in a theological miscellany (with some German glosses) originally from the small Bavarian monastery which gave it its name. The German is on a free leaf following a section on the measurement of time, and although written clearly, it is not without problems. The original provenance of the work is unknown; the use of a runic symbol and an abbreviation for 'and' is unusual, as are some individual words, causing problems with the predominantly Bavarian dialect; there are some gaps, and it is unclear whether the prayer is divided into a verse and a prose portion, or is all in verse; the meaning of the Latin title *De poeta* has been disputed, while the Latin passage following the German (in the same hand) has largely been ignored.

De poeta probably means 'of the Creator', and the German text first describes in nine alliterative long-lines the primeval nothingness, when there was only the presence of God. The whole text is written continuously, but sense demands a division after this description of the beginnings, because a direct address to God now asks for grace to resist the devil and do God's will. These lines can be arranged as verse, although not entirely satisfactorily, and may really be rhetorical prose in balanced periods, for which parallels appear later. The Latin lines which follow the German (after a one-line gap) are a stronger demand for repentance. This is not a creation-poem but a prayer, perhaps for private meditation. The request in the second part for right belief matches that in the briefer *Franconian prayer*, which also has incidental alliteration at that point. The structure is close to the liturgical collect on the one hand and to the so-called charms on the other, in both of which we find, typically, a title, a narrative portion, and then a request, followed by a Latin conclusion.

Simpler verse prayers are found later on in Old High German, composed after the new literary form of end-rhyme has established itself. Most of them postdate Otfrid's rhymed Gospel-book, and must be considered in that context. It *is* appropriate, however, to follow the *Wessobrunn prayer* with the brief (but both literary and functional) texts usually designated *Zaubersprüche* (St. LXII-LXXIV), 'charms', a term which is, however, misleading, insofar as it concentrates upon the presumed original intent of some parts of a few of the surviving texts, whilst ignoring the context in which they are actually preserved in the Carolingian and later periods. What literary histories have termed charms or blessings (without necessarily differentiating clearly) are all, in their surviving forms, a specific type of supplicatory prayer found in Old High and Low German (and in Latin and most vernaculars), in prose and verse (alliterative or end-rhymed), which occasionally preserve in a Christian context a (very) few pre-Christian elements.

In its original form a charm is a piece of prose or verse for oral pronouncement (although written versions could be used as talismans) designed to ameliorate an existing misfortune, often a medical one, by words alone. They are in the first instance, then, therapeutic rather than prophylactic. Prayers, too, can also petition God for help with existing situations, and both are similar *in aim* to the medical recipe, which uses physical ingredients to cure something that has already happened. Only a few medical recipes have survived from the early stages of Old High German; the *Basler Rezepte* (St. VII) describe medicines for a fever and a tumour, but not until the end of our period do we find larger medical collections such as the *Innsbruck* or *Zurich pharmacopoeia* (Wilhelm XI, XXV), the recipes in which are mixtures of Latin and (sometimes very little) German, and which also contain charms.

It is unnecessary to consider here any official Carolingian church proscriptions against the use of magic, since what little pre-Christian mythology our texts contain has been assimilated. The extent to which they are *German* is also limited; typically, a Latin heading will explain the purpose, a brief and sometimes corrupt German text will follow (perhaps prescribing actions), and there is almost invariably a concluding call for a number of Latin prayers, such as three 'Our Fathers'. Spoken aloud, those would far outweigh the Old High German, and would impose upon any original sense of magic the submission to the will of God. Incidentally, most of the charms would have been effective, insofar as most are concerned with traumatic or transitory conditions: bleeding, sprains, or the alarming, but temporary symptoms of epilepsy.

The *Merseburg charms* (St. LXII) *do* preserve what is clearly older material. Two brief passages of German which can be resolved into alliterative verse have been written in a tenth-century hand on a blank page of a manuscript containing liturgical material (including a fragment in German of a prayer spoken at the elevation of the host, St. LXXXIV). The first describes in three long-lines how some prisoners were released by 'idisi', valkyries, and then in a concluding line commands that someone should escape from bonds. The second, structurally more complex poem describes how Wodan and Phol (who is unidentified) were riding in a wood when the latter's horse sprained a foot. Several named goddesses (it is not clear whether we have four separate names or two sets of appositions) try to cure it, and then Wodan himself effects the cure; the piece ends with a set of poetic formulaic phrases demanding that bone be joined to bone and blood to blood. The verses are followed by a Latin prose prayer which asks for God's help for an individual (whose name can be added). This prayer is integral to the whole and makes acceptable the earlier material.

There are no headings, but although the first charm is often described as being for the release of prisoners it is more likely an allegory for paralysis or cramp. Similarly, although the second piece refers to a horse, it might apply to any sprain, and certainly the accompanying prayer refers to people. The narrative element is found in a completely Christian form later, the riders being Christ, St Peter or St Stephen, and further charms are based upon originally Christian narratives such as the piercing of Christ's side by Longinus, invoked frequently against bleeding. An Old High German epilepsy prayer may also preserve the name of another Germanic god, but here in particular the pre-Christian element is reduced to little more than an opening abracadabra-word. Such 'magic' words might be in any language: a charm at the end of the *Zurich pharmacopoeia* contains a threefold repetition of the Greek 'agios', 'holy'.

Some of these pieces *are* concerned with animals, particularly horses, but the majority have to do with minor medical conditions amongst humans. While some appear in medical texts, they are as often found in theological contexts, and the structural similarity to the collect is clear in prose pieces asking for cures from fever, weak eyes, or indeed that hailstorms be averted. A prayer for sore throats invoking St Blaise (Wilhelm XIX) reminds us that individual saints were and are associated with specific misfortunes. One late prayer from Zurich (Wilhelm XXVI), finally, has a Latin superscript announcing its theme as chastity. In the German part, the example of the Virgin Mary is followed by a request for chasteness, and there is a concluding 'amen', 'let it be'. But a final comment has a curiously medical ring: 'Diz gebet ist uilgŏt tagilich gelesin' ('this prayer is very effective if read once daily').

It is sometimes difficult in Old High German prose to distinguish between translation and glossing, as is the case with the *Diatessaron* of Tatian, a digest or harmony of the Gospels, made in Greek in the second century, translated into Latin in the sixth, and most European vernaculars thereafter. It was translated into German at Fulda, probably under the auspices of Hrabanus early in the ninth century, and the principal copy, (now in St Gallen) made by six different scribes with differing dialects. The manuscript has the German and the Latin in parallel columns, and the German text does not always match the Latin, nor indeed is that Latin version the same as other western European versions. The first impression, judged by modern standards, is that this, although not a gloss, is overly literal; but the technique is probably deliberately that of the faithful translator, the *fidus interpres*, working in the consciousness that the language of the Gospels was sacred, and therefore the German should deviate from it as little as possible.

The technique contrasts with that of an older (late eighth-century) group of translations of scriptural and other texts, principally a difficult theological treatise by Isidore of Seville, who lived in the sixth century, but whose *De fide Catholica* (*On the Catholic faith*) presents clearly the tenets of basic Christianity whilst countering arguments against it. The Isidore-group includes also parts of a sermon called *De vocatione gentium*, of another sermon by Augustine, of an unidentified work, and of Matthew's Gospel. Dialect and provenance are unclear, but there are two manuscripts, one containing the Isidore-tract now in Paris, the other, a series of fragments, from the former monastery of Mon(d)see, near Salzburg. In the Paris manuscript the left-hand page has the Latin text of Isidore's tract, the right the German, though the latter was not completed, and after a few blank pages the Latin fills both sides. The translator seems actively to have avoided Latin constructions (such as participial forms) and tries consistently to make clear who is presenting the argument at any point. There is also a clear and consistent orthographic system. In the fragments from Monsee, the translation of the Gospel is not as free, perhaps due to the desire to keep to the sacred language once again, although it is not as literal as the Tatian version. These translations again indicate the potential of High German at an early stage. Old Saxon translations are sparse, but they include a small portion of a sermon by Bede (MSD LXX) from a manuscript of the ninth century, and a fragment on the Psalms (MSD LXXI) written down perhaps in the tenth.

Religious poetry: *Heliand*, Otfrid and later pieces

Old Saxon does provide, however, a literary bridge to Otfrid in the *Heliand* (*Saviour*), a long poem on the life of Christ. Two more or less full manuscripts (one written probably at Corvey, where it may have been composed) and some fragments preserve nearly six thousand alliterative long-lines divided into just over seventy cantos. The work seems to show the influence of Fulda; the narrative is based on the Tatian Gospel-harmony, and the poet may have used a commentary on Matthew by Hrabanus himself, written around 820. A Latin preface and 34-line *versus* printed from an unidentified source in 1562 seems to link the work with Lewis the Pious, dating it to between 820 and 840, and providing an imperial *raison d'être*: to offer the Gospels 'in Germanicam linguam poetice' to the literate and the illiterate. The assumption may be made that this is a work for reading aloud to an audience of pupils able to understand the mixture of narrative and theological interpretation, perhaps ecclesiastically educated men returning to take up positions in the world. Earlier views of the text as a missionary work, Germanising the Gospels for proselytising purposes are no longer held.

The work presents and explains the many miracles ('uundarlîcas filo', 36b) of Christ. The epic elements strike the reader, but the interpretative parts are also important. Thus canto XLIII, recounting the healing of the blind men at Jericho in Matthew xx, 29–34, is followed by a canto explaining this as an image ('biliđi', 3,589a) of mankind as a whole, 'al mancunni' (3,592a), descended from Adam and Eve, who lost their real sight when they fell to the devil's wiles, and had their eyes opened to sin. The exegesis is a familiar one, going back to Gregory the Great, and Otfrid himself uses it too. The effect of the whole work, though, is to stress the power of God over the attacks of the enemy, and the conclusion to the raising of Lazarus (XLIX) epitomises this: as Lazarus was healed, so may the 'mikile maht godes' ('God's mighty power') preserve any man 'uuiđ fîundo nið' ('against the envy of the enemy').

Of course the *Heliand* 'Germanises' to an extent; it employs a Germanic poetic form, and hence in its build-up of formulaic phrases, with echoes of secular heroic poetry, it can sometimes look like more an heroic epic than is justified. But Christ does not become a Germanic warrior, nor is there really evidence of supposed Germanic delights in battle. In the struggle between Malchus and Peter, for example, which is sometimes seen as evidence for such interest, the implications of the story are spelt out very clearly indeed.

There was clearly some cross-influence between Anglo-Saxon and continental Low German biblical poetry. Part of an Anglo-Saxon poem on Genesis (now called *Genesis B*) proved to be a translation of an Old Saxon original, of which fragments have survived. The *Genesis* is close to the *Heliand* in form, and the treatment of the two poles of man's salvation, the fall and the redemption, is understandable. Surviving fragments present the fall, Cain, and Sodom and Gomorrah, using formulas that again echo heroic poetry. Before setting off to tempt Eve, the devil arms himself like a hero, and the cosmic conflict between Enoch and Antichrist, which we shall meet again in the *Muspilli*, is mentioned. Adam's complaint at the expulsion from paradise, however, is theologically interesting, as is the whole question of responsibility for the fall.

Otfrid of Weißenburg's *Evangelienbuch* (*Gospel book*) stands out within the limited amount of early German literature because it is preserved in several dedicated manuscripts. Otfrid conceived the work as it appears in the principal manuscript, now in Vienna, and in simplest terms it is a German poem of over seven thousand long-lines, narrating and expounding material from the Gospels (though not based, like the *Heliand*, on a harmony). The German poetry is at the centre, arranged in couplets of long-lines, rhyming at caesura and cadence, and with the second line indented, the work is divided into five books, the books into chapters, and there are introductory and concluding chapters in each. But the chapters have Latin titles (in red), and tables of these titles are prefaced to each book. A German dedicatory poem to Lewis the German opens the work, and a prose letter in Latin to Liutbert, archbishop of Mainz and Otfrid's ecclesiastical superior, comes next. After this is another dedicatory poem in German, to Salomo, Bishop of Constance, and another, addressed to two friends, Hartmuat and Werinbert of St Gallen, follows the work as a whole. These poems have *Latin* titles which are spelt out as acrostics and telestichs by the first and last letters of the *German* strophes. That the title is also spelt out by the last letters of the third half-line is not always clear in modern editions, however. The capital letters that begin each strophe are red, and they vary in size (Otfrid used this as a further structuring element) and there are also Latin marginal indications (which tend to become submerged in the apparatus to modern editions) in red, pointing to biblical passages. The Vienna manuscript has three coloured illustrations (the entry into Jerusalem, last supper, crucifixion), and the cover has an image of a labyrinth. It was written at Weißenburg, corrected by Otfrid himself, and from the same scriptorium came the second (virtually complete) manuscript, now in Heidelberg, and probably a fragmentary 'codex discissus'. But another copy was made (without the dedicatory poems) at the Bavarian monastery of Freising and the dialect is Bavarian, rather than Otfrid's South Rhenish Franconian. There are several distinct differences from the *Heliand*, and it has been argued both that Otfrid used, and that he deliberately avoided similarities with that work. Both works present Gospel material in the vernacular, of course, and both mix narrative and interpretation, but the form is different, archaic alliterative line against rhymed long-line couplets, as is the artistic complexity of Otfrid's work.

Otfrid was born around the beginning of the ninth century, and in his letter to Liutbert he tells that he studied at Fulda under Hrabanus, probably in the 820s, as part of the generation of Gottschalk and Walahfrid. At

Weißenburg he became 'magister scholiae', played a major role in the building up of the (now dispersed) library, and may have been involved with glossing. His name is on a Weißenburg document dated 851, and he probably died in about 870, although there is no record of his death. The dedications indicate that the *Evangelienbuch* was completed between 863, when Liutbert became archbishop, and 871, when Salomo of Constance died.

In the letter to Liutbert Otfrid gives a number of reasons for writing the poem. One is to counter German secular songs ('cantus obscenus'), but he refers also to the encouragement of friends, and to the inspiration of Latin Christian writers. This invites us to make comparisons, and of those Otfrid names, Juvencus (fourth century) produced a largely narrative Gospel poem in four books (rather than five), while Arator (fifth century) combined commentary and narrative in his metrical version of the Acts of the Apostles. Of others, Caelius Sedulius (fifth century) wrote a *Carmen Paschale* (*Easter song*) in five books, and Alcimus Avitus (d. 519) also divided his creation-poem into five books. All of these might have had a general influence, but Otfrid's source is first the Vulgate, and then commentaries on the Gospels, especially those by Alcuin and Hrabanus, who themselves drew heavily upon Jerome, Augustine and Gregory (all three of whom are named in the German work). There was an abridged reworking by Erchambert of Fulda of the commentary of Alcuin on John in the Weißenburg library, and, in another manuscript from Weißenburg, a marginal commentary in Latin excerpted from the same source has been added to the Gospel by Otfrid himself.

Otfrid's five books represent, he tells us, our five imperfect senses to be countered by the four Gospels, and contain 28, 24, 26, 37 and 25 chapters respectively, few having more than a hundred long-lines. Book III, chapter 20 on the man born blind in John ix, 1 has nearly two hundred (plus an additional chapter offering a spiritual interpretation), and one (v, 23), contrasting heaven and earth, has nearly three hundred. The books deal with the prophecies about and nativity of Christ (I), the ministry, teaching and miracles (II and III), the passion (IV) and the resurrection, ascension and last judgement (V). It remains unclear whether Otfrid is selecting Gospel passages from memory, or using either a lectionary or a Vulgate marked with pericopes for reading. His technique, however, is to integrate narrative (augmented according to the literal sense) with interpretation, and this integration can be subtle. When he is narrating the incident of Christ and the Woman of Samaria (II, 14 on John iv), for example, he introduces two words to render the Vulgate 'fons', 'well', allowing Christ to use one word, the Samaritan woman another, underscoring the difference between her literal understanding and the spiritual water that Christ is offering. More extensively, in the passage describing the arrival of the

Magi and their visit to Herod (1, 17), Otfrid not only stresses Herod's wickedness but actualises its significance: it might have destroyed *our* salvation. Later in the same passage Otfrid interrupts his narrative (the word 'mystice', 'spiritual interpretation', is inserted as a sub-heading) to explain the meaning of the gifts brought by the Magi by sketching briefly the still-familiar interpretation of the gold, incense and myrrh as indicating Christ's kingship, priesthood and death; the effect is of a reminder to an audience familiar already with the details. The following chapter (1, 18), however, uses Matthew ii,12 (that the Magi returned home by a different route) as the basis for a sermon according to the tropological sense on fallen man's need to return to his real homeland of paradise by the route of righteousness. The contrast betweeen the misery of the world and the delights of paradise is a repeated motif.

Sometimes Otfrid devotes more than one additional chapter to interpretation. The pericope of Christ tempted in the wilderness (II, 4) is followed by a short typological chapter comparing Adam's fall with Christ's successfully resisted temptation in the desert, and another underscoring again the significance of the fall for mankind by stressing the mercy of God in providing a redeemer. There are in the *Evangelienbuch* striking lyrical passages and refrains, but the meat of the work is in passages like these, or the chapters dealing with the wedding feast at Cana (II, 7–9), where a spiritual interpretation is followed by a consideration of why Christ turned water into wine rather than creating it from nothing. So, too, the story of the man born blind (III, 20–21) is again seen as referring to sinful humanity, and the relevant chapter is in the form of a prayer (ending with an 'amen') that man's inner eyes might be opened.

Otfrid shares with other Old High German poets a vivid image of the day of judgement, and stresses the impossibility of escape from a justice which is no respecter of persons in his apocalyptic description in V, 19, where a refrain underlines the good fortune of anyone who can face that doom with equanimity. Further chapters continue the theme down to the longest and most complex chapter of all (V, 23), contrasting heaven and earth, and containing prayers for mercy, just before the conclusion of the whole work. Otfrid's theme is more than the life of Christ: he is preoccupied with the return of man to the 'patria paradisi', and the note sounded in the homily based on the return of the Magi (1, 18) recurs frequently: 'uuolaga elilenti harto bistu herti' ('alas exile, how hard you are'), the exile being mankind's, into the vale of tears.

To refer to the *Evangelienbuch* as a biblical epic is misleading, as it places too great an emphasis on the narrative aspects. It is a teaching work for use with the Vulgate, and the marginal indicators refer the reader to given verses. Possibly it was designed for the schoolroom, sometimes providing only pointers to more complex exegesis. The teacher is also the preacher, however, and the interpretations are frequently homiletic. The work is intended presumably both for a listening audience, as reinforced by the frequent interpolated comments referring backwards and forwards in the text ('as I have said') and as a reading or study text, as when Otfrid tells the audience 'Lis sélbo, theih thir rédion' ('Go and read for yourself what I am telling you', 11, 9, 71). The *Evangelienbuch* is polyfunctional, narrating, teaching and commenting, and the stylistic tension between his use of voices – 'ih' and 'uuir' ('I' and 'you') – is that between the teacher and the preacher. The homiletic impulse, finally, is one of the constant features of virtually the whole of early German literature.

Otfrid's work is the first major German text to use rhymed verse, and he was aware of the novelty. His rhymes are sometimes on unstressed final vowels, or are assonantic, though only two lines are unrhymed. The origin of rhyme in German has occasioned much debate, and possible influences include the colometric style found in the Vulgate Psalter as well as in Latin prose, where recurring sequences ('cola') can demonstrate 'omoioteleuton', the word Otfrid uses for end-rhyme. He clearly knew formal works on grammar and metre and he plays on metrical terms. The Latin 'rhythmi' known as Ambrosian hymns developed rhymed short lines (especially in England and Ireland, possibly influenced by native Irish verse), while the Leonine hexameter is a longer rhymed Latin form. Otfrid used acrostic and other patterns and the dedicatory verses are all in multiples of twelve couplets, but more complex numerological patterns have been sought in the work based upon differentiated capitals. The repetitions and (sometimes varied) refrain-passages in the work also merit attention, notably in larger chapters such as v, 23.

In one major respect, Otfrid is a revolutionary: in his choice of German. This cannot be overstated, and he justifies it in the first chapter of the first book, headed (in Latin) 'why the writer wrote this book in German'. Although he is less apologetic about the barbaric nature of German (by which he means that it is unlike Latin in orthography and grammar) here than in his letter to Liutbert, there is a nationalistic note in both. To Liutbert he complains that the Franks use 'the languages of other peoples'. In 1, 1 he stresses that the Franks are just as good as the Romans and Greeks, and should not be inhibited from writing God's praise in their own language. Otfrid's desire to replace secular vernacular poetry may be in line with the cultural policy of Charlemagne's successors, but there are echoes of the nationalism implicit in the 'translatio imperii'. The *De Carolo Magno* referred, too, to the envy ('invidia') of the Greeks and Romans of the glory of the Franks. Otfrid concludes his introductory chapter by rejoicing that 'wir Kriste sungun / in unsera zungun / joh uuir ouh thaz gilebetun, / in frenkisgon nan loboton' (1, 1, 125f. 'we sang of Christ in our own language, and had the experience of Christ being praised in Frankish'). The *Conclusio voluminis totius* (*The conclusion of the whole volume*, v, 25) picks up the idea, calling for the eternal singing of God's praises by all men and angels, placing the Franks into a scheme that is not only world-wide, but eternal.

Much in the shadow of Otfrid is a small piece of Alemannic verse relating the story of *Christ and the woman of Samaria* (St. xvii) told in John iv, 6–21. Composed perhaps at the Reichenau and written down in the tenth century, it breaks off at the end of a manuscript page. It was probably influenced by the *Evangelienbuch*, although it is in a mixture of two and three-line strophes, and the appearance in smaller pieces of three-liners (which Otfrid does not use) has caused speculation that strophes of varying size were in existence earlier. The pericope is retold without commentary; Otfrid takes twice as long to reach the point where this text stops, and he distinguishes consistently between actual and metaphorical (living) water, where this text does not. There is a homely feel about the dialogue, and the Samaritana exclaims 'uuizze Christ', 'Christ knows' on one occasion. It ends at John iv, 20, leaving us the question of why this somewhat unpretentious fragment was written, although the pericope (one of the readings for Lent), was adapted separately later in the Middle Ages in English. The purpose may have been to stress that those who are not Jews can believe in Christ.

Several smaller rhymed pieces in German are probably (sometimes certainly) later than Otfrid. At the end of the Freising manuscript of the *Evangelienbuch*, following an indication in Latin that the copy was done at the behest of Bishop Waldo (883–906) by the 'unworthy scribe' Sigihard, comes *Sigihard's prayer* (St. xx), two couplets in Bavarian asking simply for God's mercy. Another (Rhenish Franconian) rhymed prayer, probably made in the late ninth century, renders into four lines of German verse the Latin prose collect *Deus qui proprium . . .* (*O God, whose nature . . .*) from the Litany of the Saints, which precedes it in the manuscript, and further prayers are directed specifically against the wiles of the devil. One, in a Trier manuscript in an eleventh-century hand uses the crude code sometimes found in glosses (St. lxxx), and another, from a different monastery in Trier and written rather earlier, has two long-lines adapted from Gregory the Great (St. lxxxi). The rhymed *Zurich house-blessing* (St. lxxv) is the bluntest attempt to keep away devils, however, challenging any demon to pronounce the word 'chnospinci'. Specific rhymed prayers ask that bees might not swarm elsewhere, or that valuable dogs might not run away (St. lxxvif.), and later still come lorical poems for protection on a journey (*Reisesegen*), a fine example of which, from Weingarten (St. lxxviii), contains gestures, each of the five fingers sending five-and-fifty guardian angels.

The *Petruslied* (*The song of St Peter*, St. xxi), which solicits St Peter's aid in gaining the kingdom of heaven, is a hymn rather than a prayer. The three pairs of rhymed long-lines with the liturgical refrain 'kyrie eleison, christe eleison' are found in a manuscript of the Genesis commentary of Hrabanus, and discussing it after Otfrid implies a judgement on its (disputed) age; but it is likely to have been composed at Freising with an awareness of Otfrid's work. That St Peter, as keeper of the gate of heaven, can intercede for the sinner is familiar enough, and is echoed closely in a Latin hymn, albeit not a rhymed or rhythmic one. The real interest of the work lies in the implicit sense of community: God is 'unsar trohtin', 'our Lord', and the prayer concludes 'pittemes . . . alla samant', 'let us pray . . . all together'. The hymnic feel is unmistakable, and the text is provided in the manuscript with musical notation. The work is less easy to associate with the dedication of a specific church than with St Peter's See in Rome, something voiced long ago by Hoffmann von Fallersleben, who noted in a description of the coronation there of Henry IV in 1084 a reference to the singing by the clergy of the parallel Latin hymn, and by the laity of a German song to St Peter with the 'kyrie'.

It is more difficult to categorise another work, again almost certainly composed under the influence of the Freising Otfrid. The Old High German metrical *Psalm 138* (St. XXII; Authorised Version 139) is very different from the tradition of glossed Psalters, being a free adaptation of the main themes in that Psalm. The Bavarian piece was composed probably in the early part of the ninth century, and the capitals point once more to strophes of two or three lines. A separate and out-of-context introductory couplet invites an audience to hear David's words to God, and this is followed by a block of fifteen lines, the last of which (the second long-line of a couplet) is repeated as a capitalised *first* line at the start of the second group of fifteen lines. The final long-line of *this* group is repeated in the same way to begin a concluding six lines. The first part follows the Vulgate fairly closely and concludes with an idea that comes later in the Psalm, that of shunning those who do murder. This idea becomes the start of the next section (which omits the request in the original that God destroy the Psalmist's enemies), and the poem goes on to ask, like so many of the prayers, for protection against evil, then takes up again the idea of God's control over man from conception onwards. The section concludes, however, with an idea from the first part of the Vulgate text: the impossibility of escaping from God. This becomes the theme of the six-line concluding prayer for God to preserve the speaker. The poem is neither a translation of the Vulgate nor, like Otfrid's work, an interpretation, but a skilful free adaptation of a confessional Psalm into a poetic prayer.

Latin poems on historical events are often panegyric in tone, and a German equivalent is found in the Old High German *Ludwigslied* (*Song of King Lewis*, St. XVI), fifty-nine rhymed long-lines written out as poetry and divided into strophes of two or three lines. This time the precise year of composition is known, but the work raises an odd question: why is it in German at all? The poem was written down in France (by a French scribe, from the look of his errors), probably in the monastery of St Amand, near Valenciennes. Next to it in the otherwise Latin manuscript is an Old French hagiographic poem in the same hand. Furthermore, the poem is about a victory over Viking invaders by a French king, Lewis III, grandson of Charles the Bald, who ruled the West Franks after the division of Charlemagne's empire. Lewis came to the throne in his teens in 879, and shared the West Frank territories (at the Agreement of Amiens in 880) with his brother, Carloman. (McKitterick (*The Carolingians and the written word*, 1989, pp. 232–5) argues that the poem is about Lewis the Younger, king of the East Franks, but this is quite untenable.) Lewis III was faced with various real problems: he needed to establish his throne, and his accession coincided with a series of attacks on northern France by the Vikings. From contemporary chronicles we know that Lewis and Carloman together defeated a would-be usurper, Boso, Duke of Provence, after which Lewis rode north and defeated a Viking force at Saucourt in Picardy in August 881, a victory that was bound to be the subject of immediate acclaim, but was of limited significance, since Lewis died almost exactly a year later. When the poem was copied, a Latin heading was added indicating that it was 'in memoriam', a sad contrast to the triumphant conclusion trusting that God would preserve the young king.

There are hagiographic overtones in the portrayal of a direct relationship between God and the king. In his dedicatory poem to Lewis the German, Otfrid, too, made references to God's aid in victory, to the loyal followers, to the king's ability to withstand suffering, his service of God, and to the hope of long life, all of which are echoed here. The *Ludwigslied* is consistently theocentric in its approach, however. The Vikings are sent by God for two reasons: to test the young king (whose premature loss of a father, we are told, has been compensated for by his adoption by God); and to punish the Franks for their sins. The Vikings themselves are not characterised at all, because they are simply instruments, and there is none of the vivid presentation of these feared invaders found in some of the annals. The notion of a divine scourge goes back to the Old Testament and continues well beyond the ninth century; Alcuin wrote to Ethelred of Northumbria interpreting the Viking raids on Lindisfarne in June, 793 as a punishment against 'fornication, avarice, robbery', precisely the sins mentioned here. God commands Lewis (we are told simply that he was away, not where he was) to 'avenge my people,' a significant formulation, and Lewis rallies his troops, joins battle and is victorious.

The poet is aware of an historical purpose, but the protagonists have no special knowledge. Lewis is not told that victory will be his, and in an address to his troops not unlike those found in Germanic heroic poetry points out that men's lives are in God's hands. They ride into battle after singing the 'kyrie', submissive to God's mercy, then, rather than confident of victory or of heaven. As an historical work the poem operates on three levels: giving the potentially verifiable facts of secular history; putting them into the theocentric framework which explains why they happened; and stressing the king's direct relationship to God as panegyric and propaganda. A somewhat repetitious amount of critical attention has been paid to the historical *context* of the poem, rather than its approach to history. Certainly it may be seen as propaganda for a young king under threat, and his birthright is underscored, but to seek specific connections with events outside the poem is of dubious relevance. Hincmar, the influential archbishop of Rheims, for example, clashed with the young king on episcopal investiture, but there are no real indications in the poem of a direct attack on Hincmar, except possibly the idea that God 'adopted' Lewis, since he had suggested that Lewis might be adopted by the East Frank Charles the Fat. Why, however, is the poem in German and not in Old French or Latin? St Amand, where the poem was probably written, had a celebrated school, attracting men from abroad, including probably this Rhenish poet. The poem may have been intended for German speakers amongst the West Franks, but the interesting suggestion has been made that it was designed as propaganda on a broader scale. The king's German counterpart, Lewis the Younger, died in January 882, leaving no absolutely clear successor. Perhaps the poem was intended to make a case to a lay nobility *in Germany* for the West Frank king as overall ruler? His demise in August of the same year rendered the question null, and the poem became a memorial.

While there was an extensive tradition of Latin hagiography in prose and verse by German writers such as Walahfrid, we know of only two saints' lives *in* German, one of which survives only in a later adaptation, so that Ratpert's life of St Gall must be considered under Ottonian Latin. We do, however, have a tenth-century strophic rhymed poem on St George in German, the *Georgslied* (St. XIX), but establishing a text is difficult. The poem was added to the Heidelberg Otfrid-manuscript by a scribe called Wisolf, who seems to have given up in mid-narrative (though he still had space available) with the word 'nequeo', 'I can't manage'. The text is garbled, the orthography eccentric (looking occasionally like dyslexia), and there are copy errors. A Latin *Vita* like one in St Gallen may be the source, and the dragon-slaying episode, incidentally, was not associated with the saint until far later. What we have is a standard hagiography of an early saint and martyr, who asserts his faith in the face of pressure and imprisonment, heals the sick, blind and lame, and also causes a column to put out leaves, brings a dead man back to life, converts the wife of the Roman emperor and banishes a demon. Galerius of Dacia (who may have had the real St George killed and who appears here as Dacianus) tries to kill him in the poem, but whenever he tries to do so, we are told in a repeated line that 'George rose up again'.

Different problems are presented by another badly preserved work, and one which, moreover, is extremely difficult to place into a literary-historical framework, chronologically and otherwise. This is the alliterative poem known as *Muspilli* (St. XIV), which seems to mean 'the destruction of the world'. The poem was copied in the spaces in a presentation manuscript of Latin theology dedicated to Lewis the German whilst he was still a prince, and although capitals give some indication of strophic patterns, the shape of the work is a problem. Although the basis is the alliterative long-line, there are also rhymes. The work has three themes: first, the battle between the forces of heaven and hell for the individual soul after death, with the implications for the afterlife of misdeeds on earth; then doomsday itself, brought about by victory of Antichrist over Elijah and the spilling of Elijah's blood, with the inescapability of the judgement stressed, and also that things will go badly for anyone who has not judged honestly; and the summoning of the quick and the dead, when Christ will appear in majesty. At this point the poem breaks off.

The two first themes have been taken as belonging originally to different poems, but this speculation is unhelpful. The theme of the work *as we have it* is judgement after death, of the individual soul and of the world, and the message is clear enough: right behaviour is needed during man's earthly life. Some aspects of the final conflict with Elijah (the poet mentions but rejects other outcomes of the battle with Antichrist) are unusual, and may indicate knowledge of apocryphal works, although the basic ideas are theologically straightforward. What is of interest is that the precise theme of judgement is both terrestrial and celestial, and the audience for this hell-fire sermon may well have had a special interest in judgement: perhaps an aristocratic audience was being reminded of the absolute nature of justice and of the fact that they would not be able to hide behind relatives at the last. An aristocratic audience, too, might have responded better to the old alliterative form associated with secular writings. Whether *Muspilli* came before or after Otfrid's Gospel-book is hard to determine, and the fact that both share an alliterative line describing paradise ('dar ist lip ano tod   lioht ano finstri' ('there is life without death, light without darkness')), need imply no more than that both writers drew on a tradition which is well attested in Latin too. There is no evidence that either poet knew the other's work, but both had a clear idea of doomsday, and we shall encounter again homiletic poems on the same theme.

The Germanic hero: the *Hildebrandslied* and *Waltharius*

The secular songs to which Otfrid objected doubtless included heroic poems, of which only one early German example survives. We know from other Germanic languages, from Latin and from later material, of numerous heroic themes from Germanic history and mythology, and we may well postulate a tradition in German of oral poetry as good or better than the religious material that we *are* able to assess. But it is less than useful to try to discuss in detail what we do *not* have, and our sole written example is a poem of sixty-nine lines in a mixture of High and Low German, preserved, though we have no idea why, in a theological document. The work is important because it is unique, but in spite of problems it is still clearly of literary value. The *Hildebrand(s)lied* (*Lay of Hildebrand*, St. 1) uses the alliterative long-line found throughout Germanic heroic poetry, and its oral origins are clear from the use of formulaic expressions. A description early in the work of the two central figures putting on their armour can be matched phrase-for-phrase in Anglo-Saxon, and other formulas are repeated within the work. Nevertheless, our manuscript is a late copy (there are mistakes in it that can only have come from a written source) and it is impossible to guess how many written stages preceded it. Preserved on the front and back pages of a manuscript, it is incomplete, though only a few lines seem to be missing. Its language, though, is impossible; an attempt has been made to render a work written in the Bavarian dialect (the alliteration only works in High German) into Low German, but with such lack of success that false forms appear. This version was copied (using some Anglo-Saxon characters) probably early in the ninth century at Fulda, but when the poem was composed can only be guessed at.

The poem deals with a battle between a father and a son set within a distorted but recognisable context, namely the east–west division of the Ostrogoths and Visigoths. From what is now south-west Russia, the Visigoths moved in the fifth century westwards to Rome and then to Burgundy and Spain, while the Ostrogoths remained in the east. The Ostrogoths under Theoderic (known in German as Dietrich) took Rome in 493 from Odoacer, but the poem and later German writings assume that Odoacer had driven Theoderic out of his rightful kingdom, after which he spent time as an exile at the court of Attila (Theoderic's *father* had been an ally of the Huns), returning to regain his lands. In our poem, Hildebrand is one of Theoderic's men, who had fled with him into exile, and, having returned, has to face in single combat the son he left behind. It is possible that the original version was Gothic, and that it passed to Italy and was taken over (judging by the names of the central characters), into Lombardic, a High German dialect that gave way in the seventh century to the local Romance language. The story might well have passed thence to Bavaria, and then northwards.

The themes are those of a warrior's reputation (felt inwardly as part of a code of honour, and expressed outwardly by gold and fine armour), and the conflict between fate and the individual, coupled with the impossibility of real knowledge. Two champions are picked to fight in single combat before their respective forces, and we are told at the outset that they are father and son. Repetition of their names and patronymics underscores a relationship of which the father becomes aware, though the son never believes it.

Much of the work is in dialogue. Hildebrand claims that if his adversary names one relative he will know all the rest, but Hadubrand names his father as Hildebrand, who left a bride and a baby behind 'without inheritance' when exiled with Theoderic. Hildebrand was a brave warrior, but Hadubrand supposes, since he was always in the forefront of battle, that he must be dead. Old men, who *are* now dead and cannot bear witness, have told him so. There is no question of actual recognition, and the leaving of a *bride* means that this is an only son. When Hildebrand now states that he is the closest of relatives, the son understands, but does not believe him. Hildebrand, furthermore, makes a mistake when he offers the son a conciliatory gift, a gold arm-ring that the narrator tells us came from Attila. To us, the ring identifies Hildebrand as a great and therefore well-rewarded warrior, albeit with some connection with the Huns. To Hadubrand, the ring identifies Hildebrand *as* a Hun. He has no reason to believe this man, and his supposition that Hildebrand is dead becomes definite when he tells us that he has heard from sailors (also unavailable witnesses) that his father *was* killed in battle. The arm-ring also reintroduces the idea of inheritance. Hadubrand has clearly inherited from his father the abilities of a great warrior, but if this gold is to be his inheritance he can gain it only by earning it, that is, by defeating and killing his father. Haduband refuses the arm-ring, identifying his adversary as an 'alter hun' ('old Hun'), and accusing him of trickery.

At this point there seems to be some textual corruption, but if we accept a small amount of editing, the son now denies that his adversary was ever the exile he claims to be. Hildebrand himself realises at this point that battle is inevitable, that 'wewurt skihit' ('cruel fate will take its course'). We do not have the ending, but the battle is brief, and it does not seem as if much is missing. Theoretically, someone could stop the battle (as happens in a reworking of the story, the *Later Hildebrandslied*, in which the wife/mother appears); otherwise the men could kill each other, or the son the father, which would show blind fate at work only. Presumably, however, the father kills the son (as in various European analogues), the presence of the two observing forces requiring that the two men fight, and the tragedy is that Hildebrand destroys his own posterity. And yet the true inheritance of Hildebrand is the song itself; he could neither cheat fate nor prove his own identity, but the song preserves his fame.

We owe the *Hildebrandslied* to the church, even if the Christian adaptations in it are insignificant. In the literature of the Carolingian age, though, it is Otfrid who is in the avant-garde, while the *Hildebrandslied* is an antiquarian anomaly, an oral work that ought logically not to have survived at all in a society whose literacy was programmatically Christian. Given that other Old High German texts were aimed at a secular, unlettered and aristocratic audience, perhaps the *Hildebrandslied*, too, was copied for some similar group, or perhaps the monks were themselves from that class.

The only comparable *long* work in our period written by a German is a Latin poem of over 1,400 Vergilian hexameters (with a large number of actual quotations from Vergil). *Waltharius* is based upon (again a distorted version of) early Germanic tribal history, of the Goths, the Franks and the Burgundians, and stresses once again the themes of bravery in battle, especially single combat, reputation, and indeed the possession of gold. The superficial Christianity of the *Hildebrandslied*, however, is much strengthened here.

There is no agreement on when, where or by whom the work was written. It has been placed in the Carolingian period and in the eleventh century, and even its ascription to Ekkehard I of St Gallen in the early tenth century is now considered unsafe. In some of the manuscripts there is a prologue by a monk who names himself as Geraldus, but since nothing is known about him, this is unhelpful. *Waltharius* was composed by a young monk (he tells us so in an epilogue) whose native language, German, is clear from his word-plays, but who might have been writing any time between the early ninth and the end of the tenth century.

Waltharius is a prince of Aquitaine, taken as hostage and brought up by Attila, together with Hiltgund, princess of the Burgundians, and Hagano, a noble youth given as hostage by the Franks in place of their prince, Guntharius. Attila did, of course, rule the Huns, and Waltharius may be identified with a fifth-century Visigoth from Toulouse. The historical Gundahari was a Burgundian, but his seat at Worms had become Frankish by the time of the poem, so that he has become a Frank, while a fictitious princess represents Burgundy. Tribute is also paid, and the hostages are brought up at the court of Attila. When Guntharius grows up, however, he revokes the tribute, causing Hagano to flee. Attila tries to marry Waltharius to a Hun princess (ensuring political stability), but Waltharius plans an escape with Hiltgund, whom he loves. They arrange for Attila and his warriors to get drunk at a feast, escape with a great amount of treasure, and Attila, waking with a hangover, can persuade no one to pursue them.

Returning through the land of the Franks, Waltharius is challenged in a pass in the Vosges by a group of twelve warriors, including Hagano and Guntharius. Hagano is torn between a reluctance to attack his old friend (also on grounds of prudence, since Waltharius is a great warrior) and loyalty to his king. Waltharius kills most of the Franks in single and combined battles and wounds Guntharius severely. The last battle is with Hagano, but after Waltharius loses a hand, Hagano an eye and some teeth, a truce is called, and a settlement made, after which Waltharius returns to his kingdom, marries Hiltgund and rules for many years.

The fighting is more vivid than in the *Hildebrandslied*, if some of the plot is a little contrived, including the abrupt ending. The role of Hiltgund is slight, although Waltharius's chaste behaviour towards her on their flight is noteworthy. Yet in spite of the language the work is a German heroic poem, in which loyalty, reputation, and the rightful possession of specific wealth (here the tribute paid originally to the Huns), as well as prowess in combat all play a part. The avoidance of tragedy in particular betrays church influence, though primitive elements are still present in Waltharius's beheading of his victims. The story was well known, and now-lost versions may have had a tragic ending, loyalty forcing Hagano to kill his friend. What we actually possess, however, is a Latin poem told (thus Geraldus's preface) for entertainment, but with pace and charm.

The division of Charlemagne's empire by the middle of the ninth century separated Germany and France, and Charlemagne's own line in Germany came to end with the disastrous rule of Lewis the Child (899–911), who was still in his teens when he died. Salomo III, abbot of St Gallen, wrote in about 904 a Latin poem lamenting the misfortunes of a country under attack from the Magyars and torn internally as well. Nor was stability restored by the election of a firm military leader, the Frankish nobleman Conrad I, who died in 918. He was succeeded, however, by the Saxon Henry I, the Fowler (919–36), and his dynasty took its name from Henry's son, Otto I, the Great (936–73). Otto claimed for Germany another imperial *renovatio*, and was crowned emperor in Rome by Pope John XII in 962. The Saxon line survived for the rest of the tenth century under Otto II (973–83) and (after some initial problems during his minority), Otto III, who died in 1002. With the death of Henry II, the Saint (1002–24), the rule of Germany passed through the maternal line to Conrad II the Salian, and a new dynasty.

Ottonian Latin literature

As regards literature in German, the tenth century is often viewed as a kind of wasteland. But material in German before the tenth century is sparse in any case, and several of the works we *do* have were copied at that time. The Latin literary traditions established in Germany under the Carolingians, however, continued vigorously under the Saxons and the Salians, especially biblical commentary and religious poetry, including sequences and hymns by Notker's followers at St Gallen. Existing annals were continued and new ones begun, some on the Saxons, such as the prose *Res gestae Saxonicae* of Widukind of Corvey, or the *Historia Ottonis* of Liutprand of Cremona (*c.* 920–70). Of special interest, though, is a collection of short Latin poems in a manuscript copied probably in Canterbury in the eleventh century, but compiled earlier in the Rhineland, and now in Cambridge, whence the title for the nearly fifty *Cambridge songs*. They include rhymed poems and several sequence-like *modi*, the most impressive of which, the *Modus Ottinc*, celebrates Otto I and his defeat of the Magyars, though it is also intended to honour his successors. The collection contains other panegyrics and coronation-poems, and there is one sequence on the life of Christ. Further pieces anticipate the 'Schwank', the humorous anecdote in verse: the *Modus Florum* is about a bragging contest, while the *Modus Liebinc* localises in Constance the folk-tale of the snow-baby, in which a returning merchant finds that his wife has a supernumary child, which she claims came from the snow. He takes the child and sells it, claiming that it melted. *Sacerdos et lupus* (*Priest and wolf*), which is described as a 'iocularis cantio' ('humorous narrative'), is a quasi-Aesopian fable of a priest's failure to catch a wolf, whilst the tale of *Unibos*, the farmer who only has a single ox, is a framework for several comic anecdotes. A much-translated poem about Heriger, archbishop of Mainz, recounts his punishment of a traveller who claimed to have visited Heaven, and one about Proterius and his daughter is a moralising piece on the avoidance of despair, a recurrent theme in later literature. Especially effective is that about Johannes, a short but over-ambitious hermit, who wants to live like an angel, but has to learn to be a good man instead.

Two poems stand out because they are macaronic, their rhymed long-lines being half Latin and then half German. One was defaced deliberately in the Middle Ages, perhaps on grounds of impropriety, and suffered again in the nineteenth century when scholars used chemicals to try and make the script clearer. *Suavissima nonna* (*Sweetest of nuns*) is apparently a dialogue between a nun and a man (not necessarily a priest, as used to be assumed), who urges the nun to come with him. She resists, but may have changed her mind at the end of the work; we can no longer tell. Easier to read, though not unproblematic otherwise, is *De Heinrico* (*Of Henry*, St. XXIII). The twenty-seven lines (in eight strophes of two or three long-lines) give an account of an incident in which Henry, Duke of Bavaria, is received by the emperor Otto, after a messenger has instructed him to do so. Otto, having apparently welcomed two men 'of that name', confers

honours on Henry and takes his advice thereafter. This looks like a reconciliation scene, perhaps involving Otto I, whose rebel younger brother,
Henry of Bavaria, was pardoned in 941. Otto did not become emperor
until 962, however, and the 'two Henrys' passage is a problem, so that the
poem may be about Henry's son, the equally rebellious Henry the
Quarrelsome, who was reconciled with the child emperor Otto III in 985
(and a child could have been told to receive the Duke as in the poem). But
there are too many possibilities for the content to be clear.

It is hard to assess the literary importance of the nun Hrotsvitha of
Gandersheim (a Saxon house in the Harz, closely associated with the
Ottonian royal family), who was born about 930 and died in the 970s. She
wrote a series of eight saints' lives and legends in Latin metrical verse, one
of them about Theophilus (an early analogue of the Faust-legend), and
also panegyrics on Otto I, but is best known for her dramatic writings. Yet
to locate the beginnings of drama in Germany in the Ottonian period is at
best misleading. Hrotsvitha's Latin plays may never have been performed,
and they certainly had no successors. In a preface to her collection of six
short theological dialogues, all about pious ladies who either convert
pagans or are themselves converted, she explains that she is imitating the
comedies of the Roman dramatist Terence, and indeed, when in her
Dulcitius the eponymous central figure tries to seduce three Christian
women, he becomes mad and embraces pots and pans instead.

The church throughout the Middle Ages objected regularly to what we
have to call histrionic entertainment. In the development of an officially
sanctioned drama it is not Hrotsvitha who attracts our interest, but a tiny
piece of dialogue once thought to have been composed at St Gallen
(specifically by a monk called Tutilo at the start of the tenth century), and
certainly known there: the so-called *Quem quæritis* trope. Tropes were a
dramatic embellishment to the Mass, developed especially at St Gallen,
although also at the French monastery of St Martial in Limoges, and there
is debate as to which was the home of this dialogue between the angel and
the Maries at the sepulchre. The angel asks 'whom do you seek', and then
announces that Christ has risen. The fragment may have been created as a
dramatic scene for use in ceremonial paraliturgical services held before
Mass, and from this small beginning developed, slowly and over a long
period, in Latin at first, with German texts coming far later, the resurrection play and the drama of the medieval church.

Notker

Notker III of St Gallen (distinguished this time by the appellation 'labeo'
('thick-lipped') or 'teutonicus' ('the German')) also felt the need to justify

writing in German. Notker (*c.* 950–1022) was a schoolmaster who wrote texts for use in the teaching of the *trivium*, and while some of his writings are in Latin, he wrote in about 1015 to Bishop Hugo of Sion explaining his essentially pedagogical use of the vernacular. Again not really a literary figure, Notker demonstrates an increasing skill in the handling of German by providing working translations of standard textbooks like Martianus Capella's *Marriage of Mercury and Philosophy*, Boethius's *Consolation of Philosophy*, and the Psalter. He favoured what has been called a 'Mischsprache', in which the Latin is accompanied sentence by sentence by a German version, plus a commentary in Latin and then German, with some Latin words untranslated as a prompt for the learner to assimilate them. Thus at the beginning of Boethius's *Consolation*, Lady Philosophy is described as having eyes 'that see beyond those of ordinary men'. Notker translates literally ('dúrhnóhtôr séhentên. tánne îoman ménniskôn séhen múge'), and adds '*Ióh* profunda dei *gesíhet* philosophia' ('and Philosophy sees also the *profunda dei*, God's profundity'). Notker's coinages and his consistent rendering of the sense are striking, and he also developed a coherent orthography for his Alemannic dialect. Notker's works were much copied (especially the Psalter), and his 'Mischsprache' recurs later in the eleventh century in the writings of Williram and continues well into the twelfth (see N. F. Palmer's edition of the 'Klosterneuburger Bußpredigten', 1989). Preserved within Notker's writings, finally, are a few brief German poems and some proverbs. Of the former, one describes the clash of warriors and the other a monstrous boar; both illustrate rhetorical devices, and are probably of classical rather than Germanic origin.

Notker was aware, finally, of an historical end that could be near. The German preface to his Boethius-translation opens with a reference to St Paul's prophecy that the day of judgement will not come until the fall of Rome, and Notker links this with Theoderic, who, as ruler of Rome, had Boethius killed. Theoderic, too, died, and the Goths were driven out, and then came the Lombards, who ruled for more than two centuries, and 'náh langobardis franci. tîe uuír nû héizên chârlinga. náh ín saxones. Sô íst nû zegángen romanvm imperivm. náh tîen uuórten sancti pauli apostoli' ('after the Lombards the Franks, whom we call the Carolingians, and after them the Saxons, so that the *imperium romanum* has now passed away, as *Paulus Apostolus* predicted').

Beside the scraps of German in the works of Notker are others which, while evidence (of a sort) for vernacular literary activity, cannot be afforded much prominence (St. LXXIX-LXXXVIII). They are usually so opaque that the over-interpretation to which they are often subjected must be viewed as suspect. Thus the nine-word *Hirsch und Hinde* (*Hart and hind*, St. LXXIX), from the upper margin of a manuscript now in Brussels, with musical notation above and a Latin line below, consists apparently of an alliterative line and a half, meaning 'the hart whispered into the hind's ear / will you, hind . . .'. The piece has been connected with folk-plays and fertility festivals, without substantial conclusions. Similarly cautious comments must be made about a number of little verses from manuscripts in St Gallen, including one that appears to be a lampoon, telling how Starzfidere returned a wife to Liubwin (St. LXXXII/2); others barely admit of *any* interpretation. There are also some proverbs (St. LXXXVI), some oddments of translation, and a few German 'probationes pennae'. One final small rhymed poem is now lost, but was once carved over a school or library, probably in the late ninth century. It was copied by the map-maker Mercator to decorate his town plan of Cologne in 1571; the *Cologne inscription* (Lb. IV, 1) promises that this is where 'reward, wisdom and fame' may be found.

Latin literature in the eleventh century

With some Latin texts we can be fairly sure that a German original lies behind them. In the *De Carolo Magno* there is an anecdote about a wit ('quidam scurra') referring in front of Charlemagne to a nobleman called Uodalrich, who lost his lands when he lost his sister; this caused the merciful emperor to restore them. An identifiable historical event lies behind this, but since the Latin prose suggests a rhyme in German, scholars have reconstructed an 'original' in Old High German, though it would be an early instance of end-rhyme indeed (MSD VIII). There are references elsewhere to rhymed Latin phrases having been declaimed 'in Teutonico eleganter' ('in neat German'), and a Latin version of the riddle of the snowflake ('the bird flying without feathers') probably had a German alliterative original. Almost certainly there are German phrases behind the Latin legend of the *Dancers of Kölbigk*, which refers to events supposedly in 1021, when some young men were doomed to dance forever by God for trying to abduct a girl. Clearest of all is the case of the German poem on St Gall by Ratpert, a fellow-student of Notker Balbulus in St Gallen, who died in about 890. His 'carmen barbaricum' ('German song') was translated into the more acceptable medium of Latin by Ekkehart IV of St Gall, who was born towards the end of the tenth and died in the mid eleventh century. Three versions, in Ekkehart's own hand, of an accented metrical Latin poem of seventeen strophes of five long-lines each survive. Ekkehart mentions the melody of the original, so that the two forms may have matched, but deducing a German original is difficult. The text contains hagiographical commonplaces, such as St Gall's mastery of the animals, his refusal of a bishopric, and the carrying of his soul to heaven by St Michael, as well as the story of the chain he wore about his body as a penance.

Latin writings in Germany in the eleventh century include the much-read commentaries of the aristocratic Bruno of Würzburg (d. 1045), and later the conservative theological writings of Rupert of Deutz (1070–1129), which stand out against the new dialectic of scholasticism. Two scholars deserve special mention. The first, Otloh of St Emmeram (c. 1010–70), translated one of his prayers for the forgiveness of sins into Old High German (St. xxxv), but against that must be set a profusion of Latin theological texts and poems, a collection of proverbs, and lives of bishops and saints, including one of St Boniface, written specifically to replace that by Boniface's kinsman Willibald in the eighth century. The second, Hermann the Lame (Her[i]mannus Contractus, of Reichenau, 1013–54), also produced a mass of Latin material, in spite of what we know from contemporary descriptions to have been serious physical disabilities. He wrote on world history, astronomy, mathematics and music, and his complex and linguistically inventive sequences are typified by the use of adapted Greek words.

An interesting pendant to the hagiography of this later period is the *De Mahumete* by Embricho of Mainz (who became bishop of Augsburg in 1064), which presents in verse various legends of Mohammed from a Christian point of view. Historians include Thietmar (975–1018), related to Otto I and later bishop of Merseburg, author of the important and lengthy *Chronicon* (containing documentation of German–Slav relations) which celebrated the new Ottonian *imperium*; and Wipo (d. c. 1050), chaplain to Conrad II. He wrote a eulogy for Conrad's predecessor, Henry the Saint, and his *Gesta Chuonradi* remains the principal source for Conrad's reign, although he is still known for the famous Easter sequence *Victimae paschalis*. Later still come chroniclers like Adam of Bremen, who wrote around 1075 a detailed history of the archbishopric of Hamburg–Bremen with a wealth of comments on the Vikings.

Religious and other poetry continued to flourish in Latin. Froumund of Tegernsee (c. 960 to c. 1008) produced epistolary poems in the tradition of Alcuin, for example, and two German poets wrote longer works of some importance under pseudonyms. Sextus Amarcius (described later as 'satiricus, amator honestatis' ('a satirist and lover of the truth')) wrote four books of *Sermones* (a title he borrowed from Horace), directly spoken verses and dialogues, dealing satirically with sins and virtues. In one poem, three songs sung by a minstrel are identifiable as from the *Cambridge songs*, including that on the snow-baby. Eupolemius, whose real name is also unknown, wrote towards the end of the eleventh century a fascinating and difficult long *Messiad* in two books, in all nearly fifteen hundred hexameters, centring upon a battle between the forces of God (here called Agatus) and evil (Cacus), after the serpent (Ophites) has attacked Adam (Antropus); when Messias, the son of Agatus is killed, Cacus's forces fail, and the righteous are redeemed.

Two final Latin poems of the eleventh century demand attention: the romance of *Ruodlieb*, and the beast-narrative known as the *Ecbasis cuiusdam captivi per tropologiam* (*The escape of a certain prisoner, moralised*. The first is a series of eighteen fragments (about 2,300 partly damaged lines) from Tegernsee of an extended version of the folk-tale usually known as 'the three points of wisdom'. In its basic form (it is found in the medieval collection of anecdotes known as the *Gesta Romanorum* and in languages as diverse as Irish and Cornish), a servant is given pieces of advice in lieu of payment; he is not to leave an old road for a new one, not to lodge where an old man has a young wife, and not to act in anger. His real payment is baked into a cake. Here, the young nobleman Ruodlieb, having served a king, is given *twelve* points of wisdom, as well as gold concealed in two loaves, and although *Ruodlieb* is clearly more ramified than the folk-tale, the witnessing by the central figure of the murder of an old man by his young wife's lover, is present. The last fragments we have are concerned with Ruodlieb's search for a wife, and as far as can be made out, the wife suggested for him has had a previous affair with a cleric. Ruodlieb sends her a messenger with a love-declaration (which contains four words of Old High German) but also with evidence of her previous indiscretions. This clearly diverges from the folk-tale, and the text we have does not cover all twelve pieces of advice, if indeed, this was ever the intention.

The *Ecbasis captivi* (1,200 Leonine hexameters, with classical borrowings) represents another genre, the animal fable in moralised Christian form. An outer plot tells how a runaway calf falls into the clutches of a wolf, who feeds it well for one night, prior to eating it. The wolf's account of his hatred of the fox now forms the content of the Aesopian inner fable (used again later in German in the writing of Heinrich der Glîchezâre), in which the fox finds a cure for the sick lion which involves flaying a wolf. Meanwhile a dog has raised the alarm with the other animals, and brings them to the wolf's lair. When we return to the outer story, the wolf is tricked into emerging, and is gored by the bull, so that the calf escapes and returns home. The promised allegorical implications are made clear: the wolf represents the wiles of the world.

Late Old High German prose

A bridge back to the vernacular is provided in the person of Williram, well born and educated at Fulda, and after that a teacher at Bamberg, who died in 1085 after thirty-seven years as abbot of the small monastery of Ebersberg. In around 1060 he produced an exposition of the biblical Song of Songs that remained influential, with one manuscript copy as late as 1523, not much more than a century before it became the object of philological study by the Dutch scholar Francis Junius in 1655. Williram's *Expositio in Cantica Canticorum* is formally unfamiliar, and its German component is limited. The major manuscripts have three sometimes ornately separated columns, the central one containing in large script the Vulgate text. The left-hand column has a Latin paraphrase in hexameters, while on the right is a prose commentary in a mixture of German and Latin. Williram sent a copy to the emperor Henry IV, with a poem expressing his general dissatisfaction with Ebersberg and hope for preferment.

The three sections belong together, although the German/Latin portion was adapted in the later *St. Trudperter Hohelied*, and was sometimes (though not often) copied independently. However, on other occasions even the German parts were translated into Latin. Williram's work is a late example of the *opus geminatum*, each part having a separate function, the hexameters enhancing and explaining, the 'Mischsprache' clarifying the text for a different audience. Its content is not original: much derives from Latin commentaries which allegorise the Song of Songs as a dialogue between Christ and the Church. Indeed, Williram claims in his preface that 'de meo nihil addidi' ('I have added nothing of my own'), and he is studiedly conservative, complaining that an excess of dialectic has obscured biblical interpretation.

More clearly literary is the brief text known as *Himmel und Hölle* (*Heaven and hell*, St. XXIX and Wilhelm IX), composed probably in the latter part of the eleventh century. Sometimes described and printed as a poem, it is, however, a prose picture of heaven and hell in balanced rhythmic units ('cola'), German rhetorical prose with occasional 'homoioteleuton'. What lies behind the composition is unclear, although it may have some link with the *Bamberg confession* (St. XXVIII), which precedes it in the manuscript. The language is remarkable, though; heaven ('God's celestial fortress') appears 'in goldes sconi, samo daz durhliehte glas, alliu durhscowig ioh durhluter' ('like translucent glass in its golden beauty, quite transparent and pure'), whilst in hell there is deathless death in 'daz richiste trisehus alles unwunnes' ('the richest storehouse of all misfortunes'), the phrase concluding a sonorous and impressive accumulation of such images.

One late translation into Old High German is of intrinsic interest. The *Physiologus* (St. XXVII) has a history going back to the second century as a description of real and mythical animals and birds. In the Middle Ages the creatures acquired religious interpretations, and the unicorn, for example, which can according to legend only be captured by a virgin, is seen as Christ. Its single horn indicates the unity of the Father and the Son, and its capture the Virgin Birth. The Old High German *Physiologus* contains only twelve chapters, and omits most of the biblical quotations found in Latin versions. It was written as a space-filler at the end of a manuscript of the writings of Alcuin (with other mythological and theological texts and some German glosses), breaking off in mid-sentence at the end of a page, but that it should be rendered into German at all depends probably as much upon interest in the animals as in the theology.

Contrary to expectations, Old High German has little to show in the way of vernacular sermons, and even the eleventh century offers only a series of fragments salvaged in part from a manuscript used in bookbinding at Wessobrunn (St. xxx, xxxii, xxxiii). These are still, like the few earlier pieces, largely from patristic sources. Of the three groups distinguished, the first has three fragments of sermons by Augustine, the second four from Gregory the Great on the Gospels, and the third some Lenten material largely from Bede. The sermons were intended either for preaching in the language, or for reading. Associated with them, and specifically with the first group, since the scribe appears to be the same, is a collection of *Geistliche Ratschläge* (*Spiritual precepts*, St. xxi), based upon Gregory's commentary on Ezechiel. Not until well into the twelfth century do we find more complete vernacular sermon collections, again designed either for reading or as handbooks for preaching. A Benediktbeuern collection from the mid twelfth century, for example, known as the *Speculum Ecclesiae* (*Mirror of the Church*), contains sermons of varying lengths, not in strict liturgical order, and sometimes with more than one for a given feast. Again they are partly from patristic and Carolingian sources, but some are from the new French school, specifically from the writings of Hildebert of Le Mans, who died in 1133, or the early twelfth-century writer Honorius Augustodunensis. However, the *Speculum Ecclesiae* and the influence of the French schoolmen take us beyond our limits.

The time of the Salian emperors Conrad II (1024–39), Henry III (1039–56) and Henry IV (1056–1106) coincides broadly with the beginning of the early Middle High German period. Changes in the language (most notably the loss or weakening of the many unstressed full vowels in Old High German) become noticeable in writing after about 1050, and there is a transition period of about a century and a half before the language settles. Although attempts were made to identify these language changes with a new spirit in German literature, there is no basis for doing so. There is a gradual increase in the *amount* of German written, but its status is still low. The period *was* one of monastic reforms (including that associated with the monastery of Cluny, in France), but there are no real effects upon German literature. One difference, however, is the shift in vernacular writing from the monasteries to the schools associated with the cathedrals. Where writers like Otloh and Williram were monks, named writers are now described often as secular priests or canons.

Early Middle High German religious literature

Virtually all of the German material in the Salian period *is* religious, and most of it develops from what has gone before. Thus the essential mixture in Otfrid of narrative and often homiletic commentary is found in the second part of the eleventh century in metrical adaptations of Genesis and Exodus. A twelfth-century all-German codex now in Vienna (whence the names *Wiener Genesis* and *Exodus*) contains the two biblical poems (written out consecutively, with rhyme-points), and between them an assonantic prose version of the *Physiologus* which is longer than the Old High German version. There has been some discussion over the form of the poems, although a short couplet style seems already to be replacing Otfrid's rhymed long-line. In content, the poems draw on the authorities just as much as Otfrid did, however. Thus the creation of Adam is expanded on the basis of medieval encyclopaedias to a detailed physical description considering even the function of his little finger for digging in the ear to enable him to hear clearly, and the poet attaches to the promise made to Eve that she will 'bruise the serpent's head' (Genesis iii,15) a homiletic excursus (derived from Carolingian Latin commentaries) of nearly a hundred lines on the theme of stopping sin as soon as it begins. If the Genesis-poet was a secular canon (as is possible), the implied audience might, however, be a lay one.

The eleventh-century material of the Vienna manuscript was reworked towards the end of the twelfth century. The new version, the Millstatt codex, has the *Physiologus* in rhymed form, and a very large number of illustrations, while a further German collective codex from Vorau in Styria (which also contains the *Kaiserchronik*) has a rather different adaptation of the first part of the Old Testament in the *Vorauer Bücher Mosis* (although the Joseph-narrative overlaps with the Vienna version), plus a number of shorter religious poems. In the same tradition is the fragmentary *Central Franconian rhymed Bible* of the early twelfth century, while the apocalyptic vision of doomsday recurs both in independent poems and in the writing of the first vernacular woman poet, Ava, probably an Austrian nun who died in the early twelfth century, and whose works cover, as did Otfrid's, both the life of Christ and the last judgement.

Shorter religious poems maintain the conservative-homiletic tone, and the year 1100 can only be an arbitrary cut-off point. One earlier poem that may be monastic *in origin* is found as a filler at the end of a manuscript of

Gregory the Great's *Moralia*. The work is known as *Memento mori* (there is no title in the original) and capitals indicate nineteen strophes of four long-lines each, though a few lines are missing in the middle. The work is perhaps by Noker (the name appears in the last line), abbot of Zwiefalten (d. 1095), and contrasts once more the perils of the world and the delights of paradise. It is addressed to 'wib und man', 'men and women', but indicates that people are, though all descended from Adam, different in ability and status. Like *Muspilli*, this poem stresses that no one (however rich) can avoid the final judgement, and again an aristocratic lay audience seems to be implied.

Another space-filler in the same manuscript is *Ezzos Gesang* (*Ezzo's hymn*). Only seven strophes were written here, but in the Vorau codex is a twelfth-century augmented reworking of it. One of the additions is a prefatory verse telling how this 'song of the miracles of Christ', was written at the behest of Bishop Gunther of Bamberg (d. 1064), with the words by a 'canonicus' named Ezzo and the (lost) melody by Wille. Even the early fragment demonstrates its poetic skill in the concentration of fall and redemption into one 12–line strophe, which takes us from the darkness at Adam's fall, through the time of the prophets, whose light shone only dimly, until in the devil's 'nebiluinster naht' ('black, miasmic night') appeared (shone) the true sun, the son of God. The word-plays and sustained balance of light and dark are effective. The earlier version is addressed to 'iv herron' ('my lords'), which is changed in the Vorau text to 'iv . . . allen' ('all of you'), so that it was clearly aimed originally at aristocratic laymen. A far later fragmentary poem, the *Scopf von dem lône* (*Poem of reward*), written probably in the late twelfth century by a secular canon at the Cathedral of St Martin in Colmar points out, with reference to the tax-gatherer Zachaeus and to St Martin, that the *rich* can also enter the kingdom of heaven (in spite of Luke xviii, 24) if they lead proper lives. The motif is unsurprising with literature aimed at a particular class, that for which *Muspilli* or *Memento Mori* was intended. *Reimpredigt* (rhymed sermon) is a term of slightly dubious validity, but the direct homiletic tone remains a key feature of early German poetry.

Some vernacular poems are problematic. That known as *Merigarto* (*The world*), from the last part of the eleventh century is in places now extremely hard even to decipher. The first part of this strophic poem (which has some Latin headings) describes seas, real and otherwise, and after another heading which refers to an unidentifiable Bishop Reginbert, goes on to say how a wise man in Utrecht had told the poet (who seems to have fled there from Bavaria in time of war) about a visit to Iceland and of its geography. The rest of the work is to do with rivers, dwelling largely on magical or thaumaturgic properties, and one of the sources of this last part is the encylopaedic work by Hrabanus Maurus (or its source,

Isidore's *Etymologies*). Frankly, very little can be made of this hydrographic enigma, although it does demonstrate the continuity of Carolingian learning.

Moving from obscure geography to clearer history, but with theology still firmly in control, the *Annolied* (*The lay of Anno*) (composed probably at Siegburg in around 1080, but which has survived only in a copy made of it by Martin Opitz in 1639) is a generically complex work, historical, panegyric and hagiographic. Anno II, the extremely powerful (though not always entirely scrupulous) archbishop of Cologne and regent for Henry IV, died in 1075 and was canonised in 1183, although the poem (the date of which is fixed by a reworked section in the *Kaiserchronik*), refers to him as a saint already. Nearly nine hundred rhymed lines in couplets, divided into forty-nine strophes, present first a brief history of the world from Adam to Anno (1–7), making clear once more the contrast between Adam's fall and the incarnation before moving on to the saints of Cologne and then to Anno, the latest saint given to the Franks. The second section (8–33) describes the four ages of the world based on interpretations of the dream in Daniel vii,1–28, taking us down to Rome, and then looking at the histories of various German tribes, Swabians, Bavarians, Saxons and Franks. The latter are the inheritors of the Trojans, since the mythical eponym Franko builds 'eini luzzele Troie' ('a litle Troy'), on the Rhine, and of the Romans, who built Colonia (Cologne). The poem now moves rapidly from the earliest stages of Christianity, and again to the Franks and Anno. The final strophes (34–49) are hagiographic, presenting Anno as the 'vatir aller weisin' ('father of orphans'), founder of monasteries (including Siegburg), and stressing his political role. After his death, healing miracles are associated with him.

The *Annolied* has some relationship with Latin genres: chronicles, hagiographic *vitae* and local historical writing. Its mixture of theological and secular harks back to the *Ludwigslied* in some respects, and there are echoes, too, of Otfrid, in the linking of the Franks with the ancient world. Otfrid simply stated that the Franks were as good as the Romans or Greeks, but the *Annolied* places them more firmly into an historical context which is, unlike Notker's, onward-looking. The divine economy of fall and redemption is present in the poem as well, however, as is the parenetic didacticism of so much early Middle High German writing; Anno entered the heavenly paradise and we should keep his example in mind. The theology is hardly new. What is different is this combination of genres in a German-language poem celebrating both a German saint and at the same time his people. It is a nice historical accident that the work was discovered by Martin Opitz, the author of *Das Buch von der deutschen Poeterey* (1624).

2

The high and later Middle Ages
(1100–1450)

NIGEL F. PALMER

Introduction

What marks out the German literature of the period 1100 to 1450 is the emergence and establishment of an autonomous German literary culture in written form, such as had not existed in the previous period. From the late eleventh century onwards it is possible to see a realignment of the relationship between German writings and Latin writings, and between written literature in the vernacular and oral tradition.

Let us take just one area as an example. The new German vernacular biblical epic in couplet verse begins in the second half of the eleventh century with the *Altdeutsche Genesis* (also known as the *Vienna Genesis*, most likely *c.* 1060–1100), continues in the twelfth century with the *Altdeutsche Exodus* (probably *c.* 1100–30), the biblical poems of Frau Ava (probably d. 1127), the *Vorauer Bücher Mosis* (*The Vorau Books of Moses*, probably *c.* 1130–40), the *Anegenge* (*The beginning*, probably 1170–80) and the *Kindheit Jesu* (*The childhood of Christ*) by Konrad von Fußesbrunnen (probably *c.* 1190–1200).[1] These major narrative texts in Middle High German provide a literary context for the *Mittelfränkische Reimbibel* (*The Central Franconian rhymed Bible*), an extensive compendium of Old and New Testament matter including stories of the martyrs and early Christian history in German verse (early twelfth-century, only fragments survive); for the *Annolied* (*The song of Anno, c.* 1077–81), where for the first time historiographical matters are addressed in German verse; and for the first European vernacular chronicle in verse, the mid-twelfth-century *Kaiserchronik* (*The chronicle of the emperors*). We know of no directly comparable traditions of written narrative literature in German before this period – notwithstanding Otfrid and the

---

[1] As far as possible titles of texts are cited in the form given in the standard reference work for medieval literature in Germany: *Die deutsche Literatur des Mittelalters. Verfasserlexikon*, 2nd revised edn by Kurt Ruh et al., 9 vols. to date (A–T), Berlin and New York, 1978–95. As a rule the dates attached to the names of people give the years when they are attested, when they are thought to have been engaged in literary composition, or in the case of princes and ecclesiastical figures the years of their rule.

shorter Old High German poems. The primary audience for which all these works were intended was to be found in the monasteries, and one of the principal functions of the German narrative poems was in all probability to provide matter to be read during meals, as was prescribed by all monastic rules. Lay brothers and those monks who had entered the order later in life, rather than as child oblates, were as a rule illiterate and could only understand readings in German. Thus it is that a body of German literature grew up that was designed for community recitation and which did not slavishly imitate Latin. It could develop its own conventions of poetic form, tonality, affective engagement with an audience and literary structure in response to the needs of a specific historical situation. The materials presented in the works named had all been gathered from authoritative Latin sources, but these works are for the most part not simply translated from Latin.

The world of oral poetry is recalled for a moment in the *Annolied*. The poem begins with famous lines directing the community to turn its backs on those songs on profane subjects which it had in the past favoured and to 'think of how we will all meet our end' – and to do so inspired by the life of Bishop Anno. This polemical passage sets the poetic life of the bishop of Cologne in a relationship to profane oral poetry, which the author condemns: 'how bold heroes fought, how they destroyed well fortified cities, how close friendships were brought to an end, how mighty kings came to grief'. Such oral tales, which might have told of the sack of Troy, the friendship of Roland and Oliver, or the downfall of King Gunther of Worms and his brothers Gernot and Giselher, formed an essential part of medieval literary culture, but in their oral form they lie outside literary history. The author of the *Annolied*, who is engaged in winning attention for his religious theme, aggressively divides the world of poetry into two, so as to divorce his own subject matter completely from the secular songs. But his polemic is equally an attestation of the proximity of the two domains, and certainly in the earlier part of the period audiences must have been aware of numerous associations between the German texts read out from books and oral tales that were told. One of the earliest secular narrative texts in German, Lambrecht's *Alexanderlied* (*Song of Alexander*), displays its affinity with the biblical epics by the repeated comments drawing attention to places mentioned in the Bible, and yet the author also compares Alexander's battle against Duke Mennes with that fought by heroes of oral poetry, Hagen and Wate, on the Wolfenwerde (in *Kudrun* called the Wulpensant) and with those described in the 'songs of the Trojans' (1331). In practice, the literary culture of the period spans and unites the religious and the secular domains in a manner that is not self-evident to the modern student. But there are tensions here, as we have seen, and the most important literary developments in the twelfth century stand in a relationship to the tensions that exist between such categories as 'oral' and 'written', 'fictional' and 'true', 'secular' and 'religious'.

The sources that might shed light on the circumstances of literary production in this period are for the most part indirect, or they are passages contained in literary works, where they have their own particular function and set out facts that need not necessarily be historically 'true'. This holds, for example, for Hartmann von Aue's self-representation as an author in *Iwein*, for Heinrich von Veldeke's account of how his work on the *Eneide* was broken off and taken up again for a new patron, or Pfaffe Konrad's statements about the composition of a Latin intermediary version of the *Chanson de Roland* in the course of his composition of the *Rolandslied* for Henry the Lion. Major works could only be written with the support of a patron, and may in some cases have been discontinued when that support failed (for example through the death of the patron). That could have been the case with Gottfried von Straßburg's *Tristan* and with the *Willehalm* of Wolfram von Eschenbach.

It must in general be supposed that the authors entrusted with the composition of written works could themselves read and write, and that, where adaptation from another language was required, they had the necessary linguistic skills. There are, however, cases of authors such as Wirnt von Grafenberg (*c.* 1210–25) and Konrad von Würzburg (*c.* 1257–87) who claim to have had access to their French sources through an interpreter. Wolfram von Eschenbach claims to have been illiterate, but that statement is more likely to be a manoeuvre to claim for himself the cultural perspective of the lay nobility than a factual statement. Patrons and audiences, however, will in many cases have been truly illiterate, or have had too scanty an education to master the task of reading right through a German literary text. Written literature was for the most part read out from the book to an audience, but by the end of the twelfth century there may already have been some private reading. The route to that skill lay through elementary instruction in Latin, such as was needed for reading prayers and the Psalter. It is not until the later Middle Ages that there is evidence of reading in German being taught as the first language. Among those who were able to read books for themselves women are likely to have been considerably more numerous than men. The scene in Hartmann's *Iwein*, where a young woman reads to her parents, or the miniature portraits of Landgrave Hermann of Thuringia and his wife Sophia of Wittelsbach in an early thirteenth-century luxury Psalter (the *Landgrafenpsalter*), where the countess alone is portrayed holding a book, are typical examples of the alignment of women and literary culture, which is frequently indicated in the sources.

Twelfth-century secular narrative

This account of 350 years of literary history will have to be selective, but as a first step let us consider, in précis, a complete tabulation of secular narrative literature in the twelfth century. Eighteen such works have survived. The *Nibelungenlied* (*Song of the Nibelungs*) and *Klage* (*Lament*), which were both composed some time around 1200, are omitted in order to allow these poems to be considered in the context of a slightly later period. The same applies to the *Lanzelet* of Ulrich von Zatzikhoven (*c.* 1194–1205). Three works that strictly speaking belong to the literary history of the later Middle Ages are counted in, the 'Spielmannsepen' *Oswald*, *Orendel* and *Salman und Morolf*, on the grounds that the surviving texts, all from the fifteenth century, are likely to derive from twelfth-century poems. The inclusion of these works, which take their name from the professional performers ('Spielleute') who were once thought to have composed them, will add a further dimension to the problem of literary chronology – and also serve to remind of a problem. Many of the twelfth-century poems continued to exert an influence, either directly or in a modified form, throughout the medieval period (and in the case of *Tristrant*, *Oswald*, the *Metamorphosen* and *Salman und Morolf* even as printed editions). Consequently the tabulation of twelfth-century texts can provide a basis for the discussion of narrative literature throughout the whole period which follows.

Kaiserchronik (*The chronicle of the emperors*), 17,283 vv., couplet verse with assonance, 2nd quarter / mid-twelfth-century (initiated most likely in the 1130s, perhaps in the milieu of Henry the Proud, duke of Bavaria 1126–39, completed after 1146, first manuscript evidence from *c.* 1160–70), Bavarian (Regensburg).

Alexanderlied (*The song of Alexander*, by Pfaffe Lambrecht), 1,532 vv., couplet verse with assonance, mid-twelfth-century, most likely from the Rhine or Mosel, but preserved only in a Bavarian copy of *c.* 1200; based on the Occitan *Alexandre* of Alberic of Pisançon.

König Rother (*King Rother*), 5,204 vv., couplet verse with assonance, not before 1152 and more probably *c.* 1160–80 (MS of *c.* 1200), probably Bavarian, most likely for the family of the counts of Tengelingen, but preserved in an early manuscript from the Rhineland.

Herzog Ernst (*Duke Ernst*, version A), fragments of 324 vv., couplet verse with assonance (version B: 6,022 vv., rhyming couplets), *c.* 1160–80 (MS fragments from *c.* 1230), central Rhineland/Hessen, but quite likely written with a Bavarian public in mind.

Trierer Floyris, fragment of 368 vv., couplet verse with assonance, *c.* 1170

(MS from *c*. 1200), from the region of the Maas, but named, like the following item, after the library where the manuscript was preserved;
based on the OF *Floire et Blancheflor*.

Straßburger Alexander, 7,302 vv., couplet verse with assonance, *c*. 1170
(MS from *c*. 1189), central Rhineland/Hessen; revising and continuing
Lambrecht's *Alexanderlied*, and drawing additionally on the Latin
prose Alexander romance (*Historia de preliis*) and *Iter ad paradisum*.

Rolandslied (*The song of Roland*, by Pfaffe Konrad), 9,094 vv., couplet
verse with assonance, *c*. 1172 (the earliest manuscript evidence from *c*.
1200), composed for the court of Henry the Lion, duke of Saxony and
Bavaria (Regensburg or Braunschweig?); based on the OF *Chanson de
Roland*.

Eneide (by Heinrich von Veldeke), 13,528 vv., rhyming couplets, the
greater part before 1174 (1172?) but then broken off and completed
shortly after 1184 (earliest manuscript evidence from *c*. 1190–1200),
originally composed for a patron in the Rhineland or eastern
Netherlands, but completed at the court of Hermann, landgrave of
Thuringia; based on the OF *Roman d'Eneas*.

Oswald, 3,564 vv. (*Münchner Oswald*), couplet verse, *c*. 1170–80 (earliest
MS from *c*. 1435), most likely Bavarian (Regensburg?).

Graf Rudolf (*Count Rudolf*), fragments of 1,400 vv., couplet verse with
assonance, *c*. 1170–90 (MS of *c*. 1200), composed in the central
Rheinland/Hessen or Thuringia; based on a lost French poem associated with the OF *Beuve de Hantone* (*c*. 1215–25).

Erec (by Hartmann von Aue), 10,135 vv., rhyming couplets, *c*. 1180–1200
(generally placed before 1190), south-west Germany, possibly, although
there is no certainty about Hartmann's patronage, to be associated with
the milieu of Duke Berthold IV of Zähringen; based on Chrétien de
Troyes, *Erec et Enide*.

Tristrant (by Eilhart von Oberg), 9,524 vv., couplet verse with assonance,
most likely *c*. 1185–95, although some authorities still place it *c*. 1170
(before the first part of the *Eneide*); earliest MS evidence early thirteenth-century, probably written in the Low German area, in Eastfalia,
but making use of the Central German written language of Thuringia
and Hessen; based on a lost OF or Anglo-Norman Tristan poem.

Reinhart Fuchs (*Reinhart the Fox*, by Heinrich), extensive fragment of 488
vv. (thirteenth-century recension: 2,268 vv.), couplet verse with assonance, *c*. 1190–1200 (MS fragment from the early thirteenth century),
Alsace; based on a version of the OF *Roman de Renart*.

Iwein (by Hartmann von Aue), 8,166 vv., rhyming couplets, *c*. 1190–1205
(after *Erec* and *Gregorius*, alluded to by Wolfram von Eschenbach
shortly after 1203; earliest MS *c*. 1225), south-west Germany; based on
Chrétien de Troyes, *Yvain*.

Orendel, 3,937 vv., *c.* 1190, surviving only in a later redaction (MS dated 1477 and a printed edition of 1512); firmly associated with Trier.

Liet von Troye (*The song of Troy*, by Herbort von Fritzlar), 18,458 vv., rhyming couplets, *c.* 1190–1217 (more likely in the earlier part of this period; earliest MS evidence from later thirteenth century), composed for the court of Landgrave Hermann of Thuringia; based on the OF *Roman de Troie* of Benoît de Sainte-Maure and likely to have been conceived as a sequel to Veldeke's *Eneide*.

Metamorphosen (by Albrecht von Halberstadt), fragments of *c.* 570 vv. from an extensive poem (preserved otherwise only in a sixteenth-century reworking by Jörg Wickram), dated 1190 (or possibly 1210?; MS fragments from the later thirteenth century), composed at Jechaburg near Sonderhausen in Thuringia, perhaps under the patronage of Landgrave Hermann of Thuringia; based on the *Metamorphoses* of Ovid.

Salman und Morolf, 783 five-line strophes, composed in the later twelfth century , but surviving only in a later version copied in the second half of the fifteenth century, probably Rhenish.

The themes of these works reflect the interests and social position of the noble and princely patrons by whom they were commissioned, and for whose households they provided not only entertainment and instruction but also a public manifestation of political aspirations.

The first identifiable centre of literary patronage is Regensburg, a prosperous trading city with important monasteries, particularly St. Emmeram and the new twelfth-century foundation Prüfening, and the focal point of both the Duchy of Bavaria and the Diocese of Regensburg. Here, in the mid twelfth century, the composition of the *Kaiserchronik* is to be sought, the first vernacular chronicle of world history in any European language, tracing the history of the Holy Roman Empire from Julius Caesar to Konrad III, elaborating the account of the early emperors with legends and adventure stories (e.g. Crescentia, Faustinian and Silvester, Lucretia) and in the latter part providing brief résumés of political events in the Empire with particular praise for the emperor Lothar III (1125–37). Henry the Proud, duke of Saxony and Bavaria (1126–38) and Lothar's son-in-law, is the individual most likely to have been the instigator of the *Kaiserchronik* project, although it was not finished until some time after his death – and in what circumstances we do not know. Some passages at the beginning of the *Kaiserchronik*, in which essential principles of the author's programme are established, are based on the *Annolied*, which had been written in the Rhineland and may have been available in Regensburg as a consequence of the links established by Kuno I, bishop of Regensburg (1126–32), who had previously been abbot of

Anno's own monastery of Siegburg just south of Cologne. The ducal court, the bishop's court and the Regensburg monasteries combined uniquely to provide a context in which a major vernacular poem could be produced in which for the first time profane historical narrative outweighed religious concerns. Certainly the historiographical conception of the *Kaiserchronik* is founded on theology, but this widely read work provided a model that pointed towards new developments.

The only other examples of literary patronage in the twelfth century to which any real certainty attaches are the dedication of the *Rolandslied* to Henry the Lion, who was the son of Henry the Proud and duke of Saxony and Bavaria (1142/55–80), and that of the *Eneide* (in this case only for the completion of the work), the *Liet von Troye* and the *Metamorphosen*, all three reflecting a strong interest in antiquity and apparently commissioned by Hermann, Pfalzgraf of Saxony and later landgrave of Thuringia (lived *c.* 1155–1217). Some of the unnamed patrons will surely have been of lower social status, but they are all to be sought among the leading noble families. Judging from the information that has survived it seems unlikely that the kings and emperors of the period, for example Lothar III (1125–37), or the Staufen rulers Konrad III, Frederick I Barbarossa (1152–90) and Henry VI (1190–97), played any direct part in the promotion of vernacular narrative poetry, although the courts of Barbarossa and Henry VI seem to have cultivated the new style of love poetry ('Minnesang').

An association can be seen between some aspects of the subject matter of the *Rolandslied*, composed in the early 1170s, and the personal history of Duke Henry the Lion. The relevant themes are the veneration of the emperor Charlemagne, given new impetus by his canonisation in 1165, the interaction between the princes of the realm (represented by Roland and the peers) and emperor, and the crusade against the heathen. Duke Henry, as the leading member of the Welf faction, a powerful family with lands in Swabia and northern Italy and from the later eleventh century dukes of Bavaria, was the most powerful of the German princes during the first half century of Staufen rule and a potential rival of Frederick Barbarossa, although for much of the period up to the 1170s he was treated as a valued political ally. His court was at Braunschweig, but the *Rolandslied* has generally been associated with his second centre of power, Regensburg. On the basis of his family and his actual power he was able to present himself as a royal person: his maternal grandfather was the emperor Lothar III, and his second wife Matilda the daughter of King Henry II of England and Eleanor of Aquitaine. We find this projection of himself both in the iconographic programme of the manuscript illumination commissioned by Henry (especially in the 'Gospel-book of Henry the Lion') and in the epilogue to the *Rolandslied*. From the 1150s onwards he was involved in battles with the Slavs, leading to extensive Christianisation and colonisation of the eastern territories adjacent to Saxony. These campaigns and his journey to Jerusalem in 1172, undertaken in the spirit of a crusade, provide a point of reference for the crusading themes of the *Rolandslied*.

Hermann of Thuringia's patronage of the *Eneide* (*c.* 1174/84) promotes the contemporary imperial ideology from a quite different angle. The *Eneide* is derived at one remove from Vergil's *Aeneid*. It tells the story of how the Trojan duke Eneas flees to escape from the victorious Greeks after the sack of Troy and is subjected to years of wandering and a series of testing adventures, including a liaison with Dido queen of Carthage, a visit to the underworld, and prolonged battles against Duke Turnus in Italy. Finally he goes on to fulfil his destiny to marry Lavine, daughter of King Latin of Laurente, and to become ruler over all Italy. Eneas and Lavine found a dynasty that extends through the Roman kings and emperors to Augustus, during whose reign, we are told, Christ was born. This conclusion, which is the invention of the German poet, had special significance in the context of contemporary Staufen politics, in which Augustus Caesar was seen as a precursor of the Holy Roman Emperor Frederick Barbarossa. Further links with the world of the present are introduced by the claim that Barbarossa found the tomb of Pallas, a young man who died fighting for Eneas, with the lamp still burning, when he went to Italy to receive the imperial crown (in 1155); and by the statement that the wedding festival of Eneas and Lavine has only ever been surpassed by Barbarossa's festival at Mainz in 1184, when his sons were knighted. Through his association with the *Eneide* Hermann could be presented as a promoter of Staufen ideology. Hermann's patronage of the *Eneide*, taken together with his commissioning of the *Liet von Troye* and his association with Albrecht von Halberstadt's *Metamorphosen*, suggests that Hermann was interested in school-orientated subject matter that brought with it the prestige of Latin learning. This ideal of a literate and learned ruler who is a patron of literature was entirely new, especially in the German context, and puts him on a par with Count Henry I of Champagne and Philipp of Flanders who were noted patrons of French literature. When later Walther von der Vogelweide states 'Ich bin des milten lantgrâven ingesinde' ('I am a member of the landgrave's retinue': L. 35,7) and when both Walther (L. 20,4) and Wolfram von Eschenbach in *Parzival* (297,16–23) present a satirical picture of life at the Thuringian court, we can be quite certain that these works were performed at the court and that there was some real interaction between the poets and the landgrave. Towards the end of his life Hermann was also the patron of Wolfram von Eschenbach's *Willehalm* and is associated with his *Titurel*.

During this period the developments in German literature shadow those in French, with a time lag of some fifteen years. Ten of the eighteen works listed above are adaptations of French (or Occitan) poems. Such borrowings were unknown before the *Alexanderlied* of Pfaffe Lambrecht, which is generally placed in the middle of the twelfth century, although there is no good reason why it could not be somewhat later. The earliest adaptations from French were made in the west, where we can assume there to have been more frequent contact with the French nobility. The dynastic links of the German princes may also have played a part in bringing a taste for French culture to the Rhine and beyond. The marriage of Henry the Lion, for example, to the English princess Matilda in 1167 marks out the route by which the *Chanson de Roland* may have been transported from the French and Anglo-Norman world to Germany. Imitation of French also has an impact on the form of German poetry: the irregular rhythmical couplet form of the *Kaiserchronik* and the early German biblical epics, which freely mixes rhyme and assonance, is adapted under the influence of French octosyllabic verse to a more regular four-beat pattern, with a tendency to restrict the number of unstressed syllables, and with pure rhyme. A progression can be plotted through the *Straßburger Alexander*, the *Eneide* (the first poem to use pure rhyme) and *Iwein* on to the poets of the next generation, where in Gottfried von Straßburg (*c.* 1200–20) and later imitators there is a strong tendency towards a strict alternating rhythm combined with consistent purity of rhyme.

It should be noted that the exploitation of French models to create a new German literature took place in the context of a bilingual German–Latin literary culture, in which poetic adaptation from Latin did not achieve a comparable status. In poems such as the *Eneide, Erec* and *Iwein* translation becomes a dynamic process that embraces a reconstitution of the meaning of the text, the subject matter being recast to take account of the new historical circumstances, reinterpreting such elements as the depiction of knightly values, regal power and interpersonal relations (love, fidelity, pity, shame). The rhetorical principles of adaptation may have been based on what was taught, through the medium of Latin, at school, but the German narrative literature of the period established itself as a distinct entity in response to that of the French and Anglo-Norman courts.

The poets of these works, where they are not veiled in total anonymity, are but names and cannot be identified with persons known from other sources. The one possible exception is Eilhart von Oberg, the author of *Tristrant* (probably *c.* 1185–95), who could be the same person as the Welf ministerial whose name is known from charters, or a member of his family. A ministerial, or *ministerialis*, was a member of a group of originally unfree men who in Germany performed military and administrative functions for a lord, a minority of whom, engaged in the service of the imperial or princely families, came to exercise power equal to that of the *nobiles*. Setting aside those poems like the *Trierer Floyris* and *Graf Rudolf* whose anonymity may be due to their fragmentary nature, it can be observed that the poems with a named author are those that are adapted from a French or Latin source. It seems that composition as literary adaptation was conceived to be a more highly personalised activity than the poetic formulation of traditional subject matter (e.g. *König Rother*). All the poets with whom we are here concerned may be presumed to have undergone clerical training, learning to read and write in a monastery or cathedral school through the medium of Latin, and with the single exception of Hartmann their social status can best be described as that of the 'clerk' (*pfaffe*). Some will have been monks or canons, whereas others will have belonged to the clergy with minor orders – the numerous group of *clerici* who performed a range of duties requiring literacy or religious training for the princes and minor nobility. It must be envisaged, however, that there was a considerable degree of 'orality' involved in their poetic production – in the mode of composition, which is not to be imagined as being performed pen in hand, and in the recitation of their work to an audience. Whether the poets prepared their own manuscripts of their compositions, or whether rather the writing out of a text in the vernacular required the skill of a specialised scribe who would work from dictation, is hard to say. Certainly there are no grounds for supposing the German poets of this generation to have been illiterate – nor is it part of their image.

Pfaffe Lambrecht, Heinrich von Veldeke and Hartmann von Aue stand out, in that they are known as the authors of several works. Lambrecht's *Tobias*, Veldeke's *Servatius* and Hartmann's *Gregorius* and *Der arme Heinrich* (*Poor Henry*) are examples of religious legends from the later twelfth century composed by the authors of secular narrative poetry. Veldeke and Hartmann, like Wolfram von Eschenbach and Gottfried von Straßburg in the next generation, are also known as the poets of 'Minnesang' (that is, the courtly love lyric). Hartmann's position among the twelfth-century authors is also quite singular in that he describes himself as a layman and a member of the ministerial class (*Der arme Heinrich* 5), and as a 'learned knight who had read this tale in books, whenever he had no better use for his time he would occupy himself with writing poetry' (*Iwein* 21–5). These passages provide rare documentation of lay literacy at a time when in Germany there is as yet little evidence of men without clerical training being able to read. In Hartmann's case, however, clerical training cannot be said to be precluded by his status as *dienstman* ('ministerial'). The notion of literary composition in German as a pastime, rather than as an arduous task that necessitated beating out the inflexible material of vernacular language on an anvil (so described in the prologue of the *Pilatus* fragment, 1–9), to meet the commission of a patron, implies that the authority of the poetic work lies with the knightly poet himself, and marks out a new conception of fictional literature.

Dominant themes of the twelfth-century poems are journeying, warfare and the bridal quest, appealing to the military and dynastic components in the ambitions of the noble families and also dominant elements of the international oral tradition, on which the German poems and their French sources could freely draw. Of these, journeying is undoubtedly the most striking single element, for it provided a framework for the traditional military subject matter of the *Rolandslied* and the *Alexanderlied*, it could be used to articulate the testing of the hero in poems such as *Herzog Ernst*, the *Eneide* and the Arthurian romance, and it is also the basic material of the wooing expedition (e.g. *König Rother*, *Tristrant, Orendel*) and of stories of separation (*Floyris, Tristrant*, the Faustinian and Crescentia legends in the *Kaiserchronik*). In the *Rolandslied* (*c.* 1172) the route of Karl's campaign embraces the whole story. Initially the Franks press on into Spain, then peace is made with the heathen emperor Marsilie through Genelun's treachery so that Karl can turn about and return to Aachen, while Roland remains and dies in battle with Marsilie; Karl then makes the journey back from Aachen to Spain to take revenge. The plot of the *Straßburger Alexander*, written about the same time, is similarly structured by military campaigns which take him back and forward across the rivers Euphrates and Strage in his struggle against Darius, then to India, and finally to Paradise. The cyclical aspect, which is already apparent in the story of Alexander, becomes the foundation of the narrative structure in tales of wooing such as *König Rother* (*c.* 1160–80). Here the unsuccessful wooing expedition for the daughter of King Constantine by proxy is followed, in a second cycle, by Rother's own expedition disguised as an exiled warrior, and then in a third cycle, after the princess has been snatched back, Rother conducts his final military expedition against King Constantine and the heathen invaders and wins the princess back once more. The parallelism of narrative cycles imposes an implicit comparison of what has been achieved in different parts of the poem on the audience. It is also an aesthetic principle creating unity.

The interpretability of structures that require the audience to relate elements in different parts of a story to one another, whether this is achieved through a pattern of cycles, through the parallelism of episodes (for example in *Tristrant*) or through polarities of other kinds (for example, Dido and Eneas's common fate as exiles, Erec and Mabonagrin as victims of love), comes to be the hallmark of twelfth-century fiction. Its most distinctive development was the Arthurian romance, a genre originating in north-western France during the period *c.* 1160–85, and in which a distinctive narrative structure was designed, that could accommodate the essentially episodic materials of oral poetry to the pursuit of a coherent literary programme. These works are no longer biographical in character, giving the whole story of a character's life (cf. *Alexanderlied, Tristrant*), but rather present an elaborately structured episode spread over some months or years and imposing its own meaning. Historical veracity is not now needed as a source of authority, and the action is set in a fantasy world cut off from the historical present. The historical position found in works such as the *Eneide* (pointing forward to the Holy Roman Empire) and *König Rother* (where the hero is revealed to be the grandfather of Charlemagne) has now been abandoned. The author may himself claim the authority for the content of his work, which is his own fiction (or in the case of a German adaptor, such as Hartmann von Aue, a work of fiction for which he assumes authority). The new position taken up by an author such as Hartmann did not embrace the originality that is expected of the author of a modern novel, but the way was now open for all the experimentation with fictionality that is to be found in the later genre of the European novel.

The originator of the literary genre of the Arthurian romance is in fact the French poet from Champagne, Chrétien de Troyes. Through the reception of his work in German, as also in Middle English and Old Norse, Chrétien came to have a quite decisive influence on the development of narrative poetry across Europe. His first surviving poem seems to be *Erec et Enide* (c. 1170, although a later date has also been proposed), followed by *Cligès* (c. 1176), *Le Chevalier de la Charrette* (c. 1177–81, completed by Godefroi de Lagny), *Chevalier au Lion* or *Yvain* (c. 1177–81), *Conte du Graal* or *Perceval* (c. 1181–90, unfinished). A Tristan romance, mentioned in the *Cligès* prologue, is lost. *Le Chevalier de la Charrette* (*Lancelot*) was apparently commissioned by Marie de Champagne, wife of Henry I, count of Champagne (1152–81, married 1164), whereas Chrétien's last work, the *Conte du Graal* was commissioned by Philip of Alsace, count of Flanders (d. 1191). His playful, often ironic authorial stance and his rhetorical skills mark him out as a writer deeply indebted to the northern French schools, but who wore his learning lightly; a sophisticated littérateur of a quite different order from any of his German contemporaries. *Erec* and *Yvain* were both swiftly adapted by Hartmann von Aue and together form the basis of the German Arthurian tradition. A second version of *Erec*, corresponding partly to Hartmann's text, but partly derived directly from Chrétien, survives only as a short fragment (*Wolfenbüttler Erec*). The *Conte du Graal* forms the basis of Wolfram von Eschenbach's *Parzival* (c. 1200–10). No German version of *Le Chevalier de la Charrette*, which introduces an entirely new element by allowing the hero to become Queen Guinevere's lover, is known, but its subject matter was passed through the *Lancelot en prose* into the German *Prosa-Lancelot*. Ulrich von Zatzikhoven's *Lanzelet* (c. 1194–1205) is based on a lost Anglo-Norman Arthurian romance unconnected to the *Charrette* (neither referring to it nor referred to by it) by a writer roughly contemporary with Chrétien. Chrétien's *Cligès*, which makes particular play with Tristan motifs, was not adapted into German until rather later, possibly in a lost version by Konrad Fleck (before 1240), and also by the continuator of Gottfried's *Tristan*, Ulrich von Türheim, of whose poem only a few brief fragments have survived. *Guillaume d'Angleterre* (*c.* 1170?), a non-Arthurian work closely related to the legend of St Eustace telling a tale of separation and reunion in the manner of the late antique romance is attributed to an author called Chrétien in its prologue, but it is excluded from the Chrétien de Troyes canon by many modern writers; it was not directly adapted into German, but it is closely related thematically to *Die gute Frau* (first half of the thirteenth century) and to Ulrich von Etzenbach's *Wilhelm von Wenden* (*c.* 1290).

Erec, the first German Arthurian romance (perhaps from the 1180s), is composed of two narrative cycles. In the first the young and untried knight rides out to seek restoration of his own honour and that of Queen Ginover after a shameful encounter with the knight Iders and his dwarf and, after a number of adventures, by defeating Iders in the sparrowhawk contest, restablishes his honour and at the same time wins himself a bride in the young noblewoman Enite, whom he raises up from a life of poverty. His achievement is validated by King Arthur and his court and celebrated in a knightly tournament, but Erec now returns to his own land to succeed his father as king of Carnant. The second cycle begins, like the first, with a personal crisis for the hero, when Enite unwittingly reveals to him that in the opinion of the court their love has turned him into a lie-a-bed. He responds irrationally, riding out with her into the countryside, compelling her to forgo her status as his wife and forbidding her to speak. He must now engage in whatever *âventiure* they encounter during this journey undertaken outside the confines of the courtly world, an unconnected series of engagements, of which the first are fights against robbers in the forest and the seduction attempt by an impassioned count corrupted by Enite's beauty. The adventures form two sub-cycles of matching episodes. During these adventures he comes to understand Enite's true fidelity, accepts her back as his wife, and achieves a new understanding of knighthood, but while returning to Arthur's court he subjects himself to the greatest test of all, the *joie de la court* adventure. Here, inspired by the true love of his wife, he overcomes an opponent who had established himself as an unassailable scourge to the land and symbolically marks out his new position as the upholder of socially beneficial knighthood. He returns to Arthur's court and then to his own land to re-establish his position as king. Through his new achievements, those of the first part of the poem have been retrospectively realigned and relativised.

Through its remarkable structural clarity *Erec* establishes narrative patterns that not only function internally, imposing on the audience a need to interpret the action symbolically and to reassess judgements already made, but also came to provide a basic double-cycle model for the genre against which later works such as Hartmann's *Iwein* (*c.* 1190–1205) and Wolfram's *Parzival* (*c.* 1200–10) have to be read. In France, where *Erec* and *Yvain* stood alongside other works that never became influential in Germany, namely *Cligès* and the *Chevalier de la Charrette*, the Arthurian romance takes on different contours, so that the genre was to develop quite differently. Hartmann's *Iwein* follows directly on from *Erec* in its aesthetic conception. Its narrative structure, with a story within the story, and its dominant motifs clearly betray the origins of the fable in the tradition of Breton lays on which Chrétien had directly or indirectly drawn. Laudine, the bride Iwein wins in the first narrative cycle, is a rationalised Celtic fairy mistress in the manner of the *Lai de Graelant* of Marie de France (*c.* 1160). The motif of the undertaking to return within a year, when Iwein, pressed by Gawein not to follow the example of Erec's 'sich verligen' ('to become a lie-abed', 2,790–8), sets out after his marriage for Arthur's court, in which the hero will of course fail, is a further link to this tradition. The poem's ethical programme, which emerges symbolically through the adventures of the second cycle and through his final achievement in the joust against Gawein while championing the Gräfin von dem Schwarzen Dorne (the Countess of the Black Thorn), culminates in his reintegration into the Arthurian court and his reacceptance by Laudine.

Hartmann's religious legend *Gregorius* (4,006 vv., *c.* 1180–1200) closely follows its French model, the *Vie de Pape Grégoire*, and yet it cannot be overlooked that it contains structural patterns closely associated with Arthurian romance. The exemplary story of sin, penance and grace, underlining how God has the capacity to grant forgiveness to the greatest of sinners, takes on a new dimension if it is read, in addition, as a double-cycle romance. The tale of how Gregorius leaves the monastery to try his fortune as God's knight in the world follows the familiar bride-winning pattern of *Erec* or *Iwein*, leading to a crisis, when he discovers that he is married to his own mother. In a second narrative cycle he sets out once more, offering his life to God when he undertakes the penance of being cast in irons on a rock in the middle of a lake in Aquitaine, where seventeen years later he is found alive by the papal legates coming to seek the man who, it has been miraculously revealed, is to be the new Pope. In *Gregorius*, however, unlike the Arthurian romance, the double cycle that articulates a dynamic ideology of human sinfulness and divine grace is set in a biographical context, beginning with parentage and birth and ending in death and salvation. The work partakes of both the fictional structures of romance and the traditional biographical pattern of the saint's life. The poem has close analogues in the legends of saints whose path to sanctity encompasses some great sin, for example incest or patricide, such as St Alban and St Julian, as well as in the legend of the anti-saint Judas.

Two central themes of the ideology that was developed in the twelfth-century German narrative poems are knighthood and love. The idea of knighthood, Middle High German *ritter/rîter, ritterschaft, ritters namen* ('knight', 'knighthood', 'knightly name'), words not attested before the eleventh century, came to embody the admiration for mounted soldiers who espoused a noble life-style and who in literature, particularly towards the end of the twelfth century, came to be associated with an ideological ideal of such values as honour, loyalty, display, generosity, pity and the social good. *Ritter* and its near synonym *guoter kneht* can designate any man who fights in armour on horseback, irrespective of whether he is, in terms of his legal status, a noble or a ministerial. The knighting ceremony referred to in a number of literary texts (e.g. *König Rother, Eneide, Nibelungenlied*, Gottfried's *Tristan*), which in Germany meant girding with the sword, is attested in the German historical sources as the ceremonial initiation of young princes, but not of non-nobles. Knightliness, in literature, comes to be synonymous with courtliness, so that women too can be called *rîterlîch* (*Iwein* 1,153, 6,135), and a knight expects to be treated in a chivalrous and courteous manner (*Erec* 4,197–204).

Throughout much of the twelfth century the German poems are greatly concerned with military ideology, but they do not promote these values under the heading of *ritterschaft*. Of central concern in a number of texts, for example in the *Kaiserchronik* (the Duke Adelger story), *König Rother, Rolandslied, Herzog Ernst* and the *Eneide*, is the ideology of vassalage, articulated in council scenes where the lord seeks the advice and assistance of his vassals before determining a course of action, and in some cases by the presentation of problem cases relating to the loyalty between a lord and an individual who owes him service. The poet of the *Rolandslied*, drawing on the ethos of the crusades, in which German participants had for the first time been involved to a significant extent in 1147 (Second Crusade), adapts his source to promote an ideal of *militia Dei*, Christian knighthood, in which warfare, traditionally problematic for the church, is sanctioned and glorified. The warrior heroes of this poem are not, however, described as *ritter*, but as *degene* ('heroes'), *chemphen* ('fighters'), *wigande* ('warriors'), *gotes helde* ('God's heroes'). Poems adapted from French models, such as the *Eneide* (but there with remarkable restraint in the latter portion), use *ritter* to correspond to *chevaliers* in their source, but it is not until Hartmann's *Erec* that the literary ideal of a knightly court culture blossoms. Here, in the German Arthurian romance, knighthood is not simply presented as a tableau, as the social and military culture of young princes at Arthur's court, but it is also problematised by the position of idealised knightly exploits in the double-cycle narrative structure. This problematisation of knighthood reflects the gulf that existed between the knightly, courtly and idealised ethical values of romance and the much harsher social reality that we know from historical sources.

Love and marriage, both separately and in combination important themes of twelfth-century poetry, undergo a development in some ways similar to that of knighthood, from being facts of life to a romantic ideal. Even as early as the *Kaiserchronik*, however, love (in marriage) is described, if only briefly, as a mutual experience based on fidelity, virtue and joy (4,335–46), and a source of strength and courtly manners (4,607–15), the basic conception that underlies the rhetorically elaborated ideal of romantic love in the Arthurian romances half a century later. The wooing expedition and its variant, the journey to recover a lost bride, form a recurrent story pattern, found in *König Rother*, *Floyris*, *Oswald*, *Orendel*, *Salman und Morolf* and *Tristrant*, associated with a political, dynastic conception of marriage, but also with such romantic motifs as 'love from afar' and 'love from hearsay', separation and reunion.

In the *Eneide*, as in the Arthurian romance, the motif of the expedition to woo a bride is replaced by that of incidental bride-winning in the context of a testing journey. Love now becomes, for the first time, a major psychological theme. It is portrayed in the *Eneide* as a compulsive force that seizes hold over an individual, potentially destructive, as it is for Dido, and yet also a powerful force for good and for the establishment of political power. The psychological condition of falling in love is accentuated here by the accompanying mythological motifs of the magic kiss and being struck by Amor's golden dart. The mythological apparatus of Venus and Cupid has a symbolic, even metaphorical function, and is closely allied to the tradition of presenting love as a personified figure, such as is later found in *Iwein*. The state of being in love is rhetorically elaborated in the *Eneide*, in descriptions, monologues, dialogues and genre scenes, and for the first time in a German context we encounter such 'Ovidian' motifs as love as a sickness, as a wound, going hot and cold, fear of telling the beloved. Here they are taken over from the French source, which was itself indebted to a tradition of studying Latin erotic literature in the schools. This style of presenting the love theme was later adopted by Eilhart von Oberg in the scene where Tristrant and Isalde drink the love potion, and where Isalde's monologue seems to take over certain formulations and motifs from Lavine's monologue in the *Eneide*. Whereas in the *Eneide* love is problematised by the contrasting fates of Dido and Lavine, in Hartmann's *Erec* love is made responsible for the crisis at the centre of the work and thus given a central place in the dynamic of the narrative structure. An idealised conception of true love ('guote minne') is proposed, and elaborated rhetorically in Enite's monologues, in which erotic passion is integrated into a superior love founded on absolute fidelity, with gender-specific roles for the man and the woman. If the historical development is seen as a progression from the *Eneide* to *Erec* to *Iwein*, then love and knighthood can be seen to have become, by the 1180s, the major themes of German courtly romance – as of the contemporary lyric. It must, however, be said that this is only part of a narrative tradition in which political and dynastic themes predominate, so that *König Rother*, where the motifs of love and knighthood are employed, but given a subordinate position, is more typical of this group of poems than Hartmann's *Erec*.

From Arthurian romance to the romance of the Grail

The Arthurian romance proved to be a genre of quite remarkable potential, even if the total number of works that can be counted as belonging to this genre in Germany hardly reaches a dozen. Wolfram von Eschenbach, who is generally thought to have lived from about 1170 to 1220 (?), followed Hartmann in choosing a 'classical' Arthurian text as the basis for his *Parzival* (*c.* 1200–10), Chrétien's *Conte du Graal*. He reproduced the narrative of his French source quite closely for long stretches of the work, but at the same time, through his additions, he created entirely new literary dimensions for the genre. This is achieved by such features as the story of Parzival's parents Gahmuret and Herzeloyde and the hero's childhood, and by the conclusion that Wolfram provided for the story of the unfinished French Grail romance, involving the hero's encounter with his half-brother Feirefiz, and the forward-looking perspectives of Prester John in India and the marriage of Parzival's son Loherangrin to the duchess of Brabant. The Arthurian romance is not here conceived as a discrete self-contained literary *exemplum*, it is presented rather as fictional historical biography and integrated, through the history of the Grail, into salvation history.

Wolfram presents the Grail, which is a chalice in Chrétien's poem, as a block of precious stone with wonderful life-giving and rejuvenating powers that was entrusted initially after the fall of Lucifer to the Neutral Angels, but is now guarded by the Grail knights, maidens and their Grail King. Its powers derive from a wafer that is brought from heaven once a year by a dove on Good Friday. At the time of the Parzival story Anfortas, the Grail King, is suffering from a terrible poisoned wound that he received in the course of an act of forbidden love-service. It has been prophesied through words that appeared on the Grail that a knight will come to the Grail Castle whose question of condolence, if put unsolicited on the first night, will cure the sick king. Wolfram's poem tells the story of how Parzival, already weighed down by previous transgressions, comes to the Grail Castle, fails to ask the question expected of him, and after years of penance undertaken in the form of knightly combat, is miraculously, through God's grace, allowed to complete the now seemingly impossible task in which he had failed at the first attempt and is himself chosen by God as the next Grail King. The romantic themes of unchaste love, knighthood (which for Wolfram is intimately linked with suffering) and the magic question are integrated into a narrative that is underpinned by a pattern of transgression, penance, grace and redemption, through which the hero's individual case is related to the larger theme of the history of man's salvation.

A particular feature of Wolfram's *Parzival* that marks a striking innovation in the narrative technique of German romance is the employment of two heroes. The adventures of Parzival are paralleled and mirrored by those of Arthur's nephew Gawan. The deeds of the two knights are so co-ordinated that each appears as a minor, background figure in the other's story, whilst coming together as foreground figures at critical points in the narrative. This development marks a new chapter in the illusionistic representation of reality in European fiction, anticipating certain aspects of the cyclical *Lancelot en prose* in France. Wolfram's treatment of this device takes as its starting point the double-cycle structures found in Hartmann's work. The principle that in a second cycle the hero surpasses his own achievement in the first is transferred to two separate figures, Gawan and Parzival, allowing a gradation of knightly/amatory achievement in the Arthurian realm and the exceptional achievement of Parzival sanctioned by God's grace in the Kingdom of the Grail.

One further aspect of *Parzival* calls for special mention as giving a new dimension to the fictional world created in poetry. The Parzival story makes use of an enormous number of named characters, the majority of whom are linked together by family bonds, so that they can be set out in two great family trees, that of the Grail family and that of King Arthur's family. This network of interrelationships is not set out explicitly, but rather it has to be inferred by the audience through the association of individual allusions. The kinship structures are functionalised by the author in that the exceptional attainment of Parzival, who is related to Arthur through his father and to the Grail King through his mother, is achieved by establishing a gradation of the Arthurian values of knighthood and the superior, religiously charged values of the world of the Grail.

Wolfram's second courtly romance was to be that of the tragic young lovers Sigune and Schionatulander, the *Titurel* (after 1217), named after the Grail King Titurel, the great-grandfather of the heroine (and also of Parzival), who is the first character to be named in the poem. As far as we know Wolfram only completed two short sections of text, 131 and 39 strophes respectively. The first describes the history of the family through three generations down to Sigune, the sorrowful circumstances of her childhood, the love of Sigune and Schionatulander and the confession of this love, after Schionatulander has set out with Gahmuret in the service of the Calif of Baghdad, to Gahmuret and Herzeloyde respectively. The second fragment tells how the hunting dog Gardevias ('Stick-to-your-path'), whose lead is inscribed with a love story, escapes from Sigune before she has read it to the end, so that she promises Schionatulander sexual fulfilment if he will retrieve it for her – a mission from which he will not return. Unlike earlier courtly romances, this poem is composed in a strophic form derived from the heroic epic, appropriate to the sorrowful subject matter of a story of love in which the erotic theme is constantly presented in relation to parting, death and mortality. Also unlike earlier romances this story has no known French source, but seems rather to be elaborated out of material from the Parzival romance for an audience that was familiar with that work.

Developments in narrative fiction 1200–1250

The first half of the thirteenth century saw a number of striking new developments in German narrative fiction that it is instructive to consider together. The German heroic epic is given written form in the *Nibelungenlied* and *Die Klage* (both datable, very broadly, to *c.* 1200), and later followed by *Kudrun* (mid-thirteenth-century). Gottfried von Straßburg's *Tristan* (datable to *c.* 1200–20) provided a more sceptical, critical variant of the courtly romance in the form of a tragic love story based on a quite different aesthetic from that of the Arthurian tradition. The German *Prosa-Lancelot*, of which only the first part can be dated pre-1250, marks the introduction of the cyclical prose romance, a form that came to dominate French literary culture, into German. Wolfram von Eschenbach's *Willehalm* (*c.* 1210–20) reintroduces the themes of French heroic poetry for the first time since the work of Pfaffe Konrad half a century earlier, and is soon followed by the poem *Karl der Große* (*Charlemagne*) by Der Stricker, a rewriting of Pfaffe Konrad's *Rolandslied*, probably composed in the 1220s.

Most of these works still draw directly or indirectly on oral tradition (which may in origin be Celtic, Romance or German) in the form of narrative patterns, principles of additive construction or in their use of traditional motifs such as the bridal quest or abduction story. With the German heroic epics the transition from oral poetry to the written epic has been effected by the authors of the surviving texts. The *Nibelungenlied* is composed in a strophic form and could be recited to a melody that was probably reminiscent of the oral lays. The poet's anonymity marks his own conception of himself as a link in a chain going back to ancient tradition, and modern scholarship gives little credence to the idea of there having been an earlier written epic which the author simply took over and revised in the second part of his poem. His poem unites the narrative cycles of the life and murder of Siegfried and of the tale of Kriemhilt's revenge, that is, the destruction at her behest of the Burgundian kings and their men (collectively called the 'Nibelungen'). This version differs markedly from the Scandinavian analogues in the Poetic Edda in that Kriemhilt (Norse *Guðrún*), now the wife of King Etzel of the Huns, takes revenge against her brother Gunther and his vassal Hagen for the murder of her first husband Siegfried, whereas in the Old Norse poems *Atlakviða* (*The lay of Atli*) and *Atlamál* (*The tale of Atli*) Guðrún takes revenge against her husband Atli (MHG *Etzel*) for the murder of her brothers Gunnar and Högni. In the *Nibelungenlied* disparate narrative elements are positioned in a bipartite epic structure, with parallel wooing expeditions and marriages, parallel invitations issued by the scheming queens Brünhilt and Kriemhilt to their festivals, and then, as the culmination of each part, catastrophe. Narrative components from oral literature are refunctionalised in a book epic with a carefully balanced and unified internal narrative structure. On the other hand, all manuscripts of the *Nibelungenlied* for which we have evidence provide the strophic epic with a sequel in couplet verse, *Die Klage*, the work of a different author. In rehearsing the events that follow on the final catastrophe at Etzelburg the *Klage* poet provides a reconciliatory perspective, whereas in the *Nibelungenlied* the narrative is brought to an abrupt conclusion with Kriemhilt and Hagen asserting themselves uncompromisingly – and tragically – in a final verbal struggle that can only be resolved in their deaths. The relationship between the composition of the two poems is unclear, and disputed: it certainly cannot be assumed that the poet of *Die Klage* was responding to the *Nibelungenlied* in its surviving form.

The *Tristan* romance, a reworking of the French version by Thomas of Brittany of this infamous story of adulterous love (a work which survives only in fragments), is presented in Gottfried's prologue as the authoritative version chosen from among many, and at various points the narrator engages in polemic against alternative variants. In the literary excursus, the first example of 'literary criticism' in a European vernacular, Gottfried establishes a relationship between his own objectives and the achievements of other contemporary German poets. The narrative structure of the poem, in common with other works derived from oral story-telling, is based on the motif of journeying to and from the court of King Mark of Cornwall: Rivalin's journey to Cornwall, Tristan's abduction and arrival in Cornwall, his first journey to Ireland in search of a cure, his second journey to Ireland to win Isolde for King Mark, the return journey (during which Tristan and Isolde are fated to drink the love potion), banishment, the journey to Arundel and his courtship of a second Isolde 'als blansche mains' ('of the white hands'), where Gottfried's version breaks off. The unfinished poem was completed in the manuscript tradition by adding, in one instance, the latter part of Eilhart's *Tristrant*, and more importantly by two continuators, Ulrich von Türheim (*c.* 1230–5) and Heinrich von Freiberg (*c.* 1290), who composed alternative versions of the ending of the poem.

Whereas the French romances of Erec and Cligès were originally conceived in opposition to the adulterous love of Tristan, the story of Lancelot develops this theme and is based around the adulterous, sinful love of Lancelot and Guinevere, the wife of King Arthur. The theme was problematic, it seems. There is no direct response in German to Chrétien's *Lancelot*, and the German *Lanzelet* by Ulrich von Zatzikhoven (*c.* 1194–1205), although full of love adventures, includes only the motifs of the abduction and rescuing of Ginover, not the adultery. Nonetheless, the French *Lancelot en prose* (*c.* 1225), a work which on account of its new form (prose rather than verse) and its potential for cyclical elaboration may be held to constitute the most significant innovation in the Romance literatures in the thirteenth century, seems to have reached Germany by the mid century in the form of a close prose rendering of the first part of the *Lancelot*, that is to say from the birth of Lancelot as far as the abduction and rescuing of Jenover ('Karrenritter-Suite'). Later, in the fourteenth and fifteenth centuries, other parts of the French cycle were translated into German prose, adding the quest for the Holy Grail, which only Lancelot's son Galaat is destined to achieve, and the total destruction of the realm of Arthur in a rendering of *La Mort le Roi Artu*.

The French heroic poems, known as the *chansons de geste*, were generally transmitted in cycles associated with particular figures such as Charlemagne or Guillaume d'Orange (that is, Count William of Toulouse, grandson of Charles Martell). Wolfram's *Willehalm*, which is incomplete, is based on one of the early poems of the Guillaume cycle, *La Bataille d'Aliscans*, but adapted to allow it to stand on its own outside the context in the cycle. The poem opens with the disastrous defeat of the Christians in a battle at Alischanz, after the Saracen prince Tybalt and his father-in-law Terramer invade Provence in an attempt to recover Tybalt's wife Arabel, who has eloped, been baptised under the name Gyburg and remarried to Willehalm. Willehalm wins the reluctantly granted aid of Lois, King of the Romans and successor to Charlemagne, and returns to meet the Saracen army for a second time. With the aid of the uncouth kitchen-boy Rennewart, who is in truth the son of the Saracen king and thus Gyburg's brother, Willehalm and his allies engage in a massive second battle in which the Saracens are defeated. Personal affairs (with strong elements of the love romance) and affairs of state (in which the true interests of the empire are betrayed by King Lois) are set in a problematic relationship to each other and to the fate of Christendom. Above all, the simple 'crusading' narrative of the *chanson de geste*, reminiscent of the *Rolandslied*, is undermined by an underlying programme of dissent regarding the conventional view of the Saracens, which acquires particular focus in the figure of Gyburg and her eloquently stated conviction that Saracens and Christians alike are all God's children and thus deserving of being spared. From the later thirteenth century the *Willehalm* was read in the context of a newly constituted cycle or trilogy, in which a rather shorter first part told of the love romance of Willehalm and the Saracen princess Arabel (the *Arabel* of Ulrich von dem Türlin, third quarter of the thirteenth century) and a third part, the *Rennewart* of Ulrich von Türheim (*c.* 1240–50), some 36,000 lines of verse, elaborates the story of Rennewart's marriage to Alise and their son Malefer who is embroiled in further battles between Willehalm and the Saracen king Terramer.

Arthurian romance in the thirteenth century

With the establishment of a tradition of secular written literature in German, the corresponding development of reading practices, public and private, and the growth of a new network of manuscript production for lay people, the writers of thirteenth-century German romance found themselves addressing a literary public who could respond to literary echoes and allusions to other German works and who would naturally relate new works of literature to what they already knew. The world of princely patrons evoked by the poet Tannhäuser in his sixth 'Leich' still sets the scene. Wirnt von Grafenberg composed his *Wigalois* for the Bavarian dukes of Andechs-Meranien and mentions the funeral of one of the dukes (probably Berthold IV, duke of Meranien 1188–1204) in his poem. At a later period a centre of patronage seems to have been the court of Ludwig II der Strenge ('the Strict') duke of Bavaria 1253–94, who is known as a patron of *Der jüngere Titurel* and *Lohengrin* (*c.* 1283–9). The claim of Der Pleier, the Austrian author of three substantial Arthurian romances (most likely *c.* 1240–70), to have written his *Meleranz* in the service of an unidentified 'frum edel Wimar' ('the worthy noble[man called] Wimar'), may be taken as an indication that the historical context of German literary production embraced not only the princely houses but also patrons of lower social standing (in this case perhaps the minor nobility).

Characteristic examples that can be used to exemplify the trends of aristocratic fiction in the thirteenth century, all from the genre of Arthurian romance, are Ulrich von Zatzikhoven's *Lanzelet* (*c.* 1194–1205), Wirnt von Gravenberg's *Wigalois* (*c.* 1210–25), *Diu Crône* (*The crown*) by Heinrich von dem Türlin (*c.* 1230), *Daniel von dem blühenden Tal* (*Daniel of the Blossoming Valley*) by Der Stricker (*c.* 1220–40) and *Der jüngere Titurel* (*The younger Titurel*), the work of a certain Albrecht (*c.* 1270). The French literary tradition still provides an important and prestigious point of orientation for these writers and their patrons. Not one of the poems is the direct reworking of a known French text, and yet in every case there is either a genuine or a spurious (in the case of Stricker's *Daniel,* a parodistic) claim to a French source – or there is internal evidence that French literary traditions have been an important influence on the author. In the case of Ulrich's *Lanzelet*, a work that is approximately contemporary with Hartmann's *Iwein*, we are told that the Anglo-Norman source manuscript was obtained from Hugh of Morville, later to be one of the murderers of Thomas Becket, who brought it with him to Germany when he was sent as one of a group of hostages to the Hohenstaufen emperor Henry VI in return for the release of King Richard Lionheart of England. Of the authors themselves we know very little. Ulrich von Zatzikhoven may be identical with a chaplain and parish priest of Lommis, near Zezikon in the Thurgau, who is attested in 1214. Only Der Stricker is known to us from further works: he is the author of an extensive oeuvre including *Karl der Grosse* and a large number of shorter couplet texts ('Märe', 'Bispel'), but we have no clues to the person behind the pseudonym, which is derived from *stricken* 'to plait, to braid'. Albrecht, implausibly identified with the poet Albrecht von Scharfenberg, who is known to us through Ulrich Fuetrer's fifteenth-century reworking of his *Merlin* and *Seifrid de Ardemont*, in the older literature, is generally held to have been a clerk; he alone of the poets named seems to have been able to handle Latin sources. For the greater part of the poem he writes under the name of Wolfram von Eschenbach, only revealing himself as 'Albrecht' at strophe 5,883.

Both *Lanzelet* and *Wigalois* follow the traditional pattern of showing how an exemplary Arthurian knight wins his bride and a kingdom, but, as in *Parzival*, the narrative model is extended back in time so that the tale begins with the hero's parents and birth. Numerous traditional structural motifs are retained, but in common with some of the other later romances the double-cycle structure is abandoned – and with it the particular significance with which the motifs were invested by virtue of their position in a structure. The Lanzelet romance is remarkable for the open eroticism of the seduction adventures which the hero undergoes in the first part before he finally wins as his bride Iblis, the heiress of Dordone, at Schatel-le-mort. Important mile-stones in this work are Lanzelet's discovery of his identity, the validation of his achievements by King Arthur, the proving of his bride ('Mantelprobe' motif), and the successful rescue mission to win the release of Arthur's knights from imprisonment by a malicious magician. *Wigalois* shows the hero's progression through a series of gradated exploits that lead him from the realm of Arthurian adventure to one of magic enchantment (an important theme in works of this period) to the world of thirteenth-century reality in the manner of the *chansons de geste*. He undergoes military feats against giants and on behalf of women in distress, an other-world experience in the land of Korntin, 'rebirth' (when he recovers from unconsciousness on the shores of a lake), his great adventure at the enchanted Castle of Glois, and finally transposition to the world of contemporary France where he avenges a wrong committed by Duke Lion of Namur by laying siege to the town. Narrative elements in this poem are closely related to the *Bel Inconnu* of the French poet Renaut de Beaujeu, and to the French prose romance *Le Chevalier au papegaut*. *Diu Crône* begins with a satirically rendered story of Artus and Ginover and the latter's abduction, and then in a long second part tells of the adventures of Gawein and his fantastic encounters with dragons and monsters, naked maidens, magicians and Dame Fortune – a medley of derivative literary motifs that may be intended to function as literary allusions. In the end Gawein comes to a wonderful castle where, in imitation of the Grail Castle in *Parzival*, he witnesses a sword and blood-filled chalice being carried into the hall, successfully poses the magic question and is then able to return to Arthur's court with the magic sword.

Daniel von dem blühenden Tal also relates a succession of fantastic and bloody adventures (the monster with no belly who kills by the gaze of a deadly severed head that he carries, a sick magician who keeps himself alive with the blood of his victims – a magic sword, a magic net, a magic skin), but these individual *âventiure* experienced by the hero are interpolated into the military, epic narrative of the war between Arthur and King Matur of Cluse, in which liberal use is made of literary motifs from the *chanson de geste* tradition. The hero is shown to win against overwhelming odds by virtue of his cleverness and rational premeditation, the latter often expressed in monologues.

The work known today as *Der jüngere Titurel* (and in the Middle Ages as *Titurel*), the most ambitious and longest of all the Arthurian romances, takes over Wolfram's *Titurel* fragments and incorporates them into a vast presentation of the history of the Holy Grail in strophic verse, foregrounding the tragic love story of Tschinatulander, the knight who dies in his attempt to satisfy the desire of Sigune to know the story inscribed on the dog-leash (the story within the story). The poem incorporates the story of Parzival, in an elaborate and self-conscious reinterpretation of Wolfram, and, at the end, the story of Prester John. The Grail is here the chalice from the Last Supper, as in French tradition and in *Diu Crône*. In the final section it is taken away from the sinful Christians of Salvaterre and transported to India. The extension of chivalric romance into a history of man's sinfulness and salvation allows this poem to be seen as the German counterpart, for the thirteenth century, of the cycle of the French *Lancelot en prose*.

Lyric poetry 1150–1300

The German lyric in the twelfth and thirteenth centuries is monophonic song, reflecting the practice of court performances, in which typically the performer would also be composer of both words and melody. The sources from which this essentially performance-orientated form of literature can be reconstructed are the great retrospective collections of Middle High German poetry that were put together in the period 1270–1350: the *Kleine Heidelberger Liederhandschrift*, the *Weingartner Liederhandschrift*, the 'Codex Manesse' or *Große Heidelberger Liederhandschrift* and the *Jenaer Liederhandschrift*.[2] Court poetry hardly ever warrants a mention in the chronicles and documents of the time, so that our knowledge of German lyric poetry in the High Middle Ages is essentially defined by the compilation history of these few sources.

The most comprehensive of the manuscripts, the Codex Manesse, compiled in Zurich in the first decades of the fourteenth century, but with poems from all over Germany as well as the Netherlands from the period 1160 to 1340, contains some 138 poetic oeuvres with about 5,240 strophes (as well as 36 'Leichs') in all. 137 full-page pictures of the poets evoke an aristocratic fantasy world of dancing, hunting, amorous genre scenes, and introspective poses suggesting the mood of poetic composition. The poets are set out hierarchically, beginning with Kaiser Heinrich (Emperor Henry VI, 1165–90), and the pictures communicate a conception of court poetry as consisting essentially of songs composed and performed by individual poet-composers and remaining the personal property of their creators. The manuscripts superimpose the conception of 'authorial oeuvres' onto collections of lyric strophes that must in many cases, at least in part, have been brought together for other reasons, such as common melodies or common subject matter.

---

[2] Recommended editions: Hugo Moser and Helmut Tervooren (eds.), *Des Minnesangs Frühling I: Texte*, 38th, revised edn, Stuttgart, 1988 (= MF) – up to Wolfram von Eschenbach, but not including Walther von der Vogelweide; Carl von Kraus (ed.), *Liederdichter des 13. Jahrhunderts*, 2 vols., 2nd edn, revised by Gisela Kornrumpf, Tübingen, 1978 (= KLM); Karl Bartsch (ed.), *Die Schweizer Minnesänger*, new edn by Max Schiendorfer, Tübingen, 1990 (=SMS).

All the named poets are men, and by contrast with France there is no evidence at all in Germany for women as the composers or performers of courtly songs. Popular poetry and the songs of itinerant *cantatrices*, who are occasionally mentioned in historical records, have not survived, and for the first surviving lyrics that are likely to have been composed by women we have to turn to the numerous German adaptations of Latin hymns and sequences, such as the *Mariensequenz aus St. Lambrecht* (*The Marian sequence from St. Lambrecht*) or the Low German versions composed by the nuns of the Cistercian convent Medingen near Lüneburg in the later thirteenth century that have been edited by Lipphardt. In the Netherlands Hadewijch of Antwerp (before 1250) composed religious songs based on the tradition of courtly love poetry, but there is nothing exactly comparable among the poems by German nuns.

The earliest German lyric poetry to have survived belongs to the generation of Der von Kürenberg, whose songs were probably composed in the 1160s, which puts the beginnings of the 'Minnesang' some sixty years later than the earliest troubadour poetry in the south of France. That this is not the whole story is indicated, for example, by the preservation of an obscene bilingual (Latin-German) love song 'Kleriker und Nonne' ('The clerk and the nun') in the mid-eleventh-century collection known as the *Carmina Cantabrigiensia* (*Cambridge songs*), and from such references as that to 'uuinileoda' ('love songs') in the eleventh-century Latin epic *Ruodlieb* or the polemic against 'troutliet' ('love songs') by the twelfth-century Austrian satirical poet Heinrich von Melk. The inception of courtly love poetry in the mid-century puts German almost exactly in line with the trouvère poetry of northern France, whereas the Occitan poetry of the troubadours (formerly called Old Provençal), which begins in the 1090s, can be seen as a precursor of both northern traditions. The style of German poetry initiated in this period runs on to the time of the Codex Manesse and beyond. The most notable landmarks are the prolific poets Reinmar der Alte (died before 1210), Walther von der Vogelweide (*c.* 1190 to *c.* 1230) and Neidhart (died before 1246). In the later Middle Ages Heinrich von Meißen, called Frauenlob (*c.* 1290–1318), and the poets of the pre-Reformation 'Meistergesang' predominate. The most individual poet of the later period, who like Walther and Neidhart is a poet of European stature, is Oswald von Wolkenstein (lived *c.* 1376–1445).

Love poetry and didactic poetry stand side-by-side in most of the surviving collections, but not in the oeuvres of the greater number of poets. The earliest named poets, Der von Kürenberg (*c.* 1160) and Meinloh von Sevelingen (*c.*1160/70), are known only as poets of 'Minnesang' (mostly single strophes that stand alone), thus attesting the erotic theme in courtly song at a time when it had not yet become established in German narrative literature. The didactic songs of Herger and Spervogel (1170s and 1180s) are also monostrophic, pointing the way to the later 'Spruchdichtung' ('didactic poetry') where this is the rule, but already in the love songs of Der von Kürenberg and Meinloh there is a tendency for the strophes to form pairs. With the oeuvre of Dietmar von Aist (*c.* 1160–80), the diversity of which poses a serious authenticity problem, a polystrophic norm, characteristically of three strophes, comes to be established. This development in the love lyric is accompanied by increasing formal complexity, notably the development of more complex strophic forms employing lines of different length, more complex rhyme schemes and the introduction of pure rhyme, whilst remaining for the most part within the constraints of the tripartite *canzone* form for the strophe. This consists of an 'Aufgesang' formed of two metrically identical 'Stollen', followed by a metrically differentiated 'Abgesang'. By the time of Reinmar der Alte, Heinrich von Morungen and Walther von der Vogelweide, whose poetic production continued into the early years of the thirteenth century, the love lyric had developed into the prestige form of courtly poetry. This is apparent not only from the formal artistry of the 'Minnesang' (most notably with Heinrich von Morungen), but also from the social status of the named poets. Whereas Meinloh von Sevelingen, Dietmar von Aist and Albrecht von Johannsdorf carry the names of noble families, others such as Friedrich von Hausen (*c.* 1155–90, attested in the entourage of Barbarossa), Rudolf von Fenis (Count Rudolf II von Fenis-Neuenburg, attested 1158–92) and Emperor Henry VI are influential nobles who had an important part to play in the world of political affairs.

French influence plays an important part in the early history of the 'Minnesang', especially in the songs of Heinrich von Veldeke, Friedrich von Hausen and Rudolf von Fenis in the 1170s and 1180s. Troubadour poetry was also an important influence, at a slightly later date (*c.* 1190–1220), on Heinrich von Morungen. Veldeke's poetry, which preserves some of its Limburg colouring, even though the manuscripts are from the south of Germany or Switzerland, is the product of a Netherlandish court society whose political links to Flanders and France were as strong as those to Germany. The indebtedness of his songs in their form, content (for example in the elaborate nature introductions) and phraseology to the northern French trouvères is to be explained by geographical proximity. That Friedrich von Hausen and a number of other Rhenish poets of the high nobility associated with the Hohenstaufen court knew the songs of their northern French and Occitan counterparts is to be explained from the extensive involvement of their generation in the Italian campaigns of Barbarossa, as well as from the proximity of the Rhineland to France. Rudolf von Fenis, named after Vinelz near Erlach in eastern Switzerland, was a count of Neuchâtel (Neuenburg) and may be assumed to have been at home in a bilingual culture. The three poets share a common alignment with Romance poetry in their diction, form and content, and numerous individual songs by Hausen and Fenis appear to show additionally a specific formal dependency on, as well as occasional verbal borrowings from, particular Romance poems. The poets on whom they draw are not the earlier troubadours from Guilhem IX, duke of Aquitaine and count of Poitiers (lived 1071–1126), to Marcabru (1130–48), who had established the genre of vernacular love poetry, but rather their own exact contemporaries, the troubadours Folquet de Marseille, Peire Vidal, Guiot de Provins and Gaucelm Faidit, and the trouvères Gace Brulé and Conon de Béthune. Morungen was influenced by the troubadour poets Bernart de Ventadorn, Guilhem de Cabastanh and Peirol. The lion's share of the borrowing is from Occitan poetry, with which the German nobles and ministerials may have become acquainted in Italy. Hard evidence of the direction of the borrowing does not as a rule exist (although Occitan into German is by far the most likely), and there is a case for seeing all the poets named as forming part of a single, multi-lingual poetic tradition.

The history of the music of the 'Minnesang' is lost to us because of the paucity of the surviving sources, but in this area too there must have been a story to tell of the impact of the Old French and Occitan songs on native German tradition. Whereas there are quite a number of early French sources (such as the *Chansonnier de Saint-Germain*, first half of the thir-teenth century) which set out the melodies of trouvère or troubadour poetry in highted neumes that can be transcribed, there are no comparable German manuscripts until the later thirteenth century. These later sources preserve the melodies of some of the earlier didactic poems (for example the 'Spruchdichtung' of Walther von der Vogelweide and Bruder Wernher in the *Jenaer Liederhandschrift*) and of Neidhart's songs, but no direct sources survive for the earlier 'Minnesang'. With a true *contrafactum*, where formal dependency on a French song with an extant melody can be demonstrated, it is possible, experimentally, to sing the German song to the French tune.[3] The situation with regard to music changes radically in the later Middle Ages, where the extant oeuvre of poets such as Frauenlob, Der Mönch von Salzburg, Muskatblut, Hugo von Montfort and Oswald von Wolkenstein consists of a combination of text and music.

Not much more is known about performance than about the melodies. Whereas for the twelfth and thirteenth centuries it can be said with

---

[3] For German *contrafacta* see Ursula Aarburg, 'Melodien zum frühen deutschen Minnesang' (1956/7), revised version in: Hans Fromm (ed.), *Der deutsche Minnesang. Aufsätze zu seiner Erforschung*, Wege der Forschung 15, Darmstadt, 1963, pp. 378–423. For the music of the 'Minnesang' see Burkhard Kippenberg, 'Minnesang', in: *The new Grove dictionary of music and musicians*, ed. Stanley Sadie, London, 1980, vol. 12, pp. 337–45.

certainty that the performance of German songs must have been monodic rather than polyphonic, it seems impossible, on the basis of scant literary sources such as the description of musical performance in the Tristan romances and the *Nibelungenlied*, to ascertain whether the performance by a (presumably) male singer was accompanied or unaccompanied, or whether both modes of presentation were usual.

The German songs are characterised, by contrast with other branches of the European love lyric, by a particular range of distinctive forms. One of these is the 'Wechsel', a song consisting of indirect exchange between two speakers who usually refer to each other in the third person. Early examples are found in the songs of Der von Kürenberg and Dietmar von Aist, and it is retained throughout the development of the 'Minnesang' as a formal option deriving from native tradition. True dialogue songs with interaction of the participants in the manner of the Romance *tenso* are not found in German until Walther von der Vogelweide. A related genre is the 'Botenlied' ('messenger's song'), often making use of the 'Wechsel' form and quite distinct from the Romance *envoi*, where the distance between lover and beloved is similarly stylised – and in this case embodied in the person of the messenger. Just as it is a feature of these specifically German traditions that the woman is given a voice of her own, addressing the messenger or 'not addressing' her lover in the 'Wechsel', there is a corresponding monologue genre in the early German 'Frauenlied' ('woman's song') or 'Frauenklage' ('woman's complaint'), a feature which strongly differentiates the German love lyric from its counterparts in the Romance languages, where women's songs are rare. An important parallel to the German songs placed in the mouth of the woman does, however, exist in the thirteenth- and fourteenth-century collections of Galician-Portuguese lyrics, which include a significant body of such *cantigas di amigo*. The classic early example of the genre in German is Kürenberg's strophe 'Swenne ich stân aleine' ('When I stand alone', MF 8,17), which stylises the expression of female sexuality with a paradoxical combination of a flush of pleasure and sorrow of the heart 'like the rose on the thornbush'. In Reinmar's elaborate song 'Ungenâde und swaz ie danne sorge was' ('Of misfortune and trouble I have had my fill', MF 186,19) the conventions of the early German 'Frauenklage' are redesigned to give expression to the frustrated desire of a woman who has felt obliged to reject her lover. In Walther von der Vogelweide's 'Unter der linden' ('Under the lime tree', L. 39,11) a woman celebrates her experience of fulfilled love in a natural setting (the *locus amoenus*) in a playful secret confession expressed through the public medium of song.

A genre that might seem to be associated with the native German forms by virtue of its tonality is the 'Tagelied' ('dawn song'), a convention according to which, typically, the parting of the lovers at dawn is presented in a third-person narrative, often using direct speech. In fact the evidence points to the 'Tagelied' being more strongly associated with the *alba* of Occitan poetry, and neither of the two earliest German examples, the bilingual Latin–German 'Si puer cum puellula' ('When a boy and a young girl') in the *Carmina Burana* collection (CB 183) and 'Slâfest du vriedel ziere' ('Are you sleeping, my beloved?', MF 31,18) in the Dietmar corpus, would seem to belong to the earliest stratum of the 'Minnesang'. Nonetheless, the dawn song seems to have acquired a much greater popularity in German than in Romance, where there are in all only about nine Occitan examples and just five in Old French. There are close links between the early German dawn songs and the Romance tradition of the *pastourelle*. The master of the dawn song in German was Wolfram von Eschenbach, who composed four songs of this type and a fifth using related motifs. These poems have a dramatic quality, making particular use of the watchman motif, here placed on the turret of a castle rather than in a natural setting, and of the personification of the dawn. This unusual form of the 'Minnesang' enjoyed a considerable vogue in the thirteenth and fourteenth centuries. Steinmar parodies the dawn song by replacing the watchman with a cowherd (SMS xix,8). Later the genre will be taken up again by Oswald von Wolkenstein.

Whereas the individual features of the native German 'Minnesang' combine to give the earliest named poets a varied oeuvre, the great mass of German love songs, like those of French and Occitan poets, are based on a single model: the male lover's monologue in which he expresses abject subservience to a beloved, his *frouwe* ('mistress', 'liegelady'), who is idealised to the point of abstraction. By comparison with the Romance tradition, from which the model is derived, the German songs increase the degree of ritualisation and spiritualisation of the lover's stance and give extra weight to the ethical dimensions of his love service, to the point where it can effectively become a goal in itself. The cult of the woman is intensified to such a degree that free borrowing of eulogistic motifs from Mariological literature was possible, as with Morungen's insistent comparisons of his lady to the sun and moon.

The essential elements of the literary model are derived from the concept of feudal service, the military service and obedience a vassal owed his liegelord, from whom he had received a fief (generally to be thought of as a piece of land) and from whom he was entitled to protection. These notions of vertical reciprocal obligations are transferred to the relationship of lover and beloved, allowing the lover to portray himself as demonstrating the constancy (*staete*) and fidelity (*triuwe*) of the faithful vassal, whilst requiring of the beloved, who is treated as a high-born lady and his *frouwe*, that having accepted his service she should show him her *hulde* ('favour'). What is significant is that this ritual gesture of wooing, which could go as far as demanding sexual favours, is as a rule not acted out to the end, but rather frozen half way, thus always preserving the tension-loaded situation of wooing. These poems articulate male desire, exploiting the tension of such motifs as separation, parting, refusal, prohibition, failure to communicate, the restrictions of social decorum (with 'society' interposed between lover and beloved). As a rule the lover is styled as a lover-minstrel whose service is made concrete in his song, a convention that may have been an invitation to performers to act out the lover's part dramatically. Whereas the feudal motifs tie the songs of the 'Minnesang' in to the tensions of the power structure of aristocratic society, the lover-minstrel motif associates love with poetry, so that love may be realised in the songs as a medium for self-expression *per se*. Seen from this point of view erotic poetry provided a vehicle for articulating, through the triangle of lover-minstrel, beloved and society-audience, a need for personal expression and a sense of the autonomy of the individual that was in conflict with the prevailing structures of early medieval society.

The most productive and wide-ranging poet of the period 1190–1230 is Walther von der Vogelweide. He styles himself an itinerant court singer, which tallies with documentary evidence of 1203 in the travel accounts of Wolfger of Erla, bishop of Passau (1190–1204, patriarch of Aquileja 1204–18). He claims to have learnt his art in Austria (L. 32,14), probably at the Babenberg court in Vienna, where he may have encountered the famous 'Minnesänger' Reinmar, and he describes the death of Frederick I of Babenberg, duke of Austria (1194–98), as a landmark in his career that resulted in his departure from the court (L.19,29). The second strophe in the 'Reichston' ('Ich hôrte ein wazzer diezen', 'I heard the rushing of water', L. 9,28) addresses the political situation of 1198, after the death of Emperor Henry VI in 1197, when Henry's brother Philipp of Swabia and the Welf contender Otto of Braunschweig struggled for the crown. This and the songs promoting Philipp's cause in the 'Erster Philippston' (L. 18,29; 19,5) show that for a time he served a patron close to the Hohenstaufen cause. These songs mark the beginning of an entirely new form of political 'Spruchdichtung' in German in which the authority of the first-person voice of the poet is involved in a wide range of political and public contexts. Often the contemporary references provide a precise historical context for the first performance of these songs. Even Walther's long religious poem, the 'Leich' (L. 3,1), contains a passage of political allusion. The song 'Ich hân mîn lehen' ('I've got my fief', L. 28,31) presents Walther triumphant at having been granted a fief by the Hohenstaufen emperor Frederick II in about 1220.

The range of Walther's 'Minnesang' is enormous. There are songs of traditional courtly love, playful teasing of Reinmar's conventions from his time at the Babenberg court, nature settings inspired by the Latin tradition, theoretical digressions on the nature of love inspired by the 'Spruchdichtung', as well as songs that throw off the liegeman-and-liege-lady conceit and experiment with the motif of a beloved who is looked down on by the world of the court aristocracy. A recurrent motif, and a hallmark of Walther's love poetry, is the insistence on mutuality and reciprocation in love. In what are probably late poems the conventional first-person role of the lover/minstrel comes to be fused with Walther's own individual profile as a court performer of some thirty years standing, and he makes play with the new motif of the aged poet who combines introspection and an awareness of mortality with a critical perspective on the changing times.

Neidhart's break with the traditional 'Minnesang' is of a quite different kind from Walther's in that his songs are founded on an entirely new set of conventions. They are linked only by individual formal elements and motifs, often parodistically employed, to the 'Minnesang' that had gone before. The case of the Neidhart songs shows more clearly than any other how inappropriate the notion of a 'genuine' authorial oeuvre is to the medieval German lyric. References to the crusades, perhaps those of 1217–21 and 1228–9, and to the patronage of Frederick II, duke of Austria (1230–46), provide external points of reference that allow an identification of the poet as a real person with links in Bavaria, and later in Austria. On the other hand, scholars are divided as to whether the Neidhart corpus should be seen as containing a thirteenth-century kernel augmented by a vast number of imitations, or whether the whole body of surviving material, including the 1,098 strophes of the fifteenth-century Berlin manuscript c, should be seen as constituting, in principle, a thirteenth-century literary oeuvre. Even if we accept that it is only the texts that have a place in literary history the problem of dating remains.

Both quantitatively and qualitatively Neidhart claims a special place in the history of the 'Minnesang'. His songs consist of 'Sommerlieder' ('summer songs'), composed in a range of strophic forms (most commonly the 'Reihenstrophe': 'dance strophe'), and 'Winterlieder' ('winter songs') composed in the *canzone* form. There are three main components in the 'Sommerlieder': dialogues between peasant girls who have set their heart on winning the knight of Riuwental at the dance, mother-and-daughter dialogues (competitive or admonitory), and the first-person voice of the knight of Riuwental (hence the name used in the older critical literature: Neidhart von Reuental). The 'Winterlieder', which came to be particularly popular, are presented for the most part from the point of view of the lover-knight of Riuwental, sometimes addressed as 'Nîthart', whose wooing of the peasant girl brings him into competition with the peasants at the barn dance. The coarseness and obscenity of the world depicted (and named) in the scenes of peasant satire turn the 'Winterlieder' into a parodistic inversion of the 'Minnesang', whereas the 'Sommerlieder' are based on an inversion of a different kind: the lyric 'Ich', which is generally only implied, is here the object of the women's desire, rather than consistently finding expression as the lyric subject. The distinctive tonality of these coarsely 'realistic' and explicit songs sets them aside from the traditional courtly literature and associates them with forms of German literature that characterised the later Middle Ages and the sixteenth century, such as the Shrovetide play and 'Schwank'.

A second departure from the traditional 'Minnesang' that, like Neidhart, points to the specific literary situation in the thirteenth century, is to be found in the work of Ulrich von Liechtenstein. Ulrich, a leading ministerial and public figure in Styria (lived 1198–1275), is the author of fifty-eight love songs, preserved in the Manesse manuscript, but also surviving integrated into an extensive literary autobiography in verse, the *Frauendienst* (*Love-service*). The underlying conceit of every song of the 'Minnesang', namely, the claim that the feelings expressed are real, is played out here in a sustained work of autobiographical fiction set in the real world, alluding to real events and based on Ulrich's own life. The culmination of Ulrich's love-service, which he had begun as his lady's page, is the fabulous journey that he undertakes, decked out as Lady Venus, from one tournament to another all the way from Venice to Bohemia. The motifs of rejection by the liegelady and turning to another woman are also elaborated in the narrative here.

Medieval German religious literature in verse and prose

The secular literature of the twelfth and thirteenth centuries, with which we have mostly been concerned so far, is underpinned by a wide range of religious writings in German. Most of this literature is anonymous and may be supposed to have been composed by monks and members of the clergy, in some cases by nuns or other members of semi-religious groups. Apart from the biblical poetry discussed above, the works with the greatest affinity to courtly literature are the saints' lives, which are mostly verse adaptations of Latin prose. There are, for example, three early lives of John the Baptist, that by Frau Ava, in whose work it forms part of a sequence of biblical poems, that of Priester Adelbrecht, and the anonymous *Baumgartenberger Johannes Baptista* (*Baumgartenberg John the Baptist*). Further landmarks in the German hagiographical tradition are Priester Arnold's *Juliane*, Heinrich von Veldeke's *Servatius*, Albert von Augsburg's *Leben des hl. Ulrich* (*The life of St Ulrich*), the *Wallersteiner Margaretalegende* (*The Wallerstein life of St Margaret*, after 1235) written for Clementia, duchess of Zähringen, and Konrad von Würzburg's versions of *Silvester*, *Alexius* and *Pantaleon* written in Basle in the 1260s or 1270s. German hymns and sequences in imitation of Latin models are exemplified by the early Mariological works, the *Mariensequenz aus Muri* (*The Marian sequence from Muri*, attested in Muri near Lucerne, in Engelberg, on the Rhine and in Admont in Austria), the *Mariensequenz aus St. Lambrecht* (*The Marian sequence from St. Lambrecht*) – actually from the house of Augustinian canonesses in Seckau (Austria), the *Melker Marienlied* (*The song to the Virgin from Melk*) and the *Arnsteiner Mariengebet* (*The prayer to the Virgin from Arnstein*) from the Rhineland. These poems all date from the later twelfth century.

German prose sermons, which represent the only literary type that can be plotted continuously from the Old High German period to the present day, can be studied from the translations of the *Bairisches Homiliar* (*Wessobrunner Predigten* – *The Wessobrunn sermons*, attested *c.* 1100), the *Speculum ecclesie* (*The mirror of the church*), the *Schwarzwälder Predigten* (*The Black Forest sermons*), the *St. Georgener Predigten* (*The St. Georgen sermons*), the Berthold von Regensburg collections and in the mystical sermons of Meister Eckhart and Tauler. In the earlier part of the period they are literary model sermons rather than transcriptions from oral delivery, which even later are exceptionally rare, but with the sermons of Berthold von Regensburg (1240–72) a new type emerges: German texts translated from the Latin collections, that were written up by the preacher himself, and imitating some of the features of this famous preacher's oral delivery. Oral literary practice, and oral performance on the basis of carefully prepared written texts, which constituted a major aspect of literary communication with almost all types of literature, are instructively documented here.

A group of texts which takes us right into the world in which literary activity was practised is that of spiritual biography and autobiography. One group of such texts consists of the collections of lives of nuns from a particular convent, such as the *Kirchberger Schwesternbuch* (*Lives of the nuns at Kirchberg*, between Sulz and Hagerloch, *c.* 1330) and the *St. Katharinentaler Schwesternbuch* (*Lives of the nuns of St. Katharinental*, from the convent near Diessenhofen in Switzerland, *c.* 1350). A second type is the individual life of a woman, such as the life and revelations of Christine Ebner (lived 1277–1356), a Dominican nun at Engelthal near Nuremberg, in which autobiographical texts recording the nun's own spiritual experiences, such as visions and auditions, came to be recast in the form of a *vita*. In the case of Elsbeth von Oye (*c.* 1290 to *c.* 1340), a Dominican nun of Ötenbach in Zurich, a first-person report of her spiritual auditions, apparently written up for the edification of her own community, has been preserved as a rough copy in her own handwriting. In the life of Friedrich Sunder (lived 1254–1328), chaplain to the nuns of Engelthal, this literary form was accommodated to the *vita* of a man. An elaborated form of the literary type is the 'autobiography', or *Vita*, of the Dominican Heinrich Seuse (d. 1366), which forms the first part of what the writer called his *Exemplar*, followed by the *Büchlein der Ewigen Weisheit* (*The little book of eternal wisdom*), the *Büchlein der Wahrheit* (*The little book of truth*) and the *Briefbüchlein* (*The book of letters*). The Dominican nun Elsbeth Stagel, who is portrayed in Seuse's *Vita* as having directly participated in the composition of the work, may also have been involved in assembling the compendium of the lives of nuns from her own convent Töss near Winterthur, the *Tösser Schwesternbuch* (*Lives of the nuns of Töss*).

These autobiographical writings, although from the fourteenth century, provide a literary context for one of the outstanding works of the thirteenth century: the *Fließendes Licht der Gottheit* (*The flowing light of the Divinity*) by Mechthild von Magdeburg. Mechthild's work is a collection of ecstatic revelations in which spiritual experience is verbalised and given literary form as dialogues, visions, auditions, allegories and narratives. The metaphorical language of love that is used here to depict religious experience, in particular for the expression of the mystical union of the soul with God her bridegroom (as in i.15), is only superficially reminiscent of the 'Minnesang': it is in fact drawn from the traditional exegesis of the Song of Songs in the Bible. This subject had previously been treated by Williram of Ebersberg and, in vigorous German prose that points forward to Mechthild's own writing, in the *St. Trudperter Hohelied* (*The St. Trudpert Song of Songs*, c. 1170, from Admont in Austria). Individual Latin writings that stand in this tradition, such as the epistle to the Carthusians of Mont-Dieu by William of St-Thierry and extracts from the writings of Bernard of Clairvaux, were translated into German by contemporaries of Mechthild. The extant version of Mechthild's work, arranged in seven books, is a mid-fourteenth-century rendering into the High German of the region of Basle on the basis of the author's Low German original, which is lost. Autobiographical fragments in the text suggest that Mechthild was a beguine in Magdeburg, that is, a member of a community of women living to evangelical precepts but not following a formal religious rule, who recorded her religious experiences in written form from about 1250, and later continued writing up her spiritual life in this form when in later life she joined a convent of nuns following the Cistercian rule in Helfta near Eisleben (c. 1270 to c. 1282). In Mechthild's writing, autobiographical motifs that typify the experiences of a semi-religious visionary (such as the burning of her writings, or her response to criticism from the cathedral clergy, as well as her religious experiences) are functionalised so as to convey a spiritual message to her audience.

One area of religious literature stands apart from the rest: liturgical drama in German. The period from the tenth to the sixteenth century saw a remarkable development of dramatic forms documented over all of Europe, uninfluenced by classical Greek and Latin drama, and themselves without appreciable influence on the more elevated tradition of the later European theatre. Medieval religious drama has its origin in certain innovatory forms of embellishment, musical additions to the authorised liturgy, known as tropes, which served to intensify the emotional appeal of particularly important moments in the Mass. An important early example is the 'Quem quæritis' from St Gall (Latin, tenth century) attached to the introit of the Mass of Easter, in which the question 'Whom are you seeking in the grave, worshippers of Christ?' receives the response 'Jesus of Nazareth, who has has been crucified, o heavenly ones.' – 'He is not here, he has arisen from the dead, as was foretold: go and announce that he is risen from the grave.' The trope, which may originally have been sung antiphonally by two choirs, came to be accompanied by mime; at a later stage the parts of the dialogue were taken over by actors, and German texts came to be included. The singing of the hymn 'Christ ist erstanden' ('Christ is risen', a four-line strophe with 'Kyrieleison') in the context of the Elevation of the Cross on Easter Sunday is attested for Salzburg Cathedral in a manuscript of c. 1160. In the course of the Middle Ages such simple forms developed into elaborate plays, initially in a mixture of Latin and German, later entirely in the vernacular. The drama was transposed from its original context in church, in the context of the liturgy (especially the Easter liturgy), into the streets and squares of the town, where it was often accompanied by a procession from one site to the next, and later into the villages. The range of subject matter was extended to include not only the events of Easter but also Christmas, the Last Judgement, the lives of saints and religious legends as well. The performers, originally clergy, came to encompass the urban laity (including members of the tradesmen's guilds), and in a village context the peasants. The performance of the liturgical plays remained almost exclusively the domain of men and boys until the sixteenth century, with the exception of certain plays performed by nuns in their own communities, where all the parts were played by women. Some of the late medieval plays had elaborate sets (such as those attested for Lucerne) and were performed over a period of several days, and they thus came to be major events in the life of the community.

The sources for medieval German drama are extremely diverse and range from reports in chronicles, civic legislation, lists of props, bills and receipts, to manuscript copies of the texts used for performance. The number of medieval German religious plays whose text survives – at least in part – today has been calculated as 162, in addition to 32 religious plays mostly in Latin with some passages in German, and 53 plays from

Germany in Latin alone (Hansjürgen Linke, 'Germany and German-speaking Central Europe', 1991). Many of these sources give only a partial account of the text that was used as the basis for performance, as is manifestly the case where only the script of an individual part has survived, or with the 'Dirigierrollen' (directors' rolls), which generally give only the opening words of each speech. The plays themselves were performed again and again, sometimes at intervals of several years, and the texts were subject to continual modification. The manuscript tradition, even in those cases where substantial texts have been preserved, can give only glimpses of the reality of medieval liturgical drama, generally preserving a 'unique' version, but almost always with extensive parallels to other extant plays in Latin or German.

The earliest liturgical play in German is the *Osterspiel aus Muri* (*Easter play from Muri*), an extensive fragment of some 538 lines of German verse preserved as a roll two metres in length and twenty centimetres wide, originally intended for use by the prompter. It comes from Muri in Switzerland. As an Easter play it concentrates on the scene with the guards at the sepulchre, the peddler who comes selling his wares in the market-place, the Harrowing of Hell, and Mary Magdalen's encounter with the risen Christ after purchasing ointments to embalm his corpse. It can usefully be compared with the *Innsbrucker Osterspiel* of 1391 (now preserved in Innsbruck, but documenting a performance somewhere in Thuringia). This Easter play, which is representative of the central German tradition, presents the discovery of the empty grave, the Harrowing of Hell (with an extensive part for Lucifer and the damned souls), the three Marys seeking Jesus, the scene where Jesus appears to Mary Magdalen, and the disciples on the road to Emmaus. The scene in the market-place where the peddlar sells his wares is particularly elaborate. The depiction of Lucifer and the damned souls provides an opportunity for extensive social satire. This play documents the fully developed liturgical play in the vernacular, sung and recited by some forty actors and requiring elaborate stage sets, and clearly a major event in the life of the community. Both the *Osterspiel aus Muri* and the *Innsbrucker Osterspiel* contain the central 'visitatio sepulchri' scene with the 'Quem quæritis' trope elaborated in German (VI,8ff. and 1089ff. respectively). Whereas we know from records that plays of this kind were performed all over Germany in the later thirteenth and fourteenth centuries, by far the greater number of surviving texts are from the later fifteenth and sixteenth centuries and fall outside the period here under review. In that period the liturgical drama flourished alongside secular plays, the 'Neidhart plays', attested from the late fourteenth century onwards, and above all the Shrovetide plays, and the late medieval religious dramas came to share a good deal of their atmosphere with these works.

Narrative fiction in the later Middle Ages

Narrative fiction in the later Middle Ages had to meet the demands of a new literary situation. Two main factors seem to have been involved, first, the gradual development of an aesthetic of private reading rather than the performance of literature as an act of public representation, and second, a process whereby literature increasingly acquired an autonomous aesthetic that was not dependent on religious considerations for its legitimation. Three areas of writing will be considered here that contribute to the new situation, namely the work of artistically self-conscious littérateurs who commanded a wide range of literary forms (principally Rudolf von Ems and Konrad von Würzburg), the new types of shorter poem in couplet verse (notably the 'Märe') designed to be read in collections, and the later medieval heroic epic. A fourth area of writing that has a particular significance for these questions, the prose romance, begins only towards the end of the period considered here and belongs therefore to the domain of the next chapter. The same holds for the writings of the 'Ritterrenaissance' of the later fifteenth and early sixteenth century, the major representatives of which are Ulrich Fuetrer (1453–96) and Emperor Maximilian. No new courtly romances in verse seem to have been produced after Johann von Würzburg's love romance *Wilhelm von Österreich*, completed in 1314, although some of the older works came to enjoy renewed popularity, especially in the early fifteenth century. The renewal of the courtly romance comes about with two of the major literary events of the fifteenth century: the German prose translations of French *chansons de geste* made by Elisabeth, countess of Nassau-Saarbrücken, in the 1430s, and Fuetrer's strophic reworking of a series of earlier romances in his *Buch der Abenteuer (Book of adventures)* composed in the years 1473–8 for the court of Duke Albrecht IV in Munich.

Rudolf von Ems (*c.* 1220 to *c.* 1255) and Konrad von Würzburg (*c.* 1257–87) take their place as ambitious and self-conscious literary authors within a firmly established tradition of German literature. The overall profile of Rudolf's narrative fiction, which proceeds from legendary romances employing hagiographical motifs (*Der gute Gerhard (Good Gerhard)*, *Barlaam und Josaphat*) to courtly romance (*Willehalm von Orlens*) to historical narratives (*Alexander, Weltchronik (The chronicle of the world)*), can be paralleled in Konrad's work by the progression from *Engelhard*, an elaborate tale of fidelity in the legendary style, to the courtly love romance *Partonopier und Meliur,* to the vast historical canvas of the unfinished *Trojanerkrieg (The Trojan War)*.

Der gute Gerhard and *Engelhard* are freely composed fictional works elaborating on a widely attested narrative type. In the case of *Der gute*

Gerhard two widespread folk-tale types are combined: that of 'the rescued princess' (in which the rescuer forgoes his claims when the princess's bridegroom is identified) and the Jewish tale of 'comrades in paradise', in which a powerful character (here the emperor Otto) learns that a seemingly inferior character (here Gerhard, a merchant of Cologne) is his equal in virtue. Konrad's *Engelhard* is based on the 'Amicus and Amelius' story, which combines the tale of friends who offer to die for one another with that of the leper who can only be cured by the blood of his friend's children, a motif reminiscent of Hartmann von Aue's poem *Der arme Heinrich (Poor Henry)*. Rudolf's *Willehalm von Orlens* is a traditionally structured double-cycle romance with the winning and losing of Willehalm's childhood beloved, Amalie, in the first part, and the fulfilling of fairy-tale conditions (including a vow of silence) to win her again in the second. In striking contrast to the Tristan story, from which individual motifs are adapted, positive political forces in society – noble kings and rulers, suitors who relinquish their claims, the king's sister who arranges the final reunion – ensure that the route though endurance and fidelity to a happy ending is guaranteed. Konrad's *Partonopier und Meliur*, based on the French poet Denis Piramus's elaboration and rationalisation of the 'fairy mistress' theme, tells in a first part of Partonopier's sustained fidelity to his secret mistress, the sorceress Meliur, who has required of him that he should promise only to encounter her under the veil of darkness for three and a half years; before this period has elapsed he breaks the promise, loses Meliur, but in the course of a second narrative cycle rewins her with the assistance of her sister Irekel. The *Trojanerkrieg,* too, which is one of the most ambitious literary productions of the thirteenth century, is based on a French source (the *Roman de Troie (The romance of Troy)* of Benoît de Sainte-Maure) and tells of the childhood of Paris, the journey of the Argonauts, the abduction of Helen and the first part of the war between the Greeks and the Trojans, breaking off at verse 40,424 during the fourth battle of the war. Special attention is paid to the love relationship of Helen and Paris. An anonymous continuator completed the poem in a further 9,412 lines of verse. Konrad's panoply of secular history in the ancient world in the tradition of the romances of antiquity stands alongside Rudolf's equally ambitious presentation of biblical history in the *Weltchronik*, including a synchronic survey of the events of secular history contemporary with those of the Old Testament. For the readers of this period the subject matter of romance and historiography had come to stand close together, as is testified by the integration of extensive extracts from both Konrad's *Trojanerkrieg* and Rudolf's *Weltchronik* into the great verse chronicles of the world, such as the *Christherre-Chronik* and the *Weltchronik* of Heinrich von München, that came to be popular in the fourteenth century.

A dominant literary form throughout the later Middle Ages, extending from the poems of Der Stricker in the second quarter of the thirteenth century to Hans Folz and Hans Sachs in the later fifteenth and sixteenth century, is the shorter couplet verse ('Reimpaardichtung').[4] The genre consists of short self-contained poems (seldom exceeding 2,000 lines), which may be moral, religious, historical or eulogistic in content, either narrative or didactic in form, and which were read and transmitted in collections. Some important categories of the couplet verse are the fables (fictitious narratives enacted by non-human figures, mostly animals, for the purpose of moral instruction), the 'Bispel' (bipartite texts with a short narrative or descriptive section followed by an exposition of the lesson to be learned), the love discourse ('Minnerede') – a popular narrative or didactic literary type only distantly related to the 'Minnesang' and of which more than 500 examples have been preserved, religious tales (including lives of the saints and fathers), and the secular short story referred to by most modern writers as the 'Märe', of which by H. Fischer's definition there are 220 examples. Similar literary forms are to be found integrated into larger works, for example in the didactic poems *Der Welsche Gast* (*The foreign guest*) by Thomasin von Zerklaere (1215/16) and *Der Renner* (*The courier*) by Hugo von Trimberg from the last decade of the thirteenth century. They stand side-by-side in the collections in which they were read, and the degree to which they were seen in the Middle Ages as distinct and productive literary categories is the subject of controversy.

The 'Märe', one of the literary types first established in the work of Der Stricker, has a particular importance in that it has been seen as a precursor of the autonomous narrative aesthetic that marks out the *Decamerone* of Boccaccio (completed in 1353) in the early Florentine Renaissance, and which has played an important part in the debate about how to define the 'Novelle'. H. Fischer's celebrated definition of the Middle High German 'Märe' is as follows: 'a free-standing and self-contained story of medium length (about 150 to 2000 verses), composed in rhyming four-beat couplets and describing fictitious events of a non-religious and worldly character'. The majority of such texts belong to the category of the 'schwankhaftes Märe' ('comic tale'), to which must be added two smaller groups, the moral/exemplary tales and the courtly/gallant tales. Fischer

---

[4] Editions are listed in the appendix to Ingeborg Glier (ed.), *Die deutsche Literatur im späten Mittelalter 1250–1370. Reimpaargedichte, Drama, Prosa* (=De Boor/Newald, *Geschichte der deutschen Literatur*, vol. III/2), Munich, 1987, 18–138, pp. 459–69. See in particular the catalogue, with plot summaries, of the 'Mären', in Hanns Fischer, *Studien zur deutschen Märendichtung*, 2nd edn, revised by Johannes Janota, Tübingen, 1983, pp. 305–542. The most useful collection is still that of Friedrich Heinrich von der Hagen (ed.), *Gesamtabenteuer. Hundert altdeutsche Erzählungen*, 3 vols., Stuttgart and Tübingen, 1850; repr. Darmstadt, 1961.

further defined the content of the 'Märe' by identifying twelve themes that account for nine tenths of all examples of this type (and of which the first three account for one third): (1) Adulterers achieve their desires by cunning; (2) Adulterers save themselves by subterfuge when discovered; (3) An adulterer is punished by the cuckolded husband; (4) A marital relationship tested; (5) Tales of seduction and sexual naivety; (6) Priapeia; (7) A lover is ridiculed (and his/her revenge); (8) Tales of mischief and artful deception (non erotic); (9) Comical misunderstandings; (10) Knightly adventure; (11) Fidelity in love; (12) Exposure of human failings (such as avarice, ingratitude, rebelliousness). These categories hold good not only for the mass of tales that are found in the collections, but also for the more extended 'Mären' such as *Moriz von Craûn*, which may be as early as 1210/15 thus antedating the 'invention' of the genre by Der Stricker, and the elaborated social satire of Wernher der Gärtner's *Helmbrecht* (third quarter of the thirteenth century). The courtly/gallant 'Mären' such as *Moriz von Craûn* and Konrad von Würzburg's *Herzmære* display an interest in the themes of knighthood and love that is comparable to the courtly romance and are completely devoid of the obscene and farcical elements which are characteristic of a majority of the texts.

Critical for the interpretation of the 'Mären' is the way in which their instructive or educative function is seen to relate to their effectiveness as literary narrative. The former will in general emerge from the lessons that the characters are made to learn in the course of the story (as when the spiteful mother-in-law is tamed by her son-in-law in Sibote's *Frauenerziehung* (*The woman's education*)) and is often made explicit, in accordance with a device common to the 'Märe', fable and 'Bispel', either at the beginning (*promythion*) or at the end (*epimythion*). The entertainment value of the 'Märe', whether it be a matter of the wit with which the events are narrated (*Studentenabenteuer* (*The student adventure*)), the hilarity of the situations (Stricker's *Der nackte Bote* (*The naked messenger*)), the shockingness of the obscenity (*Der Striegel* (*The currycomb*)), clever repetitions (*Der Sperber* (*The falcon*)), or a sudden twist at the end (*Das Häslein* (*The hare*)) is a function of the circumstances in which the text was presented to a particular audience. There is, in fact, very little in the texts that is not subordinate, in some way, to a didactic or exemplary function. Frequently, however, the various different elements in a story will point in quite different directions in a manner that is hard to reconcile, as with the exposure of the licentious instincts of the young nun in *Der Sperber* placed alongside the narrator's upbraiding of the mother superior for the shortcomings of her educational programme. In cases such as this (and, particularly, in Heinrich Kaufringer's *Die unschuldige Mörderin* (*The innocent murderess*)) there is a disparity between the implicit lessons to be learned from the story and the explicit statement of the moral. It must also be born in mind that the 'Mären' were read in collections (for example in that of the 'Schweizer Anonymus', in the Vienna manuscript Cod. 2705, or in the *Hausbuch* of Michael de Leone), in which a kaleidoscopic variety of moral lessons was assembled (with matching pairs of tales, groups of similar type, as well as groupings together with non-narrative forms). Medieval readers were not presented with consistently formulated coherent doctrine in their reading of the couplet verse, but with a range of complementary (as well as self-contradictory) insights into human life.

The later medieval heroic epic constitutes a new literary type reflecting, in written form, a tradition of oral story-telling in which Dietrich von Bern had come to be the central figure. The poems can be divided into three thematic groups, the historical/heroic epics (*Dietrichs Flucht* (*Dietrich's flight*) and *Die Rabenschlacht* (*The battle of Ravenna*), together with *Alpharts Tod* (*The death of Alphart*)), the 'aventiurehafte Dietrichepen', tales of adventure characterised by encounters with supernatural beings such as dwarves, giants and dragons (*Eckenlied, Laurin, Der Rosengarten zu Worms* (*The rosegarden at Worms*), *Sigenot, Virginal, Der Wunderer* (*The marvellous beast*), and the fragments *Dietrich und Wenezlan* and *Goldemar*), and thirdly a pair of texts that centre around an alternative 'Dietrich' figure: *Wolfdietrich* and *Ortnit* (which generally precedes in the manuscripts).[5] *Dietrichs Flucht* and *Die Rabenschlacht*, which were read as a pair, are preserved in a copy from the end of the thirteenth century, and we have evidence that around the same time the Wolfdietrich epics and adventure tales of Dietrich were already being read as a collection (the fragmentary 'Heldenbuch' now in Berlin). The 'writing up' of the Dietrich and Wolfdietrich legends was accomplished in the course of the thirteenth century, with evidence of the adventure tales from as early as about 1230 (a strophe of the *Eckenlied* preserved in the *Carmina Burana* manuscript: CB 203,4). The *Nibelungenlied* must be seen as an important model and precursor, while *Kudrun* (together with *Dukus Horant* (*Duke Horant*)) might be seen to represent a fourth thematic group within the same process of the codification of oral narrative. This process can be seen as a parallel to such phenomena as the codification of German law, hitherto passed down by oral tradition, in written form (the *Sachsenspiegel* (*The mirror of the Saxons*) of Eike of Repgow *c.* 1225–35, *Deutschenspiegel* (*The mirror of the Germans*) and *Schwabenspiegel* (*The mirror of the Swabians*) in the 1270s) and the production of charters in German (first examples *c.* 1238/40) to record agreements that had traditionally been proclaimed in German but recorded in Latin.

[5] The texts can most conveniently be studied in the edition by Karl Müllenhoff et al. (eds.), *Deutsches Heldenbuch*, 5 vols., Berlin, 1866–70; repr. Berlin, Dublin and Zurich, 1963–8.

Dietrichs Flucht, in couplet verse, and the strophic *Rabenschlacht*, whose melody is not preserved, both written towards the end of the thirteenth century, present Dietrich as a reflex of Theodoric, king of the Ostrogoths (ruled AD 455–526). His adversary, to whom he renounces his kingdom out of loyalty to his imprisoned men, is Ermenrich (based on the Ostrogothic King Ermanaric, d. 375), and his home in exile, from where he makes repeated military incursions into Italy, is the court of Etzel (the historical Attila, d. 453, king of the Huns). Motifs from Gothic history that had been preserved, and in part transposed, in the course of oral tradition are woven into a story of treachery among kinsmen and loyalty stretched to the point of total self-abnegation not unlike a French *chanson de geste*. The adventure tales of Dietrich, by contrast, which are mostly in strophic verse, place Dietrich in a fantasy world, making particular use of the international narrative motifs of militant provocation (with Dietrich either as aggressor or defendant) and liberation (Dietrich frees a captive woman from a powerful aggressor, such as the dwarf king Goldemar, Orkise the huntsman who holds Virginal captive, the cannibal monster 'der Wunderer'). In the later Middle Ages these texts were combined with the Ortnit-Wolfdietrich cycle, which tells of the ill-fated bridal quest of Ortnit (a 'Spielmannsepik' motif) and Wolfdietrich's eventual triumph over his father's faithless counsellor Sabene, in collections known as the *Dresdner Heldenbuch* (*The Dresden book of heroic tales*, 1472), Linhart Scheubel's *Heldenbuch* (*c.* 1480–90) and the *Straßburger Heldenbuch* printed in 1483 (and repeatedly until 1590).

Frauenlob and Meister Eckhart

There are two German writers in the years around 1300 who stand out for the intellectual dimensions of their work: Frauenlob and Meister Eckhart. The poet and the theologian meet in the domain of speculative philosophy, which for both of them has a neo-Platonic slant: they meet in their debt to the intelligentsia of the French schools, and in their hitherto unparalleled handling of vernacular language in German.

Frauenlob (1280–1318), whose name means 'Praise of women' and who is also known as Heinrich von Meißen, is the author of three 'Leichs' (*Marienleich, Kreuzleich* and *Minneleich* – treating Mary, the Holy Cross and love), a strophic poem in dialogue form *Minne und Welt* (*Love and the world*), seven polystrophic songs, and somewhere in the region of 320 'Spruchstrophen'. The 'Leich' is a form of particular musical and textual complexity, already practised by Ulrich von Gutenburg and Walther von der Vogelweide, in which stanzas of unequal length are arranged in a manner similar to the Latin sequence. Frauenlob appears to have been a

particularly celebrated figure among the professional poets and composers of his day and enjoyed the patronage of various German and Austrian
princes, including Wenceslas II, king of Bohemia (d. 1305). Stylistically his
work represents the culmination of a mannered form of poetry known as
the 'dunkler Stil' ('obscure style'), which has its beginnings about 1270,
and in which his most important precursor and model was Konrad von
Würzburg. It has an analogue in narrative literature in Albrecht's *Jüngerer
Titurel*. The practice of forming clusters of images to express a single
idea, combined with its opposite, namely the creation of multiple significance for a single set of images, which in Frauenlob's work is combined
with elliptical expression, unusual syntax and rare words, is derived from
the tradition of Mariological poetry, such as Konrad's long poem in praise
of the Virgin Maria, *Die goldene Schmiede* (*The golden smithy*). One of
Frauenlob's main themes, from which he derived his professional name, is
the praise of true womanhood, developed for example in the *Minneleich*,
and in the songs of the '*wîp-vrowe*-debate' (V,101ff. in the Göttingen
edition), where 'Gegenstrophen' ('counter-strophes') composed in
Frauenlob's 'Langer Ton' by other poets such as Regenbogen and
Rumelant von Sachsen, attacking his position on the status of the word
vrowe, are interposed and form part of the Frauenlob corpus. His theoretical position on the qualities of 'WIP' ('wunne-irdisch-paradis': 'joy-
earthly-paradise') and the relative qualities of 'maget' ('the maiden'),
'wîp' (after consummation), 'vrowe' (after childbirth) are underpinned by
Mariological analogues and a view of love as having an erotic-generative
function which is only fully realised in childbirth. These are new directions within medieval love poetry, and they form part of a project, in
Frauenlob's poetry, to make a place for Nature and Love within a cosmic
hierarchy, reflecting philosophical positions that are indebted to neo-
Platonism and, particularly, to the debate about the 'world soul' in the
writings of the twelfth-century School of Chartres (notably Bernardus
Silvestris). Within this conception Mary is given the status of a pivotal
figure in the cosmic and earthly hierarchy: in the *Marienleich* she is presented in a complex vision which combines elements from the Apocalypse
with a structure analogous to the *Planctus ante nescia*, the Latin sequence
that formed the basis of the thirteenth-century German 'Marienklagen'
('Laments of the Virgin'). Elements from devotional literature are refunctionalised within a new philosophical and artistic concept, in which
poems take on something of the manner of philosophical conundrums
whose sense is not intended to be immediately apparent.

   The new direction that Frauenlob gave to German poetry, which played
a considerable role in the fourteenth century and throughout the history
of the 'Meistergesang', can best be studied in the *Kolmarer
Liederhandschrift* (*The Colmar song book*), the great collection of about

4,380 strophes with their melodies that was put together in the Rhineland (probably in Speyer) somewhere around 1460. The term 'Meistergesang' is used to denote the late medieval development of the 'Spruchdichtung' that came to embrace a wide range of religious and profane subjects and is particularly associated with the later guilds of urban craftsmen who came together to practise the art of poetry (especially in Nuremberg in the time of Hans Folz and Hans Sachs). Frauenlob had an important follower in the mid fourteenth century in Heinrich von Mügeln, a poet with a not dissimilar intellectual profile to Frauenlob, in whose 'Spruchdichtung' (amounting to more than 400 strophes) and in the couplet poem *Der meide kranz* (*The garland of the Virgin*) learned themes derived from a more school-orientated view of philosophy take their place within an ethical programme that stands in the tradition founded by the 'Spruchdichtung' of such poets as Walther von der Vogelweide and Reinmar von Zweter. Mügeln makes particular use of a tradition of personification allegory, for his presentation of the virtues and the liberal arts, that is both directly and indirectly derived from the Latin philosophical epics of Alan of Lille (died *c.* 1203). In addition to his poetry, which is the oeuvre of a professional poet, Mügeln made the first Middle High German translation of a major classical Latin text in his prose rendering of the *Facta et dicta memorabilia* of Valerius Maximus completed in 1369, and composed two chronicles of Hungary, one in German prose and the other in Latin verse imitating German strophic forms.

Meister Eckhart, like Frauenlob, stands in a neo-Platonic tradition, but one derived from scholastic philosophy (Averroes, Albert the Great, Dietrich von Freiberg) and the Greek fathers (ps.-Denys the Areopagite) rather than the literary products of the twelfth-century schools. The historical location of his particular brand of intellectualism emerges clearly if one considers his career as a Dominican theologian, during which he was associated with three of the major German centres of the order, Erfurt (1270s to 1313), Strasbourg (1313–23) and Cologne (1323–8), occupying such high office as prior of the Erfurt convent (until about 1298) and vicar of Thuringia, provincial of the new province of Saxonia (1303–11), and from 1323 probably head of the 'Studium generale' in Cologne. In addition to lecturing on the Sentences of Peter Lombard in the theological schools of Paris in 1293, he was regent master (that is, professor of theology) there in 1302 and again from 1311 to 1313. In Strasbourg he was engaged with the pastoral care of nuns. In 1326 came the catastrophe. Inquisitorial proceedings on a charge of heresy were instituted against Eckhart on the basis of a list of statements which were to a significant extent extracted from his German writings, during the course of which he died (in Avignon in 1327/8). The condemnation of his views in 1329 was enacted posthumously. Eckhart's German writings, which must be seen alongside a substantial theological and philosophical oeuvre in Latin, consist of the *Rede der unterscheidunge* (or *Reden der Unterweisung*: *Talks of instruction*, often called *The spiritual counsels* in English), which is an ethical treatise addressed to members of his order and novices datable to 1294–8, the *Buch der göttlichen Tröstung* (*The book of divine consolation*), which together with the sermon *Von dem edlen Menschen* (*On the noble man*) forms the *Liber benedictus,* from *c.* 1310, and in addition more than a hundred German sermons. A set of early sermons from his Erfurt period, reflecting his concern with scholastic theology and addressed to the brethren in his own priory, are preserved in a collection known as the *Paradisus anime intelligentis*, whereas the numerous later German sermons, many of which were addressed to nuns, have had to be identified on internal evidence from the largely anonymously transmitted collections of late medieval mystical and scholastic prose-writing. In addition to these prose works, it has been argued that Eckhart was the author of the *Granum sinapis* (*Mustard seed*), a remarkable German sequence in the tradition of Dionysian mysticism, which was read together with a Latin commentary.

The later German sermons present speculative metaphysics in the context of the *cura monialium*, the pastoral care of religious women. The ideal that Eckhart presents, with mystagogical fervour, is that of 'abegescheidenheit' ('detachment'), a state of the intellect in which man achieves a mode of being analogous to God's by making himself free of all human things (such as could be exemplified from the religious practices of his audience: fasting, vigils, ecstatic visionary experience), including in particular the abnegation of the will and freedom from such categories as place and time. In this state of nothingness, which is one of absolute poverty, there comes about a union with the essential being of God in that – through a combination of apophatic mysticism with an analogical application of trinitarian theology – the divine word is born eternally in the soul of man. He calls upon his audience to identify with his own position, which is that of a testimony of the eternal truth that he is communicating, with the result that the formulation in words and textualisation of this truth is seen as part of the mystical process. In Eckhart's German writing, literary and mystical expression come together.

The early fifteenth century

Three major literary figures, whose work should be seen in the context of the complex literary situation in the period before the advent of printing in 1450, are Heinrich Wittenwiler, author of a burlesque epic poem *Der Ring* (*The ring*, *c.* 1408/10, Konstanz), Johannes von Tepl, author of the prose dialogue *Der Ackermann aus Böhmen* (*The ploughman from Bohemia*, shortly after 1400, Bohemia), and the lyric poet Oswald von Wolkenstein (lived *c.* 1376–1445, Tyrol). Wittenwiler's poem, which stands to the fore in any modern literary canon, is preserved in a single handwritten copy and had no influence whatsoever in its own day. The *Ackermann*, the earliest manuscripts of which are from just before the middle of the century, made little impact in Germany until the age of print, when it became one of the very first printed books in the German language (preceded only by a lost edition of the *Sibyllenweissagungen* (*The Sibylline prophecies*), calendars, and possibly the fable collection *Der Edelstein* (*The gemstone*) by Boner, written *c.* 1350). Oswald was a celebrated figure in Tyrol, but most of his poems and songs are preserved in just three manuscript codices in Vienna and Innsbruck that were copied and owned in the immediate circle of the poet himself and, despite his ebullient personality, there are only two contemporary references to his work.

The literary context of these writers, in which success and survival depended on access to the channels of scribal copying, is dominated above all by prose texts, mostly representing literary types that lack the autonomous aesthetic status which marks out 'literature' for the modern reader, but which in their own day were not seen as belonging to an essentially different category of writing from fictional narrative texts, works of individual poetic expression or those that stand out for their formal artistry. This means that literary works of striking aesthetic quality, such as those to which prominence will be given in this final section, take their place within a system of literary types that has to be defined by other criteria. Prose writing, which had developed in the twelfth and thirteenth century largely within the religious/monastic community and was then taken up by the friars (by the Augsburg Franciscans and the friars responsible for writing up the sermons of Berthold von Regensburg in the later thirteenth century, by the Rhenish Dominicans in the fourteenth century), is the norm from at least 1350 onwards. From 1380 to about 1475 there occurs what has been described as an explosion in the production and copying of German-language texts in prose, partly carried by religious movements with an interest in promoting spiritual reform through reading (for example, the popularisation of university-style theology in the Vienna School, books for reformed Dominican nuns, the 'Devotio moderna' promoted by the Brethren of the Common Life in northern Germany), but also reaching lay people: literate townspeople with interests that included, but extended beyond devotional literature, and also doctors, lawyers and civic officials with an interest in acquiring books relating to their professional interests. Many thousands of German prose texts were circulated in manuscript during this period, dealing with many different subject areas. Much of it is translated directly from Latin. In the following tabulation some examples of the tradition of German prose-writing before 1450 will serve to give an idea of the extent of the phenomenon:

Narrative texts in collections (profane and religious): *Der Große Seelentrost* (Low German exemplary tales, *c.* 1300); *Gesta Romanorum* (numerous translations); *Vitaspatrum* (fourteenth-century translation).

Theology, asceticism, catechetic literature: *Schwarzwälder Predigten* (later thirteenth-century); Johann von Neumarkt *c.* 1315–80 (*Buch der Liebkosung, Hieronymus-Briefe, Stachel der Liebe*); translations of major medieval writers such as Bonaventura, Bernard and Hugh Ripelin; Marquard von Lindau, died *c.* 1393 (eleven German works, including sermons, the *Eucharistietraktat* and the *Dekalogerklärung*); Otto von Passau (24 *Alten*, before 1383); Heinrich von Langenstein (*Erkenntnis der Sünde*, before 1393); Thomas Peuntner (*Büchlein von der Liebhabung Gottes*, 1428).

Bible translations: *Wien-Münchner Evangelien* (twelfth-century); *Evangelienbuch des Matthias Beheim* (thirteenth-century); *Olmützer Perikopenbuch* (thirteenth-century, widely copied); *Klosterneuburger Evangelienwerk* (1330); *Augsburger Bibel* (before 1350); *Wenzelbibel c.* 1389–92 and *Codex Teplensis c.* 1400 (both closely related to the version printed in 1466 as the 'Mentelin Bible').

Saints' lives: the prose legendaries (*Elsässische Legenda aurea*, Strasbourg *c.* 1350, *Der Heiligen Leben*, Nuremberg after 1384), as well as many individual lives.

Prayerbooks: prayerbook of Johann von Neumarkt; private prayerbooks of southern German nuns; Johannes von Indersdorf (*Gebetbuch für Elisabeth Ebran*, 1426/29).

Travel and pilgrimage literature: Mandeville's travels (translated from French by Michel Velser *c.* 1390 in Tyrol, by Otto von Diemeringen, attested 1368–99, in Lorraine); Marco Polo (translated from Latin in the fourteenth century); Odorico da Pordenone's journey to China (translated by Konrad Steckel, 1359).

Philosophy: *Lucidarius* (late twelfth-century); Boethius, *De consolatione Philosophiae* (translation by Peter von Kastl 1401, which is probably lost, also by Konrad Humery *c.* 1462/3); Thomas Aquinas, *Summa theologica* (partial translation, also as *Der tugenden buoch*).

Law: *Rechtssumme* of Bruder Berthold (before 1390); the *Processus Belial* of Jacobus de Theramo (twice translated); civic law ('Stadtrechtsbücher').

History: *Sächsiche Weltchronik* (1260–75); monastic chronicles; civic

chronicles (e.g. the *Straßburger Chronik* of Fritsche Klosener, 1362).
Natural history: Konrad von Megenberg, *Das Buch der Natur* (1348–50).
Medicine: *Bartholomäus* (thirteenth-century); Ortolf von Baierland, *Arzneibuch* (*c.* 1280); receipt collections; *Iatromathematisches Hausbuch* (an astro-medical compendium).
Pragmatic literature: Meister Johann Liechtenauer's *Kunst des Fechtens* (before 1389); Konrad Kyeser, *Bellifortis* (German recension of the treatise on warfare); *Lehre vom Haushaben* (ps.-Bernard, *Epistola de cura rei familiaris*, German translations).

In returning to the form of extended verse narrative in an age of prose Heinrich Wittenwiler reactivates the tradition of courtly romance. And yet by casting his poem in a racy style of verse strongly tinged with dialect and stylistically more reminiscent of Shrovetide plays than of the poems of the thirteenth century, he can be seen to espouse that tradition only to subvert it. The first and second sections of *Der Ring* consist of a farcical account of Bertschi's love service for the village girl Mätzli Rüerenzumph ('Pick-your-prick') from Lappenhausen. The tale progresses from the peasant tournament, the wooing of the bride (with comic serenade and love letters), and the formal approach to her family, to the marriage and wedding feast. The action of this part, which is packed with frivolities, obscenities and sexual licence (in the masturbation scene, the faked virginity, at the dance), also provides an occasion for passages of extended didacticism (love letters based on the 'Minnerede' tradition, summaries of Christian teaching, marriage guidance, practical health guidance and good housekeeping offered to the bridegroom) and lessons to be learned *ex negativo* (an ideal of beauty from the description of the wretched Mätzli, good table manners from the disgusting wedding feast). A trivial incident during the dance, when a Lappenhauser scratches the hand of a girl from the neighbouring village leads to a fight that gets out of control and ends with the Lappenhauser pursuing their neighbours back to Nissingen. In the the third section, on the Monday morning, the villages of Lappenhausen and Nissingen hold councils to take stock, with the result that war is declared. The Lappenhauser call on help from the towns of northern Italy and northern Europe, who in turn summon an international council with representatives of seventy-two towns and turn them down. However, dwarves, witches and giants side with the Lappenhauser, while literary figures such as Gawan, Lantzelett, Tristan, Dietrich von Bern and Wolffdietreich take up the cause of the Nissinger. On the Tuesday a great battle takes place, ending in victory for Nissingen and (thanks to Frau Laichedenman's treachery) the burning and total destruction of Lappenhausen. Mätzli is forgotten. On the Wednesday Bertschi departs and goes to live as a hermit in the Black Forest. Extensive pieces of didacticism are woven into the narrative of this section too, in the council scenes and in the long speech on the theoretical principles of warfare spoken by Strudel, the mayor of Nissingen. Much of the didactic material is taken over from identifiable Latin sources (for example, the *Secreta mulierum*, the pseudo-Aristotelian *Secretum secretorum*, a treatise on warfare by Johannes de Legnano, the *Moralium dogma philosophorum* of William of Conches). The scene of the wedding feast is based verbatim on a 'Märe' known as the *Bauernhochzeitsschwank* (*The peasants' wedding feast*). In addition to a wide range of literary reference some of the characters are given a new kind of 'realism' by being modelled on identifiable figures from contemporary Konstanz society. The interpretation of the work is problematic: it has been suggested that the wilfully disparate elements in *Der Ring* can best be brought into focus if it is seen as a pessimistic allegory of the world, in which the ultimate source of evil is erotic lust.

Der Ackermann aus Böhmen, which is more or less exactly contemporary with *Der Ring*, is a dialogue between an 'Ackermann' ('ploughman'), as a representation of the author (who ploughs the furrow with his pen), and the personified figure of Death, in which, for the first time in this period, we find original German prose self-consciously used as an artistic form. The author, Johannes von Tepl, is attested from *c.* 1378–1411 as town clerk and director of the grammar school in the bilingual town of Žatec (German: Saaz) in north-west Bohemia, and from 1411 to his death *c.* 1413/15 as town clerk of the New Town in Prague. The starting point for the debate is the death of the Ackermann's wife Margarete on 1 August 1400 (suggesting that the work was composed early in the first decade of the century). The work consists of artistically balanced speeches in the tradition of the 'Streitgespräch' ('disputation', cf. Frauenlob's *Minne und Welt*), rather than that of the free flowing dialogue of Boethius's *De consolatione Philosophiae*, which provided Johannes von Tepl's principal model for a dialogue between the 'author' and a personified figure, or the master-and-pupil dialogue (as in the *Lucidarius*, Seuse's *Büchlein der ewigen Weisheit* (*Little book of eternal wisdom*), Marquard von Lindau). The argument proceeds from the Ackermann's outcry at the death of his wife, presented as before a court of law, to a debate about the value of human life and human endeavour. God's judgement at the end, while upholding Death's right to take life, stresses that the Ackermann's grief was justified and that his cause was honourable, whilst also pointing to an eschatological dimension, which provides a basis for the transition to the important final chapter in which JOHANNES (the name picked out in an acrostich) prays for the soul of his deceased wife. The theme of the death of the beloved, relatively uncommon in the German lyric, is refunctionalised in the *Ackermann* as the death of the wife. An important question for the interpretation of the text is the extent to which there is in fact a transition from the theme of bereavement, which is clearly voiced in the Ackermann's initial outcry, to the broader subject of mortality, articulated through the individual's response to the death of his partner in marriage. In some aspects the value accorded here to the intrinsic value of human life and the representation of man by the Ackermann as God's finest creation seem to be precursors of Italian Renaissance ideas, as expressed for example in the *De dignitate hominis* of Pico della Mirandola (1463–94), which raises the question whether the work is at all indebted in its ideology to the early humanist writers of the fourteenth century (most notably Petrarch), who had links to the court of Emperor Charles IV in Prague. Further aspects of the work that may suggest links to early humanism, although not in themselves absent from medieval tradition, are Death's use of Stoic arguments to defend his position, and the rhetorical aspect of the speeches, to which particular attention is accorded in a Latin letter from Johannes von Tepl to his friend Petrus Rothirsch in Prague that was sent with a copy of the work. Johannes von Tepl's precursor as a writer of studied, rhetorical German prose in Bohemia was Johann von Neumarkt, imperial chancellor under Charles IV from 1353 to 1374, on whose work he draws verbatim in the final chapter. These writers' concern with vernacular prose style corresponds to the interest of the early humanists in cultivating a fine, classicising prose style in Latin, in which the attainment of eloquence and moral worth were seen as parts of a single process, whilst at the same time paralleling the concern of the Italian humanists for the vernacular.

Oswald von Wolkenstein (lived *c.* 1376–1445) was the author of some 130 songs and of two short poems in couplet verse. It is for the originality, the variety, and above all the quite remarkable personal imprint of his poetry that he stands out from among the other late medieval lyric poets, who include Hugo von Montfort (lived 1357–1423), notable for his elegy on the death of his wife Clementia von Toggenburg (who, like the Ackermann's Margarete, died in 1400), the 'Mönch von Salzburg' ('Monk of Salzburg'), whose name is attached to an important corpus of secular and religious songs and hymns associated with the court of Pilgrim II, archbishop of Salzburg (1365–96), the 'Spruchdichter' Muskatblut (1415–38), the Strasbourg author of religious poems and hymns Heinrich Laufenberg (1413–58), and also, later in the century, Michael Beheim (lived *c.* 1416–74/8). Oswald's work marks the culmination of the 'alternative' lyric tradition, which Neidhart had established in opposition to the courtly 'Minnesang', whilst using many different traditional lyric forms. The melodies have been preserved, and about one third of the songs are in parts, for two or more voices. The lyric 'Ich' of the traditional 'Minnesang' is given new contours in Oswald's songs by the use of autobiographical material, just as the traditional nature settings are reformulated using real topographical material from the poet's own milieu. But was Oswald really shipwrecked on the Black Sea and did he owe his life to an escape clinging to a barrel? Did he really spend nights of sexual frustration, when separated from his wife, in the manner so graphically described? It is clear from the extant charters relating to the public affairs of the Wolkenstein family that the overall picture given by the autobiographical material in the songs is correct, but it must also be the case that the individual events and experiences referred to are shaped on the basis of literary models and in response to the requirements of particular literary forms. In the love songs, which form the largest group in his work, particular mention is made of his *buel* ('mistress'), the 'Hausmannin', a real woman of Bressanone (Brixen) who later turned against him in a conflict over the possession of Burg Hauenstein and conspired with the enemies who imprisoned and tortured him in the years 1421–3. In 1417 he married the Swabian noblewoman Margarete von Schwangau, his love for whom is the subject of a remarkable sequence of poems in which the physical relationship of the married couple, presented with studied vulgarity, gives a distinctive slant to the popular late-medieval literary theme of marriage. Oswald makes particular use of the types of love song that have narrative content, the *genres objectifs* such as the *pastourelle*, dialogue, dawn song, erotic allegory, dancing songs. His most distinctive work, however, is the group of first-person narrative songs in which autobiographical material from his travels and political involvement is employed. In his religious poems, alongside more traditional forms, there are a number of highly individual texts relating such experiences as his imprisonment, and seemingly imminent death, at the hands of his former mistress, to an awareness of human sinfulness and mortality. This blend of religious and worldly themes presented from a distinctively personal angle, and yet with universal significance, might be seen as the hallmark of the German literature of the later Middle Ages.

3

The early modern period (1450–1720)

HELEN WATANABE-O'KELLY

This period, which begins before the Reformation and ends with the dawning of the Enlightenment, laid down the foundations of the thought and writing of the modern age and determined the future course of the German-speaking world. Germany in the modern sense did not yet exist, so the territory under discussion is the Holy Roman Empire. We must also remember that in this period most writers moved at will between Latin and German. Not until 1681 do the catalogues for the German book fairs show that more books were being published in German than in Latin.

Books and writers before the Reformation

Around 1445 in Mainz, Johann Gensfleisch (c. 1400–68), better known as Gutenberg, succeeded in printing with movable metal type. He also used paper, invented in the twelfth century, but only readily available in Germany in the fifteenth. Manuscript and print survived side by side and the boundaries between them remained blurred for a long time. Scriptoria producing multiple copies of manuscripts for sale already existed in the fifteenth century, anticipating the mass-production of the printing press, while books in the early decades were so costly as to constitute luxury items on a par with manuscripts. Books were printed on parchment and manuscripts written on paper. Many early printed books were designed to look like manuscripts, while the manuscript itself survived as a prestige tailormade item for rich, usually courtly patrons. But the book as commodity had come into being and it is no accident that the early centres of printing and publishing were important commercial towns on international trade routes: Mainz, Strasbourg, Basle, Nuremberg, Augsburg, Ulm, Cologne and Leipzig.

The emergence of the printed book has implications for both reading and writing. For the writer, the printing press meant that, instead of conceiving a work for a known patron, it was now written for an unseen and more numerous readership. Though many works, such as occasional verse or official histories, were commissioned throughout the period, in general the writer exchanged the dictates of a patron for the dictates of the market and lost face-to-face contact with an audience. Literature designed to be read took over from literature designed to be heard, though works were still often read aloud, thus again blurring the boundaries between new and old. The printing press widened the circle of potential readers immeasurably, for anyone who had money and the ability to read – two big provisos – had access to knowledge regardless of class or calling, though proficiency in Latin was necessary for access to many books.

Another kind of printing, the woodblock print, also became current in the age and contributed greatly to the development of the printed book. Not only did the illustrations increase a book's attractiveness and make its contents of interest to illiterate purchasers, the interlinking of text and picture is an important feature of the literature of the early modern period as a whole. Its early development was given vital impetus by the emergence of a large number of gifted artists such as Burgkmair, Cranach, Dürer and Graf. Thus, reading a book, hearing a book read aloud and looking at a book were intertwined activities.

Two important figures illustrate features of the literary landscape of the late fifteenth and early sixteenth centuries: Sebastian Brant (1457–1521) and Emperor Maximilian I (1459–1519). In education, career and interests Brant is typical of his times. A native of Strasbourg, he studied at the new University of Basle, one of eight founded in the Empire between 1457 and 1506. Basle at this period was in the forefront of German Humanism, that is, the new learning and new ideas which grew out of the Italian Renaissance. Brant stayed in Basle until 1501, teaching at the university and eventually becoming Dean of the Faculty of Law, working very closely with the expanding printing industry in Basle as academic consultant and editor, and writing in both Latin and German. In the former language he wrote legal textbooks and poetry, in the latter translations, didactic pieces on behaviour and morals and the work he is most famous for, *Das Narrenschiff* (*The ship of fools*, 1494). The *Narrenschiff* is the first German bestseller and went into six authorised and seven unauthorised editions in Brant's lifetime and twenty after his death. It was translated into Latin, Low German, French, Flemish and English and was adapted and paraphrased widely. The idea is that a ship full of fools sets off for an imaginary territory called Narragonia (Foolonia). There is no narrative framework as such – the work consists of a compendium of 112 separate examples of folly, ranging from downright viciousness to simple silliness and drawing on the literature of the seven deadly sins. Each of the chapters or examples consists of a woodcut, a three-line stanza and a much longer (between 30 and 200 lines) verse passage expatiating on the folly or vice depicted. The verses are pithy and amusing, full of commonsense observation of human foibles; their didactic content means that one can enjoy them and feel comfortably virtuous at the same time and the pictures are vivid and lively, not surprisingly as the artist-in-chief was Albrecht Dürer, who provided seventy-five of the 116 illustrations. Though the work is in the vernacular, the scholarly Brant still constructs individual texts according to the rules of rhetoric and peppers the texts with classical allusions. The appeal of this work should not surprise us, since it elicits the same feeling of moral outrage and superiority as the examples of human folly in a modern newspaper.

In 1501 Brant moved back to Strasbourg as legal adviser to the town council of his native city. Here the Emperor Maximilian called him in as a consultant on legal matters in 1502 and 1508. Neither noble nor churchman, versed in the new learning, famous thanks to the printing press and his career at a new university, Brant was just the sort of expert Maximilian liked to consult over the heads of his courtiers. Maximilian also used Humanist writers and scholars (for instance, Melchior Pfinzing, Marx Treitzsaurwein and Konrad Peutinger) for a series of works he either commissioned, organised, or helped to draft and which were designed to present a stylised and glorified version of his life and deeds to posterity. The project begins with Maximilian's fragmentary Latin autobiography, dictated by himself in what he called rough soldier's Latin, and moves on through the novelistic accounts of his life in German, *Freydal*, *Theuerdank* and *Weisskunig*, through the two huge woodcut series, *The Triumphal Procession* and *The Triumphal Arch*, a Latin version of the *Theuerdank* and a number of other panegyric and genealogical works, as well as a Book of Hours (*Gebetbuch*). The three 'novelistic autobiographies' are lavishly illustrated with woodcuts by such artists as Dürer and Burgkmair but, while the illustrations were printed, the unfinished prose *Freydal* was not and the prose romance *Der Weisskunig* was not printed in full until 1526. Alone of the three the verse epic *Der Theuerdank* appeared in Maximilian's day, in 1517. However, these works were not published in the modern sense. Maximilian kept their dissemination in his control and presented them to designated recipients. He also had the Book of Hours and the *Theuerdank* printed with a typeface which resembled calligraphy, he used parchment rather than paper for copies for prestigious recipients and had at least one copy of the Book of Hours decorated by hand in the margin by such artists as Dürer, Burgkmair, Cranach, Baldung Grien and Jörg Breu, thus ensuring that the printed book had the allure and the exclusivity of a manuscript. In the same way, the use of German does not mean that Maximilian intended his works for consumption by the masses. He used the vernacular because members of the aristocracy might not know Latin – or indeed how to read and write, menial tasks fulfilled by servants. Maximilian's activities show how difficult it is at this date to disentangle Latin from German, manuscript from printed book, learned from more general writing, the author as patron from the author as paid functionary from the author as individual.

By the time of Maximilian's death in 1519, Humanism had come a long way. A movement which was initially intended to revive ancient rhetoric was also centrally concerned with ethics and religion. One of the ways in which Christianity might be renewed after the dead end into which scholasticism had led it was via the wisdom of the classical writers. As Erasmus of Rotterdam (*c.* 1456–1536) maintained in his passionate defence of the study of ancient secular writers in the *Antibarbari* (begun in 1499, printed 1520), their writings were God-given. The searching out of Latin texts, and increasingly after 1500 of Greek ones, their editing, translation and publication and the study of the ideas in them led, quite against the intentions of men such as Erasmus, to a questioning of received ideas, both religious and political. Reuchlin the Hebraist, one of Brant's teachers, turned his attention to the Cabbala. In the case of Erasmus himself it led to his investigation of the Vulgate, the universally used Latin translation of the Bible by Jerome. This led Erasmus to compare the Vulgate with the Greek New Testament and to publish the latter in 1516. It was then possible to see that Jerome's translation, on which the authority of the church rested, was flawed. In his preface to the *Novum Instrumentum*, the work in which the Greek New Testament appeared, Erasmus pleads for a close study of the scriptures and for them to be available to all in the vernacular. The orientation of Humanism towards true internal piety also led to harsh satire of the inadequacies and vices of the clergy. In his brilliant verbal pyrotechnic display, *Encomium Moriae* (*The praise of folly*, 1511) Erasmus launched a comprehensive attack on all churchmen from the Pope down. Like *The Ship of Fools*, which had also pilloried abuses in the church, it was a bestseller: no less than thirty-six Latin editions during Erasmus's lifetime, quite apart from translations. While Erasmus was dedicated to bringing scholars together whatever their nationality, there was a strong undercurrent of nationalism in Italian Humanism which was taken up by Germans.

In politics this is reflected in the fact that in 1474 the phrase 'of the German nation' was added for the first time to the term 'Holy Roman Empire' on a legal document and that the full title began to be used by the Reichstag in 1512. In the world of learning it is found in Konrad Celtis's programme of national self-renewal through study of the Classics as enunciated in his inaugural lecture (given in Latin) at the University of Ingolstadt in 1492. In literature we see the same nationalism exemplified in the life and work of Ulrich von Hutten (1488–1523). Hutten was a member of the knightly class, the so-called 'Reichsritter', which at this period was undergoing an economic and political crisis. A combination of Humanist ideas and techniques with political awareness informs Hutten's writing from the first and one of his typical modes is satire, as in the *Epistolae obscurorum virorum* (*Letters of Obscure Men*, 1515–17) for which he and Crotus Rhubeanus (*c.*1480 to after 1539) were responsible. The letters purported to be written by the opponents of Johannes Reuchlin, the defender of Jewish learning and of the right of Jews to keep their libraries, and the pig Latin in which they were couched exposed the ignorance and obscurantism of these opponents. Hutten spent the years 1512–13 and 1515–17 in Italy and when he returned to Germany he began to publish a series of works damaging to the authority of the church. He brought out the Italian Humanist Lorenzo Valla's exposure of the forged document legitimising the so-called Constantine Donation, the basis for the secular power of the Pope, he published two prose dialogues between his own illness and himself (*Febris prima, Febris secunda* (*Fever the first, fever the second*, 1519)) in which he tries to persuade Fever that she would be better off with Cardinal Cajetan, the papal legate, whose loose lifestyle and great wealth would make him a better host. In *Vadiscus sive trias Romana* (Vadiscus or the Roman Trinity, 1519) he unmasks the corruption he witnessed in Rome. While all these writings were in Latin, they remained within the confines of Humanist polemics. However, in 1521 Hutten decided to put them and another called *Inspicientes, Die Anschawenden* (*The onlookers*) into German and publish them under the title *Gespräch büchlin* (*Book of Dialogues*). (The onlookers are Apollo and Phaeton looking down on, among other things, the Augsburg Reichstag of 1518.) Thus he took the controversy out of the study and into the market-place. Coming as it did on top of Luther's Reformation pamphlets, the *Gespräch büchlin* was incendiary material. Hutten was driven by a vision of a German empire freed from the claims of the papacy – something he articulates in his *Arminius* dialogue of 1519/20. He joined the Lutheran cause, not so much out of theological fervour as because he wished to harness Luther's anti-Roman propaganda to his own nationalist programme. To the same end he joined forces with the condottiere Franz von Sickingen, was defeated in battle, had to flee and died in Switzerland in 1523. His best-known work today is his so-called 'poem from the Underground' of 1521, written while he was staying with Sickingen, 'Ich hab's gewagt mit sinnen' ('I dared all knowingly').

Hutten's nationalism is related to the liberal tendency inherent in Humanism. It is manifest, for instance, in Agrippa of Nettesheim's piece on women as intellectual beings *De nobilitate et praecellentia foeminei sexus* (*Of the nobility and excellence of the female sex*, 1509) and in Erasmus's *Colloquies*, several of which challenge standard assumptions about the subordinate and domestic role suitable for women, as well as in Reuchlin's efforts on behalf of Jewish learning and spirituality.

Luther

Many social, political and economic factors have been adduced as contributing to the Reformation and to the speed with which Luther's challenge to the established ecclesiastical order took hold: the growth of the towns, the rise of German nationalism, the disparate nature of the territories within the Empire, the Turkish threat which distracted the attention of Charles V (emperor 1519–56), the precarious social and economic position of both the knightly as well as the peasant class. None of these, however, could have initiated the Reformation movement and none of them alone is a complete explanation for its spread. The new currents of thought, the scholarly examination of texts and the interest in the beliefs and value systems of the ancient world which were central to Humanism in the first quarter of the sixteenth century were at least as important. Out of them emerged that challenge to the Church launched by Martin Luther (1483–1546), Augustinian monk and professor of Theology at the new University of Wittenberg (founded in 1502), which determined the shape not only of German religion but of German society until our own day. What makes the Reformation relevant in a history of German literature is that it was sparked off and later developed by ideas expressed in writing. The use of the vernacular and of the printing press was central to that development.

Luther, having studied scholastic theology at the University of Erfurt, came to Wittenberg in 1511 where he was not only awarded his doctorate in theology but took over from his mentor Staupitz the task of lecturing on the Bible. The detailed and close reading of the biblical text and of the Church Fathers which this entailed led Luther to the conclusion that the well-established system of wiping sins away by confession and expiation was unbiblical. So too was the idea that the main route to heaven was via the sacraments, which were in the control of a priestly class. The Church had further extended its profit and loss theology by providing 'indulgences' as a substitute for doing penance and had then started an inflationary spiral by distributing them more and more often (to celebrate papal jubilees, for instance), by increasing their scope and finally by selling them. In preparing his famous lectures on St Paul's Letter to the Romans (1515–16) Luther came to the conclusion that the scholastic interpretations of the Bible were simply false, for St Paul proclaimed that man could not earn salvation by his own actions, it was a gift from God and man was justified by faith alone. It followed from this that indulgences run directly counter to the Bible (*Sermon von Ablaß und Gnade* (*Sermon on Indulgences and Grace*, 1518)). At a stroke, the idea of justification by faith made the mediation of the church in the matter of salvation unnecessary (*Von der Freiheit eines Christenmenschen* (*On Christian freedom*,

1520)). If its mediation was unnecessary, then its failings and abuses could no longer be condoned.

The other main *raison d'être* for the Church was to convey Christian teachings and the Bible to the faithful. Luther, however, appealed directly to the person in the pew over the heads of the clergy, asserting the priesthood of all believers and emphasising the corruption of the ordained priesthood (*An den christlichen Adel deutscher Nation von des christlichen Standes Besserung* (*To the Christian aristocracy of the German nation on the improvement of the Christian Estate*), *De captivitate Babylonica ecclesiae praeludium* (*A preamble on the Babylonian captivity of the Church*), both 1520). The Church had hitherto been the guardian of the sacred texts, of which the accepted version was St Jerome's Latin translation, which Erasmus had demonstrated to be flawed. The ordinary believer had access neither to Latin nor, before printing, to the actual Bible itself. He or she heard a portion of it read out on Sunday and listened to its interpretation in the sermon. To enable the faithful to carry out their priesthood adequately, they needed direct access to the Bible, so Luther set about translating it (New Testament, September 1522; the whole Bible, 1534).

Though a revolutionary in matters of theology and church organisation (*Ursach und Antwort, dass Jungfrauen Kloster gottlich verlassen mogen* (*Reasons why virgins may rightfully leave their convents*, 1523)), Luther's thinking on the nature of the state (*Von weltlicher Obrigkeit* (*On secular authority*, 1523)) and the role of government (*Wider die Mordischen und Reubischen Rotten der anderen Bauern* (*Against the murdering, thieving gangs of peasants*, 1525)) is in favour of the status quo. God has constructed the state on hierarchical lines and it behoves all classes within it to carry out His will. Unlike the Swiss Reformer Huldrich Zwingli (1484–1531), who died on the battlefield, or the preacher Thomas Müntzer (1489/90–1525), who was executed for his involvement in the Peasants' War, Luther believed in rendering unto Caesar the things that are Caesar's. His writings on marriage (*Vom ehelichen Leben* (*On married life*, 1522), *Eine Predigt vom Ehestand* (*A sermon on the married state*, 1525)) upgraded marriage as a vocation, but by emphasising the role of wife and mother as the *only* female destiny, he reduced women's sphere to the home and made them the prisoners of their own biology. By closing the convents, the only space in which women were free of that biology and in which they were licensed to study, he hampered them in their search for education and self-expression in writing, as we can see from the account by Caritas Pirckheimer (1467–1532), a Humanist scholar and prioress of a convent in Nuremberg, of her struggle to keep her convent open (*Denkwürdigkeiten* (*memoirs*, 1524)). Those women active as pamphleteers in the early decades of the Reformation such as Katharina Zell

(1497/9–1562) and Argula von Grumbach (c. 1492–1563) had to endure contumely and not only from the opposition, precisely because they were women and therefore unqualified to speak on religious matters.

How Luther's controversies developed, how some rallied to his cause and others became polarised in their opposition, how what was originally an academic theological dispute took on political overtones and led to, among other things, the Peasants' Revolt in 1525, how other Reformers such as Zwingli and later Calvin (1509–64) articulated a different version of the Reformed message and how Lutheranism evolved as a separate church in opposition to Rome is a fascinating story but not one we can tell here. But what of Luther as a writer?

He was an extraordinarily prolific one. It has been calculated that between 1518 and 1524 he was the author of one in three of all the German books published. As well as his translation of the Bible, he published at least another eighty works: sermons, pamphlets, comments on questions of the day, biblical commentaries, catechisms, hymns, not to mention his prefaces to books of the Bible, letters, etc. Luther's writings are remarkable for their stylistic energy and vividness, for he writes with directness of speech and with an ear for earthy metaphors and similes. However, he knows how to combine these with a whole range of rhetorical effects and to marshal them with the skill of the trained debater. His language and his personality overwhelm the reader, who is bombarded with invective, argument, scorn and biting satire – all in the service of deeply felt religious beliefs. Unlike Erasmus, who was writing for a network of highly educated scholars like himself, capable of understanding his classical allusions and learned jokes, Luther wanted to convince the ordinary believer. To that end he began to use the vernacular as early as 1518, something which also fitted the nationalist note he was fond of striking. But it was the printing press which gave the Reformation debate wide currency, fuelled it and created a demand for more. This encouraged both writing and printing in the vernacular.

The most influential of all of Luther's writings is his German Bible. Although there were fourteen High and four Low German versions of the complete Bible before Luther's, they are distinguished from his in that they were intended to be read with the Vulgate as a sort of crib, whereas Luther's Bible is meant to be taken on its own terms, to be the only text necessary to understand the word of God. It is an impressive work of scholarship, Humanist in its concern to return to the original sources. The first version of the New Testament, the so-called 'Septembertestament' of 1522, used Erasmus's Greek New Testament as a source. The second version of this appeared in December of the same year. Working with a team consisting of such scholars as Philipp Melanchthon, Professor of Greek at Wittenberg, Luther was able to publish the Old Testament in

1534, having learned Hebrew for the purpose. As a translator Luther is colourful and accurate, has a gift for the telling metaphor or picturesque image and an excellent grasp of the rhythm and balance of a sentence. In a pamphlet justifying his practice as a translator, *Eyn Sendbrieff vom Dolmetschen* (*Pamphlet on translation*, 1530), Luther claims that he was guided by two considerations: accuracy and a desire to write the German 'of the mother in the home, the child in the street, the ordinary man in the market-place'. We cannot take either of these claims at face value. Luther had no intention of being neutral and if accuracy in translation did not give sufficient support to his ideas, he was perfectly ready to make adjustments. He equips the various books of the Bible with prefaces or disquisitions to the faithful on how to understand the book in question. If it is not to his liking (as with the Epistle of St James or the Book of Esther), he makes clear that he does not consider it part of the canonical text! As regards his style, he uses everyday language but structures it rhetorically.

The Reformation and German literature

The effects of the Reformation on German literature were considerable. First, Luther himself exerted a considerable influence. If his Bible did not unify the German language in the overwhelming way that was once thought, his expressions and coinages have become part of the language and the vividness with which he wrote has left its mark everywhere. He initiated polemical journalism in German, aimed at a new reading public whom he addressed in the vernacular. His pronouncements on drama and its pedagogical uses made their influence felt throughout the sixteenth century and crucially influenced the cultivation of Latin drama in the schools as well as the development of drama in German, just as his initiation of the German hymn as part of his reform of church services influenced German verse and began a long and fruitful tradition of hymn writing. There was scarcely a genre which he did not touch: letters, sermons, academic writing, poems, translation, pamphlets and hymns.

Second, the controversy Luther unleashed was so heated that well into the 1540s writing in German was largely of a directly polemical kind. There was a flood of pamphlets by adversaries such as Thomas Murner (1475–1537) and Johannes Eck (1486–1543) and by supporters like Andreas Karlstadt, Hutten and Melanchthon. The debate was carried on just as fiercely in poetry, the prose dialogue, the verse epic and drama.

An example is the reaction of the dramatist and poet Hans Sachs (1494–1576) to the Reformation message. He became aware of Luther's teachings at the latest by 1518 and spent a number of years studying them. Having published nothing in 1521 and 1522 his famous verse dialogue *Die*

Wittenbergisch Nachtigall (*The nightingale of Wittenberg*) appeared in
1523. The accompanying woodcut sums up the argument: the wild beasts
of the Roman Church are preying on Christ's flock in the dark night of the
pre-Reformation era. The beasts cluster round a tree baying at the nightingale (Luther) whose sweet song announces the dawn of a new era. The
next year, 1524, Sachs published four prose dialogues, almost mini-
dramas, in which characters such as a canon, a rich man or a monk argue
out the Lutheran message. One of the discussants usually represents Hans
Sachs himself, a man of the people whose sturdy common sense and
minute knowledge of the Bible place him firmly on the side of Reform.

Another example in the tradition of folly literature stemming from
Brant and Erasmus is Thomas Murner's *Vom grossen Lutherischen narren*
(*Of the great Lutheran fool*, 1522), a verse epic accompanied by woodcuts
designed by Murner himself. Murner presents himself as the tom-cat in
monk's clothing his opponents had characterised him as (in a play on his
name) and Luther as a huge inflated fool who is concealing a crowd of
lesser fools in his belly. When they have emerged to plague the Germans,
the Great Lutheran Fool deflates to a limp parody of his former self.

Some of the most savage Reformation satire and polemic was couched
in the form of drama. In *Die Todtenfresser* (*The eaters of the dead*, 1522)
the Basle writer Pamphilius Gengenbach (*c.* 1470–1524) satirises the profit
the clergy derive from Masses for the dead by depicting the Pope, a monk,
a nun, and so on, feasting on a corpse dished up in front of them. Another
Swiss, the Bernese painter, politician and poet Niklaus Manuel
(1484–1530), is the author of *Vom Bapst und siner Priesterschaft* (*On the
Pope and his priesthood*, 1523, performed in Berne), a pageant involving
fifty speaking parts and at least another hundred supporting cast, in which
various aspects of the Pope's turpitude are presented in seven disconnected scenes. Manuel's *Der aplass Kremer* (*The indulgence-seller*,
1525) depicts an indulgence-seller being tortured by a group of peasants
until he confesses the full extent of his cynical exploitation of them.

The Reformation message is also propounded in Burkhard Waldis's (*c.*
1490–1555) Low German *De parabell vam vorlorn Szohn* (*The parable of
the prodigal son*, 1527), which gives a dramatic rendering of the gospel
story in order to emphasise the Lutheran message of justification by
faith. It initiates the flood of dramas on this theme to be found in sixteenth-century Germany. If Waldis's play is still in the medieval tradition
of episodic, epic drama, *Acolastus* (1520) by Gulielmus Gnapheus (real
name: Willem van de Voldersgroft, 1493–1568) is a polished Latin drama
in the tradition of Terence. While it too tells the story of the son who
squanders his inheritance on loose living and then comes crawling back
for forgiveness, it makes no mention of the biblical parable as such. It is
up to the audience to draw the parallel. Basic to the play is the debate

between Erasmus and Luther on the freedom or otherwise of the will, a fundamental theological doctrine in the Reformation debate. *Acolastus* exemplifies the notion, so strongly advocated by Erasmus, the Humanists and Luther himself, that Latin drama can be Christianised.

Polemical in a different way is the first martyr play in German, *Tragedia Johannis Huss* (*The tragedy of Jan Hus*, 1537) by Johann Agricola (real name: J. Schnitter, 1494/6–1566). This five-act drama depicts the show trial of Hus, the great Bohemian Reformer executed in 1415, and shows him being condemned for extreme views invented by his enemies without ever being given the chance to defend himself. The play ends with a prophet who foretells the coming of another such reformer a century later. Thomas Naogeorg (real name: T. Kirchmayer, *c.* 1508–63) wrote six plays in Latin, all deeply embued with the Reformation message. *Pammachius* (*The warmonger*, 1538), his most famous play, depicts an evil Pope, Pammachius, who has sold out to Satan, and his struggle for dominion over the virtuous Emperor Julianus, whose power the Pope wishes to usurp. In Act IV, when the papal camp is lying drunk after celebrating its victory with an orgy, we learn from Christ himself that a new spirit of renewal is stirring – where else but in Wittenberg, led by one Theophilus (Luther). Satan and the papal party learn of this and prepare to do battle against the new teaching by every means at their disposal. The play has no fifth act, we are told, because this struggle is still going on around us.

Naogeorg's *Tragoedia alia nova Mercator seu Judicium* (*The merchant*, 1541), tells of a merchant on his deathbed who despairs of salvation because of his lack of good works, until Christ and St Paul convince him of the importance of faith. *Incendia seu Pyrgopolinices* (*Conflagration or the Fireraiser*, 1541) shows the armed struggle between the Roman and Reformed camps stirred up by the warmongering Pope Pammachius and his henchman, the fireraiser Pyrgopolinices, who represents Duke Heinrich of Wolfenbüttel. Naogeorg is clearly fascinated by evil and is much more interested in portraying villains than heroes. Character-istically, his play based on the biblical Esther story is called after Haman (*Hamanus*, 1543) and his play on the last hours of Christ is entitled *Judas* (1552). *Jeremia* (1551) tells of a prophet come to reform the Jews but whose strictures fall on deaf ears. Remarkable for the energy and verve of the writing, Naogeorg's works enjoyed a wide popularity, appeared in numerous editions and were translated into German many times.

Drama 1540–1620

Post-Reformation the divisions between Catholic, Lutheran and Calvinist were given political reality in the Peace of Augsburg (1555), in which the principle of *cujus regio, ejus religio* was promulgated, that is, the religion of the ruler was to be the state religion in his territory. This led to emigration and to tensions between ruler and subject and must be borne in mind as the context for all literature of the next hundred years. Nowhere are these confessional differences more apparent than in the sphere of drama.

They emerge even in the older German pageant plays, involving huge casts of characters and performed outdoors by the citizenry, which survived in Switzerland into the 1580s. Protestant plays like Hans von Rüte's *Joseph,* performed in Berne in 1538, *Adam und Heva* (*Adam and Eve*) by Jacob Ruoff performed in Zurich in 1550, or Jos Murer's *Belägerung der Statt Babylon* (*The Siege of Babylon,* 1559) written for Zurich, are based on biblical material, while the Catholic Hanns Wagner's (1522–90) *Sant Mauritzen Tragoedia, Sant Vrsen Spil* (1581) takes rather the legends of two Solothurn saints, St Mauritius and St Ursus and emphasises their miracles.

The characteristic dramatic forms in German are the largely Protestant biblical school drama performed by schoolboys and the carnival plays of the Mastersingers performed by artisans, also usually Protestant. These two forms existed in a kind of symbiotic relationship with one another, as we shall see. Protestant biblical drama deals with a comparatively narrow range of themes usually in rhymed iambic pentameter. As school drama it stems from the Humanist encouragement of drama as rhetorical exercise. In the wake of the Reformation certain themes came to dominate. Such dramatists as Sixt Birk (1501–54), Paul Rebhun (1500–46), Thiebolt Gart (attested *c.* 1540), Jörg Wickram (*c.* 1500/05–1560/2), Andreas Pfeilschmidt (attested *c.* 1555), Jos Murer (1530–80), Thomas Brunner (*c.* 1535–71), Georg Rollenhagen (1542–1609) and Nikodemus Frischlin (1547–90) gave dramatic form again and again to the same themes and topics, many of them, such as the stories of Susanna and Tobias, directly sanctioned by Luther himself. Most of these plays are in German, though Sixt Birk began by writing biblical drama in German (e.g. *Susanna* (1532), *Joseph* and *Judith* (1539)) in Basle and then translated the plays into Latin, once he had become headmaster of the Annaschule in Augsburg in 1536. Nikodemus Frischlin wrote his biblical plays in Latin, which his brother Jakob translated some years later – *Rebecca* and *Susanna,* for instance, in 1589.

The most popular topics are those dealing with relations between father and son and with questions of filial obedience. The Prodigal Son is the favourite: Gnapheus and Waldis's versions have already been mentioned. There are plays on the same theme by Hans Salat (*Eyn parabel oder glichnus von dem Verlorenen / oder Güdigen Sun* (*A parable of the prodigal or virtuous son,* 1537)), Jörg Wickram (*Spil von dem verlornen sun* (*The play of the prodigal son,* 1540)), Jos Murer (*Der jungen Mannen*

Spiegel (*The young men's mirror*, 1560)), Wickram's dramatisation of his own novel of the same name, *Der jungen Knaben Spiegel* (*The young boys' mirror*, 1554) and many more down to Ludwig Hollonius's *Freimut* of 1603. There are dramas too on the related themes of *Absolom* by Murer (1565), and on Joseph and his brothers, for instance by Sixt Birck (1539), Thiebolt Gart (1540) and Thomas Brunner (1566). Obedience to one's father, discipline in early life and avoidance of bad company are held up as essential virtues in plots which bear witness to the importance of faith rather than works on the spiritual journey of the male protagonists. Women only appear in supporting roles as temptations to be overcome along the way.

The female population is addressed in the many plays on marriage and wifely obedience, for instance, Rebhun's *Hochzeit zu Cana* (*Marriage at Cana*, 1538), Brunner's *Isaac* (1569), the many Tobias plays (e.g. by Rollenhagen, 1576) and Frischlin's Latin *Rebecca* (1576). The Esther story, in which the meek and saintly Jewess, chosen as Ashaverus's wife instead of the rebellious Vashti, saves her people, and the Susanna theme, in which a pure wife is saved by the young Daniel from the lecherous Elders, provide pictures of the model wife and of the ideal marriage. There are Esther plays by Naogeorg (*Hamanus*, 1543), Pfeilschmidt (1555) and Murer (1567), we know of at least twenty-one Susanna plays up to 1636, of which the most famous are those by Birk (1532), Rebhun (1535) and Nikodemus Frischlin (1577). The Lutheran vision of the woman's role is reinforced by the passive female figures presented in these dramas. While a writer such as Rebhun stands out for his dramatic flair and ability to write realistic genre scenes, all these works, performed by the Protestant boys' grammar schools, resemble each other in their moral and didactic intention and in their clear aim to impose certain behavioural norms on the community which both acts in and watches the play.

At first glance, the Mastersingers' drama is completely unrelated to the biblical drama. It is always in the vernacular, put on by unlearned, usually Protestant, artisans with a cast of not more than about a dozen and in the case of the carnival plays sometimes with as few as two or three. There were noted practitioners already in the fifteenth century such as Hans Rosenblüt (active from 1427 on) and Hans Folz (1435/40–1513) but it is Hans Sachs (1494–1576) who is primarily associated with the form today. He was a shoemaker in Nuremberg, with some Latin, a thirst for learning and sufficient income from his trade to enable him to assemble a library. In that his aspirations are unthinkable before the era of the printed book, he is just as much a product of the Renaissance as such learned Nuremberg contemporaries as the scholar Willibald Pirckheimer or the painter Albrecht Dürer. Sachs learned to write verse, music and plays as a member of a Mastersingers guild. The Mastersingers ('Meistersinger') were rhymesmiths who from the middle of the fifteenth century (the earliest record is 1430 in Lübeck, 1440 in Nuremberg) organised themselves locally into what they called singing schools ('Singschulen') or guilds, which laid down strict rules for versification and musical composition which they taught in the same way that a craft guild would teach a manual skill. The Nuremberg 'Singschule', founded in 1450 at about the time 'Meistersang' established itself generally, was a particularly active one which lasted until 1774. The aim of the Mastersingers was to present all aspects of life either in song or in dramatic form: the Bible, sacred subjects, current events, well-known tales, jokes, were all versified. Sachs's considerable oeuvre corresponds to this aim. He was a highly self-conscious artist who made periodic inventories of his own works, as he tells us in his poetic autobiography, the 254–line poem, 'Summa all meiner gedicht' ('Summing-up of all my poems', 1567), and who, beginning in 1558, compiled a five-volume folio edition of his works during his own lifetime. Sachs himself divides his dramatic works, of which there are more than two hundred, in three ways: according to genre (sixty-one tragedies, sixty-five comedies and eighty-five carnival plays, the distinction between the first two being the happy or tragic ending), according to the source material used (the Bible, ancient history, the *Decameron* and other literary sources, and comic anecdotes or 'Schwänke') and according to the purpose he assigns to the various types of play: the biblical plays are meant to be 'conducive to a repentant Christian life', the secular plays should function as moral examples, the carnival plays should delight, distract and dispel melancholy. Carnival plays, so called because they were performed during the pre-Lenten season of jollification and misrule, could occasionally be serious, such as Sachs's *Der dot im stock* (*Death in the tree trunk*, 1555), a play about the penalties of greed, but the vast majority are short, humorous playlets, based on a combination of stock comic types – the adulterous wife, the jealous husband, the nosy neighbour, the naive simpleton, the lecherous priest – and pinpoint the folly and duplicity of the human race (*Der fahrendt Schuler im Paradeiss* (*The wandering student in Paradise*, 1550), or *Der gross Eyferer* (*The jealous husband*, 1553)). The humour is coarse, the behaviour exaggerated to the point of grotesquerie and the interactions between the characters often brutal. Here is where one sees the relationship of the carnival plays to the biblical drama. On the one hand they function as an outlet for the taboos the biblical drama imposes, for they license the depiction of those vices the biblical drama castigates and allow the audience to enjoy that depiction. Therefore their humour comes from the transgression of clearly understood sexual rules and from universally applicable inverted power relations, in the spirit of carnival and misrule. On the other hand, order is restored at the end and the norms invoked are precisely those of the biblical drama. The monstrous women of the carnival plays, lecherous, quarrelsome, deceitful, lazy and power-crazed, as exaggerated in their vice as the biblical heroines are in their virtue, are usually brought to book by being beaten into submission. The tyrannical Gredt in Sachs's *Kälberbrüten* (*How to hatch calves*, 1551), the lecherous wife in his *Teufelsbannen* (*The exorcism*, 1551), Jakob Ayrer's lazy and undutiful housewife Lampa in *Die Erziehung des bösen Weibes* (*The education of the wicked wife*) written at the end of the century are all disciplined by this means. The carnival plays, it is thought, were performed in inns, which means that the audience was largely, if not exclusively, male. If their wives have not learned to behave by watching biblical plays, the men are here taught their true nature and the remedy for it. Having highlighted human fallibility, it has often been said that Sachs is concerned to end on a note of tolerance, and the message for the audience, after they have derided the behaviour on stage, is to draw parallels with their own and to live and let live (*Das heiss Eysen* (*The hot iron*, 1551)). This can only happen after the correct power relations have been restored. In *Das heiss Eysen*, husband and wife are equally guilty of sexual promiscuity and deceit. But only the wife is unmasked, only she loses face, and the husband, who by his own admission is worse than she is, holds the moral high ground by forgiving her and taking her back. The carnival plays are thus the mirror-image of the biblical drama and serve the same normative social function.

By contrast with his carnival plays, Sachs's tragedies and comedies are epic rather than dramatic works, in which he is concerned to put across a story, whether biblical or secular, to those who have no means of reading it. There is often no dramatic shape in terms of complication, crisis and resolution and there seems to be no very good reason in any one instance why Sachs should have chosen drama rather than narrative poem or dialogue. The point of these plays is the narrative, as in *Die gantz histori Tobie mit seinem sun* (*The complete tale of Tobias and his son*, 1533), *Tristrant* (1553) or *Griselda* (1546).

Increasingly during the second half of the sixteenth century, however, a range of outside influences and foreign forms was patronised and encouraged by the courts. The Habsburg Emperor Ferdinand I invited the Society of Jesus, a teaching order founded in 1540 to renew the spiritual life of the Catholic church, to open a College in Vienna in 1551, though Jesuits were already in Cologne from 1544 and in Munich from 1549. Even in the 1550s the Jesuits had begun to make Latin drama central to their educational programme, taking as a starting-point the pre-existing Humanist school drama. The first Jesuit play put on in the Empire was Livinus Brecht's *Euripus*, a Catholic morality play written in the Netherlands in 1548 but performed by the Jesuits in Vienna in 1555. This internationalism is characteristic of Jesuit drama which borrowed plays from all over Europe. While the material used was fairly heterogeneous in the beginning, using biblical themes, Terentian comedy, allegorical dramas and stories of local saints as well as Humanist and even Protestant material (for instance, Gnapheus's *Acolastus*), the order was so well-organised and so centralised that a characteristic type of Latin drama soon evolved which was then to be found in all Jesuit institutions, codified in the *Ratio studiorum* or regulations for the Jesuit schools promulgated in 1599. This drama, whose purpose was to demonstrate the spiritual meaning behind the events of this world, was of central importance throughout the Empire until the 1770s. After 1551 Jesuit colleges were founded rapidly in Ingolstadt (1556), Cologne (1556), Munich (1559), Trier (1561) and Dillingen (1563) and in each of these centres drama was cultivated. By 1725 there were no less than 208 schools and colleges, of which the biggest, such as Munich, had well over 1,000 pupils. The Jesuits were the educators and advisers of the Catholic aristocracy and princes in the Empire, up to the Emperor himself. In centres such as Munich and Vienna, Jesuit theatre was closely linked to the court itself and was performed as part of court festivals. The Jesuits also had an indirect influence on Protestant drama in the vernacular, which saw itself in competition with and in opposition to the Jesuits.

After the heterogeneous beginnings mentioned above, Jesuit colleges in the Empire soon began to write their own plays. Many Jesuit plays are anonymous – it was one of the duties of the Professor of Rhetoric to write and direct these plays for performance at the beginning of the school year, in the spring and on special occasions – and, unlike Protestant and Humanist plays, were often not printed. One outstanding dramatist, however, does emerge, namely, Jakob Bidermann (1578–1639). He wrote his first and most famous drama *Cenodoxus* in 1602 but his period as Professor of Rhetoric in Munich was the most important for his dramatic activities: he wrote *Adrian* in 1606 (now lost), *Belisarius* in 1607, *Macarius Romanus* (1613) and *Josephus* (1615), *Cosmarchia* and *Philemon Martyr* (1618). There was also a famous revival of *Cenodoxus* in 1613. Bidermann's plays centre on a protagonist who is usually blind to the true nature of the world at the beginning of the play. Those, like Joseph and Philemon, who achieve insight into the wiles of the world are saved, as are those like Belisarius who come to grief but who learn from this experience, whereas others who remain wilfully blind, like Cenodoxus, are damned. Bidermann's plays were put on indoors in the lecture theatre of the college on a wide stage with various open booths at the back to represent the different settings, surmounted by an upper stage.

The Jesuit theatre was amateur theatre, analogous to the Protestant school drama, and just as the former was patronised by Catholic courts, the latter was patronised by Protestant ones. Nikodemus Frischlin

(1547–90) was both an academic at the University of Tübingen and a court poet to the Duke of Württemberg at Stuttgart. His biblical plays *Rebecca* (1576) and *Susanna* (1578) and the historical play, *Hildegardis magna* (*Hildegard the Great*, 1579), as well as *Fraw Wendelgard* (1579), were all put on at court in their original Latin. Other works were put on at Tübingen with the court present. Frischlin fell foul of the Duke in 1580 and went into exile, but tried to re-establish relations in 1585 with his best-known play *Julius Redivivus* (1582) in which Cicero and Julius Caesar come back to life and visit Germany where they are amazed to discover the German invention of the printing press and impressed by the standard of learning. This friendship between the writer Cicero and the ruler Caesar was intended to reconcile Frischlin with the Duke.

Dramatic performances at court in languages other than the vernacular were nothing unusual. For instance, the Catholic Munich court was instrumental in bringing the *commedia dell'arte*, professional but improvised comic theatre in Italian using a small number of stock comic types, to Bavaria in 1568. The Protestant courts were also the first patrons of the English strolling players. English players were first invited to the Danish court at Copenhagen in 1585 and again in 1586, recommended by the Earl of Leicester. They took up service with the Danish king who lent them to the Saxon Elector Christian I at Dresden in 1587. From then on, troupes of English players were constantly on the move across Europe, seeking their fortune away from a London rather too richly endowed with competing acting companies and increasingly coming under the sway of Puritan restrictions on the theatre. Furthermore the London theatres had to be closed between 1592 and 1594 because of plague. It was not, however, the incompetent who sought their fortune abroad. Such notable Elizabethan actors as Robert Browne, Richard Jones, William Kemp, Thomas Pope and Thomas Sackville all spent extended periods on the Continent. Members of the Lord Admiral's men performed at the Frankfurt fair in 1592 and though they and their successors regularly played during the great fairs of Europe, their travelling was restricted to the late spring, summer and early autumn and usually ceased completely in winter, which the troupes spent mostly at a prince's court. Thomas Sackville and John Bradstreet went to the court of Duke Heinrich Julius of Braunschweig at Wolfenbüttel in 1592 and Robert Browne's troupe, possibly including for a time the composer John Dowland, was based in Kassel at the court of Landgrave Maurice of Hessen-Kassel between 1594 and 1613. In central Europe from the beginning of the seventeenth century it was the Electors of Brandenburg, the Vasa kings of Poland and the Habsburgs of Bohemia and Austria who were the principal patrons of the players and who enabled them to survive for extended periods even during the Thirty Years War. The area covered by the players was enormous, stretching from Cologne in the West to Königsberg on the Baltic coast.

The players acted in English at first (up to about 1606), then increasingly in German, putting across the prose text with much visual comedy, music and dancing, but with more sophisticated acting and staging techniques than the Germans were used to. They presented the English drama of the day in simplified versions, including plays by Peele, Marlowe, Kyd, Greene, Chapman, Heywood, Dekker, Marston, Beaumont and Fletcher, Massinger and at least a dozen of Shakespeare's plays, both tragedies and comedies. Duke Heinrich Julius of Braunschweig (1564–1613) wrote eleven plays for Sackville's troupe which was in his service in Wolfenbüttel from 1592. These include the biblical play *Von der Susanna* (1593), comedies relating to social reforms he was instituting in the Duchy such as *Von einem Weibe* ([*Tale*] *of a woman*, 1593) and *Von einem Wirthe oder Gastgeber* ([*Tale*] *of a inn-keeper*, 1594) and his best-known comedy about a braggadocio, *Von Vincentio Ladislao* (1594). This theatrical activity lasted until about 1600. The Duke was thus the first German dramatist to write for professional actors performing regularly in one place. Another nobleman, Landgrave Maurice of Hessen-Kassel, built the first standing theatre in the Empire for his troupe of English players between 1603 and 1605, the so-called Ottonium. Robert Browne's men spent the years 1594–1613 in Kassel and it is clear the the Landgrave wrote plays for them himself, though the manuscript of only one is preserved (*Die Belohnung der gottes furcht (Fear of God rewarded)*).

Other influences of the English players can be seen in the work of Jakob Ayrer (1544–1605) who saw them act in Nuremberg in 1596. As well as tragedies and comedies, Ayrer wrote thirty-six carnival plays, in which one of the recurring figures is the comic Jan Bouset or John Posset, created by Sackville. Another of the recurrent clown figures is Pickelhäring, probably created by Robert Reynolds. We encounter him officially in the first of the printed collections of the English players' plays, published in 1620, and entitled *Engelische Comedien und Tragedien (English comedies and tragedies)*. It is interesting to see how this volume contains plays on such favourite German themes as Esther and the Prodigal Son alongside the foreign material.

Those courts which were patrons of various forms of drama – Kassel, Dresden and Stuttgart among the Protestant courts, Vienna, Graz and Munich among the Catholic ones – were also those in which court festivals of an increasingly elaborate and international kind, such as costumed tournaments, firework displays and later ballet and opera, were cultivated. The technical innovations introduced here eventually percolated down into spoken theatre.

Sixteenth-century verse

Modern distinctions between prose and verse, between the themes and styles proper to each and between song and poem are unhelpful when discussing the verse of this century. Many topics which we would treat in prose, were versified in the sixteenth and even in the seventeenth centuries – battles, political events or sensational local happenings. Indeed, the very large category of narrative verse includes all kinds of factual reportage and fictional story-telling. Nor is it easy to use music as a distinguishing characteristic. The most extraordinary variety of verse was sung and the term 'song' can cover anything from simple folk-songs and love songs, to political songs and ballads, to lengthy sung narratives. Musically speaking it can range from courtly polyphony to Mastersinger melodies, from hymns to folk-songs, while melodies and texts moved back and forth between secular and religious, between the court and the people.

Secular song continued to be cultivated at court and among circles of friends as it always had been, but collections of such songs were now published for the first time and so gained wide currency. The most famous and influential is Georg Forster's *Frische Teutsche Liedlein* (*New German songs*, published in five parts between 1539 and 1556 in Nuremberg). Forster went about his collecting in a systematic way, attributing the melodies, working with composers and including as many types of song as possible. His collection contains many charming love songs, ballads and drinking songs, comic and political songs but Forster's emphasis is more on the music than on the text.

Another important category of song is that of the Mastersingers. Their strict rules extended equally to the melodies and to the texts of their songs, so-called 'Meistersang', which they themselves divided into secular and religious. While the Mastersingers demanded adherence to the norm rather than individuality, one has only to read Sachs's poetry – he wrote some 4,000 Mastersongs – to hear a poet treating the characteristic themes of poets in all ages: his own emotions, his role as a poet, grief and loss, for instance. He communes with himself on the loss of a wife to whom he had been married for forty years, he discusses his own poetic oeuvre, he meditates on death and on his own state of mind. We have already seen how he put his poetry at the service of the Reformation. Once the Reformation had spread, most of the Mastersingers went over to it and the teachings of Luther influenced their verse.

The single most important development in sixteenth-century verse in German was the Protestant hymn. In his five-volume compendium of German hymn texts published between 1864 and 1877, Wackernagel prints some 3,700 Protestant examples for the sixteenth century alone and only about 450 Catholic ones. It was Luther's reorganisation of the Mass and the prominence he gave to congregational singing which launched the genre, though he may himself have been reacting to Thomas Müntzer's German translations of ten Latin hymns from 1525. Luther translated Latin hymns or provided new versions of them, he recast psalms in the form of hymns and wrote new texts and some melodies. The sixteenth-century texts best known to Germans and in translation the world over are Luther's hymns. While Luther initially envisaged a strictly liturgical function for his hymns, the genre soon developed a catechetical purpose and began also to be used in private meditation and prayer.

Naturally too, the unrest of the period gave rise to a body of political and polemical poetry, for instance, that of Ulrich von Hutten discussed above. Into the same category come the songs relating to the Peasants' Revolt of 1525, the songs of the soldier-poet Jörg Graff (1475/80–1542) or even Luther's own ballad on the burning of two Protestant martyrs, Augustinian monks, in 1523 in Brussels. The vast majority of such verse, disseminated in songs and on broadsheets, often illustrated, was, however, anonymous.

There is also a fine body of Latin poetry, written to be read rather than to be sung. Two outstanding poets are Jan Nicholaus Everaerts (1511–36), better known as Johannes Secundus, and Petrus Lotichius (1528–60). Johannes Secundus is the author of epigrams, odes, verse epistles and occasional verse but best known for his love elegies collected under the title *Basia* (*Kisses*). A selection of his work was first published after his death but from then on interest in it remained continuous until the end of the eighteenth century. He influenced such poets as du Bellay and Ronsard in France, Marino in Italy, Jonson, Herrick, Marvell, Milton and Pope in England, and Goethe was still singing his praises in 1817. He himself was following in the footsteps of Ovid, Propertius and Tibullus and was able to combine elegance of language and rhetorical mastery of style with great passion. Petrus Lotichius wrote poems famous for their elegant clarity of style which cover a wide range of subjects – friendship poems, eclogues, elegies, occasional poems of all kinds. Latin poetry of this learned kind, rather than popular vernacular verse, provided the foundation for the German poetry of the next century.

Some formal experimentation is already to be found in vernacular verse, however, from the middle of the century, when we have the first sonnets in German by Christoff Wirsung and Johann Fischart. The latter even wrote a cycle of sonnets in 1555 entitled *An Ehr und Billigkeit liebende Leser. Etlich Sonnet* (*To those readers who love honour and right. Some sonnets*). The hexameter was also introduced about the same time. These developments show a move away from verse as song text towards poetry as a written form.

Sixteenth-century story-telling

The sixteenth century may be a century of religious controversialists but it is also a century of story-tellers. But just as it is difficult to apply modern categories to sixteenth-century verse, it is equally difficult to apply them to story-telling. The demarcation lines between prose and verse as suitable media for narration are blurred, as are those between fact and fiction, literary and non-literary subject matter, entertainment and moral instruction, and different forms and lengths of narration. The question of authorship and originality is often pointless when applied to this literature, for works are frequently anonymous and borrow from each other. The ground was muddied by the Romantics with their unhelpful but regrettably long-lived term 'Volksbuch', meaning an anonymous tale emanating from the unlettered 'folk' in parallel to the folk-song. The modern search for precursors of the novel has also led to distortion.

Verse narrative

Some of the difficulties of categorisation are exemplified by the work of Sachs. He clothes in verse narrative (so-called 'Spruchdichtung') topics now dealt with in newspaper articles – the coming of the Emperor to Nuremberg on 16 February 1541 or the birth of a child with a very large head on 5 November 1556 in Dinkelsbühl – but he is just as likely to narrate an animal fable after Aesop (based on Heinrich Steinhöwel's translation published between 1476 and 1480), a biblical episode, a legend or a funny story (a so-called 'facetia' or 'Schwank'), of the sort he might as easily have turned into a carnival play. So-called 'Pritschmeisterdichtung' – the accounts of court festivals and other celebrations in verse by a kind of master of ceremonies called after his 'Pritsche', the stick he thwacked to attract attention – is another example. When Heinrich Wirre narrates the court festivals in 1563 at Pressburg, in 1568 at the Munich court and in 1571 in Vienna, he presents a versified amalgam of literary fiction, history and contemporary events. When Johann Fischart (1546–90) tells in rhyming couplets of a Zurich delegation's voyage down the Rhine to Strasbourg on 20 June 1576 to attend a shooting competition, he presents it as a latter-day voyage of the Golden Fleece and attaches to it a discourse on bourgeois virtues and values.

Then too there are satirical verse epics. The tradition of verse satire in Brant's *Narrenschiff* and Murner's *Vom großen lutherischen Narren* was carried on by such works as the 4,000–line account by Fischart of the battle between the fleas and the women (*Flöh Hatz Weiber Tratz*, 1573) and Georg Rollenhagen's *Froschmeusler*, first published 1595, an adaptation of the Greek *Batrachomyomachia*, a mock epic in pseudo-Homeric style in which the heroes of the Trojan War are replaced by mice and frogs. Such works stand in the tradition of the animal epic of which the Low German *Reynke de Vos* (*Reineke the fox*, 1498) is a noted early example.

Short prose narrative

Story-telling in prose becomes increasingly important as the century progresses. In the shorter forms, such as the comic tales called 'Schwänke' or 'facetiae', the distinction between the didactic and the entertaining, even between the secular and the religious is demonstrably blurred in many of them. These tales, when they illustrate a moral failing or demonstrate some crudity of human behaviour, clearly have a didactic purpose. They can, however, also tell of an extraordinary event or a particularly clever or witty reaction, with the aim of providing entertainment. Heinrich Bebel (1472–1518), a pupil of Sebastian Brant's in Basel and from 1496/7 Professor of Rhetoric at the new University of Tübingen, produced an important collection, *Libri facetiarum iucundissimi* (*Joyful jokebooks*, 1509–14), influenced by the 'facetiae' of Gian Francesco Bracciolini, called Il Poggio (1380–1459). Bebel's collection was expanded, republished many times and translated into German in 1558. Bebel was a Humanist who from his educated perspective highlights the grossness of peasants and lesser mortals. One of his principal imitators was the Franciscan Johannes Pauli (1450/54 to after 1522) whose collection of very short comic tales in German, *Schimpf und Ernst* (*Satire and seriousness*, 1522), was designed to enliven sermons as well as to entertain and provide moral guidance for the private reader. Many of them are concerned with the nature of folly, but where Bebel looks down on folly, Pauli wants his reader to look at his own actions and consider whether the fool is not sometimes wiser than the wise. Thus the same genre in two languages can be employed with two different agendas. Such collections continued to be compiled, composed and added to throughout the century and the authors frequently borrowed tales and motifs from one another. One of the best known is the *Rollwagenbüchlein* (literally 'Carriage book' or 'Tales for a journey') by Jörg Wickram, discussed below as a novelist. Wickram first published the collection in 1555 and in expanded editions in 1556 and 1557. A comparison of his stories with those of Pauli reveals Wickram as a much more sophisticated and self-conscious narrator and stylist. The stories, though similar in the type of comic anecdote they narrate, are considerably longer and allow the writer to develop the narrative with more detail and a much greater authorial presence. Wickram had a host of imitators and followers.

But there are other compendia which prefigure the novel in which all the tales relate to one figure or group. One of the earliest of these is *Ein kurtzweilig Lesen von Dyl Ulenspiegel* (*A merry tale of Till Eulenspiegel*) now generally thought to have been written by the Low German author Hermann Bote. The first almost complete edition to have survived comes from 1510 and the first complete version from 1515, though it is highly likely that there were earlier versions of the same stories. It follows the trickster Dyl Ulenspiegel, based on a little-known historical figure who died in 1350, roughly from the cradle to the grave. Dyl embodies a principle of misrule. He is asocial and utterly without respect for authority, whether secular or religious, but equally without any consistent plan for his own self-interest. As long as he has enough to eat and can make those who seek to chastise or correct him look foolish, he is happy. There is a curious atmosphere of childlike mischief-making about him, even in his most outrageous escapades, emphasised by the recurrent fascination with scatological humour. Similar in that it too groups anecdotes round a historical character with mythical accretions, the *Historia von D. Johann Fausten* (*The tale of Dr Johann Faust*, 1587) has advanced much further in the direction of the novel. The historical Faust lived in the early part of the sixteenth century, practised astronomy and fell foul of the law. The fictional Faust of the story is a much more interesting character. The brilliantly gifted son of a peasant, he shines at university and then becomes consumed by the passion to know for its own sake, a godless motive in itself. To this end he makes his pact with the devil. In the early part of the story, until the devil refuses to answer any more questions, he and Faust engage in a series of dialogues in which the devil is quite frank about Hell and its arrangements, the organisation of the company of devils and about the course of action Faust should have taken. But it is too late and the devil enslaves Faust by pandering to his lust and by convincing him that he is now beyond forgiveness. Though the tales of magic and trickery practised by Faust are entertaining, it is the strong Christian, indeed Protestant, message which gives the work its compelling unity of focus.

Ten years later in 1597 the *Lalebuch* (*The history of the simpletons*) appeared, followed in 1598 by an almost identical work *Die Schiltburgerchronik* (*The chronicle of the Schiltburgers*). It has been argued that both of these almost identical stories are based on an earlier common source and that the author is Johann Fischart (Peter Honegger, *Die Schiltburgerchronik und ihr Verfasser Johann Fischart*, 1982). Whatever the truth of these assertions, the works tell of a community so constantly in demand for its wisdom that it has to pretend to be foolish to get some peace. The townsfolk succeed in becoming foolish, indeed become enamoured of folly and of themselves. Since all their actions are group actions – building a town hall, welcoming the Emperor, chasing a homicidal mousedog (cats are unknown to them) – much of the satire is directed at government by committee and can be enjoyed today.

The early novel

Though the *Faustbuch* and the *Lalebuch* have an additive structure such that an episode or individual 'Schwank' could often be removed without doing much violence to the whole, they are still well on the way to being novels. The other ancestor of the sixteenth-century novel is the prose romance.

It has its inception around the year 1430 with the work of two noble-women who translated medieval French verse romances or *chansons de geste* into German prose. Elisabeth of Nassau-Saarbrücken (after 1393–1456) is the author of four translations dealing with descendants or associates of Charlemagne. *Sibille* deals with the youth of the French king Louis, the son of Charlemagne, *Loher* with his life and death, *Hug Schapler* with the story of how Hugh Capet rises from low estate to marry Louis's daughter and becomes king of France and *Herpin* with the story of how the wife of Duke Herpin saves him from execution, bears and raises their child single-handedly and goes in search of him in exile. These works, composed probably between 1430 and 1440, circulated first in manuscript and then began to be printed. With the exception of *Sibille*, they were reprinted many times throughout the next three centuries. *Hug Schapler*, the most popular of the four, is an exciting tale of rags to riches, in which a young man, through his valour and virtue, saves the queen of France and advances to be her husband and king himself in spite of his lowly descent. The other noble author was Eleonor (1430–80), daughter of James I of Scotland and wife of Siegmund of Tyrol. She is the author of one prose romance, *Pontus und Sidonia,* a lastingly popular tale of the manners and morals, reverses, and final good fortune of the prince and princess of the title. This work too was constantly reprinted up to the end of the eighteenth century.

Into the same category come such works as Thüring von Ringoltingen's *Melusine* (printed in 1471), the tale of the mermaid who brings good fortune to her husband as long as he will ask no questions as to her origins, nor try to see her naked and give her her freedom on Saturdays, when she reverts to her mermaid form. Thüring embeds all this in a saga of Melusine, the virtuous queen and mother, and the stories of her ten sons. This is just one in a whole list of prose tales, of which *Alexander* (printed in 1473), *Fortunatus* (1509), Veit Warbeck's *Magelone* (printed in 1535), *Fierabras* (1532), *Die Haymons Kinder* (1534) are others; all, except *Fortunatus,* translations or versions of earlier material.

At the same time the German novel, in the sense of an extended original prose narrative, can truly be said to begin with the Alsatian Jörg Wickram (1505–60/62) whose *Rollwagenbüchlein* has already been discussed. Wickram was born in Colmar, the illegitimate son of the patrician and local official Konrad Wickram. He began his writing career with Meistersinger songs and biblical plays on such typical themes as the Prodigal Son (1540) and *Tobias* (1550), as well as a translation of Ovid's *Metamorphoses* from the Middle High German. His first novel *Ritter Galmy* (Sir Galmy, 1539) tells of a simple knight who falls in love with a married Duchess. Both behave virtuously and resist all temptation to adultery until her husband dies. While the chivalrous atmosphere smacks of the prose romance, the emphasis on emotion, on the inner world of the characters, albeit stylised, partakes rather of the world of the Renaissance. Wickram wrote four other novels, *Gabriotto und Reinhard* (1551), *Der jungen Knaben Spiegel* (*The mirror for young boys*, 1554), *Von guten und bösen Nachbarn* (*Of good and bad neighbours*, 1556) and *Der Goldtfaden* (*The golden chain*, written in 1554 but published in 1557). *Gabriotto und Reinhard*, a retelling of an Italian source, like *Ritter Galmy* deals with love in a courtly setting and between lovers of unequal social standing, and it is again the young men who are inferior. *Der jungen Knaben Spiegel* is the first work for which Wickram invented the plot himself rather than reworking a well-known tale. A rich young wastrel is contrasted with two poor boys who rise through their industry, persistence and honesty. The support of a loyal friend is shown to be a cardinal virtue and a key factor in their advancement. *Der Goldtfaden* again tells of a disadvantaged young man who, against all the odds and through sheer merit, triumphs over the villains, succeeds in life and gets the girl he loves who is far above him socially. In all these heroes we may see a reflection of Wickram's own dubious social position stemming from his illegitimate birth, though Hug Schapler a century before went through the same social rise. *Von guten und bösen Nachbarn* is a middle-class saga of three generations of a merchant family who, by supporting each other both in their business and private life, increase their fortunes against the machinations of a wicked world. Thus, Wickram moves away from the romance and towards the novel as a bourgeois genre set in the real world.

Another important early novelist is Johann Fischart (1546/7–1590) mentioned above for his verse narratives. He also wrote a versified *Eulenspiegel* (1572), Protestant polemics against the Counter-Reformation and moral tracts on marriage and the pleasures of a country life. His claim to be a novelist rests on a work entitled *Affentheurlich Naupengeheurliche Geschichtklitterung* (the title consists of three invented and untranslateable terms containing plays on the words for adventure, monkey, whim, pleasant, history and scribble!) which appeared in three versions, each time extended, in 1575, 1582 and 1590. It is based on the first book of Rabelais's *Gargantua et Pantagruel* of 1534 and while it sometimes translates passages word for word, three-quarters of Fischart's text is original. It is not so much a story as an extended word-game in which each sentence is a bundle of alliteration, assonance, ono-matopoeia, puns, internal rhymes and lists of synonyms and neologisms, a technique familiar to us today in the work of such modernists as Joyce or Arno Schmidt.

The seventeenth century – an introduction

The context for all literary endeavour in the seventeenth century, at least until after the Thirty Years War, was the division between Catholics, Lutherans and Calvinists enshrined in the Peace of Augsburg in 1555 and which eventually resulted in the Thirty Years War (1618–48). Initially a war of religion, it became more and more concerned with the balance of power in Europe and its only positive achievement was to convince European monarchs of the inefficacy of war as a means of settling reli-gious differences. Religious difference entered also into the struggle between monarch and nobility which was so central in the rise of Absolutism as the dominant political form in the great states in the Empire, for, particularly in the Catholic states (Austria, Bavaria), the nobility was mostly Protestant. But the divisions between Lutheran and Calvinist were often as great if not greater than those between Catholic and Protestant. Parallel to the religious tensions, however, learned and literary men held fast to that concept, so often articulated in the Renaissance, of a nation bound together by a common language and liter-ature in which tolerance might reign and, beyond it, of a commonwealth of letters binding all men of learning throughout the civilised world. (The term 'men' is used here advisedly.) In the first decades of the seventeenth century, we see a series of initiatives, particularly among the Protestant intelligentsia, to advance the goals just mentioned: freedom for Protestants within the Empire under a Protestant monarch, a German lit-erature to stand beside that of the other vernaculars, the realisation of a Humanist ideal of learning and mutual tolerance. All of this was under-pinned by the drive towards inner religious renewal common both to the Reformation and the Counter-Reformation.

Seventeenth-century verse

As in the previous century, Latin verse was considered the proper craft of all educated men. No literary or scientific publication, no dynastic event, no wedding or funeral was complete without its accompanying Latin verses. In Latin, poets had at their disposal the whole range of forms and themes from the Classics through the Renaissance to their own day, so the problem for Germans in the early decades of the seventeenth century, when vying with their European neighbours, was how to write verse in German of equal stature with that which they had long been producing in Latin. Contrasting solutions to this problem from the early decades of the century are illustrated by the work of two very different poets, the Protestant Georg Rodolf Weckherlin (1584–1653) and the Catholic Friedrich von Spee (1591–1635).

Weckherlin, an official of the Württemberg court in Stuttgart, returned there in 1616 after service abroad and in the next three years designed, and wrote the official accounts of, a series of brilliant festivals which articulated an iconography for the Protestant Union, the most important Protestant power bloc between 1608 and the beginning of the Thirty Years War in 1618, when the confessional divisions enshrined in the Peace of Augsburg of 1555 finally erupted. These festivals expressed a fervent Protestant patriotism within a German tradition going back at least to Arminius. Naturally, such patriotism demanded literature of high quality in the vernacular, which resulted in Weckherlin's first volumes of poems, *Das Erste Buch Oden vnd Gesäng* and *Das ander Buch Oden vnd Gesäng* (*The first and second books of odes and songs*, 1618 and 1619 respectively). Steeped in the literature of antiquity and of the European vernaculars, Weckherlin produced here for the first time in German a varied and ambitious body of elevated verse – occasional courtly poetry, poems on the themes of love, friendship and transience, translations of classical and contemporary poetry. However, because he counted syllables according to the rules of French prosody, to our ears his verse sounds irregular and bumpy, though the range and freshness of his poetry are obvious. Weckherlin's work might have formed the basis for seventeenth-century German poetry, but he was forced into exile in England in 1620 where he died in 1653. The direct connection with his homeland and native language was therefore severed and it was many years before he caught up with poetic developments there. Though he embodied Opitz's prosodic reforms in his later poetry, when that poetry was published in Amsterdam in 1641 and 1648 under the title *Gaistlichen und weltlichen Gedichte* (*Sacred and secular poems*), it passed almost unnoticed.

From the age of ten until his death Friedrich von Spee (1591–1635) lived within the ambit of the Society of Jesus, first as a schoolboy in Cologne, then as a student and finally as a full member of the order. He was ordained in 1622, taught theology and moral philosophy at various Jesuit universities and schools, yet was always a rebel. The order even wished to expel him for his polemic against the witch-hunts, *Cautio criminalis seu de processibus contra sagas*, printed anonymously in 1631. Apart from around a hundred hymns in the Catholic hymnal, *Außerlesene Catholische Geistliche Kirchengesäng* (*Selected Catholic hymns*) and his work of edification *Das Guldene Tugend-Buch* (*The golden book of virtue*, 1649), his chief poetic fame rests on his collection of spiritual verse entitled *Trvtz-Nachtigal* (1649). The 'Defiant nightingale' consists of fifty-two religious eclogues, in which the soul, the Bride of Christ, hymns her love for Jesus the Bridegroom. This mystical love, influenced by the Song of Songs, is depicted against a background of nature imagery, which draws on biblical conceptions of the Garden of Eden, classical notions of Arcadia and the Renaissance pastoral tradition. Spee, independently of Opitz, organises his verse into naturally alternating stressed and unstressed syllables and achieves a limpid simplicity which at times resembles the folk-song. Spee's priestly purpose of providing the reader with religious edification is very different from the courtly ambitions of Weckherlin's poetry. But both Weckherlin and Spee were conscious of the latent possibilities in the German language, Spee stoutly affirming them in the 'Notes to the reader' at the beginning of the *Trvtz-Nachtigal*.

It was, however, the Silesian Martin Opitz (1597–1639) who had the clearest vision of the direction German literature ought to take. His career, like Weckherlin's, is also inextricably entwined with the Protestant cause. In 1617 while still at school Opitz had already written his first important work, a polemic entitled *Aristarchus sive de contemptu linguae teutonicae* (*Aristarchus or on the contempt of the German language*). This was a call to arms on behalf of the German language, which since Luther was the language of Protestantism. Unlike Latin, the language of Catholicism, it was free of foreign corruption. German should therefore displace Latin as the language of literature. The political intent of such sentiments is connected with the situation of Silesia itself, a Protestant territory bordering Bohemia, the seat of opposition to the Catholicising programme of the Habsburg Emperors. In 1619 Opitz went to university in Heidelberg, where he formed part of a Calvinist group hoping for a universal Protestant monarchy, a hope dashed in 1620. From Heidelberg Opitz went to Leiden in the Netherlands, another territory filled with the spirit of Calvinism and with the memory of its own wars of liberation.

Opitz first announced his vision for what German literature could become in his most famous work, *Das Buch von der deutschen Poeterey* (*A treatise on German poesie*, 1624). German could be the equal not just of the classical languages, he maintained, but of the other European vernaculars, but poets first needed to expand the possibilities of the language by translating. They should then proceed to write original works, for which he laid down ground-rules largely based on Scaliger, Ronsard and du Bellay. Opitz firmly endorsed the principle that German verse should consist of alternating stressed and unstressed syllables and that natural speech rhythms should coincide naturally with metrical ones. This is the famous 'Opitzian reform'.

Typical of Opitz was the coupling of precept with example and his first collection of poetry, entitled *Teutsche Poemata* (*German poems*) was published against his will in 1624, with a second revised and authorised collection appearing in 1625 as *Acht Bücher Deutscher Poematum* (*Eight books of German poems*). The elegance of Opitz's verse, the seemingly effortless embodiment in it of his reading in the Classics, the Pléiade and the Italian poets, lifted German poetry to a level it had not reached before and laid the ground for the subsequent poetic achievements of the century. In the *Acht Bücher* Opitz also provided models for a wide range of forms and topics: psalms, didactic, occasional and love poems, odes, epistles, sonnets and epigrams. His epic poem against war, *Trostgedichte in Widerwärtigkeit des Krieges* (*Consolatory poems amidst the desolation of war*), written in 1620 though not published until 1633, is a sustained lament against war with all its religious and political implications for Europe. Opitz was also one of the channels by which the latest literary and artistic forms reached the Empire. The importance of the models he provided for such central genres of the age as the pastoral, the opera libretto and the classical tragedy cannot be overemphasised. This aspect of his work is discussed below.

The intellectualised literary quality of Opitz's work constitutes a link with Renaissance humanism and it is obvious that his literary programme was aimed at an intellectual and political élite, both as producers and as consumers. That élite had already set out its own programme when Prince Ludwig von Anhalt-Köthen founded an organisation called the 'Fruchtbringende Gesellschaft' ('The Fructifying Society') in 1617 in Weimar. This organisation was modelled on the Florentine Accademia della Crusca, a society founded in 1592 to purify the Italian language. It is no accident that 1617 was the centenary of the Reformation, for Prince Ludwig wished explicitly to acknowledge Luther's achievements on behalf of the German language. Virtually all the important poets of the age belonged to this society – Opitz became a member in 1629 – which lasted until 1680 and at its height had some eight hundred members. During Duke Ludwig's lifetime (1579–1650) ninety-six per cent of them were Protestant, more or less equally divided between Lutherans and Calvinists. The society aimed to purify the German language, provide dictionaries and grammars for it, raise it to the level of the other European vernaculars by encouraging translation and unite men of learning across territorial boundaries and already existing institutions such as the Universities.

Opitz's most important early disciple was the Saxon Paul Fleming

(1609–40), like Opitz a learned poet but one who was able to combine the Romance and classical traditions with that of the native German song which flourished particularly in Leipzig where he studied. Fleming, who, like most poets of the age, wrote in both Latin and German throughout his life, was able to write love poetry in the Petrarchan tradition (that is, poetry in which the unattainable beloved is idealised and love itself is conceived as blessed suffering), pastoral poetry based on Opitz's *Schäfferey von der Nimfen Hercinie* (*Pastoral of the nymph Hercinie*), friendship poetry in the Renaissance mode, religious poetry and poems in which a calm neo-stoicism is the dominant mood, as in his famous epitaph written a week before his death. His German poems were collected and published posthumously in 1646 as *D. Paul Flemings Teütsche Poemata* (*Dr Paul Fleming's German poems*). Because of the extent to which Fleming used autobiographical elements in his poetry, he has often been praised in the past quite unhistorically for writing personal rather than conventional poetry. We can now see his poetry more justly in its indebtedness to the European and classical traditions and in its technical perfection but without denying Fleming his own unique and direct voice.

By 1640 both Opitz and Fleming were dead but Opitz's reforms were generally accepted among German-speaking poets. One can observe Opitz's influence in a collection such as *Musa Teutonica* (*The German muse*, 1634) by the Hamburg clergyman Johann Rist (1607–67) and in the work of poets in such diverse places as Greifswald (Sibylle Schwarz, 1621–38), Rostock (Andreas Tscherning, 1611–59) and Königsberg (Simon Dach, 1605–59). But the further technical development of German poetry is due in large part to the influence exercised on a generation of poets by the Professor of Poetry and Rhetoric at Wittenberg, August Buchner (1591–1661). Buchner introduced the dactyl and the anapaest into German prosody, but left it to his pupil Philipp von Zesen (1619–89) to promulgate the new metres. Zesen wrote the first German poetics after Opitz, *Deutscher Helicon* (*German Helicon*, 1640, further editions in 1641, 1649, 1656), as well as numerous poems, song texts, linguistic treatises. His novels are discussed below. Zesen, firmly convinced of the links between poetry, dance and song, moved away from Opitz's rather cerebral mode towards a more experimental verse, in which sound and rhythm played a large part. He demonstrated that the dactyl, both alone and in combination with other metres, could give German verse a new lightness and grace.

The 1640s generally was a period of experimentation in which Zesen's efforts were seconded by the Nuremberg group, consisting of Georg Philipp Harsdörffer (1607–58), Sigmund von Birken (1626–81) and Johann Klaj (1616–56). Klaj, also a pupil of Buchner's, moved to Nuremberg in 1644, in which year he publicly declaimed several of his

Redeoratorien (Declamations). These *tours de force* consisted of groups
of poems in diverse metres on such sacred themes as the Resurrection or
the Ascension. Harsdörffer joined Klaj in Nuremberg later in 1644 and in
the same year they founded the language academy known as the
'Löblicher Hirten- und Blumenorden' or 'Pegnitzschäfer' (Laudable Order
of Shepherds and Flowers or Pegnitz Shepherds, from the river Pegnitz
which flows through Nuremberg). Though not as important as the
Fruchtbringende Gesellschaft, the Pegnesischer Blumenorden was one of
the few literary organisations which tolerated women. The characteristic
form which this group cultivated was the prose eclogue in which each of
the three poets had a suitably pastoral pseudonym, and whose arcadian
landscape is situated on the banks of the Pegnitz. The prose narrative is
interspersed with poems and marked by linguistic play, including ono-
matopoeia, assonance and internal rhyme, and adventurous versification.
Like Zesen, Harsdörffer, Klaj and Birken cultivated the dactyl. Their first
collaborative work was written for a patrician wedding in 1644:
Pegnesisches Schaefergedicht (Pegnitz pastoral), of which there was a
further instalment in 1645. Among Harsdörffer's many other works are
his encyclopaedia in dialogue form, the *Frauenzimmer-Gesprächsspiele
(Conversational entertainments for women*, 1641–49), his poetics *Der
poetische Trichter (The poetic funnel*, 1647–53) and a series of devotional
works and narrative anthologies.

Very different from the playfulness and urbanity of the Pegnitz
Shepherds is the Silesian poet, Andreas Gryphius (1616–64). A major
dramatist as well as a poet, Gryphius was a Lutheran, who, after the vicis-
situdes of an early life dominated by the war, spent nearly ten years abroad
from 1638, first at the University of Leiden in the Netherlands and then
travelling through France and Italy. He returned to Silesia in 1647 where
from 1650 he filled the administrative post of Landes-Syndikus in Glogau.
Gryphius published his first collection of thirty-one sonnets in 1637, the
so-called *Lissaer Sonette*, in Leiden he published the first edition of his
Sonn- und Feiertagssonette (Sunday and Holyday Sonnets, one sonnet for
each Sunday and feast-day in the year) in 1639, and in 1643 the first book
of odes, sonnets and epigrams respectively. In Strasbourg in 1646 he finished his second book of odes, another two books of epigrams and a
revised version of the *Sonn- und Feiertagssonette*. Once back in Silesia, he
continued to write poems in these categories as well as quantities of occasional verse.

For all the wide range of Gryphius's poetry, he made the themes of transience and earthly suffering particularly his own. He takes what are stock
topics of the age, drawing on an international repertoire of images and
linguistic devices but creating out of this raw material a new and personal
language, seizing the attention with striking metaphors, surprising

juxtapositions and varied rhythms and rhymes. The tension between the tightly structured sonnet form, at which he excelled, and the pain and lamentation he expresses constitute Gryphius's unique voice. He uses the images of the psalmist to lament the depredations of war, the death of children and of friends, his own sickness and suffering, the ever-presence of death (as in his *Kirchhoffsgedancken* (*Meditations in a churchyard*), in which he imagines the graves opening to display the putrefaction within). This tone of lament is not to be taken merely as a realistic response to the difficulties of his war-torn existence. His pseudonym 'Meletomenus', the melancholy one, indicates his assumption of the attitude of the melancholic, who, by virtue of his melancholy, has a peculiar insight into the vanity of the world and into human failings, which in turn leads him to the divine.

A contemporary and friend of Gryphius's was his fellow-Silesian Christian Hoffmann von Hoffmannswaldau (1619–79). Though his family was much wealthier than Gryphius's, his background was similar. They both came from devout Lutheran homes, attended the same school, studied in Leiden, travelled in Europe and returned home to assume roles in civic life. Like Gryphius, Hoffmannswaldau was much involved in the political and religious fate of Silesia after the Thirty Years War. Like Gryphius, he was very productive as a writer in the 1640s. In these years he translated Guarini's *Il Pastor Fido* and Viau's discourse, *Mort de Socrate,* and began his *Helden-Briefe* or 'Heroicall Epistles', as his model Drayton called them. In these years he also wrote many of his *Geschichtreden* (*Historical monologues*), his religious and love poems and his occasional verses. While most of his work circulated in manuscript during his lifetime, he authorised one edition in 1679, at the end of his life. The selection of works in this edition shows Hoffmannswaldau to be a highly educated, sophisticated and serious moral thinker whose technical resources are as extensive as the range of his interests. Like Donne, whose work he clearly knew, Hoffmannswaldau was both a master of witty conceits and ornate language and a moving religious poet. He is thus very far from being the purely erotic poet many critics have considered him to be on the basis of those poems which appeared in Benjamin Neukirch's posthumous anthology *Herrn von Hoffmannswaldau und andrer Deutschen auserlesne und bißher ungedruckte Gedichte* (*Selected and previously unpublished poems by Mr Hoffmannswaldau and other Germans*, 1695 and 1727).

The last of the Silesian poets is Johann Christian Günther (1695–1723). Filled with classical and Renaissance concepts of the divinely inspired poetic calling and very conscious of his Silesian predecessors, he attempted to live by his poetry in an age when this was only possible for a court poet and died in the poorhouse before he was thirty. His poetry covers all the usual genres of the age – eulogies of public figures, epicedia, religious poetry, love poems – but infuses them with an intensity of personal feeling that, though often overemphasised by nineteenth-century critics, points to the later eighteenth century. Günther's sorrow at parting from his beloved, his despair at what his life had become, his gratitude towards his patrons and his awareness of his poetic vocation may be couched in the manner of Ovid or Job or Opitz but the tone of intense personal experience and the language, which has largely left Baroque ornateness behind, distinguishes and distances him from Hofmannswaldau or Gryphius.

Another dominant strain in the religious poetry of the age is mysticism. This articulates an emotional and non-rational religious experience and is therefore tangential to institutionalised religion. But whereas the Catholic Church with its stress on the sacraments and their 'magic' power and its cult of miracles and the emotional response to them provided some outlet for this kind of religious experience, it represented much more of a problem for the word-centred Protestant churches. The mystical stance of emotional, even erotic communion with God bypassed the Bible as the source of man's connection with God, and the mystical gesture of seeking, even pursuing the Beloved stood in opposition to the central Protestant idea that God gives himself to man without man in any way being able to control, far less induce this action. The fact, therefore, that Protestantism could not accommodate mysticism within it paradoxically explains why almost all the important German mystics of the early modern period, from Jakob Böhme (1575–1624) on, are Protestant. Mysticism appealed also to women, who felt themselves marginalised by the religious and literary establishment of their day, the most notable example being Greiffenberg, who is discussed below. Mystics were necessarily perceived as unorthodox, not to say deviant, and either had to live retired lives or conceal their mystical leanings. Three of the most important mystical poets were Silesian, namely, Daniel Czepko von Reigersfeld (1605–60), Johannes Scheffler, often known by his pseudonym Angelus Silesius, who later converted to Catholicism (1624–77), and Quirinus Kuhlmann (1651–89). The first two are chiefly known as the authors of religious epigrams.

Czepko, a lawyer and son of a Lutheran minister, came under the influence of Abraham von Franckenberg (1593–1652) some time in the later 1630s. Franckenberg was a Silesian nobleman and follower of Jakob Böhme's, who had withdrawn from the world to escape censure by the Lutheran authorities. Himself a religious writer, he collected a group of like-minded people around him. One of those he was in contact with was Johann Theodor von Tschesch (1595–1649), quondam adviser to Frederick of the Palatinate and also a follower of Böhme's. Tschesch composed a series of religious epigrams in Latin (twelve groups of a hundred each) and thus paved the way for the poetry of Czepko. Indeed, Franckenberg himself is known to have composed similar epigrams in German. The result is Czepko's collection of mystical epigrams in German, *Sexcenta Monodisticha Sapientium* (*Six hundred distichs or wise sayings*), written between 1640 and 1647 but unpublished for fear of Lutheran censorship. Czepko was already a published author of historical works, a pastoral epic and some religious works, yet clearly the epigrams stood outside the limits of acceptable orthodoxy.

The epigram specialises in linguistic play and paradox and in compression of thought as a means of evoking surprise, even shock. But whereas the satiral epigram wishes to jolt the reader into laughter or towards recognition of the ills of the world, as in the famous *Sinngedichte* (*Epigrams*, 1654) by Czepko's Silesian contemporary Friedrich von Logau (1604–55), the religious epigram attempts to launch the reader towards the divine, by using language to express the ineffable. The very brevity of the form, as well as its playfulness, demands the intense collaboration and concentration of the reader. Language, like the world itself, is the mirror in which God reveals himself 'through a glass darkly'.

Johannes Scheffler takes this process a stage further. He too was influenced by Böhme's writings which he got to know in Leiden where he studied medicine from 1643, finishing his studies in Padua in 1647 and 1648. On his return to Silesia in 1649, Scheffler joined Franckenberg's circle. Scheffler was still officially a Lutheran but began to fall foul of the authorities. Scheffler was then refused permission to publish an anthology of mystical writings, resigned his post as physician to Duke Sylvius Nimrod of Württemberg at Oels and became a Catholic in 1653, taking the name of Angelus, to which he later added the soubriquet Silesius. The last stage in this spiritual progression was his ordination to the priesthood in 1661. Indeed, Scheffler became an aggressive campaigner for the re-Catholicisation of Silesia. In 1657 he published *Heilige Seelen-Lust Oder Geistliche Hirten Lieder Der in jhren JESUM verliebten Psyche* (*Sacred joy of the soul or, sacred eclogues by Psyche, enamoured of her Jesus*) and a collection of 302 epigrams entitled *Geistreiche Sinn- und Schlußreime* (*Witty epigrams and couplets*). This latter formed the nucleus of the much augmented collection of over 1,600 epigrams entitled *Der Cherubinische Wandersmann* (*The cherubinic wanderer*, 1675). The *Heilige Seelen-Lust* also appeared in an augmented edition in 1668.

Formally, Scheffler's epigrams are indebted to those of Tschesch, Franckenberg and Czepko. It appears that the first two books of the *Wandersmann* were written before Scheffler's conversion and Franckenberg's death. Characteristic of them are extreme and paradoxical statements about the nature of God and of man's relation to him. Time after time the distance between God and man is overcome, the greatness of

God and littleness of man meet at the interface of time and eternity, the reader is shocked into startled reconsideration of set ideas. But the epigrams do not all deal with pure abstraction. Scheffler often uses concrete and homely images – the child crying for the mother's breast, the rose, the magnet. This tendency becomes much more marked in those books of the *Wandersmann* thought to have been written after Scheffler's conversion. Books IV and V are again more speculative and book VI, first published in the edition of 1675, is the most militant. However we attempt to assess the *Wandersmann* aesthetically, we should not forget that this is poetry with a purpose. As Scheffler tells us in the preface, his book should cause the reader to burn with the heavenly love of a seraph and contemplate God with the unwavering eyes of a cherub.

The last in the line of Silesian mystics is Quirinus Kuhlmann (1651–89). A clever young man who became a published author at the age of eighteen, he set off to study law in Jena and was destined for a brilliant academic or public career, when, like his compatriots, he went to Leiden and discovered the work of Jakob Böhme. In his lengthy prose work *Neubegeisterter Böhme* (*Newly-enthused Böhme*, 1674) he documents the extraordinary effect Böhme had on him. From now on until his death at the stake in Moscow in 1689, Kuhlmann lived the life of a wandering prophet, covering huge distances throughout Europe and meeting various non-conformist groups in England, Holland, France and Geneva. He went on abortive journeys to Constantinople and Jerusalem to convert the Sultan and the Jews respectively. Everywhere he went he fell foul of the authorities and of members of local groups and had to move on. Kuhlmann saw himself as a latter-day prophet, the 'son of the Son of God', a second Böhme, and invested every detail of his own life with symbolic significance, so that it demonstrated his divine mission. The basis for his chief work *Der Kühlpsalter* (*The cool-psalter*, 1684–85) was therefore his own life from 1670 which he treated as a hermetic code to be subjected to all kinds of numerological and linguistic analysis. Typical is the way in which a phrase in the Acts of the Apostles, iii,19, which in the Vulgate reads 'tempora refrigerii' (Authorised Version: 'the times of refreshing' but more literally 'times of cooling') was related by Kuhlmann to his own name and formed a key concept in the 20,000–line *Kühlpsalter*, whose poetry is modelled on the biblical psalter. Kuhlmann's own sense of his messianic, millenarian mission finally led him to Russia, where he was tried, sentenced and burned at the stake in 1689. At his best Kuhlmann is a poet of great linguistic verve, deep religious feeling and strong emotion. At his worst, towards the end of his life, the poetry becomes fragmentary and overexcited.

If mystical writers were by definition outsiders, so were women writers. Scarcely educated, almost always cut off from Latin, instructed by the

Reformation that their sole vocation was childbearing and denied access to many of the types of literature their menfolk read, it is a miracle that women wrote at all. Only two institutions actually fostered their creative activities: the language academies and the courts. A series of prohibitions, both written and unwritten, dictated what women might write as well as what they might read. The drama, where it was not the province of such male institutions as the Catholic orders and the boys' grammar schools, partook of the morally dubious nature of the stage, the novel purveyed lies, secular love poetry contravened conventions about the sexual purity of women. Therefore women were virtually restricted to religious verse and occasional poetry. Women produced some prose works, predominantly non-fiction, autobiographical writing and translations, if they were learned enough, with novels only making their appearance from the second half of the seventeenth century. Reading the work of women poets of this age, one is struck by the extent to which they felt themselves to be deviants, defying convention, writing out of an inner compulsion. This explains why their religious poetry often takes on a mystical tinge.

Anna Ovena Hoyers (1584–1655), the non-conformist poet from Schleswig-Holstein, was driven into exile by the Lutheran authorities. Her *Gespräch eines Kindes mit seiner Mutter* (*Conversation of a child with its mother*, 1628) and a collection entitled *Geistliche und weltliche Poemata* (*Sacred and secular poetry*, 1650) were published by her during her lifetime and her sons put together a further collection of forty-seven poems in manuscript after her death. She saw herself as following Luther's own precepts, both in her criticism of clerical abuse and in her composition of hymns for actual liturgical use, though in some of her word-play, in which she uses her own name or initials, the letters of the alphabet or the name of Jesus as a kind of code, she resembles the mystics. Another example of a woman who wrote out of inner necessity was Margarethe Susanna von Kuntsch (1651–1717). Her parents forbade her to learn Latin and French as unsuited to her station in life and it is thanks to her grandson that her verse was published in 1720 under the title *Sämmtliche Geist- und weltliche Gedichte* (*Complete sacred and secular poems*). This collection consists of religious verse on biblical or other pious topics and of occasional poetry, written for funerals, weddings and birthdays or to acquaintances and friends. Her most powerful poetry deals with the deaths of her own children (she had fifteen pregnancies but only one child who survived to adulthood), showing Lutheran submission to the will of God in conflict with unassuageable personal pain.

Hemmed in by the same restrictions was the Austrian baroness Catharina Regina von Greiffenberg (1633–94), though, unlike her female contemporaries, she was very highly educated indeed. Her step-uncle, guardian and subsequent husband, Hans Rudolf von Greiffenberg, taught her the classical languages, as well as French, Italian and Spanish. She read widely in ancient and modern history, law, politics, astronomy, alchemy, theology and philosophy as well as the European literature of her day. A Protestant living under a Catholic monarchy who had to travel long distances to practise her religion, Greiffenberg had what she considered an important mystical revelation at Easter 1651 in Pressburg after the death of her younger sister and only sibling. This revelation, which she referred to thereafter as her 'Deoglori-Licht' ('the light of God's glory'), marked her birth as a mystical poet. Her literary development was furthered by becoming a member of the 'Ister-Gesellschaft', a loose literary association, and in having as an adviser Johann Wilhelm von Stubenberg (1619–63) who made her known to Sigmund von Birken (1626–81). The unfortunate marriage she was forced to enter into by and with her guardian in 1664, his death in 1677, her subsequent legal troubles and impoverishment made her life and writing difficult and she only achieved a measure of peace on her permanent move to Nuremberg in 1680. Her first and most famous publication is the collection entitled *Geistliche Sonette, Lieder und Gedichte* (*Sacred sonnets, songs and poems*) published in 1662 by Hans Rudolf with Birken's help. Greiffenberg's characteristic method is to present the concrete in vividly sensuous terms and then to interpret it in spiritual ones, teasing out its religious significance. As with all mystics, the physical world is seen as a set of ciphers which have to be decoded in order to arrive at their spiritual meaning. She uses the tightly controlled sonnet form to brilliant effect, pushing language to its boundaries by creating unexpected compounds and emphatic prefixes. Her poems are highly charged with personal faith and deep emotion. Apart from a short pastoral dialogue written in 1662, and a lengthy poem calling for repentance and faith to ward off the Turkish threat written in 1663 but published in 1675, Greiffenberg's last decades were dedicated to the composition of four extensive series of religious meditations in prose, interspersed here and there with poems, on the incarnation and early life of Jesus (1678), His suffering and death (1683), His teachings and miracles (1693) and His life and prophecies (1693).

Drama 1620–1720

By 1620 the theatre of the English strolling players was well established and German dramatists had begun to write for it, the Latin drama of the Jesuits and other Catholic orders was in full flood, and court theatre and spectacle were becoming more Italianate. These developments continued during the seventeenth century and form the context in which German-language drama must be seen.

Until the opening of the first municipal opera house in 1678 in Hamburg, the English strolling players constituted the only commercial theatre in the Empire. Most of their activity during the war years was in Warsaw and the Baltic cities of Königsberg and Danzig, each of which was visited at least once a year from the late 1620s until the end of the war by one of a number of troupes, led variously by Robert Archer, Robert Reynolds and John Wayde. The last important native English manager of a travelling troupe was George Jolly, who was active in Central Europe, particularly Vienna during the 1650s. From extant lists of plays it is clear that up to this time the players performed their own versions of Elizabethan and Jacobean drama, as we saw above.

After the middle of the seventeenth century, however, the nature of the travelling companies changed. From now on they were led and staffed by German actors, of whom the most famous is Johannes Velten (1640–92). Velten was an educated man with a degree in theology and philosophy from Wittenberg and another in philosophy from Leipzig, so that he was entitled to call himself 'Magister'. Around 1665 he joined Carl Andreas Paul's troupe and married Paul's daughter. Velten is mentioned as early as 1668 as the leader of a troupe in Nuremberg. He aimed to raise the status of the actor and to present a repertoire of a high standard, so, as well as Gryphius's comedies, he staged works by Corneille, Molière and Calderón, some of them for the first time in German. He performed at such important courts as Dresden, Vienna and Berlin, as well as touring widely, and his influence on the development of German drama should not be underestimated. His wife took over leadership of the troupe on his death and kept it going until at least 1711 and the leading eighteenth-century managers were all descended from Velten's company.

Important though the strolling players were in transmitting an international theatrical culture, however, the scale of Jesuit theatre was incomparably greater. As we saw earlier, Jesuit drama lasted in the Empire from 1555 until 1773. Though the Society of Jesus was founded to renew the spiritual life of the old church, its aim became that of re-Catholicising the Empire and its drama one of the weapons in that struggle.

The vast mass of Jesuit drama, all in Latin, presents the spiritual journey of figures exemplary either for their goodness, their repentance at the point of death or for their wickedness. They can be historical, such as Mauritius, Constantine or Sigismund of Burgundy, or biblical, such as David, Joseph, Jephtha, Esther or Nebuchadnezzar. They can be saints, such as Ignatius Loyola, the founder of the Jesuits, or martyrs, such as Catherine, Thomas à Becket or Thomas More. Sometimes the message is presented by means of allegory, as in the Rhinelander Jakob Masen's (1606–81) *Androphilus* (1645), the story of the king's son who is prepared to endure any humiliation to rescue the unfaithful and unlovely servant –

an allegory of Christ's redemption of undeserving man. Jesuit drama also shows tendencies towards oratorio or even opera. Johannes Paullinus's *Philothea* and *Theophilus*, performed in Munich in 1643 and 1644 respectively, employed a chorus, an orchestra and as many as seventeen singers and in the last decades of Jesuit drama in the eighteenth century, full-scale operas were performed.

Jesuit drama was often not published and if it was, was published anonymously. Our most informative source from 1597 on is the so-called 'Periochen', programmes which contain plot summaries and cast lists. Rarely is the author indicated, since he was usually the Professor of Rhetoric at the college in question, who was simply ordered by his superiors to produce a drama and who ceased to be a dramatist when his superiors decreed that he turn his hand to something else. It is therefore a falsification to single out individual authors. However, some writers were more talented than others and deserve to be mentioned: the Alsatian poet Jakob Balde (1604–68) who wrote six plays for the Jesuit stage of which *Jocus serius theatralis*, (1629) and *Jephtias*, (1637) are the best known, Georg Bernardt (1595–1660), whose plays for Ingolstadt such as *Theophilus* (1621) or *Tundalus* (1622) provide a wonderful combination of comic and serious scenes in lively prose; Andreas Brunner (1589–1650) who wrote a biblical pageant play called *Nabuchodonosor* for Munich in 1635 and, unusually, a series of plays in German between 1637 and 1649/50 for Innsbruck, Jakob Masen (1606–81), who in the 1640s developed sixteenth-century Humanist school drama in comedies such as *Rusticus imperans* (*Peasant as ruler*), on the 'king-for-a-day' theme, or tragedies such as *Mauritius imperator orientis* (*Maurice, emperor of the East*), on the theme of the unjust but eventually repentant monarch, or his moral fable *Androphilus* already mentioned. Of all of these dramatists Nicolaus Avancini (1611–86) deserves the most attention because of the range and quantity of his dramatic production. Many of his plays deal with questions of tyranny and the struggle for power: *Xerxes*, *Alexius Comnenus*, for example, or *Semiramis*. Another group takes innocent women wrongfully accused of adultery, such as Genoveva or Susanna, and investigates the place of marriage within the social and legal structure. Yet another, the so-called *ludi caesarei* of the 1650s in Vienna, were magnificent spectacles in honour of the Habsburgs which employed the latest in sophisticated theatrical technology. *Pax Imperii* (*Peace in the Empire*), for instance, performed in 1650 to celebrate the ending of the Thirty Years War, presents Joseph in Egypt as a forerunner of the emperor Ferdinand III, while *Pietas victrix*, (*Piety triumphant*) performed in 1658 for the election of Leopold I, depicts the emperor Constantine as Leopold's prefiguration in a historical panorama which culminates with the Habsburg Empire. Whether he is examining the workings of the state or of the family, Avancini's point of view is clear: cosmic order is disturbed by sin and is only restored if man repents. Religion cannot be the instrument of the state, it must be its rudder.

The courts themselves produced one characteristic form which came into being in Italy around the year 1600 and came north of the Alps some twenty years later – namely, opera. The first opera on German soil is *Orfeo*, probably Monteverdi's opera of that name, performed in Salzburg at the court of Prince Archbishop Marx Sittich von Hohenems in 1618 and again in 1619. The first opera to be performed in German is *Dafne*, with music by Schütz and libretto by Opitz, translated from Rinuccini's Italian, performed at Torgau, a summer residence of the Dresden court, in 1627. The first original opera libretto in German is the religious allegory *Seelewig* by Harsdörffer (1644). The real explosion of opera, however, takes place after the war from 1660 on. An Italianate court such as Munich is thought to have staged some fifty operas from then until 1700, while the equally Italianate but much grander Imperial court at Vienna staged some seventy-five in the same period. The much smaller northern courts actively cultivated opera in German. Wolfenbüttel, for instance, staged *Seelewig* in 1654 and Duke Anton Ulrich of Braunschweig-Lüneburg wrote German texts for some nine operas (which he called *Singspiele*) on this model. Halle, Ansbach, Weißenfels and Bayreuth followed suit. Commercial opera began in 1678 in Hamburg and there were three other such centres: Braunschweig, Leipzig and Naumburg. Where court opera was a propaganda instrument designed to glorify the prince and underline the hierarchical nature of the court, commercial opera was open to a paying public. Local princes were, however, more or less actively involved in granting licences or subsidies to these opera houses. Hamburg in particular concentrated on producing German opera, though arias in Italian were permitted even here.

The development of opera is central to an understanding of drama in this period for a number of reasons: it was via the opera stage that much of the latest technology – changeable sets, lighting, special effects – was introduced into the Empire, many of the same writers were involved in writing both spoken drama and opera libretti, the prestige of opera, particularly at court, meant that other forms of drama took on an operatic dimension (for example, Jesuit drama, Hallmann's plays, the Rudolstadt entertainments by Kaspar Stieler (1632–1707), even some of Weise's plays) and courts patronised opera rather than drama.

Against this background must be seen the development of German language drama. Opitz again provided German models in competition with Latin, here more specifically with Jesuit drama. For Opitz verse tragedy was pre-eminent. He began by translating Seneca's *Trojan women* (*Die Trojanerinnen*) in 1625, thus providing a model for the martyr as protagonist which afterwards became so common on the Silesian stage. Then came his translations of Italian opera libretti, Rinuccini's *Dafne* (1627) and Salvadori's *Giuditta* (*Judith*) in 1635. He translated Sophocles' *Antigone* in 1636.

Silesian drama, which developed throughout the century and ends around 1700, largely followed these models but was also constantly influenced by Jesuit drama, established in Breslau in 1638, by the theatre of the strolling players and by opera. Its main achievement is historical tragedy in elevated verse, usually performed by one or another of the great grammar schools in Breslau. The first of the great Silesian dramatists, Andreas Gryphius, discussed above as a poet, began by translating Catholic dramas such as Joost van den Vondel's *De Gebroeders* (1639) as *Die Sieben Brüder / Oder die Gibeoniter* (*The seven brothers or, the Gibeonites*) and the Jesuit Nicolaus Caussinus's martyr play *Felicitas* as *Beständige Mutter / Oder Die Heilige Felicitas* (*The steadfast mother or, Saint Felicity*), probably between 1634 and 1636. Gryphius's first original drama *Leo Armenius* (*c.* 1646) was also based on a Jesuit original, the English Jesuit Joseph Simon's *Leo Armenus*. Gryphius as an orthodox Lutheran believed that the ruler, however evil, had been put in place by God and could never be overthrown by human agency. Thus it is wicked to depose the usurper Leo Armenius, even though he has become king by wrongful means. Leo is saved at the moment of death by dying on the steps of the altar during the first Mass of Christmas clutching a relic of the True Cross. Similarly in *Catharina von Georgien* (*Catherine of Georgia, c.* 1649–50), *Carolus Stuardus* (*Charles Stuart*, published in 1657, though begun shortly after Charles I's execution in 1649) and *Papinianus* (1659), Gryphius delineates the type of the martyr, whose greatness consists in recognising the path of virtue and in passively enduring suffering unto death in such a way as to rule out any attempt at earthly salvation or escape. Eschewing any attempt at realism or psychological nuance, Gryphius uses historical figures to demonstrate truths about salvation. Man can only triumph over the tribulations of life on earth by exhibiting a rock-like and stoic constancy (*Beständigkeit*), thus assimilating himself to the timelessness of the divine. With a wonderful mastery of the alexandrine couplet Gryphius presents us with tableaus of suffering nobly borne: Charles I in prison as a latter-day Christ dying for his people, Catharina repelling the advances of the lustful infidel Schach Abbas, Papinianus contemplating the corpses of his dead children. After each act, a chorus interprets what we have just seen, teases out its message in terms of divine salvation, the course of history or Christian redemption and confirms a truth already acknowledged by the audience.

As well as two courtly entertainments, the mini-operas *Piastus* and *Majuma* (1653), Gryphius also wrote *Cardenio und Celinde* (*c.* 1650), which employs characters of medium estate who speak a relatively simple language. It deals with the theme of virtuous Christian love versus pagan lust and is full of tension and surprise effects by means of which a moral regeneration is brought about in the characters. Gryphius also wrote three delightful comedies: *Herr Peter Squentz* (*c.* 1648), a satire on the drama of the Meistersinger and based on the Peter Quince episode from Shakespeare's *Midsummer Night's Dream*, *Horribilicribrifax* (also *c.* 1648), a comedy containing not one but two braggarts, the eponymous hero and his counterpart, Daradiridatumtarides, and a whole galaxy of other comic characters, and *Verlibtes Gespenst/die gelibte Dornrose* (*Ghost in love/beloved Dornrose*), a pair of plays written for the wedding in 1660 of Georg III, the local duke, in which a verse semi-opera alternates act for act with a dialect peasant play. The two plots are mirror-images of each other and the third social stratum is provided by the ducal couple seated in the audience. In each of these comedies, virtue is rewarded, constancy wins the day, pretence and social climbing are exposed and the status quo is restored at the end in the images of marriage and the dance. There is much linguistic comedy and some delightful comic invention.

Daniel Casper von Lohenstein (1635–83) developed the five-act Senecan verse tragedy further. He wrote only six plays, two on Turkish themes, *Ibrahim Bassa* (written while still a schoolboy in 1650), and *Ibrahim Sultan* (1673), two set in Rome, *Epicharis* (1665?) and *Agrippina* (published in 1665), and two in Africa in Roman times, *Cleopatra* (first version written in 1661, second version in 1680) and *Sophonisbe* (written in 1669). Lohenstein was fascinated by power, particularly when exercised by women. Cleopatra, the Egyptian priestess and queen, Agrippina, the mother of Nero, and Sophonisbe, the Carthaginian princess, use their sensuality to enslave men, and they embody the dangerous excesses of passion as opposed to the statesmanlike reason represented by such figures as Augustus in *Cleopatra* or Scipio in *Sophonisbe*. Agrippina is even prepared to seduce her own son to maintain power. However, all these women see the error of their ways and to an extent are vindicated by the ending of the plays but, while they die bravely, none of them embodies the kind of flawless virtue and passive stoicism of Gryphius's martyrs.

In Lohenstein's three other dramas, we come closer to the martyr play. In *Ibrahim Bassa* a Christian couple, Ibrahim and Isabelle, are persecuted by a Muslim ruler, Soliman, who is in love with Isabelle. In *Ibrahim Sultan* the eponymous hero is a savage infidel ruler who rapes the virginal Ambre. She, martyr-like, commits suicide, as does Epicharis, in the play of that name, who leads a revolt against the tyrant Nero, and kills herself after imprisonment and torture. These weak women triumph at last by the sacrifice of their lives. In the two last-named plays, Lohenstein takes the moral conflict which is at the heart of his works out of the Christian framework. His Romans, Africans and Turks choose virtue over vice, recognise the vanity of the world and learn the importance of steadfastness, without thereby necessarily having to be Christian. In contrast to Jesuit drama, Lohenstein's characters come to acknowledge a transcendental power without assenting to a Christian faith as the *sine qua non* of ethical living. Both the power of his language and the sweep of his characterisation make Lohenstein the best dramatist in German before Schiller.

The last of the Silesian dramatists is Johann Christian Hallmann (*c.* 1640 to after 1704). Hallmann, like Gryphius, began in 1662 by adapting a Jesuit play, namely, Masen's *Mauritius* and, like Gryphius, by treating the problem of the unjust prince both here and in his second play, *Theodoricus* (1666). Hallmann is often wrongly characterised as a second-rate imitator of Lohenstein, usually on the basis of his best-known play, *Die beleidigte Schönheit Oder Sterbende Mariamne* (*Beauty traduced or, dying Mariamne*) which superficially resembles a Lohenstein tragedy. But where Lohenstein is interested in the conflict in his characters between passion and reason and between politics and ethics, *Mariamne* is a study in pure evil, showing how Herod's sister, brother and son by his divorced first wife, destroy Mariamne, Josephus, Salome's husband, and Herod's marriage by implanting false suspicions against Mariamne. Herod's own lustful nature is all too susceptible to these machinations. Hallmann's characters are far more static than Lohenstein's, resembling operatic figures in that they represent various 'Affekte' or strong emotions, rather than presenting psychologically consistent personalities. His heroines are always passive beauties, whose sexuality condemns them to constant brutal attack and whose only weapon is death and passive suffering. Hallmann's choruses mostly consist of personifications of virtues and vices rather than of the gods and goddesses or emotional qualities more typical of Lohenstein. Hallmann's range, however, is far wider than Lohenstein's. *Urania* (1662) and *Rosibella* (1671) are pastoral plays on the theme of virtuous love. *Sophia* (1671) is a martyr tragedy very like Gryphius's *Felicitas*, in which an early Christian sees her three daughters (Spes, Fides and Charitas) killed before her eyes and is then invited to a banquet consisting of three plates bearing their heads and three glasses of their blood. In many of these pieces, musical interludes played an important part. *Catharina Königin in Engelland* (*Catherine, Queen of England*, 1684) is actually called 'a musical tragedy', in other words it is a libretto. In another way, too, *Catharina* represents a decisive development in Hallmann's oeuvre, in that it clearly presents Catherine of Aragon, Henry VIII's first wife, not just as a wronged queen but as a Catholic sacrificed by a heretic. Hallmann is thought to have converted to Catholicism, with the result that his works could no longer be performed by the Protestant grammar schools. After a collected edition of his work which appeared in 1684, our information about Hallmann, perhaps because of his conversion, is sparse. We know that he wrote another seven plays, now lost, but only the tragedy *Die Unüberwindliche Keuschheit Oder Die Großmüthige Prinzeßin Liberata* (*Unconquerable chastity or, the noble Princess Liberata*, 1699) was published in a very small edition paid for by Hallmann himself. Almost in the manner of a Jesuit drama, *Liberata* shows how an ethical polity must also be a Christian one, returning to the theme of just governance with which his oeuvre began. The last documented performance of a work by Hallmann took place in 1704.

A contemporary of Hallmann's who is usually seen as inheriting the Silesian tradition is the Saxon August Adolph von Haugwitz (1647–1706). He wrote two verse tragedies, *Maria Stuarda* and *Soliman* and a pastoral, *Flora*, all published in 1684. *Maria Stuarda*, Catholic martyr, stands on the one hand in the tradition of Jesuit drama, and on the other, it also relates to Gryphius's *Carolus Stuardus* and *Catharina von Georgien*. But Haugwitz, far from simply presenting his two Queens as personifications of 'virtue' and 'vice' or 'true religion' and 'heresy', embarks on an investigation of their inner feelings and the moral choice each is called on to make. Haugwitz's *Soliman* resembles Lohenstein's *Ibrahim Bassa*, in that it depicts a Muslim ruler who loves a Christian woman betrothed to another, but unlike Lohenstein's youthful effort, Haugwitz takes his cue from Madeleine de Scudéry's novel *Ibrahim ou l'Illustre Bassa* (1641) in which the infidel Soliman chooses the path of virtue and allows the Christians to go free. The conflict between passion and reason is decided in favour of reason, here as in Lohenstein's African plays the chief attribute of the admirable ruler. Haugwitz's third dramatic work, the pastoral *Flora*, was influenced by his having attended the performance of Benserade's *Ballet de Flore* at the French court in 1669. It is a vehicle for metaphysical ideas on the nature of love and its divine power to regenerate the universe. With Haugwitz and Hallmann, however, the tradition of Silesian drama, initiated by Opitz, came to an end.

Meanwhile elsewhere in the Empire, principally in North Germany and in Saxony, 'historico-political drama' came into being after the Thirty Years War. This is serious drama in German prose which can deal with historical events but whose main purpose is to discuss such questions as the structure of the state, the links between politics and ethics, the nature of princely power and the role of advisers and courtiers. Characteristic of these plays is their often colloquial and always unpoetic language and their admixture of comic scenes. A typical plot for such a play (for example, Johann Rist's *Das Friedewünschende Teutschland* (*Germany Athirst for Peace*, 1647, the anonymous *Ratio Status* 1668 or Johann Riemer's *Von der erlösten Germania* (*Germany Liberated*, 1681)) depicts

Queen Germania attempting first to cure her maladies with the help of Ratio Status, that is, Machiavellian *raison d'état*, a political philosophy based on dissimulation, realising that this is un-German and only being cured when she learns that such virtues as *pietas*, *fides*, *iustitia* and *clementia* are the adjuncts of a good ruler. The background to many of these plays is the contemporary threat posed by Louis XIV, who often appears in veiled form, for instance, as Gaile in Riemer's play and as Marcomir in the anonymous *Die Teutsche Groß-Königin Leonilda* (*The great German queen Leonilda*, 1673), whose eponymous heroine represents Leopold I. Into the same category come such works as Johann Rist's (1607–67) *Irenaromachia* (*The battle for peace*, 1630), *Perseus* (1634) and *Friedejauchtzendes Teutschland* (*Germany rejoicing in peace*, 1653), David Elias Heidenreich's *Rache zu Gibeon* (*Revenge at Gibeon*, 1662), Christoph Kormart's *Polyeuctus* (1669), *Maria Stuart* (1672) and *Heraclius* (1675), Johann Sebastian Mitternacht's *Politica dramatica* (1667), and Riemer's two plays about Mary Queen of Scots, *Von hohen Vermählungen* and *Vom Staats-Eifer* (*Marriages in high places* and *of political ambition*, 1681).

While Christian Weise (1642–1708) sometimes treats political problems in his plays, his oeuvre is much more varied. He wrote some sixty plays of which forty have survived, dramas which grew out of his work as a teacher. From 1678 until his death in 1708 he was headmaster at his own old school in Zittau, where there already existed the kind of dramatic tradition typical of a Protestant grammar school. Weise built on this, making it a central plank of his pedagogic programme. He wrote three plays every year, consisting of a biblical play, a comedy and a tragedy or political play, in the prefaces to which he articulated his programme: his pupils, future government officials, lawyers and diplomats, were to learn, through drama, the art of rhetoric, while at the same time encountering situations which might be of practical use to them. Rhetoric Weise understood as the art of speaking, which includes conversation as well as oration, and of persuasion, something he underlines in his many theoretical writings and handbooks. Weise's plays are always in prose because it corresponded to real speech. This realism is central to his theatrical philosophy. Whether he is representing the highest in the land or the peasant, his acute ear for ordinary speech allows him to write an idiomatic spoken style and he dictated his plays, the better to achieve a natural effect. In his characters and situations, he eschewed idealised characters and abstract virtues in favour of a pragmatic vision of the world and its affairs, for which an expedient solution must be found. For his themes and forms, he draws on the school drama, the Protestant biblical drama and the contemporary historical-political drama and combines these with some aspects of the theatre of the English players and of opera.

His plays could not be more different from the idealised and emotionally charged drama of the Jesuits or the Silesians. For instance, in *Der
gestürtzte Marggraf von Ancre* (*The fall of the Count of Ancres*, 1679),
the first tragedy he wrote for Zittau, set in France during the Regency of
Marie de Medici, we are shown two factions, each dominated by an
amoral desire for power, and for whom deceit and even murder are
weapons readily to hand. There is no ideal representation of virtue to
counter this portrait of evil and violence. The role played by the common
people is also innovatory, for, though the ordinary citizen is shown to be at
the mercy of political forces he does not understand, he is also capable of
influencing events by sheer force of numbers. The comedy presented in the
same year, *Der bäurische Machiavellus* (*A peasant Machiavelli*), presents
similar ideas in comic form. Machiavelli is arraigned before Apollo on a
charge of having corrupted mankind with his ideas. He defends himself by
maintaining that the villagers of Quirlequitsch, who have never even heard
of him, are the most perfect Machiavellians. In a series of wonderfully
comic manoeuvrings over the appointment of a village clown or
'Pickelhering', we are shown the truth of this. Machiavelli has proved his
point and has to be acquitted. The third play for the year 1679 was
Jephtha, the story of how Jephtha is forced to kill his own daughter Tamar
in fulfilment of a vow he made on the battlefield. One might imagine
Weise to be formally more constrained in the case of the biblical story but
this is not the case. As in such other biblical plays as *Abraham*, he uses the
biblical story as much to depict the diplomatic manoeuvrings and ceremonial usages common among princes as to point a moral. He employs the
lively prose dialogue characteristic of his entire oeuvre and mixes comic
scenes with tragic ones, in a manner reminiscent of the biblical operas performed at Hamburg. Weise, the great innovator, here picks up the tradition of Protestant biblical drama but secularises and demystifies it.

In *Masaniello*, Weise's best-known play (1682) and his best tragedy, he
depicts an uprising by Neapolitan fishermen in 1647. In the eponymous
hero, Weise created one of his few tragic figures, an honest man who never
wanted to overthrow the state but who is forced into a position of
unwanted power and then goes mad. Yet, though the fishermen's grievance
is clearly just and the means which quell it are Machiavellian, not to say
downright evil, the political message Weise's pupils must imbibe is that a
politician cannot allow disturbances in the body politic and that *raison
d'état* must be his guiding principle. The world Weise depicts is a bleak
one, in which a ruler is prepared to poison the water supply in order to
regain power (*Masaniello*) or a mother to attempt repeatedly to kill her
own child in order that her paramour shall become king (*König Wenzel*
(*King Wenceslas*, 1700)), in which peasants are drunken (*Der nieder-
ländische Bauer* (*The Dutch peasant*, 1665)) or pretentious (*Vom

Verfolgten Lateiner (*The persecuted Latin scholar*, 1696)) and therefore deserve what they get. The Old Testament world is in general less bleak, since Weise uses his material – Abraham and Isaac, Jacob's union with Leah and her sister Rachel, David, Esau and Jacob, Joseph in Egypt – not so much to present themes of divine justice and retribution but rather familial relationships, ties of friendship and affection and courtships, alongside the analysis of Old Testament history in terms of politics and diplomacy, always leavened with a large proportion of broad comedy.

In some of his later work, Weise clearly anticipates eighteenth-century drama. In *Der curieuse Körbelmacher* (*The knacky basket-weaver*, 1702), for instance, Weise sets his touching story of love and loss in a bourgeois milieu, in the urban world of merchants and craftsmen. This tragedy with a happy ending points ahead to Gottsched, Gellert and even to Lessing.

Seventeenth-century fiction

We saw the beginnings of the extended prose fictional narrative in the previous century with such writers as Wickram. In this century the novel truly emerges as a distinct genre. It can be divided into two categories, the elevated novel and the popular novel, though from what we can deduce about reading habits and book purchases in this period it seems that it was the same readers who consumed both types. The distinction resides therefore in their differing aims and styles. The elevated novel forms are the pastoral and the courtly-historical novel, while the popular novel covers such genres as the picaresque, the comic novel, the 'political' novel and, at the end of the century, the 'gallant' novel. Most of these were influenced by foreign models, so the history of the seventeenth-century German novel is thus one of translation followed by native imitation. Only the picaresque or comic novel connects with some of the forms of prose fiction of the previous century, but even here, impulses from abroad played a vital role.

The pastoral novel is the earliest of the new forms to become established. Such prototypes as Jorge de Montemayor's *Diana* (1559), Philip Sydney's *Arcadia* (1590), Honoré d'Urfé's *Astrée* (1607–27) and John Barclay's *Argenis* (1621), written in Spanish, English, French and Latin respectively, were all available in German translation by the 1620s. The pastoral novel is a love story, set in an artificial landscape which provides a Utopian alternative to the artificiality of courtly society in which the emotions of private people can be explored. The first such novel in German is the anonymous *Amoena und Amandus* (1632), probably written by the Silesian nobleman Hans Adam von Gruttschreiber und Czopkendorff. In many ways it is typical: it is a *roman à clef* which takes place in the milieu of the country aristocrat, in which action is subordinate to the expression of feeling and whose plot ends unhappily. Such successors as *Leoriander und Perelina* (1642), *Die verführte Schäferin Cynthie* (*The Seduced Shepherdess Cynthia*, 1660) by Jacob Schwieger (*c.* 1630 to *c.* 1666) and *Damon und Lisille* (1672) by Johann Thomas (1624–1679/80) exhibit similar features, which have been characterised as the beginning of the bourgeois novel. Out of the Nuremberg circle emerged the two-part novel, *Die Kunst- und Tugend-gezierte Macarie* (*Macarie Decked with Art and Virtue*, part I: 1669; part II: 1673), of which the first is by Heinrich Arnold Stockfleth (1643–1708) in collaboration with his wife Maria Katharina Heden, née Frisch (1633?-92), while the second is wholly her work. The first part shows the shepherd Polyphilus setting off into the world to seek honour and glory. He meets and falls in love with the beautiful and learned Macarie but cannot win her because he has yet to learn the emptiness of court life. The second part shows him turning away from the court and retiring to the countryside where, in a community of shepherds and shepherdesses, he finds his ideal of equality and virtue and, of course, is reunited with Macarie. Thus, a pastoral utopia where, far from worldly hierarchy and ambition, men and women are equal in spirit and can cultivate their minds and souls, stands in opposition to the court.

The courtly novel has its roots both in Heliodorus' third century Greek novel *Aithiopica* and in the prose romance of the late Middle Ages. Heliodorus' novel, first printed in 1534 and translated into German in 1559, provided a model for the detailed and subtle portrayal of relations between the sexes, placed much greater emphasis than before on female characterisation and introduced the characteristic *in medias res* beginning, subsequent flashbacks, intertwined subplots and final unravelling. Out of the prose romance had developed that best known of all tales of knight errantry, the Spanish *Amadís de Gaula* by Garci Rodriguez de Montalvo (1508), which had appeared in German between 1569 and 1595. Out of the synthesis of these two forms grew the French seventeenth-century courtly novel which provides the blueprint for the German examples.

The French novels, written by such aristocratic authors as La Calprenède and Madeleine de Scudéry with plots from ancient history, were able to show how political and individual destiny is intertwined. Focusing on high-born characters, rulers and generals and showing them in endlessly complicated love intrigues which were simultaneously and by definition political intrigues, these novels provided a model for behaviour in a courtly society. The hero is no longer the all-action tearaway of the *Amadís* but a polished courtier, as much at home at a *levée* as on a horse. The heroine is no longer merely a prop, a reward for the hero after a good day's fighting, but someone whose emotions are as central to the novel as the hero's. The virtue of the characters is constantly tested and they triumph at the end only if they have withstood the moral trials and dangers of a deceitful world.

In the 1640s there were numerous translations of these novels. One of the most important translators was Philipp von Zesen (1618–89), who lived in Paris in 1643/4 and translated Vital d'Audiguier's *Lysandre et Caliste* in 1644, Madeleine de Scudéry's *Ibrahim ou l'illustre Bassa* in 1645 and François de Soucy, Sieur de Gerzan's *L'histoire afriquaine de Cléomède et de Sophonisbe* in 1647. Yet, when Zesen came to write original novels himself, he moved in a rather different direction. His first novel was *Die Adriatische Rosemund* (*Adriatic Rosemund*, 1645) which does not strictly adhere to any one genre. It tells of the love of the German Protestant Markhold who falls in love with the Venetian Catholic Rosemund but cannot marry her because of the difference in religion. He moves far away and she retires to pastoral solitude where in the guise of a shepherdess she can lament her loss. There can be no happy outcome to the lovers' dilemma and we are left to assume that Rosemund dies of grief. A large part of the novel is set in a middle-class milieu and the problem confronting the lovers is one belonging to Zesen's own day. However, as in the pastoral, the exploration of emotion is the chief focus of the novel and the action is relatively slight, in contrast to the courtly novel with its large cast of characters, numerous sub-plots and much more intricate action.

In fact, true courtly novels are so rare in German that they can be counted in single figures. The clergyman Andreas Heinrich Bucholtz (1607–71), Professor at the Lutheran University of Rinteln, wrote two such novels, *Herkules und Valiksa* (1659) and a 'son of Herkules', *Herkuliskus und Herkuladisla* (1665). Both novels follow a noble or royal protagonist who goes on an extended and dangerous journey to find and free his beloved, with whom after many tribulations he is reunited. Bucholtz's original contribution to the genre is the addition of both a religious and a patriotic dimension. On a religious level, his protagonists are presented as perfect Christians and his plots as demonstrations of the workings of divine providence. Bucholtz's novels at times resemble devotional works in the prayers the characters utter and in the emphasis placed on religious sentiment. On a patriotic level Herkules and his son Herkuladiskus are German heroes from the period just before the founding of the Holy Roman Empire, an event which is anticipated in the novels. Bucholtz embeds his narrative in a historical framework and pays great attention to such realistic details as chronology.

Another way to christianise the courtly novel was to use biblical material. This is what Hans Jakob Christoffel von Grimmelshausen (discussed below as a picaresque novelist) does in his *Histori vom keuschen Joseph in Aegypten* (*The tale of chaste Joseph in Egypt*, 1666, second expanded edition 1670), in which he sticks closely to the biblical text presented in loose episodic fashion. Zesen, who returned to the novel twenty years after his *Adriatische Rosemund*, also wrote a Joseph novel, called *Assenat* (1670) after Joseph's wife, Assenat or Asnath. The focus of the action, however, is Joseph, whom Zesen portrays not as the ideal ruler but as the ideal princely servant. Zesen's second biblical novel, *Simson* (1679), is a less successful mixure of courtly and non-courtly narration, of biblical history and spiritual edification.

Closest to the French courtly novel are two works by an author who was himself a prince: Duke Anton Ulrich of Braunschweig-Lüneburg (1633–1714), who also wrote court entertainments, ballets, opera libretti and poems. His first novel, *Die Durchleuchtigen Syrerinn Aramena (The noble Syrian Lady Aramena)* set in biblical times in the period of the patriarch Jacob, was published between 1669 and 1673. Manuscript evidence suggests that it was begun by Anton Ulrich's sister, Sibylle Ursula (1629–71), who had translated La Calprenède and Madeleine de Scudéry and even corresponded with the latter. On her marriage and consequent departure from the Wolfenbüttel court, Anton Ulrich continued the novel which was then corrected and augmented by the Nuremberg poet Sigmund von Birken, Anton Ulrich's sometime tutor. In its 3,900 octavo pages Anton Ulrich and his sister describe a courtly world, apparently dominated by Fortuna, the goddess of chance, in which the love affairs of twenty-seven couples are depicted as fraught with uncertainty and difficulty. However, virtue and constancy win through in the end, thus demonstrating the workings of divine providence. Anton Ulrich presents the reader with disquisitions on the right conduct of a prince, on the welfare of the state and on good government in general. The fifth volume of the novel is a pastoral in which characters from the first four books as well as members of the court and the ducal family are to be found under pseudonymns as shepherds and shepherdesses.

Anton Ulrich's second novel, *Octavia Römische Geschichte (The Roman history of Octavia)*, had a much longer and even more complicated gestation. The first three books of a first version appeared between 1677 and 1679, three further volumes of an extended version appeared between 1703 and 1707 and the major part of another version appeared in 1712. *Octavia* is set in the Rome of the Emperors Nero and Vespasian and in some 7,000 pages tells the stories of twenty-four different couples. The novel covers Roman history in the years AD 68–71 and thus illustrates the spread of Christianity – Octavia is a secret Christian – while also indicating links between the Habsburg and Roman Empires, to whose glories the Holy Roman Empire of the German Nation succeeded.

Two novels which appeared in 1689, however, already prefigure the end of the courtly novel of the French type. The first of these is *Arminius*, the only novel by the Silesian dramatist Daniel Casper von Lohenstein

(1635–83), which bursts the bounds of the novel by the sheer weight of historical material it incorporates within it, and Heinrich Anselm von Zigler and Kliphausen's *Asiatische Banise*, which points forward towards the eighteenth century in its attempt to apply reason to real problems of practical politics. Lohenstein left *Arminius* all but finished at his death and it appeared posthumously in 1689–90. The full title describes Arminius as 'the Magnanimous General and valiant defender of German freedom' and states that the novel should spur the German nobility to emulate him. The novel takes the reader through a huge historical panorama to demonstrate the divine plan which lies behind all historical change, but more particularly behind the emergence of the Holy Roman Empire. The theory of the four kingdoms of the world is used, as in Lohenstein's plays, to demonstrate that the Habsburg Empire is the last and greatest of these and that Arminius, the German hero, prefigures the Emperor Leopold (reigned 1658–1705).

Heinrich Anselm von Zigler und Kliphausen (1663–97), the Saxon aristocrat who wrote *Die Asiatische Banise, Oder Das blutig- doch muthige Pegu* (*Asiatic Banise, or the bloody yet courageous Kingdom of Pegu*, 1689), has a much clearer eye for what will appeal to a broad public. His novel is a fraction the length of Lohenstein's, is set in northern Burma and packed with local colour and exotic detail. Instead of theological and philosophical problems it illustrates questions of *raison d'état* and pragmatic government within an absolutist system. The action is fast-moving and provides examples of statesmen from the villainous to the virtuous. It therefore has links with the so-called 'political' novel discussed below. The public loved it, it was still in print seventy years later and the sequel by Johann Georg Hamann (1697–1733) which appeared in 1724 went into five editions.

The best known of the types of popular novel is the picaresque, that is, the episodic, linear and often autobiographical tale of a petty criminal or social outsider who has to survive in a cruel and inimical world. Moving at a fast pace and involving a large cast of characters, the picaresque novel, which is always centred on the main character of the *pícaro* or *pícara* from whose point of view the action is seen, can be made the vehicle for social satire, moral reflection and broad comedy. This genre produced one of the greatest novels in the German language, namely, Grimmelshausen's *Simplicissimus*.

As with the other genres, the picaresque novel was launched by translations from abroad, first from Spanish, then from the French *roman comique*. Mateo Alemán's *Guzman de Alfarache* (1599–1605) was translated by the Munich Jesuit Aegidius Albertinus (1560–1620) in 1615, the anonymous *Lazarillo de Tormes* (1554) in 1617, Francisco López de Úbeda's *Pícara Justina* (1605) in 1620–7 and Charles Sorel's *Histoire comique de Francion* (1623–33) in 1662 and 1668, to name but the most important. Of these translations Albertinus's, in which the second part showed the repentant sinner and emphasised the edificatory function of the novel, was by far the most important in that it served Grimmelshausen as a model.

Hans Jakob Christoffel von Grimmelshausen (1621 or 1622–76) did not attend a university, follow any learned profession nor form part of any learned and literary grouping but spent his formative years from about 1635 until 1648 following the army as a soldier and subsequently as regimental clerk. He wrote two different types of novel: elevated novels – as well as his Joseph novel there are the courtly novels *Dietwald und Amelinde* (1670) and *Proximus und Lympida* (1672) – and the more numerous picaresque novels. Only the two courtly novels appeared under his real name, while both *Joseph* and the picaresque novels appeared under a series of anagrammatic pseudonyms. Grimmelshausen's extensive oeuvre all appeared within ten years.

His most important novel, *Der abentheuerliche Simplicissimus Teutsch* (*The adventures of Simplicissimus, a German*) appeared in 1668. For it, Grimmelshausen drew on the Spanish picaresque novel, especially on the religious dimension which Albertinus emphasised so much, on the rich folly literature in German, on the native tradition of the 'Schwank' and on the social satire of Johann Michael Moscherosch (1601–69) in his *Gesichte Philanders von Sittewald* (*The visions of Philander von Sittewald*, 1640–3). It tells the story of Simplicius Simplicissimus who begins the novel so young and untutored that he is almost at the level of a beast. He takes refuge in the forest where he is initiated into Christian knowledge by a hermit who gives him a name indicating his simplicity and foolishness. The hermit, in one of the many symbolic twists in the work, turns out much later to be his true father. A fully fledged Christian but totally ignorant of the ways of the world, the simpleton is brought by the fortunes of war to the fortress of Hanau. Here he takes a decisive step away from religion and towards the world and its temptations, and the rest of the novel is the tale of how he sinks deeper into sin against a background of the brutality of war until his final repentance, when he becomes a hermit again and the novel comes full circle. The narrative is racy, funny and exciting, told by the regenerate, older and wiser man about his younger sinful self. It provides a rich panorama of life during the Thirty Years War, it takes us across Europe and into a wide variety of situations. It includes passages of sharp social criticism, deep moral and religious insight and others of pure fantasy. It examines the nature of knowledge – of Christ, of the world, of oneself – and of folly, while at the same time it can be seen as an allegory of Everyman or Mr Christian on his pilgrimage through the world.

In subsequent works, Grimmelshausen built on this foundation. There is the so-called *Continuatio* (1669), in which Simplicissimus's renunciation of the world is shown to be less profound than it seemed, there is *Courasche* (1670), the racy autobiography of a female *pícara*, a minor character in the big novel, who combines both male and female qualities. She survives the war by selling her sexuality – 'Courasche' is the name she gives to her own private parts – but also by fighting and taking prisoners and booty. Unlike Simplicissimus, she is utterly unrepentant of her sins and ends the novel as the leader of the gypsies. She can be seen as an allegory of Frau Welt (Lady World), the female personification of the world and its temptations of the flesh. *Springinsfeld* (1670) is the tale of an old sweat who has once been Courasche's lover and Simplicissimus's servant and begins with a subtle examination of what constitutes writing and even more, what constitutes reading. The *Wunderbarliches Vogelnest I* (*The magic birdsnest*, 1672) and *II* (1675), no longer picaresque novels in the narrow sense, provide us with a broad panorama of the post-war world, which has even fewer good qualities than the war era. There are numerous shorter associated works, the so-called *Simplicianische Schriften*, but the novels listed were stated by the author himself to constitute a cycle which can only be understood as a whole.

Grimmelshausen had such a success that it was sufficient for a work to use the epithet 'simplicianisch' in the title for it to sell. Johann Beer (1655–1700) is the only other novelist of the period who can approach Grimmelshausen in inventiveness and narrative verve, though he lags far behind him in moral profundity. Beer was an Austrian, a musician and composer in the service of the Duke of Sachsen-Weißenfels, first at his court in Halle and then in Weißenfels from 1676 until his death. As well as other writings, Beer published three novels in Simplician mode: *Der Simplicianische Welt=Kucker/ Oder Abentheuerliche Jan Rebhu* (*The Simplician observer of the world*, 1677–79); *Jucundi Jucundissimi Wunderliche Lebens-Beschreibung* (*The wonderful life history of Jucundus Jucundissimus*, 1680); *Zendorii a Zendoriis Teutsche Winter-Nächte* (*Zendorius a Zendoriis's German winter nights*, 1682), *Die kurzweiligen Sommer-Täge* (*The amusing summer days*, 1683). These works resemble the picaresque novel in their episodic narrative with its focus on the eponymous hero and in the swift succession of adventures, but the tight structure, the double perspective of repentant older man looking back on a sinful life, the clarity with which the venality of mankind and the atrocities of war are delineated are missing in Beer. The novels are much more purely comic, their aim is to entertain, their world has become more middle-class and worldly success is not ruled out at the end.

Another aspect of Beer's oeuvre was influenced by Christian Weise

(1642–1708) who coincided for a few years with Beer in Weißenfels when Weise was Professor at the grammar school there from 1670–8. Weise began the vogue for what came to be called 'political' novels with *Die drey Haupt-Verderber in Teutschland* (*The three chief destroyers of Germany*, 1671), a satire also influenced by Moscherosch, in which the narrator dreams that he descends into the underworld where he meets three figures representing the ills of contemporary Germany. Weise went on to write three 'political' novels proper. The first is *Die Drey ärgsten Ertz=Narren in der gantzen Welt* (*The three worst fools in the whole world*, 1672), in which a young nobleman can claim his inheritance only when he has located the three fools of the title. The novel tells the adventures which befall him and his companions while on this search. The emphasis of the work is on teaching the reader how to assess correctly the people and events of this world, how to act with 'politique' cleverness, how to look after one's own interests and at the same time serve the common good. The contrast with Grimmelshausen's Christian values could hardly be more apparent. *Die Drey Klügsten Leute in der gantzen Welt* (*The three cleverest people in the whole world*, 1675) is a further instalment of the above, with the company now in search of the three cleverest people. *Der Politische Näscher* (*The political taster*, 1678) tells of Crescentio, a young man who almost ruins his chances in society by overestimating his own abilities. He learns from experience, however, and we are left with the notion that on the one hand social conventions and norms should be respected but that the individual is master of his own destiny and can learn from his mistakes – a far cry from the characters of the courtly novel in the grip of a Fortuna they cannot understand and cannot influence. Moderation, rational behaviour and just assessment of social situations constitute 'politique' behaviour and will bring their own social rewards.

Beer followed in Weise's footsteps with his own 'political' novels, such as *Der Politischer Bratenwender* (*The political spit-turner*) and *Der Politischer Feuermäuer-Kehrer* (*The political chimney-sweep*, both 1682). Beer is much more purely satirical than Weise and his 'political' works are designed less as models for correct behaviour than as lampoons of folly. In this and in their linear narration, the 'political' novel can be seen to be indebted to Grimmelshausen. So to some extent is the short comic novel by Christian Reuter (1665–1712), *Schelmuffskys Wahrhafftige Curiöse und sehr gefährliche Reisebeschreibung Zu Wasser und Lande* (*Schelmuffsky's truthful description of his curious and very dangerous journey by sea and land*, 1696–7). The name of the hero announces that he is a *pícaro* (in German 'Schelm'), but at the same time the novel is a spoof on the exotic travelogue, a satire on the nobility and a successful piece of comic writing in which the hero constantly unmasks himself. He tells the story of his amazing travels, the exciting adventures he meets with, the ladies who love him – and all the while it is becoming clear to the reader that he has never got further than the next village, where he has drunk his inheritance, and that he comes staggering back within a matter of days. Here too there is a dual perspective, but it is that of the reader working against the hero rather than the older hero commenting on his younger self.

If the 'political' novel marks a decisive step towards secularisation and into the eighteenth century, the so-called 'gallant' or society novel, of which Christian Friedrich Hunold (1681–1722) is the foremost practitioner, goes a stage further. Hunold, whose *nom de plume* was Menantes, was another writer with Weißenfels connections. Unable to obtain a court position, Hunold went to Hamburg and was able to capture the public imagination to such an extent with his novels that he could live for a time as a freelance writer – an indication of how much both the book trade and the reading public had increased. His novels such as *Die Verliebte und Galante Welt* (*The gallant world in love*, 1700), *Die Liebens-Würdige Adalie* (*Lovable Adalie*, 1702), *Der Europäischen Höfe Liebes- und Helden-Geschichte* (*The heroic love story of the European courts*, 1705) and *Der Satyrische Roman* (*The satirical novel*, 1706) take place in a world of operas, balls, country villas, elegant toilettes and delicate erotic intrigue. *Die Liebens-Würdige Adalie* is a representative example, for it is set at the French court and tells of a mere banker's daughter who manages to rise into the aristocracy, marry a duke and live happily ever after. The erotic scenes and scandalous goings-on among opera singers, courtiers and aristocrats must have entertained the contemporary public, even while they shocked them. *Der Europäischen Höfe Liebes- und Helden-Geschichte* is a *roman à clef* which narrates some of the best-known court scandals of the era. These are novels as entertainment, titillating, amusing and voyeuristic.

By the end of this century, therefore, literacy has increased; in 1681 for the first time the catalogues of the German book fairs show that more books were being published in German than in Latin, literature has begun the process of secularisation and the literary exploration of the inner world of the emotions is well under way.

4

The German Enlightenment (1720–1790)

RUTH-ELLEN BOETCHER JOERES

Introduction

Developments in literary historiography, especially in the last few decades, have called into question facile analyses, convenient categorisations, and underlying assumptions about the possibility of determining 'real' history. With the growing number of challenges to the belief that we in the present can establish a set of distinct truths about the past – with the doubt (propounded above all by postmodernists) about the possibility of a unified (clearly identified and defined, absolutely understood) self – and with the concomitant awareness (offered most recently by feminist scholars) that however much we can glean about the past, the usual sample that we have chosen has been narrow and limited, the writing and study of literary history have become more complex. Learning about history can no longer involve only the investigation of privileged individuals who have often been assumed to represent universally applicable characteristics and ideologies. We know that we need to broaden our study, to re-focus the lens, to think contextually.

We also know that the task of writing and thinking about history is one that cannot be marked by universalising statements. What we must acknowledge is the necessity on the part of (literary, but also other) historians for approximations and attempted assumptions. Given that every idea, every concept, even every category understood to represent some solid, dependable, credible, perhaps even absolute thing is now seen as socially constructed, as temporary, uncertain, and changeable, the most a literary historian can hope for is to provide an estimate of a time and place that she/he cannot ever fully know.

Let us, for example, consider the German Enlightenment and the *Sturm und Drang*, the short-lived rebellion that came towards the end of the Enlightenment. Literary histories have spent much energy analysing this period, which is seen by most to be pivotal in its consequences for those who lived in it as well as for succeeding generations including our own. It is certainly true that much happened in the area of German literature between 1720 and 1790 in terms of the increasing use of German as a literary (and official) language, the growth of a publishing industry, the expansion of a reading public, the development of literary forms, the accumulation of a body of philosophical ideas that were to influence other areas of Europe as well as later generations of German thinkers and writers. But it is also true that those who have written about this epoch have, in the interests of categorisation and theoretical clarification, often made broad generalisations. In a desire for sources, literary historians have tended to seize upon a text and to make the leap between it and a statement about the reality of life in the eighteenth century. In an effort to systematise the chaos that any body of written texts is bound to represent, they have also been too willing to put everything into boxes: to say, for instance, that the dialectic of the eighteenth century consisted of a thesis, namely the cool, mechanical, and rational Enlightenment, that was challenged by an antithesis, namely the fiery, irrational, rebellious *Sturm und Drang* (Storm and Stress), and that they were then resolved in the synthesis of the highbrow, brilliant, intellectual, philosophical Classical movement. Underlying this assumption is the belief that Enlightenment and *Sturm und Drang* respectively represent a movement and a reaction against that movement. It is also generally believed that a literary activity can be confined to a particular set of years, an assertion easily disproved as soon as one begins to check dates on various texts belonging, at least chronologically, to one box or another, and discovers that distinct boundaries between periods do not exist at all.

Other illusions are also being challenged. Many literary histories of the German Enlightenment written before 1975 seemed to assert that what was available to those who were literate in the eighteenth century were high-flung philosophy and lofty literary works: that 'popular literature' did not exist. Since both the gender and class of the readership have mostly remained unmarked, another assumption was that everyone was literate and lived a middle or upper-class existence, or conversely, that only highly educated men wrote: that no working-class people of either gender, and that certainly no women, were publishing. It has also been assumed that large numbers of the populace must have been participants in the philosophical and literary debates of the day, and that books and other written texts must have been widely available to that audience.

This chapter cannot deal with all of these illusions nor will it pretend to represent an all-encompassing picture of those vital and exciting seventy years. It will focus on some of the paradoxes of the epoch, complicate the picture, and introduce some points of discussion that may lead to further discussions. For that purpose, gender and class have been chosen as the primary analytic categories. Despite the broadening discussion about this century and the welcome social histories of literature that have appeared over the past few years, despite the periodic interest in class as a lens through which to examine literary history, gender and the intersection between gender and class have often been ignored. To introduce such a discussion into a literary history is to add subtlety to the picture: to contextualise in necessary and differentiating ways. This does not mean that the purpose is simply to include numbers of women and working-class men and women among the authors and works discussed, but also to employ gender and/or class as analytic lenses that can assist us in forming a necessarily approximate picture of the eighteenth century: to examine, for example, concepts like 'masculinity' and 'femininity', the understandings of which underwent significant changes in the course of the century, to think about what role they might have played in the literary and philosophical developments of the Enlightenment; to think as well about the readership and the literary market, both of which changed dramatically in size and scope during the century, especially after the 1740s; to ask about the implication of such terms as 'popular literature' and 'popular philosophy' and the effect such labelling had on readers, writers and critics.

For all its claims to clarification and clarity, to making its ideas clear and bright, the Enlightenment itself is increasingly seen as inherently contradictory. The basic meaning of the word 'Enlightenment' implied something that was optimistic, positive, progressive (in the sense of an ongoing, linear progression towards the Good and the Moral and the Happy), democratic, educational. Yet in practice, the movement was also narrow, anti-imaginative, rigid, limited, and biased. It is significant that the most visible literary product of the era of the Enlightenment was the tragedy, the so-called 'bürgerliches Trauerspiel' (middle-class tragedy), with its gloomy ending belying any positive outcome. Despite the theoretical emphasis on tolerance, general education and inclusion, demythologisation and secularisation and on the faith in 'man', individual agency and potential – such beliefs could be realised only slightly under absolutist rule (even though for much of the epoch, from 1712 to 1786, Frederick II reigned as king of Prussia and his openness encouraged those propounding the ideas of enlightened thinking and action). Theory and practice were in conflict with one another: when Adorno's and Horkheimer's *Dialectic of the Enlightenment* (1972) describes Enlightenment as 'demythologisation', they follow that up swiftly with the acknowledgement that it was also 'mythic fear turned radical'. In much of what follows, therefore, certain paradoxes and contradictions will emerge. The use of gender and class will help determine the inner unevennesses and difficulties that marked an age that has most often been seen as a shining progression.

It is interesting to realise how many beliefs that still prevail in much of western culture are derived from the Enlightenment. Despite postmodern claims, the existence of a stable, coherent and reasoning self still underlies many Western assumptions. The Enlightenment belief in reason and philosophy is still paramount, as well as the conviction that 'truth' can indeed be determined. Most of us still believe that if reason is used properly, it will benefit all of us, and philosophy, as the neutral 'science' of reason, is still considered credible and ultimately beneficial for society at large. Language, as the tool that transmits philosophy, knowledge, and reason, is still considered reliable, for 'objects are not linguistically (or socially) constructed, they are merely *made present* to consciousness by naming and the right use of language' (Jane Flax, 'Postmodernism and gender relations in feminist theory', 1987, pp. 624–5).

At the same time, given the present-day postmodern theoretical debates that see everything as constructed against a specific background of social, ideological, economic, and historical variables enmeshed in a particular time and place, such beliefs are thrown into question. To many today, the assumption of a single Truth implies élitism and a myopic view that will exclude any loose ends that do not fit. If there is such a thing as a 'tribunal of reason', to which the Enlightenment submits all claims to truth, then certain cases are likely not to be heard. If freedom implies obedience to a set of laws claiming to know what is necessary and right, then it is appropriate to ask who it is that is determining what is right. If science and philosophy are assumed to be the neutral and unbiased representatives of 'true knowledge', then does that mean that the atomic bomb or (to return to the eighteenth century) the rack, torture, witch burnings, all of which are presumably based on the 'right' reason that invents and produces instruments of torture, are right as well? If 'word' and 'thing' correspond and language is to be trusted, then are meanings immutable?

To examine the seventy years during which Enlightenment thought held sway in Germany is both to see its continuing influence and vitality and to realise its multifaceted, often problematic nature. For to investigate the German 'Enlightenment' is also to see how its beliefs were even then thrown into question, challenged, modified, revised, enhanced and augmented by the participants themselves. It is to see the period as exciting, contentious, searching, but also as flawed. It is to see a time long past in which we ourselves, and how we in the western world still often think and act and judge, are reflected.

What follows is a discussion of selected canonical and non-canonical categories, genres and texts that have been chosen to clarify and enlarge a review of German literary history between 1720 and 1790. An inclusion of some less well-known writers and texts and a different focus on the ideas these writers and texts presented will obviously preclude other more canonical texts, ideas and writers. Preceding that discussion are a brief general overview of the era and a paradigmatic case study of two philosophical texts that help to illustrate the use of gender and class as analytic categories.

Overview

Between 1720 and 1790, Germany underwent massive developments and changes. At the same time, much seemed not to change at all: the eighteenth century began with a German-speaking territory that was made up of numerous fragmented principalities forming the primary political units, and at its end it looked much the same. The absolutism that experienced its most pronounced power between 1648 (the end of the Thirty Years War) and 1805 (the beginning of the Napoleonic era) was still dominant in 1790 despite the upheavals of the French Revolution. Many of the changes that were most obvious occurred in the cultural sphere, in the development of German as the primary literary and cultural language, the rapid expansion in the numbers of those who considered writing their profession, the growing literacy rates, and the differentiation of the readership. The seventy years that will be discussed here moved, in terms of literary history, through what are variously called 'Aufklärung' (often divided into 'Früh-' and 'Hochaufklärung' (Early and Late Enlightenment)), 'Empfindsamkeit,' (Sentimentality) and 'Sturm und Drang' (Storm and Stress). Despite the implied categorisation of literary movements, all of these trends grew out of a common source, a search for what today would be called bourgeois subjectivity: a focus on the fastest growing demographic group that, by the mid-nineteenth century, would be understood as the social/economic class of the bourgeoisie ('Bürgertum'). The continuing locus of power remained the absolutist monarchies, but with the growth in educational possibilities, in literacy, in the availability of cultural artefacts such as books or theatres, and with the wide-ranging emphasis on a variety of political, social and emotional emancipations (the emancipation *from* absolutism, but also the emancipation *of* reason, feeling, emotion and imagination), a change in consciousness was possible on certain social levels.

Trends came and went during the course of the century, and emphases were transformed as various factors played a greater or lesser role in social and literary developments. The moves towards the defining of subjectivity that increased as the century progressed were already present early on, albeit in less specific form. To avoid the creation of artificial boundaries, therefore, the usual term that will be used in the following will be 'Enlightenment', unless what is called for is the more specific reference of 'Empfindsamkeit' (a term that was most often used to describe a variety of developments after 1750 that focused on the open expression of emotion and was appropriated from the English Sentimentality of Sterne and others) or 'Sturm und Drang' (understood as the brief rebellion of young male writers in the 1770s and 1780s).

The period began under the philosophical influence of Christian Thomasius (1655–1728) and Gottfried Wilhelm Leibniz (1646–1716), whose work spanned the latter years of the seventeenth and the early decades of the eighteenth centuries. The significance of their contributions as philosophers was matched by the broader impact of their influence on the adaptation of German as a literary and intellectual language. In a region in which the use of Latin had served to define and limit the size of a reading and writing public which by definition needed to be highly educated, the idea of the general education of the populace was thereby discouraged and the knowledge that was produced and transmitted was decisively shaped. As a professor of philosophy who chose to deliver his 1688 lectures in German rather than Latin, Thomasius in particular spurred the use of German as an academic language and inspired others to challenge the dominance of Latin as the medium of intellectual discourse. The replacement of Latin with German and the emphasis on accessibility and communication led logically into one of the principal ideals of the Enlightenment, namely the creation of an educational programme in the German population that would allow for the popularisation of Enlightenment ideals and the concomitant improvement in the lives of German citizens. To these ends, Thomasius provided an appropriate model; his efforts on behalf of general education and a popular philosophy that gave new authority to individual subjectivity provided a fertile ground for further developments. In many respects, he anticipated his successors by emphasising a level of subjectivity in creativity that is more like the focus on the autonomous individual in the later Enlightenment. Thomasius also specifically mentioned women as possible beneficiaries of his writings and spoke out explicitly against the persecution of witches.

The interest of Leibniz in education and cultivation ('Bildung') also provided optimistic, utopian impulses for those who followed him and led to a growing perception of the potentially political nature of didacticism. The discourse that he developed ultimately formed a basis for Enlightenment thought, a discourse tied very much to language and its use that clothed the essentially philosophical movement known as the Enlightenment in literary/linguistic garb. In an effort to resolve the contradictions between material and spiritual realms, his theory of monads suggested a harmony that would join the cosmos to the individual and lower forms to higher ones, thereby influencing the underlying optimism of the Enlightenment by giving rise as well to an emphasis on human reason and science.

What both Thomasius and Leibniz transmitted – and what Christian Wolff (1679–1754), the populariser of Leibniz, Immanuel Kant (1724–1804), Johann Georg Hamann (1730–88), Johann Gottfried Herder (1744–1803), and others developed – were concepts that centred on speaking/writing, explaining and transmitting knowledge and/or theory with the goal of ultimate action. As thinkers, their popular reception was limited; at the same time, they chose increasingly to write and speak in a language whose very use implied a larger and more heterogeneous audience. Theory thus could – at least theoretically – lead to practice. Wolff in particular stressed the need for accessibility, and his student Gottsched, who was to become a major voice in Enlightenment thought on literature, put that thinking into practice with his attempts at realising a national German politics of culture and, through his establishment of (often pedantic) rules, provided concrete examples of how one should compose literary works. Herder, who exerted a strong influence on Goethe, particularly stressed language and its unique importance in human development. Language as conducive to, and symbolic of, interaction was central to his belief in the potential for change, and his emphasis on the importance of a national language also extended into discussions on diversity and the compelling need for political discourse.

Much of such thinking was utopian, far removed from the reality of a world that in large part was illiterate, poor and hardly open to the heady ideas of philosophers. At the same time, changes occurred – in literacy rates, in the availability of books and periodicals, and in the developing public sphere of literary and political and social discourse – and at least some of the optimistic ideals of philosophers like Leibniz, Thomasius, and Herder were realised. Where changes most notably occurred was in the way in which the new cultural discourses were presented. From the early part of the century, far more affected by the optimism of Leibniz and his belief in the harmonising possibilities of the universe, to the more sceptical, more complicating later years, when the autonomous individual rather than the community implied in Leibniz's theories became the focus, the continuing thread was the defining and prescribing of a bourgeois subjectivity that reflected the growing power of the developing middle class, but also the need to understand the considerable diversity of that class.

The popularisation of philosophical discourse in the eighteenth century – essentially the move from metaphysics and natural philosophy to the more subject-based arenas of morality, empirical psychology, politics and aesthetics – did not mean that the writings of Leibniz, Thomasius, Wolff, Kant and others were readily accessible. What is innovative, however, is the manner in which these philosophers occasionally transmitted their ideas. Thomasius often presented his thoughts in the more readable essay form, for example. Moses Mendelssohn took part in dialogues, both epistolary and conversational, with his friends, the writers Lessing and Friedrich Nicolai. Kant and Mendelssohn contributed regularly to periodicals with their larger readerships. Herder published a travel journal. Despite the continuing presence of absolutism, their goal of popularising knowledge was made increasingly obvious.

In literary matters, this growing popularisation meant a spectrum moving from the more rigid ideas propounded by Gottsched, whose cultural power was considerable during the first half of the century, to rebellious young men like Goethe and Schiller and other *Stürmer und Dränger* who honed the perception of the individual into a cult of genius. It meant the development of several literary discourses, from periodicals intended to popularise Enlightenment thinking among a potentially larger and more diverse readership, to literary criticism, begun by Gottsched in his *Versuch einer critischen Dichtkunst* (*Attempt at a critical poetic art*, 1751) and expanded upon and challenged by his students and others. It meant a discourse of and about theatre, with the politically tinged hope for a national German theatre that would serve to unite the country even in its fragmented political state. It meant a discourse of subjectivity, presented at first in the attention paid to the letter, then expanded upon in the novel, the journalistic essay, the development of lyric poetry. It meant a discourse on the dissemination of knowledge that produced a growing journalistic movement and a popular philosophical writing that distanced itself from the stolid writing of traditional philosophical and theological debate. It meant a critical discourse that led to many public battles among intellectuals. Whether it was Gottsched, with his emphasis on rules and his preference for the classical writing of the French, competing with the Swiss critics Bodmer and Breitinger, with their growing interest in the worth of individual texts that would lead in turn to the individualisation so evident at the time of the *Sturm und Drang* – or with Lessing, who urged an adherence to the more freely constructed writing of Shakespeare and his successors – or whether it was Lessing himself, in bitter dispute with the orthodox pastor Goeze on issues of religious freedom – the freewheeling critical debates were accessible to a larger group of readers and writers than had existed before.

Although literary works and debates became more available to a growing readership, only a small portion of the largely rural, illiterate German population was touched by them. Nevertheless, we can use these texts as signposts towards understanding something of what Germany was like two centuries ago. And by enlarging the discussion to include genres and works beyond the standard canon, we will learn more about the contradictions that also marked the Enlightenment: how, for example, with the desired increase in reading material, that material itself began to diverge from expected paths with the development of a reading public that was far different from any of previous generations.

This seventy-year period in German literary history was marked by varied developments in both literature and philosophy in particular intellectual contexts, but always against the background of political repression, absolutist rule, limited literacy on the part of the populace at large, and little progress towards political and social democratisation. The utopia that was often dreamed and written of turned out to be both unrealisable and unrealistic and, in many senses, myopic. At the same time, the colourful and varied products of that period showed evidence of progression, variety, and, as social and literary movements always do, set the stage for the reactions and the developments of the next century.

A paradigmatic case: Kant, Mendelssohn and the lenses of gender and class

An examination of the responses of two prominent German Enlightenment philosophers, namely Immanuel Kant (1724–1804) and Moses Mendelssohn (1729–86), to the question, 'What is Enlightenment?' will serve as an introduction to some general ideas behind the movement that motivated its philosophical debates. In addition, if the lens is refocused to consider the place of gender and class within two documents that did not consciously focus on either, some of the contradictions can be made apparent that have as much to do with the lacks and gaps in Enlightenment thought as they do with the problematic dichotomies that marked the movement, especially in the tensions between a traditional understanding of the classical language of philosophy and the Enlightenment goal of popularising knowledge.

It is important to note that these two responses appeared late in the period that is the focus of this chapter, at a time when much that had been asserted and accepted was being transformed and often disputed by the rebels of the *Sturm und Drang*. The *Berlinische Monatsschrift*, in which these pieces were first published, was one of the numerous periodical journals that arose during the century; it represents an important voice of the Enlightenment, although it actually did not begin publication until 1783. Both Kant and Mendelssohn were regular contributors, as were other leading figures in the German Enlightenment and beyond the borders of Germany – there were, for example, contributions by Thomas Jefferson, Count Mirabeau, and Benjamin Franklin. Mendelssohn's inclusion was significant on other grounds, for he was a Jew, a member of a population group that then, as later, bore the brunt of brutal German prejudice. Mendelssohn was also viewed as a so-called 'popular philosopher', and although the use of the label 'popular' was less trivialising at a time when broader educational access was being encouraged, the perception of Mendelssohn as both Jew and popular philosopher marked his response. Whereas Kant's piece has been reprinted in virtually every anthology of

Enlightenment writings, Mendelssohn's is less well known. Yet in many ways it is more revealing, less cryptic, and especially helpful in its explanation of Enlightenment thinking.

Mendelssohn's article was published in September and Kant's in December 1784. Mendelssohn's essay concentrates on establishing a scheme that contextualises 'Aufklärung' (Enlightenment) and connects it with two other concepts, namely the umbrella term of 'Bildung' (cultural education) and the concept of 'Kultur' (culture): that is, he sees all three terms as vital, but whereas 'Bildung' is privileged as the originary term, with its dual implications of education and formation, 'Aufklärung' and 'Kultur' are its subordinate aspects. The central argument focuses on defining and differentiating these aspects: that is, Mendelssohn employs an approximating, indirect, inductive approach to the initial question, an interpretation of the Enlightenment not solely by itself, but within a larger context of meaning.

By seeing 'Kultur' and 'Aufklärung' as essentially dichotomous, Mendelssohn can set up a comfortable set of opposites that ostensibly cover all that it is necessary to know: whereas 'Kultur' is considered practical, as related to handicrafts, social mores and the arts, or to cleverness, industriousness and (manual) skills, or as encompassing drives, desires and habits, 'Aufklärung' is viewed as theoretical, reasoning, as centring on the larger issues of human life and human determination. An implicit ranking of the two concepts is provided when Mendelssohn declares that human determination is the goal of all of our actions and claims that that goal is essential to our survival.

Much of what follows refines these initial statements. 'Aufklärung' is aligned with the sciences; 'Kultur' is seen as being related to social relations, poetry and conversation. 'Aufklärung' is theory, realisation, criticism; 'Kultur' is practice, morality, virtuosity. In distinguishing between the role of humans as humans and as citizens, Mendelssohn has 'Kultur' claim the human as citizen, with 'Aufklärung' concerning itself with the human as human. In other words, 'Kultur' focuses on matters of the state and the citizen's role in it, but also on issues of class location and professional life: on the human being as a member of a larger group, a society with a variety of social roles and classes. On the other hand, he locates 'Aufklärung' above the particularities of class and professional status with which 'Kultur' is concerned. Such a difference may well produce conflict between the two, although he assures his readers that both concepts are essential. Nevertheless, a hierarchy is again apparent: whereas an absence of citizenship would condemn the state to non-existence, the absence of human characteristics would lower the human to the level of animal. The spectre of the loss of human-ness is clearly more serious.

Mendelssohn's text ends with an astonishingly modern warning. In introducing the theme of religion, he also opens up the possibility for the intolerance that is implicit in religions, which traditionally war with each other over their position in the hierarchy of ultimate 'truth'. This battle over supreme rightness leads him to express concern about the claims to perfection reflected in various warring religions and, by extension, in a philosophy like the Enlightenment that also implies perfection at the end of a progression of growth. Appropriately, he cites a Hebrew saying:

Je edler ein Ding in seiner Vollkommenheit . . ., desto gräßlicher in seiner Verwesung . . . So auch mit Kultur und Aufklärung. Je edler in ihrer Blüte: desto abscheulicher in ihrer Verwesung und Verderbtheit.

[*The more noble a thing in its perfection, the more hideous it is in its decay . . .* So it is with culture and Enlightenment. The more noble in their flowering, the more horrible in their decay and corruption.]

The negative results of 'Aufklärung' and 'Kultur', Mendelssohn claims, are rigidity, egotism, irreligiosity and anarchy (in the case of Enlightenment), and lushness, dissembling, weakness, superstition and slavery (in the case of culture). In the national search for happiness, perhaps the most central of Enlightenment goals, he warns, excess is to be avoided at all costs – a statement that is ironically applicable not only to his own time but also to the hideous results of extreme nationalism in twentieth-century Germany.

The accessible language in which Mendelssohn presents his arguments certainly helped in their being perceived as popular philosophy. But if a reader moves beyond the obvious messages to a more metaphorical level that takes into account various ideological changes in the latter eighteenth century, a more subtle reading also becomes possible, one that shows some of the contradictory tendencies that were also a part of a progressive movement towards the light of reason and truth. Along with the economic and social changes that solidified what came to be known as the public sphere in a place outside the home, there was a corresponding change in perceptions of gender and gender roles that resulted in rationalising the continuing presence of middle-class women in the home, in the so-called private sphere. These changes, linguistic and symbolic as well as concrete, had to do with so-called 'Geschlechtscharaktere', gendered characteristics that were connected with the specific roles and characteristics of a partic-ular gender and that gradually became institutionalised into the language as naturalised characteristics of 'masculinity' and 'femininity'. Thus, for example, traits such as 'feeling', 'modesty' and 'domesticity' were increas-ingly connected with the feminine, whereas 'reason', 'public life' and 'abstract thinking' were seen as decidedly 'masculine'.

In Moses Mendelssohn's piece, for all its talk of the – presumably neutral, genderless – human (a masculine noun in German), some of those gendered characteristics have begun to establish themselves in his language. Thus the mention of handiwork, social customs and mores, practicality, drives and feelings in the description of 'Kultur' points to traits that by 1784 would have been aligned with the feminine. 'Aufklärung', on the other hand, is seen – and privileged – as theoretical, reasoning, scientific and broadly human. In the hierarchy that is set up with this dichotomy, 'Aufklärung' is paramount, irreplaceable, essential, primary; 'Kultur' is vital, but – giving the lie to the separate-but-equal argument that accompanied the changes involved in establishing 'Geschlechtscharaktere' – less privileged. The male, male science and reason become the norm. As a Jew in a social world that did not always welcome him, Mendelssohn must also have realised that the label 'Kultur' had particular connotations for him, a man whose religion *and* culture were Jewish. The hierarchy he establishes thus has ethnic significance as well.

It is important to note that matters concerning class position are confined to the lesser concept of culture. Class (as opposed to gender) is explicitly mentioned and marks an acknowledgement both of class differentiation (between Mendelssohn himself and the 'gemeiner Haufe' (common horde) who do not understand terms like Enlightenment, 'Bildung' or culture) and the utopian hope of classlessness that is an implied goal of the Enlightenment. The implicit message is that class as a differentiating category has only a temporary place in the 'Aufklärung'. In fact, the abstract theoretical issues that are the focus of the Enlightenment hold a more privileged status than the particulars of class (or gender, or religion).

Immanuel Kant is somewhat more explicit than Mendelssohn on issues of gender and class. Proceeding in a more deductive way, he begins by declaring that Enlightenment is what he calls '*der Ausgang des Menschen aus seiner selbstverschuldeten Unmündigkeit*' ('*the human being's emergence out of his self-inflicted/self-caused immaturity*' – Kant's emphasis –) into a position of autonomous, independently thinking subjecthood. (The independent thinking referred to here is later called 'Selbstdenken' in Kant's essay, 'Was heißt: sich im Denken orientieren?') As a compelling example of that immaturity, he includes 'das ganze schöne Geschlecht' ('the entire fair sex'), that is, all women. He continues acidly:

Nachdem sie ihr Hausvieh zuerst dumm gemacht haben und sorgfältig verhüteten, daß diese ruhigen Geschöpfe ja keinen Schritt außer dem Gängelwagen, darin sie sie einsperreten, wagen durften, so zeigen sie ihnen nachher die Gefahr, die ihnen drohet, wenn sie es versuchen, allein zu gehen.

[After they [the male guardians of women] have first made their domestic pets [women] stupid and have carefully seen to it that these quiet creatures make no step outside the go-cart [baby walker] to which they have been confined, afterwards they show them the danger that threatens them if they attempt to walk on their own.]

The description of women as both uneducated (a negative trait) and naive (often viewed positively as connecting women to nature) was hardly new with Kant, but his specific mention of them here is noticeable.[1]

In his essay, Kant distinguishes in an unusual way between the public and private spheres, and by doing so, in essence implicitly excludes both women and the working class. His effort to define what he terms the public and private spheres involves a departure from the generally understood meaning of those terms. For him, the public sphere is that realm of intellectuals who write and publish their ideas; in contrast, the private sphere is the realm of work, the professional world, in which those same intellectuals in all likelihood need to remain silent and to obey those above them. Implied is the absolutist state, but in both the private and public spheres, as defined by Kant, the usually understood private sphere – the world of the personal and the domestic – is absent. According to the system of 'Geschlechtscharaktere' that was becoming acceptable at that time, it is in that absent sphere that women were expected to be. The intellectualising nature of this construction of spheres is also obvious, if only implicitly so: intellectuals were not members of the working class nor were they women. Given the popularising intentions of the Enlightenment, what might be understood here is a future in which women and the working class would ultimately benefit from the public debates of the Enlightenment, with its efforts to transform immature children into mature, autonomous adults. But those groups are shut out here. In fact, the underlying thread in Kant's analysis is his effort to press for the particular freedom of expression for intellectuals, who, he feels, ought to be allowed to publish their thoughts and ideas.

In his indirect attacks on censorship and thought control, Kant also establishes a dichotomy between words versus action, theory versus practice, in which, like Mendelssohn, he privileges the former. But his hierarchy is even less inclusive than Mendelssohn's: Kant is content to see freedom confined to the freedom to think and speak, as opposed to the freedom to act. His is, it appears, an almost non-political piece if one

---

[1] There is a more extensive and explicit analysis of gender by Kant in his 1764 essay 'Beobachtungen über das Gefühl des Schönen und Erhabenen', which is available in English translation as *Observations on the feeling of the beautiful and sublime*, trans. John T. Goldthwait (Berkeley, Los Angeles, London: University of California Press, 1960). This detailed schematisation of aesthetic characteristics is notable especially for its third section, 'Von dem Unterschiede des Erhabenen und Schönen in dem Gegenverhältnis beider Geschlechter' ('Of the distinction of the beautiful and sublime in the interrelations of the two sexes').

defines politics as involving the necessary and active involvement of the citizenry. The intellectuals who are at the centre here should, in other words, be granted the freedom to write, to publish, and, by extension, to influence at least that reasoning portion of the public who will have access to their words. That public might well include the absolutist ruler who, over time, might absorb the necessary and useful lessons of the Enlightenment and re/act accordingly. Kant's essay is in that sense utopian, far less concrete in its discussion than Mendelssohn's, yet revolutionary in the implied potential outcome. But where the two philosophers converge – metaphorically and explicitly – is in the narrowness of their perception and definition of the 'human race' that they ostensibly want to influence and enlighten. Theirs is a discussion of and to and among the unmarked: the privileged few males who were educated enough to read and understand their texts. The contradiction between pushing for broad education and, especially in the case of Kant, seeing such openness as possible while continuing to support the absolutism of the state is apparent.

At the same time, the general ideas that are expressed or implied by these two pieces are remarkable for their suggestions and implications for what might be: for their implicit support of broadly based education, for their belief in a progression that would ultimately realise liberalising goals, for Mendelssohn's astute warnings against intolerance and bigotry. In their most optimistic form, these ideas were at the root of the Enlightenment: the emphasis on freedom, education and the autonomy of the individual. There is also an implied political critique throughout, whether it is tied to vagaries of publishing or to the obvious difficulties of working for an absolutist state if one is an intellectual who wishes to speak his mind. The intolerance indicated by the narrow roles attached to women, the tendency either to ignore women or to see them only in an inferior light, and the inclination to ignore the working class or to see it patronisingly as an underprivileged group that must be brought up to the standards of the upper and middle classes are, however, other characteristics of the Enlightenment that should not be overlooked. The following discussion is undertaken with such thoughts in mind.

The letter

Briefe schreibend entfaltet sich das Individuum in seiner Subjektivität.

[By writing letters, the individual reveals himself in his subjectivity.]

Jürgen Habermas, *Strukturwandel*, 1962

In a generalising but useful statement, Reinhard Wittmann claims that whereas the seventeenth century was an era of pamphlets, and the nineteenth, the time for family journals, and whereas the twentieth has been the era of film and television, the eighteenth century was the century of letters ('Das Jahrhundert des Briefes', p.151). The letter and the critical discussions about it represent a number of ideas that were circulating during that century: the interest in individual subjectivities within a developing bourgeoisie, for example, as well as the growing emphasis on the education of women and the young, on friendship, on the broad concept of humanity, on both verbal and written communication, on the art of conversation. Letters are no more a reflection of 'reality' than any other kind of text; they too represent only a localised, limited and hardly trustworthy perspective, and the specific location of the letter-writer will make an obvious difference as to how 'reality' is interpreted. Letters have always been viewed as ways to report, first serving as the transmitters of news, as a version of a newspaper, later taking on more subtle and indirect functions. As a subject for theoretical debate during the century, letters also illustrate the growth of critical discussion itself, serving especially for the critic and writer Christian Fürchtegott Gellert (1715–69) as central to his writings on literature and education, but also of interest to other writers from Gellert to the early romantics Friedrich Schlegel and Novalis. Discussions about the letter often spill over as well into aesthetic discussions: Gellert's emphasis on naturalness in letters reflects the debates between Gottsched and the Swiss critics Bodmer and Breitinger about the role of reason versus imagination in poetic writing; Johann Eschenburg's commentary on literary forms, in fact, includes the letter under the 'Rhetorik' section of his discussion of aesthetic theory and literature (*Entwurf einer Theorie und Literatur der schönen Wissenschaften*, 1783).

But what is especially important when one looks at the letter during this century is the role that was played by gender, specifically the way in which women, who were viewed as exemplary letter-writers, were seen to be related to the form. In fact, when it was increasingly asserted later in the century that women possessed certain characteristics specific to their gender, the letter itself began to be seen as reflecting those characteristics, as natural (as opposed to cultured, a role assigned to men), as liberated from external rules, as sentimental, naive, unsophisticated, and so on.

The letter was also considered in its more essayistic form as a forum for public discussion by and about women. Barbara Becker-Cantarino sees letters as what she calls 'the school for writing women . . .' ('Leben als Text', p. 83.): the form that made room for women to write and to be accepted, even praised as writers and critics. Both women and young people were encouraged to write letters, for letter-writing was viewed as good training for the maturation process that Kant found so central to his concept of the Enlightenment. And what German women were able to do with letters was ultimately to turn them into epistolary novels, thereby taking themselves a further step out of their domestic realm into the world of publishing.

Letters also blurred the boundaries that were assumed to exist between public and private realms of life. Unlike the perception of letters that we have today, namely, private documents that are read solely by their recipients, letters in the eighteenth century were often read aloud and shared with a larger audience. Since they were usually written with that audience in mind, they resembled other literary forms that are always written with an eye towards a public. The letter was also viewed as an object of communication as well as of self-expression, a dialogue as well as a monologue. It therefore usefully represents another eighteenth-century interest, namely conversation, an art that was also cultivated in a gendered context in the literary and other salons that were frequently founded by women. A number of the critical writings about letters indeed describe them as conversations in writing and make the two activities complementary.

Christian Fürchtegott Gellert served both a practical and theoretical purpose in his writings on the letter. Like other Enlightenment thinkers, he hoped that humanity could be improved by a broad and accessible education and he offered pragmatic rules that could serve as useful steps towards that goal. Women were prominent in this discussion in part because they were clearly in need of education. A leitmotif that echoes throughout the century is also evident in Gellert's writing, namely, his differentiation between scholarship and education: women needed the latter, but by no means the former, and letters, as contained and limited forms, were thus appropriate for them. The concept of subjectivity that is touched upon here is highly constructed, even circular in its argumentation: letters reflect women because women, as constructed, are 'natural'. But both letters and women also need to be 'trained', that is, shaped and properly formed. Gellert's feminine markers serve as codes to gender his discussion but also to create hierarchies.

The writers whose letters are available for us to read today are almost uniformly middle-class Germans from the mid to late eighteenth century. They represent the context that Jürgen Habermas describes in his *Strukturwandel der Öffentlichkeit* (*Structural transformation of the public sphere*, 1962): an era of individuality and subjectivity, but also a time during which the remaking of the social world, especially that of the bourgeois family, was underway. Caroline Christiane Lucius (1739–1833), for example, a correspondent of Gellert's, uses her letters to speculate on the form and her role in producing it; she does not have the permission or the authority to write theoretical treatises like Gellert's and instead thinks conceptually within the letters themselves. There she defines a letter as her emissary to others, as a form that is given a shape by her that it then retains. She speaks of how her own role may possibly deviate from societal expectations. She writes of the mask of a letter-writer and says that it may well be more noticeable and more extreme when a woman is writing to a man and thereby obliged to exhibit the coquetry and self-deprecation that are expected of her. By making the form her vehicle to present her theoretical ideas and her way of communicating with friends and family, Lucius has her theory become complementary to her practice: the woman, with the baggage of gendered social roles, caters to those expectations but is able to use them for her own aims. There are positive as well as negative results of such a configuration: on the one hand, women could be seen as agents representing a style that is imitated and adapted by men, but on the other, the very act of male expropriation indicates that the locus of control is not with the women but rather with the men who could occupy the public sphere, in this instance the sphere of publishing and criticism.

Nevertheless, women's letters were read, imitated, and in some instances published. Even as early as the late seventeenth century, German women were known as exemplary correspondents: the letters of Lieselotte von der Pfalz (1652–1722) did not appear until the following century although her reputation as a correspondent was established early on, but those of Sophie von La Roche (1730–1807) were known during her lifetime, most particularly the fictionalised didactic letters to the young woman Lina that were published in La Roche's periodical journal *Pomona*. Particularly interesting were exchanges of letters between various eighteenth-century wives and husbands: Meta Moller (1728–58) and Friedrich Klopstock (1724–1803), for example, Luise Mejer (1746–86) and Heinrich Christian Boie (1744–1806), Eva König (1736–78) and Lessing, Luise Kulmus (1713–62) and Johann Christoph Gottsched. Aside from the ever more common use of the form and the occasional self-reflexive discussions of that form by the various correspondents, there is the informational value of these exchanges. The letters reveal the context of their lives, but they also serve as the instruments through which these women and men deliver critical opinions on matters considered appropriate for their gendered position as well as on general cultural, literary and social topics.

What is also apparent, however, is the ambiguous subject–object dichotomy that was created by the growing interest of male critics and authors in the epistolary form and the feminisation of that form with the dual purpose of seeing it as a way to educate women and at the same time to place the women in a particular subject category. It is not at all unusual to come across references to letters in which the form itself is coupled with a discussion on women: an anonymous piece, *Anweisung zum Briefwechsel des Frauenzimmers mit Frauenzimmern* (*Instructions for correspondence between females*, 1777), for example, not only aligns women with letters, it uses sample letters to educate women in what seems to be a decision to use (the more limited, more easily understood) example rather than (the abstract, therefore more difficult) theory. That lessening of possibility is evident as well in the letters accompanying the piece, which suggest that the education of women should be limited. The comparison between women and letters thereby takes on larger consequences as the century progresses. Prescription becomes increasingly apparent, and the message urging a control on women's intellectual education before they become 'unnatural' is readily discernible.

It is perhaps an exaggeration to say that the history of German women's writing in the eighteenth century can be told through an examination of letters, the theories surrounding them, the authors of them, and the literary form that emerged and was increasingly propounded by them as the century drew to a close, namely the epistolary novel. Nevertheless, the letter, as a form of personal narrative, serves as an important exemplar of the ongoing search for bourgeois subjectivity that occupied the century as a whole and that had as its underlying purpose the creation of bourgeois man, an undivided, optimistic, autonomous individual who would represent the positive progressive ideas of Enlightenment thinkers. To investigate a topic such as women and letters in the eighteenth century, then, is to see the problematic side of a search for bourgeois subjectivity, its myopia, its deliberate or unintentional avoidance of 'loose ends' such as those centering on gender or class, the fallacy of a discussion that claims objectivity but is full of bias, blind spots and gaps. Here it is principally gender that exposes the ambivalences; in other instances it will be class (here the unmarked middle class is usually unremarked upon by both men and women). But the altruism of the Enlightenment extended only so far when it came to questions of the power and authority to speak, to name, and to label and define. Women were called upon in the discussion about letters both as active models to be imitated and passive bodies to be educated. That conflation is remarkably apt for depicting the dichotomies and silences in eighteenth-century German thought.

The novel

Just as the eighteenth-century letter represented a form of personal narrative, that is, a way in which a subjectivity was openly searched for, constructed, and presented, the novel in the same era echoed a similar goal, the presentation of a self within the context of society. The so-called 'gallant novels', the heroic adventure stories of the seventeenth century, were gradually replaced by works closer to the moral education that was emphasised in the eighteenth century, and in their own way, the new novels, often epistolary, often autobiographical, occasionally even what we might call psychological, reflected the increasing involvement with the individual both as he (or occasionally she) could be identified and defined and – given the novel's place as a social form – related to the social context around him/her.

The novel is often characterised as a portrait of 'life' as well as society, even though it is obvious that such representation is filtered by many influences that shape the picture that is presented. As the form was coming into its own, it was affected by the transformational process that revised perceptions of gender and class, particularly in the ways novels extended into mystification and metaphor in their separation of female and male worlds. But the picture was not entirely ideological and metaphorical: it was economic as well. Not only did economic circumstances help bring about the changes in the status of the middle-class home and family; with those changes also came a new and growing reading public consisting in large part of middle-class women who were interested in novels and represented a market whose demands and interests needed to be met.

With its lack of a lengthy noble tradition, the novel could be viewed as an innovative form that was pliable, transformable, and in many ways useful for the goals of the Enlightenment. The gradual reinterpretation of the genre in light of its newly established role as a popularising vehicle that could entertain as well as educate, drew increasing attention to it. And despite the slowness of technical improvements, the steady growth in literacy rates and book production benefited novels in particular. Although distribution was limited and eighty per cent of the German population was still rural and, if it could read at all, no doubt read only the Bible, a novel by a popular author was able to reach a far larger audience than had been the case before. An edition might comprise only 2,000 to 3,000 copies, but the increasing presence of lending libraries would allow for a reading audience that might be ten times that size. And with a growing reading public, the number of writers also expanded: in 1766, for example, it was estimated that there were 2,000 to 3,000 writers, but by 1806 the number had expanded to approximately 11,000.

Despite increasingly positive reception of the novel, still as late as the 1780s the perception of the genre was far from uniformly positive. Eschenburg's *Entwurf einer Theorie und Literatur der schönen Wissenschaften*, for example, gave minimal attention to novels near the end of his volume, devoting only nine pages to them (and including in the same section sub-sections on short stories and fairy-tales). But not long before Eschenburg, Friedrich von Blanckenburg had published his anonymous *Versuch über den Roman* (*Remarks on the novel*, 1774), with its extended analysis of Goethe's *Die Leiden des jungen Werthers* (*The sorrows of young Werther*) and its privileging of the novel as the narrative of the individualising process. The development of the form was a European-wide phenomenon. From the early years of the century, English and French novels in particular enjoyed a strong popularity among German readers: Daniel Defoe's *Robinson Crusoe*, for example, was translated in 1720, and German translations of the novels of Samuel Richardson, Henry Fielding, Jean Jacques Rousseau and Laurence Sterne were always eagerly awaited. What the English and French did with their novels, the Germans tended to imitate: the so-called 'sentimental novels' of the latter half of the century arose under the influence of Richardson and Sterne, and the epistolary form was appropriated from Richardson.

To describe 'the novel' as a single form is incorrect. Although it responded thematically and otherwise to the growing audience of bourgeois readers, it also reflected the inner contradictions and disagreements that marked the discussions of the Enlightenment. Novels were written both for and against a middle-class audience; in fact, as the century progressed, they became the site for rebellion against the precepts and beliefs of their age. The outcries against the rigidities of rationalist thought that emerged in the later years of the century could be found in sentimental novels as well, which on occasion represented the bourgeois individual in battle with the (often sexual) drives that plagued and threatened to ruin him. Here was an opportunity to do as the theorists of the letter did: that is, to include 'Woman' in her newly propagated gendered role as one who would sublimate those drives and who would occasionally triumph in her position as preserver of the home and family and the representative of morality.

Just as in the 'middle-class tragedies', eighteenth-century novels focused increasingly on the home and the family and on the corresponding dangers of the public world outside that home. The developments that led to a change in the function of the home from an economic unit of self-sufficient labour to an isolated abode of privacy and love and retreat helped to create an atmosphere in which novels that echoed such developments could be read and appreciated. Novelists were increasingly willing to participate in the moralising and didactic atmosphere of the eighteenth century by departing from the initially seedy aspects of the form and becoming instructional, moral, reasoning, focusing on accounts of nuclear families and love and marriage, topics both pleasing and familiar to the readership, and perhaps also normative in that they offered models of how the new bourgeois individuals should (or should not) live.

To trace the history of German novels between 1720 and 1770 is to move from the pietistic and moralising overtones of novels like Johann Gottfried Schnabel's utopia *Insel Felsenburg* (*Island Felsenburg*, 1731), which along with many other *Robinson Crusoe* imitations was published after Defoe's work was introduced to German readers, to a veritable onslaught of novels after mid-century that began increasingly to reflect the sentimentality of the later Enlightenment with its emphasis on human welfare and the pity and tolerance that are expected to lead ultimately to equality and brotherhood. Whereas earlier stages of the Enlightenment privileged the lack of contradiction and a linear move towards a goal of human happiness – Schnabel's island is a utopia of reasonable praxis – it was increasingly thought that such a vision could descend into the mechanistic, the unimaginative and the rigid, concealing but not eliminating contradictions. The often repressive and doctrinaire emphasis on self-control was apt to fall apart if the question of sexuality was raised, for example, in the struggle of the individual with the anarchy of his emotions and passions, increasingly acknowledged, but also seen as needing to be suppressed. The discussion of bourgeois subjectivities began to recognise the power of irrationality, and novels also reflected these particular conflicts.

The following discussion will concentrate on four paradigmatic examples of eighteenth-century German novels that appeared between mid-century and the mid-1780s. As the earliest of these, Christian Gellert's *Leben der schwedischen Gräfin von G**** (*Life of the Swedish Countess of G*, 1747–8) illustrates the beginning of a transformation of gender roles. Sophie von La Roche's *Geschichte des Fräuleins von Sternheim* (*History of Miss von Sternheim*, 1771) is both epistolary and otherwise characteristic of the sentimentality of Richardson and Rousseau. Her concern with the concepts of 'Herz' ('heart') and 'Geist' ('mind, spirit') offers up the duality that became typical of the later Enlightenment, albeit in intriguing gender-specific ways. Following quickly on *Sternheim*'s heels is Goethe's *Die Leiden des jungen Werthers* (*The sorrows of young Werther*, 1774), no longer as purely sentimental as its predecessor, also epistolary, but with different ramifications and nuances. Finally, there is Karl Philip Moritz's *Anton Reiser* (1785), an autobiographical novel that Moritz himself labels 'a psychological novel' and that presents individual subjectivities that are not as purely bourgeois as was usually the case, for Moritz's protagonist emerges from the *petite bourgeoisie*.

It is important to begin with Gellert's *Leben der schwedischen Gräfin von G****. Gellert was not only the major theorist of the letter; his novel, published anonymously and narrated by a female persona, represents the growing concern with social roles and gendered characteristics that was to flourish during the second half of the century. His accessible style and lively prose, his concentration on 'private' as well as 'public' matters, his didactic message, and his rationally constructed characters mark a developing stage in novel-writing that takes it a considerable distance beyond the earlier adventure novels. The fact that his novel was published anonymously was no doubt caused by the still bad reputation of the genre, which had not yet become the educational tool that Enlightenment thinkers envisioned. The changing geographic location and the occasionally questionable relationships among various characters echo past sensationalisms, and Gellert's heroine is also a member of the – albeit impoverished – aristocracy (although she marries a bourgeois man). With the growing secularisation that accompanied Enlightenment thought, however, his novel takes over the role of earlier *Erbauungsliteratur* (homiletic literature), acquiring a moral function, becoming itself a source of moral strength and knowledge. That the novel does not use Germany as a site for the narration also adds to the distancing helpful for developing the more universalising nature of a moralising function.

The typification of its characters provides a didactic framework for Gellert's novel. This is decidedly not a *Bildungsroman*: the Countess, for example, whose personality is described at the outset and then in greater detail as the novel progresses, does not change; she only becomes more revealed to the readers. The text is nevertheless subtle: in the gradual revelation of character, the readers are presented with considerable information about social roles and prescribed personalities. The typification serves to concretise and impress upon readers the universal nature of human characteristics. Particularly in the case of women, whose depiction emphasises such traits as passivity, composure, moderation, quiet, even indifference and silence in an idealising fashion, it is made clear that these are desirable and valuable traits for them. What is implicit, in another reflection of the changing times, is a female readership who will benefit from such insights and who are, in fact, explicitly addressed at the outset of the novel.

The novel also broaches topics and ideas that reflect the interests of an age intent upon changing its focus from the abstract to the concrete, from the Almighty to the individual citizen/human being within a social world. Despite its sprawling nature, its *Decamerone*-like presentation of many individual stories, and its weak narrative structure, it reveals the assumptions, ambivalences and uncertainties of its time. In the matter of class, it echoes not only succeeding novels like La Roche's *Sternheim* but also Lessing's tragedy *Emilia Galotti*, both of which depict an ongoing tension between the ruling aristocracy and the struggling middle class. It is in the particular sphere of function, however, that its prescriptive and didactic nature comes most to the fore. The themes of education and the purpose of education for women, for example, comprise most of the narrative, indeed from the very outset, where the educating of the Countess is described as extending beyond the usual limitations, but certainly not very far, as her guardian describes it to his wife:

. . . das Fräulein lernt gewiß nicht zuviel. Sie soll nur klug und gar nicht gelehrt werden. Reich ist sie nicht, also wird sie niemand als ein vernünftiger Mann nehmen. Und wenn sie diesem gefallen und das Leben leichtmachen helfen soll, so muß sie klug, gesittet und geschickt werden.

[. . . The girl will certainly not learn too much. She should only be clever and certainly not learned. She is not rich, so only a reasonable man will take her. And if she is to please him and to help make his life easy, then she must be smart, well-mannered, and adroit.]

The enormous influence of men on the educating and supporting of women is made immediately apparent. Thus it is not surprising to see the Countess also described as passive: although she is depicted as actively involved in the education of children, what is emphasised are the innate characteristics, the natural gifts, that make her what she is. What she absorbs from men, whose presence in her life puts her at an advantage, is almost by osmosis. There is an echo of change: her eventual marriage to an honourable bourgeois man is a triumph not because of his class but because of his moral strength. But the Countess's passivity continues throughout; she is simply moved from man to man, from her father to her guardian to her husband, whose death essentially ends the novel, as if there is nothing else to say, now that she cannot continue to be identified through her connection to a male model/teacher/protector. Although all the characters are buffeted by the forces of history and fate, the men continue to be typified as patriarchal, ruling figures controlling not only women but the material means to maintain power. The establishment of a hierarchical gendered social order is thus underlined.

The adventures of the Countess von G*** are far more than events to titillate the novel's readership. Gellert's novel is meant to educate, but in particular ways that send a mixed message, for there were limits to the imaginative possibilities that were implied by the autonomy and development of the bourgeois individual. If there was to be a model, it was to be a middle-class male who would possess androgynous characteristics, at least to a certain degree – who could, in other words, weep and see the moral education of women as a task he would gladly take on – and whose dominance and superiority would never be put into question. And so a novel bearing the name of a woman, with a female narrator, purporting to be the life-story of that woman, must be seen above all as a prescriptive message about the woman-as-supporter, the woman as helpmate, as separate-but-equal: in other words, like Sophie, the woman who would be described by Jean Jacques Rousseau in the Fifth Book of his 1762 novel *Émile*.

Like Gellert's novel, Sophie von La Roche's (1730–1807) first novel, *Geschichte des Fräuleins von Sternheim* (*The history of Lady Sophia Sternheim*, 1771) was published anonymously. In her case, however, the reasons were obviously related to her gender: *Sternheim* is called the first 'Frauenroman' (women's novel) in many literary histories, and Sophie von

La Roche was one of the few German women to publish in her day. The result of her anonymity, however, was a widespread belief (at least for a time) that C. M. Wieland, whose name appears on the title page, was the author. La Roche's novel was published after Richardson's *Clarissa* and Rousseau's *Émile* and was certainly affected by both, in its epistolary form and the device of having the letters come from a variety of correspondents. Her positive portrayal of things English and French also has little of the dichotomous rigidities that had been in evidence when Lessing and Gottsched, among others, had argued about the relative merits of English and French ideas and writings (for instance, in Lessing's seventeenth *Literaturbrief*).

The novel portrays a woman who, despite her aristocratic origins among the landed gentry, represents bourgeois prescriptive thought on women. La Roche provides a vehicle for further solidifying a perception of gendered social roles, presenting us with a heroine whose traits are recognisable in most instances as belonging to what was increasingly depicted as the normative female. The presence of Wieland offers a concrete form of patriarchal control: despite his obvious support of her effort, his preface, his footnotes commenting on and in some cases correcting the text, his discussion of La Roche's difficulties with form and method of writing, and his statement that women are not by nature meant to be professional writers results in the representation of La Roche as somehow a writer against her will.

It is facile to read this novel, as many have done, as a mere imitation of La Roche's literary and philosophical models – to accept uncritically everything from Merck's (and probably Goethe's) review of 1772 calling it not a novel but 'eine Menschenseele' to the opinion of Rolf Grimminger, who implies that La Roche simply imitated those male writers who had preceded her (Hansers *Sozialgeschichte*, vol. III, 1980, p.687). One need only compare Sophie Sternheim and her apparent model Clarissa: for example, although both Sophie and Clarissa are marked by ideological and, on occasion, physical confinement, Sophie travels abroad. Clarissa dies, a victim; Sophie lives on, in triumph, in a position with some power (although she chooses among her two suitors and marries one, the other stays on to educate one of her sons, thereby freeing her up for the educating of young girls that she has undertaken). Clarissa forgives Lovelace, the man who brutally raped her; Sophie does not forgive Derby (who, as far as we can tell, never succeeded in raping her). Clarissa's activity consists of letter-writing; Sophie travels, teaches young girls, sets up schools, debates issues of intellect and marriage, and fantasises about other roles she might play. She is able to combine the Rousseauean concepts of *amour de soi* and *amour propre*, a natural and healthy self-esteem along with the self-love generated by others' impressions. She reads and discusses books and ideas. She is contrasted to men who do not possess her obvious strength. She even exhibits an occasional ambivalence about what her social role should be.

Where limitations arise is far more in the degree to which variations are permitted, in the obvious controlling of how far Sophie is allowed to go. This is a utopia, perhaps, but a conservative one. The division between knowledge and intellect is drawn here as well: women may learn, we are told (they may be smart), but only within the bounds of what is appropriate for them to learn (they may not be intellectual). The emphasis is on the application of learning to practical activities: knowledge needs to have a goal, cannot be thought about as mere abstraction. Although such an idea is hardly foreign to the general Enlightenment emphasis on education that should be useful as well as pleasurable, the gender specificity here makes clear that there are boundaries to women's learning that contrast with men's intellectual possibilities.

Against this ambiguous background, the limitations in the social role of women are in tension with the powerful account of a woman essentially on her own, dealing with perils and temptations and managing nevertheless to survive, primarily because of her inner strength and the skills she has acquired. Even when the lines are drawn – even when, for example, Sophie is seen as not capable of intellectual activity – she continues to act as if that limitation could in some ways be breached. Whereas money seems to be the decisive factor in Gellert's novel (as it was in *Clarissa*, making Clarissa, who could not control her own inherited wealth, the ultimate victim), Sophie breaks out of her privileged moneyed position by losing her inheritance, by identifying overtly with the poor, and by actively combatting her fate. She represents an outwardly apparent obedience matched by an inner self-assertion that is revealed through her activities. Although her self-assertion never goes beyond gender to class – she continues, despite her explicit efforts to connect herself with the poor, to see herself in a classed position markedly different from those beneath her – but in the matter of gender she consistently pushes out boundaries.

Goethe's *Die Leiden des jungen Werthers* (1774) echoes La Roche's work in many ways. It too is an epistolary novel, focusing on domestic issues related to love and family and describing the gendered role characteristics that were familiar by this time. But whereas La Roche's novel is still part of what we might call the We-Generation, the altruistic stage of the Enlightenment that stressed broad education and the assisting of others, *Werther* is a product of the Me-Generation, the growing interest in individual ego, in the rebellious individual, the *Genie* who became the focus for the young male writers of the *Sturm und Drang*. Whereas there are several correspondents in La Roche's novel who provide the readers with a multiplicity of viewpoints and voices, *Werther* is essentially a monologue, the hero's letters a reflection of a single rebellious and suffering soul.

The nuances have multiplied. If there is overt criticism of the aristocracy, then, in the mouth of a character as unstable as Werther, it comes across as conflicted, as tied to his own resentments against a class to which he does not belong. If gender roles are presented – Werther's beloved Lotte is first seen by him in the midst of a family, surrounded by younger brothers and sisters whom she is feeding – they are made more complex by the sense of gender-crossing in Werther as well as in Lotte. If madness and suicide – certainly a state of disorder that would not complement the order of Enlightenment thinking – are seen as destructive, Werther speaks of them in less negative terms. If reason and analytical thinking are considered good – here they are also considered rigid, myopic, and even blind on occasion. In fact, if La Roche's novel can be seen as an occasionally contradictory presentation of Enlightenment thinking, then *Werther* seems to have challenged all the rules, created disorder and confusion, and broken the mould. We know, in fact, that the resulting suicides of many young men dressed like Werther in blue and yellow and the satires written on the novel and the general upheaval created by it indicate the ambivalence arising from its reception. As an extreme critique of the problems raised by earlier, more analytic Enlightenment thought, Goethe's novel can tell us a great deal about the contradictions inherent in that intellectual movement.

Whereas Gellert saw the letter form not only as reflecting an individual soul but also as a communicative means to connect that individual constructively and creatively with others – as does indeed occur in La Roche's novel – *Werther* turns the form in upon itself, re-forms it into something like a diary, makes an audience unimportant, superfluous, and possibly unnecessary. Here a single ego dominates. Yet that male ego takes on characteristics that must have confused anyone who had accepted the idea of gendered social roles and traits. Werther is, first of all, the letter-writer, at a time when women were frequently seen in that role. He is also highly emotional, sentimental, childlike, particularly aware of the subtleties and complexities of arguments, like women, who were often seen to centre upon concrete details. He seems, in other words, to possess both female and male traits. He can argue rationally, as he illustrates in his discussion with Albert about suicide; despite his depiction as the ultimate ego, his awareness of relationships is the driving force of the novel. He is able to express passions directly and unequivocally. It is this mixed nature of his character – as well as of the character of Lotte, who is often more rational than Werther, who thinks in terms of logical planning more than he does, and who chooses the more rational Albert to marry – that makes Werther interesting, intriguing and unusual.

What the novel represents aside from the confusion of gendered traits is a reaction against the rationalism that had marked earlier generations of Enlightenment thinkers. The privileging of differentiation in the novel might, in fact, be seen as an offering by example of other possible ways to think about issues. The Rousseauean love of nature that Werther echoes also implies a love of something not easily controlled. The emphasis of *Sturm und Drang* proponents on the creative genius who ignores rules altogether allows for a widened discussion of passion, something only alluded to in La Roche's and Gellert's novels. The presentation of characters whose thinking runs along a spectrum from sentimentality to rationalism and who are not at all dichotomous is a major step along the way to making the novel form more sophisticated and nuanced. Here the novel is more than just an overt depiction of society; here it has entered into formerly forbidden areas, passion, sexuality, pathology, and become a psychological study of a bourgeois individual.

In 1785, as the century headed inexorably towards the chaos and the explosions of change brought on by the French Revolution, Karl Philipp Moritz (1757–93) published the first volume of *Anton Reiser*, his slightly disguised autobiographical novel. Parts two and three appeared in 1786 and part four in 1790. In many ways it reflects the transformations in the novel that have been illustrated thus far: the increasingly complex nature of personal characterisation, including the possibilities for gender role-bending; the overt discussion of class; the continuing search for an identifiable subjectivity; the growing interest in an autobiographical narrative as a way to construct and present a self. Moritz also presents his protagonist as a child, who is extremely dependent for a number of years, and who is in that way 'feminised'. It is that facet of the novel that creates a conflation between the gendered characteristics ascribed to women and the child/young adult Anton Reiser, who is depicted as an outsider, not because of his gender, but primarily because of his class: unlike the protagonists of the other novels discussed here, Anton Reiser is a member not of the secure middle class, but of the world of manual workers and the *petite bourgeoisie*. Like the women who write and like female characters in general, Anton Reiser finds it necessary to mark his identity in more overt ways than is the case when gender and class are dominant.

In the subtitle, Moritz labels his novel psychological, reflecting its autobiographical focus and his editorship of the *Magazin zur Erfahrungsseelenkunde* (1783–93), the most important journal of empirical psychology of his time. The mix between autobiographical narrative and fiction is noticeable throughout: the novel centres on the intersection between real and unreal in its protagonist's life in which an escape into the unreal (through reading or theatre or dreams or simple role-playing) is often the only way to survive the grim reality of his surroundings. In anticipation perhaps of the approaching new century, which would find itself concerned with the scientification of so much of the world, the novel at times borders on a scientific treatise. In a novel in which the narrator is only rarely heard, Moritz's belief that it is important to theorise even within a work of fiction about human traits and tendencies is reflected, and a sociological perspective as well as a sense of class consciousness and psychological probing are provided.

What makes Moritz's novel distinctive for its time are the implicit intersection of gender and class and the exploitation and contradiction that accompany them. As a member of a lower class who at the outset is described as 'von der Wiege unterdrückt' ('oppressed from the cradle onwards'), Anton is perforce confined, just as Clarissa (who is hardly poor, but who is a woman) is framed by the confinement of her existence. Like women, Anton is taught that confinement is appropriate, indeed in many ways desirable, thereby making a positive trait out of a negative circumstance. His efforts to escape the horrors of his daily life frequently centre on the sort of role-playing that Sophie Sternheim also engaged in. And for the narrator to describe Anton's desire to be an actor as 'bloß die Neigung ohne den Beruf' ('just the desire without the calling') is to damn his ambition just as surely as the ambitions of women were discouraged and mocked.

Among the novels discussed here, it is only in *Werther* that sexuality plays a more pronounced role. Moritz's novel also lacks a representation of sexuality – Anton's only connection with such is indeed 'feminine', for it is said that he is 'pregnant' with a poem when he writes poetry. But otherwise, sexuality seems in this work not to be a trait of lower-middle-class men like Anton. In fact, Anton's expressed attraction to *Werther* centres above all on its depiction of the intimate confessions of a lonely man, whose sexlessness (in an echo of the characterising of women as sexless) is most important to Moritz's protagonist.

At the same time, to see Anton as entirely feminine would be to overlook the privileges that even he, the exploited and underprivileged, possesses as a male. His surname is emblematic of the privilege of movement, for the freedom that Kant propounded as essential to the Enlightenment is – at least as freedom of movement – more possible for Anton than it could ever be for Clarissa, for example. His education, despite its woeful inadequacies, goes far beyond that offered the women of his time. Even his intense involvement with himself is in a sense like Werther's ego-based view of the world, the sign of a certain authority and certainty.

Anton's class nevertheless marks him as an outsider, and once materialistic factors have been taken into account – once it is apparent, as this novel makes clear, that class status can be oppressive – the unproblematic, unified bourgeois self begins to become fragmented and contradictory. As a feminised male who is also poor, Anton Reiser can be seen as a portent of an era in which the positive, sure, and unambiguous belief in the power of the secularised, unified individual would be thrown into doubt. Even the ego-centred genius hero of the *Sturm und Drang* is superseded here, in a novel that more than most shows evidence of how the genre had come into its own as a complex, sophisticated, and highly flexible form that reflected, shaped, and challenged its times.

It is not only *Anton Reiser* that bears a striking similarity to – and was indeed often called – an autobiography; both *Sternheim* and *Werther* can also be seen on some level as autobiographical narratives. As a result in part of a traditional pietist use of the autobiography and the diary – but also as a reflection of the general Enlightenment interest in the individual in a far more definite way than the Pietist practice, which produced an 'I' only to conflate it with the 'We' of the religious community – it is not surprising that both the autobiography and the novel gained popularity in the second half of the eighteenth century, overlapping with one another in their search for authenticity. The self-assertion that is represented by the autobiography was parallel to the self-in-the-world focus of the novel, and in both instances the stress on the individual allowed the author to work out publicly the facets of a personality.

Although the majority of autobiographies were written by men from the middle class (culminating in the publication of Goethe's *Dichtung und Wahrheit*, 1811–33), the autobiography, like the autobiographical novel, allowed a space for other groups as well. Ulrich Bräker's *Lebensgeschichte und natürliche Ebenteuer des Armen Manns im Tockenburg* (*Life story and natural adventures of the poor man in Tockenburg*, 1789) and Heinrich Jung-Stilling's autobiographical volumes depicting his youth, apprenticeship and domestic life (1777–89) represent voices of the *petite bourgeoisie*. Like Moritz, Jung-Stilling pays particular attention to the significance of familial context in his youth, thereby lending a psychological tone to his story. Bräker, in an echo of Rousseau's *Confessions*, emphasises the difference and uniqueness of his personal story and provides valuable details about his development and the determining factors of his class position.

Class is an important analytical factor in these early autobiographies; gender is less pronounced. The only autobiographical text written during this period by a woman, but not published until 1791, after her death, is *Lebensbeschreibung von Friderika Baldinger von ihr selbst verfaßt* (*Autobiography of Friderika Baldinger written by herself*). Sophie von La Roche edited and saw to the publication of this short text by her late friend. What is most telling about Baldinger's autobiographical sketch is the by-now familiar topic of women and intellectual activity: Baldinger's bluntly painful statements about the limits of her education, her overt dependence on men (a brother, a husband) for her access to educational training, and the resulting ambivalence about herself offer a graphic record of her clearly difficult position.

Although the detailed realism of Bräker's text, the multifaceted class depiction of Jung-Stilling's personal narratives, and the eloquent frustration of Baldinger's memoir are eventually superseded by the paradigmatic middle-class autobiography of Goethe, these texts show evidence of the search for self that bourgeois Germans were openly and frequently giving witness to. But whether the autobiographical narratives were labelled novels or autobiographies, they are rich in possibilities for gender and class analysis. The very meaning of the generic term – the writing of a self – implies the opportunity to represent and assert oneself as autonomous, as worth acknowledgement and recognition.

Drama

With the growing insistence on a national language and the development of a national culture, theatre took on different parameters from those of the previous century. Long before Schiller wrote his essay on theatre as a moral institution ('Die Schaubühne als eine moralische Anstalt betrachtet', 1784), even before Lessing composed his writings on German theatre as a national force (*Hamburgische Dramaturgie*, 1767–9), others were offering ideas about the purpose of theatre and the drama. The move from early Enlightenment classic tragedies and the so-called 'sächsische Typenkomödien' (Saxon comedies of type) to 'weinerliche Komödien' (sentimental comedies) and bourgeois comedies and tragedies reflected, in fact, the growing development of Enlightenment thought: a philosophy that in addition to its interest in the bourgeois subject also wished to disseminate ideas about a universalising, trans-class nobility of thinking and action. But the progression evident in the evolution of German drama – from the court, from noble heroes who fall, and from the rigidities of social hierarchies, to the family – from the dying Cato (Gottsched) to *Miss Sara Sampson* (Lessing) – is a revision in the representation of class and gender. As the novel moves from galant adventures to domestic depictions, from 'public' to 'private', so the drama depicts a feminisation of culture, from the gendered characteristics ascribed to men to those ascribed to women.

The transformation was neither sudden nor clearly demarcated. Nor did it become permanent, as the discussion below about *Sturm und Drang* dramas will make clear. The feminisation was also not brought about by women themselves. With the exception of Luise Gottsched, who adapted and wrote a number of comedies, the theatre director Friederike Karoline

Neuber (1697–1760), and the actresses who performed in the plays, women were almost entirely absent. Nevertheless, the move from a focus on absolutism towards the family, or on the king and the nobility towards the private bourgeois sphere, is remarkably sustained throughout much of the century.

Although he was primarily known as a theorist – his 1730 *Versuch einer critischen Dichtkunst* can be considered the first significant statement of what might be called an Enlightenment aesthetic theory – Johann Christoph Gottsched (1700–66) was also a playwright, adaptor and poet. His first drama, *Sterbender Cato* (*Dying Cato*, 1732) presents a response to what he called the 'Verwirrungen' ('confusions') of the German stage in the first half of the eighteenth century. Gottsched's efforts as writer and critic were essentially on two fronts: encouraging the development of a specifically German literature and setting up literary models for the Germans, namely, the Greeks (particularly Aristotle) and the French (especially the French classicists Racine and Corneille). Thus his tragedy on Cato's suicide encompasses the didactic, moralising elements that Gottsched thought were important for the Enlightenment stage along with a strong echo of its French model, the play by Deschamps. Addison's influence is also discernible.

The drama, written in rhymed Alexandrines, is stiff and awkward, full of cardboard figures who are meant to represent types: the freedom-loving Cato, the power-hungry and brutal King Pharnaces, the wily Caesar, the dutiful female figures whose roles are slight and stereotypical. At the same time, there are interesting contextualisations: it is clear, for example, that Cato's resistance to Caesar is also a resistance to absolutist rule, and the fatal presence of letters that are introduced at critical moments in the plot reflect the eighteenth-century interest in that form. When Cato responds to Caesar's request that he surrender his power and then share it with the words 'Mein Schicksal heißt: Sei frei!' ('my fate is to be free!') – when, in fact, the word 'freedom' appears as often as it does here – there is a coded message that this search for autonomy is occurring against a backdrop of absolutism. Certainly the sense of the free individual and of developing subjectivity is present in such sentiments: Cato therefore chooses suicide over his subjection to Caesar. Gottsched's drama helped underscore his strong belief in the power of the theatre to bring about social change and broader education.

Yet it was not just the male Gottsched who was active in this area: Gottsched's wife Luise Adelgunde Victorie Kulmus wrote and adapted several comedies that were more flexible and accessible than her husband's dramas. Although Luise Gottsched is best known for her adaptation *Die Pietisterey im Fischbein-Rocke* (*Pietism in a crinoline*, 1736), she wrote other comedies that echo Gottsched's aesthetic ideas and express her own theatrical sense. Her talents were primarily in the realm of the satirical, whether in her Germanised attack on pietism (the French original depicted an attack on Jansenists), or on superficial intellectuals, both male and female (*Pietisterey*, but also *Der Witzling*), or on broader, less period-defined vices like greed (*Das Testament*), for example. Although her characters represent positions and lack the depth and breadth of actual figures, it is the intentional didactic purpose and not a failure in dramatic skills that prompted Luise Gottsched to write this way. As the initial and primary representative of the so-called Saxon comedies, she followed her husband's rigid aesthetic categories and did not allow her comedies to exhibit the more complex nature of Gellert's 'weinerliche Komödien', with their mix of tragedy and comedy.

At the same time, there are contradictions, especially in the matter of gendered characteristics of women. In several of her plays, for example, the relationship between women and intellect is addressed. It is obvious that Luise Gottsched – who herself was constantly engaged in intellectual projects – nevertheless complies with the generally accepted difference between 'clever' and 'intellectual' in terms of women representing the former, men the latter. The women in *Pietisterey* who spend their time reading books by various Pietists and who think that their utterances about Pietist debates should be recorded and published, are thus ridiculed. The hierarchical division between women and men leads to the message that if the father/patriarch is away, women become endangered, primarily at the hands and minds of other men. It is only with the return of the father that things resume their proper rational virtuous state, which in this instance includes a retreat from intellectual reading.

In the area of theatre we once again encounter Christian Fürchtegott Gellert. His insistent presence in the areas of letters, letter theory and novels, his continuing acknowledgement of women, and his inclusion of 'female' characteristics in all areas of his writings are complemented by the domestic focus of his dramas. His 'rührende/weinerliche Lustspiele' with their copious shows of emotion present a move away from the earlier more materialist Enlightenment mentality (Luise Gottsched's *Das Testament* is a particularly good example of such thinking with its narrative on inheritances and their connection to the rest of life). It is also important to note that Gellert himself was a member of the *petite bourgeoisie*, at some distance from Gottsched's upper-middle-class location, and was representative of a move by less privileged groups against the aristocratic power élite.

Comedy and satires are strongly in evidence during the eighteenth century. Although many literary critics see Lessing's *Minna von Barnhelm* as the only canonical comic drama of its time, to look at it in isolation is to miss some of the insights that are to be found in a reading of Luise

Gottsched as well as Gellert and Lenz. The comedy as such, whether in the more rigidly defined form prescribed by Gottsched or the modified forms of Gellert and Lenz, provided accessibility to an audience that the playwrights wanted to educate and inform. The less satirical 'weinerliches Lustspiel' (in England it was called the 'sentimental comedy', in France 'comédie larmoyante') was an open appeal to the emotions of the viewers in an anticipatory move towards Lessing's emphasis on what he called 'Mitleid', translated generally as pity or empathy but focused on the intersubjectivity between characters and audience, on a sharing of emotions, a 'suffering-with'.

Gellert's most famous play, the 1747 *Die zärtlichen Schwestern* (*The tender sisters*), is a three-act comedy that departs from both Gottscheds' dramatic models particularly in its mix of comedy and tragedy and anticipates the later comedy/dramas of Lenz. Gellert was the principal representative in Germany of this sub-genre, and this play is its most pronounced example. It presents the story of two sisters who seem at least temporarily to represent differing positions in terms of their views on marriage. Whereas Julchen echoes the Enlightenment focus on freedom, her sister Lottchen, an ideal Enlightenment figure who possesses virtue, reason/rationality and morality, is a voice for love above and beyond freedom. The mystification of women's gendered characteristics has clearly begun: what Lottchen tries to convince her sister of is the need for women – her sister as well as herself – to exhibit the appropriate feminine characteristics of modesty, virtue, and the willingness, indeed the eagerness, to carry out the prescribed female role of wife and mother. The characteristics that a woman should not strive to attain are also outlined, including the impossibility – in fact, the undesirability – of a woman's becoming learned. The difference between love and friendship is also explicated, with women representing the former, not the latter: Julchen, in other words, cannot become friends with Damis, her lover, for it is not an accepted status for her.

That the play ends differently than one might expect is perhaps in part because of Gellert's own awareness of the nuances that emerge in developing subjectivities. Lottchen's position is revealed to be less than certain, and with the acknowledgement that the man whom she loves and whose marriage to her has been a certainty from the outset is less than worthy, there is a reversal, with Julchen now in the role that she had rebelled against and more than willing to become Damis's wife, and with Lottchen in possession of her freedom. The ambiguous last line is hers: although she blames not love but the foolishness of her lover for her single state, she nevertheless comments: 'Bedauern Sie mich.' ('Feel sorry for me.') The audience is left with a lesson that is expected to move them, and the differentiating particularities that were to become more dominant with the development of the 'middle-class tragedy' are already in place. In fact, the ambivalence of Gellert's play reflects the contradictions that the Enlightenment, in its effort to provide rules and mores and enlightening insights, tended not to make explicit. By his time, and despite the continuing typification of characters like Julchen and Lottchen, issues of individuality and particularity were beginning to be more pronounced.

The move in drama from aristocratic to bourgeois ideas often produced narratives focusing specifically on women, whose names – like the names of the heroines of novels – began to appear increasingly in the titles of the plays. In this regard, Gotthold Ephraim Lessing (1729–81) provides a good illustration. To consider Lessing as playwright is to think both of the range and versatility of his plays and his contribution to general Enlightenment thinking about the place of the theatre in German cultural life. His *Miss Sara Sampson* (1755), considered the first 'middle-class tragedy', has a heroine whose struggles centre on gender roles: she, like the protagonist of *Emilia Galotti* (1772), is portrayed as a victim of preconceptions about class and gender. In both dramas, the patriarchal family that represented the turn to the domestic dominates and leads to the sacrifical deaths of both heroines. It is less a matter of class; women are the targets, the victims, the objects of power struggles that they cannot win. Their lack of agency is as central to these dramas as it is to Richardson's *Clarissa* (which may, in a way, have served as a model for them): certainly the motif of confinement as it is related to women is dominant, a confinement that can be read as protective and stifling and, in the cases of Sara and Emilia, as fatal. The visible, tangible representation of the appropriation of the female results in reification, even in fetishising, and not in a harmonising resolution.

Nevertheless, Lessing's choice of female heroines thereby makes them central. The presentation of the woman as victim (or by extension as fallen heroine, replacing the fallen heroes of earlier dramas) and as daughter in configuration and in conflict with the father/patriarch could not help but draw the observer's/reader's attention to the gendered nature of Lessing's ideas. The fact that Lessing thereby problematises the family as the apparent locus of good is made apparent on the bodies of women, who are not always the beneficiaries of the domestic life. In the case of *Miss Sara Sampson*, Sara is both a figure embodying virtue and a woman whose characterisation exhibits some nuance. Mellefont, her abductor, is no Lovelace, he is, in fact, aware of his guilt at having taken Sara away from her old and ailing father. If there is a villain, it is Marwood, the former mistress of Mellefont, who is evil, who provides the poison that eventually (and slowly and agonisingly) kills Sara and the knife that Mellefont, in despair, uses to kill himself, but who is also intriguing in the ways that she breaks down any monotonic definition of the woman. Sara, in this context, represents the contradictions of a reality that can only be endured if there is a consciousness of another world. Any other interpretation would make her death seem pointless: she has gained the forgiveness of her father, who is in need of her and who is even willing to accept as his son the rogue who has taken her away. One critical explanation, namely, that her fate has to do with her 'seduce-ability' ('Verführbarkeit'), is cynical in its reduction of Sara to a mere symbol. And yet there is perhaps no better interpretation: Sara, as a symbol, can serve as a reified example of virtue who will lose out no matter what she does. The new pessimism of the bourgeois tragedy receives a vivid initiation in this drama.

Emilia Galotti, which in many ways resembles the earlier play, also echoes its pessimism. Emilia, like Sara, is not purely bourgeois, but rather on the edge of the aristocracy, and like Sophie Sternheim a victim of aristocratic desires. At the same time, the Prince who tries to win her is an enlightened monarch who seems more nuanced than Mellefont in the earlier drama. What is outwardly the same, namely the configuration of father and daughter, is, however, perverted into the ultimate power of the patriarchy: rather than see his daughter led into perdition, Odoardo Galotti stabs her to death. The role of the woman is reduced to that of victim, robbed of all agency, robbed even of the long dying scene of Sara Sampson, who at least is given time to say all that she wants to say.

It is in Lessing's comedies that he presents women who are not victims. In his comedy *Minna von Barnhelm* (1767), whose plot prefigures those of many Mozart comic operas, it is the female protagonist Minna who represents wit and cleverness as well as the practical common sense that women, in their domestic roles, were expected to have. In contrast, Tellheim, her impoverished lover, becomes a parody in his insistence on honour and pride. Despite what is clearly meant to be a sympathetic portrayal of his woes, the driving force is Minna, the representative of newer ideas who chooses love above honour and challenges Tellheim's unquestioning acceptance of outdated virtues, thereby indicating to the spectator/reader that there are nobilities that go beyond the power of political or other status. The didactic message of the need for reason and for the flexibility of creative thinking is as tangible here as it is in Lessing's critical writings on theatre.

The lightness of touch evident in *Minna* is less present in *Nathan der Weise* (1779), subtitled 'ein dramatisches Gedicht' ('a dramatic poem'), that is, labelled neither comedy nor tragedy and thereby freed of the expectations of either designation. The drama's polemics involve a barely concealed attack on the reactionary Pastor Goeze whose religious orthodoxy and intolerance were key to Lessing's decision to write *Nathan*, which he wrote after several years of searing debate with Goeze and others. What is intriguing about this drama is not its strongly analytical, highly structured framework, but rather the secularisation that permeates it despite its overt discussion of religion. The use (in a tribute to Lessing's friend Mendelssohn) of a Jew as central and wisest figure does not lead to Judaism's being privileged. Nathan's parable of the rings, the narrative focus of the drama, which centres on the three major world religions, leads instead to a more humanistic conclusion, a world-vision that echoes the Enlightenment search for an autonomous subject who will benefit from the lessons of religion but who will ultimately move beyond that instrument of education. The play's presentation of the utopian message of human potential is especially illustrative of Enlightenment ideals at their most progressive and far-reaching.

But the contradictions of the Enlightenment, with its focus on the determination of subjectivity, come to light if one considers the category of gender. If *Nathan* concerns autonomous individuals, those individuals, whether Jew or Muslim or Christian, are understood to be male. The play is essentially a patriarchal portrait, for the women – Daja, the Christian housekeeper in Nathan's house, Sittah, the Sultan's sister, and Recha, Nathan's adopted daughter – are secondary, present at the behest of their employer/brother/father. Daja is not as bigoted as the Christian Patriarch of Jerusalem; Recha, the child of an enlightened father, is positively presented; Sittah speaks eloquently; but their positions are secondary, their subjectivities hardly autonomous. The notion of universal human freedom that Kant saw as central to the Enlightenment project is lacking: not in the area of class or of religion or of nationality, certainly not for the male characters, but for women.

The distant locations of three of these plays (*Emilia Galotti* takes place in Italy, *Nathan der Weise* in Jerusalem, *Miss Sara Sampson* in England) allow for a more detached philosophical approach. *Minna von Barnhelm*, on the other hand, firmly anchored in Prussia with all the contextualisation that that location implied, offers a more specifically German (or Prussian) tone and set of lessons. The same can be said for Schiller's early drama *Kabale und Liebe* (*Conspiracy and love*, 1784), whose female heroine Luise Millerin (after whom the play was initially named) is, like Sara and Emilia, ultimately a victim of the absolutist court and the feudalistic thinking that emphasises class differences and the power of the aristocracy. Luise Millerin's very name is indicative of her bourgeois status, and here too, the configuration of father/patriarch and daughter becomes central to the conflicts of the drama: a problem of generational difference as well as the difference of attitude between one who can imagine love with a member of a higher class and one who cannot. That Ferdinand, the son of a court official, loves Luise, whom he ultimately poisons before poisoning himself, underlines the victimised status of this woman, who serves as a passive symbol of noble ideals – virtue, above all – who, however, must die despite her innocence.

Schiller's drama is a good example of the continuing traditions that the Enlightenment and the *Sturm und Drang* shared: at least in terms of the heroine, there is little to separate Luise from her predecessors in Lessing's dramas. That Schiller sees to it that the father of Ferdinand is enlightened by the experience is a pale victory. What continues to be acceptable is the role of women as symbolic property to be dispensed with by the ruling patriarchs (in these three instances, the fathers), as stereotypes with few individual characteristics. Theatre is intended for didactic purposes, not for the mimetic presentation of reality, and if there are subtleties of character – as there most certainly are if one thinks of the ambiguities of Odoardo Galotti, Emilia's father, or the shortcomings of Tellheim, Minna's beloved, or the less-than-evil traits of Sara's abductor Mellefont – they are mostly gendered male.

The didacticism that was essential in the Enlightenment's popularising function began to fade by the time of the explosive theatre activity of the *Sturm und Drang*, when the concept of the theatre as a location for moral education and altruism was replaced by individualism. Writing itself was increasingly considered a personal and highly subjective activity. Just as in *Anton Reiser*, the sense of nuance, differentiation, and fragmentation became more pronounced in the matter of defining the individual. Just as the progression from the serene Sophie Sternheim through the troubled Werther to the complex Anton Reiser represented nuancing change and new insights, the development from the stereotypic characters who educated and entertained theatre audiences to the figures whose uncertainties filled the dramas of the late eighteenth-century playwrights represented both refinement and ambiguity. The social implications of didactic instruction were transformed into the introspective and idiosyncratic world of the *Sturm und Drang* rebels, who in their rebellion gained a certain freedom in how they chose to represent themselves or their subjects in their writings. The social function of literature, the so-called *Wirkungsästhetik* (aesthetics of effect), became less clear in the rush towards individualisation despite the growing presence of social protest.

Goethe's (1749–1832) and Schiller's (1759–1805) early plays provide a revealing mirror of the philosophy of *Sturm und Drang*, with its emphasis on individual subjectivities, genius and social rebellion. Among the dramas emerging from these years, Goethe's *Götz von Berlichingen mit der eisernen Hand* (*Götz von Berlichingen with the iron fist*, 1771–3) and Schiller's *Die Räuber* (*The robbers*, 1781) can serve as exemplars of the sprawling, Shakespearean theatre of the latter years of the Enlightenment. They represent different stages of that period, given the decade that separates them. Karl Moor, the principal figure in Schiller's *Räuber*, is less consistent and more ambiguous and complex than Goethe's Götz, who shares Moor's propensity for violence and revolt but who also echoes the Enlightenment beliefs in orderly, evolutionary change. Götz in himself is also more linear and predictable than Moor. The two men share a critique of absolutist rule, but Götz maintains a consistent loyalty to the Emperor and accepts the idea of a hierarchy of power and his particular place in it. They are both, in a sense, criminals, for they act outside the law: Karl, the idealist leader of a band of robbers who even speaks on occasion of 'Robin'; Götz, who engages in battle when and where it seems right to him and who cannot envision a life without combat or, at the very least, hunting. But whereas Moor and his gang participate in murderous, nihilistic acts, Götz, a husband, father and patriarch, is intent upon maintaining what he has and fighting purposefully for himself and his Emperor. Both men, most notably Götz, are seen as being ennobled by their actions; much of what we learn of them is through the admiring statements of others. Both fight evil and attempt to do good, although that good is always bound up in some way with violent moves that represent the imposing of their individual will upon a variety of situations. Both also act as members of groups (Karl's robber band, Götz's various friends and followers) and so there is a sense of community at the same time that the individual stands out as supremely central, or, if viewed another way, as representative of the extremes of autonomy, individual behaviour and complete freedom.

Although Goethe's play focuses primarily on the tensions between court/church and individual landowners like Götz, who remains a vital force throughout and whose death ends the play, Schiller's drama is more extended, depicting the continuing battle between various individuals, especially between father and sons (Karl and his brother Franz) and between brothers. In both plays, the Aristotelian unities are abandoned. Schiller's drama has multiple focuses and, though Goethe's play is centred on Götz, it depicts battles fought on behalf of a variety of causes, from the ongoing attempts of the princes to gain territory to the uprisings of the farmers. Violence, emerging often from the insistent emphasis on the place and power of individual wills, is the thread that holds both plays together.

It is not surprising that, given the gendered expectations of the late eighteenth century, women are barely present in such plays and, when they do appear, they are stereotyped: the loyal Amalia, the only female figure in Schiller's play, who alternates between her obedient and loving service to Karl's father and her ongoing love for Karl; the compliant, always nurturing and sustaining Marie and Elisabeth, Götz's sister and wife, whose actions are focused entirely on the well-being and furtherance of their brother and husband; the evil Adelheid, who uses her considerable intelligence to seduce Götz's former friend Weislingen and to mould him to her aims of power and prestige and away from the honest nobility of Götz. Women move these dramas along in useful ways: it is Marie whose goodness persuades Weislingen (who is by that time dying of Adelheid's poison) to release the dying Götz from the execution that is awaiting him; it is Amalia who, in her loyalty to Karl, physically hits and drives away Karl's scheming brother Franz who is threatening to rape her. But particularly in the case of Schiller's play, the value and worth of male characters are at least on occasion measured by their attitude towards women. The nihilists Spiegelberg and Schufterle, members of Karl's robber band, come to no good end, and it cannot be an accident that they are frequently shown to be contemptuous of those who are weaker than they, specifically of women. Franz's continuing mistreatment of Amalia is also seen in negative contrast to Karl's love and respect for her. Reflecting the mystification of women that was common during the century, women represent objects to be protected as well as the embodiment of values to be respected, even imitated.

In an initially pseudonymous review of *Die Räuber* that Schiller published in 1782, the playwright's own concern with gendered issues emerges, albeit through the slightly satirical mask of a reviewer who is highly critical of the drama. What emerges is the 'reviewer's' discomfort with the heroic aspects of Amalia, who does not fit the proper description of 'woman', as the reviewer understands it, namely 'das sanfte leidende, schmachtende Ding – das Mädchen' ('the gentle, suffering, languishing thing, the girl'). He is only accepting of the figure who emerges in full character once she is directly connected to Karl: 'Sie glänzt in seinem Strahle, erwärmt sich an seinem Feuer, *schmachtet* neben dem *Starken*, und ist ein *Weib* neben dem *Mann*.' ('She shines in his light, she warms herself at his fire, she *languishes* next to the *strong man*, and is a *woman* next to the *man*') (Schiller's italics). What the reviewer wants is a female figure who is realised through her connection with an other, with a man; it is only through such a connection that her own profile can become apparent. The social construction of women is thus made apparent, and here the emphasis on relationships seems intended to limit the potential power of a woman's position: to see her value as that of supporter, not autonomous individual, not as the agent of her own actions.

Class plays a role in these dramas, at once marked by the presence of ennobled figures of any class (a prime example is Georg, the young servant of Götz, who is more like a son to him than his own son) and by the sense that, in both plays, acts are performed with a concern for the poor and downtrodden. Karl and his robber band carry out Robin Hood-like feats, or like to see themselves in such a light, and Götz finds that he cannot lead the rebellious farmers not because of their class position, but because of their rampant violence. At the same time, there is an acknowledgement of the hierarchy that Götz supports: he claims repeatedly that he will remain loyal to the Emperor, although he rebels against the warring princes who separate him and his Emperor. The idea of the nobility of the individual points towards a trans-class nobility that can no longer be tied to a particular social group: the fall of Karl Moor and Götz might echo the fall of aristocratic figures in earlier dramas, but we are firmly in the realm of bourgeois values that will extend beyond the classed values of the aristocracy (to which both essentially belong, as members of the landed gentry) and the bourgeoisie. What these plays involve is the development of the *Genie*, the exceptional, creative, compelling individual who provides the force and cohesion of the plays in which he appears. There are no more Emilia Galottis or Sara Sampsons. Amalia, like Emilia, is killed at her behest by someone close to her (Emilia by her father, Amalia by Karl), but in the Lessing play it is a class issue – the protection of the honour of the bourgeois girl from the aristocratic seducer – whereas in Schiller's play, at least according to the 1782 'reviewer', Karl kills Amalia because he loves her too much to abandon her. In his decision to stay with the members of his robber band rather than with Amalia, he chooses (at least for the moment) brotherhood over the love of a woman. Gender and class actually both play a role at the end: after he has killed Amalia, Karl returns to his robber band, but only long enough to announce that he will surrender, so that a poor man with eleven children will gain a reward by turning Karl in. In the new ambiguity of figures like Karl and Franz Moor, both of whom exhibit multiply complex personalities, Schiller represents a rebellious departure.

J. M. Reinhold Lenz's *Der Hofmeister oder Vorteile der Privaterziehung* (*The tutor, or the advantages of private education*, 1774) carries its rebellion into a consideration of class. Läuffer, the tutor whose erotic involvement with the daughter of his employer leads both to her pregnancy and his self-castration, vividly symbolises the problematics of class, while the role of women in Lenz's comedy remains that of virtually silent symbols, so much so that in the last scenes where the fate of the daughter Gustchen is being decided, she does not speak at all, is only spoken for and about. Matters of class differences range from the *petit-bourgeois* status of Läuffer to the vaguely enlightened position of the privy councillor, who nevertheless represents an aristocratic view, to the brutality of Gustchen's father the Major, who shoots Läuffer and drives his daughter to a suicide attempt.

The social critique of Lenz's play, which moves back and forth from comedy to flirting on the very abyss of tragedy, offers types and stereotypes much as Lessing and Schiller did, but the biting satire and the heavy irony provide subtlety and differentiation. The ironic subtitle indicates a focus on a very particular sub-class, namely the private tutor, ill-paid, mistreated, exploited (above all by the aristocracy that hired him), forced to move from place to place to make a living. Here the clashes are not between the bourgeoisie and the court/aristocracy, but rather the intelligentsia and those who have financial and political power over them.

Nothing develops in discrete ways, and in any discussion of Enlightenment drama, it should be kept in mind that in 1788, two years before the era that is the subject of this chapter ended, Goethe's classical drama *Iphigenie auf Tauris* appeared. Another, and different didacticism was emerging, a reaction was setting in even before the excesses of the French Revolution would bring about the backlash that made the German *Klassiker* so sceptical of social change, so reactive against what they viewed as the dangers of ego and individualism represented in the chaos of the revolution. Although the family as desirable and exemplary social unit remains a central symbol, it is the negative aspects that are paramount here: namely, what happens if a family is torn apart by dissension (or worse). The moralising, popularising tone of Enlightenment philosophy is rarefied, placed on a lofty, no longer bourgeois and domestic level. Iphigenie is triumphant, saves her brother and herself, but in a context that is neither immediate nor accessible and that implies an élitism that once again will narrow the potential audience.

As a literary genre in the Enlightenment, the drama had the particular advantage of being direct, immediate, visible, of being both educational and entertaining. The progress in the development of German theatre in the eighteenth century was a result no doubt of the functions that the drama and the theatre were seen to fulfil within the intellectual projects of the day. The position of the bourgeois citizen could be developed, transmitted, and made clear, particularly in his counterposition to absolutism. Class could be shown in increasingly revealing ways on the stage. The visible representation of Enlightenment convictions and ideas was particularly effective in the theatre. And given the obvious talent of dramatists like Luise Gottsched, Lessing, Schiller, Goethe and Lenz, given the ongoing discussion of theatre, the theory in addition to the practice, given the eager reception of theatre by an enthusiastic public, a German theatre was well on its way to being established. The national theatre about which Lessing and others dreamed was not yet possible in a country as fragmented as Germany continued to be. But the obvious progress and increasing levels of sophistication made the German theatre look very different by 1790 than it had around 1720.

Against a background of a still powerful absolutist tradition, however, even the more individualised narratives represented by the title figures of Lessing's and others' dramas are primarily representative of broad and fairly vague humanistic ideas and ideals. The deficiencies of the real world in which writers lived were such that the specificity of a controversial debate about human freedom was an unlikely occurrence. Especially in the case of literature there was a sense of starting out anew. And given the still small reading (and viewing) public, there was also little that could be taken for granted. In essence, then, the German drama, from the Saxon comedies through the sentimental comedies up to and beyond the bourgeois tragedies and the sprawling dramas of the *Sturm und Drang*, gained considerable importance in these seventy years. But the context of a highly fragmented state, a low rate of literacy, limited access to cultural events and many internecine struggles, affected the results.

Poetry

In the midst of a great storm in Goethe's *Werther*, when the title figure and Lotte are at the moment of realising their love, Lotte lays her hand on Werther's, looks into his eyes, and says a name: 'Klopstock!' Such a code word would have been transparent to contemporary readers, who would know that the reference is to Germany's best known and most revered poet of the day, specifically to his ode 'Die Frühlingsfeier' ('Celebration of Spring'), which was written and published in 1759 and appeared again in a collection of Klopstock's odes in 1771, not long before Goethe's novel burst on the scene. The meeting of souls that that one name implied gives some indication of the power of Klopstock, whose four-volume heroic-spiritual epic *Der Messias* (*The Messiah*, 1751ff.) was accompanied in its 1782 edition by an essay entitled 'Von der heiligen Poesie' ('About sacred poetry'), which emphasises both the value and sacred nature of poetry. That this poetic union takes place in Goethe's novel between two individuals, that the *Seelengemeinschaft* or spiritual communion that is brought about implies an equality of feeling as well as of minds, indicates the role of poetry at this point in the century: as an almost sacred transmitter of emotions and thoughts between subjective beings who are autonomous but who are united by a literary form.

Such was not always the case. 'Lyrik' as an all-encompassing genre was not understood as such until later in the century; it tended instead, under the label of 'Poetik', to encompass a variety of texts from poetic tales to didactic poetry to elegies, heroic odes and lyric poetry. Poetic forms in their great variety reflected the change in ideas from poems by such empirical writers as Brockes and Haller, in which the bourgeois emphasis on the empirical and practical, the revelations of the Pietists, and various other threads dominated, to lyrical poetry, the liberation of subjectivity, and the focus on the individual in the latter years of the century. The development of lyrical forms reached a climax in the early love and nature poetry of Goethe, in which the overt political statements characteristic of an earlier anti-absolutist mode were replaced by the more subtle assertions of emotions and subjectivities. Accompanying such developments was a growing interest in the cultural power of individuals. Gottfried August Bürger's (1747–94) poems, for example, were openly political on occasion but they were also concerned with the 'Volk', who were to become objects of study for Goethe and Herder long before the collections of so-called 'Volkslieder' were undertaken by others in the nineteenth century.[2]

Gelegenheitsgedichte, occasional poetry, served a practical purpose for eighteenth-century poets whose existence was still often dependent upon the financial support of the aristocracy and the court. An occasional poem written, for example, to celebrate a wedding or a birthday of a royal or aristocratic figure would earn its author a fee. It would also be written in a formal, ritualistic way, not likely to be original or unique, with a prescribed viewpoint that would mask whatever 'real' feelings the poet might harbour towards the figure he or she was addressing. Poets belonged occasionally to the aristocracy, but more often than not they tended to be members of the *bourgeoisie* or the *petite bourgeoisie* who were by no means independently wealthy. Although not many poets supported themselves and their families entirely through their writing as Anna Luise Karsch (1722–91) did, the situation created by a class difference between the poet and those whom he/she was addressing no doubt influenced the nature of the poetry produced.

Occasional poetry was not the only sub-genre in vogue. More intellectual and reflective of the growing interest in the empirical sciences and in the specific power of the senses was the empirically framed poetry of men like Barthold Heinrich Brockes (1680–1747) and Albrecht von Haller (1708–77). Brockes's *Irdisches Vergnügen in Gott* (*Earthly pleasure in God*, 1721–48), a massive poem cycle whose subject matter ranges from descriptions of the seasons to minute depictions of nature and from philosophical musings to accounts of toothaches and descriptions of human anatomy, is a good example of the combination of useful education and pleasure that Enlightenment thinking propounded. The exactness of detail is coupled with the wide-sweeping moralising thinking that has a poem like 'Das Große und Kleine' ('The great and the small') move from describing the heavens to the worm that the figure finds with the help of his magnifying glass, and then end with the summarising, comforting thought that since God is to be found in all earthly manifestations, large and small, so too He is in man. The confident undercurrent of most of

---

[2] For an interestingly negative commentary on this mix of politics and lyricism, see Friedrich Schiller's 1791 essay, 'Über Bürgers Gedichte'.

these poems, the sense that they describe a world that is planned, orderly and incapable of absurdity, complement the optimism of Leibniz and Wolff, the pre-established harmony where individuals have their particular and appropriate places and roles.

Unlike Brockes, Albrecht von Haller supplies more questions than answers in his often melancholy poetry, which seems more an echo of the fatalistic Baroque than a bright look at a new and progressive world. His poems are also often heavily empirical, full of details of nature (as well as many footnotes providing scientific backing for his assertions), and strongly didactic. Perhaps his most famous poem is 'Die Alpen' (1729), a paean to the glories of the Swiss Alps and their inhabitants. Aside from the scientific detail, the description of the flora and fauna of the Alps, and the sense of empirical authenticity that is transmitted by Haller's prefatory note that his insights and discoveries were based on the personal experience of a journey through the Alps in 1728, there is also a nostalgic look at an apparently classless society in which all are equal: thus a footnote states,

Man sieht leicht, daß dieses Gemälde auf die vollkommene Gleichheit der Alpenleute geht, wo kein Adel und sogar kein Landvogt ist, wo keine möglichen Beförderungen eine Bewegung in den Gemütern erwecken und die Ehrsucht keinen Namen in der Landsprache hat.

[One can easily see that this portrait revolves around the complete equality of the residents of the Alps, where there is no aristocracy, not even a provincial governor, where no possible advancements change people's moods and where the lust for honour does not even exist in the local language.]

The pursuit of happiness that was central to the Enlightenment is portrayed here in its purest and most idealistic form: thus the didactic message of Haller's poem is both utopian and practical, since its overlay of nature detail is as immediate as its larger discussion of the proper location for the human being, for whom virtue and rationality are more important than earthly riches. The fact that Haller's Swiss farmers represent a class that is neither aristocratic nor specifically bourgeois may provide a sheen of progressiveness; at the same time, the transmitted message that poverty is good seems hardly more than a levelling assertion that one must be satisfied with one's station in life. Lines congratulating the poor on their removal from the temptations of wealth or the description of humans who seem content in their ignorance present a picture of an archaic and indeed rigidly classed world.

A transition to the poetry of love and nature that began to dominate as the century progressed was offered by the so-called Anacreontic poets, whose new lyricism culminated in the poetry of Friedrich Gottlieb Klopstock (1724–1803). Before Klopstock, however, there were others, members of the circle around Gottsched, whose odes became more and more personal, aesthetic, removed from the politics of anti-absolutist thought. Among the Anacreontic poets there were also women, including the so-called 'anakreontisches Mädchen' ('anacreontic girl') Johanne Charlotte Unzer (1725–82), whose anonymously published poems focus on love and friendship. Unzer, who often marked her gender explicitly, also wrote polemic verse that complained about the lack of education for women and the few opportunities for women poets.

It was Klopstock, however, who stood out more than any other German poet during the century. The widespread admiration for him continued long after the publication of his *Messias*; in fact, it seems in many ways to have resulted in a personality cult that produced imitations of his poetry as well as poetic descriptions of those who read his poetry. In his essay 'Von der heiligen Poesie', his discussion of the 'Genie', the genius, and of the need for 'Genie' to be joined with 'Herz' indicate how prescient his ideas were. He also related genius and heart to morality: 'Der letzte Endzweck der höheren Poesie, und zugleich das wahre Kennzeichen ihres Werths, ist die moralische Schönheit.' ('The final goal of higher poetry, and at the same time the true mark of its worth, is moral beauty.') And there is also an emphasis on moral truth, for Klopstock is a religious poet who sees the need for a connection to the timeless and immortal, who therefore chooses to make Christ the hero of his heroic epic. His writings move away from the immediacy of the occasional poem into a realm of the universal and the philosophical.

At the same time, he acknowledges the private being, the world of the family and the home, as well as different literary models: thus he supplants the Greeks, the Romans and the French with the English, poets like Edward Young and his 'Night thoughts' (1742–5). Klopstock brings about an increasing involvement with the subject, a movement towards the 'I', that nevertheless remains highly intellectualised. His effort to unite feeling and reason, to incorporate nature in ways that no longer focus on the scientific, empirical detail of Haller and Brockes, his redefining of religion to encompass nature found resonance in those who read him and inspired many who followed him, from Goethe to the poets of the so-called 'Göttinger Hain', who appropriated his form of the ode.

While Klopstock was gaining in popularity, poets like Christoph Martin Wieland (1733–1813), who produced a body of writings that ranged from the lyric to the epic to the journalistic and essayistic, were also becoming known. Wieland's unusually frank treatment of the intersection between sexuality, women and gender roles can be seen in his poetic narrative *Musarion, oder die Philosophie der Grazien* (*Musarion, or the philosophy of the Graces*, 1768). Although the epic swarms with muses and goddesses, with female imagery and prescriptive messages about women, what is emphasised is the sensual woman, seen always from the perspective of a male narrator or a male character: thus Musarion, the title figure, is depicted as a hetaera whose seduction is the goal of the smitten Phanias, a young Athenian nobleman. The third book of the poem centres primarily on the seduction, told in light and cheerful fashion with only a subtle level of didacticism. Musarion is shown to be clever, but her role is that of the anti-learned, the anti-intellectual figure who wittily mocks the two philosophers who are Phanias's mentors; she represents experience, not ideas, and is privileged for it.

At the same time, both in *Musarion* and another poetic narrative, *Idris und Zenide*, there is intriguing nuance. Musarion, who is besieged by Phanias, is also described as being 'ihrer selbst gewiß . . .' ('sure of herself'), and this self-certainty causes her to be cautious rather than foolish when it comes to giving in to Phanias, who sees her resistance to his efforts to seduce her not as 'Tugend' ('virtue'), but rather as 'Eigensinn und Grillenfängerei' ('stubbornness and crazy ideas'). Musarion's caution is presented admiringly by the narrator, who has her demand proof of Phanias's intentions and reassurance that his passion is more than a mere fleeting game. Virtue, for Musarion, is to be experienced and lived as well as discussed. And she wins out in the end, thereby teaching Phanias a lesson.

Idris und Zenide (1767) goes even farther in its effort to present a female-specific viewpoint. This romantic poetic epic is highly erotic. But what is more unusual and innovative are several passages in the First Canto, in which not Zenide but rather the young knight Idris is presented via the female gaze of a young nymph as he bathes in full nakedness. Here is the opposite of the mood of *Musarion*, with its warning to men that they need to respect women, who are implied to be on a less-than-equal footing with them; here, in an equality of eroticism, the nymph is allowed to appropriate what is the male gaze: to see the naked male body, to desire it, and to give voice to those desires.

Women poets did not echo such eroticism. Like Unzer, they confined their gendered comments to protests about their status as women and/or poets, or they imitated their male counterparts, producing didactic, Anacreontic or occasional verse. At the same time, and no doubt in light of the growing female readership, the eighteenth century produced several women poets, among them Anna Louise Karsch (1722–91), who enjoyed varying degrees of public acknowledgement. What is notable about Karsch, aside from the fact that she supported herself by her writings, that she was received by Fredrick II in a well-reported audience, and that she was revered by male writers and philosophers from Mendelssohn to Goethe, is her class status. She was born into poverty as the daughter of an innkeeper and spent much of her life fighting the dual agonies of poverty and a lack of formal education.

That she enjoyed considerable fame for what was essentially a body of work consisting almost exclusively of occasional poetry gives some indication of the value allotted that form in the eighteenth century. At the same time, she wrote other poems that, when read through the lenses of gender and class, provide insight into the woman who was alternately praised and mocked as a 'natural' poet, that is, as one who could not reason but could write. 'Das Harz-Moos' ('Moss in the Harz Mountains', 1761), for example, is on the surface a fairly traditional poem about nature. But its combination of the subjective with the philosophical lifts Karsch's poem into a symbolic realm. Its first two stanzas depict in specific details the power of God in his creation of nature; it is the third stanza that offers a personal and political commentary:

> Doch andre Blumen sterben bald,
> Das fein gebaute Moos bleibt, wenn sie schon gestorben,
> Tief unter Schnee noch unverdorben.
> Wie ähnlich ist es mir! tief lag ich unter Gram
> Viel schwere Jahre lang, und als mein Winter kam,
> Da stand ich unverwelkt und fieng erst an zu grünen.
> Ich mußte, wie das Moos, dem Glück zum weichen Tritt,
> Dem Thoren zur Verachtung dienen.
> Einst sterb ich! Doch mein Lied geht nicht zum Grabe mit!

[Although other flowers die soon, / The finely structured moss remains; when they are already dead, / It is still unspoiled deep under the snow. / How much it is like me! I too lay buried deep under sorrow and grief / For many hard years, and when my winter came, / I stood there unwilted and began at that point to turn green. / Just like the moss, I had to serve as the soft tread for fortune, / As the object of contempt for fools. / I will die sometime! But my song will not go into my grave with me!]

Those women poets who attained fame were also often considered exceptional in ways that bordered on labelling them intellectuals. Christiana Mariana Ziegler (1695–1760), for example, for whom Gottsched served as mentor and supporter, was made the first female member of the 'Deutsche Gesellschaft' in Leipzig, and her acceptance speech had as its topic 'Ob es dem Frauenzimmer erlaubt sey, sich nach den Wissenschaften zu bestreben' ('Whether it should be allowed to women to aspire to scholarship'); she was also the first German woman to be crowned as a poet laureate by a university, namely, the University of Wittenberg, in 1733. Sidonia Hedwig Zäunemann (1714–40) was also crowned an imperial poet by the University of Göttingen in 1738. More than Karsch, both women spoke up publicly for their sex, Ziegler in particular stressing the need for education for women, and Zäunemann

writing openly and positively about the importance of women's autonomy, most especially in her poem 'Jungfern-Glück' ('the happiness of an
unmarried woman'), which is remarkably modern in its privileging of the
freedom of unmarried women and its overt comments on the physical
abuse women are likely to suffer in marriage. Ziegler, whose poetry was
occasionally used in the libretti of Bach's oratorios, also asserted her independence and individual competence and thereby echoed the strivings of
the Enlightenment towards an autonomous subject.

That women poets like Ziegler, Zäunemann and Karsch were exceptions may well have had to do with the developing nature of German
poetry, which for much of the century was philosophical, didactic, and
dependent to a large extent on a level of intellectual training that German
women did not possess. But as the century progressed, as the Anacreontic
poets began to write of love and the private sphere of individuals, as
Klopstock became famous, as both Werther and Lotte were seen as equal
participants in his poetry, the picture began to change and to move away
from the idea of poetry as primarily an intellectual tool to transmit
philosophical lessons.

Given the dominant position allotted by literary historians and critics
to Goethe and Schiller, it is startling to find neither one represented in Karl
Otto Conrady's otherwise thorough 1968 collection of eighteenth-
century German poetry. Conrady is not alone in his criticism of scholars
who have attempted to give Goethe prominence as a poet in the years
before 1790, given that most of his poems were published at a later date:
Wolfgang Promies, for example, comments succinctly: 'Für das Publikum
blieb der lyrische Neutöner Goethe im 18. Jahrhundert daher das
Ungewohnte, weil nicht Gekannte.' ('For the public, the lyric innovator
Goethe thus remained unusual in the eighteenth century, because he was
unknown.') (*Hansers Sozialgeschichte*, vol. III, p. 599.) In the case of
Schiller, with a few exceptions, his poetic production before 1789 was not
particularly distinguished: a number of relatively dense early poems on a
variety of topics, a series of love poems that are usually designated as the
'Laura' cycle, and several long philosophical poems towards the end of
that era, in particular 'An die Freude' ('Ode to Joy'), the paean to classical
Greece 'Die Götter Griechenlands' ('The gods of Greece') and 'Die
Künstler' ('The artists'), written around 1789.

Despite the later publication dates for many of Goethe's poems, from
our perspective it is interesting to note the variety of those texts, both in
their form and content. Emerging from this era were such divergent pieces
as 'Prometheus', with its arrogant, egotistical assertion of the creative
power of the individual human being, and 'Grenzen der Menschheit',
('Limits of humanity') the restrained acknowlegement of limits that is like
a programmatic text for German Classicism. 'Prometheus' (written in

1774), with its contemptuous remarks towards the diety, who is compared to a boy who is envious of humans, ends with a powerful assertion of ego:

> Hier sitz' ich, forme Menschen
> Nach meinem Bilde,
> Ein Geschlecht, das mir gleich sei,
> Zu leiden, weinen,
> Genießen, und zu freuen sich,
> Und dein nicht zu achten,
> Wie ich.

[Here I sit, create people / In my image, / A race that is like me, / Made to suffer, to weep, / To enjoy and to be glad / – And to ignore you, / Just as I do.]

But barely seven years later came 'Grenzen der Menschheit' ('Limits of mankind', 1781), with its humility, with its title already indicating limitations and its last stanza reading as follows:

> Ein kleiner Ring
> Begrenzt unser Leben,
> Und viele Geschlechter
> Reihen sich dauernd
> An ihres Daseins
> Unendliche Kette.

[A narrow ring / Limits our life, / And many generations / Are continuously being linked / To the endless chain / Of their existence.]

The great variation in Goethe's early pre-Classical poems – from simple love poems, to a series of ballads, to occasional poetry, to nature and philosophical poems and to great hymns like 'Prometheus' – provides a compelling indication of his involvement in the poetic developments of the century. Poetry was a vehicle for him and others not only to experiment with form and content, but also to express emotions and political and social commentary in an accessible, direct fashion. When looked at in gender-specific fashion, there seems to be little in the way of positive ideas that Goethe can express about women if he cannot place them on a pedestal. 'Der Adler und die Taube', ('The eagle and the dove') for example, describes the hunt of an eagle for its prey, its crippling injury at the hands of a hunter, and then its response to a male dove, who urges the eagle to be satisfied with its confinement on the ground, whereupon the eagle, mightily depressed at the thought, can only respond, '. . . du redest wie eine Taube'. ('. . you speak like a female dove'). But there is also 'Vor Gericht' ('On trial'), a ballad that depicts a strong and resistant woman, pregnant, but resolutely refusing to reveal the name of the father despite the legal and religious pressures that are placed upon her.

The *Sturm und Drang* poetry and other writings that emerged before

1790 represented in their contempt for formal learning something of a return to the anti-scholastic philosophy that had flourished earlier in the century. Haller's 'Die Alpen', for example, also expressed a resistance to rhetorical rigidities and the narrowness of intellectual thinking. Perhaps that can offer an explanation for the exclusively male nature of *Sturm und Drang*, for only the privileged, educated upper and middle classes, who were primarily male, could or would rebel against the gaining of formal knowledge at a time when other elements of the population were beginning to urge such privileges for themselves.

Schiller's most notable poetry of this era was not in the realm of nature/love poetry, but focused rather on abstract ideas. 'Die Götter Griechenlands', originally published in 1788, offers an elegiac portrait of classical Greece, contrasting it to the modern, Christian era, which is depicted as centred on death and darkness. Words like 'entgöttert' ('deprived of divine attributes') and 'entseelt' ('lifeless') (as in 'das entseelte Wort', the opposite of the dynamic *logos*) are contrasted to fidelity, truth, beauty, colour, brilliance. At the end, the contrast between life, which must end, and art, which must continue, is noted: 'Was unsterblich im Gesang soll leben, / Muß im Leben untergehn.' ('What is immortal in poetry should live but must disappear in life.') A complementary poem, an aesthetic discussion of art and artists and life, is 'Die Künstler', composed in 1788–9, which focuses in particular on the humanisation of the higher forms of nature through art. Although Schiller later discounted the poem and its overly didactic tone, its philosophic messages, particularly the mission of artists to further the dignity of human beings, remained present in his thinking: 'Der Menschheit Würde ist in eure Hand gegeben – / Bewahrt sie! / Sie sinkt mit euch! Mit euch wird sie sich heben!' ('The dignity of humanity is placed in your hands – / Watch over it! / It falls with you, and with you it will rise!') The poem's basic motif centres on the revelation of truth through beauty and the presentation of essences in the forms, sounds and pictures of art, that is, the power of the aesthetic and those – the artists – who represent it. Art is thereby ennobled and justified; more importantly, the artists themselves, the human individuals who create the art, are given a status that emphasises their own agency and significance.

In remarkable contrast to his philosophical and aesthetic musings, there is 'Männerwürde' ('Dignity of men', 1782), in which Schiller provides a definition of men that is in counterpoint to his 'Würde der Frauen' ('Dignity of women', 1796). The gendered characteristics that emerged in the latter years of the eighteenth century are uncritically and unproblematically presented: to be a man is to be free, creative, powerful, proud, and, in particular, able to exert sexual power over women. Thus there are stanzas like the following:

Und wohl mir, daß ichs darf und kann!
Geht's Mädchen mit vorüber,
Rufts laut in mir: Du bist ein Mann!
Und küsse sie so lieber.

Und röter wird das Mädchen dann,
Und's Mieder wird ihr enge.
Das Mädchen weiß: Ich bin ein Mann!
Drum wird ihr's Mieder enge.

Wie wird sie erst um Genade schrein,
Ertapp ich sie im Bade!
Ich bin ein Mann, das fällt ihr ein –
Wie schrie sie sonst um Gnade?

[And it's good for me that I may and can do as I wish! / If a girl walks by me, / A loud cry emerges inside of me: 'you are a man!' / and then I kiss her as I wish. / And the girl will blush then / and her bodice will get tighter. / The girl knows I am a man, / And because of that her bodice will become tighter. / Oh, how she will first cry for mercy / If I come upon her in her bath! / I am a man, that will occur to her / – Why else would she cry for mercy?]

The arrogant strength of the man contrasts with the productive, but controlled and orderly activity of the women who are praised in the later poem. One might attribute the earlier poem to youthful rebellion, to the playful, chaotic spirit that was characteristic of the male figures in the era of *Sturm und Drang*. At the same time, the perception of gender roles presented in these two poems and the cavalier acknowledgement and acceptance of male violence in 'Männerwürde' should be duly noted as part of the context in which ideas about gender were discussed and understood.

Periodicals and literary criticism

Given the efforts to popularise Enlightenment ideas, it is logical that those writers and philosophers who subscribed to such a goal would look for ways in which to reach as large an audience as possible. For unlike the class-based élitism of the previous century, when the focus of writers was directed towards the small and privileged portion of the population that was educated and, unlike the élitism that emerged towards the end of the eighteenth century, an élitism of the intellectual and the artist represented most graphically in so-called Classicism – the proponents of the Enlightenment were primarily interested in communicating their ideas in an idealistic educative process that would ultimately create a public sphere of moral, virtuous and right-thinking citizens *and* readers. One instrument of such an educating process was the periodical journal.

The influence of England was felt from the outset. The earlier German periodicals were named – in a literal translation from the English label given to, among others, Addison's and Steele's moral weeklies like the *Tatler* and the *Spectator* – 'moralische Wochenschriften'. In an effort to communicate and popularise, the weeklies were directly and simply written, full of homiletic language encouraging the readers to be moral and virtuous, and addressed to the middle-class citizen whom the Enlightenment was intent upon reaching and defining. Communicative literary forms like the essay, the tract, the dialogue and the fable predominated. Wide-ranging discussions on taste, on imagination, on various literary forms, were paramount. But the overwhelming purpose remained the education of a readership that was marked by gender and class, for although the literate population in Germany did not encompass all middle- and upper-class men, the groups that were newest to literacy were primarily women and lower-class men. Despite the relatively high cost of the weeklies, they were widely read – if not copies that their readers had bought, then copies distributed by the rapidly growing number of reading societies.

According to Wolfgang Martens, whose 1968 study of the 'moralische Wochenenschriften' remains a standard work, middle-class women were meant to be a major audience addressed by the weeklies, which dealt with general questions and did not specifically address intellectuals. In the spirit of the Enlightenment, with its dual goals of mediating useful knowledge and providing pleasure, the message of the weeklies stressed the realms to which women could aspire, namely the roles of good mothers, clever housewives and pleasing friends.

Another important development emerged from the general goal of the periodicals to create a connection to, and dialogue with, a company of readers. Given the literary works that appeared in ever greater numbers as the century progressed, and given the Enlightenment goal of prescribing and encouraging ways to think about that knowledge, it is not surprising that literary and artistic criticism also began to flourish. This process can be observed in literary periodicals early on, when Gottsched held considerable cultural power and propounded his belief in rules and in the role of what were then called the 'Kunstrichter' ('judges of art') to observe how those rules were being followed in a literary work. Following him came the Swiss critics Bodmer and Breitinger, and later Lessing and others, who transformed Gottsched's perception of taste (in which good taste was synonymous with the following of rules) into a more individualised, subjective act in which feelings were privileged (in Lessing's case, this is connected with his emphasis on the role of *Mitleid*), readers themselves became critics, and the bourgeois reader would see him or herself as possessed of a self-consciousness that was separate from the aristocracy, but equal to it.

As the century progressed, literary journals replaced the moral weeklies and began to provide wide-ranging reviews of the new literature. The emphasis on connection and dialogue is often apparent even in the form: the *Briefe, die neueste Litteratur betreffend* (*Letters concerning the newest literature*, 1759–65) of Lessing, Nicolai and Mendelssohn, for example, use the letter, thus giving the review a more conversational tone and an accessible, familiar, dialogic language. Lessing also published the *Hamburgische Dramaturgie* (1767–69), a theatrical journal that offered his views on drama and the theatre and clarified his own role as a critic. Nicolai founded and oversaw the *Allgemeine Deutsche Bibliothek* (*ADB*, 1765–92; 1793–1806), the review journal that began with a stated goal of considering all new books in German, but that could not carry out that goal once the growing flood of books overwhelmed it.

With the development of literary criticism, some of the contradictions of the Enlightenment also became apparent. When Nicolai and his assistants realised that their aim of creating a homogeneous literary public sphere by means of the *ADB* was unrealisable, it was not just the mass of books that was too much for them to acknowledge – it was the varying nature of those books, and of the reading public that was demanding them, that made their goal impossible. The paradox of the Enlightenment is in part grounded in the good intentions that are countered by the inevitable results that occur when uniformity and universalising are assumed to be possible and correct. The gap between the educated élite and the growing number of readers whose tastes did not always conform to the prescribed tastes of Gottsched or Lessing was inevitable and led to other developments: to the superindividualism of the *Sturm und Drang*, with its stress on feeling, subjectivity and the autonomous individual, but also to the pristine, removed *Klassik*, which retreated into art and avoided the popular by ignoring it. Thus, the original purpose of the periodical as a transmitter of knowledge and as an instrument to help form the literary public sphere became mired in reality, in the paradox of worthy but narrow goals and inevitable ruptures in a far too normalised picture.

At the same time, journalism, mass communication and literary criticism emerged from the growth of periodicals. The goal of reaching a large audience led to the creation of what was a division into elitist culture and mass/popular culture. Although the Enlightenment may have seen the world too simply and optimistically, it also inspired moves towards the modernity that (despite postmodernism) is with us still. In its plan to enlighten by means of periodical literature women and others who were less fortunate, it had a considerable effect, even encouraging Sophie von La Roche to found and edit her own periodical in the 1780s and thereby stimulate other women to do the same. La Roche's *Pomona für Teutschlands Töchter* (*Pomona for Germany's daughters*, 1783–4)) is explicitly addressed to women, and although it too reflects the ambivalences of Enlightenment thought on gender, it gives important proof of the presence of women in the literary market. It was widely read and openly welcomed, at least among the middle- to upper-class women and men to whom it was meant to speak. Providing a mixture of poems, letters, short stories and essays, its aim of educating and informing Germany's 'daughters' is clear. Perhaps it is most interesting in its ambivalences, in the differences between, for example, the normalising letters to Lina, a young woman whom La Roche educates in the proper role of women, and some of the so-called 'moral tales' that are more subtle in their analysis of women. 'Liebe, Freundschaft und Misverständniß' ('Love, friendship and misunderstanding'), for instance, begins with a standard story of a bright young woman who learns all she can and hopes to marry an educated man who can teach her more, but it ends with her abandoning her plans for marriage and instead becoming a teacher in a school for young girls. Even when her suitor finds her years later, she is firm in her choice of her life's activity and now stresses friendship over love.

Closing note

This has been an experiment in examining old material with a new(er) eye. It is meant to enter into conversation with the ways in which we view literary history. If it has shown that issues of gender and class were present in both actual and metaphorical ways in much of the German Enlightenment, it was not intended to present an unproblematic portrait, either of the Enlightenment itself or of the middle-class German women or lower-middle-class German men who were also participant observers in it. It is, in fact, the very contradictions themselves that provide a more differentiated view. The bright and optimistic ideas of the Enlightenment were challenged and also occasionally proven to be facile or narrow; it was not always a matter of omission, but also of commission. An example is certainly the overt limitations of eighteenth-century thought when it came to defining women not as intellectual, but as clever ('klug'). It was not a matter of omitting them; it was, rather, an inclusion that drew strict and narrowing boundaries. To be smart and not intellectual not only implies a limitation on opportunities (university training, for example), but also on the assumptions about women's intellectual capabilities.

The concept of freedom also had so much in the way of structured control attached to it, whether by means of the absolutist rulers or the church or simply the underlying conservatism of those who were propounding it, that we cannot interpret such an idea as implying the liberty we might think it would encompass. The interest in developing bourgeois subjectivities certainly included thoughts of autonomy and personal choice, but as to how connected such an interest was to real circumstances, one need only think of the always problematic relationship between theory and practice. If the Enlightenment allowed for progress, its emphasis on theories (no matter how flawed in practice) of education, culture and the popularisation of ideas nevertheless significantly benefited those, both women and men, who were on the margin.

5

Aesthetic humanism (1790–1830)

NICHOLAS SAUL

Introduction

These years, which begin with Johann Wolfgang von Goethe's maturity and end approximately at his death in 1832, used to be called the Age of Goethe. There were good reasons for this: the period contains most of Goethe's major works, all of which display his characteristic tendency to embody the conflicts of the age refracted through his own, subjective experience and so claim representative status. Of course, this involved accepting Goethe's absolute pre-eminence and taking only his view – for example, that Romanticism, one of the most widespread cultural tendencies of the age, was sick, so that Goethe's Classicism had to fight it. In truth, even though Goethe remains the epoch's outstanding writer, this kind of monolithic model no longer explains what we know of the literary situation and its development.

For example, the Enlightenment did not, as Goethe's own Classic–Romantic dualism suggests, simply end with the onset of polemics against its rationalistic tendencies around 1795–6. August von Kotzebue (1761–1819), whose works dominated the German stage (including Weimar) from 1790 to well beyond his assassination, was a slavish (and, in a sense, masterly) imitator of Lessing's Enlightenment dramas, to say nothing of Wieland, the father and son team of Voß, and a host of popular novelists. There emerged too a newly coherent body of literature by women such as Caroline Auguste Fischer and Karoline von Günderrode. Nor is the epoch any longer clear cut. In the *Biedermeierzeit* (Age of the loyal subject – 1815–48) an archetypal Romantic like Clemens Brentano assimilates central values of Restoration. At the other end of the time-scale the Romantics Novalis and Friedrich Schlegel not only negated the Enlightenment, they consciously retained many of its fundamental convictions (intellectualism, progress). Even the traditional opposition of Classicism and Romanticism will not quite do any more. This used to be defined by their different ideals of personality: rounded harmonious stability versus destabilised yearning for infinity. But that only covers up common ground. The mutual antipathy of Schiller and the Romantics belies shared basic convictions (alienation from prosaic modern existence, the aesthetic state, the historical view of poetics). Goethe, for his part, worked with the exotic Romantic Zacharias Werner and the outsider Kleist as late as 1807–9. As for Kleist, he does not fit well into any contemporary category. Some locate him, if anywhere, in the postmodern age of decentred uncertainties. Indeed, many see early Romanticism as postmodernism *avant la lettre*. Nowadays this process of deconstruction has gone so far as to present Goethe himself as the great outsider of his own time (Nicholas Boyle, *Goethe. The poet and the age*, 1991).

So where, if not in Goethe, might the unity of our period lie? No other individual or school can compete with him for the role in so diverse a period, though a case has been made for Tieck (Roger Paulin, *Ludwig Tieck. A literary biography*, 1985). If the unity of our period is not to be found in literature, it must be found elsewhere. This chapter argues that literature's role from 1790 to 1830 was in general to respond creatively to historical events, both political and cultural. Two events, one political, one cultural, stand out before 1790. Both sought to realise the grand humanistic project of Enlightenment. The most significant political event is the success and failure of the French Revolution, with its proclamation of individual self-determination and equality and demand for constitution and republic. In one way or another it provokes all major political developments in Germany during this period, from the anti-revolutionary Wars of Coalition (1792–1807), the collapse and abolition of the Holy Roman Empire and French occupation of Prussia (1806ff.), the War of German Liberation (1812–15) and the replacement of the Empire by the restorative German Federation (1815), to the reactionary Karlsbad Decrees (1819) and the 'Vormärz' period before the 1848 revolution. Each event drew a literary response (usually a call for peace or war). All evoke the Revolution. The biggest cultural event is secularisation, the decline and fall of traditional religion following the challenge to externalised religious authority by secular reason which is Enlightenment's signature, and which in Germany found its most far-reaching expression in the abolition of sacred institutions by the 'Reichsdeputationshauptschlüsse' of 1803. The literature of this time always resonates with the sense of religious loss.

Both Revolution and secularisation provoked crisis. The Revolution proclaimed human rights and was welcomed warmly by Johann Gottfried Herder and Georg Forster, who were all too conscious of Germany's political contradictions. The middle class or third estate, to which they and most writers of the age belonged, was the cultivated class in Germany, the vehicle of Enlightenment and of public opinion, the indispensable administrator of the state apparatus and creator of wealth. It was, however, in 1790 generally excluded from political responsibility by the persistence of feudalism in the contractualised and rationalised form bequeathed to

Germany by Frederick the Great and Joseph II. German intellectuals in general sympathised with the political aims of the Revolution, but its violent methods soon alienated virtually all German support. It was rejected as a model for Germany. This merely intensified social frustration, which was hardly eased by the widespread reception of Edmund Burke's conservative *Reflections on the Revolution* (1790). Only with the abolition of the Holy Roman Empire and occupation of Prussia by Napoleon in 1806–7 were wide-ranging emancipatory political and social reforms carried through during the period from 1807 to 1812 by the ministers Freiherr vom Stein and Fürst von Hardenberg. Secularisation, for its part, destroyed the logical absurdities of positive religion, yet offered no coherent alternative. With its dualistic world-view and focus on the other world as goal and fulfilment, traditional Christianity was in the eighteenth century still the major source of meaning in most individuals' lives. Since the principle of *cuius regio, eius religio* institutionalised by the Treaty of Westphalia after the Thirty Years War (1648) had led in every part of Germany to a community of interest between the state and its established church, the collapse of traditional forms of piety worked together with Revolution to shake people's inner *and* outer orientation. Both revolution and secularisation were, unsurprisingly, often treated as manifestations of one problem.

The period around 1790 is thus a transitional phase. Prior to the establishment of a new, recognisably modern order, provisional syntheses of the new, which avoided the contradictions of the Revolution yet retained its general aims, had initially to bypass the existing political structures. The Berlin salon, a social forum which flourished from around 1790 to around 1806, can serve as the epitome of this phase. Generally organised by the wives of wealthy professional Jews, it offered a unique, new form of personal encounter on other than the received terms for all comers: women, as yet struggling to translate emancipation into the terms received from Enlightenment; Jews, only privately free in the age of religious orthodoxy; the nobility and the cultivated middle classes, otherwise segregated. The salon, like an aesthetic idea made real, prefigures the new order. But it was a precarious synthesis of opposites, which soon broke up under the pressure of nationalist patriotism and intellectual reaction after 1807. Our age, like the salon, is fundamentally an unstable equilibrium, the uneasy transition between two orders, the old and the new regime. The period 1770–1830 has aptly been called the *Sattelzeit:* an epoch, like a saddle, straddling old and new. To this we owe too the simultaneous co-existence of several heterogeneous literary trends.

The notion of German literature as response to history unifies the epoch on one level. However, a collective literary response can only be made on the basis of some deeper consensus, even if it is emergent and

ragged. This chapter sees that underlying consensus as a new, anthropologically orientated vision of human fulfilment, which continues the
Enlightenment project, yet differs clearly from it, and is not without its
own contradiction. Human fulfilment, in the wake of the Revolution and
secularisation, was to be realised through *aesthetic* means. On this
account writers, irrespective of school, saw the realisation of the new
anthropological idea as their common project. It is no coincidence that
the *salons* were in essence literary circles. Gotthold Ephraim Lessing's *Die
Erziehung des Menschengeschlechts* (*The education of the human race*,
1781) and Friedrich Schiller's *Über die ästhetische Erziehung des
Menschen* (*The aesthetic education of humanity*, 1795) exhibit how the
emergent consensus grew.

Lessing purports to answer the Enlightened secularist attacks of
Hermann Samuel Reimarus on the Bible's shaky reputation as vehicle of
a universal revelation. Biblical revelation, he says, is not an instantaneous
conferring of ultimate truth, but more like education, a progressive
unfolding. God is the teacher, the Bible the book, history the period of
humanity's education. Seeming contradictions or omissions in the Bible
are really skilful accommodations of the message to human understanding at a given point in its maturation. The plausible analogy has,
however, a sting in the tail. For *after* maturity teacher, textbook, and
education become dispensable. It is thus no accident that Lessing uses
the same metaphor to defend religion as Kant for his definition of
Aufklärung (Enlightenment) of 1784, as 'Ausgang des Menschen aus
seiner selbstverschuldeten Unmündigkeit' ('emergence of humankind
from its self-imposed tutelage'). Finally he predicts the coming of a new,
anthropocentric millennium, with its *new* New Testament. Whilst
seeming to save the Bible, Lessing has really disposed of it. He frees
humanity from biblical and, probably, Christian authority. He breaks the
link of state and religion (but not the authority of the state), and he has
not written part three of the Bible, nor told us what it should contain. He
resolves the religious crisis of the age only to this extent. His successors
had to provide a substitute from whatever (secular) materials lay to hand.
There were plenty of writers prepared to try. Metaphors signalling a
text's intention to be the new Gospel are among the most common in the
literature of the age.

In his remarkable letters *Über die ästhetische Erziehung des Menschen*,
with their intrinsic reference to *Die Erziehung des Menschengeschlechts*,
Schiller provided a convincing alternative both to the religious crisis
bequeathed by Lessing and the socio-political dilemmas of the
Revolution. As the Terror set in and German opinion, never more than
cautiously approving of the Revolution, swung towards reaction, Schiller
had begun a political pamphlet in defence of Louis XVI. That he then,

after the King's execution on 21 January 1793, started the work which became the *Ästhetische Briefe*, might seem escapist. They contain that seemingly most unpolitical of things, a theory of beauty, which claims that aesthetic beauty is 'freedom in appearance' or the apparent self-determination of things. Escapist they are decidedly not. For the *Ästhetische Briefe* link the new aesthetic theory with Schiller's holistic anthropology, the expression of his lifelong concern to harmonise what he saw as the fundamental dualism of human nature. This anthropology is the base from which he launches his critique of the age and the Revolution. In it, art has become nothing less than the chief agent of anthropological therapy.

The letters diagnose the age as sick. It was not always thus. Greek antiquity, Schiller claims, is characterised by wholeness, a unity of striving between individual and state, which is represented by the harmony of individual personalities. If totality is the character of Greek culture, fragmentation is that of modernity. Increased reflexivity has imposed narrow specialisation in all spheres of life, from social and political structures to the inner economy of the personality. Of course, the impulse to impose rational on natural order, freedom upon necessity (the 'Formtrieb'), is fundamental to human nature. Yet modernity forgets that people, just as fundamentally, possess a 'Stofftrieb', are natural (sensual and imaginative) beings. Thus, when institutional compulsion – revolution in France, reform in Germany – is applied to create an ideal ethical state, the lack of mediation between form and sensuality generates only perversions of human nature. The uneducated ('savages') know only violent means to achieve the moral goal. The educated ('barbarians') let their ethical consciousness be dominated by sensuality. Either way people are instrumentalised. In a rounded anthropological approach, says Schiller, intellectual form must be harmonised with sensual content. But how? Through beauty, as 'living form'. For 'living form' connotes 'freedom in appearance', the aesthetic object's property of *apparent* self-determination which enables it *as* sensual experience seemingly to overcome the capricious dictatorship of natural forces. The experience of beauty thus answers simultaneously the sensual demand for material satisfaction (life) and the demand for autonomous rule characteristic of ethical consciousness (form). In this realm of beautiful appearance people are freed from the one-sided dictatorship of form or matter. What is free, has no purpose beyond itself. It plays. Schiller calls the new, artificially generated disposition which creates that yearned-for harmony of dualistic human nature the 'Spieltrieb' ('play impulse'). Only in this mode of holistic aesthetic experience is humanity entirely humane. The lost classical ideal has been realised in a modern form. However, whilst aesthetic experience so defined is intrinsically purposeless – and Schiller sometimes sees it as the actual mode of human fulfilment – it also has a function. As the revelation of freedom in an aptly sensual mode it is the *only* way for sensual human beings to become aware of their latent capacity for self-determination. Aesthetic education, then, is the alternative to failed reform and failed revolution.

Schiller does not shrink from the logical consequence: the postulate of the aesthetic state, in which – irrespective of political system – all objects and all communication, between the sexes, in society (he means the *salon)*, in the sciences, in politics, are systematically beautified. His journal *Die Horen* (*The hours*, 1795–7), in which the *Ästhetische Briefe* appeared, was the first vehicle for the project of aesthetic humanism and became the age's most influential organ. Its intention, to integrate writers from different disciplines and readers from diverse areas of special interest under the common aesthetic ideology reflects the analysis of fragmentation as the central problem of the age. Even the style of the letters exemplifies how aestheticisation serves the purpose of *haute vulgarisation*. Schiller makes his formidably abstract language perform graceful rhetorical dances enacting the magic of 'freedom in appearance', so that (in theory) even the most resistant reader should experience what he might not grasp intellectually. This might suggest intellectual intoxication. Yet Schiller's expectations are sober. He sees the Revolution's ideals as being realised for the time being only in the realm of beauteous appearance, and envisages more than one century as being required for completion of the task. Nevertheless the *Ästhetische Briefe* prompt a major shift in the mentality of contemporary writers. Schiller does cite the Kantian slogan of Enlightenment – *sapere aude* (dare to know). But the Enlightenment's demand for human fulfilment as intellectual self-cultivation has been superseded by a new vision of anthropological wholeness, in which the fact of corporeality is recognised and given new value. Aesthetic discourse, with its fusion of the spiritual and the sensual and its sovereign, purposeless autonomy, has become the universal means to that end. German writers begin, as they would for a generation, to talk of 'Lebenskunst', life in terms of art. The Berlin salon, the court circles at Weimar, and the Bohemian groupings of the Jena Romantics would seek to translate this aesthetic vision into social fact. This is the sense in which Heinrich Heine's name for our epoch, 'Kunstperiode' ('epoch of art'), is apt. Heine interpreted the aesthetics of autonomy, as we have expounded them in this, their classical text, as connoting the hermetic isolation of literature from its environment, as if in an ivory tower of sovereign disdain for prosaic reality. How false this assumption is, must already be evident. The same paradoxical commitment to changing the real world applies to virtually all the autonomous, aestheticist literature of our epoch. Yet in the identification of aestheticism as the dominant note of the epoch Heine is as right now as he was then.

But aestheticism is not the only sense in which the *Ästhetische Briefe* are epoch-making. Schiller's text also offers a religious solution. The 'Spieltrieb', for all that it is both fulfilment of humanity and means to education, is an artificially created faculty. It connotes, then, the remaking of humanity *by* humanity. Thus it stands most aptly for the Copernican shift from theocentric to anthropocentric meaning entailed by secularisation. The trained theologian Schiller leaps to equate his aesthetic regeneration with the analogous Christian event of baptismal rebirth: 'Beauty is our second creator', he says. Lessing's need for the new evangel is now in the process of being met by an aesthetic religion. Schiller does not develop his implications – others would do that for him.

Johann Gottfried Herder (1744–1803) illustrates in a mild variant the general acceptance of Schiller's paradigms. He too wrote humanistic letters in response to the Terror, the *Briefe zur Beförderung der Humanität* (*Letters on the furtherance of humanity*, 1793–7). Like Schiller Herder accepts the Revolution in principle but rejects violence, so that 'Bildung zur Humanität' ('cultivation towards humanity'), this time in the form of national renewal, is the task. As in Schiller, fragmentation is the basic problem. Germany is broken up, a cultural and political jumble of religions, sects, dialects, provinces, governments, customs and laws. But fragmentation of language, which Herder sees as constitutive of national identity and as medium of education, is the problem's chief expression. Inner cultural heterogeneity and feudal social structure have led the nobility to adopt foreign languages and artists to imitate foreign models, especially in the theatre. German has become the language of servants. The German character has thus been catastrophically alienated from itself. A centre is needed. But Herder's cure is not a physical capital and a unified state. That would damage the regional interests which promote healthy antagonisms. He proposes a *paper* capital, a national focus for its writers' 'industry of mind' ('Geistes-Industrie'). They – primarily by reference to Germanic cultural models from the past – would teach, cultivate, and develop public taste in unhindered (and uncensored) communication. Thus, if Herder's diagnosis of the problem after the Revolution accords with Schiller's, so too at this level does his solution: the communicative ideal of a literary renewal, centred on individuals, circumventing institutions, and modelled on an idealised past. Greek and German ideals would compete in the following decades.

But into what literary environment did this new consensus emerge? Another revolution – of reading-habits – was occurring in the last quarter of the eighteenth-century. The book-market expanded between 1740 and 1800 by about three hundred and fifty per cent, although the Napoleonic Wars did depress production temporarily after 1805. This increase easily outpaced population growth. In 1775 the Enlightenment writer and publisher Friedrich Nicolai estimated the German population at around twenty million. It still only numbered twenty-two million in 1800 and twenty-nine million in 1806. Not all of these could read: in 1770 at most fifteen per cent of Germans over the age of six, in 1800 perhaps still only twenty-five per cent. And not all of them did read. Until industrialisation, following the Stein–Hardenberg reforms, began in earnest in the 1820s, Germany remained an agrarian nation. In 1800 three-quarters of the Germans still lived on the land. Countryfolk for the most part ignored the reading revolution. They still lived and read in the rhythm of the church or the natural year, reading and re-reading (or hearing) a thematically limited selection of devotional or chapbook literature. Educated city-dwellers, dotted around the nation without a capital, comprised the reading public. Nicolai guesses at a mere 20,000 in 1775, and Jean Paul signals the fact of the reading revolution when he estimates 300,000 in 1800. These comprised in part the 'Dienstadel' (the aristocratic stratum of the bureaucracy and army officers), but mainly middle classes or *Bürger,* ranging in profession from ministers of the Crown, to government offi-cials (usually lawyers by training), teachers, students, preachers, mer-chants, doctors, academics, and the like (and their wives). They rarely bought books in quantity, for books were far more expensive than today. Educated men subscribed instead to reading clubs (*Lesegesellschaften*) which allowed them to read and discuss in a common room. These – by contrast to the mixed salon – are a pioneering form of republican culture in Germany, the rare instance of a self-constituting and autonomous middle-class institution. There was a correspondingly vast growth of such institutions in the epoch: by 1800, at least one in every town. In 1811 Berlin supported twenty-seven, Dresden sixteen.

But what did the middle-class citizen read? Periodicals outweighed books in most reading clubs. This in itself typifies how the Enlightened middle class subscribed to the idea of progress. They read newspapers and practical journals, relevant to everyday problems and covering for example educational issues or learned specialist disciplines. Perhaps half, such as Nicolai's *Allgemeine Deutsche Bibliothek* or Wieland's *Teutscher Merkur,* would offer general reading. The book-holdings were similarly factual and informative in character, dominated by reference works, history and the like. In 1790 sophisticated literature as such was poorly represented. By contrast to the countryfolk the urban citizens, then, pos-itively consumed literature. They would read extensively, but only once, and only for a purpose. Schiller's intended reader, learned and well-trained but unremittingly prosaic, is clearly recognisable in these out-lines.

There *was* a relative increase in the reading of poetic literature of a kind. As the townsfolk, in the wake of secularisation, gave up reading their devotional literature, they turned increasingly to fiction. But this dynamic was centred on another main reading institution, the commercial circulating library (*Leihbibliothek*). That did not mean high literature. Kleist found, when he inquired about the contents of the circulating library at Würzburg in 1801, that Goethe, Schiller and Wieland were never requested and not stocked. When they were not keeping abreast of the latest developments in cameralistic theory, then, people preferred to read, in private, the eighteenth-century analogue of the modern thriller, the Enlightenment Gothic novel, such as Christian August Vulpius's *Rinaldo Rinaldini* or Karl Grosse's *Der Genius* to the work emanating from Weimar, Jena or Berlin. If they went to the theatre, as Goethe discovered in Weimar, they preferred Kotzebue and Iffland. Those who did read high literature in their select circles of cultivation, used them, in this age of secularisation, like devotional literature. As Novalis's use of Goethe's *Bildungsroman Wilhelm Meisters Lehrjahre* testifies, they read and re-read them. However these years, especially from 1815 to 1830, were, as Wilhelm Hauff's satire *Die Bücher und die Lesewelt* (*Books and the reading world*) shows, typified by the vast rise in popularity of disposable trivial reading. The circulating library was also the main source of literature for women (and servants). A certain type of novel – the Enlightenment genre of the epistolary novel by and for women – gradually came to be classed as the women's genre.

All this had consequences for the serious writer's self-understanding. There were more authors than ever before, perhaps two to three thousand in 1800. As the drastic decline in the number of book-dedications demonstrates, they had largely freed themselves from the usually problematic situation of court patronage. Yet they now had to find an entrepreneur to publish them and enough readers in the market-place. Thus the influence of the patron over taste and production was replaced by that of the publisher and the public. Market-share had to be established by demonstrating an acceptable originality. Then it had to be kept. The result was a simultaneous counter-tendency towards normalisation of the literary 'product' and against experiment. By 1800 the trivial novel thus took over seventy-five per cent of the literary market. The novel-factories in which, rather like Scott or Dickens, Ludwig Tieck and Wilhelm Hauff laboured, are the consequence. Unsurprisingly, the end of the century is characterised by a growing gulf between serious writer and public. Tieck's comedy *Der gestiefelte Kater* (*Puss in boots*, 1797) is typical, in that here the reading classes are brought onto the stage of an avant-garde play, and their philistine incomprehension is a major lever of humour.

In defence of their newly won autonomy authors had only a limited number of possible remedies. They could seek to square the circle by appealing to the mass-audience in some writings and the elite in others (or even both in the same work). Tieck (until the last decade of his life) and Jean Paul remained independent authors in this way. Alternatively, authors could and did increasingly seek to circumvent the publisher, generally with little success. Lessing and Novalis made plans for founding their own publishing houses, and Kleist attempted it. Additionally, authors, like most of the allegedly escapist Romantics, could practise a civil profession and write in their leisure time. Novalis was primarily a mining engineer. Goethe trained as lawyer and worked most of his life in government. Schiller and A. W. Schlegel were glad to take on university professorships. Johann Peter Hebel was a headmaster. E. T. A. Hoffmann was an eminent lawyer and judge, Joseph von Eichendorff a Prussian administrator. Kleist tried and failed several times to keep a job. If unmarried, women writers needed another source of income. Karoline von Günderrode was a 'Stiftsdame', a kind of lay nun. Caroline Auguste Fischer ran a school and a circulating library. Authors who chose not to follow this route – such as the middle-class Friedrich Hölderlin, and, finally, the minor aristocrat Kleist – were forced into miserably paid professions such as private tutoring, or into penury. Lastly, unless like Clemens Brentano or Goethe they came from wealthy families and had independent means, authors could still accept courtly patronage. Schiller, Adam Müller, Zacharias Werner, Friedrich Schlegel, Tieck and even August von Kotzebue and Goethe all finally returned to the old model and accepted courtly support in one form or another, since they could not live on their earnings from writing. Thus when Schiller concludes that the aesthetic state in reality exists only 'in a few select circles', he underlines not only the secularised consciousness of mission possessed by the aesthetic writers of the age, but also their equally profound sense of alienation from the present literary environment. The poet, Schiller wrote to Goethe in one of their earliest letters, was the only true human being. Herder's author is equally disillusioned and remote. He relies on the written word addressed to an invisible ideal community of readers scattered throughout Germany. Goethe's essay *Literarischer Sansculottismus* (*Literary Sansculottism*, 1795) expresses the common analysis most clearly. The German public has too long been educated under foreign influence to serve as a guide for the development of German writers, so that too many talents – he is thinking of Schiller – are compelled to pander to bad taste simply to survive in the market-place. It is a wonder that Germany possesses as many good writers as it does, and Goethe, with a view to the Revolution, does not wish for Germany the kind of dramatic historical upheavals which are one condition of classical literature. In fact, Germany's classical literature came about without that social background and the communicative centre they all wished for was found in Goethe's own Weimar.

Weimar classicism

In 1794 Goethe received a letter from Schiller which, he said, inaugurated a new epoch in his life. They had known each other since 1788, and Goethe had recently agreed to contribute to *Die Horen*. Yet relations had never been more than polite. They seemed opposites. Goethe thought Schiller too idealistic, passionate and extreme, Schiller thought Goethe too aloof, sensual, and, as a poet, too intimidating a reminder of his own limitations. But his letter is an offer of friendship of a particular kind. It is based on a rapprochement of their convictions on the task of the poet, and thus contains just a hint of future co-operation. Weimar classicism, the original and most powerful expression of the epochal consensus, results from the letter's brilliant success.

In it Schiller offers new sympathy for Goethe's approach. The mature Goethe had derived from Spinoza's pantheistic philosophy a characteristic method of intuitive apprehension of particular objects as revelations of the divine, or totality. From Schiller's Kantian perspective such evaluations had been unacceptable. For the Kantian, personification of nature as a creative source working through objects to a particular end is an idea, a fiction, generated by the subject's reason for the sole purpose of guiding the understanding. To identify that with the sensual object – as Goethe seemed constantly to do – was, in 1794, a basic error. Schiller, we know, thought the poet's task was to idealise nature, to make the individual object symbolise a general, and in this sense objective, human law, a project which – especially when contrasted with the plastic immediacy of Goethe's work – led to a certain abstract quality in his poetry. The letter represents Schiller's self-critical recognition of this, but also – precisely on this account – that Goethe's way is a valid *alternative* to his own. For Goethe, he now sees, is no sensual enthusiast. He is, in the technical sense, a genius, one of those rare, favoured children of nature whose spontaneous, yet disciplined intuitions follow the law already without need for speculative reflection, and whose poetry objectifies that intuitively grasped law without generating the empty fantasies otherwise produced by such minds. Goethe's realism, then, appears from this perspective as the fully-fledged colleague of Schiller's idealism. They are complementary opposites. If the letter acknowledges Goethe's pre-eminence as genius-poet, the theoretical incisiveness of Schiller's Goethe-interpretation makes clear who is the dominant thinker.

Schiller and Goethe co-operated not only on *Die Horen*, but also on every aspect of the theory and practice of their production until Schiller's death in 1805. That means a series of major works which mark every worthwhile German text in the epoch. Goethe responded so positively because the letter came at the right time in his own development. He was only in Weimar for the sake of his long-term campaign (prompted by Herder) to renew German literature, the outcome of which was still undecided in 1794. The landmarks on his journey illustrate the point. His autobiography *Dichtung und Wahrheit* (*Poetry and truth*, 1811–14) records how the young, middle-class Goethe in Frankfurt am Main opted – in opposition to the utilitarian mentality of the day – for the poetic profession. The question was, what to put in the poetry? Conventional religious themes were an exhausted vein. The nation, apart from the initial attraction of Frederick the Great's feats, was nowhere to be found. Hence Goethe began his lifelong search for meaning in the only other empirical source available – the emotions and impressions of his personal experience. His works are in this sense 'fragments of a great confession'. Such personal poetry of protest at middle-class circumstance and official religion is intrinsically experimental. It goes in search of meaning through itself and understanding through others. That meant initially the middle-class readership. But Goethe soon discovered their limitations. For example, the middle-class hero of *Die Leiden des jungen Werthers* (*The sufferings of young Werther*, 1774) tries in his repressive religious, political and social environment to live out the faintly Bohemian, poetic alternative he finds in works of literature, and fails. He thus seems to suffer representatively for Goethe and his generation, and was taken as a figure of protest and identification. In truth, Werther misuses literature wilfully to transform reality into whatever fantasy happens to suit his fundamentally escapist subjectivism, whilst changing nothing. The novel in fact subverts its figure of protest and attacks its middle-class German readers.

The readers did not take the point, and Goethe took the logical step. In autumn 1775 the poet of middle-class protest accepted the Duke of Sachsen-Weimar's shilling as court-poet and tutor. Princely patronage removed the need to compromise with public taste, whereas Sachsen-Weimar, although an independent state, was almost laughably small and politically weak. The move to Weimar thus freed Goethe from two kinds of poetic servitude and allowed him to continue poetic experiments in relative peace. These became attempts at realising what Goethe came to call the objective or the classical. Yet the first decade at Weimar did not solve the problem. Goethe's situation before Schiller is characterised by his difficulty in finishing any serious work. Between 1776 and 1786 he began *Wilhelm Meisters theatralische Sendung* (*Wilhelm Meister's theatrical mission*), *Iphigenie auf Tauris*, (*Iphigenia in Tauris*), *Torquato Tasso*, *Faust* and *Egmont*, but completed none of them. Some of Goethe's creativity went into his work as minister, for roads, mines and the university at Jena. More went into his increasing interest in natural science, ranging from the theory of colour, to mineralogy, and plant and animal morphology. Both of these activities connote a shift towards the objective, and are thus milestones on the path to Schiller and Weimar classicism. But they are only symptoms of and compensations for the poetic problem, not its solution. The lack of one drove Goethe to Italy for the most famous unsanctioned sabbatical in German literary history from 1786 to 1788.

In Italy, as the *Italienische Reise* (*Italian journey*, 1816–17, 1829) describes, he seeks an art which transcends subjectivism, is open to plastic, sensual immediacy, and yet does not abandon his own idealistic tendency. He rejects introspection as a fatal tautologous illusion, formulating instead his lifelong conviction that self-knowledge is achieved only through observation of the subject's interaction with the objective world. He polemicises against Christian art, with its desire to transcend the concrete, sensual present and willingness to portray human mutilation, and studies antique, classical portrayals of the objective, idealised human form in sculpture. In Palladio, the Renaissance classical architect, he seems to discover the analogue of the modern classicism he strives for in poetry. Finally he calls himself reborn (the parallel with Schiller's metaphor of aesthetic baptism is not coincidental) and starts to complete the poetic torsos of the first Weimar decade.

Torquato Tasso, conceived in 1780, finished in 1789, marks the circle through which Goethe has moved. This 'Werther intensified' is decidedly subjective. But with its iambic pentameter blank verse and harmonious symmetry of form, *Tasso* represents a new synthesis. Intended as an objective, classical model for the new German theatre, it is one of the first examples of self-reflexive literature *about* literature. The passionate, pathologically sensitive Tasso is in his element at Duke Alfons's ideal Renaissance 'Musenhof', which sees itself as representing a frankly élitist maximum of humanistic culture. There is a precarious harmony between the inner world and the outer mode of his existence, from which he necessarily draws material, inspiration, and recognition. Here, Tasso need only be himself, write as he sees fit, and dedicate his work to his master. *Jerusalem Delivered* is aimed at this seemingly ideal courtly readership, and the loose parallel to Goethe's situation in Weimar is clear. But Tasso comes undone when his fiery temperament conflicts with the court mentality. In truth, the courtly audience does not understand his work, but sees him merely as an obstacle to personal success, an adornment of the court's representative culture, or a means to pleasurable self-affirmation. Thus *Torquato Tasso*, despite the poetic rebirth of the Italian journey, reveals the still unsolved problem of Goethe's own situation before Schiller. The middle-class world has been abandoned. The courtly now proves equally inadequate. A new audience, if it does not exist, must therefore be made.

Die Horen, Schiller's attempt simultaneously to elevate and to unify the fragmented and small readership of intellectual periodicals in Germany, must on this ground alone have appealed irresistibly to Goethe. Number six in 1795 is the most perfect example of the classical consensus at work. It contains the final instalment of the *Ästhetische Briefe,* which Goethe had read with admiration during their composition, and of which the ninth letter, with its picture of the classical poet, contains his portrait. But this issue also contains Goethe's *Römische Elegien (Roman elegies),* written in 1790 and withheld until now. The beautiful cerebrality of the *Ästhetische Briefe* is thus here complemented by the intellectualised sensuality of the *Elegien,* so that the issue, taken as a whole, encapsulates both the mutual co-operation of the two poets, with their characteristically different (theoretical and intuitive) approaches to the problem, and, in itself, the intended cultivation of human wholeness. In the *Römische Elegien* Goethe takes a classical metre (distichs of alternating hexameter and pentameter) to celebrate a particularly vivid aspect of his Roman period during the Italian journey: the discovery of sexuality, something notably repressed during the first Weimar decade, devoted as it was to the austere muse Charlotte von Stein. Here erotic love offers asylum in a warm southern climate to the persecuted northern poet. Spontaneity of desire and immediacy of fulfilment are seen as the recovery of antique wholeness. But, says the poet pointedly to his learned German readers, the celebration of eroticism is also study. In the fifth elegy he records with only a trace of higher frivolity how his tactile nights with Faustina actually further his visual study of antique form by day. The insight so obtained passes by another act of synaesthesia into the poetry, as he taps out the hexameters on his lover's back. In this realisation of the Italian experiences, the poetic rhythms not only represent, they enact objectively the sensual embraces described, and chiastic structures echo the dancing rhythm of Schiller's letters. Nor should we forget that this is a northern poet reviving a dead genre, and writing as a poet *about* poetry, so that the *Elegien* are truly, in Schiller's sense, a remarkable synthesis of modern reflexivity with antique spontaneity. The woman's role in this poetic achievement of wholeness is, however, notably passive.

Goethe had been the outsider in the literary market with *Werther* and the outsider at court with *Tasso.* The edition of collected works in 1790 had signalled his return to the market-place, and he seemed with the inclusion of the *Römische Elegien* in *Die Horen* at last to have found his element. Now, with his *Bildungsroman Wilhelm Meisters Lehrjahre* (*Wilhelm Meister's years of apprenticeship,* 1795–6), which he in turn passed to Schiller for critical assent, he adapted the market's major genre to the common cause of aesthetic education. It was to establish the epoch's dominant novel-paradigm.

The discontinued precursor of the *Lehrjahre*, *Wilhelm Meisters theatralische Sendung*, had been another reflection in literature about literature, which launched a young *Bürger* on the Goethean mission of creating a national theatre. The *Lehrjahre* ironise that mission. Here, Wilhelm's development features the familiar conflict of poetic humanism and middle-class professionalism. His encounters with women at various levels of sophistication symbolise gradual maturation and seem to culminate in the aesthetic mission. As a *Bürger,* defined solely by his work, Wilhelm becomes convinced that the theatre (an alternative synthesis of work and art) offers the only realistic medium of (evidently Schillerian) self-cultivation. When his pioneering production of *Hamlet* is swiftly removed from the repertoire for more commercial plays, Wilhelm recognises at last that the success is owed not to real talent but to fortuitous projection of his own character onto a similar, fictive personality – a vessel too weak to contain the vigorous growth planted in it by fate. Of course, his goal of a national theatre has been the projection of all that onto the limited possibilities of the real theatre and public. This seems like the end of the project of aesthetic education before it has begun.

It turns out that a secret Society of the Tower – plot-machinery adapted from the popular novel – has manipulated Wilhelm's life to just this end. As he is initiated into its higher truths, a rainbow (like that which greets Noah as he renews the covenant with God after the baptismal Flood) suggests that the Society is the modern renewer of the divine covenant, possessor, no less, of Lessing's promised new evangel. But what is the new evangel? The Society is philanthropic and idealistic, but also unrepentently practical and utilitarian. Typically, Lothario is a modern democratic capitalist with patriarchal leanings who believes in purposeful risk-taking investment, equal taxation for the common good and equal rights of ownership as a motivation to productive activity. All members of the society (by contrast to Wilhelm's vision of individual wholeness) have accepted the division of labour and fragmentation of personality that is the signature of modernity. Only *as* a society, in mutual complementarity, do they represent a fully rounded humanity. The theatrical mission has retained its philanthropic orientation and secularised religious intensity, but it seems, as Novalis said, to have become an 'Evangelium der Oeconomie' ('gospel of utility').

Art does however have a place. The sale of the family art-collection by Wilhelm's father had signalled the anthropological poverty of his early life. That the Society, in the person of Natalie, should be revealed as its present custodian, suggests that the aesthetic ideal has been recuperated into the Society's ideology. Natalie, the 'beautiful Amazon' who first appears on horseback in a man's coat and devotes herself to social service, suggests that the synthesis of the beautiful and the useful in an *internal-*

ised mode (by contrast to the theatre) is the mainspring of the Society's utilitarian mission. She becomes Wilhelm's betrothed and the novel seems, after all, to have arrived at a solid, more-or-less Schillerian position.

Yet hidden in its glossy surface are contradictory indicators. In the end, the Society disperses around the globe to continue the good work. Wilhelm does not join them. It turns out that his *Bildung* has still come to nothing. The most intense irony involves the epoch's most resonant symbol of poetic humanism. As the hint of masculinisation in the term 'Amazon' suggests, Natalie evokes the humanistic ideal of androgynous wholeness. This symbol of human fulfilment through mutual complementarity derives from *Genesis* (Adam, before the removal of the rib and the race's expulsion from paradise, is androgynous) and Plato's *Symposium* (where the comic poet Aristophanes uses it to explain sexual desire). For all that Natalie remains wan and the irony lies in the fate of another, the epoch's most famous androgyne, young Mignon. Wilhelm's constant companion, this girl in a trouser suit prefigures Natalie's role. But above all she personifies, with unequalled textual charisma, living poetry. When she expires in the Society's innermost sanctum, the 'Hall of the Past', it becomes clear that she and its ambiguous utopia are mutually exclusive. The Society's intended homage – Mignon is embalmed, made into her own monument and integrated into the Society's art-collection – is crassly tragi-comic. Living poetry and the synthesis of the beautiful and useful which is the classical remedy for modernity's ills in fact do not mix. Goethe remains to this extent an esoteric outsider of the classical consensus. Did we not know the intensity of co-operation between Goethe and Schiller that went into it, we should see the *Lehrjahre* as a critique of the *Ästhetische Briefe*. The ambiguities are, however, so deeply buried, or so irreducible, that few contemporary readers could fathom them. The novel's frequent reception – critics speak of Wilhelm Meister's brothers – is thus a chain of productive misunderstandings.

But the vast majority did not read *Wilhelm Meisters Lehrjahre*. Typical of the novels they read instead – by such as Benedikte Naubert, August Lafontaine, Karl Grosse or Heinrich Zschokke – is *Rinaldo Rinaldini der Räuber Hauptmann. Eine romantische Geschichte unsers Jahrhunderts* (*Rinaldo Rinaldini, robber captain. A romantic tale of our century*, 1799–1800) by Christian August Vulpius (1762–1827). *Rinaldo*, perhaps the age's bestseller, was once a byword for triviality, but is not without merit. It is, for a time, an exciting adventure tale featuring an anti-hero, modelled on Schiller's Karl Moor, with more than one dimension to his personality. Once a simple goatherd, Rinaldo is educated for higher things. However his fiery temperament leads to insubordination and murder, so that he must become a robber. Inwardly noble (albeit ruthless), he plunders only the rich and powerful. No woman is safe from his wooing. Otherwise fearless, his great enemy is his troubled conscience. He yearns to return to the innocent idyll of his youth but is doomed, Macbeth-like, to continue on his path in the identity not his own. *Rinaldo* takes up central obsessions of the age. One of the robbers is an Amazon, Fiorilla, who bravely goes to her death for him. Rinaldo too has his androgynous Mignon, Rosalie. Most prominent in the second half is however Rinaldo's semi-religious sense of fatal powerlessness. The sinister 'Old Man of Fronteja', an omniscient seer, adept of the Egyptian mysteries, magician and revolutionary, seems to have manipulated Rinaldo's life. He urges Rinaldo to lead a revolution against the French occupation of Corsica, but at last – perhaps provoked by Rinaldo's loyalty to the King – kills him. (Vulpius later resurrected him for a continuation of the novel.) Rinaldo thus – satisfyingly for the readers – combines revolutionary ideals with final rejection of revolution and religious piety with a sense that all religion is a fraud. Finally, all this palls. Vulpius cannot resist repeating familiar effects (erotic *frissons* and sudden unmaskings of Rinaldo's incognito), so that the thin veneer of engagement with fundamental themes is soon exposed as such.

Hermann und Dorothea (1798), inspired by Johann Heinrich Voß's Enlightenment epic *Luise* (1782–4) and hexameter idylls from the 1770s such as 'Die Leibeigenen' ('The serfs') and 'Die Freigelassenen' ('The emancipated ones'), is Goethe's first attempt seriously to treat the French Revolution and popularise the classical epic. Where however Voß, rejecting even the mildest patriarchal versions of feudalism, had extolled revolutionary ideals in the cause of peasants' emancipation from tyrannical Junker lords, Goethe portrays the Revolution as a threat. Here the left bank of the Rhine is in French hands and, whilst the French have been expelled from Georg Forster's Mainz, a column of German refugees, driven away by the chaos of war, limps in the fierce late autumn heat past the prosperous Rhenish home of Hermann's family. Calling to mind the fragile nature of human institutions – they themselves suffered a disastrous fire a mere twenty years since – the good *Bürger* succour the needy. Hermann, son of the local innkeeper (and named after the great German general, conqueror of the Romans in AD 9), suddenly realises he has fallen in love with a lone woman refugee, the Amazonian Dorothea. He must act before the column moves on. Thus the main drama involves overcoming his father's resistance to the unexpected betrothal. This gives Goethe the opportunity for heart-warming portrayals of family solidarity, the constructive support of neighbours and the mediation of the local pastor, all of which symbolises the essential solidity of traditional German socio-political values and institutions in the face of cultural crisis. Dorothea, it turns out, is alone because her first betrothed, misled by noble ideals, died in the tumult of Revolutionary Paris. Her espousal of the solid *Bürger*

Hermann symbolises the renewal of old values. The Revolution is thus portrayed as an error, an ideal which paradoxically unleashes the animal in human nature. The Rhine must remain Germany's bulwark. Goethe's counter-Revolutionary ideals – family values (the Amazon Dorothea sees her role as housewife), stability, and continuity – reveal his basic conservatism (not to be identified with reaction), and tendency (evinced by the parallel with the fire) to see the Revolution in terms of natural science rather than as historical necessity. This charming and deceptively complex idyll was Goethe's only strictly classical work to be popular.

What, in the meantime, was Schiller's poetic contribution to the classical humanist project? As far as he was concerned, the novelist was (with the exception of Goethe) only the half-brother of the true poet. While Goethe wrote the novel, then, Schiller wrote the plays. That did not mean plays embodying the kind of beauty the *Ästhetische Briefe* talked of. It meant tragedy, and a refinement of his aesthetics. In the *Ästhetische Briefe* he had posited that the idea of beauty was never quite realised as such. Either form or matter predominates, so that beauty, in 'melting' or 'energetic' realisation, tends to relax or excite. The *Ästhetische Briefe* however managed to treat only the former. *Über das Erhabene* (*On the sublime*), published in 1801 but dating from the late 1790s, fills the gap, where the bracing effect of energetic beauty should have come, with a theory of tragic affect. This, Schiller now says, necessarily complements beauty and functions as the next stage in the aesthetic education of humanity. For beauty, he claims, only gives us one kind of freedom: enjoyment of our latent disposition to freedom *in* nature, but not active freedom, the transcendence by ethical action *of* nature. The sublime is precisely that feeling. It occurs only in situations of extreme conflict, so that where beauty is harmony, the sublime presupposes disharmony. For example, the structure of a wild gigantic mountain range, or the vast ethical chaos that is history defy comprehension and throw the mind back on its innermost resources. Reason, its highest faculty, forms in reaction the idea of infinity, so that this very act, whilst not overcoming nature *as* nature, is the realisation of our own inner freedom and fundamental independence *of* nature. Hence opposite emotions typical of Aristotelian tragedy are simultaneously generated. When we confront the tragic spectacle of an heroic individual crushed by fate, fear or terror is accompanied by moral pleasure at the inner triumph of personality over physical catastrophe. In this, the sublime is a fuller realisation of human destiny than the experience of beauty. This concession to dualism is the Ariadne's thread of the superb historical tragedies Schiller produced in constant consultation with Goethe from 1799 to 1805 and so defines Schiller's contribution to the classical project. If *Wilhelm Meisters Lehrjahre* offer the paradigm of the novel for the epoch, *Wallenstein* (1799–1800), *Maria Stuart* (1801) and *Die*

Jungfrau von Orleans (*The Maid of Orleans*, 1801) do the same for tragedy.

The eponymous hero of *Wallenstein*, the great general of the Thirty Years War (1618–48), seems an odd choice for a Schillerian tragic hero. He is a titan, but not a sublime character. A materialistic calculator, who, imprisoned in his symbolic observation tower, depends on the astrologer Seni's advice, he is perhaps Schiller's attempt to follow Goethe's thematic realism. The astrology motif, as Goethe saw, skilfully opens up a dimension of universal significance to the otherwise earthbound action. The play's central issues are, however, political and ethical. The political issue (not coincidentally at the time of the Wars of Coalition) is German unity, projected onto a Baroque scene. Wallenstein, general of the imperial Catholic party, fights for the old order against the Protestant armies of Gustavus Adolphus. Yet his very being threatens all that. This echo of the rising general Bonaparte is modern: cynical, pragmatic, and religiously indifferent, a disciple of nature and determinism. He is loyal only to himself, and his self-legitimating power is the standing army, whose loyalty to him is an equally pragmatic mixture of admiration for his leadership qualities and reliance on his track record. When Wallenstein ostensibly negotiates peace with the Swedes, he is really toying with high treason. He will negotiate detailed agreements, although he will not put them in writing, and even then, with Hamlet-like reluctance born of final uncertainty, avoids translating word into deed. Ironically, when mere suspicion of intent is confirmed, this makes him as guilty as if he had done the deed (a telling parallel with the Terror). It thus compels him to attempt it. The rebellion fails, but signifies, for all that, the effective destruction of imperial authority. The old order prevails. No one believes in it, but no one can change it. *Wallenstein* enacts the identity-crisis of modern Germany.

The two generals Piccolomini provide the moral foil to this. Having consulted the planets, the constitutional doubter Wallenstein nevertheless also demands from his generals a written pledge of unconditional loyalty to himself. Since the actual document differs from the original (a complementary pledge of loyalty to the Emperor is omitted), the idealistic Max Piccolomini refuses. His father Octavio, accepting fatal compromise, both signs and betrays Wallenstein, but Max, ironically, is bound by loyalty and love for Wallenstein's daughter Thekla. He rejects both Wallenstein and Octavio. Choosing honourable death in battle, he accepts fatal necessity but overcomes it on a higher plane. Max thus embodies the sublime. When Wallenstein can fathom neither Max's loyalty nor Octavio's disloyalty, the world seems out of joint to his calculating realism. All that remains is for him to be betrayed and murdered by Buttler's men. There seems no alternative to Max's idealistic self-sacrifice, Octavio's unscrupulous principle, and Wallenstein's brutal pragmatism. The resultant spectacle of awesome historical chaos is the sense in which the play as a whole evokes the tragic sublime. It is the essence of Schiller's philosophy of history.

Maria Stuart, a drama of strong women, reaffirms idealism and is thus the clearer paradigm of the historical drama that will dominate the epoch. Maria has acquiesced in Darnley's murder, prevented Bothwell's conviction, and intrigued to depose Elisabeth. But she has not plotted Elisabeth's death, which is the ground of her condemnation. The source of tragedy is Maria's fatal combination of charismatic beauty and moral weakness. If Mary is the woman who yearns to be queen, Elisabeth is the queen who yearns to be a woman. She lives the interests of state, unable or unwilling to marry, and thus suffers perpetual sexual jealousy of Maria, which is sublimated into moral contempt. An inkling of this prompts her (Wallenstein-like) calculating indecision. Maria must die. But Elisabeth is tortured by pragmatic and (unlike Wallenstein) moral scruple. The confrontation of queens in Act III is decisive. Maria, abandoning political ambition, humbly pleads for her life. Elisabeth provokes her rival, but is finally crushed by the spectacle of Maria's passionate and glowing womanhood. She signs the death warrant, but even then (again, like Wallenstein) leaves unclear whether the clerk Davison is to turn word into deed. As Leicester – Maria's lover all along – leaves for France, Elisabeth's political triumph is accompanied by her moral and sexual destruction. *Maria Stuart* is classically symmetrical in structure. Two acts of hope and two of despair ring the central confrontation. Maria (passionate, beautiful, weak yet strong) and Elisabeth (calculating, plain, strong yet weak) are complementary opposites. Elisabeth's rise to political greatness contrasts with her slide into moral corruption, Maria's fall from worldly power with her inner purification and moral elevation. The play is also brilliantly theatrical. Beheaded just off-stage, Maria's spiritual presence, channelled through the betrayer Leicester, palpably fills the deserted stage. It is the essence of the sublime.

Die Jungfrau von Orleans. Eine romantische Tragödie (*The Maid of Orleans. A romantic tragedy*, 1801) anticipates deep changes in the Apolline cosmopolitan humanism of the Weimar writers after Schiller's death. It features another strong woman, but is far more Shakespearean (with battles, a ghost, miracles, and so on). In invaded and divided France, the simple peasant girl Johanna recognises her divine mission to transcend nature, assume a manly role, defend Orleans and unify the nation. She succeeds, but again the conflict of womanly nature and political role prompts tragedy. The mission entails sexual abstinence, yet she falls in love with the English knight Lionel, and is expelled from the French forces. In a terrifying symbolic storm she accepts and overcomes her guilt. Captured, she breaks her chains. As the French finally triumph, she dies, not at the stake, but transfigured by the national flags draped over her.

Schiller, we see, is still occupied by women at odds with their traditional role. Johanna is even more Amazonian than Elisabeth. More important, the sublime has modulated here to accommodate a religious and patriotic accentuation, in which medieval France is a thinly veiled modern Germany. Johanna's death and transfiguration are a secularised and militarised self-sacrifice by one of the common people to redeem a divided nation. Aesthetic education, symbolised by the troubadour King Réné, has been consigned to a by-way of history. Equally significant, as Johanna's struggle to establish the legitimacy of her legendary mission with her own side suggests, is the play's function as a pioneering reflection on the power of myth in modern culture. Zacharias Werner and Clemens Brentano will take up this thread. In the Wars of Liberation, other Romantics – Theodor Körner, Friedrich de la Motte-Fouqué, and Kleist – will show the extremes to which the synthesis of religious, mythical and patriotic energies could be taken.

Against this background, what of Enlightenment and women's writing? The educated classes quite liked Schiller on stage. They liked Goethe less (especially *Iphigenie* and *Tasso*). But they loved August von Kotzebue. The very title of his 'Schauspiel' (a sentimental comedy) *Menschenhaß und Reue* (*Misanthropy and contrition*, 1790) evidences Kotzebue's Enlightenment humanism. Misanthropy much engaged philanthropic Enlightenment thinkers, notably the philosophical doctor Johann Georg Zimmermann, whose popular, anthropologically orientated *Über die Einsamkeit* (*On solitude*, 1784–5) had influenced Goethe's portrait of Tasso. Zimmermann himself treated Kotzebue for melancholy, and Baron Meinau, the problematic hero of the play, reads *Über die Einsamkeit*. The heroine Eulalia exemplifies Kotzebue's debt to Lessing. She, like Sara Sampson, is a guilty and contrite woman, but will not accept forgiveness. Married at fourteen, she leaves Meinau for another (who leaves her). Meinau, still in love, gives his children into care (they resemble Eulalia) and retreats into melancholy solitude. But he remains a secret philanthropist. Eulalia enters service with a Count as the middle-class 'Madame Müller' and becomes a paragon of virtue. When chance and their common philanthropy cause their paths to cross again, it would seem reasonable to remake the marriage. Yet Kotzebue puts up theatrically effective hindrances. Quite apart from Eulalia's brittleness, Meinau (like Lessing's Tellheim) makes honour an obstacle to reconciliation, and the Count's brother Major von der Horst is determined, irrespective of class-barriers, to marry her. The knot is untangled when it turns out that Meinau and the Major are old friends. The Major renounces his claim, arranges for the ex-partners to meet and, since words fail, produces the children. Both practical and principled objections to the reconciliation are thereby dissolved in general goodwill, and the play ends with the moving tableau of a family embrace. *Menschenhaß und Reue* typifies Kotzebue's good and bad qualities. The situation is well established and skilfully resolved. No one had rescued marriage from adultery on stage before, and audiences were pleasantly shocked. Yet the imperative of a happy ending precludes real engagement with the issues. Meinau convinces neither as misanthrope nor depressive. No utopian marriage across the class-barrier with 'Madame Müller' could ever have occurred, and the moral problem of forgiveness/divorce is merely dissolved. Thus Kotzebue was rightly attacked for lack of a moral standpoint whilst people continued to attend his plays in large numbers. They were ideal entertainment for 'barbarians'. Kotzebue's 230 plays (he lost count) dominated the stage, together with those of the Berlin state theatre director August Iffland, for the entire epoch. Against this, then, aesthetic education had to compete.

One would expect the emancipatory anthropology of classicism to promote women's creativity. Goethe's and Schiller's works are full of strong women. Almost every positive female figure in *Wilhelm Meisters Lehrjahre*, from the Chlorinde admired by Wilhelm in Tasso's *Jerusalem Delivered*, to Mariane in her officer's uniform, Therese in her hunter's suit, Mignon and Natalie, possesses androgyne or Amazonian attributes. Women are even admitted to government in the actors' republic of *Wilhelm Meisters Lehrjahre*. Goethe's Iphigenie personifies the strong woman whose words, unlike men's swords, redeem an entire cursed generation. Hermann's Dorothea takes a sabre to some robbers when the menfolk draw back. Eugenie, in Goethe's *Die natürliche Tochter* (*The natural daughter*), is an energetic horse-riding Amazon who personifies the ideal state. We have seen how Schiller features such women. Yet when we seek these idealizing tendencies in the sphere of productivity, the classical view changes. In Schiller's ostensibly humorous poem 'Die berühmte Frau' ('The woman of renown', 1789), one husband complains to another about his wife. The man whose wife has merely been unfaithful, is lucky. Far worse, his own wife has become a successful writer who neglects him, her household duties and her children to bask in fame. The marital paradise is destroyed. It is all contrary to nature, she is 'A *strong* mind in a *frail* body, / A hybrid thing of man and woman'. There is a limit, then, to the Amazonisation of women in classical humanism. Women, it would seem, can *be* ideals, or be *portrayed* as ideals, but they cannot *write* them, or – unless we count Mignon – be portrayed *as* writers.

Intended to distinguish true artists from false, the collaborative theory of dilettantism (1797–9) makes the Classicist exclusion of women from aesthetic creativity explicit. The dilettante, whilst cultivated, is merely a passive recipient of the aesthetic message. Unfortunately, he fancies himself capable of production. Dilettantism has positive side-effects (it improves self-expression), but it also, fatally, sets imitation in place of originality. Dilettantish works express only content or typify mere mechanical perfection. This seems innocuous, but when Goethe and Schiller establish the category 'women's dilettantism' they disqualify the entire sex from aesthetic originality. In this, they reflect the anthropology of Wilhelm von Humboldt's influential essay (also in *Die Horen*) *Über den Geschlechtsunterschied und dessen Einfluß auf die organische Natur* (*Sexual difference and its influence on organic nature*, 1795). Here Humboldt preaches the androgynous ideal of complementarity. Yet he also defines essential differences. The male is all disharmonious striving, form and concentrated productive energy, the female harmonious wholeness, matter and enfolding receptivity. Thus the male monopolises productivity, and Humboldt continues the Rousseauistic tradition of emphasising the abstract equality of the sexes whilst prescribing different 'natural' roles for them. The aesthetic analogue of this anthropology is the dark side of classical humanism.

By and large the women of our epoch, with only the Enlightenment traditions of woman as model of natural virtue or monster of unnatural wit on which to draw, had to accept such classification. Publication was possible only under the category of dilettantish production and usually, as with Sophie La Roche's *Geschichte des Fräuleins von Sternheim* (*The history of Lady Sophia Sternheim*, 1771), after a man's preface (here, Wieland's). Women wrote much, but only in these received terms, for and about women, and, in general, in the lesser form of the (usually epistolary) novel. Wilhelmine Karoline von Wobeser's anonymously published *Elisa oder das Weib wie es seyn sollte* (*Elisa, or woman as she ought to be*, 1795), a didactic novel of female manners, is typical of the 'women's genre', and, with four editions by 1799, the most successful. Here we have the 'woman's' theme of marriage and the triumph of Elisa over adversity. Elisa renounces her beloved in favour of a loveless marriage. She rescues that marriage after her husband's adultery for the children's sake. In the process, she educates both men to moral perfection. Elisa is thus the paradigm of Enlightenment womanhood as internalised by Enlightenment woman. A rationalist, she is cleverer than anyone in the novel save her father. She rejects the doctrine of personal immortality and approves the Revolution's ideals of freedom and equality, but, like Schiller and Goethe, rejects institutional in favour of individual change, so that the ideals are to be realised through individuals living out exemplary virtues. From the philosophical insight into her place in the great chain of being derives the definition of her destiny as the imperative to do the maximum good under the given conditions of her womanly nature. Fulfilment for Elisa involves nothing more than acceptance of her nature, subordination to the man in marriage (whatever his weaknesses and whims may be), and perfect role-playing as wife, housekeeper and mother, with all concrete action limited to the wife's cultivation of the man. Wobeser (1769–1807) followed her own philosophy when, on marrying in 1799, she ceased further publication. Writing and marriage are mutually exclusive. Wobeser's lack of participation in public life before or after, like most women writers, ensured her future obscurity.

Many thought Wobeser's novel the work of a man. The publicist Christian August Fischer sought to profit with a sequel, *Ueber den Umgang der Weiber mit Männern* (*Conduct for women in masculine company*, 1800), in which the role-models are refined still further. It is therefore fitting that one of the outstanding woman writers of the epoch, Caroline Auguste Fischer (1764–1842), should be his ex-wife. She left Fischer in 1809 to build an independent (but failed) writer's existence. Before abandoning the profession in 1820, she wrote fine epistolary novels, from the sentimental *Gustavs Verirrungen* (*Gustav's progress*, 1801), to the novel of courtly intrigue *Der Günstling* (*The favourite*, 1808) and the *Künstlerroman Margarethe* (1812), plus *Kleine Erzählungen* (*Short stories*, 1818). All display a feminist talent for exposing anthropological stereotypes. The ironically titled *Die Honigmonathe* (*The honeymoon*, 1802), written shortly before she married, takes up the standard 'women's' themes, but is a lively and subversive engagement with the dominant stereotypes. It stands at the apex of the developments in sexual politics we have described. Julie and Wilhelmine, termed a 'schöne Seele' and an Amazon, represent the two stereotypes of female behaviour: the submissive Elisa-like figure, and the apparently dominant, masculinised rebel. Wilhelmine (named perhaps after Goethe's hero) is an enemy of men and marriage, who compares the role demanded by *Elisa* of women with the slavery of blacks in America, whom planters reconcile to their fate with the promise of a reward in heaven. There are traces of protest in Julie: she complains how hard it is to write whilst performing domestic duties. But Julie (perhaps named after Rousseau's heroine) accepts her received, 'natural' role as the moral perfecter of the coarser sex and, under protest from Wilhelmine, marries. The emergence of a handsome rival rouses her sensuality after all. The death of both men and Julie's subsequent celibacy defuse the conflict, but this suffices to undermine the stereotype. The Amazon fares no better. Having accused Julie of betraying her sex, she warms increasingly to marriage, produces a theory that no marriage should be contracted for longer than five years (which uncannily anticipates Goethe's thoughts in *Die Wahlverwandtschaften*), and finally marries a young countryman. Too little is done to motivate Wilhelmine's decision. Fischer evidently offers no alternative. But she also accepts neither stereotype. In this, she steps quite outside the conceptual framework of the age.

Jena romanticism

If Schiller's *Horen* is the centre of classical humanism in courtly Weimar, the rival literary journal *Athenaeum* (1798–1800) of August Wilhelm and Friedrich Schlegel, whose base was in the nearby university town of Jena, is the centre of the sister movement Romanticism. With the exception of the philosopher Johann Gottlieb Fichte and the Berlin poets Ludwig Tieck and Wilhelm Heinrich Wackenroder, everyone who was anyone in early Romanticism wrote for *Athenaeum:* chiefly the Schlegels, their wives Caroline and Dorothea, Friedrich von Hardenberg (Novalis), and the theologian, preacher and philosopher Friedrich Schleiermacher. Schiller was their great bugbear. There had been much early collaboration with the classicists. August Wilhelm wrote essays on Shakespeare and prosody for *Die Horen,* and Friedrich, known as a scholar of classical poetry, wished to. Goethe took August Wilhelm's advice when crafting the distichs of the *Römische Elegien.* But Friedrich's disrespectful reviews of *Die Horen* and Schiller's *Musenalmanach* of 1796 highlighted tactlessly the abstract quality of Schiller's lyrics, so that Schiller broke relations with both. Hence *Athenaeum,* which scarcely mentioned Schiller, was founded. At bottom, the Schlegels wished to break the classical alliance and appropriate Goethe to their own version of the aesthetic consensus. Goethe, at least in the early numbers of *Athenaeum,* is thus held up as a model. After Schiller, the early Romantics are his greatest champions, so that Goethe between both groups is for this brief moment truly the centre of German literature at the time.

Schiller is nonetheless formidably present in the explosion of creative energy which is early Romanticism, notably through his Rousseauistic essay *Über naive und sentimentalische Dichtung* (*On naive and reflective poetry,* 1795–6), which develops the familiar contrast of antique and modern, harmonious and divided human nature into an historical typology. A child, for example, is naive. It exists solely to exist, in harmonious spontaneity indifferent to what is outside its sphere. The contrast with sophisticated adult consciousness amuses the prosaic understanding. But reason is deeply affected. It grasps that the child exemplifies a kind of perfection which the reflective adult has lost forever. Classical Greek culture, as in the *Ästhetische Briefe* and Schiller's elegy 'Die Götter Griechenlands' ('The gods of Greece', 1787), exemplifies in history the childlike unity of culture and nature. Alienated modern humanity yearns for the naive, as a sick man for health. But it is also an aesthetic category. For Schiller now makes the poet into the committed advocate of the lost natural unity in the historical process (a role as cultural outsider he still plays). Modern poetry can either continue bearing witness to nature by being true to the lost unity, or it can avenge the loss. Only the first, poetry of sensual presence, is naive. The second (nothing to do with *Empfindsamkeit)* is 'sentimental': reflective poetry of ideas. We recognise the classical duo in the typology, which is to this extent ahistorical. The reflective poet has an aesthetic problem. Where the naive poet objectively imitates nature, the reflective poet, divided as he and his world are, can only imitate the *idea* of the lost object. He must elevate prosaic reality to the status of the lost ideal from his inner, speculative resources (this is the origin of nonmimetic poetry). What kind of sentimental poet he is depends on his emotional relation to the lost ideal. From this flows a whole generic system. If he tends to negate reality, he prefers the satiric mode, which includes both tragedy (inner overcoming of threatening circumstance) and comedy (harmonisation of adversity). If he inclines to the once and future ideal, the mode is elegaic, which contains the idyll (recovery of the lost ideal) and the elegy proper (mourning for its loss). The sentimental idyll is the positive goal of modern poetry. Schiller's essay thus culminates in a programme of cultural progress led by the poet, in a characteristic three-phase rhythm of ideal, alienation and recovery at a higher level. This secularised and poeticised version of a familiar Christian figure, the lost and future paradise, dominates Romantic thinking on the historical role of the poet.

Romanticism has many sources, including Novalis's reception of Fichte's 'Wissenschaftslehre' ('theory of knowledge') and Tieck's of Herder's plea for the renewal of Germanic folk literature. But Friedrich Schlegel (1772–1829) is the mainspring, and his reception of Schiller more vital. He takes over the conviction of poetry's historical mission, the search for the new, sentimental Elysium. Of it he and Novalis make a myth which dominates the thinking of Romantics and connected figures such as Kleist, Hölderlin and Jean Paul. But Schlegel did not see himself primarily as a poet. Even more important is the new concept of the creative critic which he derives from Schiller's opposition of classicicity and reflection.

Schlegel too saw the model of modern humanity in 'naive' Greek culture and the lost ideal as embodied by classical Greek literature. But Schlegel also derived from the Göttingen classical scholar F. A. Wolf a lesson for modern theorists. For Wolf had argued that the core texts of Greek literature, the *Iliad* and *Odyssey*, were in fact not uniquely by Homer. His originals had been compiled, edited and modified by other poets and the so-called 'Diaskeuasten' (reflective critics). From this Schlegel drew a momentous conclusion: that much of Homer's poetic perfection was owed to the reflection of those critics, whose creativity had been greatly undervalued. Classicism and reflectivity are thus intimately connected even at their origin. Schlegel identified with the 'Diaskeuast'. Schiller's notion of the 'sentimental' was based on his conviction that reflectivity, as the character of modernity, meant gain as well as loss. Schlegel's notion of the critic is the radicalised modification thereof. This is the deeper source of his rivalry with Schiller, but also the foundation of Romanticism, for Romanticism's major concepts are nothing more (nor less) than the product of Schlegel's critical reflection on the role of poetry as defined by Classical Humanism. Despite the sometimes bitter polemic Romanticism is thus in substance not opposition to Classicism so much as insistent radicalisation of its convictions and achievements. Theory is the engine of early Romanticism. Paradoxically, this love of reflection is also a continuation of Enlightenment intellectualism.

All this occasions a new Romantic understanding of text and genre. Homer's canonical work, if not finished when he wrote it, must have been a fragment. It is thus not a static object embodying the ideal, so much as a dynamic object constantly progressing towards further perfections, a process primarily motivated by critical discourse. The relationship between text and criticism becomes an unending yet progressive dialogue of equals, neither of which alone is 'Poesie'. The act of reading acquires productive dignity. The critic is a reader who recreates the original in a further refinement. Poetry can only be criticised by poetry. The classical notion of text as closed and unified is thus replaced with a more open, romantic concept (modern in quite another sense), in which the centre is constantly being displaced. Correspondingly, the received notion of single authorship is relativised, and the Romantics set up 'Sympoesie' or 'Symphilosophie' as their radicalised version of the co-operation between Schiller and Goethe. *Athenaeum* is its first literary fruit, the Jena, Berlin and Dresden literary circles its social realisation.

Even more radical: a fragment is most perfect when it also signals its inevitably fragmentary character. Such absolute poetry is more than either Schiller's naive poetry or sentimental idyll. There are two ways of achieving this. Acceptance of the inevitable disproportion between intended and actual meaning suggests a short, epigrammatic form – Chamfort and Lichtenberg are models – which through implication and provocation stimulates the otherwise passive reader productively to complete the text. The Romantic 'Fragment', a new kind of aphorism, is the result. Every fragment, says Schlegel in the 'Fragment' which (as 'Poesie der Poesie') defines the genre, must be self-contained and inwardly perfect, like a rolled-up hedgehog (*Athenaeums-Fragmente*, No. 206). Rolled up, it is a living microcosmic symbol of totality. Yet its spiny exterior provokes to further reflection. Fragment-collections, immensely complex generators of ideas usually by several hands, are one basic form of expression in early Romanticism. They are the Romantic alternative in modern, shaped prose to the *Xenien* in Goethe's and Schiller's classical monodistichs, and have the same publicistic function. Schlegel's first attempt at the new genre were the *Kritische Fragmente* (1797). *Athenaeum* contains over 450 sympoetical *Athenaeums-Fragmente* (1798), followed by Novalis's *Blüthenstaub* (*Pollen*, 1798) and Schlegel's *Ideen* (*Ideas*, 1800).

Another way to signal fragmentary status is Romantic Irony. Ordinary rhetorical irony signals at a given point that the opposite of the ostensible meaning is intended. Since Romanticism understands the entire text as an inherently unstable structure of constitutive provisionality, Romantic Irony demands its creative self-destruction, which occurs through the mirroring of the text by the text *as a whole*. This is a radicalised modern version of classical Socratic irony, the paradoxical mode of knowing the limits of human knowledge in which Plato's wisdom culminates. Schlegel, emphasising equally the humoristic disproportion connoted by this deflationary practice and its absolutist pretentions, calls it 'transzendentale Buffonerie' ('transcendental buffoonery') (*Kritische Fragmente*, No. 42). A direct line can be drawn from here to postmodern textual theory, although it is wrong to ascribe the postmodern sense of metaphysical void to the yearning for metaphysical plenitude which Romantic Irony connotes. The Romantic concept of text is like Romanticism itself: Janus-faced, the part-modern, part-traditional product of the *Sattelzeit*. However, Romantic Irony is not a genre, and not aphoristic fragments but novels, says Schlegel, are the Socratic dialogues of our age (*Kritische Fragmente*, No. 26). The romantic novel, their favourite genre, is the Romantics' embodiment of Schlegel's postulated self-reflective absolute poetry. Schlegel does not mean a conventional novel like *Rinaldo Rinaldini* or *Elisa*. A *Kritisches Fragment* (No. 62) had already asked why there were theories of each individual genre, but no absolute generic theory of poetry. This the famous *Athenaeums-Fragment* No. 116 provides. It is a startling contrast to the normative theories of drama, novel, fairy-tale and novella Goethe and Schiller were producing, and, above all, to Schiller's notion of the sentimental idyll as the task of modern poetry. Where Goethe and Schiller discriminated painstakingly, Schlegel mixed. Romantic poetry, he says, is progressive universal poetry. It synthesises all the previously separate genres (epic, lyric, dramatic, rhetorical and other). It is subjective and objective, confessional and realistic, tragic and comic, classical (in the narrow sense) and modern. Above all it is self-reflective, for in this sovereign self-referentiality lies the perfection of poetry and what Schlegel on the basis of his Homeric studies can call 'grenzenlos wachsende Klassizität' ('limitlessly expanding Classicicity'). The absolute book which the ironic Romantic novel is has been conceived, if not yet born.

Schiller had already shown that one modern poet, Goethe, could embody naive themes in a sentimental form. But where he drew no conclusions from this ahistorical mixture of ancient and modern, Schlegel saw in

Wilhelm Meisters Lehrjahre the exemplary synthesis of classicism and reflectivity needed to confirm his theory. Hence Goethe preoccupies the *Athenaeum* in 1798. The French Revolution, Fichte's 'Wissenschaftslehre', and Goethe's *Meister* are the three greatest tendencies of the age. In his attempt to be Goethe's 'Diaskeuast', the *Athenaeum* essay *Über Goethes Meister* (*On Goethe's 'Meister'*, 1798), he argues that the novel embodies a classical message (wholeness of personality) in a modern form. Even in its treatment of aesthetic education it is self-reflective and ironic. This, and the capricious combination of tragic and comic elements in the last two books, makes Goethe's novel in generic terms much more than a conventional novel. It is the sovereign play of the author's poetic intellect with itself, the self-celebration and therefore the maximum of 'Poesie'. We can see here how Schiller's innocuous stylisation of the poet as the missionary healer of modern humanity has become an autonomous myth of 'Poesie'. Schlegel must have seen that this does justice neither to Goethe's novel nor Romantic theory. *Athenaeum* thus contains in *Brief über den Roman* (*Letter on the novel*, 1800) another, the last definition of the Romantic novel, as *the* Romantic book. It transcends genre and embodies a sentimental theme in a fantastic form, the arabesque or hieroglyph. That is, material is to be ordered into complex symbolic forms which allude ironically to the inexpressible absolute rather than attempt prosaically to embody it. Goethe is not mentioned. *Brief über den Roman* and *Lucinde* mark a parting of the ways for him and the Romantics which lasts until after Schiller's death in 1805.

Lucinde (1799) is Schlegel's attempt at a model Romantic novel. When Julius unexpectedly finds Lucinde absent, he decides to embody their love in writing. The text is thus both poetic compensation for the lost idyll and ironically reflects the conditions of its own production. Julius exercises his sovereign right to order material as creative caprice sees fit, but the form is not chaotic. A central section, *Lehrjahre der Männlichkeit* (*Apprenticeship to manhood*), narrates his progression (as Wilhelm Meister's brother) through a series of affairs with women who lead him towards the goal of 'Lebenskunst', until Lucinde perfects his life and art. This is ringed symmetrically by non-narrative sections (six before, six after), which embody variations on Julius's and Lucinde's love in diverse genres (dialogue, idyll, letter). The resultant representation of love is the first Romantic arabesque. It develops the digressive technique established by Laurence Sterne in *Tristram Shandy* and adapted by Jean Paul.

If *Lucinde* treats the conventional theme of marriage, its heroine seems quite different from Elisa or Natalie. Lucinde partners Julius equally through all modes of human expression, from indulgent sensuality to abstract intellectuality. Strikingly, the *Dithyrambische Fantasie über die schönste Situation* (*Dithyrambic fantasy on the most beautiful situation*) shows the lovers mimicking each other's behavioural roles in search of androgynous perfection. As lived wholeness this love is their organ of religious experience. Lucinde is even allowed to be an artist in her own right. Julius's feminised perspective is symbolised by his writing the novel with Lucinde's quill. In intention, then, this is the epoch's most enthusiastic enactment of the androgynous ideal. Yet woman's traditional gender role still dominates. Lucinde's love makes her, after all the sensuality is done, into a conventional muse, priestess of the new erotic religion. She willingly abandons art and takes on the mother's role when a child arrives. She is therefore more a projection of masculine wishes than a truly emancipated figure. Moreover the mode of fulfilment this *Künstlerroman* portrays is, finally, a regression to the aesthetic existence Wilhelm Meister had already overcome. In this *Lucinde* dictates the mode of all other Romantic novels.

Friedrich von Hardenberg (Novalis) (1772–1801) shared the myth of poetry and critical reverence for Goethe. Friedrich Schlegel's friend and co-practitioner of 'Symphilosophie', he is early Romanticism's major poet and philosopher and set the movement's religious and political tone. His inspiration to develop the characteristic early Romantic stance of intellectual sovereignty came from Fichte. Fichte's speculative *Grundlage der gesammten Wissenschaftslehre* (*Foundation of the complete theory of knowledge*, 1794) had postulated a metaphysical absolute, which constitutes by self-division the mutually opposed, intrinsically alienated realms of empirical subjectivity and objectivity. The subject is inspired to strive against alienation by a privileged experience of origin in 'intellectual intuition', an ultimate mode of self-knowledge. Of Fichte's sovereign intuition Novalis makes a mode of ecstatic perception which transcends the boundaries of prosaic everyday consciousness (where subject and object are rigidly opposed) and transports the subject to a paradoxical absolute standpoint whence all boundaries are overcome. He calls this de-centred state at first 'Selbsttödtung' ('metaphorical suicide'), later, 'geistige Gegenwart' ('spiritual presence'). It makes present in the prosaic everyday the absent yet yearned-for absolute. Poetic writing, through imaginative evocation of the absent totality, is its means of construction and communication. In its overcoming of reflective thought, this poetic philosophy is deeply irrationalist. It is why Enlightenment rationalism is attacked in *Athenaeum*. Yet it is not so much opposed to Enlightenment as designed to encompass Enlightenment within a higher unity. From the discovery of this sovereign standpoint (the 'new land' of his pseudonym) derive Novalis's sense of mission and concept of the poet as stranger. After him the Romantic novel becomes less a static hieroglyph and more a narrative pilgrimage to identity in our hidden origin and end. Yet despite his rhetoric, Novalis's religion is as much human self-redemption as

Schillerian aesthetic experience, albeit with de-centring consequences. For this reason the absolute designs he projects onto empirical data are always self-consciously experimental notions with provisional validity signalled by Romantic Irony. Novalis seeks to apply this method of poeticisation (soon called 'Romantisirung') to all fields of human experience. Here his and Schlegel's ideas of absolute poetry meet.

The first is poetry itself. The hero of Novalis's Romantic novel *Heinrich von Ofterdingen* (1800), which tells self-reflexively of a medieval courtly-love poet's apprenticeship, is another aesthetic brother of Wilhelm Meister. Novalis's literally encyclopaedic notion of the artist's education is wider than Schlegel's. But, as in Schlegel, the key experience is love – of Mathilde, another ideal of womanly harmony. The novel's major achievement is, however, its unique structure. Heinrich's youthful dream of ecstatic self-transcendence, nature redeemed, and love discovered is literally enacted in the subsequent narrative, so that (for the reader) dream, reality and temporal spheres merge on a plane of indifference. The absolute standpoint of boundless presence, the synthesis of the finite and the infinite into a paradoxically totalised perspective, has been constructed. This self-celebratory realisation of the poetic paradise is Novalis's riposte to what he saw as the anti-poetic message of *Wilhelm Meisters Lehrjahre*.

But 'Poesie' can be applied to more than just poetry. The early Romantics were more committed than Goethe and Schiller to political thought. Schiller had resigned before the spectacle of moral chaos that is history. He supported the nationalist revival with *Die Jungfrau von Orleans* and *Wilhelm Tell* (1804), but the aesthetic state alluded to in the *Ästhetische Briefe* remains his basic political position. Goethe accepted the fact of the Revolution as marking a new phase in world history, but doubted the lasting value of such a catastrophic interruption of natural evolution, and limited his poetic comment to slight satires on minor aspects of the Revolution such as *Der Groß-Cophtha* (*The great Copt*) and *Der Bürgergeneral* (*The citizen general*) or expressions of generalised sympathy such as *Hermann und Dorothea* or *Unterhaltungen deutscher Ausgewanderten* (*Entertainments of German refugees*) and the resignation of the unfinished *Die natürliche Tochter* (*The natural daughter*). Novalis's *Glauben und Liebe oder der König und die Königin* (*Faith and love, or the King and the Queen*, 1798) and *Die Christenheit oder Europa* (*Christendom, or Europe*, 1799) reflect the early Romantics' will to come to terms with the Revolution from their absolute perspective.

The fragmentary essay *Glauben und Liebe* audaciously attempts to romanticise King Frederick William III (1770–1840) and Queen Luise of Prussia, but prefigures dark chapters of German political theory. Democracy, says Novalis reflecting on the French experience, tends to anarchy, and written constitutions intrinsically limit definitions of human rights. Monarchy, on the other hand, promotes unity and harmony but tends to despotism. The alternative is another Romantic radicalisation of Schiller: the poetic state. The King is to be a messianic, representative ideal, the Queen a complementary Natalie-figure. As such they (in theory) both represent their subjects more adequately than elected individuals and inspire unity. Hence the royal family is the microcosm of the state, and the system synthesises all that is good in monarchy and republic. Sadly, since the entire structure rests on a poetic projection of faith onto the royal pair, despotism or worse results if they fail to conform. This criticism of representative democracy and attempt to replace it with the notion of an élite, *aesthetically* representative person or class is characteristic of all Romantic political thought.

Die Christenheit oder Europa turns the poetic state into a theocracy and radicalises Schiller's view of political history. Here the medieval papacy is presented as a lost Schillerian idyll. It embodies visibly a principle of harmonious unity transcending political structures. But all history follows a dialectical rhythm. Rationalistic and individualistic perversions of religion (Luther) fragment the unity. The confessional anarchy of the Peace of Westphalia culminates in the French Revolution's apocalyptic failure to establish an order of things which is the image of anthropocentric perfection. But when the pendulum of historical dialectic reaches its maximum it must swing back. Thus Revolution, Novalis correctly predicts, occasions its opposite: religion's spontaneous rebirth, as the logically necessary sense of totality. A new Catholicism will synthesise modern individualism and the recuperated idyll and make peace in Napoleonic Europe. This is a kind of answer to *Wallenstein*, but also to Edmund Burke. Novalis accepts Burke's conservative view of historical development. But by historicising the Revolution he turns Burke against himself. The Revolution is now integrated into a unified interpretation of history, as an unpleasant phase of natural development through which humanity must pass towards perfection. Hence Novalis is modern and progressive. But his projection of ideal solutions onto traditional forms (monarchy and papacy) betrays deep conservatism too. In this, he is truly of the *Sattelzeit*. Of course *Die Christenheit*, as an allusion to Lessing's *Die Erziehung des Menschengeschlechts* suggests, is also Novalis's new New Testament. His romanticised Catholicism, which takes from the real thing only the need for physical embodiments of religious devotion and confessional unity, was, after half a century of polemic against *l'infâme*, greeted with amazement. But it promoted both Romantic medievalism and countless Romantic conversions (or reversions), from Friedrich and Dorothea Schlegel in 1808, to Adam Müller, Joseph Görres, Clemens Brentano and Zacharias Werner. Hereafter Romanticism is typically (and wrongly) opposed to the Classical ideal of heathen antiquity.

Novalis also inaugurated the Romantic fascination with death. *Hymnen an die Nacht* (*Hymns to the night*, 1800), a spiritualised answer to 'Die Götter Griechenlands', translate the experience of self-loss into Orphic terms. The poet's descent into the inner world involves the recovery in imaginative, anamnesic presence of the lost beloved. Novalis's Eurydice (based on his first fiancée, Sophie von Kühn) thus functions as a mediator of transcendence in parallel with Christ. The poet yearns for the fulfilment of the love-death. Schleiermacher's *Über die Religion* (*On religion*, 1799) adopted the notion of plural mediation as an instrument of religious eclecticism. Novalis's rhetoric of mediatory self-sacrifice was appropriated by trivialising perpetrators of 'Novalismus' such as Graf Friedrich Heinrich von Loeben and patriotic poets like Theodor Körner during the Wars of Liberation.

In 1797 Friedrich Schlegel, by now living symphilosophically with Schleiermacher in Berlin, had introduced Ludwig Tieck (1776–1853) to the rest of the early Romantic group. Tieck and Novalis became inseparable, and Tieck edited Novalis's posthumous works (1802). It was not the first time he had done such a duty. In 1796 he had edited the collaborative *Herzensergießungen eines kunstliebenden Klosterbruders* (*Heartfelt outpourings of an art-loving friar*) of his Berlin friend Wilhelm Heinrich Wackenroder (1773–98), followed in 1799 by *Phantasien über die Kunst* (*Fantasias on the theme of art*). This work, which contrasts the aesthetic wholeness of Renaissance artists with the divided person of the (fictive) modern musician Joseph Berglinger, has close affinities with the Romantic novel. It is a heterogeneous collection of texts on aesthetic themes, with some variety of genre. As art about art, it is thematically self-reflective and draws formative energies from reflection. If the theme of androgynous love is missing and the overriding perspective is not unified enough for the *Herzensergießungen* to be a Romantic novel, we have here, nonetheless, the first monument to the Romantic religion of art. The tone of Wackenroder's aesthetic criticism – reverential humility and resignation before the task – differs markedly from Schlegel's reflective sovereignty. But his use of lyric poetry as medium of critical discourse exposes as superficial the contrast with Schlegel (for whom, we know, criticism is 'Poesie der Poesie'). Wackenroder's main target is the rigorously analytical aesthetic criticism of the Enlightenment. But there is a difference of focus between Schlegel and Wackenroder which points to later Romanticism. Schlegel aims at interpretative perfection, Wackenroder at the mysterious process of aesthetic creation itself. Art is the product of divine inspiration. It promotes the highest human perfection and unfolds the wings of the soul. Yet the very sovereignty of art, which seems to free humanity from earthly contingency, can also, Berglinger sees, be regarded as freedom from divine authority. As the tortured artist hovers in a state of corrupt innocence between ecstatic de-centred transcendence and mere self-idolatry, Wackenroder exposes the intrinsic duplicity of aesthetic experience so defined. The problem of the artist in this form will dominate Romantic novels and novellas in the movement's next phase, especially in E. T. A. Hoffmann, August Klingemann (Bonaventura) and Jean Paul.

Tieck further collaborated with Wackenroder on *Franz Sternbalds Wanderungen* (*Franz Sternbald's wanderings*, 1798), another tale of aesthetic education promoting a Romantic programme of allegorical art. The son of a Berlin master rope-maker, he (like Friedrich Schlegel) opted to write for a living, and underwent an apprenticeship at Friedrich Nicolai's publishing house, so that his first work is marked by the restrictive norms of the market-place. The early novel *William Lovell* (1796) is still in the epistolary form beloved of the Enlightenment, and features a devilish conspiracy in the same tradition, but its radical perspectivism and near nihilism indicate profounder things to come. Tieck's oeuvre is, however, large and many-sided, from novels of various kinds to novellas, criticism and editions. His novella *Der blonde Eckbert* (*Fair Eckbert*, 1796) uncovers the dark side of Romantic chiliasm. For Heinrich von Ofterdingen, dream became reality. For Eckbert, who slowly realizes that his marriage to Bertha is incestuous and his whole life is based on wrong, nightmare and reality merge. *Der Runenberg* (*The rune mountain*, 1801–4) transforms Novalis's theme of descent into nature's heart through a mine shaft into another nightmare. The farmer Christian is strangely drawn from his world of culture into archaic nature. The symbolic tension between his wife Elisabeth and a mythical, witch-like Queen of nature at last destroys his marriage and drives him to madness. Like Wackenroder's Berglinger, these creations point forward to the crisis of later Romanticism. However Tieck's dramas are his weightiest contribution to early Romanticism. Both Schlegels had attempted Romantic tragedies with *Alarcos* and *Ion*. Neither work had been accepted by the Weimar theatre-goers, whose catcalls Goethe had had to quell in person. In 1798 Tieck and A. W. Schlegel had begun what is still the most popular German translation of Shakespeare, whose capricious creativity, combination of nature with irony and mixture of tragedy and comedy had made him into a model nearly as significant as Goethe for the Romantics. But only Tieck in the first generation of Romantics was capable of combining Romantic aesthetic principles with effective dramatic presence. The comedy *Der gestiefelte Kater* (*Puss in boots*, 1797) and the tragedy *Leben und Tod der Heiligen Genoveva* (*Life and death of Saint Genevieve*, 1800) dramatise, respectively, Romantic Irony and medievalism.

The feline hero of *Der gestiefelte Kater* is of course a vehicle for social satire. But his role as means of aesthetic attack is much more significant. This does not mean only the play's disdainful abandonment of realism through the return to folk and fairy-tale motifs. Many comic traditions, especially *commedia dell'arte,* had emphasised the humoristic potential of a character's ironic abandonment of role. Here, however, Tieck radical-ises traditional techniques of undermining illusion. He brings the audi-ence on stage, so that self-reflective comment is built into the action. Their bovine reaction to the unexpected ruthlessly and amusingly exposes their ossified notion of taste. The poet himself must plead grovellingly for understanding. Later, when the characters debate the play's comic merits, re-write the script, and even the scenery (through the rehabilitated Hanswurst) begins to speak, his position becomes much more serious. The play itself has slipped out of its role. *Der gestiefelte Kater* thus exploits the traditional subject as a means to conduct dialogue with the public, to reflect in poetry on poetry in the dramatic mode. Its achieve-ment lies in Tieck's successful combination of real comic humour with Romantic principle. Here again, the close (if short-lived) bond of early Romanticism and Classicism is revealed by the Poet's concluding plea for comprehension. It is a 'Xenion'.

Genoveva, if no less effective, is more of an armchair drama. It enjoyed cult status amongst the early Romantics, and Goethe approved. Spurred on by Herder's call for literary renewal through readoption of Germanic models and Novalis's medievalism, Tieck was the first Romantic seriously to revive medieval and early modern genres as well as themes. He edited *Minnelieder aus dem schwäbischen Zeitalter* (*Courtly love songs from the Swabian epoch*, 1803). *Genoveva* – contemporaneous with Schiller's *Jungfrau* – attempts to revive martyr drama, a genre popular until killed by Lessing's refusal in the *Hamburgische Dramaturgie* (1767–8) to allow martyrs true tragic status. Tieck thus adapts for ostensibly devotional ends a German chapbook version of St Genevieve's sufferings. Tragedy in Schiller's sense is duly ignored. In Lessing's sense it is restricted to Golo's forbidden love for and persecution of the pure heroine during her husband Siegfried's enforced absence. Framed by St Boniface's lament for modern unbelief and exhortation to follow Genoveva's example, the play however only masquerades as devotional literature. Genoveva's inability to identify with the saints in her *Vita sanctorum* betrays that her piety is really modern nostalgia for faith now lost. Behind the piety is the Romantic religion of erotic love, exemplified by the Moorish king Abdorrahman and his androgynous wife Zulma. Tieck's real concerns are the psychological subtleties of Golo's transformations and Genoveva's Emilia-like innocent ambiguities, and the innovative mixture of narrative and lyric concealed beneath the apparently simple medieval structure.

The vanguard of women's emancipation seems generally to cluster around centres of alternative culture. The Berlin salons were just such an environment. Established about 1790 by more or less assimilated Jewish women such as Henriette Herz and Rahel Varnhagen von Ense, they provided a uniquely tolerant, humanistically orientated forum which survived into the 1830s. Here culture was the sole qualification, so that otherwise segregated social classes might mix and women and Jews make themselves a social existence. As a forum of integration and catalyst of change the salon thus played as important a role in our epoch as the university or the reading society. Friedrich Schlegel met his future wife Dorothea at Henriette Herz's salon. Schleiermacher based his theory of Romantic sociability *Versuch einer Theorie des geselligen Betragens* (*Essay on social conduct*, 1799) as the catalyst of individual cultivation on his experiences here. Progressively minded women – Dorothea Mendelssohn-Veit-Schlegel, Caroline Michaelis-Böhmer-Schlegel-Schelling, Sophie Mereau-Brentano, Bettine Brentano-von Arnim, Karoline von Günderrode, Rahel Levin-Varnhagen von Ense and many others – seem also on this account to have been drawn to the Romantic movement, much more so than can be said of the Classicist grouping. (*Athenaeum*, unlike *Die Horen,* contains a well-intentioned review of Godwin's life of Mary Wollstonecraft.) Romantic women were perhaps the first group of women writers successfully to combine spring-cleaning with the aesthetic *causerie*. But little of their work found its way into print and less into major genres. The exception is Karoline von Günderrode (1780–1806), who, under the genderless pseudonym Tian, produced work, in an unmistakably Romantic mode of weighty intellectuality, in the recognised elevated genres of lyric, drama, and also novella. Dorothea Schlegel (1764–1839) alone produced a Romantic novel, although she felt obliged to present it anonymously under Friedrich's authoritative editorship. Much Romantic women's work was channelled into private, essentially confessional avenues such as letters and diaries, so that, as with Caroline Schlegel (August Wilhelm's wife), its literary status was only claimed much later. The same holds for Rahel Varnhagen's autobiographical writings, published by her husband after her death. Alternatively (Caroline Schlegel again), the partners worked sympoetically together, but the woman's contribution was absorbed into her partner's work or communal dialogues such as *Die Gemählde. Ein Gespräch.* Tieck's daughter Dorothea seems to have done much of the later Shakespeare-translation credited to her father. Yet even here, as with Sophie Mereau-Brentano (an established author before she met her husband) and Bettine Brentano-von Arnim, marriage to a poet seems often enough to have involved the Wobeser-model: willing or unwilling renunciation of writing. Bettine's writing commences only after Arnim's death in 1831.

Dorothea Schlegel makes much play in the afterword of her unfinished *Florentin* (1801) of its dilettantish character. Elsewhere she insists it was written to subsidise Friedrich's writing career. Florentin is a typical

Romantic stranger to the world, searching for, yet not finding his identity, so that he lives in the state of constitutional unfulfilment which for Romantics is reality. As with *Franz Sternbald* and *Heinrich von Ofterdingen*, the plot is thus analytic. Much space is taken by ironically reflected flashback narrative of his childhood. Schlegel takes up Novalis's theme of the family as political model, and Wackenroder's of the artists's alienation in a capitalistic culture. Here however gender issues are given a specifically feminine accentuation. Walter, a would-be marital tyrant, is obviously derived from the 'women's novel'. In a more Romantic vein, the painter Florentin's typically Romantic aesthetic partnership with his wife is also the platform for launching discussion of gender problems. His joy at impending fatherhood is cut short by his Roman wife's decision to abort the child. He becomes the first divorced Romantic hero, and the forbidden question of abortion (remarkably enough in a literature which idolised the child) has been tabled. Unusually, Florentin still lacks an obvious mate at the end. Female characters are consistently given different accentuations. Clementina, a kind of feminised Mentor, prefigures Goethe's Makarie. Juliane, on the other hand, cross-dresses for a premarital adventure of gender-identity with her fiancé Eduard and Florentin into uncharted territory. She even sympathises with the predicament of Florentin's ex-wife. But the limit of Schlegel's feminism is Juliane's final recognition of her natural dependency on men.

Karoline von Günderrode's work, a feminist confrontation with the age's poetic conventions, is marked by Novalis's religion of self-loss and rhetorical glorification of death. Technically the most gifted woman poet and philosophically the most sophisticated, 'Tian' was able to publish through the mediation of her lover Friedrich Creuzer, a Romantic professor at Heidelberg. There are two collections of experiments in various genres, *Gedichte und Phantasien* (*Poems and fantasias*, 1804) and *Poetische Fragmente* (*Poetic fragments*, 1805), plus assorted contributions to journals and anthologies. Her major achievement is the anti-Voltairean *Mahomet, der Prophet von Mekka* (*Mohammed, prophet of Mecca*, 1805). This classicising drama follows Schiller's *Die Braut von Messina* (*The bride of Messina*, 1803) in using an antiphonic chorus to reflect the prophet's inner state. Mahomet's role as the visionary mediator, whose ambition is to fuse all religions into a new synthesis, reflects study of Schleiermacher and Novalis. But he is also tortured by doubt as to the validity of his subjectivist visions. With its effective central metaphor of the inexorably growing tree, *Mahomet* is thus another dramatisation of an essentially modern subject's struggle for faith and, like Wackenroder, points to later Romantic nihilism. The contrast of word and sword as means of redemption echoes *Iphigenie* and *Tasso*, and the inclination to the sword anticipates the literature of the Wars of Liberation. Gender issues are also central for Günderrode. The dramatic fragment *Hildgund* (c. 1804) presents an Amazon, determined to break out of her role as temple-maiden and, Judith-like, to murder the oppressor Attila. The ballad 'Don Juan' (1803–4) is a feminist appropriation of the myth. The Queen, unusually, captures the Don's affection and ends his interest in other women. Absorbed into the Romantic ideal of absolute love, his death is overcoming and fulfilment rather than loss.

Variations

If courtly Weimar, university Jena and salon Berlin are German literature's centres of gravity, not all the major writers felt comfortable in this triple orbit. Both Friedrich Hölderlin and Jean Paul traversed and left these centres. In 1800 Friedrich Schlegel, echoing Schiller's lament for the gods of Greece, had focused his generation's sense of deficit and fragmentation on the need for a new mythology to serve moderns in the way the old had served the ancients. In fact Hölderlin (1770–1843), fellow-countryman of the Swabian Schiller, friend of Hegel and Schelling, anticipated Schlegel's wish (and Novalis's attempts to fulfil it) by several years. The mythification of poetry in the Romantic style is the *locus* of Hölderlin's work, yet it also focuses almost exclusively, in hymnic and finally elegaic intensity, on the Greek gods of Schiller's lost classical idyll. Thus Hölderlin, like Goethe (they are the age's greatest lyric poets), stands as a characteristic variant of the consensus between Romanticism and Classicism.

Hyperion, oder der Eremit in Griechenland (*Hyperion, or the hermit in Greece*, 1797–9) is a lyrical *Bildungsroman* set symbolically in *modern* Greece around 1770, the time of its revolt against Russo-Turkish colonialism. Hyperion, as the introduction tells us, is an elegaic hero, torn between acceptance of alienated modernity and yearning for the glories of Greek antiquity, torn also between word and deed as means to recover the lost ideal. Problems of sentimentality thus dominate this epistolary novel of reminiscence. In search of a society which embodies objectively the conceptualised ideal Hyperion traverses Greece, but encounters only barbarians, savages, or revolutionary enthusiasts such as Alabanda. At last, like one of Zimmermann's melancholics, he becomes a mountain hermit. Diotima, named after the woman who teaches Socrates what beauty is, rescues him from depression. As the embodiment of beauty – Hyperion calls her pure 'Gesang' ('song') – she is the aesthetic revelation of divinity. Another ideal of feminine wholeness and harmony, she heals his divided personality. They become an androgynous oneness. Against her wishes Hyperion joins Alabanda in violent revolt against Russo-

Turkish rule (an evident parallel to the Revolution). The brutality of his idealised peasant soldiers soon disillusions him. After Diotima's death the novel thus becomes the search for her recuperation and for intellectual reconciliation with his fate. A pantheistic nature is the healing force and poetry the instrument for channelling it. An epiphanic moment of communion with Diotima's voice in the ether, captured in lyrical Orphic prose in the last pages, overcomes his loss and suffuses other oppositions with the sense of oneness, so that *Hyperion* is revealed as a *Künstlerroman,* with reflexivity of the Goethean rather than the Schlegelian kind. Hyperion has become the poet of the sentimental idyll, keeper of the flame for future generations, and the novel's flashback structure is the enactment of this process of self-understanding as an eccentric path.

Hölderlin's progress as the mythopœic proclaimer of pantheistic reconciliation in the age of Revolution is marked by increasing consciousness of the tragic fate of the poet. Twice Hyperion had considered suicide. Hölderlin's next major project, the lyric tragedy *Der Tod des Empedokles* (*The death of Empedocles*, 1798–9), treats the ancient philosopher who is said to have committed suicide by leaping into the flames of Mount Etna. There are three incomplete versions which cannot be unified. It can be said however that here again the central figure is a poetic philosopher, who is overwhelmed by the Romantic myth of intuited oneness with the divine. As with *Hyperion*, there are obvious responses to the issues of the Revolution. Diotima had finally counselled Hyperion to become the mentor of his people. Empedokles takes on this role, so that the text can be seen in this too as the extrapolation of *Hyperion*. But not so much death, as the attainment and mediation of authentic life for which the suicide metaphor stands, is the theme of *Empedokles*. In all three versions Empedocles' visionary union with the life of the gods and attempt to realise through the word a unity of nature and state entail conflict both with the secular and sacral establishments of Agrigento and in his own personality. After *Hyperion* it is noticeable that Diotima-figures, as mediations of the divine, are absent from Hölderlin's work. Susette Gontard, the model for Diotima, broke contact in 1799 and died in 1802.

After 1799 Hölderlin pours out hymnic and elegaic lyric poetry, in strictly classical triadic forms, with a highly artificial, Klopstockian syntax known as 'harte Fügung' and with uniquely plastic imagery. It is dominated by the theme of hubris (Hölderlin's equivalent of Romantic Irony) and the poetic self-reflection entailed by the ever-intensifying conflict of his prophetic consciousness with historical reality. Among the hymns, 'Der Archipelagus' ('The archipelago', 1800–1) celebrates the Greek landscape as focus for union of nature and spirit. This birthplace of heroes and classical culture is no more, but the poet recalls the later rebirth of Attic culture from the ruins of Persian occupation, and celebrates his role in the modern, godless world as anamnesis of the absent divine. 'Die Wanderung' ('Migration', 1801) celebrates, like the elegy 'Studgard' (1800), the experience of belonging. But even blessed Swabia cannot hold the poet, who wanders to the Caucasus, promotes a marriage of German and Greek cultures, and brings the synthesis home. *Hyperion* had included a memorable Schillerian castigation of the Germans for their supine tolerance of oppressive circumstance. 'Germanien' (1801) reverses this tendency. It praises Germany as the elect renewer of Greek cultural tradition in the West, and ends with a hymn of mystic patriotism for the German language, but also notes the nation's defencelessness. 'Wie wenn am Feiertage' ('As on a feast day', 1799–1800) imagines the thunderstorm as an element of mediation between the natural and the divine and posits the poet as earthly voice of divine nature and instrument of historical mediation (with more than a hint at the Revolution), but culminates in a paralysing consciousness of hubris. 'Friedensfeier' ('Rite of peace', 1801–3) is Hölderlin's visionary response to Napoleon's festivals of peace during 1801. At a ritual festival after the storms of recent history a gathering of gods, including the yearned-for Christ (who may be the 'Fürst des Festes' ('Festival prince')), sanctions reconciliation, and the poet envisions the imminent millennium. Perhaps Hölderlin's greatest lyric achievements are the elegy 'Brod und Wein' ('Bread and wine', 1800–1) and the hymn 'Patmos' (1802–3). 'Brod und Wein', with its many echoes of Novalis, makes explicit the poet's Romantic syncretism. As ever, classical antiquity is praised as the lost idyll. Humanity lives at present in the epoch of night. But the poet's task is recall of what was and will be. The God who will come is present in the memorials of bread and wine, and his coming will silence Napoleon's guns. He is Jesus, but also Dionysus. 'Patmos', named after the island on which John the Evangelist died, is a hymn on the lost and regained authority of the Bible in the age of secularisation. Hölderlin retained his involvement with Revolutionary movements, but after the return from France in 1802, his mental equilibrium became increasingly upset. Placed in a clinic, he was released to spend the rest of his days in the famous tower in Tübingen, a fitting symbol for his imprisonment in a broken psyche. He continued to write, since poetry, as David Constantine says, was his home, but that later poetry exhibits in its pseudonyms and restriction to pure plastic imaging a withdrawal to inner recesses. Goethe and Schiller had supported Hölderlin where possible, but found his poetry too abstract and lengthy. His work was only later recognised by Romantics such as Brentano.

Johann Paul Friedrich Richter (1763–1825), known after 1793 as Jean Paul, is the great outsider of the epoch. His work, whilst invariably in prose and usually narrative, is extremely variegated. It ranges from early mono-dimensional satiric and idyllic writings to the amply proportioned, multi-faceted novels which are his main works – *Die unsichtbare Loge* (*The invisible lodge*, 1793), *Hesperus, oder 45 Hundsposttage* (*Hesperus, or 45 dog-post days*, 1795), *Leben des Quintus Fixlein* (*Life of Quintus Fixlein*, 1796), *Blumen- Frucht- und Dornenstücke, oder Ehestand, Tod und Hochzeit des Armenadvokaten F. St. Siebenkäs* (*Still lives of blossom, fruit and thorns, or marriage, death and nuptials of F. St. Siebenkäs, advocate of the poor*, 1796), *Titan* (1800–3), *Flegeljahre* (*Fledgling years*, 1804) and *Der Komet* (*The comet*, 1820–2) – and occasional writings such as *Das Kampaner Tal* (*Vale of Campano*, 1797 – a meditation on immortality), *Vorschule der Ästhetik* (*Pre-school of aesthetics*, 1804), *Levana oder Erziehlehre* (*Levana, or theory of education*, 1807) and *Politische Fasten-Predigten* (*Political Lenten sermons*, 1817). From 1795 he was one of the nation's most popular authors. Despite this he has several Romantic features. He is a deeply religious writer, whose major concern is to infuse the alienated everyday with spiritual presence. His works are formally complex and eccentric. He sees poetry as the vehicle of highest insight. He is obsessed with problems of the self, death and immortality. Above all, he is a great humorist: the reflective intrusion of the narrative ego into the fiction, often as 'Jean Paul' in person, is a hallmark of his style. It both underlines the discrepancy of ideal and real and, sometimes, overcomes it. Much, however, also links Jean Paul to Classicism. He lacks the Romantic sense of poetry as myth and sense of poetic mission. His writing is a poetic anthropology designed to harmonise the dualism of spirit and matter in human nature, and his novels tend loosely to follow the structures of the *Bildungsroman*. But much also links him to the Enlightenment tradition. His continuous digressions and relative concern for forward motion of plot betray that Jean Paul is closer to Sterne than Friedrich Schlegel. He is also steeped in the emotional tradition of *Empfindsamkeit*, and his work typically contains numerous virtuoso projections of sentiment onto landscape. Jean Paul's work thus embodies bewildering polarities, from enraptured religious ecstasy to coldest nihilism, from satirical distance to emotional dissolution, from sober realism to pure aesthetic play. The common denominator of all this he shares however with all writers of the age: consciousness of division.

Die unsichtbare Loge, a novel of education in the tradition of Wieland's *Agathon* (1766–7) and Karl Philipp Moritz's *Anton Reiser* (1785–90), is Jean Paul's first mature work. There is a story, Gustav's remarkable education *ab ovo* as Jean Paul's ideal of the 'hoher Mensch' ('higher person'). He lives and is taught for the first eight years of his life in a catacomb, by a Pietist known as 'der Genius', and told that his emergence into the upper world is both death and, through the encounter with God, rebirth. This evokes profound resonances of Platonic philosophy. A moving description of his first, blinding experience of the sun signals Gustav's lifelong orientation towards higher things and his status – analogous to the heroes of Novalis and Hölderlin – as 'Fremdling'. Thereafter Gustav's progress through different levels of tutelage, is typically complex, although the intended contrast of ideal and real is evident. However, the constant presence of 'Jean Paul' (he is Gustav's next tutor) leads to frequent humoristic digressions on the theory of education, marriage, the feudal structure of German politics (Jean Paul never wavered in support of the Revolutionary goals), German provincial manners, and the Shandy-esque process of narration. The reflection on narrative as process is intensified by 'Jean Paul's' illness and abandonment of narration (his sister Philippine takes over), and by the thematisation of a parallel novel about Gustav within the novel by the court poet Oefel. *Die unsichtbare Loge* is unfinished, but that is hardly the point. Jean Paul's novels, like the Romantic novel, are constitutionally fragments, with this one basic divergence: that Jean Paul's novels are not hieroglyphs of a higher reality, so much as consoling records of fragmentation.

Jean Paul's major novel *Titan* is the product of his engagement with Weimar Classical Humanism. He had worked on it from 1792, but lived in Weimar for over a year from October 1798, where he met Goethe, Schiller, Herder and, in nearby Jena, the leading early Romantics. The Romantics suspected him of elevated hypocrisy, and the Classicists rejected his eccentric, constitutionally disharmonious humour. *Titan* contains Jean Paul's response. Albano, a 'hoher Mensch', is destined to become ideal ruler of the adjoining principalities Hohenfließ and Haarhaar, but must first realize his true identity (he was exchanged at birth), be fittingly educated and overcome the intrigues of the two courts. Albano aspires to Plutarchian greatness. He laments the decline of modernity, is classically educated, and an artist. But he also studies law, since, despite a certain extremism, he is determined to become a whole man. He is narrowly dissuaded from fighting in the French Revolution. Thus this 'hoher Mensch' is intended as a synthesis of the characteristic yearning for transcendence and a disposition to practical activity. The major factors in his education are, however, as in *Wilhelm Meisters Lehrjahre*, a succession of 'titanic' lovers: Liane, Linda and Idoïne. The first two are fatally one-sided. Liane's yearning for transcendence is too strong, so that she succumbs, symbolically, to consumption. Linda is another Amazon. Like Fischer's Wilhelmine, she possesses manly intellect and learning and despises marriage. Like Liane, however, she suffers from symbolical (here night) blindness. This leads to her seduction by the sublime villain Roquairol and departure from the scene. The climax of the series is Idoïne. Liane's double, she is a princess of neighbouring Haarhaar, but her practical orientation makes her Albano's perfect mate. *Titan* is the only novel by

Jean Paul to possess such an harmonious, 'closed' ending. The two most fascinating characters are Roquairol and Schoppe, each a polemical instrument. The former is intended as an attack on what Jean Paul saw as the formalistic aestheticism of the Weimar classicists. He intimately confuses art and life. Early acquaintance with extremes of passion and intellect combines with his aestheticism to make him a cynical nihilist who has lived his life out – in imagination – long before death, so that for him existence is living death, tolerable only as ironic play with living figures in search of thrills. Schoppe, one of Jean Paul's many eccentric humorists, is an attack on the Fichteanism underlying early Romanticism. As a Fichtean, Schoppe cannot distinguish between his ego and the objective realm it generates. Existence becomes a hall of mirrors. He perishes when he encounters his double (Siebenkäs, from the novel of that name). Schoppe's demise marks Jean Paul's commitment to realism. *Titan* as a whole is a profound commentary on the deepest tendencies of the age, but the new synthesis it offers is (perhaps unwittingly) closer to Goethe and Schiller than Jean Paul thought. The *Vorschule der Ästhetik* provides the later theoretical explication of these ideas, but also contains the most famous definition of humour in German literary history, as the inverted sublime.

Humanism to nationalism

The aesthetic consensus in this form was not to last. The years 1806–15 see Romanticism, as its vehicle, spread and dominate the literary scene in many centres, from Berlin and Jena to Heidelberg and Stuttgart, Dresden to Vienna and Prague, and Kassel to Munich. But it is transformed by two major factors: the demonic achievements of Napoleon, and a change in the personal constellations.

The titan Napoleon changed the political face of Europe. In 1799 he had transformed Revolutionary into Imperial France. After the repeated failures of the traditional European monarchies' Wars of Coalition, the provisions of the Peace of Lunéville (1801) enacted one of Napoleon's major strategic aims: the dissolution, after a thousand years, of the Holy Roman Empire. It was formally abolished on 6 August 1806. The Holy Roman Emperor Franz II was reduced to mere Emperor Franz I of Austria. As a counterweight to Austria, the Rhenish states were transformed into the Napoleonic fiefs of the 'Rheinbund'. The left bank of the Rhine was, after Napoleon's victories and the peace of Campo Formio (1797), to remain in French hands for twenty years. The 'Reichsdeputations-hauptschluß' (1803) dissolved the Prince-Bishoprics of central Germany, abolished most of the Free Towns and secularized the monasteries – with their artistic treasures – on the French model. Prussia was to play the key role in the ensuing historical drama. As was possible under the Empire, it had concluded a separate peace with Napoleon at Basle in 1795. This, at the price of humiliation and passivity, guaranteed its security for the next eleven years, and made Austria and Britain Napoleon's chief opponents. But when Napoleon's offer to give Hanover to Britain in 1806 provoked the bystander Prussia beyond self-control, its ill-advised uprising resulted in catastrophic defeat in October 1806 at the battle of Jena-Auerstädt (Goethe's house was within ear-shot) and French occupation of the entire state. With Prussia's collapse and territorial decimation the old order had finally disappeared. The Revolution had consumed Germany. German law was replaced in many states by the *Code Napoléon*.

As for the personal constellations, with the deaths of Novalis in 1801 and Schiller in 1805 – Wackenroder had died in 1798 – the cement that held together both Classical and Romantic groupings dissolved. Friedrich Schlegel began a period of wandering until 1810, when he settled, via Jena, Berlin, Paris and Cologne, in Vienna. August Wilhelm moved via Berlin, Coppet (*chez* Mme de Staël) and Vienna to Bonn. Tieck's wanderings, blighted with illness and writer's block, took him via Munich to Dresden in 1819. Fringe members of the early Romantic group, such as Clemens Brentano (1778–1842) and Ludwig Achim von Arnim (1781–1831), migrated to other burgeoning centres of Romantic culture, such as Heidelberg. Of the outsiders, Hölderlin's state was irremediable after 1806 and Jean Paul, choosing marriage to a non-titanic woman, settled in remote Bayreuth. On the Classical side, Wilhelm von Humboldt went to Rome as Prussian ambassador, and Schiller's demise coincided with Goethe's own bout of serious illness. Goethe emerged from gloomy Olympian isolation only in 1807.

The German response to Napoleon was reaction in several forms. With the end of the old Germany, proponents of Enlightenment and Revolution, both of which Napoleon represented, now lost all prestige (even if, like J. H. Voß, they were dyed-in-the-wool patriots). In Prussia defeat crystallized the already given sense that the state was inwardly decadent and required renewal. A major reform of Prussia's laws and institutions in the spirit of classical humanism was the result, and Prussia came therefore to lead the German resistance to Napoleon. Between 1807 and 1812 Friedrich Wilhelm III's chancellors, Freiherr vom Stein and Fürst Karl August von Hardenberg (an uncle of Novalis), emancipated the citizenry of the towns, the peasants and the Jews from their places in the received feudal order, and greatly modified the relation of the aristocracy to the army and agriculture. The definition of ministerial responsibility gradually reduced monarchic power. There followed the far-reaching introduction of freedom of trade and general liability for tax. The central symbol of this process was Berlin university, founded on his return from Rome in 1810 by Wilhelm von Humboldt. Fichte was its first rector. Inspiring scholars from across Germany joined the enterprise, from Schleiermacher to the legal historian and philosopher Carl Friedrich von Savigny (Brentano's brother-in-law), the physicians Christoph Wilhelm Hufeland and Johann Christian Reil, the 'Naturphilosoph' Henrik Steffens, the philosophers Friedrich Wilhelm Joseph Schelling and Karl Wilhelm Solger, the theologian Wilhelm Martin Leberecht de Wette and the philologists Friedrich von der Hagen and Friedrich August Wolf. In the university's founding documents, Schleiermacher's *Gelegentliche Gedanken über Universitäten im deutschen Sinn* (*Occasional thoughts on universities in a German context*, 1809) and Humboldt's *Über die innere und äussere Organisation der höheren wissenschaftlichen Anstalten in Berlin* (*On the internal and external organisation of the higher institutes of education in Berlin*, 1810), the university in its Enlightenment role, as a place of narrow specialist training, is emphatically rejected. Instead, it is advocated that research and teaching be intrinsically linked, and, above all, that wholeness of the student's person be cultivated. Berlin university translates the age's theoretical humanism into institutional fact. Hegel was later to join it.

Together with the transformation of institutions came the intellectuals' attempt to raise the level of popular culture through public lectures. A form hitherto rare, they proliferate in all centres after 1802. August Wilhelm Schlegel held successful *Vorlesungen über schöne Litteratur und Kunst* (*Lectures on high literature and art*) at Berlin in 1801–4. There too Fichte gave lectures on *Die Grundzüge des gegenwärtigen Zeitalters* (*Contours of the present age*, 1804–5) and *Die Anweisung zum seligen Leben* (*Admonition to a blessed life*, 1806). In Dresden, Adam Müller gave *Vorlesungen über die deutsche Wissenschaft und Kunst* (*Lectures on German science and art*, 1806), and the influential Romantic natural philosopher Gotthilf Heinrich Schubert lectured on *Ansichten von der Nachtseite der Naturwissenschaft* (*Views of the dark side of natural science*, 1808). Friedrich Schlegel gave lectures on art history to the brothers Boisserée in Cologne, and lectured later (like August Wilhelm) on literary history and history in Vienna. The high point of this trend is Adam Müller's *Zwölf Reden über die Beredsamkeit und deren Verfall in Deutschland* (*Twelve addresses on rhetoric and its decline in Germany*, 1812), which self-reflexively take rhetoric as rhetoric's subject. They echo Herder's *Humanitätsbriefe*. But where Herder was resigned to the dominance of the printed medium in the national system of communication, Müller condemns it, denies the influence of any but the greatest authors through print, and advocates the living spoken word as the medium of national cultural renewal. Müller's renewed rhetoric is not a mere art of persuasion aimed at the passions. It is the art of higher communicative exchange orientated towards integration of opposites. An address is an enacted dialogue between speaker and listener, which leads not to the replacement of one standpoint by another, but to the provisional synthesis of both on a higher plane, which is in turn superseded. Thus he rejects French-style measures such as standardisation of German, a German Academy and a single German capital as means of synthesising particular and general in the national language, and advocates the productive clash of dialects. Pulpit eloquence too experienced a rebirth at this time. The Reformed Schleiermacher, like his Roman Catholic counterpart Johann Michael Sailer in Bavaria and his Lutheran counterpart Franz Volkmar Reinhard in Saxony, reaped the rewards of the religious renewal sensed by the early Romantics. As a means of influencing the cultivated and unculti-vated classes, they raised pulpit oratory to heights of sophistication undreamt of by the dry rationalist preachers of the Enlightenment.

Analogous shifts are observable in literature around this time. The sen-timental generation now focused its nostalgia less on classical antiquity and more on the German past. After the turn of the century Clemens Brentano and Achim von Arnim, both of whom had tried their hand at a Romantic novel (*Godwi*, 1802 and *Hollin's Liebesleben* (*Hollin's life of love*, 1802)), followed Tieck's example and applied symphilosophy to the sentimental Herderian task of rescuing and strengthening Germany's cul-tural heritage. Brentano had already returned to the chronicle form for his next major narrative, the *Chronika des fahrenden Schülers* (*Chronicle of the travelling scholar*, 1805–6). But their folk-song collection *Des Knaben Wunderhorn* (*The boy's magic horn*, 1806–8) is a great store of often deceptively simple lyrics from the age now recognized as bygone, usually featuring elemental emotions (love, joy, regret, guilt). Arnim's afterword to the first volume, *Von Volksliedern* (*On folk-songs*), praises in true Herderian style the poetic creativity of that indefinable author 'Volk' (the people). He makes the scholarly class, with their love of the abstract and of foreign models, responsible for the relative decay of the folk-song. Goethe, to whom the work was dedicated, reviewed it enthusiastically and recommended that every household buy it. It was enormously influential in reviving a sense of 'authentic' German identity. But the *Wunderhorn* is also the active appropriation of a lost heritage by modern consciousness, so that the authors did not shrink from including their own works, exten-sively modifying the originals or including part of an eighteenth-century sermon by Abraham a Sancta Clara. The same is true of others' work in the field. Arnim and Brentano also published the Romantic painter Philipp Otto Runge's fine low German reconstruction of *Von dem Machandel Bohm* (*The juniper tree*) in their Heidelberg journal *Zeitung für Einsiedler* (*Tidings for hermits)* in 1808. The brothers Jacob and

Wilhelm Grimm, who worked, for a time, with Brentano in Göttingen and Kassel, are scholars rather than poets. However, they responded to Arnim's arguments, and share the basic Romantic epistemology – the sense of poetry as the vehicle of highest truth. It is this which guides their collections of *Kinder- und Hausmärchen* (*Domestic and children's fairy-tales*, 1812; seven editions by 1857). Here too we have the yearning for basic, 'original' poetic forms coupled with the unabashed admission that the surface textuality stems from the Grimms themselves. The same mentality guides the Grimms' studies in German myth, law, language and philology. In Karlsruhe, Johann Peter Hebel (1760–1826), a Christian teacher, revived with his *Schatzkästlein des rheinischen Hausfreundes* (*The Rhenish family friend's little treasure chest*, 1811) the rural form of the 'Kalendergeschichte'. These are finely crafted miniature anecdotal tales, intended to accompany the reader with reflections transcending time in the course of his daily business, told in plain, yet characteristically provincial German, often studded with proverbs.

All this, in one way or another, is prompted by the political disaster of Napoleon, which translates the poetic and intellectual achievements of the first Classic–Romantic generation into a more-or-less popular and, for the first time, national culture. It was a different matter with high litera-ture, for which Schiller's death in particular was a body blow. The Romantics, however, saw that Schiller's death opened up new possibilities of co-operation with Goethe. Now that Friedrich Schlegel had disqual-ified himself through conversion to Roman Catholicism, two writers in particular saw themselves as Schiller's successor.

It seems astounding that one of these should have been the East Prussian Friedrich Ludwig Zacharias Werner (1768–1823). He is the most gifted Romantic dramatist, the only one whose plays were successfully performed, both publicly, in Berlin and Weimar (under Iffland and Goethe), and privately, in Mme de Staël's Coppet (under August Wilhelm Schlegel). Werner deplored the state of popular theatre after Schiller's death, and never hid his ambition, after Napoleon had cost him his post in the Prussian administration, to take Schiller's place. As a dramatist, he follows Schiller. His plays almost always use historical matter to evoke some variant of the Schillerian sublime's transforming power. All this would have appealed to Goethe. But Werner's reading of Schleiermacher and Novalis established his fundamentally mystical and untragic orienta-tion. He felt that Schiller's 'Greek' notion of the individual crushed by fate should be overcome by the 'Romantic' notion of the individual transcend-ing fate. All of this was to be embodied in a suitably plastic theatrical lan-guage, and this, as so often in our epoch, he found in the historical institutions of Roman Catholicism. Hence Werner, in this influenced by A. W. Schlegel's new translation of Calderón's martyr dramas, used the historical drama to preach the familiar catholicised aestheticism. To this Goethe, with his ingrained suspicion of speculation, fantasy and mysticism, could scarcely be expected to relate.

Werner won Iffland's favour with the masonic drama of ideas *Die Söhne des Thals* (*The Sons of the Vale*, 1803–4), a colossal two-part history play in twelve acts. As he says, it hovers between *Genoveva* and *Wallenstein*. The mythifying tale of the destruction and rebirth of the Knights Templar under Jacob von Molay in 1306–14, its plot owes much to the Enlightenment popular novel. The Order of Templars is devoted to humanity's salvation in a corrupt century. Yet it too is corrupt. Molay's task is to grasp that the order's mission paradoxically requires its destruction, purification and renewal, by the Sons of the Vale, an even more secret society which manipulates the course of sacred history. He and Archbishop Wilhelm (of the Inqusition) are the most interesting figures, Jacob for his progress from madness to insight and joyful acceptance of self-sacrifice, Wilhelm for the moral conflict imposed upon him by fate as destroyer yet preserver of the Order. Jacob's progress is intended as Schillerian, but his transfiguration undermines authentic tragedy. Its message is trivial Romanticism, but *Die Söhne des Thals* abounds with spectacular effects.

Werner went on to write *Martin Luther, oder die Weihe der Kraft* (*Martin Luther, or the sanctification of power*, 1806), which daringly presents a Romanticised Luther and Katharina von Bora on the German stage for the first time and took Berlin by storm, but his true vein, as suggested by Molay's sanctification, is the synthesis of the Schillerian sublime and Romantic transcendence encapsulated in the Calderónian motif of martyrdom. Thereafter he produced a series of martyr dramas – *Das Kreuz an der Ostsee* (*The cross on the Baltic*, 1805), *Attila, König der Hunnen* (*Attila, King of the Huns*, 1807), *Wanda, Königin der Sarmiten* (*Wanda, Queen of the Sarmites*, 1807), *Cunegunde die Heilige, Römisch-deutsche Kaiserin* (*Saint Cunegunde, Holy Roman Empress*, 1808), and *Die Mutter der Makkabäer* (*The mother of the Maccabees*, 1814–8). All feature poetic priest-figures, present women in the familiar role of love-priestesses, and mix skilful versification, authentic theatricality and messianic fervour with an ever-intensifying focus on the ritualised destruction of the human body.

Nonetheless, when Iffland recommended him, the call came from Weimar. Like Schiller in 1794, Werner, when he arrived at Weimar on 2 December 1807, made an 'epoch' in Goethe's life. What moved Goethe in 1808 to put on *Wanda* in Weimar is clearly its elegant structure and well-motivated conclusion, and, above all, its theme: sexual relationships. For *Wanda* is that figure which dominates Goethe's writings of the 1790s: an Amazon, leader of the Sarmites, and always in the vanguard of battle.

Here however, as in Schiller, sexuality threatens a woman's exercise of power, which is sustained only by the transfer onto her nation of the unfulfilled erotic passion for a lost lover, and guaranteed by an oath. But Rüdiger of Rügen has loved Wanda since their time at Libussa's court in Prague, and will, if necessary, fight for her hand. Only too late in this analytical drama does Wanda realise that her lost lover is none other than Rüdiger. She is thus compelled to fight Rüdiger, kills him and, in a spectacularly operatic finale, leaps from her funeral pyre into the great River Vistula. The moral of this classicising play is thus deeply Romantic: Wanda is, finally, another Romantic priestess of love and the fulfilment of love is in death. Like Schiller's *Jungfrau*, it is the explicit confirmation of the epoch's misogynist anthropology.

Co-operation between Goethe and Werner (beyond the composition of newly fashionable sonnets) was possible only if one of them changed. Werner sought Goethe's tutelage. His attempt at a classical drama, the one-act *Der 24. Februar* (*The 24th of February*, 1809), is his least typical and most renowned work. Here all mysticism seems to have been banished. It is the thrilling analytical reconstruction of a Swiss family's tragic redemption from what seems to be an inherited curse. Goethe must have liked the subtle play of illusion and reality, and how the catastrophe merges analytical retrospect and present action. But *Der 24. Februar* is still anti-classical. It is not a drama *of* fate, but *about* fate, the (Schillerian!) concept of which is finally exposed as superstition – the only genuine murder occurs, *after* the clock has struck midnight, on 25 Febuary. The son Kurt, moreover, is a Christ-like figure, whose sacrificial death finally expiates the guilt. The play is thus at bottom another martyr drama. Goethe may or may not have sensed this. In any case, he delayed performance of the play until after Werner's final departure from Weimar in 1809. Werner had lost his favour, it is said, through a comparison, over dinner, of the full moon with the Eucharist. His journey took him to Rome, conversion to Roman Catholicism on Maundy Thursday 1810, and ordination in Aschaffenburg in 1814 – steps which made any reconciliation impossible.

The other writer to approach Goethe in 1807 was Heinrich von Kleist (1777–1811). This, like Goethe's interest in Werner, was a grave miscalculation. If Goethe participates in the epoch's consensuality at least to the extent of being its great outsider, Kleist is its great deconstructer. All his works engage critically with the various modulations of the humanist consensus. Yet they leave nothing, save the fact of engagement, in their wake. With a commitment matching only Schiller's and Friedrich Schlegel's, Kleist sought to live the ideal of *Bildung*. From an ancient Prussian military family, he found true humanity incompatible with the soldier's life. After several attempts, he found no other profession, save that of poet, acceptable. Initially wedded to Enlightenment – he was closely attached to Wieland – Kleist was visited around 1800–01 by uncertainty as to the possibility of all scientific knowledge. He (implausibly) makes Kant responsible for this, by suggesting that mediation makes all knowledge constitutionally unreliable. But precisely this crystallised his will to live as a poet and commitment to aesthetic discourse. This is the thread which links Kleist to his age. Yet it also separates him. For his poetic career is marked by anything but a Romantic confidence in the utopian designs of the poetic imagination. The common denominator of almost all his works is the search for unambiguous truth in the medium of aesthetic discourse, often symbolised by (the aptly Kantian) motif of a legal process.

Die Familie Schroffenstein (*The family of Schroffenstein*, 1802) destroys Romanticism's cherished anthropological and epistemological ideals. Two branches of one family live on opposing sides of the mountain and become embroiled in a version of *Romeo and Juliet* which echoes Rousseau's contract-theory of the state, the Terror, and Wallenstein's brooding mistrust. But the major targets are the Romantic vision of the state as family and the ideal of marriage – Kleist makes the cross-dressed androgynity of the two lovers into the very occasion of their murder.

In 1807 Kleist settled in Dresden, which became for the next few years a centre of Romantic culture. He and his symphilosophical friend Adam Müller founded the aesthetic journal *Phöbus,* and Kleist, with Müller as mediator, set about winning Goethe's favour. But *Amphitryon* (1806) is even more anti-consensual than *Die Familie Schroffenstein.* Here the figure of the *Doppelgänger* who is both husband and god enacts Kleist's constant theme of uncertainty, this time in an ostensibly comic vein. Both Amphitryon, the Theban victor at Pharissa, and Sosias, his servant, who must bring the good news to Thebes, are duplicated by Jupiter and Mercury respectively. Hence both men lose their identity and Amphitryon's wife Alkmene, in a night lasting by divine command seventeen hours, unwittingly betrays her husband. The theme of self-loss is pushed to the limit of tragedy, as Alkmene, compelled to choose, always prefers the wrong person. However, as Goethe recognised, the true emphasis of the drama lies at the level of theology. As Alkmene heartrendingly tries to distinguish man and god, Jupiter demonstrates the inevitably anthropomorphic nature of all religious experience. It seems impossible to distinguish self-idolatry from transcendence. When Jupiter quotes the angel of the Annunciation to reveal the coming birth of Hercules, Kleist's deconstructive identification of heathen antiquity and Christian modernity is plain. Thus, despite the attack on Romantic religion, Goethe rejected *Amphitryon* in the same terms as Werner's work. It was unatheatrical because 'mystisch'.

Goethe also read *Der zerbrochne Krug* (*The broken jug*, 1807). It is

Kleist's last comedy. Here the central motif, derived from an etching in his Swiss friend Zschokke's house (it connotes loss of virginity), is a frame on which to hang weighty mythological connotations. The clubfooted village magistrate, Oedipus and Adam in one, must discover who broke the jug in Eve's bedroom the previous night. The joke is, that Adam, despite his best efforts at concealment and condemnation of Eve's fiancé Ruprecht for the crime, inevitably identifies himself as the perpetrator of an attempted seduction (when the jug was also broken). All attempts to avoid discovering the truth thus have the opposite effect. Adam, like his namesake, eats of the tree of knowledge, and so destroys his paradise; like Oedipus, he finds out the truth, but destroys himself thereby. Goethe was impressed, but again doubted the play's theatricality. When the play was put on in Weimar, its fundamental problem – the need to promote humour by prolonging the dialectical process of investigation as far as possible – brought its downfall.

But it was *Penthesilea* (1807) which led to the parting of the ways. As usual, Goethe emphasises its untheatricality. But this alone cannot explain his outrage. More likely he recognised the play's destruction of the epoch's fundamental ideal. For *Penthesilea*, like *Wanda*, treats love and sexuality from the perspective of the Amazon. Penthesilea, Queen of the Amazons, who leads a utopian female state founded on women's destruction of male violence, is struck during the seige of Troy by star-crossed love for Achilles. It is time for the erotic Festival of Roses, when the Amazons capture males suitable for procreation. When Penthesilea is captured by Achilles, she rises to defeat him again, this time with her emblematic dogs. There is an astonishing account of how love, lost honour, and *libido* lead her to savage the corpse. Such a portrait of female sexuality is unparalleled in the high literature of the epoch. Having lost control of her body, she then, full of remorse, loses control of her mind. She fashions a dagger of sheer thought, and kills herself. But this, as the lack of any metaphysical framework à la Werner reveals, is not a 'conventional' Romantic love-death. The total dissociation by love of Penthesilea's anthropological harmony of mind and body is a direct contradiction of Schiller's and Goethe's humanistic ideal. The point – unlike that of *Wanda* or anything else in the epoch – is thus uniquely two-edged: that love, the hope of healing for unfree men and women, is possible, but only at the price of mutual destruction. It is certainly impossible within the framework of the Classic-Romantic anthropology. Here, then, Kleist's deconstructive fury has transcended the age's dominant paradigm. The attack is continued in Kleist's late essay *Über das Marionettentheater* (*On puppet theatre*, 1810) where an argument is made that true aesthetic grace is possible only in inanimate objects (such as puppets) or animals, and not in the characteristically reflective human race.

After theatrical disaster at Weimar, Kleist courted popularity by publishing two volumes of *Erzählungen* (*Stories*, 1810). All create a world which no longer makes sense. *Das Erdbeben in Chili* (*The earthquake in Chile*, 1807) reflects on the Revolution and cocks a snook at Schiller's aesthetic utopia by emphasising the instability of things. *Die Marquise von O...* (*The Marchioness of O...*, 1807) deconstructs sexual morality with a Goethe-parody. In *Hermann und Dorothea*, the innkeeper recalls – in transparent sexual imagery – how good came of ill when he rescued his future wife from her father's burning house and sealed their successful marriage with an imposed kiss. Kleist radicalises this imagery. After the storm of a burning citadel by Russian troops, the unconscious Marchioness is raped in her father's house by Count F., who later becomes her beloved husband. But Kleist complicates the telling. His narrator coyly substitutes a dash in the text for the rape itself. Moreover the Count had rescued the Marquise from rape by his own troops minutes before the crime. His sudden insistence, months later, on the Marquise's hand in marriage, thus puzzles the reader until a confessional dream makes all clear. However, the main interest is the Marquise's perspective. She apparently cannot recall the rape, especially since the Count seems to have rescued her from abuse. When her guardian angel is exposed as a devil, her innermost convictions are cruelly refuted, and the slow shifts in her position, from assent to his suit, to rejection and then assent again, only underline the foundationlessness of human convictions.

A treatise and a novel signal Goethe's increasing alienation from the bewildering *Zeitgeist*. As ever in such circumstances he turned first to natural science. His *Farbenlehre* (*Theory of colour*, 1810) denounces Newton's analytical and mathematical method as useless for grasping the living truth of nature. The alternative is a pantheistic myth based on his notion that the totality of nature is revealed through privileged sensual intuition. The colour theory thus – strangely mirroring the tendencies of the age – assumes fundamental antagonistic elements of light and darkness and suggests how these generate colours by interacting in translucent media. More convincing are his observations on seeing. He notes how the eye, confronted with bright light or colour, spontaneously generates the complementary opposite on the retina. Thus the individual strives but fails to encompass totality. The empirically orientated scientific establishment ignored his work. It was too close to Romantic 'Naturphilosophie'.

Die Wahlverwandtschaften (*Elective affinities*, 1809–10) treats the traditional novelistic conflict of love and marriage in a still more antagonistic, but equally mythical mode. The four main characters seem to obey a chemical law of substances' propensity to combine and re-combine, but only in fantasised adultery, where illusion asserts a fatal power over reality. Charlotte, in love with the Captain, becomes unexpectedly pregnant by her husband Eduard. This hardens Charlotte's commitment to marriage, but only complicates Eduard's determination to break it. His return from the Napoleonic wars so unsettles Ottilie, with whom he is in love, that she causes the 'adulterous' child to drown. Charlotte at last accepts divorce, but Ottilie decides that the perfection of her love for Eduard is to renounce him. All further moves exhausted, the four remain on the estate in an eery semblance of normality. When Ottilie starves herself to death, Eduard too pines away. Goethe seems in this irreducibly ambiguous work to advocate Romantic passion. Eduard and Ottilie are presented as an androgynous ideal, and their death mimics the Romantic love-death. Yet the espousal of Romantic myth is not Goethe's, but his narrator's, who, having attacked the lovers in Part 1, wilfully glamorises them in Part 2. That, however, hardly makes the novel into an apology of marriage. Faced with this perspectivism, we do well to remember the colour theory, with its doctrine that we strive, but fail to grasp totality. *Die Wahlverwandtschaften*, with its oscillating sympathies, is a kind of *moral* 'Urphänomen' embodying the unending struggle of passion and law. The marriage is also Goethe's metaphor for the age. The estate constantly resonates to the noise of outside events, from the wars to the dissolution of feudalism, which signal the birth of a new order. But that is radically undermined. The marriage, scarcely made, is shown to be dying. The child, scarcely born, drowns. The love of Eduard and Ottilie is sterile. So the whole novel is shot through with new beginnings doomed from infancy. It is a gloomy and frightening snapshot of Germany in these years of transition. The Romantics admired its bleak aesthetic achievement. Ottilie's renunciation of her sensuality, surrounded by Catholicising imagery, seems to have prompted Werner's conversion to orthodox Roman Catholicism. But the moralistic Arnim's counterblast, his Romantic novel *Armut, Reichtum, Schuld und Buße der Gräfin Dolores* (*Poverty, wealth, guilt and repentance of Countess Dolores*, 1810), shows how an adulterous marriage is saved.

As resistance to Napoleon intensified, nationalist attitudes became extreme. Fichte's *Reden an die deutsche Nation* (*Addresses to the German nation*, 1807–8) are typical. Delivered in a Berlin still under French occupation, they project Fichte's familiar notion of the ego's absolute sovereignty onto the historico-cultural plane of the German nation. As the ego defines itself philosophically by the reflection of what it is not, so Germany establishes its identity by distinguishing Germanness from otherness. The *Reden* thus posit the uniqueness of the German nation as an ethical and metaphysical entity. Germany's mission – the cultural and political domination of Europe (by merit) – is threatened. Germany requires inner self-renewal by a return to origins. A programme of popular education is to bind the individual ever more closely to the state, which monitors the nation's historical mission. Finally, Fichte demands that the author serve the same cause. It was an inspiring call from the pre-stigious mentor of early Romanticism. The preachers followed suit. Schleiermacher, in particular, gave memorable series of (subtly left-wing) patriotic sermons on German salvation in Halle and later in Berlin. Worse, however, was to come. With its well-understood need of scape-goats, the nationalist mentality, in defining what it was, also defined what it was not. The prime example here are the statutes of the 'Christlich-Teutsche Tischgesellschaft' (Christian-German Dining Club'), founded by Brentano and Arnim at Berlin in 1811. Despite including the cream of the Berlin intelligentsia – the founders, Müller, Kleist, Savigny, Fichte, the architect Schinkel, the general Clausewitz, the composer Zelter, plus leading members of the nobility and the military – its ideology is star-tlingly narrow. Only male Christian Germans are eligible for membership. Women (even Bettine von Arnim) and Jews (even if converted, and despite their imminent emancipation) are excluded. Thus Arnim and Brentano propagate a new anti-Semitism. *Des Knaben Wunderhorn* had included Arnim's version of a standard anti-Jewish story, 'Die Juden in Passau' ('The Passau Jews'). At this time the salons of Rahel Varnhagen and Henriette Herz begin to be cold-shouldered by right-thinking Christian Berliners. But nationalism found opponents even within. In 1811 Brentano gave his biting satirical lecture *Geschichte des Philisters vor, in, und nach der Geschichte* (*History of the Philistine before, in, and after history*) in the 'Tischgesellschaft'. This tirade opens with anti-Semitic insults, but concentrates on the Philistines (also banned from membership). It is not entirely clear who they (in the Bible the enemy of God's people) are. Lack of nationalist fervour is not a criterion. One of Brentano's Philistines is the linguistic purist Voß, who memorably recommended that 'kunstschal-lend' replace 'musikalisch' in the German vocabulary, and fought a bitter battle with Brentano and Arnim over their love for the (un-German) sonnet-form. Elsewhere we hear that Philistines are by nature leathery, deeply egoistic, bound to their prosaic habits and incapable of true faith or true national identity. The Philistines, then, are the enemy within, the comfortable German burghers.

When the Wars of Liberation began after Napoleon's débâcle in Moscow in 1812, Fichte's extremist call for absolute poetic subservience to the nationalist cause was answered by nearly every living German poet. The mutually exclusive tension of word and sword, we saw, is a *Leitmotiv* of the age's literature. Now, when Theodor Körner (1791–1813), son of Schiller's Dresden friend (and contributor to *Die Horen*) Christian Gottfried Körner, joined Friedrich Ludwig Jahn's élite volunteer corps of Lützower Jäger ('Lützow Rangers'), word and sword became one. Körner's postumously edited anthology *Leier und Schwert* (*Lyre and sword*, 1814) contains war songs intended for communal singing and designed to reinforce a common consciousness. Henceforth the imagery of religious self-sacrifice, appropriated in easy literary secularisation for the nationalist cause, predominates. Körner's poetry emphasises only how far the hard-won terrain of aesthetic autonomy (with its protection of the self against external determination) has been re-colonised by unreflecting activism. The same holds for war poets like Jahn (1778–1852) and Ernst Moritz Arndt (1769–1860). As Körner's war poetry appropriates the language of classical humanism, so the military cult of the body by 'Turnvater' Jahn appropriates its apology of corporeality.

Körner's drama *Zriny* (1812) is a transparent allegory of the German situation. In 1566 the Turkish Emperor Soliman seeks to crown his ebbing life with its highest triumph. Only the Hungarian fortress Sigeth, manned by Graf Zriny's small garrison, stands between him and Vienna. Emperor Maximilian commands Zriny to sacrifice all in desperate defence of the Christian nation. 'Das Vaterland darf jedes Opfer fordern' ('The fatherland may demand any sacrifice') is his intoxicated reply. The rest of the play merely enacts the citadel's inevitable fall. There is an effective contrast between the totalitarian methods used by cruel Soliman-Napoleon to send his soldiers to their death, and the willing self-sacrifice of Zriny's people. Equally impressive is the visual imagery, which involves the Christians withdrawing into ever deeper recesses of the fortress as successive ring walls are taken, until they are cornered in the cellar, murder the women to spare them dishonour, and unexpectedly blow up the entire fortress. Thus defeat is victory and death is life. The spectacular finale, with its triumphant assertion of the self's inner freedom, is intended to evoke the sublime. Yet that aesthetic has been perverted. There never was any Schillerian moral problem to overcome. In truth, the play evokes only delight in a ritualised process of self-destruction glorified by the familiar love-death imagery. Killed on patrol with his unit, Körner (as he wished) not only lived but died the ideology of his writings. No less than six per cent of the entire Prussian population entered active service during the Wars of Liberation 1813–15.

Three writers stand outside this trend. Kleist ostensibly joined in the fervour with his dramas *Die Hermannsschlacht* (*The battle of Hermann*, 1808) and *Der Prinz von Homburg* (*The Prince of Homburg*, 1811). But in each the nation is in fact problematic. In *Die Hermannsschlacht* Kleist as usual confuses our expectation. Hermann, the renowned German leader who annihilated the Romans in the Teutoburger Wald in AD 9, is for Kleist neither charismatic hero nor anti-hero, but an amoral anti-colonialist plotter and terrorist of the most modern kind. He double-deals the Romans under the noble Varus by leading them into a trap. But he also fools his (mostly contemptible) German allies, and provokes the passive Germans by inciting atrocities, allegedly committed by the Romans, himself. Here, then, ethics and the search for truth are subordinated to the lie and the overriding need for total war. Success is Hermann's only merit. Otherwise, he and his state are as suspect as what they seek to replace, and the bloodthirsty play sparks anything but warlike enthusiasm.

Remarkably, since it features a Prussian prince's abject fear of death, *Der Prinz von Homburg* was intended to win Kleist the Prussian royal family's favour. This time the historical precedent is the Prussian victory over Sweden in 1675 at Fehrbellin. The play might seem to be the usual glorification of Prussian military prowess and exhortation to greater feats. In fact, it undermines the otherwise sacred bond of Prussian state and subject. Carried away, Homburg – not for the first time – disobeys the Great Elector's explicit battle orders. The Prussians still triumph, but Homburg is arrested and condemned to death, for he has transgressed the law which is the foundation of Prussia's very existence. As a result his personality crumbles shamefully. Offered mercy at the price of injustice, Homburg at last decides to glorify the law by accepting his fate. Meanwhile, the entire army is in revolt against this application of the law. His generals remind the Elector that he himself prompted Homburg's lust for patriotic glory the night before, when Homburg was in a (suggestible) state of somnambulist trance. The sentence is commuted. Thus – in stark contrast to Körner – the state's demand for death is defeated, and the law on which Prussia is built is subverted by humanistic pleas.

Jean Paul stayed loyal to the ideals of the Revolution and Enlightenment. His writings of this time, formed in that secularised version of the sermon beloved of Romantic publicists – *Friedens-Predigt an Deutschland* (Peace-sermon to Germany, 1808), *Dämmerungen für Deutschland* (Dawnings for Germany, 1809), *Mars' und Phöbus' Thronwechsel* (Phoebus's succession to Mars, 1814) and *Politische Fastenpredigten* (Political Lenten sermons, 1810–17) – do not demonise the French occupiers of Germany. Instead they preach moral strength, faith and resistance rather than violent overthrow, emphasise Germany's status as cultural rather than political power, and, in the tradition of Kant's *Zum Ewigen Frieden* (Perpetual peace, 1795), yearn for a German republic to replace the unlamented Empire at the heart of a war-free Europe under the rule of law.

Goethe's literary relationship with German nationalism was still more complex. The author of 'Prometheus' made no secret of his admiration for Napoleon as titan of world history. When Goethe tried to write war songs, the ink refused to flow. He did his best to satisfy the public by distributing copies of *Hermann und Dorothea*. Iffland received a festival drama *Des Epimenides Erwachen* (Epimenides' awakening), which was, however, staged only in 1815. But at a time when most writers used the drama and the lyric to preach self-sacrifice in the cause of national redemption, Goethe bucked the trend. *Aus meinem Leben. Dichtung und Wahrheit* (*Towards a life. Poetry and truth*, 1811–14; fourth part, 1827), which treats Goethe's life from 1749–75, takes up an unfashionable, indeed, non-literary genre, and focuses not on the nation, but – in what must have seemed irresponsible self-preoccupation – his own personality. Contemporary letters attest to Goethe's intense alienation from the public and his view that this, paradoxically, is his most constructive contribution to the national cause. *Dichtung und Wahrheit* on one level seeks to modify Goethe's image. By and large he was still known as the author of *Werther*. But it also follows soul-baring confessions from St Augustine to Rousseau. Goethe was far from sovereign self-control at this time, and the encounters with the *Zeitgeist* had disorientated his sense of personal identity too, so that *Dichtung und Wahrheit* also performs the classic autobiographical task of self-insight. Yet Goethe's revolutionary definition of the genre sees the individual as intrinsically a product of his contemporary context, so that the Goethean autobiography achieves its task of self-knowledge only by interpreting the entire epoch as well. Hence *Dichtung und Wahrheit* is Goethe's coded protest against the tendencies of the age. Two of the early books exemplify the technique. Book 3 looks at Goethe's early youth in Frankfurt 1759–63. But its true subject is a hymn of praise to the urbanity of the French army then occupying his home town. Book 5 lovingly ridicules the coronation of the Holy Roman Emperor at Frankfurt in 1763–4 so as to destroy the political icon – the Empire – which Napoleon's opponents in the Wars of Liberation most dearly yearned to restore. How this went down with the 'Franzosenfresser' ('Francivores') of the day we can imagine. Increasingly, as his focus on world literature and the renewed Orientalism of the *West-östlicher Divan* (*West-Eastern divan*) attest, Goethe began to look for readers and reading-matter beyond German-speaking lands or beyond contemporary times.

Restoration

Napoleon and his system were broken by the monumental 'Battle of the Nations' at Leipzig on 16–18 October 1813, which was to make a lasting impression on the German psyche. The Bourbons' return to Paris marked the beginning of the Age of Restoration. The Peace of Paris restored the borders of 1792, so that the left bank of the Rhine became German once more. The Austrian Chancellor Metternich's Congress of Vienna (1815) ordered Germany and Europe anew. In Germany, Austria lost the Netherlands but made territorial gains to the South and East, in Upper Italy, Dalmatia and Galicia. Prussia made gains to the South and West, with part of Saxony and, above all, Westphalia and the left bank of the

Rhine. As Austria grew out of the German core lands, Prussia expanded into them. The Congress's principles – restoration of the pre-Napoleonic *status quo,* legitimism (the assertion of its rights by the French monarchy and of their sovereign authority by the victorious monarchies), and the European balance of power – removed most of the achievements of Revolution. Germany still lacked a truly constitutional monarchy. The Holy Alliance, initiated by Tsar Alexander, and enthusiastically supported by Friedrich Wilhelm III of Prussia and Franz I, pledged itself to Christian patriarchal rule within and interventionism against opposed tendencies without. Against the wishes of Arndt, the Romantic publicist Joseph von Görres (1776–1848), and even Freiherr vom Stein, the Holy Roman Empire was not reborn. The Congress constituted instead the 'Deutscher Bund' ('German Federation'), with thirty-eight founding members and a Federal Parliament in Frankfurt am Main, to which however only delegates of the governments, not their subjects, belonged. As with the Empire, the Eastern dominions of Prussia and Austria did not form part of the Federation. Germany was thus still fragmented, without effective central direction of power, and exposed to the Prussian–Austrian dualism. Conservatism ruled, democratic, liberal and nationalist energies were repressed. Hegel's philosophy, which, with its notions of history as the realisation of the idea, and of the individual (no matter how titanic), as the mere instrument of reason's higher cunning, seemed to legitimate existing circumstances, was now dominant in Berlin. Slowly, the process of industrialisation, encouraged by the Stein–Hardenberg reforms, commenced. The age of managed stability yearned for by all – *Biedermeierzeit* – had dawned, if not in the form all wished. The federation was to last until 1866.

This was an age of resignation, both political and otherwise, and repression. The party most disappointed by the outcome of the Congress of Vienna was that of the German nationalists. Their opposition crystallised henceforth in the universities. The first 'Burschenschaft' (patriotic student club), devoted to the ideals of honour, freedom and fatherland, was founded on 12 June 1815 in Jena by former Lützower Jäger, followers of Jahn, and students. They adopted as their colours those of the rangers – black, red and gold. Others rapidly followed. Five hundred met at the Wartburg festival in October 1817, on the anniversary of the Reformation. Books, including those of Kotzebue and Haller, were burnt, as was the 'Bundesakte' or Deed of Federation, and ringing speeches were made in the name of freedom. The members of the Holy Alliance feared another Revolution. When Kotzebue, who in the meantime, true to his lack of fundamental convictions, had become an (innocuous) agent of the Tsar, was assassinated as a 'spy' and 'seducer of youth' on 23 March 1819 at Mannheim by the student Karl Ludwig Sand, the reactionary Karlsbad decrees were forced through the Federal Parliament and into the Deed of Federation, with severe restrictions on the universities' freedom, and press censorship. This instrument of repression was used ruthlessly to persecute oppositional thinkers for the next thirty years.

The Romantics, whose instinctive conservatism and historicism had, nevertheless, always attacked the establishment, were generally in opposition. Görres's *Kotzebue und was ihn gemordet* (*Kotzebue and what murdered him*, 1819) is a typical late Romantic gesture. Published in Ludwig Börne's *Die Waage* (*The balance*), it is, although at bottom theologically motivated, a stinging attack on both despotic repression from above, which he sees as symbolic of the old order, and violent agitation from below (the new order). The murder is a sign of the times. The princes, who have denied Germany its just reward after the struggle, are responsible. Görres's flight to Strasbourg for the next eight years is a sign of the enforced powerlessness of the literary word for the rest of the epoch. If the literature of the Wars of Liberation marked the steady colonisation of the autonomous literary language created by Goethe, Schiller and the Romantics for other, mainly propagandistic ends, then the period after 1815 continues and concludes this process. All writers now experience the loss of aesthetic autonomy in an age of disappointment, both as literary and as philosophical phenomenon, and their writings express individual strategies of facing the problem.

At this time of religious revival – Napoleon's fall was generally seen as a judgement of God – Clemens Brentano typifies the turn towards established religious authority anticipated in a sense by Novalis and Friedrich Schlegel and finally taken by nearly all later Romantics. The tension between poetry and life had always been a basic feature of his writing. His early career, including the marriages to Sophie Mereau and Auguste Bußmann, is the attempt to live the aestheticist utopia contained in *Lucinde*, which he calls the 'free poetic existence'. This belief in the ego's ability to create the earthly paradise from its own imaginative resources is slowly undermined after Mereau's death (1806). With it, apparently, goes his will to practise poetry, and the return to the historical institution of religion. The cradle Catholic Brentano (and Arnim) formed close links in 1816 with the Pietistic grouping in Berlin around the 'Spittelkirche' ('Hospital Church') of the aged Lutheran pastor, Justus Gottfried Hermes, who semed a mythical embodiment of old and simple truths. Brentano's confession and reversion to practising Catholicism followed on 27 February 1817.

But first there came a flowering of his poetry in crisis. Brentano, one of the great literary gossips of the day, had gleefully reported Kleist's feeling of humiliation at having to earn his living by writing in the popular novella-form. In fact, the novella was to become one of the dominant literary genres of the nineteenth century. Arnim had published his *Wintergarten* in 1809, Tieck (emerging from writer's block) his collection of early and later novellas as *Phantasus* (1812–16), Fouqué his *Undine* in 1811, and Adelbert von Chamisso his *Peter Schlemihls wundersame Geschichte* (*The marvellous tale of Peter Schlemihl*) in 1814. Hoffmann's *Fantasiestücke in Callots Manier* (*Fantasias in the manner of Callot*) appeared in 1814, followed by *Nachtstücke* (*Nocturnes*, 1815) and *Die Serapions-Brüder* (*The Brethren of Serapion*) in 1819–21. Goethe's *Die Wahlverwandtschaften* was based on a planned novella, and his continuation of the *Bildungsroman, Wilhelm Meisters Wanderjahre* (*Wilhelm Meister's years of wandering*, 1821–9) is in essence a modified collection of novellas. Brentano too, after his failure to conquer the stage with his Tieckian ironic comedy *Ponce de Leon* (1804) and his patriotic Habsburg drama *Die Gründung Prags* (*The foundation of Prague*, 1815) turned to the once-despised form. Two novellas typify the transition he, and Romanticism, were undergoing.

Brentano's *Die Schachtel mit der Friedenspuppe* (*The box with the peace doll*, 1815) appeared in the Viennese journal *Friedensblätter* (*Journal of peace*), and was intended to influence the Congress. Set in 1814, it tells how a crime, committed during the Revolution in France, comes to light in Germany, as a column of refugees from Moscow passes through an estate resembling Arnim's. The box is a fatal object. Used to hold a stillborn baby as part of a *citoyen's* plot to usurp an aristocrat's inheritance, this Pandora's Box symbolises the root of all Revolutionary evil. Unwittingly, the German Baron has brought it home, where the refugees, betrayer and betrayed, recognize it, quarrel, and are brought to justice. The hero is the Prussian 'Gerichtshalter' (an official with investigative as well as judicial duties). Intuitively he discerns truth and falsehood in the refugees' stories and metes out justice, the foundation for lasting peace. This contrastive tale thus glorifies traditional German patrimonial law at the expense of the *Code Napoléon*. The 'Gerichtshalter', who applies creative intuition to discover factual truth, is of course Brentano's ideal artist in disguise. He links poetry productively with life, so that the novella is an attempt to discover a use for poetry in an increasingly utilitarian age. In *Die Geschichte vom braven Kasperl und dem schönen Annerl* (*The history of brave Casper and pretty Anna*, 1817), derived from a folk-song in *Des Knaben Wunderhorn*, the reflection on poetry in poetry is again used to justify poetry's use-value. This time we have as narrator a Romantic poet (and collector of folk-songs). He is ashamed of his seemingly vacuous profession, but is spellbound by an aged, seemingly forlorn peasant woman. This mythical figure embodies everything he is not. Thanks to her naive faith, she is at one with herself and the world. The poet, on the other hand, is torn between desire for faith and its lack. He willingly accepts the providential opportunity to serve her, by putting her unsophisticated words into the form of a petition to the Duke: Annerl, who has been dishonoured, killed her illegitimate child and will shortly be executed, is to lie with her former beloved, the proud suicide Kasperl. This, then, is another attempt to link Romantic poetry, in the service of an end, with life. But it all goes wrong. Asked only to plead for honourable burial, the poet in fact bids (too late) for clemency. Not only, then, does poetry fail to serve life, it insensibly perverts the (Christian) message.

After 1817, Brentano made his choice, abandoning publication of all autonomous poetry. The self-censor began to evolve into what Heine (pejoratively) termed a corresponding member of the Catholic propaganda. The charismatic spiritual director of many later Romantic poets, Bishop Johann Michael Sailer, may have influenced him with his critique of Wackenroder's aesthetic religion *Von dem Bunde der Religion mit der Kunst* (*The covenant of religion and art*, 1808), in which he argued that the role of art was to propagate religious truth. In any case, Brentano emblematically left salon Berlin on 14 September 1818 to spend most of the next six years at the bedside of a stigmatic nun, Anna Katharina Emmerick, in obscure Dülmen (near Münster). His task was that of the clerk the poet of *Kasperl und Annerl* had wished to become. For Emmerick was felt to have authentic visions of the Passion, and Brentano – for whom inner poetic revelation is now replaced by authoritative and externalised religious vision, backed by the empirical 'evidence' of her wounds – produced thousands of pages of notes purporting to reproduce her descriptions of the ecstatic trances. The editing of these visions became his (unfinished) life's work. Only one volume, *Das bittere Leiden unseres Herrn Jesu Christi* (*The bitter tears of our Lord Jesus Christ*, 1833), appeared in his lifetime. It became, and remains, a widely read work of devotional literature, and is far from lacking in poetic merit. That is no accident, for recent work has demonstrated the extent to which these ostensibly clerkly dictations are the esoteric continuation of Romantic poetry by other means. Brentano continued to publish profane works – the classic humorous novella *Die mehreren Wehmüller und ungarischen Nationalgesichter* (*The several Wehmüllers and Hungarian national physiognomies* – first published 1817, republished 1833) and the masterly fairy-tale *Gockel, Hinkel und Gackeleia* (1838) are examples – but these all appeared explicitly to raise money for good causes.

Zacharias Werner's fate is analogous to Brentano's. He too experienced conversion as the rejection of essentially anthropomorphic religion and bent his poetic gifts to serve the old religion. He retrained in homiletics, had sensational success as a preacher to the educated classes (and crowned heads) from 1814 to 1816 in Vienna, and ended up as St Clement Maria

Hofbauer's assistant. Adam Müller, Friedrich Schlegel and Friedrich Gentz became propagandistic functionaries of Metternich's restorative apparatus.

E. T. A. Hoffmann's reaction to the loss of autonomy focuses on problems of narrative and rationality. Like Werner, Hoffmann lost his job in the Prussian administration in 1806. But this distinguished lawyer was also a multi-talented artist. He had a successful career as Kapellmeister at Bamberg (where he put on one of the first modern German performances of Calderón). When the Wars of Liberation ended his musical career, he became an eminent liberal judge in Restoration Berlin, but continued to write – initially, fashionable novellas. However *Die Elixiere des Teufels* (*The devil's elixirs*, 1814–15) and *Lebens-Ansichten des Katers Murr* (*The life and opinions of Murr the cat*, 1820–2) are major Romantic novels. Hoffmann has much in common with the Jean Paul, who contributed the preface to the *Fantasiestücke*. But his writings express much more radically the crisis of poetry and of the sovereign Romantic ego in an age which refuted their very possibility. For all that, they – like Brentano's and Werner's – remain committed to the Romantic ideal.

For Hoffmann not religion, but the new depth psychology – prompted by Fichte's redefinition of the ego to include hidden origins – undermines poetic autonomy. He admired Moritz's *Anton Reiser*, with its notion that the psyche is programmed by unconscious structures formed during childhood. More important are Gotthilf Heinrich Schubert's Dresden lectures of 1808, *Ansichten von der Nachtseite der Naturwissenschaft*, and *Symbolik der Träume* (*Symbolism of dreams*, 1814), which treat trance, dream and somnambulism as manifestations of the unconscious. Schubert sees such states as experience of a sixth sense, which bestows spiritual insight on a physical organ. But they are also deeply suspect, for they enable the body to take over the mind. This *Die Elixiere des Teufels*, a novel of schizophrenic loss of autonomy and reflection on art in art, takes up. Here the monk Medardus's artist's autobiography is supposed to heal his divided psyche by crystallising his lifelong struggle for possession of Aurelie with his *Doppelgänger*, the vicious sensualist Viktorin. In fact, the process of therapy is problematised. As Medardus describes the first appearance of his *Doppelgänger*, the narrative slides into the (historic) present. The past comes alive in the present, Viktorin, symbol of diabolical physicality, usurps the writer Medardus's consciousness, and the autonomy of the subject – and artist – is lost. The reader must share the schizoid perspective. The therapeutic effect of poetry on the psyche has thus failed, the Romantic ego has become the plaything of the unconscious, and so has the project of *Bildung*. Hoffmann's novellas develop the theme. *Der Magnetiseur* (*The Mesmerist*, a *Fantasiestück* of 1814), in which the Mesmerist Alban turns out to be a demonic artist-figure with a

vampire-like appetite for young women's souls, reflects on the misogynist
anthropology underlying Romantic aesthetics. *Der Sandmann* (*The
sandman*, a *Nachtstück* of 1815) treats the madness of the artist
Nathanael, who is gradually overcome by an Oedipal childhood complex
and commits suicide. The focus is, however, on his social isolation, as
neither he, nor the narrator of the tale, manages to communicate his
vision to ordinary burghers like his fiancé Clara – or the reader. The division between artist and public, overcome by the patriotic literature of the
Wars of Liberation, has opened up again. *Nachtwachen von Bonaventura*
(*Nightwatches of Bonaventura*), now assumed to be by the minor dramatist August Klingemann, had already taken the sense of Romantic narrative insecurity, isolation and irrelevance to suicidal extremes in those
strange years of 1805–6.

If these works focus on dissonance, *Kater Murr*, Hoffmann's masterpiece and one of the great poetic achievements of the nineteenth century,
is a hymn to compensatory humour. It attacks smug Restoration
'Bildungsbürgertum'. Murr, a relative of Tieck's Puss-in-boots, has (like
Goethe) written his poetic autobiography for the benefit of youth. The
astonishingly well-read Murr is blissfully unaware of the satirical disproportion between ambition and achievement. More important is the other
narrative strand. Murr, so the editor 'E. T. A. Hoffmann' tells us, has used
the proof-sheets of another work, the biography of the Romantic composer Kreisler, as scrap paper. Unaccountably, these have been printed
with his autobiography in seemingly random order. Thus we have two
texts: the seamlessly readable autobiography of the cultivated cat, and the
Künstlerroman of the authentically tortured Romantic artist, which –
having been recycled by the cat – remains a tattered fragment. The latter,
in a sense, is the more valuable document. It records the life of a moody
musical genius and his conflict with the banal mentality and power structures of the feudal court. Thus if Murr's life naively identifies real and
ideal, Kreisler's makes the ironic distance of the two painfully obvious.
The work's achievement lies however in the way meaning is expressed
through its fragmented form. Narrative in *both* strands is out of control.
Its traditional task – closure, or imposition of significance on chaotic life-
data – has become impossible. But Hoffmann is not defeatist. In fact, the
two narrative strands are not unrelated parallels, but criss-cross and
mirror one another. *Taken together,* they rescue us from resignation. As
Kreisler's sublime love-duet with Julia is mirrored by Murr's roof-top cat-
erwauling with Miesmies, so his duel with an adjutant is mirrored by
Murr's scrap with a spotted cat. Hence savage irony modulates into the
characteristic attitude of the later Hoffmann: consolatory humour. This,
however, is not the sovereignty Medardus has lost, but a comforting substitute in bad times. Hoffmann demonstrated much moral courage during

the persecution of the 'demagogues'. He represented Jahn, when the Karlsbad decrees were invoked against the patriot, and also served as a force for moderation on the King's commission of inquiry into the troubles. His late fairy-tale *Meister Floh* (*Master flea*, 1822) satirises (as Knarrpanti) the man Friedrich Wilhelm III entrusted with pursuit of the demagogues, Carl Albert von Kamptz.

Mimili. Eine Erzählung (*Mimili. A tale*, 1815) by H. Clauren (Carl Gottlieb Samuel Heun, 1771–1854) typifies the *Biedermeier* taste for light reading and the gap, satirised by Hoffmann, which opened again between high and popular literature. First published in the literary journal *Der Freimüthige* (*The free speaker*), it was extended successively until 1819. This is ostensibly the idyllic tale – in the tradition of Haller, Geßner, Voß, and Goethe's *Hermann und Dorothea* – of the Prussian officer Wilhelm's love for the naive Swiss girl Mimili (Wilhelmine), whom he meets on his travels in search of peace after the first War of Liberation. The experience of sublime mountain scenery – reminiscent of Goethe's *Briefe aus der Schweiz* (*Letters from Switzerland*, 1796) – coincides with Mimili's appearance to produce love at first sight. This innocently coquettish yet cultivated ideal seems a heaven-sent reward for the heroic bearer of the Iron Cross. The stern yet kindly father requires them to wait a year before marriage, and all is well until Napoleon returns from Elba. When the patriotic Wilhelm seems to have perished at Waterloo, Mimili too sickens, so that even the narrator, who is skilfully kept in ignorance, presumes them dead. However, both pull through, marry and live happily ever after. In fact, this is a skilful exploitation of restorative taste. The evocation of the recovered sentimental idyll and its characters is totally schematic and familiar, so that identification with them is easy, and the predictable happy ending affirms received patriotic and religious values. Clauren caters for male interest with adventurous battle-scenes and female interest with expert descriptions of Mimili's provincial fashions. But the work's most striking feature – and that to which the Romantic publicist Wilhelm Hauff in his *Kontrovers-Predigt über H. Clauren* (*Polemical sermon on H. Clauren*, 1827) most strongly objected – is its calculated appeal to eroticism. Countless times Wilhelm must restrain himself – usually by an appeal to the values incorporated in his Iron Cross – from exploiting the delights offered by Mimili's lovingly described heaving bosom and shapely calves, so that the text is both sub-pornographically titillating and satisfyingly moral. *Mimili* sold nine thousand copies in three years and Clauren produced twenty-five volumes of collected works to the same recipe by 1851, many published in his journal *Vergißmeinnicht* (*Forget-me-not*) (named after the flower Mimili gives Wilhelm at their first parting). In his satire *Die Bücher und die Lesewelt* (*Books and the reading world*, 1828) Hauff attacks the *Biedermeier* world of popular reading and finds that we have returned to the state Kleist found at Würzburg in 1801. A lending librarian says of his customers: 'They want to be entertained; each, of course, in his own way.' Literature is merely a pastime. Görres's reflection on *Deutschland und die Revolution* (*Germany and the Revolution*, 1819) is a substitute for a sleeping draught. Travelogues and scientific works have disappeared. Jean Paul, save for rare interest by *cognoscenti* in *Das Kampaner Tal* and *Titan*, is ignored. Cheap translations of historical romances by Walter Scott, James Fenimore Cooper and Washington Irving dominate. There is no public today for a German Goethe or Schiller: 'The public has lost faith, confidence and pleasure in our literature.' They read almanachs and journals such as *Der Freimüthige*. Above all, ladies love H. Clauren: 'That is after all the taste of the age.' Hauff himself capitulated to the *Zeitgeist* with his (probably unintended) parody of Clauren *Der Mann im Mond* (*The man in the moon*, 1825) and Scottian historical romance *Lichtenstein* (1825), not to mention his large production of novellas.

Two novellas, Hoffmann's *Des Vetters Eckfenster* (*My cousin's corner-window*, 1822) and Tieck's *Des Lebens Überfluß* (*The luxuries of life*, 1839) exemplify the inner decay of Romantic aesthetics against this background. The cousin is a poet, even in his illness a figuration of the dying Hoffmann, and his lofty window, looking down on a crowded Berlin market-place, symbolises the sovereignty of the Romantic poetic ego in its last years. Hoffmann's Romantic compositional technique is enacted before our very eyes, as the cousin conjures poetry from the prosaic reality in the square. But the point of the tale is a memory, the poignant meeting between the poet and an avidly reading flower-girl. Proudly, he reveals that he is her favourite author, only to be deflated by a naive admission: until now she had never known that the books from the lending library had authors. If it is encouraging that his works are read, it is all the more crushing that their intended effect is negated by the use readers make of them. This is less Romantic Irony than admission of the Romantic vision's growing irrelevance. Tieck followed the trend. Like Hauff's friend, the critic and poet Willibald Alexis (Wilhelm Häring) Tieck wrote historical novels in the manner of Scott and Manzoni (*Der Aufruhr in den Cevennen* (*The uprising in the Cevennes*, 1826), *Vittoria Accorombona* (1840), and moved much closer to realism. *Des Lebens Überfluß* (1839) is his testament to Romanticism. A Romantic couple, he a poet, she a housewife, share a garret next to, but hidden from, a busy Dresden thoroughfare. One freezing Christmas, their funds run out. They depend for food on their aged servant and for warmth on Heinrich's destruction, plank by plank, of the timber staircase to their flat. Disconnected from reality yet miraculously sustained by Heinrich's writings, they live on. When the owner returns, reality – prefigured by a satirical dream in which human dignity is measured by money – destroys the idyll. Since Heinrich resists eviction, the people fear Revolution is breaking out. However a *deus ex machina* restores their finances, and Heinrich becomes a successful writer. If Romanticism is here attacked for its lack of contact with reality, so materialistic reality is attacked for its unwillingness to support Romanticism.

Romanticism lived on, but only in the sense that its practitioners physically survived in an age orientated increasingly towards utilitarianism, entertainment and realism. The Catholic Joseph von Eichendorff (1788–1857) – a contemporary of Friedrich Schlegel, Brentano, Werner and Hofbauer in Vienna – is the archetypal late Romantic, holding fast to his aesthetic, whilst history moves on. His novella *Das Marmorbild* (*The marble statue*, 1816–17) echoes the ambivalence of Brentano's attitude to poetry, as the innocent youth Florio wavers between the heathen beauty of Venus and Bianca's authentic Christian life. *Das Schloß Dürande* (*Château Durande*, 1835–6), which sees the French Revolution as sparked by fanaticism in the people and foolish exploitation by the nobility, echoes Brentano's diagnosis in *Die Schachtel*. His *Taugenichts* (*Good-for-nothing*, written 1817–21, published 1826) is a frothy little masterpiece, in which a personification of poetry triumphs, more by luck than judgement, over his philistine environment. Eichendorff's last Romantic novel, *Dichter und ihre Gesellen* (*Poets and their apprentices*) appeared as late as 1834.

In the late 1820s, as the radical literary movement 'Das Junge Deutschland' (Young Germany), which advocated literature as an instrument of social and political polemic, grew more voluble and influential not only the Romantics, but Goethe too seemed to have become irrelevant. Wolfgang Menzel's *Die deutsche Literatur* (*German literature*) – no doubt as a consequence of his policy of publication in the Wars of Liberation – attacks Goethe as an egoist and political quietist. Heine's *Die romantische Schule* (*The Romantic school*, 1833) polished the legend of Goethe's aesthetic autonomy as an ivory tower of political indifference. Goethe, in the meantime, had made his compromises with the age. *Sankt-Rochus-Fest zu Bingen* (*The feast of St Roche at Bingen*, 1817) celebrated a popular festival for the restoration of the Roman Catholic chapel on the Rhine after the secularist depredations of the French. At a time of bitter polemic against Werner and Friedrich Schlegel, he even uses a Catholic hagiographical sermon as the vehicle for a Goethean message of reconciliation and consolation. But his publication of Heinrich Meyer's *Neudeutsche religios-patriotische Kunst* (*Modern German religious-patriotic art*, 1817) with its denunciation of Romantic allegorical art in favour of Classical plastic art, made the final break with Romanticism. In the *Ästhetische Briefe*, Schiller had argued that only the artist was immune to the modifications of time, and recalled inspiringly how, in the age of

Roman decadence, artists had preserved true humanity in aesthetic form for posterity. The works of Goethe's old age follow just this principle. He holds fast to the classical project in this age of change and disappointment, crystallises the doctrine of 'Entsagung' ('renunciation') and produces, in his last works, an aesthetic testament. *Wilhelm Meisters Wanderjahre* (*Wilhelm Meister's journeyman years*, 1821–9) concludes the ironic novel of self-cultivation in a way which both anticipates modern novel aesthetics, and is open to the tendencies of the age, yet preserves the classical heritage. It is no longer a coherent narrative, but a collection of novellas loosely linked (if not integrated) by the frame of Wilhelm's wanderings. The open form (like *Kater Murr*) signifies the new inadequacy of personal lives and narrative closure. Wilhelm retains his original motivation – aesthetic love of humanity – but has given up aesthetic for medical therapy. He experiences varied domains of human activity, from Jarno (now the mining expert 'Montan') and the domestic industries of spinning and weaving, to the astronomical mystic Makarie, and the Pädagogische Provinz, a vast educational foundation. The failure to grasp Mignon is condemned. But other embedded text-types dominate: masterly novellas – from *Die Flucht nach Ägypten* (*The flight to Egypt*) to *Die pilgernde Törin* (*The wandering fool*), *Der Mann von fünfzig Jahren* (*The fifty-year old man*) and *Die gefährliche Wette* (*The dangerous wager*) – but also letters, aphorisms, journals and diaries. All reflect the framework narrative. They hinge on Goethe's favourite theme of 'Schein' and 'Sein', exposing a subjective impulse to personal fulfilment as an error, and underscoring the lesson of renunciation. This novel is saturated more than any other text of its time with the objective reality of its age. The domestic workers' livelihood is threatened by the onward march of machines, the culture of humanity by de-personalised empirical science (symbolised by Wilhelm's forced anatomisation of a beautiful suicide's arm). The message is always the same: this is the age of one-sidedness and inhumanity. But Goethe is neither reactionary nor escapist. The weavers and spinners can join emigration projects, and Goethe accompanies the critique of modern science with the notion that aesthetic models might replace dissection. Above all, the individual must develop 'secular piety', think in terms of a global social mentality, and contribute through renunciation and goal-orientated labour. This highly self-conscious novel interprets itself. But its radical experiment in form makes it still a test for the reader.

Faust, a treatment of the legendary Renaissance alchemist and charlatan, accompanied Goethe all his life. The milestones of its development are simultaneously those of Goethe's own history of publication: the *Fragment* appears in his first collected works (1790), Part 1 in his second (1808), and Part 2 (1829–31) in the *Ausgabe letzter Hand*. But Faust is not Goethe, not even a poet. Instead, as his translation of St John's Gospel testifies ('In the beginning was the word' becomes 'In the beginning was the deed'), he is the representative figure of western European humanity, no less. *Faust* is thus, in a sense, the ultimate literary secularisation. The Prologue in Heaven suggests he is a new Job. But the accent is on 'new'. This child of Enlightenment lacks metaphysical interest, and the pact he makes with Mephistopheles hinges only on his ability to sustain his 'striving' against the attempts of the devil (whom we must see as a projection of modern consciousness) to satiate it. Striving, in turn, connotes at last the Western – sentimental – commitment to impose human values on the otherwise meaningless natural world. In Part 1, it is focused on Faust's person. He demands the microcosmic totality of human experience. What he gets, ironically, are a student drinking bout, an unconvincing rejuvenation of his appearance, and a domestic tragedy – the seduction, impregnation and execution of naive Gretchen. Only in Part 2, composed largely after 1825, does the work unfold its greatness. The structural principle changes, from the strongly integrated episodic scenes of Part 1 to five classical acts, which are, however, linked in the serial way typical of Goethe's late style. As in the *Wanderjahre*, Faust's experience is now saturated with the tendencies of the age – from the invention of paper money (presented as the final triumph of 'Schein' over 'Sein'), to revolution and reform (the competing natural theories of Vulcanism and Neptunism), the Northern longing for union with classical beauty (Helen of Troy), Byron's Romanticism (Euphorion, child of Faust and Helen) and, finally, the technological colonisation of the world (Faust's land-reclamation project). Here Faust the creator – Goethe, after Lessing, breaks with tradition – transcends tragedy. He does not go to hell. One can argue that he does not so much say 'Verweile doch, du bist so schön' ('Linger yet, you are so beautiful') (and so give up striving), as envisage a circumstance in which he would say it. But Faust is redeemed in the end, to undergo metamorphosis and tutelage under higher spirits, for his continuing faith in human creativity. He never learns 'Entsagung'. No children survive him. But he makes his indelible mark on the world. This may be the sum of the epoch. But it must now be clear from Goethe's constant isolation since 1790 that Heine's repeated characterisation of this period as the 'Goethe'sche Kunstperiode' could scarcely be more wrong.

One end of the epoch is heralded by Bettine von Arnim's literary overcoming of its disadvantaging female anthropology. Bettine (1785–1859) was privileged – imbued with Romantic unconventionality and encouraged to cultivate her mind and write. Marriage to Arnim in 1811 postponed this until his death – thanks both to his opposition and her own internalisation of convention. Her first book, *Goethe's Briefwechsel mit einem Kinde* (*Goethe's correspondence with a child*, 1835), is a fictionalised edition of her correspondence with Goethe from 1807 until his death.

It resembles a women's epistolary novel, but is in truth a woman writer's autobiographical search for identity through confrontation with the epoch's most prominent writer and the doomed paradigm of female creativity – Mignon – he had institutionalised. Bettine, with her eroticism, athleticism and spontaneous lyricism, had always been stylised as a living Mignon. We hear of Amazonian horse-riding and a journey to Weimar through war-torn Germany disguised as a man (complete with pistol). Bettine exploits this identification with Mignon to enter the inner circle of the poet whom she had been taught to venerate, and takes on for him the function of child and muse typical of the epoch's literary anthropology. However, this muse steps out of her role. Bettine composes a fictive dream, in which she dances before Goethe as Mignon before Wilhelm: 'alles, was Du kaum ahndest, das zeige ich Dir im Tanz, und Du staunst über die Weisheit, die ich Dir vortanze' ('everything you scarcely dreamt of I show you in the dance, and you are astonished at the wisdom I dance before you'). Having appropriated the image of the woman incapable of writing, Bettine refutes it *ipso facto*. *Goethe's Briefwechsel mit einem Kinde* echoes many Young German criticisms of Goethe. His conservatism in the matter of Jewish emancipation is critically mirrored in Bettine's correspondence on Dalberg's emancipation of the Frankfurt Jews. His reluctant militancy is contrasted with Bettine-Mignon's willingness to fight with the betrayed Tirolean rebel Andreas Hofer against Napoleon. Much of Bettine's social engagement – for the poor in *Dies Buch gehört dem König* (*This book belongs to the King*, 1843) – also echoes Young German concerns. But Bettine's other work which followed in rapid succession – the epistolary autobiographical novel *Die Günderode* (1840) and *Clemens Brentanos Frühlingskranz* (*A vernal wreath for Clemens Brentano*, 1844) – continue the engagement with the anthropological stereotype of women's writing in the Romantic age.

The other end of the epoch is the novel *Wally, die Zweiflerin* (*Wally the doubter*, 1835, discussed in Chapter 6) by the Young German Karl Gutzkow (1811–78). The twin themes of this polemic – woman's sexuality and religious crisis – reflect what is to come in the mirror of what has passed. *Wally*, the story of two lovers' struggle for freedom and self-realisation, is the counterfeit of *Lucinde*, and the epitaph of that attempted revolution, in which woman's Romantic yearning for freedom in religion and love results in total domination by male fantasy.

The epoch had begun with the decay of old values, imposed in the name of divine or rationalist authority. It flourished in the hope of a new order emanating from the creative activity of the individual subject, a *poiesis* in the true sense of the word, which transforms reality into the image of humane perfection which is itself aesthetic. It ended, fittingly, with the realisation that the transforming power of the aesthetic has its own dialectic. The aesthetic may transform the terms on which the subject engages with reality, but is itself transfomed by reality. On this basis, the new epoch, dominated by mistrust of the aesthetic and consciousness of the self's subordination to external, material and economic forces, starts.

6

Revolution, resignation, realism
(1830–1890)

Gail Finney

Revolution: 'Junges Deutschland' and 'Vormärz'

The nineteenth century was a time of enormous change in Europe, and nowhere was this truer than in Germany. Emerging from the Congress of Vienna in 1815 as a confederation of dozens of small states, Germany at last achieved nationhood in 1871. Similarly, the nineteenth century saw Germany move from a largely feudal, agrarian economy to capitalist means of production in a steadily more industrialised society. The middle class gradually emerged as a dominant force, first in conflict with the declining feudal nobility and then in tension with the rising proletariat.

The most volatile decades of this period were those between 1830 and 1850, when 'revolution' was a catchword of the day. The temper of the times is reflected in German literature, philosophy, music and art, which testify to at least four major kinds of revolutions: socio-political, sexual, religious and aesthetic. Regarding the first of these, the Revolutions of 1830 and 1848 were of paramount influence. Although Germany did not bring about a revolutionary upheaval in 1830, the 1830 'July Revolution' in France, which replaced the Bourbon Charles X with the 'Citizen King' Louis Philippe and significantly strengthened the economic and political power of the bourgeoisie, added impetus to the German opposition to absolutist rule. Absolutism was personified in Klemens Metternich (1773–1859), the Austrian statesman who arbitrated the Congress of Vienna and, as prince, oversaw the so-called Holy Alliance, formed in 1815 between Russia, Austria and Prussia. Metternich's name still symbolises the forces of reaction, since his regime functioned through a rigid system of censorship, espionage, imprisonment and exile that touched virtually all liberal-minded intellectuals. Oppositional professors were removed from their positions; liberal presses, newspapers and periodicals were banned or unduly pressured; no protesting citizen's voice was safe.

By 1848, Europe had had enough of Metternich's oppression. France led the way, when in February economic difficulties combined with political discontent to spark the first of a series of uprisings throughout central and western Europe. In March the German bourgeoisie and proletariat revolted and succeeded in calling a national assembly or parliament in the

Paulskirche in Frankfurt, composed for the most part of middle-class academics and intellectuals, to draw up the constitution for a united, democratic German nation. The effort was short-lived, however, collapsing by 1849 in the face of the renewed authority of rulers in Prussia, Baden, Cologne, Breslau, Dresden and various German principalities.

The French July Revolution of 1830 and the Revolution of 1848 were significant factors in the identities of the literary movements known as 'Junges Deutschland' (Young Germany) and 'Vormärz' (Pre-March) respectively. 'Vormärz' is the retrospective designation for literature of the 1840s which is oriented around progressive concerns that culminated in the Revolution of March 1848. The term 'Junges Deutschland' is usually ascribed to the *Ästhetische Feldzüge* (*Aesthetic campaigns*, 1834) of Ludolf Wienbarg (1802–72), whose works were banned the following year. The *Ästhetische Feldzüge*, which urge an aestheticisation of politics, begin with a dedication to a 'young Germany' rather than the old one, which is in need of overthrowing; Wienbarg specifically attacks the old German nobility, German scholarliness, the university, and the court as stuffy and unhealthy.

Hence the adjective 'young' in the coinage 'Young Germany' connotes the liberal, the modern. Yet 'Junges Deutschland' was never a self-consciously unified group of writers. Names associated with it include Theodor Mundt (1808–61), Ludwig Börne (1786–1837), Ferdinand Kühne (1808–88), Georg Büchner (1813–37), Heinrich Heine (1797–1856), Karl Gutzkow (1811–78), Heinrich Laube (1806–84), Ernst Willkomm (1810–86) and Wienbarg. But these writers were not all living in the same city in the early 1830s, the period during which the movement's activity was at its height; Heine and Börne were not even in Germany, but rather in self-imposed exile in Paris. Nonetheless these writers are united by certain central features, such as the politicising effect of the July Revolution. Gutzkow sums up this influence in his *Jahrbuch der Literatur* (*Yearbook of literature*, 1839), where he confesses that two months before the Revolution of 1830 he had no conception of European politics and did not even read a newspaper – this from a man who was later to work as a journalist. By 1832 we find him claiming that it is absolutely necessary for German literature to be politicised.

Both 'Junges Deutschland' and the 'Vormärz' are to be seen in a pan-European context. 'Junges Deutschland' is comparable to the 'Giovine Italia' in Italy, 'Das junge Europa' in Switzerland, or 'La Jeune France', and revolutionary literature is found in a number of European countries in the 1840s. But the oppressive grip of the Metternich regime is everywhere evident in the German-speaking realm, where writers often remain unheard or heard only briefly before they are banned. The opposition to 'Junges Deutschland' is personified in Wolfgang Menzel, who during his tenure as editor of a literary journal in the 1830s and 1840s took every opportunity to denounce liberal publications. His attacks gave significant impetus to a government decree suppressing the works of Gutzkow, Laube, Heine, Wienbarg and Mundt in 1835. With its most important voices silenced, the Young German movement was at an end.

Although 'Junges Deutschland' loosely spans the period from 1830 to 1835 and the publications of the 'Vormärz', defined by its anticipation of the Revolution of 1848, appear throughout the 1840s, the two movements manifest a number of common concerns. To mention one small but representative example, in his *Briefe aus Paris* (*Letters from Paris*, 1832–4) Börne sums up the vicious circle involved in the crucial issue of freedom of the press: freedom of the press is not a victory, not even a battle, but rather only a weapon; yet how can one win without a battle, and how can one fight without weapons? On the same theme, though in a very different tone, the 'Vormärz' writer August Heinrich Hoffmann von Fallersleben (1798–1874) mocks censorship, in particular the censoring of newspapers, in his 1842 poem 'Wie ist doch die Zeitung interessant!' ('But isn't the newspaper interesting!'), in which he satirically recounts the trivial events documented in the daily papers: the delivery of the princess's baby, the return of the king, the early arrival of spring, to the exclusion of weighty but politically charged issues.

Probably the most significant factor linking 'Junges Deutschland' and the 'Vormärz' is the phenomenon in Germany of particularism, or the existence of several dozen small duchies and principalities rather than one united German nation. The opposition to feudal absolutism and the desire for a unified democratic state go hand in hand between 1830 and 1850. These concerns, together with the related causes they spawn, are treated by writers of 'Junges Deutschland' and the 'Vormärz' alike, although in general the former issue is more prevalent in the writings of 'Junges Deutschland' and the latter more evident in the publications of the 'Vormärz'. Büchner's political pamphlet *Der Hessische Landbote* (*The Hessian courier*, 1834) is typical in using graphic imagery to attack the differences between the princes, for whom life consists only of leisure and affluence, and the peasants, who function as tools of their rulers and whose days are filled with labour and deprivation. Referring to the phenomenon of absolutist particularism, Büchner claims that Germany has thirty-four tyrants and vehemently advocates unification of these individual states.

As became evident to the world following the fall of the Berlin Wall in 1989, the inevitable result of the desire for unification is nationalism. This was certainly the case in nineteenth-century Germany. Yet it is important to keep in mind that nationalism was a liberal tendency in the nineteenth century, since the goal of unification was a democratic state, something the Germans had never experienced. Liberalism and democracy were ringing catchwords during the 1830s and 1840s. In his novel *Das junge Europa* (*Young Europe*, 1833–7), Laube vehemently praises democracy in contrast to the despotic governments in control at the time and celebrates the power of the individual as against the general will of the mass. For him, the state should exist for the individual rather than vice versa. Such sentiments are not uncommon in these decades.

One of the most significant developments of the 'Vormärz' is that poetry becomes a frequent mode of expression for political views. In a work entitled *Die politische Poesie der Deutschen* (*German political poetry*, 1845) the liberal literary historian Robert Prutz criticises the characteristically German split between politics and literature, especially poetry. He sees the primary opponents of political poetry to be the aristocracy, who have a vested interest in maintaining the status quo, and those who advocate an apolitical, classical aesthetics according to which poetry belongs to the realm of the ideal, loftily suspended above the events of the day. The apoliticism Prutz attacks is related to that satirised throughout the 1840s in many so-called 'Michellieder', poems mocking the complacent, well-meaning but slow, philistine, apolitical German, generically referred to as 'the German Michel'. The thrust of poems addressed to the German Michel can loosely be summarised by a line found in two examples by August Heinrich Hoffmann von Fallersleben and Georg Herwegh: 'Schlafe! was willst du mehr?' ('Sleep! What more could you want?'). By contrast, Prutz's new viewpoint, alive and sensitive to contemporary affairs, is typical of the writers of the 'Vormärz', whose poetry is filled with political themes such as nationalism.

Poetry registers, for instance, one of the major rallying points for German patriotism at the time, the so-called Rhine crisis of 1840. A dispute about the border of the Rhine arising between Prussia, which had been given lands along the river in the settlement of the Congress of Vienna, and France, unleashed a wave of anti-Gallic sentiment and a poetic outpouring in Germany that year. One of the most fervent of the poems written in response, Nicholas Becker's 'Der deutsche Rhein' ('The German Rhine'), emphatically repeats that 'they' won't get the 'free German Rhine', and compares the French to greedy ravens.

The most famous, or infamous, patriotic poem of the 1840s is Hoffmann von Fallersleben's 'Lied der Deutschen' ('Song of the Germans'), the first stanza of which acquired particularly dark associations through its appropriation by the National Socialists, beginning 'Deutschland, Deutschland über alles, / über alles in der Welt' ('Germany, Germany above everything, / Above everything in the world'). Heralding and then celebrating the Revolution of 1848 itself, numerous poems bid farewell to the old German Reich by focusing on the black, red and gold of the new republican flag. The following stanza of Herwegh's 'Aufruf' ('Appeal') is a particularly apocalyptic example:

> Deutsche, glaubet euren Sehern,
> Unsre Tage werden ehern,
> Unsre Zukunft klirrt in Erz;
> Schwarzer Tod ist unser Sold nur,
> Unser Gold ein Abendgold nur,
> Unser Rot ein blutend Herz!

[Germans, believe your prophets, / Our days are becoming cast in iron, / Our future is rattling in bronze; / Black death is our only reward, / Our gold is merely the gold of evening, / Our red a bleeding heart!]

In more down-to-earth terms, the refrain of Ferdinand Freiligrath's 'Schwarz-Rot-Gold' associates black with gunpowder, red with blood, and gold with the flame of battle.

In their frustration with class inequities writers of the day also call attention to the condition of the poor, especially in the workplace. In *Dies Buch gehört dem König* (*This book belongs to the king*, 1843) the writer Bettina von Arnim (1785–1859), who gathered extensive material on the poor, paints a horrifying picture of the 'Poor Colony' in Hamburg, where 2,500 people live, in filth and near-starvation, in 400 rooms. A moving passage of Willkomm's novel *Weiße Sklaven* (*White slaves*, 1845) describes how adolescent children, working eleven-hour days for low pay in the hot, damp, oily atmosphere of a textile factory, suffer from persistent respiratory, eye and skin irritations. The 'Vormärz' writer Georg Weerth's poem 'Arbeite' ('Work!') evokes the needs of workers' families that force them to keep going without rest despite the body-breaking, numbing nature of the work and the low returns it brings, and attacks the managerial attitude that compares labourers to cattle.

The critique of absolutist rule and its inequities and the condemnation of workers' exploitation come together and find one of their pithiest and most famous formulations in Heine's poem 'Die schlesischen Weber' ('The Silesian weavers'). This powerful poem is spoken almost entirely in the collective voice of the textile workers, who reveal that they are weaving a threefold curse into the shroud of Germany: on the God who has betrayed them with vain hopes; on the rich man's king who lets them starve and be shot like dogs; and on their false fatherland, filled with shame and corruption. Inspired by an actual revolt of textile workers in Silesia, an area northeast of Berlin and now part of Poland, Heine's poem also looks ahead to the Revolution of 1848, which would seek to overthrow precisely the kinds of political and social ills the poem so dramatically evokes.

An interesting counterpoint is provided by a poem on the same theme by Louise Aston (1814–71), an outspoken champion of women's rights, 'Lied einer schlesischen Weberin' ('Song of a Silesian weaver'). Spoken by a female worker, the poem dramatises the plight of poor women forced to sell themselves to their wealthy employers to stay afloat financially. Her father having been killed by a forest warden while trying to shoot game to feed his family, the young woman is now the main source of support for her sister and invalid mother. Although the girl's concern for her family wins out over her moral compunctions at the factory owner's proposition, the poem ends with an evocation of her despair at what she has done and an intimation of its possible dire consequences. The poems by Heine and Aston thus offer complementary perspectives on the plight of the textile workers, the one poem aggressive and ominous in tone, political in stance, and focused on the collective, the other lyrical, concerned with moral rather than political complexities, and personal.

Despite Heine's sympathy with many of the causes of 'Junges Deutschland' and the 'Vormärz', it should be noted that he also offers a corrective to numerous ideas promulgated by his fellow writers in Germany, perhaps most extensively in his satirical verse narratives *Atta Troll. Ein Sommernachtstraum* (*Atta Troll. A midsummer night's dream*, 1843) and *Deutschland. Ein Wintermärchen* (*Germany. A winter's tale*, 1844). In the figure of Atta Troll, the crude, unkempt, 'tendential bear', Heine satirises the political poetry of the day, in particular that of Freiligrath, lambasting it as overly enthusiastic, filled with pathos, and drowning in generalities. *Deutschland. Ein Wintermärchen*, inspired by Heine's trip home to Hamburg after thirteen years in exile in Paris, encapsulates his love–hate relationship with the country of his birth: although he participates in the attacks on censorship and on other injustices of Metternich's regime, he humourously scoffs at the cult of 'Germanness' embodied in the Middle Ages, notably in Cologne cathedral, and reincarnated in the struggle with France for the Rhine. As a Jew and a cosmopolite, Heine has a rare perspective on the patriotism so predominant in Germany in the 1840s.

A number of the writers of 'Junges Deutschland' and the 'Vormärz' were influenced by the thought of Friedrich Engels (1820–95) and Karl Marx (1818–83), the social and economic philosophers whose works not only offer a radical critique of class inequities but suggest an alternative. Partly under the influence of Ludwig Feuerbach (1804–72) Marx and Engels rejected the thought of Friedrich Hegel (1770–1831), who represents the culmination of German idealist philosophy. But they took over Hegel's dialectical method and incorporated it into their philosophy of historical materialism, which holds that ideas are always the product of economic and social conditions: the base, or economic structure of society, conditions the superstructure, or the forms of the state and social consciousness. Their *Manifest der kommunistischen Partei* (*Manifesto of the Communist Party*, 1848) argues that in order to change the way people think, one must change their economic and political reality. A major object of critique in the *Manifest* is the bourgeoisie, who, the authors contend, are devoted to the acquisition of money and place an exchange value on everything and everyone. Marx and Engels see the constant self-enrichment of the bourgeoisie as leading to the increasing poverty of the proletariat, in contrast to the feudal system, in which the serfs were taken care of. The authors believe that the dependence of the proletariat on the bourgeoisie will lead to the downfall of the latter and the victory of the former in a communist revolution. In their view the primary cause of economic disparity is the institution of private property, which the communists seek to abolish. But the framework of Marx and Engels's hopes was a larger one: a desire for the wholescale removal of the exploitation, tyranny and domination of one part of humanity by another.

Concomitant with the revolutionary political thinking so prominent in Germany in the 1830s and 40s is a twofold sexual revolution, affecting both sexuality and women's rights. Wienbarg's celebration in the *Ästhetische Feldzüge* of vitality and emotion over the acquisition of positivist knowledge, of life over thought, is a step on the way to the advocacy of increased freedom in matters of sexuality. Similarly, Prince Hermann von Puckler-Muskau, who supported the writers of 'Junges Deutschland' although he had a problematic relationship with some of them, writes in his *Südostlicher Bildersaal* (*Southeastern portrait gallery*, 1840) in opposition to utilitarianism and in favour of pleasure, which he claims should be the only occupation of human beings. Mundt's *Charaktere und Situationen* (*Characters and situations*, 1837) attacks the prudishness so common, in his opinion, in Germany, which he feels is destroying the German language.

This emancipatory tendency appears in even more radical guise concerning affairs of the heart. In his 'Vorrede zu Schleiermachers "Vertrauten Briefen über die Lucinde"' ('Preface to Schleiermacher's "Intimate letters about Lucinde"', 1835), Gutzkow's provocative preface to his edition of Schleiermacher's defence of Friedrich Schlegel's controversial novel, Gutzkow urges readers not to be ashamed of passion, not to view morality as a state institution and to let their romantic unions be sanctioned by pleasure rather than by the church. In like manner, a character in Willkomm's novel *Die Europamüden* (*Those weary of Europe*, 1838) encourages freethinking and ingenuity in love, observing that habit is a deadening force in amorous matters, and goes so far as to refer to love as a secular religion. Similarly, Laube's *Das junge Europa* depicts in the princess a sexually emancipated woman who takes full pleasure in (extramarital) lovemaking and feels no shame about her enjoyment.

Writers of 'Junges Deutschland' also take a stand on women's rights. In his *Briefe eines Narren an eine Närrin* (*Letters of a male to a female fool*, 1832) Gutzkow laments the lack of educational opportunities available to women, a criticism echoed in his portrayal of the title character of his novel *Wally, die Zweiflerin* (*Wally the sceptic*, 1835), discussed below. In the *Briefe* he points out the contradiction in the fact that people scorn women if they overstep their bounds and at the same time want to see in them more than spineless creatures. Yet Gutzkow also claims that women are their own worst enemies, raging against each other in envy and jealousy and thereby undermining any sense of solidarity from within and unity from without. Comparably stereotypical and condescending thinking is evident in his pronounced desire to use the weight of his rhetoric to represent his addressee as her advocate and champion.

A similar pattern is found in Wienbarg's thinking on women's emancipation. In his *Wanderungen durch den Tierkreis* (*Travels through the zodiac*, 1835) he proceeds sympathetically through a litany of injustices against women: men have ruled the world for 6,000 years; their silly deeds have been called world history; women have rarely held positions of power, but instead have been accused of causing bloody wars and the destruction of kingdoms and cities through their faithless beauty. But after asking women what their response will be, *his* response is to offer himself as their spokesman.

Fortunately, women also spoke for themselves. In terms of writings on women's rights, the 1840s was the most productive decade in German history prior to the turn of the century, so productive that one can speak of the first women's movement in Germany, at least on paper. One of women's primary causes in the 1840s was inequality in matters of education, since in this period formal schooling was not available for girls past the age of thirteen or fourteen. Not only was it generally thought that girls had no need of secondary and higher education, since a girl's presumed destiny was to become a wife and mother; it was also considered desirable to keep girls as childlike as possible for as long as possible as a guarantee of their spiritual purity, and knowledge obviously counteracted childishness. Not surprisingly, several intelligent and enterprising women rebelled against this state of affairs. Fanny Lewald (1811–89), a highly gifted woman born to a respected Jewish merchant family in Königsberg, is a moving example. Following the completion of her formal schooling, because she was not married and her father considered it unfitting for her to earn money, Lewald was forced to live at home for some twenty years with nothing to occupy her but sewing, knitting and piano lessons.

After Lewald finally began writing and left home for Berlin, she eventually became one of the first women in Germany to live from her pen. Her novels, among them *Clementine* (1843) and *Jenny* (1843), were hugely popular in their day, but the work that offers probably the fullest insight into the times is her three-volume autobiography, *Meine Lebensgeschichte* (*The education of Fanny Lewald: an autobiography*, 1861–2). Here Lewald records the envy she feels as a girl when, despite her superior performance in grammar school, she watches the boys attend the high school from which she is excluded. She laments the overprotection of girls, the way they are shielded from learning about the passions of love, the degree to which they are preserved in a state of eternal childlikeness until marriage. She further criticises the fact that girls are raised solely with an eye to marriage, since as she well knows, marriage is not the destiny of every young girl (Lewald did eventually marry, but not until her mid-forties). Even in the 1840s Lewald is not opposed to marriage; we find her title character Clementine claiming in convincing terms that the ideal would be to share all one's joys and sorrows with a beloved partner and thereby lead life in a double fashion. Lewald simply believes that a girl is better off educated, whether she marries or not.

Another fervent champion of women's education is Louise Otto (1819–95), usually known by her married name Otto-Peters. One of the most important of the early women's rights advocates in Germany, Otto-Peters founded both the *Frauen-Zeitung* (*Women's Newspaper*) in 1849, designed to promote solidarity among all women, and in 1865 the 'Allgemeiner Deutscher Frauenverein' (Public German Women's League), aimed at improving opportunities for women's education and for their right to work. Her newspaper was also in sympathy with the liberal ideals of 1848, reporting on political prisoners and protesting against the condition of victims, and was banned in 1852. Like Lewald, Otto-Peters objects to the fact that just when a girl would be truly ready for education, it ceases. But she adds a socio-political component, contending in her essay 'Die Teilnahme der weiblichen Welt am Staatsleben' ('Women's participation in affairs of state', 1847) that women's education is in conflict with governmental and social circumstances and that girls should instead be taught subjects like world history, science and physical education, not merely 'feminine' subjects such as sewing, music and foreign languages. In the opinion of Otto-Peters the latter subjects help train girls to be dolls for men rather than companions. In *Kathinka* (1844) she couches these ideas in particularly graphic terms, comparing the 'binding' of the female character in the West to hinder women's autonomy and progress to the crippling Chinese practice of binding girls' feet to keep them small and beautiful.

Much of Otto-Peters's writing is coloured by a pronouncedly nationalistic rhetoric; for her the broadest purpose of education, male and female, is to instill a sense of Germanness in pupils. Although such an emphasis on Germanness and the *Volk* is unavoidably tainted for us today, it exists in Otto-Peters's writings side by side with a strong commitment to the proletariat, whose education she considers especially important if a revolution of the proletariat against the bourgeoisie is to be avoided. In her discussion of women's right to hold a job, in the essay 'Mein Programm als Mitarbeiterin einer Frauenzeitung' ('My programme as contributor to a women's newspaper', 1849), she pays particular attention to lower-class women; if denied the right to work for a living, she writes, they will be thrown into prostitution, a public form of the scandal that so many other women suffer privately in loveless marriages.

Given her fervent commitment to women's rights and her sympathies with the lower classes, it is interesting to observe that Otto-Peters's views on revolution anticipate those of many feminists during women's movements at both the turn of the century and in the late 1960s in Europe and the United States: revolutions tend to be made by men, and those men tend to overlook the causes of women. Her poem 'Für alle' ('For all') offers a succinct description of this phenomenon: 'Dem Männerrecht nur galt das neue Ringen, / Das Frauenrecht blieb in den alten Schlingen' ('The new struggle was on behalf of the rights of man; / The rights of woman were caught in the old toils'). It is hence not surprising that despite her liberal views Otto-Peters sees revolution as something to be avoided.

To differentiate between the situations of French and German women in the first half of the nineteenth century, it has been customary, especially among male literary historians, to hold up the lives of George Sand and Charlotte Stieglitz as paradigms: on the one hand the flamboyant, free-thinking and free-loving novelist, on the other hand the woman who in 1834 committed suicide in an effort to inspire her husband Heinrich to creativity as a writer. A notable example occurs in the novelist Karl Immermann's *Die Jugend vor fünfundzwanzig Jahren* (*Young people twenty-five years ago*, 1839), where Immermann presents Stieglitz as typically German and Sand as typically French. But this rather simplistic dichotomy is undermined by the fact that a number of other German women viewed Sand as a model and source of inspiration. Many wrote poems to her, such as the writer Ida von Reinsberg-Duringsfeld, whose empathic 'An George Sand' ('To George Sand') contains the stanza,

> Doch Jene, die dich richten und verdammen,
> Was wissen sie von dir und deinem Geiste?
> Schlug in ihr Herz, das öde, das vereiste,
> Ein Funken je von deines Herzens Flammen?

[But those who pass judgement and condemn you, / What do they know of you and of your spirit? / Were their desolate, frozen hearts ever touched / By a spark from the flames that are in your heart?]

Louise Aston, mentioned above as the author of the 'Lied einer schlesischen Weberin', not only writes a poem celebrating Sand as 'Das *freie*

Weib, das keinem fremden Wahn, / Das nur dem eignen *Geiste* untertan' ('The *free woman*, subservient to no external delusion, / But rather only to her own *spirit*'); Aston also self-consciously imitated Sand's behaviour, often wearing men's clothes and smoking cigars in public. Following a bad marriage to an industrialist Aston became fairly emancipated in her love life, rebelling against the double standard which dictates monogamy for women only and advocating free love. The conclusion of her poem 'Lebensmotto' ('Motto for life') sums up her philosophy: 'Freiem Lieben, freiem Leben, / Hab' ich ewig mich ergeben!' ('Free love, free living, / To these I have given myself for eternity!')

According to her own testimony in *Meine Emancipation: Verweisung und Rechtfertigung* (*My emancipation: banishment and justification*, 1846), Aston was eventually banned from Berlin because she had expressed ideas threatening to middle-class order and stability. Doubtless these included her belief, also documented in *Meine Emancipation*, that women must demand from this new era a new right, the right to a free personality, guided not by external influences but by its own inner laws. Aston returned to Berlin in time to mount the barricades in 1848 and remained for the sad aftermath of the revolution, as poems like 'Barrikadenklänge' ('Sounds from the barricades') and 'Berlin am Abende des 12. November 1848' (Berlin on the evening of 12 November 1848') attest. Her novel *Revolution und Contrerevolution* (1849) has been called the first and only novel of the Revolution of 1848, and one written from the perspective of a politically active woman.

A similar plea is made by the Countess Ida Hahn-Hahn (1805–80), an especially colourful personality among this group of truly unusual women writers. Where other women wrote poems to George Sand, Hahn-Hahn is often called the German Sand. An aristocrat without much education whose father fell on hard financial times, she entered an arranged marriage with her cousin that soon became disastrous, involving frequent arguments and even violence. She was divorced after three years and began travelling widely, going as far as the Orient with her unmarried companion, a baron, thereby breaking new ground on two fronts: travelling as a woman and in the company of a man not her husband. Such behaviour led earlier literary historians such as Otto von Leixner writing in 1916 to speak of a 'dämonischer Zug' ('demonic streak') in Hahn-Hahn's nature.

But perhaps the most striking turn of events in Hahn-Hahn's life was her conversion to Catholicism in 1850, at the age of forty-five, and her subsequent establishment of a convent, where she spent the last twenty-five years of her life. The reasons for her rejection of the world are complex, but they likely include her disillusionment with the Revolution of 1848, her dismay at the materialist orientation of communism, and her grief and loneliness after the death of her companion in 1849.

Although Hahn-Hahn continued writing after her retreat into the convent, these later works are highly religious in nature, and her reputation rests on her status as the leading female author of popular novels in the first half of the nineteenth century. Advocacy of a woman's right to develop herself is a foremost theme of her fiction. Emphasising the crucial importance of social conditioning over nature, a character in her novel *Der Rechte* (*The right one*, 1839) urges that girls be sent to the university and boys to the sewing school and kitchen for three years so that women can learn what they are really capable of and men can discover what oppression is. *Zwei Frauen* (*Two women*, 1845) criticises the notions that women should not think or have a will of their own; that they should be worshipped as in the Middle Ages, a practice in fact tantamount to subordination; and that a woman acquires a place in society only through a husband, regardless of how beautiful, intelligent, or wealthy she is.

Emphatic arguments for women's equality are made also by Luise Mühlbach (Klara Mundt) (1814–73), a supporter of Young German writers whose particular interest in the work of Theodor Mundt led to their correspondence and eventual marriage. Taking as her chosen model not George Sand but Aphra Behn, in her 1849 novel centring on the exotic seventeenth-century English writer Mühlbach presents Behn as testimony to the fact that women are born with the same abilities, mental power and energy as men and should therefore not suffer subordination and slavery to them.

A further topic treated extensively by women writers in the 1840s is marriage. In view of her own painful experience with matrimony, it is not surprising that Hahn-Hahn devotes considerable attention to the flaws of this institution. Her most famous novel, *Gräfin Faustine* (*Countess Faustine*, 1840), bears autobiographical traces in its portrait of a loveless union in which the marital partners essentially go their own ways while remaining married. At one point the title character exclaims at the strangeness of men who imagine that God created the female sex in order to serve them and that half of humanity exists to be brutalised by the other half. The treatment of women as 'slaves whom men have bought' leads in Faustine's opinion to the phenomenon where, in her words, 'Heut lassen sie sich eine Brutalität gefallen, um dafür morgen einen neuen Hut zu bekommen' ('Today they put up with an act of brutality in order to get a new hat for it tomorrow'). In a dialogue in Hahn-Hahn's *Aus der Gesellschaft* (*From society*, 1838) a character known as the baron presents the female character Ilda with several reasons why women marry: to have a stable position in society, to bear a great name openly and proudly, to be in the protection of a faithful friend, to enjoy the pleasures of domesticity and to have beloved children. With reference to her own situation, she refutes every reason, one by one.

But the most extensive critique of marriage to emerge in these years is found in *Das Wesen der Ehe* (*The essence of marriage*, 1849) by Louise Dittmar (1807–84), one of the least known of nineteenth-century German women writers. Until the late 1980s even the dates of her birth and death were unknown, but during the last few years the persistent research of Ruth-Ellen Boetcher Joeres and of Christina Klausmann at the Feministisches Archiv und Dokumentationszentrum in Frankfurt has yielded helpful information about her life and works. Dittmar is distinguished from her fellow women's rights advocates in at least two major ways: by the extent to which her writings are informed by politics and philosophy, and by the radically critical nature of her analysis. Asking rhetorically in *Das Wesen der Ehe* why there exist so many unhappy marriages, formed because of coincidence or external need, and so few, indeed hardly any, happy ones, based on an inner necessity, she answers very simply: because of the economic and political dependence of women. She is ahead of her time and milieu in her recognition that social institutions and the relations between the sexes are mutually dependent entities, that change in the one requires change in the other. Her unusually keen awareness of women's particular problems, of the difficult nature of interactions not only between men and women but among women, also sets her apart; Joeres goes so far as to call her 'the most perceptive of contemporary German thinkers on the question of women in society' (*Out of line*, 1989, p.297).

Worth mentioning as a kind of pendant to the early women's rights movement in Germany is the phenomenon of the bluestockings. Originating in mid-eighteenth-century England to refer to women with marked literary interests who often held evening parties or formed clubs to which eminent men of the day were invited as well, the term supposedly derived from the unconventional habit of a man attending one of the clubs of wearing blue worsted stockings instead of the usual black silk stockings. In the early decades of the nineteenth century the term gained currency in Germany as well, as is evident in Annette von Droste-Hülshoff's (1797–1848) one-act play *Perdu! oder Dichter, Verleger und Blaustrümpfe* (*Lost! or writers, publishers and bluestockings*, written in 1840 but published 1900). Known primarily for her poetry and short fiction, Droste-Hülshoff tries her hand at comedy here to give dramatic form to an actual occurrence concerning the completion of a book by herself and her companion Levin Schücking when the project was neglected by Freiligrath. The autobiographical element of the woman writer is complemented by Droste's experience in Münster with a group of literary ladies and gentlemen who met regularly to read and critique each other's writing, some of whom (including Droste herself) lend their features to the play's bluestockings. A later, likewise humorous treatment of the bluestocking is found in Marie von Ebner-Eschenbach's poem 'Sankt Peter und der Blaustrumpf' ('Saint Peter and the bluestocking'), in which St Peter ultimately decides to allow a bluestocking into heaven because she tells him that, even if she failed as a freethinker to observe the rites of the church, she always kept God in her heart.

By 1850, if Germany was probably no longer a place where a woman would sacrifice her life to inspire her husband to write, in contrast to America and elsewhere it had not yet witnessed any women's conventions or the founding of women's leagues, and most of the strong voices speaking up in favour of women's rights quietened down after the failure of the Revolution of 1848. Yet much progress had been made towards the significantly more emancipated state of affairs that would reign at the end of the nineteenth century, the situation so dramatically described by the woman character at the end of Marie Janitschek's poem 'Ein modernes Weib' ('A modern woman'), just before she shoots down the man who has wronged and then insulted her: 'So wisse, daß das Weib / Gewachsen ist im neunzehnten Jahrhundert' ('Then learn, that women have grown during the nineteenth century').

The religious revolution occurring in the 1830s and 1840s is closely bound up with the sexual one. A foremost example of this link is Gutzkow's short novel *Wally, die Zweiflerin* (*Wally the sceptic*, 1835), a telling document of the crisis of faith beginning to manifest itself throughout much of Europe at the time. As indicated above, Gutzkow's quasi-psychological study of the title character, who as a fairly undistinguished young woman anticipates the protagonists of naturalist literature, explicitly refers to some of the issues that occupied his women's rights contemporaries. In her often-quoted letter to a friend in the eleventh chapter of the novel's first book, for example, Wally complains of the chance nature of women's actions, the fact that nothing is demanded of women and nothing depends on them; their uselessness resembles for her an unconscious, vegetative state.

But the more serious reasons for Wally's ennui and malaise are religious in nature: her doubts about the meaning of religion, the role of the church in marriage, the existence of God. In the chapter mentioned above, the narrator describes her as suffering from a 'religious tic' that manifests itself in a pathological curiosity which suffocates her. In one of the novel's most controversial scenes the themes of sexuality or sensuality and religion come together, as Wally fulfils the request of the man she loves, Cäsar, briefly to display herself naked to him on the day she is to marry another, unloved man for reasons of convention. A further manifestation of Gutzkow's challenge to Christian conventions are the novel's numerous instances of suicide, the most sensational being that of Wally's brother-in-law who, mad with unrequited love for her, shoots himself before her eyes. The question of whether suicide can ever be justified on ideological grounds – in particular the case of Charlotte Stieglitz – had been one of the points of departure for the novel. Terminally shaken by her reading of Cäsar's 'creed', which presents religion as the result of human despair at the purposeless of life, Wally stabs herself in the heart. The pathos and melodramatic quality of the book's plot are paralleled by its often hyperbolic, heavily sentimental style.

Gutzkow's *Wally* had one of the most turbulent receptions in nineteenth-century literary history. Published in August 1835, it was banned in Prussia a little more than a month later, and other states soon followed suit. Spurred on by the fiercely conservative energies of Wolfgang Menzel, who denounced the book as immoral and sacrilegious, the controversy over *Wally* was largely responsible for the wholesale ban on the works of Gutzkow, Wienbarg, Laube, Heine and Mundt in December 1835. To add injury to insult, Gutzkow was sentenced to four weeks in prison for his affronts to Christianity. One of the most influential religious thinkers of the 1840s is Ludwig Feuerbach, whose radical theology put an early end to his academic career. His unorthodox views on Christianity come to the fore in *Das Wesen des Christentums* (*The essence of Christianity*, 1841), where he defines God as a projection or externalisation of the human being, the inner self made visible; in his opinion the polarity between the human and the divine on which religion is based is an illusory one. In *Das Wesen der Religion* (*Lectures on the essence of religion*, 1845) Feuerbach contends that Christianity has distracted people from their problems on earth. In holding up the fulfilment of unfulfillable wishes as its goal, Christianity has neglected feasible human desires; in diverting attention towards the promise of a better and eternal life after death, it has discouraged people from working to improve their lives while here; it has given people the heavenly happiness they wish for in their imaginations but not what they want in reality, an earthly, moderate happiness. Going further, he claims that where theism promotes envy, resentment and jealousy, atheism is liberal and generous, granting everyone his or her will and talents.

The similarity to Marx's religious thinking is evident, in particular to his famous characterisation of religion as the 'opium of the people', the illusory happiness which must be abolished if people are to attain real happiness, in his 'Zur Kritik der Hegelschen Rechtsphilosophie' ('Toward the critique of Hegel's philosophy of right', 1844). But Feuerbach's orientation was not practical and social enough for Marx. In his 'Thesen über Feuerbach' ('Theses on Feuerbach', written 1845, published 1888) Marx insists that Feuerbach, with his speculative, contemplative orientation, fails to see that religious sentiment is a social product, that what causes human beings to invent heaven, the holy family, and so on, is a dissatisfaction with earthly conditions. For Marx, the purpose of philosophy should be not merely to interpret these conditions but to change them. Once such change occurs, there will be no further need for religion. Marx's socio-political and religious critiques come together in 'Der Kommunismus des *Rheinischen Beobachters*' ('The communism of the paper *Rheinischer Beobachter*', 1847), where he claims that Christianity favours a class system: it glorified ancient slavery and medieval serfdom and is now defending the oppression of the proletariat.

Feuerbach is also important for Louise Dittmar, whose radical thinking extends into the religious realm as well. Her *Lessing und Feuerbach* (1847) consists of a collection of Lessing's theological writings which she analyses through the lens of Feuerbach's theses. Like her *Der Mensch und sein Gott in und außer dem Christenthum* (*The human being and his God in and outside of Christianity*, 1846), it was written with the encouragement of the so-called Montag-Verein in Mannheim, a group of men and women who began meeting in 1847 to discuss religious questions from a critical perspective. This organisation was part of a much larger-scale oppositional movement growing up in Germany against traditional Christianity at the time. Dittmar's lectures to this group in 1847, which were published the same year under the title *Vier Zeitfragen* (*Four burning issues of the day*), represented an unusual and enormously courageous step for a woman to take. Her appearance there is in the spirit of her critique of religion, which highlights the minimal role women have played in Christianity since antiquity. Dittmar advocates instead an alternative religion based on truth, reason and sexual equality.

No discussion of the revolution in nineteenth-century religious thought would be complete without a look at one of the foremost influences on twentieth-century philosophy and literature, Friedrich Nietzsche (1844–1900). Born in 1844 as the son of a Protestant clergyman, Nietzsche began already as a teenager to reject Christian beliefs. As the titles of two of his major works indicate, *Jenseits von Gut und Böse* (*Beyond good and evil*, 1886) and *Zur Genealogie der Moral* (*Toward a genealogy of morals*, 1887), he is preoccupied with questions of morality, by which is meant Christian morality: how does morality come about, and how might it be transcended? His rethinking is so far-reaching that it often constitutes a virtual philosophy of negation or inversion. Beginning *Jenseits von Gut und Böse* with the observation that philosophers have always sought truth, he rhetorically asks why they do not look instead for untruth. Similarly, *Zur Genealogie der Moral* effects a 'transvaluation of all values' in its critique of Christian ethics, throwing into question the qualities Christianity has held to be good, such as pity, weakness, self-sacrifice, submissiveness, asceticism and guilt.

In a passage which foreshadows Freud's *Das Unbehagen in der Kultur* (*Civilisation and its discontents*, 1930), the sixteenth section of the second essay of *Zur Genealogie der Moral* hypothesises that as human beings evolved from animals and their consciousness took over, their instincts, not allowed free play, were internalised (Freud would talk of repression or sublimation) and the human awareness of the instincts turned in on themselves led to the birth of 'bad conscience'. This split between instinct and morality, Nietzsche argues, produces culture or civilisation, but also a feeling of alienation from our original nature. Hence he longs for a new kind of man (for Nietzsche, the ideal being is definitely masculine) who can transcend human nature, accommodate the instinctual realm, and embrace will, power and domination instead of the Christian virtues. With the end of the twenty-fourth section of the second essay, which heralds this man of the future as the Antichrist, the overturning of Christian values begun in the 1830s and 1840s by thinkers like Gutzkow and Feuerbach is complete.

In a discussion, finally, of the aesthetic revolution occurring in Germany in the first half of the nineteenth century, it is illuminating to consider innovations not only in literature but in music as well. Nietzsche's thinking provides a link to one of the leading figures in the development of music drama, Richard Wagner (1813–83). The momentous effects of Nietzsche's first encounter with him in 1868, when Nietzsche was twenty-four and Wagner fifty-five, are evident in Nietzsche's first book, *Die Geburt der Tragödie aus dem Geiste der Musik* (*The birth of tragedy out of the spirit of music*, 1872). In contrast to the long-standing German tradition of idealising ancient Greek culture as rational, harmonious and sublime, a tradition represented by such writers as Winckelmann, Wieland, Goethe and Schiller, Nietzsche argues that in order fully to appreciate Greek culture one must recognise not only its Apollonian aspects but also the Dionysian forces, frenzied, uncontrolled, potentially cruel and destructive, reflected in the festivals of Bacchus. According to Nietzsche's theory, Greek tragedy grew out of the synthesis between Apollonian principles and the spirit of music embodied in the Dionysian chorus. In his view, a contemporary analogy is found in the operas of Wagner.

Although Nietzsche later became disenchanted with Wagner, as is documented in *Der Fall Wagner* (*The Wagner case*, 1888) and *Nietzsche contra Wagner* (1895), his analogy is instructive in talking about Wagner's notion of the *Gesamtkunstwerk* (total work of art). In his reconstruction of old Germanic and medieval legend and mythology in operas such as *Der fliegende Holländer* (*The flying Dutchman*), *Tannhäuser*, *Lohengrin*, *Der Ring des Nibelungen*, and *Tristan und Isolde* (all written in the 1840s and 50s), Wagner revolutionises opera above all through the unity with which he imbues it. Sets, costumes, gestures, facial expressions, choreography and, most importantly, orchestral accompaniment, song and recitative blend and harmonise to produce the maximum emotional effect. The most concise expression of Wagner's unifying technique is perhaps the leitmotif, or phrase of music repeatedly associated with a particular character, object, place or mood, which he developed to an unprecedented level of complexity. The literary equivalent of this technique became enormously widespread in European realist fiction, used by novelists such as Dickens, Flaubert, Turgenev and, most notably, Thomas Mann.

The aesthetic revolution which Wagner effected in music drama is paralleled by manifold experiments in literature as well. Behind much of the innovation is the need to rebel against the inescapable model of Weimar classicism as epitomised by Goethe. There exists among writers the conviction that Goethe's death in 1832 brought with it the end of an era, '[d]ie Endschaft der "Goetheschen Kunstperiode"' ('the end of the "Goethean artistic epoch"'), as Heine formulates it in *Die romantische Schule* (*The romantic school*, 1836). This caesura is an ambivalent one, leading on the one hand, as will be seen in Part 2, to the resigned sense that Goethe's example cannot be surpassed.

On the other hand, many writers, such as those affiliated with 'Junges Deutschland', view Goethe as something to be overcome. A number of them oppose his loftiness, his preoccupation with themes from the distant past, which is directly at odds with the orientation of 'Junges Deutschland' towards contemporary political affairs. In *Aus meinem Tagebuche* (*From my diary*, 1830) Börne criticises Goethe as one who, although virtually inviolable in his blessed, privileged and powerful position, was unconcerned about the people and about the rights of other German writers and thought only of himself. Börne contends, moreover, that Goethe's writings will remain without effect, since they are lacking in wit and their sensible teachings are no longer useful. Similarly, Charlotte Stieglitz, as quoted in Mundt's commemoration of her, refers to Goethe as an 'absolute king' in his relation to his audience and finds the distance he maintains from the public to be inappropriate to the times. Commenting in his *Reisenovellen* (*Travel novellas*, 1834–7) on Goethe's egotism, Laube observes that he has never liked him, just as he has never liked Jupiter, another notorious egotist. Finally, in one of the most famous formulations of the scepticism towards Goethe prominent in these years, in *Die romantische Schule* Heine compares Goethe's works to the statue sculpted by Pygmalion: although the statue was brought to life, it could not bear children, just as Goethe's beautiful words, as the product solely of art, are infertile in that they do not inspire action.

Since the drama is the pre-eminent genre of Weimar classicism, it is in the theatre, in reaction against classical norms, that we witness some of the most radical aesthetic innovations of the first half of the nineteenth century. *Scherz, Satire, Ironie und tiefere Bedeutung* (*Jest, satire, irony and deeper significance*, 1827) by Christian D. Grabbe (1801–36) represents an interesting transition between the self-conscious romantic irony of Ludwig Tieck's fairy-tale play *Der gestiefelte Kater* (*Puss in boots*, 1797), which repeatedly undercuts theatrical illusion by calling attention to its own fictionality, and the contemporary orientation of 'Junges Deutschland'. In *Scherz*, an exaggeratedly complicated plot framed within a Faust-satire serves as a vehicle for numerous mocking references to writers of Grabbe's day, most of whom are now unknown; in the end the playwright himself appears, only to be lambasted by one of the characters for his stupidity in creating this play in which he satirises other writers although he is worthless himself.

In substituting sharp humour, ironic wit and lavish playfulness for the emotionality of the sentimental comedy, Grabbe contributes another hue to the spectrum of German comedy, one that is further enriched by Büchner's comedy *Leonce und Lena* (1842). The play can be seen as a lighthearted variation on the critique of absolutism at the heart of *Der Hessische Landbote*: in Prince Leonce of the realm of Popo, drowning in boredom and melancholy, compared with a 'Buch ohne Buchstaben, mit nichts als Gedankenstrichen' ('book without letters, filled with nothing but dashes'), his lips 'languid from yawning' (Act 1, scene 3), Büchner satirises the virtual cult of romantic *weltschmerz* so prominent in these years (discussed in part 2 of this chapter). Leonce's father King Peter is a grotesque caricature of a ruler, having to force himself to remember his subjects; the president of the state council calls the royal word a 'nonentity' (III, 3), and much of Peter's language consists of the nonsensical satirisation of German idealist philosophy, specifically that of Kant and Fichte: Peter's compares his cuffs with morality, his trouser fly with free will.

When it is revealed that Princess Lena of Pipi, the woman with whom Leonce has fallen in love, is the same woman that his father has arranged for him to marry, Leonce's friend Valerio's comparison of the bridal couple to marionettes is far from arbitrary: in its emphasis on the role of chance and coincidence in determining human lives, the play embodies a philosophy of determinism, bordering at times on nihilism, that takes it far beyond the comic mode and the 1830s. Yet Büchner is careful to intimate the concretely social nature of the problems the couple overlooks as they marry and take over the kingdom, problems previewed already in the play's epigraph: 'Alfieri: "E la fama?" Gozzi: "E la fame?"' ('Alfieri: "And fame?" Gozzi: "And hunger?"')

Büchner's serious plays are as forward-looking as his comedy. *Dantons Tod* (*Danton's death*, 1835), set in 1794 and faithful to details of the turbulent period following the French Revolution, stands on the face of things in the tradition of the Schillerian historical drama. Yet it breaks with the aesthetics not only of classical Weimar but of Aristotelian theatre in general. One of the most significant manifestations of this break is the subordination of action to character; revelation and analysis of character are more important to Büchner than the careful, and often contrived, construction of dramatic action. His character study focuses on Danton and Robespierre and the differences between them. Although both had been active in the revolution, Danton has become disillusioned with it and pessimistic about the effectiveness of political activity, and eventually the tide turns against him. His fatalism, based in contrast to that of Leonce on actual experience, reaches its climax at the play's end just before he is executed, in his often quoted statements that the world is chaos, nothingness is the world-god yet to be born, and the guillotine is the best physician. The modernity of the play's theme is complemented by its unconventional language, which in contrast to the refined language of classical drama is highly lifelike and heterogeneous, even including obscenities. Further breaks with tradition include the play's large and diverse cast, encompassing all social classes, and its failure to adhere to the Aristotelian unities of time, place and action.

More radical still in terms of the aesthetics of drama is Büchner's final work, *Woyzeck* (written 1836–7; published 1877). Consisting not of acts but of a series of episodic scenes, the play was unfinished at Büchner's death and survived in several versions which differ among other things in the order of the scenes. The play portrays the fate of the barber and soldier Woyzeck, a simple but passionate man who is victimised from every side, ordered around and humiliated by his captain, exploited for scientific experiments by the doctor, and betrayed by his beloved with a virile drum major passing through town. Since she is the only thing that gives his life meaning, he is shattered by her infidelity and murders her. The play looks ahead to expressionist drama though its episodic structure, its visually graphic imagery, and its use of types rather than individual characters. Yet in its focus on a proletarian figure, its depiction of human beings as determined by their heredity and milieu, its analysis of a troubled psyche, and its attention to the power of sexuality, *Woyzeck* anticipates the theatre of naturalism. Büchner's oeuvre is unique in nineteenth-century drama.

Resignation: 'Biedermeier' and its counter-currents

A discussion of 'Junges Deutschland' and the 'Vormärz' does not take into account the currents of reaction and resignation that predate and then exist alongside the revolutionary fervour of the 1830s and 1840s. In the political realm, the reactionary forces exerted by Metternich's regime, extending from 1815 to 1848, eventually thwart progressive efforts towards the establishment of a unified democratic government in Germany. In literature and the other arts, one finds a corresponding rejection of contemporary issues and political engagement in favour of the selection of historical subjects or past authors as models, a focus on provincial life, a turning to fairy-tale or fantasy, or a preoccupation with nature.

When the term 'Biedermeier' is used to characterise the period from 1815 to 1848, it usually refers to these more conservative, backward-looking trends in the arts. In 1855 the German humorous poets Ludwig Eichrodt and Adolf Kussmaul began publishing poems by Eichrodt and by the south German schoolmaster Samuel Sauter under the title *Gedichte des schwäbischen Schulmeisters Gottlieb Biedermaier und seines Freundes Horatius Treuherz* (*Poems by the Swabian schoolmaster Amadeus Solidcitizen and his friend Horace Trueheart*). Although these poems, one of which is a song of praise to the potato, are in large measure parodic, the fictitious schoolmaster's name came in its altered spelling to be associated with many of the qualities embodied in the poems attributed to him. Qualities connoted by the term 'Biedermeier' include the withdrawal into the private sphere of the home and family, even into a kind of domestic, homebaked cosiness; the respect for traditional, middle-class values such as stability and order, moderation and modesty, and the preservation of the status quo; and, reflecting the meaning of 'bieder', virtues like honesty, competence and uprightness. The renunciation of dangerous yet promising possibilities in favour of an accepted, secure course of action – a prominent theme in German literature – is especially common in Biedermeier.

Biedermeier literature, with its focus on the domestic sphere, is fond of depicting social events and performances in the home such as parties, balls, games and musical evenings in the parlour. Images appropriate to the style might include an intimate coffee hour, a garden gnome, an elderly man in nightcap and dressing gown, a woman darning socks, or a kitten drinking milk from a bowl. Phrases that have come to be linked with Biedermeier include 'sammeln und hegen' ('collecting and tending'), which reflects the conservative, nurturing qualities associated with the style.

In the second half of the nineteenth century the designation 'Biedermeier' was far from wholly positive, connoting a way of being that was lacking in imagination, prosaic or philistine, and restricted and narrow in its contentment with the everyday. The term came by the turn of the century to refer to the post-Napoleonic style of interior decoration, especially furniture, with its simplicity, solid workmanship, and functionalism rather than ornamentation and elegance, and showing a preference for floral designs and rounded lines. The term also came to apply to painting, where it typically refers to idyllic genre compositions and scenes in benevolent natural settings, such as gardens, that convey an impression of peace, goodness and safety.

Given the political, rebellious orientation of the writers of 'Junges Deutschland' and the 'Vormärz', it is clear why 'Biedermeier' as an umbrella designation for the period 1815–48 is problematic. More recent scholarship has pointed to the defensive, fearful nature of the apparent idyllicism of Biedermeier and has suggested that the tranquil surface is a barrier against the chaotic, even demonic forces lying beneath. Seen from this perspective, Biedermeier works appear more closely allied with the political literature of the time.

One of the main reasons for the withdrawal of many German writers into the past or the private sphere is the sense that their era has somehow 'missed the boat', that the great individuals have lived before them and the significant events of history have already occurred. This particular kind of *weltschmerz* is a European phenomenon, colouring literary texts from several national traditions in the years between 1815 and 1840, and reaching its height in the 1830s. The Byronic hero, brooding and melancholic, rebellious, seeking intense experience of every kind, is a forerunner of numerous literary personae who are frustrated by the lack of outlets for their discontent. Julien Sorel, protagonist of Stendhal's *Le rouge et le noir* (*The red and the black*, 1830), chafes at his position as one old enough to remember Napoleon but too young to have served under him; instead Julien must make do with the boredom of life in Restoration France. In like manner, in his autobiographical novel *La confession d'un enfant du siècle* (*Confession of a child of the century*, 1836) Alfred de Musset attributes the malaise and pessimism felt by many young people at the time to the fact that they are confronted with the closed door of the restored Bourbon monarchy rather than the grandeur, excitement and hope that had been embodied by Napoleon. Analogous sentiments are found in German literature, for similar reasons. A character in Theodor Mundt's novel *Moderne Lebenswirren* (*Modern confusions*, 1834) laments the state of ennui, indifference, restlessness and purposelessness that has rendered his heart a graveyard; although he longs for activity and conflict and would like to make history, he is stuck away in the provinces, in the misery of small-town life. His problem: he harbours the 'polyp of the times', which infested him after the July Revolution and has since been eating away at him like a cancerous tumour. In his metaphor, the *zeitgeist* is making him ill.

A comparable sense of disillusionment and disappointment is felt by many German intellectuals and writers who do not share Mundt's liberal political views. As Joeres points out in her introduction to *Wally* (1974), this generation's sense of inadequacy is exacerbated by the striking number of deaths of talented writers and thinkers in the 1820s and 1830s: the romantic writer Jean Paul Richter (1825); the composer Carl Maria von Weber (1826); the romantic theorist Friedrich Schlegel (1829); the philosopher Georg Wilhelm Friedrich Hegel (1831); the composer Carl Friedrich Zelter (1832); Rahel Varnhagen, whose Berlin salon was a meeting place for many of the intellectual lights of Germany (1833); the theologian Friedrich Schleiermacher (1834); and the statesman and philologist Wilhelm von Humboldt (1835).

Towering above all these is the death of Goethe in 1832, which casts a long and inescapable shadow. A good deal of Biedermeier drama and fiction is written with the difficult double awareness that Goethe is the model par excellence and yet at the same time inimitable. Hence we often find an orientation towards the past in two senses: both turned back towards themes from history and turned back towards Goethe. Both are present in the work of the Austrian writer Franz Grillparzer (1791–1872). His dramas include what one might call small-scale plays, which contain very few characters and are neo-classical in style, as well as large-scale plays in a more elaborate, theatrical mode.

Representative of the first group are the tragedies *Sappho* (1818) and *Des Meeres und der Liebe Wellen* (*Hero and Leander*, 1831). Both resemble Goethe's neo-classical dramas in that they are written in unrhymed iambic pentameter, or blank verse; consist of five carefully structured and balanced acts; focus on a handful of characters; and adhere to the Aristotelian unities of time, place and action. Both plays revolve around the conflict between public duty and private happiness in love. In *Sappho* this conflict takes the form of the tension between the artist and society, one of the most prominent themes in German literature from the late eighteenth century onwards, treated by writers like Goethe, Wackenroder and Tieck, Novalis, Brentano, Hoffmann, Eichendorff, Mörike, Büchner, Thomas Mann, Rilke and Kafka. *Sappho* is especially indebted to Goethe's drama *Torquato Tasso* (1790), with whose title figure Grillparzer strongly identified. Grillparzer's play is in essence a psychological study of the greatest of the early Greek lyric poets, who was born on the island of Lesbos around 600 BC and belonged to a society of girls. Although only fragments of her work survive, it was enormously influential on later love poets.

Grillparzer's *Sappho*, whose premiere at the Burgtheater in Vienna was a great success and led to his tenure as court dramatist, begins at Sappho's moment of triumph, her return home after winning the laurel wreath for her poetry in Olympia. Her happiness is amplified by her love for the younger man she has brought back with her, Phaon. Yet her plan to substitute domestic wifely joys for her career as a poet founders on Phaon's inability to love a woman he admires and exalts. When Sappho realises that he has fallen in love with her maidservant, a simpler and more conventionally feminine girl, she recognises that she has failed in her duty to the gods by subordinating her poetic calling to her personal happiness, and in a dramatic conclusion she throws herself from a cliff into the sea.

Des Meeres und der Liebe Wellen also features a woman devoted to a sacred calling, in this case Hero, who as priestess to Aphrodite must remain unmarried. The echo of Goethe's *Iphigenie auf Tauris* (*Iphigenie in Tauris*, 1787), whose title character is priestess to Diana, is evident. In Grillparzer's treatment of the classical myth, Hero's religious and social duties are externalised in the person of the priest, who in the third act impresses on her the crucial importance of another kind of 'Sammlung' valued in Biedermeier literature, 'composure'. Realising that Hero has lost her composure, and is in danger of sacrificing her calling because she has fallen in love with the impetuous youth Leander, the priest extinguishes the lamp that is to guide Leander across the sea to her tower. On discovering his corpse, Hero dies of a broken heart. Grillparzer shows particular skill in demonstrating Hero's psychological progression, in the scene in her tower between herself and Leander, from resistance to the desire to see him again as soon as possible.

Both *Sappho* and *Des Meeres und der Liebe Wellen* reflect Grillparzer's fascination with the concept of fate, which appears in these dramas as the force prompting a decision between two equally valid value systems, one human and one divine. In contrast to Goethe's notorious avoidance of tragedy, for Grillparzer the clash of values cannot be harmoniously resolved. The pessimistic stance of resignation conveyed by these plays is typical of Grillparzer's work and in part grows out of the manifold disappointments of his life, which include the suicides of his mother and brother, the fact that none of his love relationships resulted in marriage, and the failure of his comedy *Weh dem, der lügt* (*Thou shalt not lie*, 1838), which caused him to give up the theatre.

Another way to interpret fate in *Sappho* and *Des Meeres und der Liebe Wellen* is as a lack of balance. A reading in the spirit of Biedermeier would suggest that greater balance or mediation between the two conflicting forces, less polarity or extremity, might have prevented disaster. The extreme nature of Hero's calling as a priestess, for example, is symbolised by her confinement to a lofty tower above the sea, cut off from the world. The doomed nature of the split between divine duty and conventional life is reinforced by the gender of the two heroines. Since the natural course of life for Sappho and Hero as women would have been to marry and have children, their initial decision to renounce this destiny singles them out and exalts them at the same time as it presages the difficulty of attempting to change their minds at a later stage.

Grillparzer's heterogeneous dramatic heritage further distinguishes his theatrical oeuvre from that of Weimar classicism. Products of the metropolitan theatre tradition of Vienna, his plays reflect the influence of Shakespearean tragedy, of the Viennese popular theatre, and of the drama of the Spanish and German Renaissance and Baroque, in addition to the plays of Weimar classicism. Always aware of theatre as performance, Grillparzer is more attuned to the visual aspects of drama than are Goethe and Schiller. Hence he carefully attends to imagery, gestures and spatial relationships, which possess great theatrical weight. In *Sappho*, examples include the association of Sappho with heights and Phaon with low places; Sappho's crimson mantle, golden lyre, and dagger; and numerous theatrical entrances and exits.

Even more theatrically grand are Grillparzer's plays in the Shakespearean manner, such as *Konig Ottokars Glück und Ende*, (*King Ottokar, his rise and fall*, 1825) and *Ein Bruderzwist in Habsburg*. (*Fraternal strife among the Habsburgs*, completed 1848 and published 1872). Though also written in blank verse and similarly constructed, these tragedies deal not with classical subjects but with figures from Austro-Hungarian history, and they span a much greater range both chronologically and geographically than *Sappho* and *Des Meeres und der Liebe Wellen*. Grillparzer's primary interest in these dramas is in character as reflective of differing world views. *König Ottokar*, set in thirteenth-century Bohemia, portrays the defeat of the Napoleonic title figure, a power-hungry, bossy, rude individualist, by Rudolf von Habsburg, a supporter of justice and order, friend of the people, and self-proclaimed embodiment of the German national spirit. Since the fall of the historical Ottokar led to the rise of the Habsburg dynasty in Austria, the play gave Grillparzer occasion to celebrate this event. Alongside considerable local colour and allusions to Shakespearean characters like Macbeth, Lady Macbeth and Ophelia, the drama displays affinities with Spanish and German Baroque drama, such as the use of emblematic imagery and a heavily didactic conclusion.

Ein Bruderzwist in Habsburg retains the locale of *König Ottokar* but moves the scene up several centuries to the years just prior to the Thirty Years War. A virtual antitype to Ottokar, who thwarted the church by divorcing his first wife, the emperor Rudolf II is depicted as a committed Catholic and monarchist who values art, science and religion over politics, peace over war, and passivity over activity. In a variation on the ancient theme of the fraternal feud, which was especially popular during the tumultuous *Sturm und Drang* (Storm and Stress) period in German literature, Rudolf is ultimately brought down by his brothers, who do not share his pacifistic inclinations. As in *König Ottokar*, Grillparzer uses a historical sequence of events to make an oblique comment on a contemporary situation, in this instance the turmoil of the Revolution of 1848. Like

Rudolf II, Grillparzer's tendency is to withdraw from the violence of the outside world into the life of the mind.

A similar figure is the focus of Grillparzer's best-known prose work, the novella *Der arme Spielmann* (*The poor fiddler*, 1847). A psychological study of Jakob, an eccentric street musician in Vienna, as viewed by the narrator, the novella employs a frame narrative technique which anticipates the frequent use of this device in realist fiction: the narrator's perceptions of Jakob as a curious anthropological specimen are offset by the internal narrative in which the fiddler tells his own story. Here it is revealed that this is no ordinary street person, but rather a man of good family whose father mistreated and rebuffed him because of his slowness. He is distinguished also by his gentle, benevolent character, which however emerges as something of an anachronism in his fast-paced, materialistic urban milieu: his timidity holds him back both professionally and personally, standing in the way of a union with Barbara, the woman he loves. As is frequent in Biedermeier literature, the work ends with an image of heartbroken renunciation rather than fulfilment.

Der arme Spielmann is striking in its mixture of disharmonious elements. Certain aspects appear to support a religious interpretation: the fiddler explains his dissonant music to the narrator by claiming that he is 'playing God' ('God' is a direct object here), he dies from a chill caught while saving others from a flood, and Barbara's placing of his violin opposite a crucifix on the wall after his death suggests a symbolic parallel with Christ. Yet the novella abounds in images of alienation which point forward to a world view that would exclude salvation after death. Jakob is an outsider spatially, temporally and metaphysically: in mid-nineteenth-century Vienna, the narrator is taken aback by the Latin phrase the fiddler utters; he typically makes his way against the stream of the crowd; the only time he kisses Barbara he is separated from her by a glass door; the music he produces is dissonant and incomprehensible; the room he shares is divided down the middle by a chalk line which marks off his neat, orderly space from his roommates' slovenly side, in the same way that Jakob separates himself from the chaos of contemporary life by retreating into his music and his anachronistic kindness. Just as his fiddling can be seen to prefigure atonal music, the text's many images of alienation, intimating the darker insights beneath the placid surface of Biedermeier, link Grillparzer's novella to modernist literature.

Another writer attempting to come to terms with the shadow of Goethe is Karl Immermann (1796–1840), most self-consciously in his voluminous novel *Die Epigonen* (*The epigones*, 1836), which offers perhaps the fullest exploration of the sense of being born too late that is so pervasive at this time. The title signals the phenomenon examined through many levels of society and put into words by Wilhelmi, the character whose voice most closely resembles the author's: 'Wir sind, um in *einem* Worte das ganze Elend auszusprechen, Epigonen, und tragen an der Last, die jeder Erb- und Nachgeborenschaft anzukleben pflegt' ('To sum up the whole wretched situation in one word, we are epigones, and bear part of the burden that tends to cling to every successive generation'). The word 'epigone', from the Greek word for 'one born after', originally had no neg- ative meaning; in Greek legend the 'Epigonoi' were the sons of the Seven against Thebes, who were able to conquer the city which had defeated their fathers. It is through Immermann's usage that that word acquires its pejorative definition, referring to an imitative, unproductive generation inferior to the one preceding it.

Correspondingly, Immermann writes in the tradition of the Goethean *Bildungsroman* while at the same time oppressed by the sense that Goethe had already perfected the genre in *Wilhelm Meister* (*Wilhelm Meisters Lehrjahre* (*Wilhelm Meister's apprenticeship*, 1795–96) and *Wilhelm Meisters Wanderjahre* (*Wilhelm Meister's journeyman years*, 1821)). For the Goethean concept of 'Bildung', or self-cultivation, dies hard for nine- teenth-century German writers. It is difficult to overestimate the impor- tance of this concept in the history of German literature. In a language realm where statehood was attained so late, culture often served as a sub- stitute for political activity. This compensatory mechanism is given express formulation by the writers of Weimar classicism. Goethe's essay 'Literarischer Sansculottismus' ('The production of a national classic', 1795) explains that the lack of a national centre, national literary canon and national style has of necessity caused German writers to find their subjects in other times and places; the dichotomy between a here-and-now orientation and the favoured historical themes of Weimar classicism is recognisable. In like manner, Schiller writes in the *Xenien*, 'Zur *Nation* euch zu bilden, ihr hoffet es, Deutsche, vergebens; / Bildet, ihr könnt es, dafür freier zu Menschen euch aus.' ('You Germans hope in vain to estab- lish yourselves as a *nation*; / Cultivate yourselves instead, strive to become free human beings – this you are capable of.')

With his epigonal consciousness Immermann follows the pattern of *Wilhelm Meister*, bringing his young protagonist Hermann into contact with diverse sectors of society and leading him through a variety of amorous encounters in a highly convoluted plot, full of intrigue and mystery. Yet on closer inspection *Die Epigonen* emerges as a parody of numerous aspects of *Wilhelm Meister*. The episodes with the forest crea- ture Flämmchen can in the end be seen as a critical comment on aspects of early German Romanticism as embodied in the figure of Mignon in *Wilhelm Meisters Lehrjahre*. Similarly, whereas aristocrats play a key role in the learning process of Wilhelm Meister, in *Die Epigonen* the nobility is heavily satirised as anachronistic. The attempt of the duke and duchess to put on a medieval tournament, complete with joust, is a comic failure. Although Hermann moves from this milieu to the salons of Berlin with ease, he seems to have no real goal. In contrast to Goethe's Wilhelm, whose every encounter and experience makes some contribution to his developing humanity, Hermann becomes progressively more confused. Furthermore, the manner in which he is drawn into relationships and used without full knowledge of the circumstances renders him less autonomous than the hero of Goethe's *Bildungsroman*. Finally, whereas Wilhelm Meister integrates himself into a concrete social milieu at the end of Goethe's novel by becoming a doctor, Hermann withdraws from contemporary society by deciding to turn the factories he has inherited back into farmland and live on this 'green spot' or 'island' with his wife-to-be for as long as progress allows him to.

Immermann's down-to-earth treatment of *Bildung* reflects the transition from the neo-classical Goethean ideal of attained virtue to the nineteenth-century reality of 'Bildung als Besitz', or cultural knowledge as material possession. *Die Epigonen* testifies to the 'collecting' ethic of Biedermeier, which prizes the accumulation of cultural artefacts, often from abroad, both in private homes and in museums. This is one of the ways in which Immermann's novel is as much, if not more, a *Zeitroman* (novel of the times) as a *Bildungsroman*. The transitional nature of the era it portrays is evident on many other levels as well and is even articulated by Wilhelmi, whose move from servant at the duke's to husband of the middle-class salon hostess Madame Meyer typifies the growing social mobility of the times:

Ja, wir leben in einer Übergangsperiode ... Auf alle Weise sucht man sich zu helfen, man wechselt die Religion, oder ergibt sich dem Pietismus, kurz, die innere Unruhe will Halt und Beistand gewinnen, und löst in diesem leidenschaftlichen Streben gemeiniglich noch die letzten Stützen vom Boden.

[Yes, we live in an age of transition ... People are trying to deal with it in all kinds of ways, they are changing their religion, or giving themselves over to pietism, in short, their internal agitation is seeking stability and support, and in the process of this passionate search usually knocks down the last props that hold them up.]

Alongside Immermann's depiction of the decaying aristocracy, who struggle to retain their status while losing their land, the novel contains the first description in German fiction of a capitalist and industrial business. In view of Immermann's strikingly early portrayal of the factories of Hermann's uncle, complete with clattering machines, smokestacks pouring forth coal fumes, and mention of the pale faces, sunken cheeks and hollow eyes of the workers, Hermann's decision to retreat into a retrograde utopia at the novel's end is hardly surprising.

In contrast to *Die Epigonen*, in the Austrian writer Adalbert Stifter's

(1805–68) *Bildungsroman Der Nachsommer* (*Indian summer*, 1857) the contemporary world is scarcely visible. Where the bulk of *Die Epigonen* is devoted to depicting the multiple layers of German society in Immermann's day, virtually all of Stifter's massive novel focuses on the cultural education of the young Heinrich Drendorf. Freed from the necessity of earning a living by his father's income as a merchant in Vienna, Drendorf decides to concentrate on his geological studies. On one of his expeditions through the mountains he comes on the estate of the Freiherr von Risach, who becomes his mentor. With the aid of the objects in his house, which with its numerous collections resembles a museum more than a place of residence, Risach, whose demeanour, values and biography bear unmistakable signs of being modelled on Goethe, instructs Drendorf in science, art, music, drawing and other disciplines.

In keeping with the classical ideal of the *cultus agri* (cultivation of the land) as a metaphor for the *cultus animi* (cultivation of the spirit), Risach's cultivation of Drendorf's abilities is symbolised by the process that culminates in Risach's garden. The garden in general, representing the control of nature and the withdrawal into a private realm, can stand as a virtual emblem of the Biedermeier ethic. Risach's highly stylised garden, with its smooth trees, meticulously pruned vegetation, labels on the plants, and absence of insects and other annoyances, is more akin to a work of art than a natural space. As such it externalises the extremely artificial manner of dealing with emotion which the novel portrays. This approach to feeling is exemplified in the relationship between Drendorf and Natalie, whose name reflects one of the many influences of *Wilhelm Meister* on *Der Nachsommer*. Progressing with infinite moderation, their liaison stands in marked contrast to the youthful relationship between Risach and Natalie's mother Mathilde, which, we learn, was characterised by impatience and passionate feelings. In keeping with the renunciatory mode so common in Biedermeier, that relationship remained unfulfilled, leaving Risach a lifelong bachelor.

To the present-day reader, the narrative technique of *Der Nachsommer* appears as stylised and artificial as Risach's estate and its collections. The novel's style and vocabulary are lacking in colour, the plot contains little action or emotion, description and dialogue abound. The characters' wooden speech and ritualistic gestures, especially obvious in the slowly developing relationship between Drendorf and Natalie, render them similar to marionettes. The novel's style can be seen to reflect the difficulty of shoring up this island of control and order in the face of the world outside – for example, the reality of urban life in mid-nineteenth-century Vienna – which is glimpsed only occasionally in the novel. A telling remark by Risach helps explain the idealised nature of the narrow sphere circumscribed by *Der Nachsommer*. Talking to Drendorf about his current platonic relationship with Mathilde, whose husband has died, he says that they are living 'einen Nachsommer ohne vorhergegangen Sommer' ('an Indian summer without a preceding summer'), an expression that in German negates itself. Hence Risach's estate emerges as a utopia, a symbolic didactic model of the best way to manage both nature and emotion.

Advocating moderation, harmony and gentleness on both the human and the natural levels, *Der Nachsommer* extensively illustrates the principles laid down in the preface to Stifter's collection of short stories entitled *Bunte Steine* (*Coloured stones*, 1853), which can be seen as a manifesto of the Biedermeier ethic. Thwarting conventional associations, Stifter characterises natural phenomena such as the wafting of a breeze, the trickling of water, the growth of grain, the breaking of waves in the ocean, the brilliance of the sky, and the shimmering of stars as 'great'; by contrast, phenomena like thunderstorms, lightning, volcanoes and earthquakes are 'smaller, more insignificant'. This categorisation accords with his definition of the 'gentle law' which in his opinion should guide the human race: the law of justice and morality, the law that works according to the common good and dictates mutual respect, admiration and love among human beings. One recognises the similarity of Stifter's law to Kant's categorical imperative and to the ethic of neo-classical humanism, as epitomised in Goethe's works, in general.

Given women's exclusion from higher education in Germany in the better part of the nineteenth century, it is not surprising that we have no *Bildungsromane* by women from that period comparable to *Wilhelm Meister*. Yet much of the work of Fanny Lewald, discussed earlier as an advocate of women's education, establishes her as a follower of Goethe. Margaret Ward's analysis of the influence of Goethe's *Die Wahlverwandtschaften* (*Elective affinities*, 1809) on Lewald's early novels *Clementine* (1843), *Jenny* (1843) and *Eine Lebensfrage* (*A vital question*, 1845) sheds new light on the prevalent theme of renunciation. Ward explores the tension in these novels between renunciation, which Goethe stereotypically associates with the feminine and with Ottilie in *Die Wahlverwandtschaften* in particular, and Lewald's new ideas about women's self-realisation.

Similarly, Konstanze Baumer goes so far as to claim that Lewald conveys the impression of a 'female Goethe' in her life and work (1989). Baumer refers above all to Lewald's travels to Italy and her recording of them in *Meine Lebensjahre* (*The education of Fanny Lewald: an autobiography*, 1861–2), the second and third volumes of which bear the Goethean titles *Leidensjahre* (*The years of suffering*) and *Befreiung und Wanderleben* (*Liberation and the wandering life*). As with Goethe, Lewald's arrival in Italy, as recalled in her autobiography, was intended to signal the beginning of a new life, a rebirth. In contrast to Goethe's situation, however, the primary purpose of Lewald's travels was to further her writing career. Similarly, whereas Goethe, as the internationally known author of *Werther*, attempted to keep a low profile in Italy, Lewald sought the limelight and seized every opportunity for social interactions. Baumer observes that in her later years Lewald, her self-confidence having grown because of her success as a writer, even adopted Goethe's style of staging this elevated sense of herself and of speaking in aphorisms. Since the quality of her work can scarcely be compared with his, one can truly speak here of an epigone in Immermann's sense.

The turning away from contemporary urban life in favour of the simpler forms of existence offered by the country, a choice represented as we have seen by the conclusion of Immermann's *Die Epigonen* and by the whole of Stifter's *Der Nachsommer*, is typical of a tendency towards provincialism that manifests itself in a number of other German-language works in the 1830s and 1840s. In contrast to the liberal currents of nationalism discussed earlier in connection with the writers of 'Junges Deutschland' and the 'Vormärz', these works are set in a village or rural milieu that celebrates peasant morality and a regional *Heimat* or homeland. One of the best-known examples is the section of Immermann's novel *Münchhausen* (1838–9) treating the Oberhof, a (fictional) prosperous farm in Westphalia. The other half of *Münchhausen* details the adventures of the title figure, supposedly a descendant of the notorious tale-teller of the same name, and his servant Karl Buttervogel, a kind of Sancho Panza to his Don Quixote. Written much in the manner of the eighteenth-century self-conscious novel, even down to the inclusion of an appearance by Immermann himself, this section of *Münchhausen* is highly satirical in tone, abounding in literary and other cultural references.

Interspersed with and counterbalancing the books on Münchhausen are those concerning the Oberhof. This half of Immermann's novel can stand on its own and soon began to be published independently under the title *Der Oberhof* (*The Oberhof*). This utopian alternative to the disjointed, uprooted way of life represented by Münchhausen is epitomised in the owner of the farm and the protagonist of the Oberhof books, the Hofschulze. He and the other inhabitants of the Oberhof embody values like modesty, autonomy, a sense of community, adherence to tradition, resistance to change and the upholding of external order. As in *Der Nachsommer*, the tenaciousness with which the status quo is preserved reflects the threat of dissolution from the inside that hangs over this increasingly anachronistic way of life. Like *Die Epigonen*, *Der Oberhof* ends with the spotlight on a bridal couple, in this case a couple from two different social classes, giving the harmonious conclusion larger symbolic significance.

Although *Der Oberhof* long proved to be more popular than *Münchhausen* as a whole, publishing the Oberhof books separately neglects the socio-critical dimension of the novel, since Immermann intended these books to be read as a kind of antidote to the mendacious, unstable world depicted in the section treating Münchhausen. This consideration, along with the fact that Immermann was himself not a provincialite but a city-dweller, helps explain the sentimental, idealised character of much of *Der Oberhof*.

The idealisation of peasant life comes into its own in the *Dorfgeschichte*, or tale of village life, which appears around 1840 as an autonomous literary genre in Germany, Austria, Switzerland and other European countries. This development can be seen in general as a reaction against growing industrialism and urbanisation; in Germany and Austria the particular combination of regionalism and folksy pro-German feelings conveyed by the *Dorfgeschichte* is no doubt bound up with Germany's frustrated pursuit of national unity. The founders of the 'Dorfgeschichte' are the Swabian Berthold Auerbach (1812–82) and the Swiss writer Jeremias Gotthelf (Albert Bitzius, 1797–1854). Although he is now largely unknown, Auerbach's works were enormously popular in his day, above all his *Schwarzwälder Dorfgeschichten* (*Black Forest village stories*, 1843ff.). They reflect the influence of Johann Peter Hebel's *Schatzkästlein des Rheinischen Hausfreundes* (*Treasure chest of the Rhenish family friend*, 1811), a collection of anecdotes, short stories and humorous tales characterised by unsentimental good sense and folk wisdom.

One of the best known of Auerbach's *Schwarzwälder Dorfgeschichten*, 'Der Tolpatsch' ('The clumsy fellow'), is a vivid regional portrait, evoking the provincial spirit of Swabia through its use of dialect, local place names and songs, and minutiae of village life. The narrator, a fellow villager of Aloys, the title figure, describes in earthy detail and with folksy language Aloys's clothing, the pipe he smokes, the stages involved in making his shirt, from picking the hemp to spinning, bleaching and sewing. The peasant milieu comes alive especially in the narrator's portrayal of Aloys's farming duties, such as feeding the cows and cleaning stalls; even the manner in which he stacks manure is praised. The depiction has an undeniably sentimental strain, mentioning the way the calves lick Aloys's hands and endowing the farm animals with an understanding of human affairs. The regionalism of this story and its celebration of the notion of *Heimat*, far removed from the universal humanism of Weimar classicism, have been seen to anticipate the 'Blut und Boden' (blood and soil) ethic central to National Socialist ideology a century later.

If the peasant milieu is idealised in Auerbach, however, it is not idyllicised; harshly realistic elements impinge on the placid village tableau.

While Aloys is in the military attempting to lose some of his awkwardness, a local ladies' man seduces his girl and, it is implied, impregnates her, inciting Aloys to a murderously violent brawl with his rival. The thoughts of *vanitas* in a peasant vein that then come to Aloys reflect the didacticism of the typical *Dorfgeschichte*, aimed both at the peasant readership who identify with the personages of the stories and at the larger urban audience of the tales, on whom the social criticism is not lost. Although Aloys's decision to emigrate to America at the end of the story points to a trend of the times, his pride in his accomplishments in the new world is mixed, significantly, with nostalgia for his lost homeland.

With Gotthelf the peasant scene shifts from Swabia to Switzerland. The author of several novels set in rural Switzerland, he is perhaps best known for his novella *Die schwarze Spinne* (*The black spider*, 1842). Its metaphysical cast, reflecting Gotthelf's other career as a pastor, renders this novella unique among nineteenth-century village tales. The work stands out in regional literature also by virtue of its highly refined narrative structure, which like *Der arme Spielmann* and many realist novellas employs the technique of the frame or embedded narration. As is often the case with this device, a symbolic object serves to link the various narratives. In *Die schwarze Spinne* a black window jamb on a house in the framing story, set in the author's times, triggers the grandfather's tale, set some six hundred years in the past. His listeners hear a terrifying story of sin and retribution revolving around an old motif, a pact with the devil: in return for help with their labour, the local peasants promise the devil, disguised as a hunter, the soul of an unborn child. Their spokesperson is Christine, whose cheek the devil kisses to seal the pact. When his end of the bargain is not upheld, the devil infests the region with a plague of destructive black spiders, spawned from a master spider in Christine's cheek. Only the sacrifice of a pure woman, who loses her life in trapping the spider in the window jamb, saves the peasant clan from extinction.

A secondary frame narrative conveys a similar sequence of events occurring nearly two hundred years after the first. The didactic message to the listeners is clear: the guilt for the sacrifice of one soul weighs heavier than the salvation of many, and he who worships God has nothing to fear from the devil or his incarnation in the black spider. The novella abounds with religious touches: the names Christine and Christen are among the only ones mentioned; prayer is a frequent and crucial activity; the framing narrative takes place on a Sunday. But *Die schwarze Spinne* is much more than a fictional religious tract. The story's heterogeneity – its realistic descriptions of Swiss peasant life alongside elements like the gruesome portrayal of the spider's physiognomy or the lightning flash caused by the devil's kiss – results in a fascinating and gripping narrative that lends new sophistication to the village tale.

A further manifestation of the tendency of Biedermeier writers to turn away from contemporary life, especially the urban world, is the interest in fairy-tales and fairy-tale dramas that flourishes from the 1820s through the middle of the century. With their folksy quality and focus on the German people these nineteenth-century fairy-tales carry on the tradition begun by the brothers Jacob and Wilhelm Grimm, whose *Kinder- und Hausmärchen* (*Grimms' fairy-tales*, 1812–15) represent a major achievement of the Romantic period. The publication of these stories, purporting to be a collection of tales transmitted by the German *Volk*, or simple people, is at least in part a nationalistic reaction to the humiliation of Germany by Napoleon.

Among noted epigones of the Grimm brothers is Ludwig Bechstein (1801–60), whose *Deutsches Märchenbuch* (*Popular German tales*, 1845) is a collection of fairy-tales consciously designed to serve as an instrument of family life. Although the tales are also clearly intended to entertain, Bechstein's collection is much more pedagogical than that of the Grimms. The overriding goal of each tale is to provide children with a lesson or moral, to teach a particular virtue: be critical of greed and materialism, smile even when you're suffering, and so on. By comparison with the Grimms' work, the tales in Bechstein's collection are watered down, more everyday in character; they are distinctly of the children's playroom, whereas the Grimms' tales belong to literature. In general, Bechstein's fairy-tales are more harmless than the Grimms', revealing less cruelty, fewer details about punishments inflicted. When present in Bechstein, such details have a didactic function, whereas the Grimms depict cruelty because it exists in life. One might well see an analogy between Bechstein's collection and the Biedermeier garden, which not only domesticates and tames nature but endows it with an indoor quality.

Biedermeier writers who tried their own hand at writing fairy-tales include Eduard Mörike (1804–75), with his collection entitled *Das Stuttgarter Hutzelmännlein* (*The wizened old man from Stuttgart*, 1852). More memorable are the numerous fairy-tale or magic plays stemming from the first part of the century. The most prominent of these were written by the Austrian actor and dramatist Ferdinand Raimund (1790–1836). Raimund first attempted tragedies but, failing in this mode, found his ideal genre in the *Volksstück* (folk play), of which the magic play is often a sub-category. The *Volksstück* reflects Austria's heterogeneous theatrical tradition, manifesting influences from both *commedia dell'arte* and the Austrian and Spanish Baroque drama, while yet conveying, as the term *Volksstück* suggests, the regional spirit of the people. The primary aim of the *Volksstück* is to entertain, but in the politically repressive Metternich era it often contains veiled social criticism that can find no other outlet. The *Volksstück* flourished in the suburban theatres of

Vienna, the main ones at the time being the Theater in der Leopoldstadt, the Theater in der Josephstadt, and the Theater an der Wien. These theatres represented not a counter-tradition to court and city theatres like the Burgtheater but rather an established part of the Viennese theatre world. They were designated *Volkstheater* primarily because they offered cheaper tickets and held performances on Sundays and holidays.

Together with his compatriot Johann Nestroy (1801–62), Raimund developed the genre of the *Volksstück* to its height. Raimund's most successful *Volksstück* in his lifetime was *Der Alpenkönig und der Menschenfeind* (*The Alpine King and the misanthrope*, 1828), subtitled 'A romantic-comical fairy-tale in three acts'. The title points to the opposition that drives the play's action. The Alpine King, a benevolent figure from the world of the fairy-tale who resides in an ice palace complete with Alpine spirits, wears a long tunic and an emerald crown, and has a white beard, takes on the task of curing Rappelkopf, a wealthy estate owner who represents a psychological case study in his hatred and paranoid mistrust of everyone, especially women, and his violent, destructive temper. The Alpine King effects Rappelkopf's cure by assuming his appearance and behaviour and, in essence, reflecting himself back to him; Rappelkopf becomes so put off by his misanthropy that he transforms himself. Hence the fantastic figure of the Alpine King can be read as the allegorical externalisation of Rappelkopf's process of self-recognition.

This play presents an interesting intertwining of Biedermeier fairy-tale surface with elements that transcend complacency and convention. For example, the naive statement by the chambermaid of Rappelkopf's daughter that she cannot understand how anyone with such a large fortune, a good-natured wife, a well-brought-up daughter, and a pretty chambermaid can be a misanthrope directs audience attention all the more to the complexity and difficulty of Rappelkopf's hostile personality. Similarly, the stereotypical Biedermeier attitudes towards relations between the sexes demonstrated by Rappelkopf's daughter and her maid, who are obsessed with physical beauty as the major lure for men and therefore the only thing that makes women valuable, are ironically offset by the fact that Rappelkopf's current wife is his fourth. Perhaps most striking in its realism is the portrayal of the family of coalburners whose hut Rappelkopf buys. This destitute family, complete with alcoholic father, childbeating mother, marital discord, starving children, one of whom is hunchbacked, and ailing grandmother, would in today's parlance be characterised as highly dysfunctional, and Rappelkopf's purchase renders them homeless as well. In socio-economic terms, Rappelkopf's purchase of the hut so that he can have a place to be alone and laugh at the folly of mankind can be seen as a microcosmic enaction of capital buying out labour, a further element that takes the play considerably beyond the fairy-tale realm. Fairy-tale and magic plays by other Biedermeier authors, such as Nestroy's *Der böse Geist Lumpazivagabundus oder Das liederliche Kleeblatt* (*The evil spirit Lumpazivagabundus, or the dissolute threesome*, 1833) and Grillparzer's *Der Traum, ein Leben* (*A dream is life*, 1834), also exploit the psychological and socio-critical potential of the fantastic framework. The frequent characterisation of the Biedermeier spirit as 'Heiterkeit auf dem Grunde der Schwermut' ('cheerfulness based on melancholy') is perhaps nowhere better illustrated than in the fact that Raimund, like Stifter, died by suicide.

Another manifestation of the Biedermeier tendency to avoid direct confrontation with the contemporary world is a preoccupation with organic nature. Writers like Nikolaus Lenau (1802–50), Eduard Mörike and Annette von Droste-Hülshoff testify to the continuing metaphoric power that nature holds for the poet. Lenau and Mörike can be seen to represent a transition from the romantic to the Biedermeier view of nature, from a conception of nature as an embodiment of the divine or transcendent to a much more down-to-earth understanding of the organic world. For Lenau, nature often serves as a mirror of human emotions, which for his personae are usually of a melancholy cast. A languorous mood pervades his poems; 'müde' ('weary') is a recurrent word. Employing the technique of personification, which is particularly prevalent in romantic poetry, in the poem 'Bitte' ('Entreaty') he endows the night with human characteristics in presenting it as the means for the poetic persona's escape. A similar device is used in 'Aus den Schilfliedern' ('From songs among the reeds'), where the day is described as weary, the willows as sad and the birds as dreamy, all as a reflection of the persona's grief at separating from his beloved. In 'Blick in den Strom' ('Staring into the stream') the poetic 'I' merges with the natural world, imagining that his suffering soul sees itself flowing by in the stream into which he is staring.

Mörike, who produced some of the most beautiful poems in the German language, is also fond of personifying nature. In his often anthologised 'Um Mitternacht' ('At midnight') the night is depicted as a mother who climbs up onto the land, dreamily leans against the mountains, and is sung to by nearby springs. The poem creates a picture of perfect balance and serenity in its portrayal of midnight as the hour when the scales of time are equally balanced, poised between night and day. Yet this mood belies the existential disquiet that infiltrates many of Mörike's other poems. 'Im Frühling' ('In springtime'), for instance, presents the natural world as a repository of memories into which the persona can escape from the nonspecific malaise caused by an unsatisfactory present:

> Ich sehne mich, und weiß nicht recht, nach was:
> Halb ist es Lust, halb ist es Klage;
> Mein Herz, o sage,

Was webst du für Erinnerung
In golden grüner Zweige Dämmerung?
- Alte unnennbare Tage!

[I feel longing, and I'm not really sure what for: / It's half desire, half complaint /
Oh tell me, my heart, what kind of memory are you weaving / In the golden twilight of green branches? / – Old, unutterable days!]

Mörike's strategy here is typical of the apolitical tendency of Biedermeier
writers to idealise the past because the present does not strike them as
something that can create a future.

Mörike's existential fears are especially visible in 'Denk' es, o Seele'
('Oh, soul, remember this'), the poem with which his novella *Mozart auf
der Reise nach Prag* (*Mozart on the way to Prague*, 1855) ends. The poem
encapsulates the presentiment of an early death which Mozart is shown to
have in the novella through the use of evocative elements from the natural
world, a pine sapling and a rosebush intended, according to this meditation, to grow on his grave and two black colts who will draw the coach carrying his coffin. The use of nature to convey a mood of impending death is
characteristic of the Biedermeier treatment of death, which is in general
more abstract than in romanticism.

The progression from a romantic to a Biedermeier view of nature
becomes complete with the poems of Droste-Hülshoff. In contrast to the
telescopic perspective of many romantic nature poems, in which the gaze
glides over expanses of landscape or the persona hears evocative sounds in
the distance, her poems take a microscopic or binocular stance.
Manifesting the Biedermeier tendency towards intimate description, she
attends to the nuances of the landscape, the tiny plants and animals popu-
lating it, their subtle noises and movements. In contrast to the generalised
vocabulary of romantic poets like Eichendorff, in whose work the elements mountain, forest, stream and field recur again and again as generic
terms, Droste-Hülshoff selects a particularised vocabulary in rendering,
for example, the heath and moor country near Lake Constance, where she
spent a good deal of time at her sister's castle at Meersburg.

'Im Grase' ('In the long grass') is representative of Droste-Hülshoff's
technique. Written from the perspective of one lying or sitting in the grass,
the poem laments the transience of all life by comparing the fleetingness of
time with delicate aspects of nature – the kiss of a sunbeam on the lake in
mourning, the song of the migrating bird that drifts down from the sky
like pearls, the flash of the shimmering beetle. Similarly, the perceiving
consciousness of 'Der Weiher' ('The pond') moves in close enough to the
pond to see the colours of the dragon-flies quivering above it, to catch
sight of the water spider's dance, to hear the lullaby of the reeds. In
Biedermeier fashion Droste-Hülshoff humanises nature, endowing it with

ethical, even religious, significance; interestingly, in describing the pond as 'So friedlich, wie ein fromm Gewissen' ('As peaceful as a pious conscience'), she compares the natural object with a human feature rather than the other way around, which is more common (for example, Heine's 'Du bist wie eine Blume' ('You are like a flower')); nature is the point of departure, but it is anthropomorphised.

Beneath the Biedermeier exterior conveyed by these poems, however, beats the heart of a passionate woman with distinctly feminist inclinations. These come clearly to the fore in her famous poem 'Am Turme' ('On the tower'), which until recently had been canonised as one of the few emancipatory statements by a German woman writer in the nineteenth century. Although such statements are, as we have seen, not as rare as was once believed, the poem is still striking in its presentation of a woman standing on a tower balcony in a storm, her hair blowing wildly in the wind, comparing herself to a maenad or bacchante as she gives vent to her desire for vitality, freedom and power – all of which are denied to her as a woman in her time and place. Hence the poem climaxes in her wish to be a man instead of the polite, well-behaved child she is treated as. Similarly rebellious feelings motivate her poem 'Der kranke Aar' ('The ailing eagle'), in which an eagle with broken wings proudly claims that it would prefer to be a wounded eagle, crippled by the eagles above it, than a hen living comfortably in a stove vent. Unable for reasons of background, health and temperament to adopt the convention-thwarting, quasi-androgynous way of life of a George Sand or a Louise Aston, Droste-Hülshoff uses poetry as an outlet for her frustration.

Droste-Hülshoff's sensitivity to organic and human nature reaches its culmination in her novella *Die Judenbuche* (*The Jews' beech tree*, 1842). Set in the mid eighteenth century in Westphalia, Droste's homeland, the story is based on an actual occurrence, a device that was increasingly to be used to promote verisimilitude in the narratives of poetic realism and realism. Although a detective story, the tale is at the same time very much a nineteenth-century novella, complete with a central, symbolic object that is often announced, as here, in the title. Moreover, the novella demonstrates an awareness of the role of heredity and environment in influencing human beings that would increase in literature throughout the century, reaching its height around 1900 in naturalism.

The reader senses that Friedrich Mergel, born of a drunkard father who beats his wife and dies when Friedrich is nine, raised in chaotic conditions, will come to no good. True to form, he winds up being suspected of two murders. In portraying Friedrich's complex psychology Droste-Hülshoff employs the motif of the *Doppelgänger*, popular in romantic writers such as Hoffmann, Tieck and Chamisso, in the person of Johannes Niemand, a mysterious figure who seems, in the manner of a Mr Hyde, to personify

Friedrich's evil side. Although Friedrich runs away from his village after the second murder, twenty-eight years later he is drawn back as if by guilt. Taking on the identity of Johannes Niemand, he hangs himself in the beech tree beneath which the body of the second murdered man, a Jew, had been found.

Such a brief summary does not do justice to the rich texture of this novella. The contrast between its highly objective mode of narration and the chilling nature of the events recounted parallels its mixture of detailed realism and the evocative symbolism of its leitmotifs. The novella is fascinating also in the ambiguity that surrounds both Friedrich's identity and his guilt for the two crimes. The power of religion, both Catholicism and Judaism, in the lives of the villagers is palpable throughout. Yet the novella's concern with questions of justice and injustice has as much to do with the law of public opinion and the notion of community as with the dictates of scripture.

Realism: from Keller to Ebner-Eschenbach

The nineteenth century is the great era of realism in the West. In Germany, one of the foremost genres of realism is the novella. The Biedermeier novellas *Der arme Spielmann*, *Die schwarze Spinne*, and *Die Judenbuche*, which have been discussed, share features with novellas written from 1850 onwards. Because the novella is such a prominent genre in the German tradition, German writers and critics have been fond of theorising about it. Many of these theories proceed from features reflected in the etymology of the term 'novella', the word for 'something new' in Italian. A seminal example is Goethe's 1827 definition, recorded in Eckermann's *Gespräche mit Goethe* (*Conversations with Goethe*, 1836), of the novella as an unheard-of event that has taken place. Another major addition to the theory of the novella is Tieck's statement in his *Vorbericht* (*Preliminary report*, 1829) about the importance of a turning point in the story, the point from which its plot is fully reversed, in a completely unexpected manner.

Later nineteenth-century theorists, such as Friedrich Theodor Vischer, emphasise the streamlined quality of the novella. Writing in his *Ästhetik oder Wissenschaft des Schönen* (*Aesthetics, or the science of the beautiful*, 1857) that the novella is to the novel as a ray of light is to the entire radiant body, he observes that the novella depicts only a slice of the total picture, a segment of a human life, a situation rather than a series of situations. Interestingly, he notes too that the tragic is more suited to the novella than to the novel. Other writers draw parallels between the novella and the drama. Theodor Storm, creator of some of the most powerful novellas in

German, not only calls the novella the sister of the drama but attributes its brief form to its poetic character. In the introduction to the *Deutscher Novellenschatz* (*Treasury of German novellas*, 1871) Paul Heyse formulates what is often referred to as the 'falcon theory', based on a tale in Boccaccio's *Decamerone* in which a falcon plays a decisive role, to emphasise the importance in every novella of a specific object that distinguishes it from a thousand other stories. Finally, in his *Beiträge zur Theorie und Technik des Romans* (*Contributions to the theory and technique of the novel*, 1883) Friedrich Spielhagen compares the novella with the drama because of the concise, economical quality of both, by contrast with the novel, which is propelled by adding events and characters. Spielhagen writes as well about the element of character in the novella. The novella, he explains, deals with complete characters, and because they determine the outcome of the conflict, the traits of the characters involved are of primary interest to the reader. It should be noted that all these elements and features concern an ideal type of the novella; it is rare for an actual novella to possess each of these traits.

Referring to the decades between 1850 and 1890, the German tradition often talks of 'poetic realism' rather than realism *per se*. This practice doubtless has much to do with Otto Ludwig's use of the term in his theoretical writings of the 1850s. Yet his definition of poetic or 'artful' realism – a mode of writing that seeks to create a self-enclosed totality by achieving a middle ground between idealism and naturalism, between the writer's subjective mind and the objective truth of things – is quite a loose one that could apply to a good deal of art.

There is nonetheless a tendency for many German-language writers in the mid nineteenth century to idealise or poeticise the world they depict, for reasons stemming from Germany's particular cultural and socio-political heritage. As we have seen, the legacy of Weimar classicism, with its strong proclivity for idealism, is highly influential. Moreover, the lack of a unified German nation is a significant factor. Particularism, or the existence of several small principalities, continues to further a provincialism similar to that prevalent in Biedermeier literature. The lack of a national capital of the order of London or Paris which would have meaning for an entire reading public hinders the development of the dialectical tension between capital and province so central to realist fiction in England and France. Finally, the strength of the pietist tradition in Germany, with its focus on the private realm as the arena of worship, further contributes to a privatised view of the world that runs counter to the more public orientation of realism.

In the course of the nineteenth century, however, increasing industrialisation and urbanisation, major influences on the realist tradition in other European countries, leave their mark on German literature as well, even before the founding of the Second German Empire in 1871. Manifestations of realism in German fiction include a concern with money, morality and middle-class values; a growing interest in human psychology; new means of treating historical topics; and narrative experimentation.

One of the most significant contributors in the first of these areas is Gottfried Keller (1819–90). Because of his attention to the importance of money and material things, Keller is often compared to the French realist novelist Honoré de Balzac. Yet Keller's work is unmistakably coloured by his Swiss homeland, although he writes in standard German interspersed with Swiss expressions. His landmark *Bildungsroman, Der grüne Heinrich* (*Green Henry*, 1854–5; second version 1879–80) is oriented on the Goethean model while at the same time giving a distinctly realistic cast to the genre. Heinrich Lee's nickname derives from the colour of his clothing, his inexperienced nature, and the colour symbolic of hope, a quality with which Keller repeatedly associates his protagonist. In the highly autobiographical plot Heinrich loses his father at an early age and is very close to his mother, has difficulties in school that culminate in his expulsion, continues his education on his own, including a forty-day marathon spent reading Goethe's works, endeavours to be a painter but fails, and lives by part-time work.

In the classic manner of the *Bildungsroman*, Heinrich is constantly trying to find a philosophy and a purpose in life. His quest takes place through experiences in five main areas: love, religion, art, homeland and politics. His amorous encounters embrace a dichotomy common in literature: on the one hand the dark-haired, sensual Judith, associated in unsubtle fashion with apples, to whom Heinrich is physically attracted, on the other hand the pale, blonde, pure Anna, whom he idealises in a nearly religious manner. Although the two types are combined in Dortchen Schönfund, whom he meets later in the novel, Heinrich marries none of the three; it is suggested that the guilt he feels towards his mother, whom he has left alone at home, is a significant barrier to a successful relationship with a woman. In the novel's first version Heinrich returns home to find his mother dead, and he dies soon after; in the second version his mother dies just after his return. Keller's own sense of guilt is strongly intimated.

Heinrich's religious experiences are distinctly autobiographical, his introduction to the work of Feuerbach through Dortchen Schönfund echoing Keller's exposure to the philosopher's lectures on materialism in Heidelberg in the late 1840s. Feuerbach's work helps to orient Heinrich's thinking away from conventional notions of divinity and towards the here and now, just as it moved Keller in the direction of agnosticism. Other significant influences on Heinrich's cultural education include his acquaintance with different periods and types of painting. His own frustrated career as a painter, progressing from landscapes to portraits to an abandonment of art altogether, seems to be a necessary stage in his growth from a rather dreamy, self-absorbed young man to a much more pragmatic, other-oriented human being who, in the second version of the novel, ultimately takes a job in the civil service.

No matter where he is or what he is doing, Heinrich's homeland is never far from his mind, an element that points to the strong strain of regionalism or provincialism still characteristic of German-language fiction in the mid nineteenth century. But an aspect of this novel that distingushes it is the importance of politics here, a feature absent from most *Bildungsromane* with the exception of Thomas Mann's *Der Zauberberg* (*The magic mountain*, 1924). Keller's critical attitude towards the Swiss form of democracy and towards the narrowness of his countrymen, albeit mitigated, like much else, in the novel's second version, parallels his liberal sympathies in the late 1840s. Heinrich's progress through all these areas of experience is aided by his encounters with the reflections or caricatures of himself which he sees in the situations of others. His development from a state of loneliness, disappointment and suffering to the attainment of an active life, integrated into society, follows the model of *Wilhelm Meister* rather than the pattern of withdrawal traced by *Die Epigonen* and *Der Nachsommer*.

Keller is one of the most successful writers of short fiction among the realists. His powers are especially visible in *Die Leute von Seldwyla* (*The people of Seldwyla*), which appeared in two volumes, in 1856 and 1873–4. Seldwyla, a name deriving from the Middle High German word 'saelde', meaning 'blissful or sunny', is a fictitious, quintessentially Swiss town. Although each novella is self-contained, together the stories convey a composite picture of this community as viewed by an ironical but fatherly observer. All the novellas are to varying degrees didactic, reflecting the heritage of the Swiss educators Rousseau and Pestalozzi. The title figure of *Pankraz, der Schmoller* (*Pankraz, the sulker*) is taught by life not to sulk; in *Frau Regel Amrain und ihr Jüngster* (*Regula Amrain and her youngest son*) Frau Amrain is if anything overactive in her pedagogical endeavours with her son. Titles such as *Kleider machen Leute* (*Clothes make the man*) point to the quasi-moralistic character of the stories. Yet such a brief summary omits mention of the humour which infuses these novellas and which distinguishes Keller from other realists writing in the German language.

One of the less humorous and more sentimental of the novellas in *Die Leute von Seldwyla*, *Romeo und Julia auf dem Dorfe* (*A village Romeo and Juliet*), is also one of the best known and loved. In this provincial, peasant version of the Shakespearean model, the lovers Sali and Vrenchen are less 'star-cross'd' than the victims of a present feud, the fight between their fathers over a piece of land. When their battle escalates to the point that Sali throws a stone at Vrenchen's father, leaving him an idiot, the misfortune of the young lovers is sealed: their sense of family honour prevents them from marrying, yet the code of bourgeois morality by which they live does not allow them to be together unmarried. The fact that the piece of land over which their fathers ruin themselves is fallow and desolate, however, says much about Keller's attitude towards such notions of honour. In an ending that is therefore more sad than tragic, Sali and Vrenchen drown themselves after consummating their love on a hay barge.

The realistic framework of the novella, which Keller based on a newspaper account, encompasses a symbolic substructure in the sequences treating the so-called 'black fiddler' and his milieu. Unlike the bohemian outsiders of romantic literature, such as Eichendorff's *Taugenichts* (good-for-nothing), who are typically wanderers, this figure spends his time at the 'Paradiesgärtlein' (Paradise Garden), an inn that serves as a haven for homeless people, the poor, unmarried lovers, off-beat artists and others who live at the margins of society. Keller calls into question the strict division between outcast and proper citizen in two ways: in the fact that the piece of land disputed by the two fathers originally belonged to the black fiddler, and in the fact that Sali and Vrenchen spend a few hours dancing at the Paradise Garden on their final day together.

Stylistic manifestations of Keller's realism include his great attention to visual detail, exhibited in his painstaking descriptions of property, food and clothing. All three are important to realist writers in general as a means of conveying a character's station, but they have special meaning for Keller as one who has known poverty. His skill in demonstrating the small-town bourgeois mentality that treasures material things is particularly evident in the passage in the novella *Die drei gerechten Kammacher* (*The three righteous combmakers*) in which he catalogues the contents of the lacquered chest of Züs Bünzlin, the woman being courted by all three combmakers; the long and minute list includes a nut containing a tiny image of the Virgin Mary behind glass and a cherry stone with a minuscule set of bowling pins inside.

The novellas comprising *Die Leute von Seldwyla* combine many of the romantic aspects of the novella around 1840 with its emphasis on the notion of *Heimat*, and infuse them with Keller's particular kind of realism. The provincial mentality still prevalent in the German-language realm in the mid nineteenth century is encapsulated in the fierce competition and suspicion among the three combmakers in the novella of that title, one being from Saxony, one from Bavaria and one from Swabia. The transition from particularism to the imperial period in Germany makes itself felt in Keller's late novel *Martin Salander* (1886), whose portrayal of

Swiss society disintegrating beneath the destructive influence of capital has considerable applicability to the new German empire as well.

The workings of capital in Germany itself are the subject of the most popular German novel in the later nineteenth and early twentieth century, Gustav Freytag's (1816–95) *Soll und Haben* (*Debit and credit*, 1855). On one level the novel is an *Entwicklungsroman* (novel of development) focusing on the fortunes of the young Anton Wohlfart, whose name ('welfare') predicts the felicitous path he will follow. His development runs parallel with that of the Jew Veitel Itzig, his former schoolmate; while Anton works as a clerk in a firm in Breslau, in training to become a merchant, Veitel is an informal apprentice to Ehrental, a shady Jewish moneylender. Throughout the novel the middle-class values associated with Anton – hard work, discipline and honesty – are contrasted in blatantly anti-Semitic fashion with the shiftiness, niggardliness, cruelty and crudeness of Itzig and Ehrental. The bourgeoisie is further cast in a positive light by contrast with the nobility, represented by Anton's fellow employee Fink, who eventually marries the girl Anton loves, and by her father the Freiherr von Rothsattel, who ruins himself financially through speculation and overspending.

In his attention to the nuts and bolts of money and business, signalled already by the novel's title, Freytag is more like Balzac than probably any other German writer. In tone Freytag is even more akin to Dickens, whose lovable but philistine bachelor figures are paralleled in the clerks with whom Anton Wohlfart works. The novel's realistic aspects also include its allusions to contemporary events and figures, such as the development of industry and the telegraph system and the Polish wars of liberation against the Tsar, and the name Rothsattel is surely intended to evoke that of Rothschild. The growing urbanisation of the times is reflected in Anton's and Veitel's move from the provinces to the capital; in an interesting reversal of the country–city dichotomy so common in earlier German literature, the Rothsattels decide to leave their rural estate and move to Breslau because they fear their daughter is growing up too wildly and without proper manners in the country. Although Freytag's milieu is Silesia, which did not occupy a central place in the minds of many Germans, he creates a work whose social realism gave it enormous appeal among his countrymen.

But the first German novelist of social realism on a European scale is Theodor Fontane (1819–98). Writing after the founding of the Second German Empire in 1871, a monarchy with Otto von Bismarck as its first chancellor, Wilhelm I of Prussia as its first emperor and Berlin as its capital, Fontane is the first major German writer to orient his fiction around a national nexus of social relations with which a large part of the population can identify. As in the case of *Soll und Haben*, Fontane's novels teem with topical references, but in this instance to people and places familiar to larger numbers of readers. His characters talk of personages and events such as Napoleon III and his wife Eugenie; Richard Wagner; the Franco-Prussian War of 1870–1, whose favourable outcome for the Germans facilitated the founding of the empire and contributed enormously to the new sense of German strength and national identity; and above all of Bismarck, the personification of the nascent state which Germans had so long wished to have. As in the great novels of French, English and Russian realism, in Fontane's fiction the reader knows at every point who and where the characters are and when their actions are occurring. Precise descriptions of settings and places are common, and no setting is more common than Berlin, where Fontane lived intermittently during his life. The flavour of Berlin localities and dialect adds local colour to his novels, just as his satire of Prussian customs and manners adds spice. One of the great masters of dialogue in the German language, he creates countless conversations satirising the superficiality, cultural pretension, hypocrisy and gossip of the population in the growing metropolis and capital.

Fontane's Berlin novels fully engage the realist themes of money, morality and middle-class values. The importance of class considerations in the new German society is graphically portrayed in the novel *Irrungen, Wirrungen* (*Trials and tribulations*, 1888), which presents a romance between Lene, a virtuous *petit-bourgeois* girl, and the Baron Botho, which falls victim to class differences. The pattern is reminiscent of Keller's *Romeo und Julia auf dem Dorfe*: separation follows a final idyllic period spent together, including in this case a 'paradisiac' night at an inn, a daring insertion on Fontane's part, in view of the couple's unmarried status. Although Botho marries a woman of his own class, it is clear that his heart still belongs to Lene. In demonstrating the need for Botho wistfully to subordinate his emotional inclinations to social codes, Fontane sounds once again the note of resignation so prevalent in nineteenth-century German literature.

The fact that Botho's mother exerts significant pressure on him to marry within his own class for the sake of the family's assets anticipates the role of the title character of Fontane's *Frau Jenny Treibel* (1892). In charting Jenny Treibel's quest for a profitable match for her weak-willed son Leopold, this novel portrays the full-blown development of the nineteenth-century process, intimated in Immermann's *Die Epigonen*, by which culture acquires the status of property: *Bildung* becomes regarded as *Besitz*. The novel can be seen to be propelled by the tension between these two entities. Hence the daughter of a schoolteacher, whose association with cultural knowledge is reflected in his constant citation of the classics, is unsuitable for Leopold in the eyes of Frau Jenny Treibel, for whom *Besitz* is paramount and *Bildung* should signal material value.

Valuing material things and surface attributes at the expense of inner, spiritual qualities, Jenny Treibel is representative of the new, money-oriented middle and upper classes that were becoming increasingly prominent in Germany after 1871, when industrial development and reparations from the French brought a wave of wealth to the fledgling empire. Fontane is especially adept at portraying the type of the *noveau riche*, the ambitious social climber who feels that wealth should purchase standing in the proper circles.

Fontane's first Berlin novel, *L'Adultera* (*The woman taken in adultery*, 1880), depicts the world of Berlin high finance as represented by Kommerzienrat van der Straaten, described as a good businessman but a questionable person who regards his wife as something to be proud of rather than happy about. These attributes of van der Straaten lay the foundation for the activity announced in the novel's title. Insofar as marriage is one of the most basic of social institutions and the family is microcosmic of society, the theme of adultery appears throughout literature as a symbol for the thwarting of the social order at large. The treatment and fate of this theme in a realist novel say much about the realistic quality of the work. In *L'Adultera*, van der Straaten is not only an unsympathetic person but twenty-five years older than his wife Melanie. Living out the implicit prediction embodied in the copy of the Tintoretto painting entitled *L'Adultera* which van der Straaten buys, Melanie becomes unfaithful to her husband, beginning her affair in true turn-of-the-century fashion in a hothouse. Although she succeeds in leaving her husband, Fontane demonstrates the power of society's moral codes in the treatment she receives after returning with her lover from Italy, where she has borne his child: not only her friends but her two children by van der Straaten snub her.

Another perspective on issues of morality and adultery is provided by Fontane's *Effi Briest* (1894–5), the scope of which ranks it with great European novels of adultery such as Flaubert's *Madame Bovary* and Tolstoy's *Anna Karenina*. Here the seeds of disaster are planted when Effi, a wild, tomboyish, romantic, unconventional girl who would rather run than do embroidery and who feels more like a child than an adult, is married off at the age of seventeen to the thirty-eight-year-old Baron Innstetten. The seeds are watered when she is repeatedly left alone at their out-of-the-way estate in Pomerania while Innstetten is immersing himself in his work; when home he is often too tired or, unaffectionate by nature, disinclined to give his young wife the kind of amorous attention she needs. Hence Effi falls easy prey to the advances of Major von Crampas, a somewhat frivolous ladies' man who delights in thwarting convention. As is typical of Fontane, their affair is conveyed in the subtlest fashion.

In contrast to Melanie in *L'Adultera* Effi, plagued by guilt and having no desire to exchange Crampas for Innstetten, eventually breaks off her affair. As occurs so often in literature, however, her lapse is discovered through love letters some six years later. Despite the time that has passed, because of the perceived injury to the social order and to his honour Innstetten insists on challenging Crampas to a duel, and the latter is fatally wounded. Like Melanie in *L'Adultera*, Effi is cut off from her child and from her associates in society by the overweening power of convention. In one of the novel's most moving scenes, Effi manages to see her daughter and is shocked and dismayed to see the child, trained by Innstetten, behave in her extreme propriety like a puppet.

Fontane points out the absurdity of this situation in a number of ways. Whereas genuine love exists between Melanie and her lover, Effi fell into her affair with Crampas out of ennui; she never loved him and had forgotten him by the time Innstetten discovered his letters to her. As the author demonstrates, Innstetten's life too is hollow following the separation from Effi. If Fontane is resigned that convention must win out, he manifests unmistakable scepticism at the hypocrisy of this society and clear sympathy with Effi's predicament. The novel strongly suggests that the instinctual fidelity of animals and servants is truer than the societal overlay wrought by middle- and upper-class convention.

A further interest of realist fiction is human psychology. Nineteenth-century literature manifests an increasing awareness of the subjectivity of perception, for example, a concern that becomes instrumental in affecting the shape of fiction at the turn of the century and in modernism. Otto Ludwig's (1813–65) poetic realist novel *Zwischen Himmel und Erde* (*Between heaven and earth*, 1856) explores this issue from the vantage point of the family as microcosmically representative of differing personality types and ways of controlling emotion. On the placid surface of the novel the slater Apollonius Nettenmair lives together with the widow of his brother Fritz, Christiane, and her children. The mystery still unsolved by the townspeople is the question why Apollonius never married her following Fritz's death some thirty years earlier.

In a flashback narrative we learn the unsavoury truth beneath the idyllic appearance of things: Fritz had arranged Apollonius's absence in order to deceive and steal his intended bride Christiane. Yet even after Apollonius sees that Fritz brutalises Christiane and the two have become alienated from each other, even after Fritz dies in trying to bring about Apollonius's death, and despite the fact that he and Christiane still love each other, Apollonius subordinates his desire for her to the word of honour he had given himself to protect his father's house and family. This obsession has become a compulsion, and that compulsion will stand in the way of his happiness for the rest of his life. The subjective nature of perception is demonstrated in the notion of family honour, which means precisely opposite things to Apollonius and his father. Apollonius's sense of family honour will not allow him to marry his brother's widow, whereas for his father, concerned with appearances, it is improper for Apollonius to live in the same house with Christiane without being married to her.

The interest in the role of heredity and environment evident in *Zwischen Himmel und Erde*, manifested in Apollonius's compulsive fear of becoming in some way like his brother because of their similar background and genetic makeup, increases in the course of the nineteenth century and reaches a climax in Naturalism. Marie von Ebner-Eschenbach's (1830–1916) realist novel *Das Gemeindekind (The child of the parish*, 1887) attempts to come to grips with the question of the role of heredity and environment in shaping human psychology in ways controversial at the time. *Das Gemeindekind*, Ebner's only full-length novel and best-known work, shares with much of her short fiction its setting in her native Moravia. Her psychological interest here centres on the workings of children's minds and on child development, set within the framework of issues of class and social equity. The title refers to the child protagonist Pavel Holub, who from the age of thirteen on is supported by the community after his father is hanged for murder and his mother is sentenced to ten years in prison for supposed complicity.

Whereas Pavel's younger sister is adopted by a wealthy baroness and eventually sent to a convent to be educated, he is rejected by all but one of the worst families in the town. Already a difficult child, he declines through the mistreatment and exploitation he receives from the townspeople, avoids school, steals, and is eventually suspected of murder himself. The childless Ebner's insight into child psychology is reflected in her awareness that children think differently from adults, manifested for example in an incident in which Pavel terrifies the baroness by impulsively pushing her chair out from under a chandelier to protect her after he learns that she is finally sending him to visit his sister.

As if to thwart the deterministic doctrines of naturalism and the novel's epigraph by George Sand, 'Tout est l'histoire', the benevolent influence of his sister helps to cultivate the good seed in Pavel and turn him towards an upright way of life despite the many factors working against him. Ebner ends the novel on a feminist note: when Pavel is at last reunited with his mother following her release from prison, he learns that she had let herself be sentenced although she was innocent, simply because she was afraid to contradict her husband.

Although Ebner was an aristocrat, she knew the value of women banding together to support their causes. Having spent most of her life in or around Vienna from her marriage in 1848 on, she was a member of the 'Verein der Schriftstellerinnen and Künstlerinnen in Wien' (League of women writers and artists in Vienna) from 1885 until her death in 1916.

She worked on behalf of a number of women's rights causes and was regarded as a symbol of the turn-of-the-century feminist movement. Her feminist sympathies are especially evident in works such as her late one-act plays *Ohne Liebe* (*Without love*, 1891) and *Am Ende* (*At the end*, 1897).

Feminist perspectives are evident as well among realism's new means of treating historical subjects. Louise von François's (1817–93) historical novel *Die letzte Reckenburgerin* (*The last von Reckenburg*, 1870), set at the turn of the nineteenth century, contrasts the fates of two women destroyed by marriage with the life of a successful single woman. Much admired by Gustav Freytag, who discovered it, and by François's friends Ebner-Eschenbach and Conrad Ferdinand Meyer, the novel was republished in numerous editions before lapsing into obscurity. As recently as 1986 it was described by Thomas Fox as 'the outstanding novel by a German-speaking woman of the last century'. One of the novel's unhappy female figures is an elderly countess living at the Reckenburg castle in Saxony. Divorced years before by a frivolous prince who squandered her fortune, she attempts to forget her bitterness by recouping the worth of the estate, and becomes close to the title character, her namesake Hardine von Reckenburg, after inviting her to the castle. The countess is so impressed by Hardine's prudence and diligence that Hardine feels the countess intends for her to marry the prince's son.

Meanwhile Dorothee or Dorl, a lower-class girl who had been taken in by Hardine's family and had grown up with her, languishes in boredom and loneliness during the long absence of her fiancé and eventually succumbs to the advances of the very prince whom Hardine is supposed to marry. Yet when Dorl has a child by him, Hardine selflessly conceals the secret and sees to the child's education after Dorl gives it up. Dorl in turn is treated like a child by her husband, and her feelings of guilt over her hidden affair and son help to drive her insane. These turbulent personal events are set against the background of the Napoleonic Wars.

In contrast to the countess and Dorl, Hardine survives psychically intact, achieving a considerable degree of emotional and intellectual satisfaction. After inheriting the Reckenburg castle on the death of the countess, she devotes herself to improving the estate, educating herself where necessary. She adopts Dorl's grandchild and remains silent about its origins even though this throws her own reputation into doubt. Unlike Dorl, she lacks beauty and feminine charm; her competence is associated with a certain masculine quality. Like François, she never marries. Although the extent of Hardine's self-denial stretches credibility at times, as do some of the novel's coincidences, the autobiographical parallels between Hardine and the author have been used to support what Linda Worley calls the 'Entsagungsmodell': confronting the biographies of unmarried nineteenth-century women writers (Droste-Hülshoff is another famous example) critics have often created the fiction of a life lived out in selfless devotion to others, renouncing without bitterness the domestic joys that conventional femininity brings.

It should also be noted that *Die letzte Reckenburgerin* was appreciated for its patriotism – not surprisingly, in view of its publication date and the time in which it is set; not for nothing does it bear the subtitle *Lebensgeschichte einer deutschen Frau (Life story of a German woman)*. It deals as well with issues of class, presenting the main characters as representative of their particular social group. The images of the aristocracy and lower classes emerge distinctly tarnished, especially by comparison with the depiction of middle-class values. Yet in its focus on female psychology and its insight into male-female relations, François's novel has more in common with nineteenth-century literature by women writers in other countries than it does with contemporaneous works by German male writers.

One notable feature which *Die letzte Reckenburgerin* shares with much fiction by François's male contemporaries is its complex narrative structure. Consisting for the most part of Hardine's autobiographical account, the story is not told chronologically but retrospectively, through flashbacks. This technique links it to some of the most narratologically sophisticated historical novellas by Theodor Storm (1817–88) and Conrad Ferdinand Meyer (1825–98). For instance, Storm's first chronicle novella, *Aquis submersus* (1876), uses the device of the frame narration to lend a degree of objectivity to the historical tale recounted. As in *Die schwarze Spinne* the narrative is set in motion by a significant object, or objects, in this case two ageing portraits which the frame narrator discovers in a village church in an area that strongly resembles Storm's homeland near Husum in Schleswig. One portrait depicts a man of fierce visage in a priest's collar; the other is of a dead boy, said to be the man's son. The narrator's curiosity is even more aroused by the letters CPAS in a corner of the boy's portrait. The interior narrative is prompted by a second painting of the boy which the narrator happens on in a house in town. When he asks the residents about it, they give him a chronicle manuscript by their seventeenth-century ancestor Johannes, who painted the picture.

Johannes's manuscript, flavoured with touches of seventeenth-century German, comprises the greater part of the novella and reveals the mystery of the paintings. It tells the frustrated love story of Johannes and Katharina, whose brother forces her to marry a wealthy but cruel nobleman. Hence Johannes and Katharina manage to spend only one night together. When they see each other by chance five years later, their reunion is so passionate that their young son – product of their single union – drowns in a nearby pond. Katharina's husband, the priest of the picture, forces Johannes to paint the dead boy's portrait as a warning. The meaning of the letters is now revealed: 'Culpa Patris Aquis Submersus' ('Vanished beneath the waters through the guilt of the father').

A short summary of this novella cannot do justice to its emotional power. In addition to its realist criticism of the pitfalls of class snobbery, which separates two rightful lovers and hence brings unhappiness on them and theirs, the story makes a larger comment on the transience of life and even of art, which is eventually subject to the same laws of decay as the human experience it is intended to preserve. The encapsulation of memory through objects which are themselves transient is also a theme of Storm's best-known novella, *Der Schimmelreiter* (*The rider on the white horse*, 1888), in which the memory of Hauke Haien, former dikegrave and innovative dike-builder, is evoked by the local superstition that his ghost can be seen riding along the dike on his white horse. The novella offers one of the most effective mixtures of fantastic and realistic elements in nineteenth-century German fiction. The story of Hauke, set against the vivid backdrop of the North Sea landscape Storm knew so well, is told in a triple-frame narration designed to prevent penetration of, and subjective identification with, the protagonist.

Meyer is distinguished from his fellow realist writers by the cosmopolitan character of his fiction. Reflecting his travels through France, Italy and elsewhere, his eleven novellas, published between 1873 and 1891, take place in Sweden, France, Italy and England, in addition to his native Switzerland. He has a penchant for historical milieus, setting his tales in eras ranging from the ninth to the seventeenth centuries. He often uses history as a distancing mask through which to depict contemporary events and personages, such as Bismarck, whom he views as a Renaissance man; when portraying actual figures from the past Meyer is not always historically accurate, since character is a foremost consideration and he occasionally exaggerates certain features to make a point.

A further distancing technique Meyer uses is the frame, as in the novella *Das Amulett* (*The amulet*, 1873), where a secondary narrator comes to take precedence over the authorial narrator. As with many of Meyer's novellas the context is religious; the central conflict here is that between Huguenots and Catholics in sixteenth-century France. The narrative is introduced by an authorial narrator who claims that the subsequent account is his translation of old seventeenth-century documents. These contain the Swiss Protestant Hans Schadau's first-person story of his youth, including the story of the Saint Bartholomew's Day Massacre of the Huguenots by the Catholics in Paris in 1572. But this account is qualified by the fact that it is filtered through memory, since it was not set down until 1611, prompted by Schadau's visit to the father of a Catholic countryman who had died protecting Schadau during the massacre. Neither the author nor the primary narrator make judgements; it is up to the readers to judge Schadau by noting contradictions in his narrative. For example, in the end he calls on the amulet, the distinguishing object or 'falcon' of this novella, in trying to save his wife, although as a Protestant he had earlier made fun of the use of holy medallions.

This technique is typical of Meyer's fiction, in which ambiguity is a recurrent reminder that it is impossible to see into the mind of another, that all knowledge of other human beings must rely on our necessarily subjective perceptions, and that there can therefore be no absolute judgements. One of the most elaborate examples of Meyer's technique is *Die Hochzeit des Mönchs* (*The marriage of the monk*, 1883–4), in which the story-teller is no less than Dante, entertaining his patron Can Grande at his court in Verona. Not only does Dante's ambiguous way of telling the shocking story of the title figure leave uncertain the real reason the monk breaks his vows; his narrative is further confused by the fact that his listeners constantly call into question details of his story as well as by the fact that he gives the characters of his tale the names of members of his audience, thereby further blurring the dividing line between the innocent and the guilty. In his awareness that narrative omniscience is an illusion and his emphasis on the subjectivity of perception, Meyer looks ahead to literary modernism.

Following its florescence in Weimar classicism, the drama undergoes something of a lull in the nineteenth century, taking a back seat to the novella, the *Bildungsroman* and lyric poetry. Alongside the relatively strong dramatic tradition in Austria, represented by writers such as Grillparzer, Raimund and Nestroy, the major figures in German drama between Weimar classicism and naturalism are Büchner and Friedrich Hebbel (1813–63), both of whom bring a new realism to the German stage.

In terms of theatre history Hebbel's most significant play is *Maria Magdalena* (1844), which has been called the first modern tragedy of family life in German. In the preface to the play, written after its completion, Hebbel echoes his earlier essay 'Mein Wort über das Drama!' ('My views on the drama!', 1843) in characterising art as the highest form of history-writing and drama as the supreme literary genre. In his view, which is strongly influenced by the Hegelian notion that history progresses dialectically, drama should focus on transitional periods of history. Greek tragedy, he claims, was the product of the progression from a naive to a reflective world view, just as Shakespearean drama grew out of Protestantism and liberated the individual. Drama should demonstrate a dialectical progression to a healthier, higher stage of history, although dramatic characters are sometimes defeated in the process.

With reference to *Maria Magdalena* these theories should be seen in juxtaposition with Hebbel's thoughts on the bourgeois tragedy, a prominent genre in the German theatrical tradition. Represented notably by

Lessing's *Miss Sara Sampson* (1755) and *Emilia Galotti* (1772) and by Schiller's *Kabale und Liebe* (*Love and intrigue*, 1784), the bourgeois tragedy presents the middle-class family as microcosmic of its class. Conflicts between the middle and upper classes are typically depicted in the seduction or attempted seduction by an aristocrat of a middle-class daughter whose honour is defended by her father; hence the father-daughter bond is a crucial element of the genre. The mother is often a weak figure, possibly even partial to the aristocratic seducer.

Hebbel, describing the bourgeois tragedy in his preface as a genre that has become discredited, feels that it should present not external conflicts, between classes, but rather inescapable conflicts within a class and within individuals. This process of interiorisation represents a significant step in the history of German drama. *Maria Magdalena*, Hebbel's attempt to renew the bourgeois tragedy, depicts a world that is ailing, itself in need of a move forward to improved health. As an illiterate cabinet-maker the family father here, Meister Anton, has descended in class standing from his predecessors in Lessing and Schiller. Yet like them he is dominated by his concern for honour, which in his case is virtually equivalent to appearances. His wife is an invalid who dies on hearing that her son is supposedly a thief. His daughter Klara has let herself be seduced by Leonhard, a soulless, opportunistic clerk, because she thought that the man she really loved, the secretary, had forgotten her. Pregnant and desperate, she feels impelled to marry Leonhard to preserve her honour and that of her father, who has sworn to kill himself if she dishonours him. Yet Leonhard abandons her when he learns that her dowry will not be what he had been expecting.

Not surprisingly, several of these dismal characters wind up dead at the play's end: Leonhard is killed in a duel with the secretary, whom he has fatally wounded, and Klara drowns herself – convinced that for her father, she is better off dead than dishonoured. Hence she emerges, as a believer in an outdated moral code, as the victim of a progression from one historical era to another. Yet the play's biblical title, with its reference to a sinner who repents, enlarges its context both temporally and spatially. Other elements look forward to twentieth-century theatre. The fact that Meister Anton's son turns out not to be a thief renders his wife's death absurd, a mode revisited at the end of the play when Meister's famous realisation that he no longer understands the world moves the tone from one of social criticism to one of existential confusion and despair.

The play's language is also quite modern in its verisimilitude. Relations between Klara and Leonhard are described in highly intimate terms, and Meister Anton's speech is colourful and uninhibited. The technique of characters talking past each other, which occurs frequently in twentieth-century drama, appears here as a sign of inadequate communication.

Although the form of *Maria Magdalena* is fairly conventional, in that it consists of three acts with scene divisions and basically adheres to the classical unities of time, place and action, its content was in many ways shocking. The play was rejected by the Hoftheater in Berlin because of the element of Klara's pregnancy, although the theme of the unwed mother who kills her baby had been a prevalent theme in German literature during the *Sturm und Drang* period (one thinks above all of Gretchen in Goethe's *Faust*) and would again achieve prominence in Naturalism.

Maria Magdalena is Hebbel's only major play to be set in contemporary times. Others take place in the biblical era, such as *Judith* (1841) and *Herodes und Mariamne* (1849); *Agnes Bernauer* (1852), set in fifteenth-century Bavaria, is a *Ritterdrama* (drama about chivalry), taking its place in this tradition alongside Goethe's *Götz von Berlichingen* (1774), Kleist's *Käthchen von Heilbronn* (1810), and Grillparzer's *König Ottokars Glück und Ende* and *Ein Bruderzwist in Habsburg*, discussed above. In many ways Hebbel's theatre represents a middle ground between the idealism of Weimar classicism and the determinism of naturalism, insofar as he explores the idea of guilt-free tragedy: the individual who does not fit into the world order either because she is unusual – extraordinarily beautiful like Agnes Bernauer – or because she has outgrown older values, like Judith and Mariamne, or because she is the victim of older values, like Klara in *Maria Magdalena*. In Hebbel's presentation these individuals must be sacrificed so that the course of history can progress. Although they are destroyed, their demise occurs only after they have accomplished something that moves history forward, such as Judith's murder of Holofernes. Thus, while Hebbel's dramas originate in a particular historical period, in symbolic terms their relevance is much larger; they are both timely and timeless.

As one would expect, realist poetry is particularly evocative of the material world. Theodor Storm has been ranked among the greatest lyric poets in the German language. Even his patriotic poems, such as 'Gräber an der Küste' ('Graves on the coast'), tend to be evocative or elegaic rather than tendentious. Best known are the lyrics depicting the landscape of his North Sea homeland. With their images of grey sea, grey city, seagulls and dreamy fog, poems like 'Die Stadt' ('The city') and 'Meeresstrand' ('The seashore') form a small counter-tradition to the romantic celebration of the forest so prevalent in German literature.

Keller's poetry, both political and otherwise, is coloured by his secularism. Many of his poems of the 1840s share in the democratic, patriotic fervour that we have seen to characterise his German countrymen at the time. Yet a number of his poems treat the perennial poetic themes of love, nature and death. Keller's poetry cannot be touched on without mention of the poem 'Abendlied' ('Evening song'), a nineteenth-century treatment of the *carpe diem* motif. Focusing on the sense of sight as the means to take in as much of the world as possible, as long as this is possible, the poetic persona closes the poem with an imperative that epitomises Keller's undying appreciation for the visual realm: 'Trinkt, o Augen, was die Wimper hält, / Von dem goldnen Überfluß der Welt!' ('Drink, o eyes, as much as your lashes can hold / Of the golden profusion of the world!')

The most significant poet among the realist writers is Meyer. Like his novellas, his poems, filled with images, places and personages from other times and locales, reflect his foreign travels. In terms of the history of lyric poetry, he is to be credited with creating the *Dinggedicht* (object-poem), which would later be refined by Rilke and others. Rather than projecting human emotions onto inanimate objects in the manner of the pathetic fallacy so common in romanticism (for example, the 'weeping willow'), Meyer strives to depict the object from its own point of view, as it were, as objectively as possible. Well-known examples of this technique are his poems 'Zwei Segel' ('Two sails') and 'Der römische Brunnen' ('The Roman fountain'). Although the harmonious relationship between the two sails suggests that they are meant to symbolise lovers, the poem concentrates throughout on the sails themselves and their mutual imitation; the confessional mode is absent. Similarly, the poem inspired by a fountain in the gardens of the Villa Borghese in Rome lacks all reference to a lyrical 'I', intimating instead an understanding of the inner workings of the fountain itself. Meyer's *Dinggedichte* effect a break with *Erlebnisdichtung*, or the poetry of personal experience, which had dominated the German tradition since the 1770s, and represent a move towards symbolist poetry. In both his fiction and his poetry, then, Meyer perfected the realist technique while transcending it.

7

From Naturalism to National Socialism
(1890–1945)

RITCHIE ROBERTSON

Introduction

The history of modern German literature cannot be detached from the social and political history leading from the authoritarian but relatively benign empires of Wilhelm II and Franz Joseph II to defeat in war, the establishment of fragile democratic republics, and the rise of a tyrannical, warlike and eventually genocidal Third Reich which left all of Central Europe in a state of devastation unmatched since the Thirty Years War. The exiled Thomas Mann told a New York audience in 1937: 'It is in a political form that the question of man's destiny presents itself today.' Some authors, like Mann, arrived by complicated routes at a defence of democratic and liberal humanism; others placed their hopes in a conservative revolution or in the dictatorship of the proletariat. A literary history, however, must attend not only to authors' explicit political choices but, still more, to the visions of society articulated in their imaginative works. And here we shall find a network of images, visions, beliefs and rhetorics which cut across political divisions, often in unexpected and disturbing ways, to give this rich and bewildering period a complex unity. As the late J. P. Stern showed in *The dear purchase* (1995), the highest achievements of modern German culture can be traced to the same imaginative matrix as many assumptions of the new barbarism. Hitler's emergence was not inevitable, but the widespread acceptance of his rhetoric was not anomalous.

If any writer placed his stamp on this period, it was Friedrich Nietzsche (1844–1900), whose descent into madness in 1889 coincided with the beginning of his literary impact. He attacked the shallow complacency of Wilhelmine Germany and demanded the restoration of heroic and tragic values. Against scientific rationality he preached the fascinating power of myth, represented especially by Wagner's music-dramas. 'Without myth,' he declared, 'every culture loses its healthy, natural, creative vigour' (*Die Geburt der Tragödie* (*The birth of tragedy*, 1872), sec. 23). The return to myth in twentieth-century literature produces exciting visions of a transfigured human life, but is also disturbingly close to the Nazis' malign attempt to realise the myths of the Aryan race and the millennial Reich. From utopian fantasies one turns with relief to writers who used realism to explore ordinary lives in contemporary society, and with particular admiration to those who exploited the imaginative appeal of myth while also using it critically as an instrument of inquiry. Pre-eminent among these is Thomas Mann, who at the end of our period evoked an ultra-German myth in *Doktor Faustus* (published in 1947) in order to examine the involuntary complicity of artists with the inhuman.

Myth seemed to counter the authority of science, which was at its height around 1890. The materialism popularised in *Kraft und Stoff* (*Power and matter*, 1855) by Ludwig Büchner (1824–99, brother of the dramatist, and much better known in the nineteenth century) persuaded many people that the freedom of the will and the immortality of the soul were illusions. The Darwinian theory of evolution, propagated in Germany by Ernst Haeckel (1834–1919), seemed to transfer humankind from God's care to the animal kingdom. The survival of the fittest in the struggle for existence confirmed the amorality of the universe and, as 'social Darwinism', helped to legitimise unfettered capitalism. These doctrines seemed equally compelling and depressing. Arthur Schnitzler, then a medical student, noted in his diary for 28 April 1880: 'To my sorrow, I find the materialists' outlook more and more plausible.'

Nietzsche won readers by accepting the negative findings of science while opposing its positive claim to authority. Science, he maintained, had cleared away religious and metaphysical theories, delivering the death-blow to a Christianity which had been mortally weakened by the Enlightenment. It disclosed an amoral and hence innocent universe in perpetual flux, which, like an aesthetic object, had only the 'meaning' that man conferred on it. Among the many 'post-Christian' ideas and ideologies, Nietzsche lent his authority to three in particular: to vitalism, aestheticism and authenticity.

Vitalism offered an antidote to scientific rationality and its pessimistic implications. The concept of 'life' rapidly acquired a mantra-like authority. 'Life', declared Oswald Spengler (1880–1936) in the 1922 peroration to *Der Untergang des Abendlandes* (*The decline of the West*), 'is the first and last thing, a microcosmic version of the cosmic flow.' 'Life' connoted organic growth and evolution; fertility, procreation, creativity; the interplay of creation and destruction. Recalling his earlier distinction, drawn in *Die Geburt der Tragödie*, between Apolline serenity and Dionysiac energy, Nietzsche claimed in *Götzen-Dämmerung* (*The twilight of the idols*, 1889) that the Greeks had expressed this concept of ever-renewed life in the cult of Dionysus: '*Eternal* life, the eternal return of life; the future promised and affirmed in the past; the triumphant Yes to life, beyond death and change; *true* life as the collective survival through procreation, through the mysteries of sexuality . . . All this is meant by the word Dionysus.'

Such heady rhetoric appealed to those who, like Hofmannsthal's Lord Chandos, sought 'a state of continual intoxication, in which all existence appeared to me as a great unity'. This unity was expressed in 'Jugendstil' painting through organic motifs of branches, undulating lines and naked bodies. Irrational vitality seemed to be located especially in the female body: Nietzsche personified life as a woman; many dramatists took a dancing woman – Wedekind's Lulu, Hofmannsthal's Elektra, Hauptmann's Pippa – as the symbol of primordial energy. 'Life' demanded expression not in intellectual abstractions but in sensuous images and myths. Vitalism was a major source of the ambivalent mythopoeia that so dominates German literature in this period.

Another was aestheticism. German philosophy from Schiller to Schopenhauer assigned a central place to art. Writing in this tradition, Nietzsche maintained that, in an empty universe without meaning or certainty, the only consolation was to be found in art: 'for only as an *aesthetic* phenomenon is existence and the world eternally *justified*' (*Die Geburt der Tragödie*, sec. 5). And by denouncing conventional morality and religion as mere disguises for the Will to Power, Nietzsche opened up a vast intellectual space to be occupied by art. Many writers at the turn of the century, especially but not only those who espoused 'decadence', wanted an aesthetic view of life to supersede religion and morality; and it is the most honest writers who explore this outlook in all its consequences, while in some others we shall discover a strange alliance between aestheticism and fascism.

Traditional morality seemed likewise due for replacement by a doctrine of personal authenticity based on the will. According to Nietzsche, the omnipresent Will to Power found expression equally in the 'master morality' of life-loving aristocrats and the 'slave morality' of life-denying Christians; though he remained ambiguous about whether 'master morality' was a theoretical construct or a blueprint for a future society. Value and even truth (Nietzsche thought it true to say) were fictions imposed on reality by the will of the strongest. Evolution would eventually produce an 'Übermensch' or 'Superman' who would joyfully affirm the life-process. Anyone capable of such affirmation could create his own values and live by moral standards infinitely more demanding than those of conventional morality. Nietzsche – the son of a Protestant clergyman – echoes St Paul and Emerson in envisaging a morality of unremitting effort directed at self-overcoming. Such a morality is inevitably self-centred, dismissing concern for other people as inauthentic. Actions are evaluated by their difficulty: 'What does not kill me, strengthens me.' This morality of authenticity achieved through strenuousness permeates modern German literature and thought. Robert Musil ironises it in *Der Mann ohne Eigenschaften* (*The man without qualities*, 1930, 1933) by making his

Nietzschean devotee, Clarisse, urge her husband to murder his best friend and thus become a genius. Heinrich Himmler, knowing Nietzsche only at several removes, nevertheless betrayed his influence when, instructing the SS to undertake the extermination of the Jews, he praised their hardness acquired by 'enduring' the sight of innumerable corpses.

Naturalism

The copious theories of the Naturalists were animated by scientific enthusiasm. Scientists, declares Heinrich Hart in his essay 'Die Moderne' ('Modernity', 1890), are the pioneers of modernity, and poets must draw on their findings and imitate them in observing reality instead of obeying tradition. Wilhelm Bölsche, in *Die naturwissenschaftlichen Grundlagen der Poesie* (*The scientific foundations of poetry*, 1887), maintains that to a poet familiar with Darwin the smallest everyday events can acquire new interest as illustrating the laws of evolution. In the most eccentric of these manifestos, *Die Kunst: Ihr Wesen und ihre Gesetze* (*Art: its nature and laws*, 1891), Arno Holz affirms that art can become a perfect imitation of nature. But most Naturalists did not go that far, either in theory or practice. They called for fearless investigation of reality in order to present people with healthy ideals and foster Germany's national rebirth. Their links with Socialism (which in any case was banned from political activity between 1878 and 1890) were few and hesitant. Their main journal, *Die Gesellschaft* (*Society*), founded in 1885 by M. G. Conrad, promised that an 'intellectual aristocracy' ('Geistesaristokratie') would present 'genuine, natural, German nobility'.

Naturalist prose is surprisingly inventive. Its masterpiece, *Bahnwärter Thiel* (*Linesman Thiel*, 1888) by Gerhart Hauptmann (1862–1946), provides a detached, circumstantial account of an inarticulate man bound sexually to his brutally physical second wife, whom he murders after her neglect causes the son of his first marriage to be run over by a train. The story looks back to Büchner's *Lenz* and forward to Expressionism in projecting Thiel's powerful sensations into the surrounding landscape and especially into the train, described like a snorting monster whose glowing eyes turn rain into blood. Very different are the sketches *Papa Hamlet* (1889) and *Der erste Schultag* (*The first day at school*, 1889) by Arno Holz (1863–1929) and Johannes Schlaf (1862–1941). They avoid narratorial commentary, concentrating on descriptive detail and mundane dialogue, but the narrative perspective shifts with bewildering agility. In *Der erste Schultag* it moves between the sadistic schoolteacher, two terrified boys, and even a trapped bluebottle; in *Papa Hamlet* the failed actor's compulsive quotations from *Hamlet* are ironically echoed by the narrator. This dexterity anticipates the irony of the early Thomas Mann.

Naturalism was introduced to the Berlin theatre by the great director Otto Brahm (1856–1912) and his society the Freie Bühne. Brahm staged Ibsen's still scandalous *Ghosts*, Hauptmann's early tragedy *Vor Sonnenaufgang* (*Before sunrise*, 1889), and the Naturalist showpiece *Die Familie Selicke* (*The Selicke family*, 1890) by Holz and Schlaf. The last depicts the misery of a Berlin family whose father returns from the pub just in time to witness the tear-jerking death of his eight-year-old child on Christmas Eve; dialogue, however inconsequential, is minutely reproduced in so-called 'Sekundenstil'. More harrowingly but more rewardingly *Vor Sonnenaufgang*, set in Hauptmann's native Silesia, shows a *nouveau-riche* farming family riddled by alcoholism and adultery; the daughter, Helene, hopes to be rescued by Alfred Loth, a social reformer, but Loth rejects her because her unhealthy heredity conflicts with his doctrinaire eugenic principles, whereupon she commits suicide. The hereditary alcoholism on which the tragedy turns is medically absurd (as is Oswald's 'softening of the brain' in *Ghosts*), but the play's rural setting and occasional dialect create a ballad-like atmosphere admired by one of its most appreciative reviewers, Theodor Fontane.

The outstanding Naturalist drama, however, is Hauptmann's *Die Weber* (*The weavers*, 1892), dealing with the unsuccessful uprising of starving Silesian weavers in 1844. Like Büchner, Hauptmann adhered closely to his sources; but while the common people in *Dantons Tod* form a Shakespearean background to the agonisings of the revolutionary leaders, Hauptmann places the people, as a collective body without dominant individuals, in the foreground of his play. Its episodic structure goes back to the realism of the *Sturm und Drang*. We see weavers being paid miserably by the factory-owner Dreissiger; then at home, lamenting their increasing poverty; then in the inn, gradually contemplating rebellion. After the attack on Dreissiger's house in Act IV, the focus shifts to the intriguingly ambiguous figure of the pious, long-suffering old weaver Hilse, who refuses to join in the revolt but prays for the weavers' safety before being killed by a stray bullet. An appeal for revolutionary solidarity? The police thought so when they banned the play's public performance lest it create Socialist propaganda. But the court which later authorised its performance observed that the cost of tickets would prevent it from influencing the working classes.

Other Naturalist plays borrow techniques from Ibsen. Their restricted setting, described in elaborate stage-directions, represents the milieu that has shaped the characters and from which the only escape is death, while their unity of time lets them concentrate on a catastrophe that arises when tensions latent in a family are released by the arrival of a stranger. They are remarkable for treating a wide range of contemporary issues, especially problems of sex and class. Hauptmann examined the plight of unmarried mothers in *Rose Bernd* (1903), whose theme of infanticide recalls the *Sturm und Drang*, and later in *Die Ratten* (*The rats*, 1910); Max Halbe (1865–1944) showed youthful love being threatened by moral and legal prudery in *Freie Liebe* (*Free love*, 1890) and by religious fanaticism in *Jugend* (*Youth*, 1893); Arthur Schnitzler (1862–1931) treated a similar theme in *Liebelei* (*Dalliance*, 1896), and in *Freiwild* (*Fair game*, 1897) attacked the assumption that actresses were 'fair game' for sexual exploitation; Hermann Sudermann (1857–1928) mocked the aristocratic duelling code in *Die Ehre* (*Honour*, 1889). In her affecting play *Dämmerung* (*Twilight*, 1893), 'Ernst Rosmer' (Elsa Bernstein, 1866–1949) juxtaposed a 'New Woman', a dedicated doctor, with a frivolous but pathetic female dilettante, while in Hauptmann's *Einsame Menschen* (*Lonely people*, 1891) another educated woman involuntarily destroys the family life of a self-centred idealist, in a conflict recalling Ibsen's *Rosmersholm*.

Hauptmann's long and extraordinarily versatile career brought him the Nobel Prize in 1912. An early high point was the comedy *Der Biberpelz* (*The beaver coat*, 1893), whose Berlin working-class heroine, Mutter Wolffen (an ancestress both of Brecht's Mother Courage and Zuckmayer's Captain of Köpenick), swindles Prussian officials and self-satisfied towns-folk. Hauptmann's attraction to symbolism and myth is already apparent in *Hanneles Himmelfahrt* (*Hannele goes to heaven*, 1894), which presents the visions of earthly terror and heavenly reward that pass before a four-teen-year-old girl dying in a Silesian poor-house. This mythopoeic ten-dency finds its supreme expression in the homespun yet compelling imagery of *Und Pippa tanzt!* (*And Pippa dances!*, 1906), where Apolline clarity, symbolised by the delicate products of a glass-factory, confronts the Dionysian energy of the brutish and sinister old glass-blower Huhn; the dancing girl Pippa suggests the indestructible soul.

Hauptmann's interest in myth was strengthened by his visit to Greece in 1907. In *Griechischer Frühling* (*Greek spring*, 1908), an important docu-ment of Germany's fascination with Greece, he maintained that Greek myth and theatre arose from the soul of the people ('Volk') and opposed the Christian attempt to dissociate humankind's spiritual life from its earthly setting. But, like Hölderlin a century earlier, he was equally fasci-nated by the myths of Dionysus and of Christ, and sharply aware of their affinities. Hauptmann's mythic novels, though, are mediated by detached and somewhat sceptical narrators. In *Der Narr in Christo Emanuel Quint* (*Emanuel Quint, the fool in Christ*, 1910), a Silesian carpenter, sincerely seeking God, is driven by his disciples' faith into proclaiming that he himself is Christ. This unwieldy novel is most persuasive in its imagery: Quint experiences God among the mountains, where he sees divinity symbolised in the rising and setting sun; descending into the lowlands, he is harassed by the police and by over-zealous disciples, and returns to the mountains only to die in a blizzard on the St Gotthard pass. In two shorter, more successful works Hauptmann described a return to a Dionysian sense of mystical unity with nature, experienced by the young priest who rediscovers pagan cults in *Der Ketzer von Soana* (*The heretic of Soana*, 1918) and by a self-sufficient community of women in *Die Insel der großen Mutter* (*The island of the great mother*, 1924).

The myths sanctioned by the Wilhelmine state appealed to Hauptmann less. His *Festspiel in deutschen Reimen* (*Festival play in German rhymes*, 1913), commissioned to celebrate the centenary of the War of Independence, annoyed patriots by gently guying Frederick the Great and by letting 'Athene Deutschland' utter a closing hymn to peace. Hauptmann's fame, and his sceptical distance from state institutions, made Thomas Mann propose half-seriously in 1922 that he be crowned King of the Weimar Republic. Alas, when the Nazis assumed power, Hauptmann several times emerged from seclusion to lend them official support, though they always treated him with distrust. But a deeper response to Nazism may be found in his last great work, the *Atriden* tetralogy (written 1940–5, published as a whole in 1949). The first and longest part, *Iphigenie in Aulis*, shows a nation brought by hardship under the sway of terrible gods whose will is interpreted by a power-crazed priest and performed by the spineless Agamemnon. Faced by a collective hysteria that demands the revival of human sacrifice and a war of obliteration against Troy, Agamemnon agrees to kill his daughter Iphigenie. She is saved by the goddess Artemis, only to become a bloodthirsty priestess in her turn. This pessimistic rewriting of Goethe's *Iphigenie* can hardly be an anti-Nazi allegory, since it was performed under Nazi rule in 1943, but its relentless power suggests that Greek myth enabled Hauptmann to express symbolically the barbaric realities of the 1940s.

Their concern to supply the 'Volk' with healthy ideals linked some Naturalists to the conservative proponents of rural literature or 'Heimatdichtung'. These drew inspiration especially from Julius Langbehn's reactionary treatise *Rembrandt als Erzieher* (*Rembrandt as educator*, 1890), which imagined Germany as a nation of aristocrats and peasants. M. G. Conrad wrote in 1902: 'The mystery of art rests on the mystery of the blood and the soil.' The immensely popular 'Heimatroman' genre, promoted especially by the periodical *Deutsche Heimat* (*German homeland*, 1900–4), opposed modernity (unreflectively identified with mushroom cities, Socialism, and the domination of cultural life by Jews and decadents) and praised the German farmer as timeless representative of the people, rooted in his native soil ('Scholle', literally 'clod', becomes a magic word) and endowed with healthy, irrational instincts. Naturalist techniques of social analysis are present in the novel *Der Büttnerbauer* (*Farmer Büttner*, 1895) by Wilhelm von Polenz (1861–1903), a conservative indictment of modernisation. An elderly farmer gets into debt and falls prey to Jewish businessmen, who are represented as unscrupulous (like those in Fontane's *Der Stechlin*, 1898); he loses his property and finally hangs himself, while his son becomes acquainted with the modern economy in which labour is only a commodity and employer and worker are linked only by the cash-nexus. The prototypical 'Heimatroman', however, is *Jörn Uhl* (1901) by Gustav Frenssen (1863–1945). It is set in Schleswig-Holstein (celebrated by Langbehn as the heartland of the German peasantry), amid a fateful, supernatural atmosphere indebted to Theodor Storm (who is mentioned several times). Jörn Uhl is a Hauke Haien without hubris. After countless misfortunes, culminating in the burning-down of his farm, he becomes an engineer and helps build the Kiel Canal. But the dissolution of rural life, shown by Polenz as a socio-economic process, is here transposed into terms of fate, while the solemn, formulaic style and the avoidance of dialect (in contrast to Polenz) move the novel further from Naturalism towards timeless myth. By 1939 *Jörn Uhl* had sold 463,000 copies, but Frenssen's success was surpassed by Hermann Löns (1866–1914) with his much cruder *Der Wehrwolf* (*The wolf fights back*, 1910), which evokes the history of the Wulf family, stretching from prehistory to the present, as the virtually timeless setting for its narrative. During the Thirty Years War, Harm Wulf becomes leader of a guerrilla band who protect the remnants of their communities and avenge the atrocities committed by marauding soldiers. The success of this monotonous adventure story (565,000 copies sold by 1939) meant that a grossly simple morality, expressed in an artificial, folksy style with a narrow emotional range, was accepted as the hallmark of 'Deutschtum'. The 'Wehrwölfe', widely misunderstood as 'werewolves', helped to inspire the paramilitary movements of the 1920s which provided the core of National Socialism.

Sexuality and the self from Wedekind to the Brothers Mann

In promoting frank discussion of sexuality, Naturalism converged with the new quasi-science of psychoanalysis being developed by Sigmund Freud (1856–1939). Structurally, Freudian analysis resembles a Naturalist drama in gradually tracing present troubles back to their source in family conflicts. By overcoming repression, the 'talking cure' discloses the triangle relating child, mother and father in sexual attraction and antagonism, and thus generates a cathartic shock of self-knowledge. Hence psychic life centres on sexuality and is largely opaque to the subject. While many earlier writers – Goethe, Novalis, Büchner – had imagined the self as multilayered and enigmatic, Freud systematised this conception and thereby rendered unsustainable the liberal individualist view of the self as secure, bounded, knowable and controlled by reason.

Similar explorations were undertaken by many writers influenced by Naturalism, even when they employed anti-Naturalist methods. The most astonishing play in Naturalism's wake was *Frühlings Erwachen* (*Spring awakening*, 1891), subtitled 'A children's tragedy', by Frank Wedekind (1864–1918). From a plot outline, it might seem merely to extend Naturalist techniques into a new area, that of adolescent sexualities and adult hypocrisy. Fourteen-year-old Wendla, shielded from sexual knowledge by her sentimental mother, is seduced by the schoolboy Melchior, and dies from a failed abortion (though her epitaph attributes her death to anaemia); another schoolboy, Moritz, crushed by soulless academic pressure, commits suicide because he has failed an exam; Melchior is sent to a reformatory from which he escapes. But Naturalist presentation, with rational discussion of social ills, is only one of several dramatic modes in which the action is represented. Such authority-figures as the headmaster Sonnenstich, the prison officer Dr Prokrustes, and Pastor Kahlbauch, are puppet-like caricatures recalling the Doctor and the Captain in Büchner's *Woyzeck*. The many fairy-tale motifs, such as the repeated image of the dryad, the tale of the headless queen, and the outdoor settings by rivers or in woods, belong to the revived Romanticism of the 1890s (as in Hauptmann's embarrassing fairy-tale play *Die versunkene Glocke* (*The sunken bell*, 1896)). And Melchior's final encounter in a churchyard with Moritz's ghost and the enigmatic Masked Man anticipates the anti-realist inventions of Expressionism. Under all these mutually relativising perspectives lies a vitalism that finds expression in the imagery of spring and nature and in the sexual urge illustrated by Wendla's and Melchior's copulation in a hayloft during a thunderstorm, by the homosexual love of two other schoolboys, and by the promiscuity of Ilse, who reports sensationally on bohemian life in the nearby city. Finally the Masked Man seems to guide Moritz into a future where a Nietzschean will to survive compensates for his detachment from all conventional beliefs.

Wedekind moved further into myth with his Lulu plays, originally an unmanageable 'Monstretragödie' which he divided into *Erdgeist* (*Earth spirit*, 1895) and *Die Büchse der Pandora* (*Pandora's box*, 1904). The former is a tightly constructed social comedy, the latter sagging and inconsequential. As the allusion to the Earth Spirit in *Faust* implies, the heroine Lulu represents life as an unself-conscious, amoral, spontaneous force: she occasions the deaths of successive husbands, but her dancing symbolises joyful art, and her unspoilt emotion rebukes and temporarily frustrates social hypocrisy, notably when she avenges Schön's degrading treatment of her by forcing him to make her his wife instead of his mistress. In commercial society, however, this life-force becomes a commodity and a victim: Lulu only escapes white slavery by becoming a street-walker in London. There she is murdered by Jack the Ripper, who combines bourgeois penny-pinching with animal-like violence. Wedekind suggests Lulu's depths by identifying her with the mythic temptresses Eve, Pandora, Helen of Troy (connoted by her nickname 'Nelli') and the water-nymph Melusine.

This mythicisation of woman found many less ambivalent echoes among men who feared that the feminist movement would produce sexless, insubordinate bluestockings. It coalesced with Strindberg's portrayal of women as destructive demons on whose sensuality the intellectual male was tragically dependent. The most influential misogynist text of the time, *Geschlecht und Charakter* (*Sex and character*, 1903) by Otto Weininger (1880–1903), which denies women (and Jews) any intellectual or moral capacity, was admired by Karl Kraus, who declared in a famous aphorism: 'Des Weibes Sinnlichkeit ist der Urquell, an dem sich des Mannes Geistigkeit Erneuerung holt' ('Woman's sensuality is the primal source where man's spirituality finds renewal'). Kraus, a friend of Wedekind's, organised the first (private) performance of *Die Büchse der Pandora* in 1905, though he thought that Wedekind, in celebrating woman's sensuality, underrated man's creativity. This mythic dichotomy reappears in the novels of Kafka: thus in *Der Proceß* (*The trial*, written 1914) the animal-like Leni drags Josef K. to the floor and seduces him, thereby distracting him from such intellectual concerns as his lawsuit.

Other dramatists besides Wedekind were inspired by the critical spirit of Naturalism to explore sexual matters via satire, though, like him, they came into conflict with official censorship. Another Munich bohemian, Oskar Panizza (1853–1921), displayed his medical training and his anti-Catholic animus in his polished play *Das Liebeskonzil* (*The council of love*, 1895). This presents a decrepit God flanked by an asthmatic Christ and a worldly, lubricious Virgin Mary. Incensed by the wickedness of Renaissance Italy, God employs the Devil to punish mortals; the Devil sires a daughter, a *femme* literally *fatale*, who spreads syphilis among humankind, starting with the Pope. This brilliant blasphemy earned Panizza the admiration of fellow-writers (including Fontane and M. G. Conrad) and a year's imprisonment. Schnitzler ironically depicted Viennese sexuality in *Reigen* (*Round dance*, written 1896–7, privately published 1900), whose ten scenes each centre on a sexual encounter between one partner from the preceding and another from the following scene. The prostitute who appears in the first scene closes the circle by reappearing in the last, while the central (fifth) scene is set in a marital bedroom of a couple, each of whom is being unfaithful to the other. Here

Schnitzler is both moralist and ironist, registering Viennese manners and everyday hypocrisies in witty detail, but hinting that all the characters are helplessly carried on a sexual merry-go-round whose ultimate model is the medieval dance of death. Even in 1920 its first complete performance provoked a scandal.

Though Schnitzler put much effort into heavyweight domestic and historical tragedies, some of his best plays deal lightly but profoundly with the relation between acting and reality: notably the historical comedy *Der grüne Kakadu* (*The green cockatoo*, 1899) and the deathbed farce *Die letzten Masken* (*The last masks*, 1902). His own favourite among his plays, *Professor Bernhardi* (1912), shows the liberal conscience under pressure. By taking a principled stand against religious obscurantism, the Jewish doctor Bernhardi enters upon a public controversy that embroils journalists, a two-faced politician and professional rivals from his own clinic, and focuses many of pre-1914 Vienna's social tensions. This ironic masterpiece shows not only a wonderful dramatic economy and ear for dialogue, but an understanding, scarcely rivalled in German literature, of institutions and institutional pressures.

Similar brilliance is evident in Schnitzler's best fiction, along with increasing scepticism about the integrity of the self. *Leutnant Gustl* (1900) is the first German story to use the stream-of-consciousness method pioneered by Edmond Dujardin and later developed by James Joyce. It consists entirely of the comically banal thoughts of an Austrian army officer who seems, under his absurd code of honour, obliged to shoot himself because he has been insulted by a baker, someone too humble to fight a duel with. Death is also close at hand in Schnitzler's second, much more sombre stream-of-consciousness narrative, *Fräulein Else* (1924), which explores the reactions of a highly strung nineteen-year-old girl when pressured by her mother into asking a middle-aged family friend for a large sum to save her father from prosecution for embezzlement. The 'friend' consents in return for seeing Else naked. This offer makes brutally explicit the assumption behind Else's upbringing: that her sexuality is an object for display, alien to herself. She exposes herself naked in public and then commits suicide. Such stories bear comparison with Freud's case histories, especially with that of 'Dora'. Freud, in a famous letter of 14 May 1922, called Schnitzler his 'Doppelgänger'. Both are sceptical heirs of the Enlightenment, committed to rational inquiry into irrational experience. *Traumnovelle* (*Dream story*, 1926), a mixture of realism and gothic romance, confronts its protagonist with the alarming omnipresence of the irrational and mysterious, and offers ways of living with this awareness; while *Flucht in die Finsternis* (*Flight into darkness*, 1931), from within its protagonist's consciousness, chronicles his helpless descent into paranoia and suicide.

Schnitzler wrote only two novels. *Der Weg ins Freie* (*The road to the open*, 1908) is a loose combination of two fictional types: the exploration of individual consciousness, including dreams, and the 'novel of good society' familiar from Fontane. The central character is the aristocratic composer Georg von Wergenthin, who eventually discovers a 'way into the open' from his rather futile existence. At a number of social events – informal gatherings in people's homes, parties, outings – he meets numerous Jewish types and arguments occur which expose different aspects of the Jewish problem. The Jewish characters are themselves seeking a 'way into the open' from their increasingly fragile assimilation, but neither Zionism nor Socialism seems to offer one; nor does the agonised introspection of the main Jewish character, the playwright and intellectual Heinrich Bermann. The imperfect integration of Georg's story with the lives of his Jewish acquaintances itself expresses the separateness of Gentile and Jewish communities in turn-of-the-century Vienna. Schnitzler's second novel, *Therese* (1928), adopts the form of a linear chronicle, reflecting the plotlessness of life, to recount the biography of a governess, with sympathetic attention to her sexual and emotional frustrations. After innumerable jobs and several brief, unrewarding affairs, Therese is fatally injured by her illegitimate son, now a criminal; that she takes her death as punishment for loving him insufficiently gives her, but not the reader, a sense of narrative closure. *Therese* must count among the best novels by men about women from this period, surpassed only by Arnold Zweig's *Junge Frau von 1914* (*Young woman of 1914*, 1931).

Women themselves, however, were encouraged by Naturalism and feminism to produce arrestingly truthful accounts of female experience. Pride of place belongs to Gabriele Reuter (1859–1941) for her novel *Aus guter Familie* (*From a good family*, 1895), which tells with discreet irony and pathos how a lively and intelligent young woman is smothered by the overprotective love of her unimaginatively respectable parents, to whom any destiny other than marriage to a rich husband means failure. The plot is episodic, keeping the focus on Agathe's consciousness of her increasingly desperate situation. Helene Böhlau (1859–1940) shows less dexterity in *Halbtier!* (*Half-animal!*, 1900): the narrative perspective is somewhat unsteady, and the theatrical catastrophe is less inevitable than Reuter's ending. But the novel is compellingly passionate and plausible in indicting spoiled, self-centred men for treating women with an ostensible reverence that hides calculating contempt, and for degrading them to the status of domestic animals – its dominant metaphor. The problems of emancipation are treated frankly by Lou Andreas-Salomé (1861–1937), who is important not only as the confidante of Nietzsche, Rilke and Freud, but as a talented writer, in her stories *Fenitschka* and *Eine Ausschweifung* (*A debauch*; both 1898). In the first, a young man has his feelings educated by contact with a Russian female university graduate, a refreshingly sincere and spontaneous person, who considers genuine love incompatible with marriage; while in the second, the female first-person narrator realises early in life that woman's conventional love for a man is masochistic, and that she would sooner renounce love than follow this course. Another independent woman, Franziska Gräfin von Reventlow (1871–1918), argued that the women's movement aimed to destroy femininity, and in her semi-autobiographical novel *Ellen Olestjerne* (1903) showed a young woman struggling to free herself from her repressive family, learning from Ibsen to value her individual integrity, gaining an artistic and erotic education in bohemian Munich, and finding fulfilment as an unmarried mother with a Nietzschean confidence in life. This engaging novel, best in describing Ellen as tomboyish child and rebellious schoolgirl, owes something to Theodor Storm (a friend of the Reventlow family) for its atmosphere of passionate yearning. Ricarda Huch (1864–1947), in her day Germany's most famous woman writer, established a reputation with *Erinnerungen von Ludolf Ursleu dem Jüngeren* (*Recollections of Ludolf Ursleu, Junior*, 1892) which now seems strange, given the novel's romantic plot and overblown style; she may be remembered rather for her exemplary role as an early university graduate, for her critical and historical writings, and for her courageous resistance to Nazi harassment.

The possibilities of satiric drama, explored by Wedekind and Schnitzler, were taken further by Carl Sternheim (1878–1942). His model was Molière, whom he understood as criticising bourgeois vices by the standard of genuine bourgeois values. Rejecting Naturalism, Sternheim makes his characters speak in a tense telegraphese which brilliantly exposes their passions and pretensions. In the first and best of his series 'Aus dem bürgerlichen Heldenleben' ('From the heroic life of the bourgeoisie'), the hilarious comedy *Die Hose* (*The knickers*, 1911), the civil servant Theobald Maske is no mere caricature of the bourgeois, despite his philistinism, his aversion to anything exotic (including the giraffe at the zoo), and the efficient regularity which he extends from his work to his domestic life, including bi-weekly adultery. His physical appetites illustrate the vitality which helps him effortlessly to frustrate the feeble attempts on his wife Luise made by two lodgers, a Nietzschean windbag and a Wagnerian hypochondriac. More grimly, he also asserts his control over Luise, nullifying her last romantic dreams and trapping her for ever in a mechanical domestic routine. Greater resourcefulness is shown by Thekla, the heroine of Sternheim's most popular comedy, *Bürger Schippel* (*Schippel the bourgeois*, 1913): against a background of *petit-bourgeois* snobbery, Thekla both ironises and enjoys a night of love with the local Prince, but settles for a dull but docile husband who will give her (and the Prince's child?) a secure future.

Wilhelmine Germany was treated with varying degrees of irony and satire in the early work of the brothers Mann. Heinrich Mann (1871–1950) soon escaped his Lübeck background and steeped himself in Italian life and French literature. In an amusing early novel, *Im Schlaraffenland* (*In the land of Cockaigne*, 1900), he transfers Balzacian realism to Berlin and shows an unscrupulous social climber reaching dizzy heights but finally being defeated by an adroit plutocrat (rather as the artistic entrepreneur in Wedekind's *Der Marquis von Keith* (1900) is brought down by a businessman). *Professor Unrat* (1905) is more grotesque. Its protagonist is a pedantic and sadistic schoolmaster who also typifies Wilhelmine authoritarianism. But, like Theobald Maske, he is a complex caricature, for his improbable liaison with the singer Rosa Fröhlich partially humanises him, and by opening a gambling-den after his dismissal from his post he not only exacts revenge but exposes the moral fragility of 'respectable' society. *Der Untertan* (*The loyal subject*, completed 1914, published 1918) moves on the border of realism and satire. It follows Diederich Hessling, a monstrous bully and power-wor-shipper, as he extirpates liberalism from his small German town by allying himself with the equally power-hungry Socialist, Napoleon Fischer. But it also shows how Diederich's authoritarian upbringing encourages him to prop up his intrinsically feeble character by compulsively playing a patriotic role and identifying with the Kaiser.

Heinrich Mann proclaimed his positive, democratic ideal in *Die kleine Stadt* (*The little town*, 1909), a fast-moving novel set in a delightful Italian town where no one ever seems to do any work. The arrival of an operatic troupe brings into the open the conflict between the conservative and progressive forces, led respectively by the priest Don Taddeo and the advocate Belotti; the resulting upheavals, verging on civil war, bring the townspeople to a cathartic reconciliation in a common commitment to humane values. The erotically charged presence of the actors recalls pre-Christian myth: the advocate remarks that a temple of Venus once occupied the town's site, and his favourite oath, 'beim Bacchus', invokes Dionysus. The novel's form is democratic: it has no dominant character, but consists mainly of crowd scenes – a theatrical performance, a riot, a fire, a gathering in the cathedral. However, Mann's vision of Dionysiac democracy may not quite convince. Women receive only subordinate or symbolic roles, notably the actress, significantly named Italia, who arouses the passions of advocate and priest. And the disturbing volatility of the crowd announces a theme that will preoccupy later, less optimistic writers from Freud's 'Massenpsychologie und Ich-Analyse' ('Group psychology and the analysis of the ego', 1921) to Canetti's *Masse und Macht* (*Crowds and power*, 1960).

The early fiction of Thomas Mann (1875–1955) uses irony more subtly and ambivalently than Heinrich's. At first glance Thomas Mann may seem heartlessly detached in his treatment of such figures as the deformed recluse who commits suicide when scorned by the statuesque Frau von Rinnlingen (*Der kleine Herr Friedemann (Little Mr Friedemann*, 1897)), or an eccentric solitary who kills a pet dog when its vitality resists his solicitude (*Tobias Mindernickel*, 1898). In fact these are sensitive studies of lonely people thwarted in their need to love. Aesthetes who place beauty above humanity are treated sceptically. The protagonist of *Beim Propheten* (*At the prophet's*, written 1904, published 1914) doubts if the apocalyptic proclamations of 'Daniel' (based on the Munich poet Ludwig Derleth) show genius: 'What is missing? Perhaps a touch of humanity? A little emotion, yearning, love?' The affected aesthete Spinell in *Tristan* (1903), who sacrifices Gabriele Klöterjahn's life to satisfy his fantasies, is clearly inferior to her warm-hearted philistine husband. In the confessional story *Tonio Kröger* (1903), the hero's problem is to reconcile the icy detachment supposedly required of artists with the attachment to his burgher origins that he expresses by defiantly wearing a suit in bohemian Munich. A visit to his home town (recognisably Lübeck) convinces him that his position between two worlds best nourishes his creativity, which is rooted in a secret love for the robustly unintellectual burghers who will never read his books.

Mann's great novel *Buddenbrooks* (1901) depends on the balance between involvement and detachment, expressed in a restrained irony which moves effortlessly between the narratorial standpoint and the viewpoints of the major characters. The story is modelled, often closely, on the Manns' own family history. The 'decline of a family' announced in the subtitle follows two narrative tracks. In the realist narrative, spanning the period 1835–75, the patrician Buddenbrooks' corn-exporting business fails to adjust to the economic changes exacerbated by German unification, and their burgher ethos of 'Leistung' or achievement loses out to the bourgeois efficiency of the vulgarian Hagenströms. In the psychological narrative, derived from Nietzsche, the declining business sense of successive Buddenbrook generations represents an increase of 'Geist' ('spirit') at the expense of vitality; this ends with the weakly, musical Hanno, whose frail constitution exposes him to an early death from typhoid. The nodal point where both narratives meet is Thomas Buddenbrook's ill-fated decision to buy the Pöppenrade crop in the ear: this is an attempt both to emulate the risky speculations of modern finance, and to demonstrate the strength of his will. These interwoven narratives correspond to two literary methods. One is the minute recording of detail that caused Mann later (in *Betrachtungen eines Unpolitischen* (*Reflections of an unpolitical man*, 1918)) to call *Buddenbrooks* 'perhaps Germany's first and only Naturalist novel'. The other (which Mann implausibly claimed to borrow from

Wagner) is the arrangement of such details into recurrent leitmotifs, deepening the novel's poetic texture and providing a sense of inevitability and of authorial control. The danger of this method, which Mann in some later works did not wholly avoid, is that too perfect an artistic control can destroy the illusion of a non-symbolic, pre-existent reality; but the firm substantiality of *Buddenbrooks* helped make it the most successful bestseller of the period (1,305,000 copies sold by 1936).

Two remarkable subsequent works treat the dangers of confusing life and art. The story *Wälsungenblut* (*The blood of the Wälsungs*, 1921) centres on the twins Siegmund and Sieglinde, the ultra-sophisticated offspring of a Berlin Jewish family; Mann wrote the story in 1904 but withdrew it from publication on belatedly realising that it might embarrass the Munich Jewish family he was about to marry into. The twins, driven by a need for love that their oppressively artificial environment does not satisfy, end up committing incest like their Wagnerian namesakes. Long an embarrassment, this story is now recognised as among Mann's most brilliant. It pales, though, beside *Der Tod in Venedig* (*Death in Venice*, 1912), which is Mann's most personal work after *Tonio Kröger*: both narratives are based on Mann's own homosexual infatuations. The protagonist Gustav von Aschenbach is likewise trying to reconcile burgher virtues with artistic talent. The novels and essays which have made him a public figure are the products of a heroic self-discipline recalling Thomas Buddenbrook's cult of achievement; but in them, instead of exploring ethical problems, he preaches a loveless, unforgiving moralism. Since his forefathers, unlike Mann's, were Prussian administrators and officers, he also typifies the rigidity of Wilhelmine Germany. Aschenbach's Apolline self-control is challenged when he visits Venice, a sinister place where the unacknowledged cholera epidemic is reducing public order to Dionysiac chaos (very different from the creative turbulence of Heinrich Mann's Italian town). This corresponds to the chaos within Aschenbach. His infatuation with the beautiful boy Tadzio first sets his creative juices flowing (allowing Mann to reflect on the illicit sources of artistic inspiration) but then erodes a self-discipline that was not founded on self-knowledge. After a dream about Dionysiac phallus-worship, he abandons restraint and pursues Tadzio shamelessly before finally dying from plague. This immensely rich Novelle is remarkable for its dual use of myth. Venice becomes a soulscape, expressing Aschenbach's psychological states; but the detached narrator also uses myth to explore critically the artistic and moral aporias by which Aschenbach is trapped, and to warn the liberal subject of the consequences of ignoring the sexual and imaginative forces within the self.

Poetry and aestheticism from George to Rilke

If Naturalism subjected the confident materialism of bourgeois society to aggressive examination, the aestheticism of the *fin de siècle* criticised it more radically by invoking art both as a standard of judgement and an alternative reality. Two consequences were possible. Some writers, inspired by Nietzsche, developed aestheticism into a philosophy of life to which ethics and politics were subordinate. Others passed through aestheticism to reject it in favour of ethical or political commitment.

German poetry in 1890 was still dominated by the Romantic lyric. New impulses came from Detlev von Liliencron (1844–1909), who evoked landscapes and warfare with sensuous vigour and without chauvinism, and from the bold erotic verse of Richard Dehmel (1863–1920). The most important innovator, however, was Stefan George (1868–1933). In the late 1880s George visited Paris, met Verlaine, and attended Mallarmé's soirées; on his return to Germany he undertook to graft Symbolist poetry and the aesthetic outlook onto the Romantic tradition. Poetry required priestly dedication; it must have no message, but gain its effect from metrical and musical form, which should be severe and economical. In his journal, the *Blätter für die Kunst* (*Pages for art*, 1892–1919), he declared: 'In der dichtung – wie in aller kunst-betätigung – ist jeder der noch von der sucht ergriffen ist etwas >sagen< etwas >wirken< zu wollen nicht einmal wert in den vorhof der kunst einzutreten' ('In poetry, as in all artistic activity, anyone still desirous to "say" or "bring about" anything is not worthy even to enter the forecourt of art'). To reinforce this élitism, George adopted a distinctive spelling, punctuation, and typography. Like Mallarmé, he tried to purify the language of his tribe, avoiding foreign loan-words; his native neologisms make his poetry often dense and opaque.

Perhaps the best way to appreciate George's poetry is to distinguish personal from prophetic utterances. His more personal poems, including songs, recount in veiled language and delicate rhythms his gradual acceptance of his homosexuality, and his unavailing attempts to escape from loneliness. His early poem-cycle *Algabal* (1892) is a major *fin-de-siècle* work in its fascination with the decadence of the Roman Empire. Its protagonist, the Emperor Heliogabalus, derives aesthetic pleasure from his artificial paradises and from casual bloodshed. But George also explores the limitations of aestheticism. Algabal's narcissism is revealed as an incapacity for relations with other people: repelled by relationships with women, he finds himself destined to love only a marble statue. Isolation reappears in the poems 'Flurgottes Trauer' ('Meadow-god's sorrow') and 'Der Herr der Insel' ('The lord of the island') from *Die Bücher der Hirten-*

und Preisgedichte (*The book of pastorals and paeans*, 1895), and an emotional narrative is subtly conveyed through landscape description in *Das Jahr der Seele* (*The soul's year*, 1897). In Munich in 1903, George formed an intense but innocuous relationship with a fourteen-year-old boy, Maximilian Kronberger, who soon afterwards died of meningitis. George's grief for 'Maximin' found expression in the fine, understated elegy 'Weh ruft vom walde' ('Woe calls from the wood', in *Der siebente Ring* (*The seventh ring*, 1907)), but the remaining 'Maximin' poems extravagantly mythicise the boy into a divinity, comparing him to Christ and Alexander the Great.

Increasingly, George abandons the aesthetic cult of form and compensates for his isolation by casting himself as a seer, fated to be misunderstood and scorned. 'Des sehers wort ist wenigen gemeinsam' ('The seer's word is shared by few'), he writes in *Das Jahr der Seele*. He celebrates such isolated heroes as Dante, Goethe and Nietzsche, and expresses contempt for the vulgar commercialism of Wilhelmine Germany. His interest in Romance literatures (including his translations from Dante and Baudelaire) and in traces of the Roman Empire in Germany (see 'Porta Nigra' in *Der siebente Ring*) represents an implicit opposition to official Germanic nationalism. Even before the First World War he published apocalyptic visions of cities overthrown in a blazing cataclysm and tens of thousands killed in a 'holy war' (*Der Stern des Bundes* (*The star of the covenant*, 1914)). 'Einzug' ('Triumphal entry') in *Der siebente Ring* proclaims the accession to power of the lowly born, who will burn and kill as a prelude to a new world; this was apparently adopted as a marching song by the Social Democrat troops in Bavaria in 1919, evidence that fantasies of attaining utopia through violence appealed to both Left and Right.

George commented on the war and its aftermath in a series of poems, written between 1914 and 1922 and published in *Das Neue Reich* (*The new empire*, 1928), which are among his most impressive and alarming prophetic utterances. The heavy tread of George's vatic poetry now fits the magnitude of the events evoked. 'Geheimes Deutschland' celebrates the 'secret Germany' surviving beneath modernity. The long poem 'Der Krieg' ('War', 1917), written when Hindenburg was expected to gain victory, denounces the chauvinistic clichés which have plunged Germany into a war with nothing to celebrate:

> Zu jubeln ziemt nicht: kein triumf wird sein •
> Nur viele untergänge ohne würde . .

[Rejoicing is unsuitable: there will be no triumph, / Only many deaths without dignity . . .]

After defeat, 'Der Dichter in Zeiten der Wirren' ('The poet in times of tumult', 1921), in a final crescendo, prophesies the arrival of a charismatic leader with a small band of followers who will restore order, raise the people's banner ('das völkische banner'), and establish the New Empire. No less frightening are the mythic poems 'Der Gehenkte' ('The hanged man'), foretelling a new historical epoch in which the swastika will replace the cross, and 'Der Brand des Tempels' ('The burning of the temple'), where an outworn civilisation awaits its destruction by a young barbarian leader. These powerful poems do not express sympathy with National Socialism, which was still in its obscure beginnings; but they illustrate the widespread rhetoric of crisis which assumed that defeated Germany could only be saved by the most extreme political solutions.

George's original *cénacle* surrounding the *Blätter für die Kunst* developed into a small group of minor poets, scholars and critics. Their most talented poet, though inferior to George, was Karl Wolfskehl (1869–1948), whose best work exploits the tension between his conception of himself as a poet-priest evoking Greek myths and his identification with the painful exile of his Jewish ancestors. The authority of the 'Master' over his little senate moved many to abject devotion, a few to irritated defection. The latter included the distinguished literary critics Friedrich Gundolf (1880–1931) and Max Kommerell (1902–44). George's circle was one form of the 'Männerbund', the male-bonded group resting on sublimated homoeroticism, which many men in early twentieth-century Germany thought an attractive social formation, since it preserved close personal ties and deference to authority within mass industrial civilisation (and conveniently ignored the question of women's equality). The pre-war Youth Movement, which sent thousands of 'Wandervögel' hiking through the German countryside, was another example, praised as exemplary by Hans Blüher in a book (*Die Rolle der Erotik in der männlichen Gesellschaft* (*The role of eroticism in male society*, 1917)) whose many enthusiastic readers included Kafka and Thomas Mann. But the solidarity of George's 'Bund' could have far-reaching effects: former members led by Claus von Stauffenberg, with 'secret Germany' as their watchword, came close to assassinating Hitler on 20 July 1944.

George failed, however, to secure the allegiance of Hugo von Hofmannsthal (1874–1929), whose precocious verse had drawn his attention. Aware of George's authoritarian character, Hofmannsthal, though he contributed to the *Blätter für die Kunst*, remained at a distance. Besides, Hofmannsthal's doubts about aestheticist aloofness are already evident in such early works as the poem 'Mein Garten' ('My garden'), where his debt to French Symbolism is most obvious, and the verse playlet *Der Tor und der Tod* (*The fool and death*, 1893). Here Claudio's sterile and selfish aesthetic seclusion is invaded by Death, who, however, gives him the only intense experience he has ever had and thus both punishes and rewards his aestheticism. Hofmannsthal's few great poems, mostly written between 1894 and 1896, express in haunting, tremulous rhythms and repeated questions an apprehension at the passing of time and the proximity of suffering: in 'Manche freilich . . .' ('Many, it is true . . .') the easy life of the privileged is shown to be obscurely linked to the misery of those confined 'at the roots of tangled life', imprisoned but close to life and growth. In the story *Das Märchen der 672. Nacht* (*The tale of the 672nd [Arabian] night*, 1895) the Merchant's Son leaves his luxurious though faintly sinister retreat only to find a humiliating death in a sordid, labyrinthine city.

Hofmannsthal finally renounced aestheticism in the fictive 'Ein Brief' (1902), purportedly a letter from the English nobleman Lord Chandos to Francis Bacon. After reviewing his semi-mystical literary projects, Lord Chandos announces that he cannot write or speak coherently, that abstract words decay in his mouth like mouldy mushrooms, that his gloom is only lightened by moments of mystical identification with humble beings and objects, and that he seeks a new language for such experiences. Though the Chandos Letter has often been understood as expressing a linguistic crisis, such an interpretation is belied by Chandos's fluency and by Hofmannsthal's continuous literary productivity. Rather, its problem was later defined by Hofmannsthal, in a letter of 14 February 1921 to the Austrian poet Anton Wildgans, thus: 'How can the solitary individual succeeed in linking himself though language with the community, indeed, in being indissolubly linked with it whether he will or no?'

To reach out to society, Hofmannsthal henceforth concentrated on two genres: prose and drama. His prose writings of 1902–14 have been underrated. The mordant cultural criticism of *Die Briefe des Zurückgekehrten* (*Letters on returning home*, 1907–8) and the visionary travel writing of *Augenblicke in Griechenland* (*Moments in Greece*; written 1908–14, published entire in 1917) stand out, but his greatest prose work is the unfinished 'Bildungsroman' *Andreas oder die Vereinigten* (*Andreas or the united*; written largely in 1912, published posthumously in 1932). It consists of two episodes: one set on an Alpine farm, where the immature hero Andreas encounters extremes of good and evil and undergoes Chandoslike experiences of mystical identification; and the other in Venice, where Andreas meets a split personality, divided into the pious Maria and the playful Mariquita (modelled on the case history recounted in Morton Prince's *The dissociation of a personality* (1906)). From Richard Alewyn's reconstruction of Hofmannsthal's intentions, it seems that love was to have brought psychic harmony to Andreas and his divided lover. But Hofmannsthal's psychological insights are perhaps too complex and painful to admit of harmonious resolution.

Initially, Hofmannsthal's drama also benefited from his psychological reading. *Elektra* (1904), based on Sophocles, is set in Mycenaean Greece, but its heroine's hysteria follows the case of 'Anna O.' in the *Studies on hysteria* (1895) by Freud and Breuer. The brooding intensity of this play dwarfs most of Hofmannsthal's other dramas. Hofmannsthal, like Brecht, adapted other plays with great eclecticism; and his long collaboration with Richard Strauss, beginning with the opera *Elektra* (1909), also produced *Der Rosenkavalier* (*The Knight of the Rose*, 1911), *Ariadne auf Naxos* (1912), and *Arabella* (1933). These libretti convey Hofmannsthal's thoughtful conservatism, focusing especially on marriage as a stable institution that survives through the partners' adaptation and self-renewal. Marriage is also the theme of his post-war comedies. In *Der Schwierige* (*The difficult man*, 1921), undoubtedly the finest social comedy in German, the civilised and subtle Austrian nobleman Hans Karl, despite seeming permanently bewildered, defeats his go-getting relatives and stumbles into marriage with the woman for whom he felt destined. And in *Der Unbestechliche* (*The incorruptible*, 1923) a young aristocrat's shaky marriage is repaired by the machinations of his loyal, all-powerful, Jeeves-like servant Theodor.

Hofmannsthal also sought social impact through public forms of drama. The mystery-plays *Jedermann* (*Everyman*, 1911) and *Das Salzburger große Welttheater* (*The Salzburg great theatre of the world*, 1922), both expressing his unease about capitalism, were directed at the Salzburg Festival by Max Reinhardt (1873–1942), who was famous for his anti-Naturalist, dream-like productions. In helping to found the Salzburg Festival in 1920, Hofmannsthal was trying to provide the new Austrian Republic with a usable past in the form of the Catholic Baroque tradition. However, the *Welttheater*, based on Calderón, offers inadequate and anachronistic answers to present-day social unrest. In *Der Turm* (*The tower*), Hofmannsthal adapted another Calderón play more boldly to project contemporary turmoil into the seventeenth century. This play exists in several versions: the richest, though the untidiest, is the first (1925). Here an old monarchy, riddled by oppression and inflation, needs absolute renewal. The charismatic figure of Sigismund overcomes his father the King in a quasi-Expressionist confrontation, leads the poor to victory, but falls victim to a demonic woman; the play ends with the pastoral utopia of the Children's King. This play, one of the strangest products of Hofmannsthal's imagination, addresses a problem familiar from Schiller's *Die Räuber* and Kleist's *Michael Kohlhaas*: can the renewal of society be achieved through revolutionary violence? Hofmannsthal's pessimism rings truer than the explicit prophecy in his Munich speech of 1927, 'Das Schrifttum als geistiger Raum der Nation' ('Literature as the nation's spiritual space'), about an imminent conservative revolution; he did not live to see his expectations travestied.

Hofmannsthal's early aestheticism was shared by the 'Jung Wien' or

'Young Vienna' circle to which he and Schnitzler belonged in the 1890s. Their chief spokesman was the versatile man of letters Hermann Bahr (1863–1934), who argued in *Die Überwindung des Naturalismus* (*Overcoming Naturalism*, 1891) that art needed to abandon the Naturalistic fictions of a knowable external reality and a continuous self, and focus instead on the sensations and impressions of which consciousness was composed. Peter Altenberg (the pseudonym of Richard Engländer, 1859–1919) supplied a verbal counterpart to artistic Impressionism in his sketches of Viennese life, beginning with *Wie ich es sehe* (*As I see it*, 1896), which not only convey atmosphere through colour and sound but use unorthodox punctuation to suggest unspoken emotional nuances. The finest piece of Impressionist prose is the short novel *Der Tod Georgs* (*The death of Georg*, 1900) by Richard Beer-Hofmann (1866–1945). There is virtually no action. We are admitted to the consciousness of the hero, Paul, at four moments of an emotional crisis: a summer evening when his friend Georg is staying with him; an elaborate dream that night in which Paul intuits Georg's death; a few days later, when Paul is travelling by train to Vienna to bring back Georg's coffin; and several months later, an autumn day on which Paul at last overcomes his sense of bereavement. Paul's inner life is explored through memories and sense-impressions, and the latter especially are conveyed in rich, sensuous, and melodious language, so that they serve as metaphors for emotions. Beer-Hofmann illustrates the preoccupation with death, found also in Hofmannsthal's poetry and Schnitzler's early stories *Sterben* (*Dying*, 1892) and *Die Toten schweigen* (*Dead men tell no tales*, 1897), which lends substance to aestheticism but also challenges it.

Beer-Hofmann's novel points beyond aestheticism when Paul overcomes grief by rediscovering his Jewish identity. Here and, above all, in the gripping metaphysical drama *Jaákobs Traum* (*Jacob's dream*, 1918) Beer-Hofmann testifies to his own metamorphosis. His contemporary Theodor Herzl (1860–1904), the founder of Zionism, likewise developed from a dandified journalist into a political visionary. Herzl's play *Das neue Ghetto* (1894) depicts what he considered the Jews' untenable position in Gentile society; his utopian novel *Altneuland* (1902) presents the Jewish state of the future. The rejection of aestheticism for ethical commitment took many other forms and partly explains the extraordinary creativity of early twentieth-century Vienna. Examples range from the ultra-Kantian rigorism of Weininger (who urged abstention from sexuality even though the human race would die out) to the rejection of architectural ornamentation by Adolf Loos (1870–1933); the introduction of mathematical rigour into music by Arnold Schoenberg (1874–1951); the Tolstoyan asceticism of Ludwig Wittgenstein (1889–1951); and the ethically founded linguistic purism of Karl Kraus (1874–1936), discussed below.

Two great Austrian writers used their early novels to explore the Nietzschean view of the world as an aesthetic phenomenon. Robert Musil (1880–1942) set *Die Verwirrungen des Zöglings Törleß* (*The confusions of the schoolboy Törless*, 1906) in an Austrian military academy where two boys (precursors, Musil said much later, of the Nazi dictators) torture and abuse a third. For Törless, an onlooker at these perversities, they form part of the irrational reality denied by the rigidly conventional outlook of his teachers and parents, along with his ineffable moments of mysticism and the imaginary numbers which prove to be the foundation for the 'rational' disciplines of mathematics and philosophy. These experiences are later described in Nietzschean language as the 'poison' which saves Törless from dull normality and gives him the refined, amoral perceptions of an aesthete. Equally disturbing is *Die Aufzeichnungen des Malte Laurids Brigge* (*The notebooks of Malte Laurids Brigge*, 1910), the only novel by Rainer Maria Rilke (1875–1926). Instead of narrative, it consists of jottings, arranged by principles of association and contrast, ascribed to a young painter leading a completely isolated life in Paris. There is a development, however: initially shocked by the ugliness of Paris and its poor, Malte learns to see and describe his surroundings aesthetically. Rilke's favourite example of aesthetic seeing is Baudelaire's poem about a rotting corpse, 'Une Charogne', praised both in the novel and in a letter of 19 October 1907 where Rilke, using Nietzschean language, tells his wife: 'Artistic contemplation had first to overcome itself sufficiently to see even in horrible and seemingly only repulsive things that which is [das Seiende] and, with everything else that is, *counts*.' Malte's development illustrates two other ideas dear to Rilke. He conquers his fear of death through envisaging it as the goal always latent in one's life, and replacing the impersonal death practised in modern cities with a conception of one's own death as the foundation of individuality. And he distances himself from his family's oppressive affection while cultivating an intransitive love, an outpouring of emotion without an object. This produces a curiously introverted novel in which the protagonist never speaks to another character; but it let Rilke exhaust the consequences of aestheticist self-absorption while exploring possibilities of intersubjectivity in his poems.

The aestheticist outlook is important – some would say all-important – to Rilke's poetry. The plangently musical *Stunden-Buch* (*Book of hours*, 1905) addresses a God whom, we are told, humankind is collectively creating, like builders working on a medieval cathedral. In an aesthetic variation on the idea (ultimately derived from Feuerbach) that God is humanity's projection, Rilke suggests that God is humanity's work of art. Later in the book, bold alliteration and rhyming poeticise the sufferings of the urban poor. Rilke, like George, regards the contemporary world with disgust: he yearns, in Langbehnian imagery, for a pastoral utopia ('Alles wird wieder groß sein und gewaltig' ('All things will once again be great and mighty')), and mourns the passing of the aristocratic eighteenth century in his many poems about deserted parks and pavilions. Sometimes he shows the ill-judged hero-worship characteristic of a timid recluse, as in the sixth of the *Duineser Elegien* (*Duino elegies*) and in the embarrassing 'Fünf Gesänge' ('Five songs') written amid the general war-fever of August 1914 (and regretted soon afterwards); and late in life he praised Mussolini. But Rilke shows a more sensitive conservatism in deploring the abstractness of the modern world, the power of money, and the shallow ideology of secular progress that leads people to repress their awareness of death. His poetry, written in opposition to his age, attempts to reclaim and celebrate abiding humane values.

After the *Stunden-Buch*, Rilke wanted to compose a more monumental, visual poetry. His ambitions were schooled by his encounters with the poetry of George, with the sculpture of Rodin (whose secretary he became, and on whom he wrote a monograph), and in 1907 with the still lifes of Cézanne. From 1903 onwards he developed a new style, exhibited in the *Neue Gedichte* (*New poems*, 1907 and 1908). Here lyrical subjectivity is disciplined into firm rhythms (often iambic pentameters) which are saved from rigidity by fluid enjambements; many poems describe a concrete object, animal or person in almost painterly terms, often with vivid colours ('Die Flamingos', 'Rosa Hortensie', 'Blaue Hortensie' ('The flamingos', 'Pink hydrangea', 'Blue hydrangea')). But these are not neutral descriptions. Some explore what Wordsworth called 'unknown modes of being': the consciousness of a caged animal in the earliest, 'Der Panther', and the depersonalised feelings of the dead Eurydice in the great mythic poem 'Orpheus. Eurydike. Hermes'. 'Letzter Abend' ('Final evening') finds objective correlatives for the intense, unspoken emotion hovering between two lovers. The descriptive poems emphasise the interaction between observer and observed through constant references to eyes, gazes, mirrors, reflections and smiles. Places like the square at Furnes ('Der Platz') or a rococo pavilion ('Der Pavillon') are described as still saturated with the emotions of their long-dead occupants: thus the associations made by the observer are projected into the objects themselves. These procedures anticipate the programmatic poem 'Es winkt zu Fühlung fast aus allen Dingen' ('All things almost summon us to feeling', 1914), which conflates the external space traversed by the beholder's gaze with the subjective space of emotion:

> Durch alle Wesen reicht der *eine* Raum:
> Weltinnenraum. Die Vögel fliegen still
> durch uns hindurch. O, der ich wachsen will,
> ich seh hinaus, und *in* mir wächst der Baum.

[The *one* space extends through all beings: / The world's inner space. The birds fly silently / Through us. O, wanting to grow, / I look out, and the tree grows *in* me.]

Space ('Raum') is among the dominant metaphors of the *Duineser Elegien* (1923), the poem-cycle that Rilke began in 1912 and completed in a burst of inspiration in February 1922. Access to this great poem has not been helped by philosophical commentators. It makes meaning not by deploying independently existing concepts, but by boldly deviating from standard language and thus inviting us to experience reality anew. Thus Rilke blurs the distinction between concrete and abstract ('Die Adern voll Dasein' ('Veins full of existence')), uses the copula 'sein' without a predicate ('die Bäume *sind*' ('the trees *are*')), coins new words and collocations ('den, mit steigernder Stille, / weithin umschweigt ein reiner bejahender Tag' ('surrounded, in gathering silence, / By the far-flung hush of a pure affirmative day')). This last quotation also illustrates the enchantingly sensuous assonance which Rilke uses with prodigal freedom.

The *Elegien* and their companion-piece, the *Sonette an Orpheus* (*Sonnets to Orpheus*, 1923), create modern myths and set them in a soulscape of emotional space. The mythic Angel of the Elegies represents an emotional intensity contrasted with the half-hearted and transient feelings available to humankind. The Angel inhabits the realms of both life and death, while Rilke's sombre brooding on death invites us to accept it as the necessary complement to life, and to regard mourning as the source of art. Though the Elegies are largely about art, they are not merely the autobiography of the poet: artistic experience is just one form of the enrichment of consciousness to which Rilke invites us. Thus the Fifth Elegy takes the pitiful street-acrobats depicted in Picasso's 'Les Saltimbanques' (rather as Kafka treats circus performers with respect in his shorter fiction) as instances of successful art; but beyond that, the thrilling moment in which they bring off their precarious balancing act provides a model for fulfilled experience. In the later Elegies, Rilke, while still insisting that life is incomplete and painful, enacts the humanist gesture of rejecting the Angel: if, no longer distracted by the false allure of transcendence, we attend to immediate experience ('Hiersein'), we shall find that life is infinitely rewarding; but to appreciate and praise it we must rescue it from transience by transferring it into our emotional space, recreating it invisibly. By attributing such praise to Orpheus, the archetypal poet, who has experienced both life and death, the *Sonette* seem to remain within the aestheticist ambit. Many, however, express a quietly beautiful, semi-mystical sense of oneness with nature that invites comparison with the philosophical ruminations of Martin Heidegger (1889–1976) on how humankind may find itself at home in this world.

New poetries from Trakl to Ball

Around 1912, new energies invade German literature. Instead of recording individual anxieties, poets now present themselves as the mouthpiece of collective humanity. For the literary innovations of 1912–20, it is impossible to avoid the loose but convenient term 'Expressionism'. Originally applied to the colourful, anti-mimetic paintings of artistic groups like 'Der blaue Reiter' ('The blue horseman') in Munich and 'Die Brücke' ('The bridge') in Dresden, it was first transferred to literature in 1912 by the critic Kurt Hiller (1885–1973). It owes its currency especially to 'Kasimir Edschmid' (Eduard Schmid, 1890–1966), who in literary manifestos, notably 'Über den dichterischen Expressionismus' (1917), described it as a subjective, visionary, spiritual art. Applied widely to literature, it becomes vacuous; applied more narrowly, as here, it at least has heuristic value in highlighting some formal similarities (while obscuring others) among outwardly diverse poems, plays and prose works.

The so-called 'Expressionist decade' witnessed intense literary activity among small groups based in major cities like Berlin, Munich, Dresden, Leipzig, Vienna and, during the war, Zurich. Their focal points were cafés (the Café des Westens and later the Romanisches Café in Berlin, the Café Stefanie in Munich); clubs which organised readings and lectures (notably the Neue Club, founded in Berlin in 1909 by Kurt Hiller and 'Jakob van Hoddis' (Hans Davidsohn (1887–1942)), whose members included Georg Heym; theatres (Max Reinhardt's experimental theatre group 'Das junge Deutschland', which lasted from 1917 to 1920, and Karlheinz Martin's short-lived 'Tribüne' of 1919, specialised in presenting Expressionist plays); and literary magazines. The most important of the latter were Herwarth Walden's *Der Sturm* (*The gale*, 1910–32), Franz Pfemfert's *Die Aktion* (*Action*, 1911–32), and René Schickele's *Die weißen Blätter* (*White pages*, 1913–21); in the 1920s, with the decline of Expressionism, the first two became primarily political. These foci helped Expressionists to think of themselves as engaged in a single undertaking, which was defined in manifestos and underpinned by reference to documents like Wassily Kandinsky's *Über das Geistige in der Kunst* (*On the spiritual in art*, 1912), with its plea for an abstract, anti-materialist art, and Wilhelm Worringer's *Abstraktion und Einfühlung* (*Abstraction and empathy*, 1908), a history of non-representational tendencies in art.

The term 'Expressionism', however, has the drawback of seeming to equate minor talents who were borne along by the bandwagon with the new generation of astonishingly original poets: Else Lasker-Schüler (1869–1945), Ernst Stadler (1883–1914), Georg Heym (1887–1912) and Georg Trakl (1887–1914). Many of Trakl's poems were published in the

Innsbruck periodical *Der Brenner*; he prepared only two slender volumes for publication: *Gedichte* (*Poems*, 1913) and *Sebastian im Traum* (*Sebastian dreaming*, 1915). Trakl was affected by the pensive lyrics of his fellow-Austrian Hofmannsthal: he likewise favours parks and gardens as settings, with evening to heighten the melancholy mood. But Trakl also owed much to Rimbaud's poetic practice of arranging sensuous vocabulary in patterns unrelated to experience. Hence the 'blue deer', 'green flowers' and 'black angels' that populate Trakl's poetry. A typical Trakl poem contains a sequence of short, descriptive statements, seldom with any empirical reference or obvious internal coherence. Often they evoke intense sadness, terror, or foreboding, but they are not simply metaphors for psychological states. Their recurring images are not ciphers with fixed values; even their prominent colour terms have shifting associations. In contrast to the poems of George, Hofmannsthal or Rilke, and to most previous poetry, Trakl's poems have no backbone of conceptual thought. They communicate powerfully, but they cannot, in any accepted sense, be interpreted.

Nevertheless, a semi-private myth of decline can be discerned in Trakl's poetry. A Salzburg Protestant, he uses religious images, especially that of Communion, to convey a state of spiritual purity, sometimes even, as in the exquisite 'Ein Winterabend' ('A winter evening'), a harmony between earthly nature and divine grace:

> Golden blüht der Baum der Gnaden
> Aus der Erde kühlem Saft.

[The tree of grace blooms golden / From the earth's cool sap.]

Often nature retains an autumnal beauty and piety. But Trakl's landscapes are visited only by black, pale or fallen angels. In the desolation of 'De profundis', dominated by 'God's silence', the body of 'the gentle orphan' is found decaying in a thorn-bush. Death is omnipresent (e.g. 'Siebengesang des Todes' ('Sevenfold song of Death')). The lost peace of childhood has given way to a feeling of guilt, associated with the shadowy figure of 'the sister' and hints of incest; night will swallow up 'the accursed race' ('Traum und Umnachtung' ('Dream and darkening')). Certain poems hint at a redemptive myth of androgyny, focused on 'the golden figure of the she-youth (Jünglingin)' ('Das Herz' ('The Heart')). But Trakl's vision of history also ends in decay and destruction. The pastoral simplicity of ancient times ('Abendländisches Lied' ('Occidental Song')) has long been destroyed by the 'stone cities'. 'Vorhölle' ('Limbo') provides a nightmarish vision of Vienna, while in 'An die Verstummten' ('To those who have fallen silent') the 'madness of the great city' includes hunger, money, a stillborn child, crippled trees, and the harshness of artificial light, all subject to 'God's wrath', while humanity bleeds to death in darkness. This decline culminates in the First World War: Trakl's horrific experiences on the Eastern Front, which almost certainly drove him to suicide, find expression in the magnificent poems 'Klage' ('Lament') and 'Grodek'.

Ernst Stadler was killed at Ypres, aged thirty, after two months of brave and reluctant fighting, and ten months after publishing *Der Aufbruch* (*Setting forth*, 1914). In this collection he repudiates the chilly formal perfection of George and Hofmannsthal which had overshadowed his poetic beginnings, and exemplifies a new, energetic, life-affirming poetry. Its long, surging lines with often complicated rhyme-schemes (encouraged, but probably not inspired, by the long lines of Whitman and Verhaeren) enact his urge to discard constraints, to identify with the sufferings of the poor, and to penetrate the living heart of reality:

> Selig singend Schmach und Dumpfheit der Geschlagenen zu fühlen,
> Mich ins Mark des Lebens wie in Gruben Erde einzuwühlen.

[Singing blissfully, to feel the disgrace and misery of the defeated; /
To burrow into life's marrow as though into tunnels of earth.]

'Tage II' ('Days II')

'Life', which for Hofmannsthal's Lord Chandos was a mystical, static unity, is for Stadler best conveyed in dynamic images of dam-bursts and warfare; it is apprehended by the emotions and the blood, and represented by churned-up soil ('Form ist Wollust' ('Form is pleasure')) and the 'maternal womb' of the sea ('Meer'). Many poems evoke erotic experience, a source of exaltation and guilt: among the most vivid are 'Lover's seat' [*sic*], 'In der Frühe' ('In the early morning') and the excessively phallic 'In diesen Nächten' ('In these nights'). Vital energies are expressed through contemporary imagery in the deservedly famous 'Fahrt über die Kölner Rheinbrücke bei Nacht' ('Crossing the bridge over the Rhine at Cologne by night'). Stadler's empathy with the poor emerges best when he describes shop assistants leaving work in 'Abendschluß' ('Ending work for the day'), but it is denied to Jews: 'Judenviertel in London' ('Jewish quarter in London') depicts Whitechapel with unrelieved revulsion. Despite his commitment to modern subject matter, pastoral nostalgia is evident in the sensuous 'Sommer' ('Summer') and the beautiful, sharply observed 'Kleine Stadt' ('Small town'), which, albeit with unmatched skill, shares the anti-urbanism of the 'Heimatroman'. To the English-speaking reader, Stadler recalls his contemporary, the young D. H. Lawrence: both write with arresting freshness in opposition to stale conventions; both may be thought occasionally to go too far in asserting the rights of the senses.

By contrast, the poetry of Georg Heym is firmly set in the contemporary city. The misery and horror of Berlin are sometimes described almost naturalistically (in 'Berlin' and 'Die Vorstadt' ('The suburb')), with emphasis on sickness, blindness and deformity, but without the compassion shown by Stadler or Rilke. Often Heym transforms terrors into mythic visions. Reviewing *Der ewige Tag* (*The everlasting day*, 1911; followed by the posthumous collection *Umbra vitae* (*The shadow of life*, 1912)) soon after Heym had been drowned while skating, Stadler noted that Heym's affirmation of life was based on full awareness of its threats and terrors. To express these, Heym occasionally revives classical myths ('Styx'), but mostly invents his own. His city is haunted by vampires and griffins; gigantic horned demons roam its streets, and a paunchy pagan god threatens it with destruction. Humankind appears only as an anonymous muddy mass, as corpuscles flowing helplessly through the city's blood-stream, or as hordes of the dead waiting anxiously in the morgue or being dashed down the infernal river. Instead, inorganic objects are filled with a grotesque, uncanny life: personification makes a crane into Moloch, the moon a hangman, death a brutal boatman; and frenzied activity occurs above the city, where the hosts of the dead sweep past as clouds, winds rave, and lurid sunsets bathe the streets in sinister light.

These terrifying visions are fitted into a strictly regular verse-form (iambic pentameters in cross-rhymed quatrains) and a language that purports to be merely descriptive. Heym adapted his verse from Baudelaire's city poems, cultivated his visionary power by reading Rimbaud, and was inspired especially by Van Gogh to aestheticise his visions through the striking use of colour: thus in 'Nach der Schlacht' ('After the battle') the battlefield becomes a painterly composition with red and blackened blood and the white entrails of a horse against the green meadow. When emotion is expressed, it is often gloating over visions of destruction. In the January 1911 issue of *Die Aktion* Heym condemned the decadence of the too peaceful world: 'Enthusiasm, greatness, heroism. Formerly the world sometimes glimpsed these gods' shadows on the horizon. Today they are stage puppets. War has vanished from the world; perpetual peace is its wretched inheritor.' The Agadir crisis of September 1911 stimulated Heym to evoke a cataclysm in 'Der Krieg' ('War'). Alongside this yearning for violence (shared by T. E. Hulme in Britain and Marinetti in Italy), two poems modelled on Rimbaud's 'Ophélie' evince sadistic misogyny: 'Die Tote im Wasser' ('The dead girl in the water'), where the girl's corpse is ejected from a sewage outlet, and 'Ophelia'. (The popularity of this motif, also found in Gottfried Benn's 'Schöne Jugend' ('Beautiful youth') and Brecht's 'Vom ertrunkenen Mädchen' ('On the drowned girl'), should prompt an inquiry into the precarious construction of masculinity among the 'generation of 1914'.) In such poems, the detachment expressed by Heym's rigid pentameters seems like a deliberate suppression of feeling, and it is a relief to discover a few late poems, written under Hölderlin's influence, whose sensitive verse-movement and intimate subjects open up a richer world of emotion. 'Deine Wimpern, die langen' ('Your long eyelashes') and 'Mit den fahrenden Schiffen' ('With the journeying ships') modify the dominant impression of a hugely talented poet who anticipated the fascist sensibility later exhibited by Ernst Jünger.

From Heym's willed toughness one turns gladly to the poetry of Else Lasker-Schüler, the greatest woman writer of our period. Her life was a sad one, overshadowed by the premature deaths of her dearly loved mother and her gifted son; both her marriages – first to a Berlin doctor, then to the literary editor 'Herwarth Walden' (Georg Levin) – were unhappy. After her second divorce, she led a bohemian life in Berlin and Munich, where her oriental costumes and impulsive behaviour gained her a reputation for eccentricity. Having suffered physical ill-treatment by the Nazis, she moved first to Switzerland and then, in 1939, to Palestine. Throughout her life she remained childlike in her love of play and disguises, her frankness and her emotional vulnerability. She constructed an exotic fantasy-world in which she figured first as Tino of Baghdad, later as Yussuf, Prince of Thebes, and gave her friends sobriquets: thus Gottfried Benn, with whom she was briefly in love, features in several poems as 'Giselheer'. Her poetry attempts to construct a private domain of feeling, not unlike the soulscape of Rilke's *Elegien*. Its rich imagery includes, as in Trakl, an idiosyncratic use of colours, where blue often symbolises spiritual purity and 'golden' represents erotic fulfilment. It also expresses emotions with a child's disconcerting directness: for example, 'Verinnerlicht' ('Brought inward') begins bluntly, 'Ich denke immer ans Sterben. / Mich hat niemand lieb.' ('I keep thinking about dying. / Nobody loves me.') Her love-poetry is best illustrated by 'Ein alter Tibetteppich' ('An old Tibetan rug', from the collection *Meine Wunder* (*My miracles*, 1911)), where the precious and exotic central image is placed in a poetic cosmos of amorous stars and the beloved is addressed with sensual playfulness. Like Rilke and Kraus, Lasker-Schüler wanted in poetry to regain an 'Ursprung', a lost paradise: 'the primal light, the loving face of the origin', as she writes (perhaps influenced by Jewish mysticism) in the essay 'Paradiese'. Yet this poetic home ('Heimat' is another favourite word) is threatened by loneliness and fear that make her long for 'God's blue spaces'; these feelings find their most poignant expression in her last collection, *Mein blaues Klavier* (*My blue piano*, 1943).

Lasker-Schüler's writings show her developing awareness of her dual, German–Jewish identity. Her most 'German' work is *Die Wupper* (*The River Wupper*, 1909), a basically Naturalist drama of class conflict, written partly in the dialect of her native Rhineland, and steeped in a lyrical atmosphere. Encouraged by Martin Buber's vitalist conception of Judaism, she distanced herself from assimilationism and celebrated the

'wild Jews' of the Bible in *Hebräische Balladen* (*Hebrew ballads*, 1913).
Her first visit to Palestine in 1934 provided material for her charming,
occasionally absurd travel-book *Das Hebräerland* (*The Hebrews' land*,
1937), which represents modern immigrants to Palestine as renewing the
identity of the ancient Hebrews. Her search for remnants of the primitive
makes her impressions of Palestine a counterpart to the accounts of
Greece by Hauptmann and Hofmannsthal.

Among consciously Expressionist poets, the path-breaking achievements of Stadler and Heym hardened into a period style, with eye-catch-
ingly contemporary subject matter, extravagant and grotesque similes and
metaphors, and dynamic verbs. This style tends towards verbal inflation
and violence, seen most markedly in the poetry of Johannes R. Becher
(1891–1958), the McGonagall of Expressionism, who ended up as
Minister for Culture in the German Democratic Republic. The predominant mood of rhetorical declamation was inspired not only by
Stadler but, still more, by Franz Werfel (1890–1945), whose *Der
Weltfreund* (*The friend of the world*, 1912) won many hearts with its
hymnic assertions of universal brotherhood. Werfel's real literary achievement, however, came much later with his fiction (discussed below).
Similarly, Gottfried Benn (1886–1956) had to outgrow the stomach-
turning descriptions of rat-eaten corpses and cancerous bodies provided
in *Morgue* (1912) before writing his worthwhile poetry.

Some poets left only the beginnings of what might have become a major
achievement. Van Hoddis, who in 1912 became incurably insane, was
inordinately admired by contemporaries for his poem 'Weltende' ('End of
the world'), a fragmented sequence of bald statements, mostly drawn
from newspapers, connected only by a sense of foreboding; but its triviality and bathos make it far inferior to Lasker-Schüler's poem of the same
title, or to Heym's apocalyptic visions. There is more promise in the often
witty poetry of Alfred Lichtenstein (1889–1914), an early war casualty; his
'Gebet vor der Schlacht' ('Prayer before battle'), in which a soldier prays
that his comrades will be killed instead of him, is at least preferable to the
bellicose effusions of non-combatants. The thorough-going Expressionist
August Stramm (1874–1915), who in the love-poems of *Du* (*You*, 1915)
had devised a concentrated, dynamic language of pure emotional intensity, transferred this technique to his war poetry (*Tropfblut* (*Dripping
blood*, 1919)), relying almost solely on violent nouns and verbs in order to
communicate raw sensation. Poetry needs reflection as well as sensation,
however, as is indicated by the more measured and precise war poems of
Wilhelm Klemm (1881–1968). A still greater achievement is that of Anton
Schnack (1892–1973), the only German war poet, apart from Trakl, who
rivals the best work of Rosenberg, Gurney and Owen. His *Tier rang
gewaltig mit Tier* (*Beast strove mightily with beast*, 1920) contains sixty

sonnets, in long lines reminiscent of Whitman and Stadler, which summon up the grotesquely ravaged landscapes of the Western Front, often with sombre magnificence, and contrast them with lyrical memories of peacetime. This sense that a residuum of ordinary life survives amid the desolation nourishes the profound humanity of Schnack's poetry.

For some writers who fled from military service to neutral Switzerland, the war seemed less tragic than absurd, the proof that Western civilisation and humanism were bankrupt. They responded with the anti-art of Dada (meaningless syllables supposed to suggest primitive magic). At the Café Voltaire in Zurich they put on spontaneous performances in unintelligible language, which they thought appropriate to an incoherent and irrational world that could only be grasped intuitively. Their main literary talents were Hans Arp (1887–1966), who also wrote in French, and Hugo Ball (1886–1927). Arp's early poetry, notably the parodistic elegy 'kaspar ist tot' ('kaspar is dead'), is amusing and inventive, though for emotional depth one must wait until his poetry of the 1940s and 1950s. Ball's sound-poems – for example, 'Wolken' ('Clouds'), which begins 'elomen elomen lefitalominal / wolminuscaio / baumbala bunga / acycam glastula feirofim flinsi' – can be shown to make a kind of sense; but this itself suggests that the Dadaist project was self-defeating. If its productions are anything more than forgettable jokes, they rejoin the institution of art which the Dadaists rejected. In their anarchic cult of spontaneity they anticipated the 'happenings' cultivated by the Grazer Gruppe and the Wiener Gruppe, as well as the confusion between jokes and art that plagued the international avant-garde of the 1960s.

Prose visions: Kafka, Döblin, Jahnn

Even before the war, a widespread mood of apocalyptic foreboding demanded new styles of visionary writing. This mood dominates the poetry of Heym, the paintings of Ludwig Meidner, and the auto-biography of the psychiatric patient Judge Daniel Schreber, *Denkwürdigkeiten eines Nervenkranken* (*Memorials of my nervous illness*, 1903), which illuminates the unconscious mind of Wilhelmine Germany and later received opposing interpretations from Freud and Canetti. Schreber's fantasies include threats to Germany from Catholics, Jews and Slavs, and culminate in the extinction of humankind apart from himself. Alfred Kubin (1877–1959) evoked destruction in *Die andere Seite* (*The other side*, 1909), a gothic narrative reminiscent of Hoffmann and Poe, accompanied by Kubin's sinister illustrations. Its narrator emigrates to a 'Dream State' founded in Central Asia by Patera, an eccentric multi-millionaire who wishes to stop progress. The conflict between Patera and

the modernising American corned-beef king Herkules Bell leads to the
Dream State's gradual dissolution amid mass hysteria, crumbling buildings, animal invasions and collective suicide. Equally striking is Ball's
Dada novel *Tenderenda der Phantast* (written 1914–20, published 1967).
Superficially a cascade of humorous nonsense, it presents Ball's own
development from Expressionism via Dada to religion and also provides a
picture of his age: a Zarathustra-like prophet proclaims a new God; in
1914, intellectuals show their ineffectuality; amid growing anti-Semitism,
a Jewish journalist is tried for blasphemy in 'Satanopolis'; and the inven-
tors of Dada retreat to the 'Grand Hotel Metaphysik' which hovers above
a landscape of mass death and decay.

Sharing the mood of cultural despair, Expressionist prose writers
discard mimesis and follow Hofmannsthal's *Ein Brief* and Rilke's *Malte* in
transferring attention to how subjective consciousness constructs its
reality. They favour short, vigorous, paratactic sentences, with emphasis
on sensuous nouns and active verbs. Such a concentrated style can be sustained only in Novellen or in very short novels like *Bebuquin* (1912) by
Carl Einstein (1885–1940), which uses a choppy, aphoristic style, sometimes modulating into lyricism, to inquire into the limitations of rationality. Its reflections are awkwardly integrated into an often amusing
sequence of surrealistic events, culminating in carnivalesque frenzy,
madness and death. Einstein's friend Gottfried Benn thought this work
the literary equivalent of abstract art; it now seems whimsical. Stronger
emotion emerges in Benn's sequence of Novellen, *Gehirne* (*Brains*, 1916).
Their protagonist, Dr Rönne, dissects corpses – a metaphor for intellectual analysis and disgust with civilisation. In increasingly dense and elliptical prose, he deplores the historical process whereby the basic urges of
hunger and love were supplemented in Northern Europe by the urge for
knowledge, and abandons himself to vivid day-dreams of sensual life
amid mythic southern landscapes. By contrast, Heym in 'Das Schiff' ('The
ship') uses an exotic setting for a spine-chilling gothic tale. The
Expressionist interest in insanity is most powerfully exemplified in
Heym's 'Der Irre' ('The madman'), which defamiliarises everyday settings
(a country road, a department store) by adopting the perspective of a
psychopath. (Both stories appeared in the posthumous collection *Der
Dieb* (*The thief*, 1913).) More contrived is the much-analysed *Die
Ermordung einer Butterblume* (*The murder of a buttercup*, 1910) by
Alfred Döblin (1878–1957): the guilt-ridden delusions of the protagonist,
who, having accidentally decapitated a buttercup, identifies it with a
woman, serve only to satirise the bourgeoisie's hostility to nature.

Franz Kafka (1883–1924) has been plausibly characterised by Walter
Sokel as a 'classical Expressionist', though his literary roots lie rather in
the *fin de siècle*. The atmospheric prose of Altenberg helped inspire his

first book, *Betrachtung* (*Contemplation*, 1912), which contains such brief
sketches as 'Der Fahrgast', where the juddering platform of a tram
becomes emblematic of the passenger's uncertain place in the world.
Another important model was the Swiss prose-writer Robert Walser
(1878–1956), who resembles the early Kafka especially in his humorously
sinister schoolboy novel *Jakob von Gunten* (1909). What Kafka himself
considered his literary breakthrough occurred in September 1912 with the
taut, dramatic story *Das Urteil* (*The judgement*, published 1916). The
sober realism of its opening modulates into a father–son conflict typical
of early Expressionism: the father, inexplicably restored to vigour, charges
the son with obscure depravity and sentences him to death by drowning.
In *Die Verwandlung* (*The metamorphosis*, written December 1912, published 1915) another inexplicable event, Gregor Samsa's transformation
into an unspecified insect, occasions similar conflicts which likewise end
with the protagonist's submission. From these dramatic narratives, Kafka
moved in 1916–17 to a different type of short fiction, exemplified in the
collection *Ein Landarzt* (*A country doctor*, 1919): short parable-like tales,
often centring on the irruption of an unfamiliar reality (the unearthly
horses in 'Ein Landarzt', the bestial nomads in 'Ein altes Blatt' ('An old
manuscript')), and sometimes recounted by a humorously untrustworthy
narrator, as in 'Ein Bericht für eine Akademie' ('A report for an academy').
This shift of focus from narrative to narrator is extended in late, reflective
stories like 'Forschungen eines Hundes' ('Investigations of a dog', written
1922), a meditation on the limitations of knowledge. 'Ein Hungerkünst-
ler' ('A starvation artist', written 1921, published 1924), which displays the
ascetic feats of an artist misunderstood and disliked by the public, may be
read as a reflection on the esoteric character of much modern art; while in
Kafka's last story, 'Josefine, die Sängerin oder das Volk der Mäuse'
('Josefine the singer or the mouse nation', 1924), the narrator meditates
with melancholy and ironic humour on the social role of the artist and her
ultimate superfluity. Kafka's short stories, fragments and aphorisms owe
their excellence not least to his infallible ear for language, which makes
them at once pellucid and enigmatic. His aphorisms also reveal Kafka as a
profound religious thinker, concerned with sin and redemption but
exhibiting a Nietzschean morality of strenuousness in refusing to contemplate any solution short of uncompromising self-sacrifice.

Although Kafka's three novels are incomplete and scarcely revised
drafts, their depiction of conflict between perplexed protagonists and
obscure authorities has appealed especially to those readers for whom religious belief seems both impossible and indispensable. Often they seem
less like literature than like new myths, cobbled from the debris of discarded religions. Though the basic narrative of conflict is similar in all
three, the mode differs. In *Der Verschollene* (*The missing person*; written

mostly in 1911 and first published as *Amerika*, 1927) Karl Rossmann's encounters with successive parent-surrogates retain a Chaplinesque humour, though he repeatedly finds himself unfairly accused of wrongdoing, and finally he is admitted to the paradisal 'Teater von Oklahama' (*sic*; Kafka was hazy about American orthography and geography). *Der Proceß* (*The trial*, or better *The lawsuit*; written 1914, published 1925) is tragic: increasingly obsessed by his unexplained guilt, and unable to benefit from the riddling warnings of the Court Painter and the Chaplain, Josef K. finally submits to execution. But his fate is ambiguous. He may well be morally obtuse to the point of inauthenticity (Kafka was familiar with Nietzsche) and engaged in a self-destructive defence against self-knowledge; yet the external squalor of the Court coexists strangely with its apparently absolute and implacable moral authority. Doubts about authority become more explicit in *Das Schloß* (*The castle*; written 1922, published 1926), where K. challenges the villagers' traditional servitude to the Castle. Village society is treated with some realism: K. develops a deep emotional relationship with Frieda, but sacrifices it to his obsession with the Castle, which – dominating the village yet inaccessible from it, abandoned by its owner, Graf Westwest, and occupied by ill-behaved yet charismatic bureaucrats – resembles the empty abode of a defunct divinity. Like the late Rilke, Kafka seems to be rejecting any transcendent authority and suggesting that humankind should not seek the divine but concentrate, whatever the difficulties, on domestic and social life on this earth. If so, K. fails in both endeavours, and the novel is again tragic, though its presentation of human relationships distinguishes it sharply from the virtual solipsism of *Der Proceß*.

Living in Prague, and working as an official in an insurance company until incurable tuberculosis obliged him to retire, Kafka had relatively little contact with other writers. Though Musil and Rilke admired his work, the only major writer among his own acquaintances was Werfel. His loyal friend, biographer, and editor, Max Brod (1884–1968), churned out innumerable mediocre works, but did write one memorable novel, *Tycho Brahes Weg zu Gott* (*Tycho Brahe's path to God*, 1916). Here the ageing Renaissance astronomer Brahe is tormented by the enigmatic personality of his more gifted younger colleague Kepler. Brod said much later that Kepler was based on Werfel, but in the text he more resembles Kafka, and the book's power probably results from Brod's success in articulating his ambivalence towards Kafka. The following generation of German writers from Czechoslovakia, however, produced some remarkable fiction which has only recently been rescued from obscurity; it often treats Kafkaesque themes in a realistic mode. Ludwig Winder (1889–1946) adopted a clipped, headlong Expressionist prose for *Die jüdische Orgel* (*The Jewish organ*, 1922), which concerns the conflict between a rigidly overbearing orthodox Jew and his weak son who takes to crime but cannot shake off his Jewish heritage and ends as a saintly eccentric. Read more sceptically, the novel recounts his inability to become independent of the authoritarian parent (father, Judaism, God) whom he must either obey or defy. The outstanding book of this group is *Kinder einer Stadt* (*Children of one town*, 1932) by Hans Natonek (1892–1963), an ultimately metaphysical novel with three main characters. The ambition of the Jewish journalist Dowidal, the self-abnegating sainthood of the Catholic Waisl, and the compulsive womanising of the aristocrat Epp, are all revealed as distractions from the search for personal truth. Natonek's simple, understated style is also reminiscent of Kafka.

If Kafka and his successors seem to create from the scantiest materials, two other outstanding prose-writers, Alfred Döblin and Hans Henny Jahnn, were inspired by Expressionism to revel in sometimes uncontrollable excess. Döblin is an extraordinarily powerful and adventurous novelist. Though acknowledged as a teacher by Grass and Koeppen, he is still insufficiently appreciated. A Socialist, he rejected the liberal individualism that we have seen under threat in Schnitzler and Thomas Mann, maintaining that the individual was being superseded by collective humanity congregated in modern cities. The insignificance of the individual would be compensated by the freedom resulting from technological advances and liberation from religious illusions. In his novels, inspired by Homer, Dante and Cervantes, with a dash of Italian futurism, he sought to revive epic by a panoramic, cinematic style, pictorial and vivid, unimpaired by authorial reflection or psychological analysis. Rejecting the cheap pleasures of plot, which merely spur the reader on to finish the book, he strove to make each episode self-sufficient. His first major novel, *Die drei Sprünge des Wang-lun* (*The three leaps of Wang-lun*, 1915), based on Chinese history, is less impersonal than Döblin's programmatic essays suggest. Its hero, founder of the pacifist sect of the Truly Weak, alternates between a Taoist doctrine of passivity and violent insurrection, both of which prove futile. Similarly, the historical novel *Wallenstein* (1920) contrasts the amoral energy of Wallenstein with the mystical detachment attained by the Emperor Ferdinand, and places both in an overwhelmingly sensuous world without meaning or transcendence, in which insistent animal imagery makes human beings, with their turbulent appetites, appear part of the natural, elemental world. Döblin excels in describing mass journeys: the Protestants' exodus from Bohemia, the Swedish fleet crossing the Baltic. Under his impassive, Flaubertian, god's-eye gaze all experience, however painful, becomes an aesthetic spectacle. His imagination finds new scope in the science-fiction novel *Berge Meere und Giganten* (*Mountains, seas and giants*, 1924), which explores the transformative and destructive potential of technology. Like Spengler in *Der Untergang des Abendlandes*

(*The decline of the West*, 1918, 1922), Döblin foresees giant cities ruled by technocratic supermen. In the twenty-seventh century they undertake to defrost and colonise Greenland by reactivating the Icelandic volcanoes and thus harnessing the earth's internal energies. The departure of the vulcanologists' fleet from the Shetlands and the succeeding disquisition on geology, a wonderful instance of the 'poetry of fact' that Döblin demanded, are among his finest passages. Naturally, technocratic hubris produces unforeseeable disasters, and Döblin's future terminates in a return to pastoral primitivism.

By common consent, the masterpiece among Döblin's voluminous fictional output is *Berlin Alexanderplatz* (1929), which turns away from his earlier work by reinstating the narrator and the individual. An omniscient, anonymous narrative voice, resembling by turns a ballad-singer, a boxing commentator and a polymath, comments on the action; it reduces tension by announcing future events, moves in and out of the characters' minds, and conveys the diversity of modern city life by montage (the mechanical juxtaposition of incongruous components), parody and defamiliarisation – techniques suggested partly by Joyce's *Ulysses*. Thus Döblin juxtaposes advertising symbols, newspaper announcements, weather reports and tram timetables; intersperses literary and biblical quotations with Berlin dialect; or describes two men drinking at a bar as 'two large, fully grown animals wrapped in cloth' and speculates on how long the sunbeam that illuminates them spent travelling through space. Franz Biberkopf, the hero, is presented as good-hearted, violent, and almost incorrigibly stupid. He inhabits eastern Berlin, where Döblin had practised as a doctor. In his semi-criminal world, women are only instruments mediating relationships among men, and Biberkopf's most important relationship is the homoerotic one with the hardened criminal Reinhold, who maliciously causes Biberkopf an injury and then murders his girlfriend Mieze. These blows of fate drive Biberkopf into insanity in which he encounters the personification of Death. His recovery leaves him sadder and cannier. But the ending is problematic. Biberkopf's appalling sufferings, attended by biblical imagery (Job, Abraham and Isaac, the Whore of Babylon), seem to require a religious interpretation which Döblin, who became a Catholic only in 1941, could not yet provide. Another fictional pattern seems present: as Goethe's Gretchen redeems Faust and Wagner's Brünnhilde redeems Siegfried, so the pure-hearted prostitute Mieze seems to redeem Biberkopf by her violent death which precipitates his crisis and quasi-spiritual rebirth. These clashing myths, however, enhance the book's fecund vitality.

Hans Henny Jahnn (1894–1959) earned early notoriety with the prize-winning play *Pastor Ephraim Magnus* (1919), whose tortured declamations on perverse sexuality make Wedekind look tame. Much better is the free-verse tragedy *Medea* (1926), loosely based on Euripides but set in a pagan universe charged with sexuality: the chorus of slaves invokes the sun-god as a young bull, and the text, with its outbursts of erotic fury, is pervaded by images of stallions and mares, which for Jahnn symbolise noble, amoral, sensual nature. The anglophone reader will be reminded of the later Lawrence. In the novel *Perrudja* (1929) this pagan world-view is anchored in rural Norway, where Jahnn and his male lover spent 1915–18 avoiding German military service. An astonishing passage (reminiscent of Heym's myth-making) evokes a hermaphroditic god unleashing spring storms which are followed by the perennial outburst of vital energies. Through its hero, a timid and reclusive millionaire, the novel also explores a fragile, polymorphous sexuality that finds successive foci in Perrudja's cult of his horse Shabdez, in his male friends and lovers, and in his terrifying wife Signe. Its innovative use of free indirect speech betrays Jahnn's enthusiastic response to Joyce. Jahnn's later novels, like Döblin's, must probably remain cult books because of their intimidating length, but *Perrudja*, though prolix and towards the end absurd, is accessible and rewarding.

Expressionist drama and epic theatre

Of all Expressionist genres, drama most sharply illustrates the revolutionary break with the past, conveyed by a rhetoric of crisis, which forms the mythic structure of modernity. The dramatic crisis typically occurs in the life of the hero. Following Strindberg's *To Damascus* (1898–1901), many Expressionist plays pursue the hero's spiritual development through a series of stages ('Stationen'). Partly under the influence of Wedekind (whose *Frühlings Erwachen* was first performed only in 1906, with Wedekind himself playing the Masked Man), characters are reduced to types: we never learn the names of the Son and Father in *Der Sohn* (*The son*, 1914) by Walter Hasenclever (1890–1940), or of the Cashier in *Von morgens bis mitternachts* (*From morning to midnight*, 1916) by Georg Kaiser (1878–1945). The abstract and non-mimetic language labours to be concentrated, oratorical, ecstatic. Monologues and choruses are favoured; characters interact only by uttering alternate monologues. This limits the Expressionists' portrayal of society to the self-centred individual and the undifferentiated mass. Conflicts are similarly abstract: youthful, revolutionary energies oppose an ossified, dehumanised society, though the radical impulse comes from utopian anarchism more often than from revolutionary Socialism. The conflict is often between the generations, as in *Der Bettler* (*The beggar*, 1912) by Reinhard Johannes Sorge (1892–1916), where the insane authoritarian Father, obsessed with technological fantasies, is killed by his son; or in *Der Sohn*, where the Father drops dead of a well-timed heart attack. (The latter play may have been partly inspired by the much-publicised case of Otto Gross, the radical psychoanalyst, whose father, a famous criminal lawyer, had him imprisoned for alleged insanity.) In *Von morgens bis mitternachts* it is the omnipotence of money that frustrates the spiritual regeneration of the Cashier, and in *Gas I* (1918) Kaiser caricatures the military-industrial nexus as a group of evil father-figures who mislead the gullible masses into manufacturing poison gas. The First World War is attacked in the frenzied declamations composed by Fritz von Unruh (1885–1970) in *Ein Geschlecht* (*A dynasty*, 1917) and, much more impressively, in Hasenclever's *Antigone* (1917), where Antigone's self-sacrifice and the burning of Thebes herald a utopia that is credible in the only possible way – poetically: 'Der Wind steigt aus den Trümmern, / Die neue Welt bricht an' (The wind is rising from the ruins, / The new world is dawning).

The revolutionary atmosphere of 1917–19 fostered such 'dramas of annunciation' ('Verkündigungsdramen'), in which political conflicts are addressed symbolically, and salvation is seen in a regenerated community under a charismatic leader. Their redemptive ideals match the early messianism, drawn from German Romanticism and Jewish mysticism, of Walter Benjamin (1892–1940), who in 'Zur Kritik der Gewalt' ('Critique of violence', 1921) invoked divine violence to break the cycle of history; and the utopian communism of Georg Lukács (1885–1971), whose heretical *Geschichte und Klassenbewußtsein* (*History and class consciousness*, 1923) imputed to the proletariat the potential for redeeming humankind from capitalist alienation. Drama's utopian conclusions are mostly vacuous, as in Kaiser's *Hölle Weg Erde* (*Hell road earth*, 1919); and though Kaiser calls for a new, regenerate human being ('der neue Mensch'), such people figure in his plays only when they are already dead (*Die Bürger von Calais*, 1914) or not yet born (end of *Gas I*). The most popular such drama was *Die Wandlung* (*The transformation*, 1919) by Ernst Toller (1893–1939). Revulsion against the war made audiences receptive to such crude shock effects as its dance of skeletons and its monologues of limbless cripples. Its hero, Friedrich, undergoes a spiritual transformation from naive militarist to revolutionary leader. One now smiles at stage-directions like 'Schreitet ekstatisch zur Tür hinaus' (Strides ecstatically out of the room), but despite its bombast the play is disturbing in depicting a charismatic leader whose spiritual authority (gained at the expense of others, as in the symbolic mountain-climbing scene where Friedrich abandons his friend in order to secure his own spiritual advancement) is exercised upon an undifferentiated, united, applauding crowd. Hitler was similarly to convince crowds by mythicising his frontline service into an authentic experience that validated his claims to leadership.

The visionary ambitions of Expressionist drama exceeded the limits of the theatre and were perhaps best realised in films like Robert Wiene's *Caligari* (1919) and Fritz Lang's *Metropolis* (1927). The few plays that stand out as convincing works of art are concentrated in time and space and relatively restrained in language. In his concise, lyrical *Der brennende Dornbusch* (*The burning bush*, 1913), the painter Oskar Kokoschka (1886–1980) treats the polarity of the sexes by subordinating his protagonists to the archetypal imagery of moon and sun. Kaiser's *Die Bürger von Calais*, despite immense monologues, holds the attention by postponing revelations: which six burghers of Calais (besieged during the Hundred Years War) will sacrifice themselves for their fellow citizens; and, since seven volunteer, which one will be saved by arriving on the scene last. When Eustache de Saint-Pierre, the spokesman for pacifism, fails to arrive, the townspeople first think he has betrayed them, then realise that he has committed suicide in order to purify the others' motives. This sacrificial death gives meaning to the communion meal of Act II and the carvings of Christ's death and resurrection visible on the cathedral portal throughout Act III. Reinhard Goering (1887–1936), in his single-act *Seeschlacht* (*Naval encounter*, 1917), presents five sailors in the gun-turret of a battleship, tensely awaiting the Battle of Jutland (31 May 1916). The compressed, sinewy language serves to express their different attitudes, especially in the dialogue between the unthinkingly patriotic First Sailor and the rationalist Fifth Sailor who gradually reveals his belief in human solidarity and his resolve to mutiny. When battle starts, however, its intoxication defeats his intentions, and in his dying words he wonders why he fired instead of disobeying. Toller's *Masse Mensch* (*Masses and man*, 1922) draws on his experience of the Munich Soviet, which was proclaimed on 7 April 1919, hijacked by Communists six days later, and soon afterwards brutally suppressed by a combination of government and Freikorps forces. The female protagonist, Sonja Irene L. (the name means 'wisdom' and 'peace'), breaks away from her authoritarian husband and joins the workers' revolution. Her personal monologues alternate with mass choruses, expressing the plight of the individual who becomes disillusioned with mass politics and realises that the mass is a perversion of the 'Volk'. Advocating love and non-violence, she comes into conflict with 'The Nameless One', who calls for violent revolution, revenge against state violence, and brutal action ('die harte Tat'), while she charges him with sacrificing present-day people to his doctrine and to the future. Here Toller, like Goering, conveys the tragedy resulting from the clash of noble intentions with hard realities.

On the fringes of Expressionism stands the powerful dramatist Ernst Barlach (1870–1938), whose dramas of spiritual seeking and renewal benefit from being set in firmly imagined North German villages. The best is *Der arme Vetter* (*The poor cousin*, 1918), where holiday-makers on Easter Sunday are stranded in an inn waiting for the steamer taking them back to Hamburg; the bar-room becomes a place of carnal revelry presided over by 'Frau Venus', while the heroine, Fräulein Isenbarn, gradually rejects her materialistic fiancé for her 'spiritual bridegroom' Hans Iver, whose suicide implies resurrection. The concrete setting, the dense, perplexing language of Barlach's characters, and their often puzzling reactions to one another, both suggest the recalcitrance of the material world and allow glimpses of another and mysterious reality.

All Expressionist drama, however, is put in the shade by the forty-odd plays of Bertolt Brecht (1898–1956) and the single, huge drama by Karl Kraus, *Die letzten Tage der Menschheit* (*The last days of mankind*, 1922). Kraus already had a controversial reputation as a journalist and polemicist. His periodical *Die Fackel* (*The torch*), which he founded in 1899 and wrote single-handed from 1910 onwards, gained him some detractors (e.g. Schnitzler) and many passionate devotees (e.g. the young Canetti). Kraus was also widely known for his public readings from his own work and from Nestroy, Offenbach, Shakespeare and German lyric poetry (his 'Theater der Dichtung').

Kraus's campaigns against sexual hypocrisy and artistic ornamentation are inspired by a combination of moral honesty, aesthetic modernism and social conservatism. For him, the degeneracy of the modern world is typified by journalism, which has replaced thoughts with opinions and artistic utterance with slogans and clichés. Hence he attacks the inflated style ('Desperanto') of the Berlin journalist Maximilian Harden (1861–1927) and blames Heine, in a misguided essay which influenced Heine critics down to Adorno, as the originator of modern journalese. Kraus's compressed and brilliant satirical style excels in dismantling clichés, as in his attack on chauvinistic bombast, 'In dieser großen Zeit' ('In these great times', 1914). Initially Kraus opposed the degenerate liberalism which he saw embodied in the power of the press and of finance capital, and on which he blamed the First World War. From 1918 on he supported the Social Democrats and the First Austrian Republic. The Socialists, however, seemed too inept to counter the threat of Hitler, and in 1934 Kraus transferred his support to the Christian-Social Chancellor Dollfuss and his attempt to establish a Catholic corporate state as a bulwark against Nazism. At no time was Kraus attracted by Fascism: his conservatism (like that of his Austrian predecessor Grillparzer) was directed elegiacally towards the past, and he did not believe that a revolution of the right or the left could benefit humankind. Kraus's conservatism corresponds to his deeply religious sensibility which his satirical persona often conceals. In 1911, turning his back on his Jewish origins, he was baptised a Catholic. He deplored the hubris of 'the technologico-romantic adventure' which aimed at the conquest of nature and, he thought, met its nemesis in the sinking of the 'Titanic'. His counter-image was that of the 'Ursprung', the original paradisal state which he celebrates in the enigmatic poem 'Zwei Läufer' ('Two runners').

The gigantic satirical drama *Die letzten Tage der Menschheit* exposes the horrors of the First World War: not just the physical suffering, but the trivial callousness of the politicians, officers, and (above all) journalists who conducted it. In Kraus's fusion of ethics and aesthetics, the linguistic corruption fostered by journalism is the index of imaginative failure and moral decay. Kraus's superb ear for dialogue, and his association of language and morality, place him in an Austrian dramatic tradition that runs from his admired Nestroy via Schnitzler to Peter Handke. Many of his countless characters have historical originals, and their utterances have documentary sources. In this, and in its abrupt scenic contrasts, the play looks back to Büchner's *Dantons Tod*. The Grumbler ('der Nörgler') comments on the action, a distancing device that anticipates Brecht. Though selections have been successfully staged, the play really demands cinematic treatment, especially in the penultimate scene when a drunken dinner of bloodthirsty officers is interrupted by apparitions of the war's victims. Expressionistic symbolism triumphs in the powerful apocalyptic epilogue, 'Die letzte Nacht' ('The last night'): we see dying soldiers, fleeing generals, voyeuristic war-correspondents, and hyenas; the Lord of the Hyenas (based on the newspaper proprietor Moritz Benedikt) proclaims himself the Antichrist; the Death's-Head Hussars and the inventor of poison gas boast of their achievements; finally a Voice from Above announces that the earth is to be destroyed by a bombardment from Mars. In Kraus's poetic cosmos, though, humankind's vileness defeats even God, who ends the play by quoting the words of Kaiser Wilhelm II on the war – 'Ich habe es nicht gewollt' ('I did not want it to happen').

Brecht's plays vary widely in style and provenance: he ransacked world literature for material and stimulus. He criticised Expressionist dramas in 1920 as too abstract, 'proclamations of humanity without human beings'. In order to outdo the Expressionist Hanns Johst (1890–1978), whose portrayal of the misunderstood genius Grabbe in *Der Einsame* (*The lonely one*, 1917) seemed too idealistic, Brecht's first play *Baal* (written 1918) depicted a robustly physical, amoral hero who indulges his own sensual appetites and celebrates them with seductive lyricism. The episodic form and natural settings show the impact of *Woyzeck* and *Frühlings Erwachen*. Baal's rejection of society, ending in his solitary death, takes individualism to an extreme, but also, as Hofmannsthal recognised in his prologue to the 1926 Vienna production, proclaims the abolition of the individual. The play particularly associates women with nature. For Baal, good sex repeats the Flood, but a woman after use is a faceless lump of flesh, and he shows small concern when his women drown themselves. Baal's real relationship (modelled on that of Rimbaud and Verlaine) is the homosexual one with Ekart, whom he eventually strangles from jealousy. These erotic and aquatic motifs strikingly resemble the imagery of proto-fascist Freikorps novels, described by Klaus Theweleit in *Male fantasies* (1977–8), in which women, symbolised by floods and swamps, represent a threat to the overriding power of male bonding.

Brecht's early poetry, especially the exciting verse collected in *Hauspostille* (*Domestic breviary*, 1927), similarly celebrates fierce energies in a violently sensuous cosmos of endless growth and decay, close to the imaginative worlds of Döblin and Jahnn. Nature appears ambivalently, sometimes as womb-like intimacy into which one can dissolve ('Vom Schwimmen in Seen und Flüssen' ('Of swimming in lakes and rivers')), sometimes as actively hostile ('Von des Cortez Leuten' ('Of Cortez' people')). As in *Baal*, amoral, instinctual drives are powerfully celebrated ('Ballade von den Seeräubern' ('Ballad of the pirates')). The layout of *Hauspostille* parodies a breviary, but God features only as an irritant ('Bericht vom Zeck' ('Report on the tick')), and religion, though in tones of elegiac regret, as a delusion ('Gegen Verführung' ('Against Temptation')).

Between 1926 and 1930 Brecht studied the works of Marx, Engels and Lenin. Marxism provided a basis for his opposition to bourgeois society; its collectivism overcame the aporia of individualism explored in *Baal*; and, unlike the implausible spiritual transformations demanded by Expressionism, it seemed to offer practical instructions for changing society. Instead of the official dogma of mechanistic materialism, however, Brecht adopted the unorthodox intellectual Marxism of Karl Korsch, who argued that ideas had a real function in transforming society. Korsch's influence helped Brecht to develop a committed theatre, intended to change the audience's consciousness by showing that the social arrangements they took for granted were contingent and alterable. The means of changing consciousness was to be 'epic theatre', which Brecht gradually approached by directing and adapting plays in Berlin. An important influence was the Communist director Erwin Piscator (1893–1966), who specialised in adapting novels to produce an epic drama that foregrounded social and political conditions. Brecht helped with Piscator's 1928 adaptation of Hašek's *The good soldier Švejk*, one of Brecht's favourite novels.

Epic theatre was not to stage an action but to tell a story. As in Döblin's epics, which Brecht admired, each section was to be self-sufficient: instead of tensely awaiting the outcome, the audience should scrutinise each incident. The actors should not 'be' their roles but play them in a conspicuously artificial way for which Brecht found precedents in classical Chinese and Japanese theatre. Instead of being entranced, the audience should remain detached, alert and critical. Characterisation is subordinated to intellectual inquiry: hence Brecht's dramatic characters, with neither the psychological depth claimed by the liberal subject nor the rampant individualism of Baal, are, in Marx's phrase, 'ensembles of social relations'. Instead of being distinguished by their language, all speak in the same lucid, sober style. Often the action culminates in a court scene (for example, the chalk-circle test in *Der kaukasische Kreidekreis* (*The Caucasian chalk circle*), the report to the Control Chorus in *Die Maßnahme* (*The measures taken*).

In *Die Dreigroschenoper* (*The threepenny opera*, 1928), on which Brecht collaborated with the composer Kurt Weill and the translator and writer Elisabeth Hauptmann (1897–1973), the Marxist critique is still shallow. The opera, which transfers the action of Gay's *Beggars' Opera* to Victorian times, made a hit by titillating respectable audiences through representing them as criminals. Commitment is most explicit in the didactic plays ('Lehrstücke'), written between 1929 and 1934, and in *Die heilige Johanna der Schlachthöfe* (*St Joan of the slaughterhouses*, written 1929–31), whose rancorous dialectical wit closely recalls Shaw's *Major Barbara*. The most challenging of these plays, *Die Maßnahme* (1930), displays, especially in its original version, the zeal of the convert. With its choruses in praise of the Communist Party and the Soviet Union, it preaches the abject submission of the individual conscience to the dictates of the supposedly omniscient and infallible Party. Its characters have discarded their individuality in the Party's service before undertaking agitation in China. One, the Young Comrade, refuses to suppress his compassion in the interest of the Party's long-term goals, strips off his mask, endangers the mission, and must, despite his comrades' humane scruples, be killed. The play's power comes from reviving a familiar theme in German tragedy (and German history), that of the necessary crime. Like the September Massacres in *Dantons Tod* and the judicial murder of Hebbel's Agnes Bernauer, the death of the Young Comrade is enjoined by reason of state as a necessary sacrifice to the future.

In exile, Brecht took a deliberate and salutary step backwards to naturalistic drama in *Furcht und Elend im Dritten Reich* (*Fear and misery in the Third Reich*, 1938), whose twenty-four self-contained scenes, based on eye-witness and newspaper reports, make a compelling indictment of National Socialist terror; in his Spanish Civil War drama *Die Gewehre der Frau Carrar* (*Señora Carrar's guns*, 1937); and in the first version of *Leben des Galilei* (*Life of Galileo*, written 1937–9). He then returned to epic theatre, but with differences. In earlier Marxist plays (*Die heilige Johanna*, *Die Mutter* (*The mother*, 1932), *Frau Carrar*), the central figure is able to understand her situation and master it by adopting militancy, whereas in his later plays the central figure is obtuse (Mother Courage) or perplexed (Shen Te) and the audience is given an increasingly active role in drawing the conclusions unavailable to her. And instead of his previous near-contemporary settings (Chicago in *Die heilige Johanna*, revolutionary Russia in *Die Mutter*), Brecht ranges widely in time and space, so that his plays' relation to the present becomes allegorical. In the final version of *Galilei*, written in 1945–7 after the dropping of atomic bombs on Japan, Brecht distorts history to make Galileo typify the irresponsible scientist. In *Mutter Courage und ihre Kinder* (*Mother Courage and her children*, written 1939) the Thirty Years War serves to allegorise the self-destructive irrationality of capitalism; the worm's-eye view adopted precludes any historical interpretation of events. In *Der gute Mensch von Sezuan* (*The good person of Sechuan*, written 1938–42), the Chinese setting has no essential relationship to the action, which through the division between Shen Te and Shui Ta represents the splitting of the personality that supposedly results wherever capitalism operates. And in *Der kaukasische Kreidekreis* (written 1943–5) the arbitrary judgements of the 'poor man's judge' Azdak are timeless and utopian, recalling the ancient motif of the world turned upside-down.

Brecht's commitment to Marxism clouded his understanding of contemporary history. He lacks the grasp of politics that we find in Shakespeare or Schiller. Instead, he reduces politics to business dealings, which he treats as intrinsically bad (especially in his lifeless novel *Der Dreigroschenroman* (*Threepenny novel*, 1934), which demonstrates his incapacity for that essentially liberal genre). This very German aversion to politics prevents Brecht from comprehending Hitler or Stalin. He sees Hitler, not as a charismatic dictator with popular support, but as a plebeian front-man for desperate capitalists, and caricatures him in the *Svendborger Gedichte* (*Svendborg poems*, 1939) as 'the house-painter', in *Schweyk im Zweiten Weltkrieg* (*Švejk in the Second World War*, written 1941–3) as a swollen bogey-man, and in *Der aufhaltsame Aufstieg des Arturo Ui* (*The stoppable rise of Arturo Ui*, written 1941) as a Chicago gangster. As for Stalin, Brecht's efforts to justify the Soviet purges – in his guarded conversations with Walter Benjamin, in poems like 'Ist das Volk unfehlbar?' ('Are the people infallible?'), and in the posthumously published allegory *Me-ti. Buch der Wendungen* (*Book of changes*) – are a sad spectacle.

Although Brecht's intellectual framework has failed the test of time, his plays survive without it. Nor does their vitality depend on the gimmickry of 'alienation': *Der kaukasische Kreidekreis* works well without prologue or epilogue, and the bereaved Mother Courage notoriously invites empathy, despite Brecht's efforts to make her repulsive. The plays' excellence lies in their spiky wit (stimulated by Brecht's early acquaintance with the Munich comedian Karl Valentin) and, above all, in the tension arising from the edgy antagonism always latent among Brecht's characters. The songs are often the best things in his plays, lending emotional depth to an otherwise trivial action: 'Die Seeräuber-Jenny' ('Pirate Jenny') in *Die Dreigroschenoper*, 'Das Lied von der Moldau' ('The song of the Vltava') in *Schweyk im Zweiten Weltkrieg*.

If any play stands out, it is surely *Mutter Courage*. Its flavourful language stems from its grounding in literary tradition (Grimmelshausen's *Courasche*, Schiller's *Wallensteins Lager* and Döblin's *Wallenstein* are among its models); business dealings are successfully integrated into the action without dominating it; and perhaps the greatest moment in all Brecht's drama is the self-sacrifice of Courage's dumb daughter Kattrin, who saves the town of Halle from destruction at the cost of her own life. She is one of the young heroines who, like Döblin's Mieze, remain mysteriously unaffected by their surroundings: the prostitute Shen Te retains her heart of gold, Grusche the kindness that makes her rescue the abandoned baby. The redemptive power of these figures, impelled by maternal feelings without experiencing motherhood (even Shen Te, though pregnant, does not become a mother during *Der gute Mensch*), springs from the mythic regions of Brecht's imagination.

Brecht's later poetry has, at least in Germany, exercised as much influence as his plays. After *Hauspostille* he tended to use rhyme only in satires and developed a lucid poetry, appealing to the intellect rather than the senses, in unrhymed lines of irregular length; dynamism comes from enjambement, which introduces expectancy and tension between the beginning and the conclusion of a statement. Such poetry can be rather grey, though, and Brecht's most admired poems return to traditional lyric stances. 'An die Nachgeborenen', which concludes the uneven *Svendborger Gedichte*, expresses qualified penitence for the inhumanity evident in *Die Maßnahme*. The group of 'Steffinische Gedichte', fine snapshots from Brecht's Danish and Finnish exile, ends with a witty sonnet. By contrast, the many satires on Germany and America suffer from lack of humour (sour mockery is no substitute), while his precariously privileged position in the GDR after 1948 hardly encouraged lyrical honesty. In the famous cycle of twenty-two short poems inspired by Chinese verse, *Buckower Elegien* (*Buckow elegies*, written 1953), constant undertones of distrust and unease become loud in 'Böser Morgen' ('Bad morning'), where Brecht seems to acknowledge his pusillanimous failure to support the Berlin workers' uprising of 17 June 1953.

In the wake of Expressionism, several gifted dramatists outdid its achievements by combining its formal flexibility with sharp realism. Brecht should not overshadow them, though his ruthless adaptation of her work nearly wrecked the career of his lover Marieluise Fleisser (1901–74).

Fleisser revived the 'Volksstück' (play about rural or small-town life) and gave it critical bite. Her *Fegefeuer in Ingolstadt* (*Purgatory in Ingolstadt*, 1926) recalls *Frühlings Erwachen* in its presentation of teenage sexuality and malicious surveillance, but gains a dimension through the Catholic imagery centred on a schoolboy misfit whose sufferings parody Christ's. The other exponent of the critical 'Volksstück' was Ödön von Horváth (1901–38), above all in *Geschichten aus dem Wiener Wald* (*Tales from the Vienna Woods*, 1931), which exposes the myth of 'Vienna's golden heart' and shows, with a Krausian ear for language, how everyday clichés can express abysmal callousness. Carl Zuckmayer (1896–1977) satirises an easier target, Prussian militarism, in *Der Hauptmann von Köpenick* (*The captain of Köpenick*, 1931), though Hindenburg's presidency lent immediacy to this familiar subject. The Communist Friedrich Wolf (1888–1953) makes his characters speechify rather than talk, but in his exile play *Professor Mamlock* (1934) he agitates his puppets rapidly enough to make memorable the contradiction whereby only the ostracised Jewish surgeon Mamlock retains a Prussian sense of responsibility. There is more human depth, though, in the play about Georg Büchner, *Gesellschaft der Menschenrechte* (*The Society for the Rights of Man*, 1927) by Franz Theodor Csokor (1885–1969), which probes the moral ambiguity of the revolutionary.

Fiction for the Republic

Defeat in the First World War was a traumatic shock. In September 1918 the German and Austrian military effort rapidly crumbled under determined Allied assaults. In November 1918, with naval mutiny in Kiel and revolution in Munich portending general disintegration, the Kaiser abdicated and a republic was proclaimed. The Weimar Republic (so called because the National Assembly met in Weimar to draw up its constitution) survived revolts from left and right, cataclysmic inflation, and even the French occupation of the Ruhr after Germany failed to pay the punitive reparations imposed by the Treaty of Versailles. The international economic recession after 1929 hastened its downfall. Its replacement by National Socialism was not inevitable, however: the Nazis' electoral support actually declined during 1932. Hitler benefited from the irresponsibility of the arch-conservatives Hindenburg and Papen who thought that by making him Chancellor in January 1933 they could keep him under control. Far from it: the Reichstag fire gave Hitler a pretext to suspend civil liberties, call new elections in which the Nazis received a clear but not overwhelming majority, obtain dictatorial powers, and govern by terror.

In Austria, meanwhile, the First Republic established by the Treaty of Saint-Germain represented the German-speaking rump of the former Habsburg Empire. It suffered from antagonisms between Social-Democratic Vienna and the conservative provinces, where support for Italian or German Fascism was especially strong among the paramilitary Heimwehr organisations. In 1933 Chancellor Dollfuss, caught between the seemingly equipollent threats of Nazism and Socialism, suspended parliament and proclaimed an authoritarian corporate state. The Civil War of February 1934, intended to pre-empt an alleged Socialist coup, left some 1,500 Socialists dead and ended their party's activities; but it did not free Austria from German aggression, culminating in the Anschluss of March 1938 (accompanied by anti-Semitic outrages from the Viennese populace) which turned Austria into the 'Ostmark'.

These disasters should not obscure the promise the republics offered for a more democratic society. This gave literature new tasks. Day-to-day issues received comment from satirical journalists – Kurt Tucholsky (1890–1935) in Berlin, Karl Kraus in Vienna. But the democratic genre is the novel, a protean form whose powers of self-renewal belie the perennial reports of its death or decline. Realist fiction helped readers to grasp their society by offering insight into other people's experience and bringing social issues engrossingly to life; while modernist techniques served the intellectual analysis of society. It is debatable which tendency produced more enjoyable and durable novels; but since academic critics have favoured modernism, its claims are due for sceptical treatment, while realist fiction deserves sympathetic re-examination.

Realist and modernist techniques are combined in two immense novels that stand out as articulating different aspects of liberalism and attempting different summations of modern life: Thomas Mann's *Der Zauberberg* (*The magic mountain*, 1924) and Robert Musil's *Der Mann ohne Eigenschaften* (*The man without qualities*, 1930, 1933). Both are set before the First World War; both carry a heavy intellectual freight; both have an allegorical relation to their contemporary world, as the action is largely confined to small, secluded groups – the denizens of a Swiss sanatorium and of some Viennese salons – through whom the great questions of the day are refracted.

Der Zauberberg has a complicated prehistory. Mann began it in 1913 as a humorous counterpart to *Der Tod in Venedig*. A young man visiting a cousin in a sanatorium comes within sight of death through the dubious diagnosis of tuberculosis, which detains him there for seven years, and through his erotic infatuation with an alluringly Oriental Russian woman. This project was interrupted by the war, which Thomas Mann, like most German intellectuals, supported, interpreting it as the final showdown between German 'Kultur' and shallow Anglo-French commercialism. His chauvinistic essay 'Gedanken im Krieg' ('Thoughts in wartime', November 1914) drove his brother Heinrich, one of the war's few opponents, to reply with the essay 'Zola' (November 1915), which praises France's public-spirited intellectuals in contrast to their time-serving German counterparts. This thinly veiled attack on Thomas's stance estranged the brothers until 1922. Even after the war was lost, Thomas justified himself at length in *Betrachtungen eines Unpolitischen*, which opposes Germany's profound Romantic heritage to that of the French Revolution, but invites the response that the Germans' supposed 'unpolitical' attitude means compliance with authoritarian politics. However, alarmed by the assassination of the German Foreign Minister, the Jewish industrialist Walther Rathenau, in 1922, Thomas came round to supporting Weimar democracy, a change announced in his lecture 'Von deutscher Republik' ('Of a German Republic', 1923).

Marked by these developments, *Der Zauberberg* became an intellectual 'Bildungsroman'. Its ironic narrative voice accompanies the journey that its robustly ordinary hero, Hans Castorp, takes through illness, eroticism, philosophical reflection – in short, the German Romantic heritage. He has questionable guides in the Italian Settembrini, proponent of a sometimes laughable Enlightenment tradition, and the Jewish Jesuit Naphta (based on Lukács), who unites the extremes of Right and Left in proposing that Communist dictatorship will restore medieval theocracy. Their brilliant arguments enable Mann to acknowledge the sinister appeal of anti-liberal values, including the horrifying thrill exerted by the ideas of murder and terrorism; the hypocritical half-truth of associating capitalism with freedom; and the shallowness of some projects for reforming humankind, such as the encyclopaedia of suffering on which Settembrini is working. But the ultimate superiority of Settembrini's liberalism over Naphta's extremism is dramatised in their duel and driven home by the explicit advocacy of life over death stated in the chapter 'Schnee' ('Snow') and vividly embodied in Hans Castorp's allegorical hallucination. Finally, the intellectual antitheses are relativised by Mynheer Peeperkorn, a great comic creation (modelled on Hauptmann): the contrast between his over-whelming presence and his vacuous utterances makes him a representative of Dionysiac vitalism, of 'life' itself, but also vulnerable to the novel's saving irony.

Der Zauberberg is intended as a democratic novel. It presents an average hero (in contrast to Aschenbach) and uses him to make its intellec-tual content readily assimilable. It goes beyond politics to greater choices: above all, to the opposition between a secular and a religious view of life. By focusing on the dramatic conflict of two world-views, it embodies the liberal conviction that, since no individual is in secure possession of the truth, truth must be approached through argument. Dramatic confrontation is also what Mann the novelist does best. His indulgence in arch loquacity, however, prolongs *Der Zauberberg* inordinately, thus reinforcing the confusion of length with significance that dogs German fiction down to Grass and Johnson. There is more drama and a lighter touch in two outstanding 'Novellen': *Unordnung und frühes Leid* (*Disorder and early sorrow*, 1926), in which a history professor has difficulty adjusting to the currency inflation and family tensions brought by contemporary history, and *Mario und der Zauberer* (*Mario and the magician*, 1930), a searching portrayal of the dictatorial power exercised by a hypnotist in Fascist Italy.

In Musil's *Der Mann ohne Eigenschaften* we encounter one of the most fascinating, original, witty and richly stocked minds in German literature. The same agile, stringent intelligence is apparent in Musil's political essays, which are among the best in German. His novel serves liberalism by focusing on the consciousness of Ulrich, whose acute awareness of possibility and contingency distances him ironically from the narrow ideologies that most people mistake for reality. Regarding reality as provisional, he takes a 'sabbatical from life' and observes a rich array of bogus prophets and polymaths and gushing devotees of higher things, demanding or proclaiming new certainties ('Rückkehr zu den inneren Urtümern', in Musil's brilliant, untranslatable phrase). Equally hostile to their verbiage and to the latent violence of philosophical systems, Ulrich practises an approach to experience called 'essayism' that is both experimental and rigorous. A trained mathematician (like Musil), he wants to apply scientific precision to such evanescent realities as emotions and mysticism. Far from being reductive, Musil employs a wealth of metaphor to capture the most fleeting emotional nuances. His novel works best when essayistic reflections are interwoven with social comedy.

Compared to *Der Zauberberg*, however, *Der Mann ohne Eigenschaften* suffers from its lack of an overarching narrative. In a much-quoted passage, Ulrich opines that life is now too complex for the simplifying illusion of narrative sequence. But any ambitious attempt to fictionalise the present will face forbidding complexity; Musil is perhaps merely apologising for failing to control his material. He could not finish the novel, which peters out into innumerable drafts. This does not greatly matter: it can best be enjoyed by repeated dipping. Serious ambiguities, however, arise in Part 3, ominously entitled 'Ins Tausendjährige Reich' ('Into the millennial kingdom'). Here the social comedy becomes an intermittent background to two contrasting attempts to enter a new reality which is no longer provisional. The unstable Nietzschean Clarisse, who enthuses about redemption through murder and madness and is especially fascinated by the sex-murderer Moosbrugger, is treated with appropriate irony. But there are disturbing similarities with the attempts made by Ulrich and his long-lost sister Agathe to sublimate sibling love into mysticism. Though these passages are deeply touching and mysterious, they also represent a search for authenticity and a devaluation of ordinary, non-mystical experience. Even Ulrich's ironic detachment succumbs to the appeal of millennial fantasies.

Thomas Mann wrote to the novelist Jakob Wassermann on 3 April 1921 that the German novel would always be personal, confessional and metaphysical, never a democratic instrument of social criticism. Fortunately he was wrong, but confessional novels, firmly in the Romantic tradition, were indeed written by Gustav Sack (1885–1916), Joseph Goebbels (1897–1945) and Hermann Hesse (1877–1962), and throw a disturbing light on the anti-democratic mentality of many young Germans.

Sack's *Ein verbummelter Student* (*A failed student*, 1917) constantly echoes Novalis and Eichendorff, and its many extracts from the hero's lyrical diary recall *Werther*. Erich, the student drop-out, is surrounded by crass philistines; he responds ardently to nature, but despises the worn-out cult of the 'Jewish God'; and he is afflicted by insatiable yearning, which he tries to satisfy in erotic experience, in imagination, in industrial labour; finally he looks forward to a destructive war, 'a twilight of humanity, a jubilant annihilation'. The young Goethe is even more clearly echoed in the rhapsodic passages of Goebbels' diary-novel *Michael* (1929), whose student hero denounces the bourgeoisie, Jews, capitalism and liberalism, and maintains that the true German, like himself, is a Faustian soul and a God-seeker. His love for a blonde female student ends when he finds her too bourgeois, and he transfers his devotion to Hitler, in whom he sees a prophet and a strong man who will shape history. Abandoning his studies to become a miner, Michael finds a substitute family in Hitler, Mother Earth, and the German 'Volk'. With its quasi-religious language of striving and redemption, this novel reveals much about the appeal of National Socialism.

This may seem strange company for Hesse, one of the few outspoken pacifists of the First World War. But in adopting the confessional genre, he also retained its ideological implications. His pseudonymous *Demian* (1919) captivated contemporaries by portraying an adolescent questioning conventional values and exploring a dark, hidden side of life. It combines watered-down rhetoric from Nietzsche and Jung (Hesse had undergone Jungian psychoanalysis) with the solipsism of Romantic 'Bildungsromane' like Novalis's *Heinrich von Ofterdingen*. Other characters exist only in relation to the hero, Emil Sinclair, who uses up a series of mentors, internalising their lessons and passing on. Even his mysterious, charismatic schoolmate Demian, after dying in the war, is absorbed into Sinclair's cannibalistic psyche, where his image survives, in the novel's chilling last words, as 'Freund und Führer' (friend and leader). *Der*

Steppenwolf (1927) again recalls the Romantic novel by the elaborate narrative framework surrounding the self-explorations that its depressive hero, Harry Haller, conducts via the virtual reality of the Magic Theatre. He learns to laugh at his own solemnity, but also tests himself through a series of fantasy-experiences culminating in murder. Though not condoned, murder here again features as the ultimate in authenticity, because in it one confronts the dark side of one's personality and the horror of life: 'Life is always frightful. We cannot help it, yet we are responsible', says the Mozart figure, thus banalising what for Kafka had been a scarcely endurable tragic insight. Egotism likewise structures *Das Glasperlenspiel* (*The glass bead game*, 1943), set in the remote future. Here the life of the mind has been translated into a cerebral game, played by an élite order of initiates, whose object is to produce aesthetically satisfying patterns. The hero, Josef Knecht, having risen to become Master of the Game, tires of its artificiality and longs to experience 'reality', which he identifies with 'risk, difficulty and danger'; he becomes a lowly private tutor to a handsome boy and dies (like a more athletic Aschenbach) while swimming across a cold lake in pursuit of his pupil. Though Hesse was widely revered as a benevolent guru, his imagination maintained a Nietzschean polarity between an unsatisfying aestheticism and an alluringly sensual and violent 'reality'.

The novel as a 'democratic instrument of social criticism' flourished in the hands of Arnold Zweig (1887–1968) and Lion Feuchtwanger (1884–1958). Zweig, long active as a Socialist and Zionist writer, achieved success with *Der Streit um den Sergeanten Grischa* (*The dispute over Sergeant Grischa*, 1927), based on his wartime experiences on the Eastern Front. This centres on an unsuccessful campaign to prevent the unjust execution of a Russian prisoner of war, but introduces a rich cast of characters, including a sardonic portrait of General Ludendorff as 'Albert von Schlieffenzahn'. Arguably, Grischa himself is too much the object of others' good (and bad) intentions; but Lenore Wahl, the heroine of *Junge Frau von 1914* (1931) is roused to activity by the war, especially when her lover, coarsened by military service, rapes her and obliges her to procure an abortion. The rape scene is presented from both viewpoints. Again, Lenore's enforced self-emancipation takes place against a detailed social background: that of wartime Berlin, where assimilated Jews, typified by her father, reluctantly learn that Germany regards them merely as useful aliens. Zweig drew the obvious conclusion by setting his next novel, *De Vriendt kehrt heim* (*De Vriendt returns home*, 1932), in Palestine, and showing European Jewish settlers forging a new identity by fighting against insurrectionary Arabs. The portrayal of Arabs is problematic, as was Zweig's attitude to Palestine: exiled there, he felt out of place, and he returned to (East) Germany the day the State of Israel was proclaimed.

Perhaps Zweig's finest novel is *Das Beil von Wandsbek* (*The axe of Wandsbek*, 1947), a study, set in Nazi Germany, of the moral insensitivity that can lead decent people into brutality. A Hamburg butcher whose trade is slack agrees to earn extra money by executing four Socialists. When word gets out, the neighbours boycott his shop. This ostracism, combined with their growing doubts about Nazism, drives the couple to suicide. Zweig allows the fatal axe to accumulate supernatural associations without detriment to his dense portrayal of Hamburg in 1937–8. He shows the range of attitudes to Nazism among ordinary people: opportunists, fanatics, disillusioned Socialists, and good-hearted but malleable people who believed Hitler's promises and are gradually becoming disillusioned. A sub-plot among intellectuals conveys Zweig's understanding of Nazism. Being committed, like Schnitzler and Freud, to the rational analysis of irrational phenomena, Zweig blames Nietzsche as a precursor of Nazism and finds the key to Hitler's character in Freud's analysis of the paranoid fantasies of Judge Schreber.

Feuchtwanger excels in exploring ambition. His historical novel *Jud Süß* (1925), on the rise and fall of the eighteenth-century financier and politician Josef Süss Oppenheimer, was inspired by the assassination of Rathenau, but bears at most an indirect relationship to his own times. At the centre of the restless political intrigue stands the gigantic figure of Süss, a Jew who, like Rathenau, attains wealth and power in Gentile society but always remains insecure. His downfall and imprisonment lead him to a strange kind of sanctity. Still better is *Erfolg* (*Success*, 1930), which vividly evokes Munich in the years 1921–4, leading up to the failed putsch by Hitler, here portrayed as 'Rupert Kutzner', leader of the 'Wahrhaft Deutsche'. The novel focuses on a case of politically motivated injustice. Feuchtwanger skilfully pilots a sizeable cast of memorable characters through many short, dense, dramatic scenes, interspersed with occasional detached commentary, and thus builds up a vivid picture of Munich and its social and political turmoils. In 1933 Feuchtwanger went into exile. His major exile work is another study of ambition and power, the *Josephus* trilogy (1932–45), set in ancient Rome and Palestine. The third part includes a memorable portrayal of the Emperor Domitian, who radiates the icy fascination of absolute power. This may well convey Feuchtwanger's considered response to Stalin, whom he met (and shamefully adulated) in 1937.

Another underrated realist is Franz Werfel (1890–1945). His novel *Barbara oder die Frömmigkeit* (*Barbara or piety*, 1929), though occasionally mawkish, centres on a stirring account of the revolutionary turmoil in post-war Vienna, in which Werfel was uncharacteristically involved. But his masterpiece is *Die vierzig Tage des Musa Dagh* (*The forty days of Musa Dagh*, 1933), based on the true story of how a small Armenian community successfully, though with appalling hardships, resisted the Turkish genocide which destroyed most of their people. Its central figure, Gabriel Bagradian, is an expatriate intellectual who discovers his life's meaning by rejoining and helping his nation; but he is never fully accepted, and meets a lonely death as his compatriots are rescued. Far from endorsing 'völkisch' simplicities about blood and soil, the novel conducts a stringent and convincing inquiry into the actual conditions of community and leadership. Werfel rivals Feuchtwanger's political insight when he confronts the German Armenophile Johannes Lepsius with the ruthless Young Turk leader Enver Pasha, who displays 'the Arctic face of power'. Of the many dialogues with power in German literature, from Goethe's *Egmont* and Schiller's *Don Carlos* onwards, this is among the most gripping.

The modernist fiction of Hermann Broch (1886–1951) begins with the trilogy *Die Schlafwandler* (*The sleepwalkers*, 1931–2), an attempt to analyse the period from 1888 to 1918. Yet its typical characters – the romantic lieutenant Pasenow, the accountant Esch with his anarchic utopian fantasies, and the calculating opportunist Huguenau – never assume a life independent of their author's theses. In its third volume, Broch tried to sidestep problems of narrative integration by telling several parallel stories illustrating aspects of contemporary anomie, and by including long, undigested expositions of his version of cultural pessimism. The result is one of modernism's most remarkable museum pieces. More ambitious still is *Der Tod des Vergil* (*The death of Vergil*, 1945), recounting the last eighteen hours of the poet's life in lyrical prose. This exercise in stream of consciousness, with sentences three pages long, has ardent admirers; but a style that relies, not on the energies of syntax, but on the accumulation of compound adjectives and participial phrases, easily becomes wearisome, and in Vergil's long dialogue with Augustus the Emperor lacks the presence of Feuchtwanger's Domitian or Werfel's Enver. Far more readable is the novel now known as *Die Verzauberung* (*The spell*, written 1937), an allegory of Nazism, in which a foreign agitator comes to dominate an Austrian mountain village, persecutes scapegoats, and leads a hysterical crowd in a ceremony of human sacrifice. Its insights into mass psychology make this novel a worthy counterpart to Thomas Mann's *Mario und der Zauberer*. Doubts arise, though, when we notice that Broch has adapted the 'Heimatroman' genre to provide a timeless natural setting, evoked with impressive lyricism; for the genre's antihistorical assumptions weaken the allegory by making his village dictator seem a brief disturbance to an everlasting cyclical order.

Although the enhanced realism of Heimito von Doderer (1896–1966) is best seen in his huge novels *Die Strudlhofstiege* (*The Strudlhof steps*, 1951) and *Die Dämonen* (*The demons*, 1956), he began writing in the

1920s, and the genesis of *Die Dämonen* goes back to 1929. Like Musil (whose work he perhaps enviously disliked), Doderer is concerned with obsession. He contrasts politically or sexually obsessed characters, enmeshed in a 'second reality', with those who retain their 'Apperzeptionsfähigkeit', their openness to experience, their awareness of the world around them. His most substantial pre-war novel, *Ein Mord den jeder begeht* (*A murder everyone commits*, 1938), has a thoroughly ordinary hero who awakes to life by investigating the violent death of his sister-in-law, and finally discovers that he himself unwittingly caused it. This combines the familiar theme of authenticity – self-knowledge means realising that one is a murderer – with a disturbing moral incoherence that may be connected with Doderer's flirtation with Nazism. He joined the Party in 1933 and left it, courageously, in 1938. Thereafter he rejected politics, admitting that this was itself a conservative stance.

Doderer's two great novels are above all richly sensuous portrayals of Vienna. The detective-story plots are mere pretexts for mobilising vast numbers of characters from different settings. *Die Strudlhofstiege* is named after an ornate stairway, just north of central Vienna, that connects two levels and thus serves both as a governing metaphor and the scene of crucial episodes. *Die Dämonen* leads up to the riot outside the Palace of Justice in 1927, which Doderer implausibly attributes to an anarchic mob and to the machinations of the criminal Meisgeier, who represents the same demonised lower-class type as Musil's Moosbrugger and Hofmannsthal's Gotthelf (in *Andreas*). But Doderer's questionable political judgement is a trivial fault compared to his evocation, through initially bewildering but carefully planned narrative convolutions, of innumerable intersecting lives in minute and persuasive detail.

Many novelists of the 1920s, reacting against Expressionist rhetoric, practised a dispassionate, critical realism that was labelled 'Neue Sachlichkeit' ('New sobriety'). 'Nothing is more startling than the simple truth, nothing is more exotic than the world around us, nothing is more imaginative than sobriety', wrote the Communist journalist Egon Erwin Kisch (1885–1948) in *Der rasende Reporter* (*The galloping reporter*, 1930). Diverse, highly readable novels resulted. The fate of the unemployed is recounted with cynical comedy by Erich Kästner (1899–1974) in *Fabian* (1931), and with humour and pathos by 'Hans Fallada' (Rudolf Ditzen, 1893–1947) in *Kleiner Mann, was nun?* (*What now, little man?*, 1932), where the reliance on lifelike dialogue recalls Fontane. The journalist 'Gabriele Tergit' (Elise Reifenberg, 1894–1982) amusingly describes the power of the media in *Käsebier erobert den Kurfürstendamm* (*Käsebier conquers the Kurfürstendamm*, 1931). Some novels transfer their focus from the individual to the social group. This applies to *Jahrgang 1902* (*Class of 1902*, 1928) by Ernst Glaeser (1902–63), which depicts the war-fever of 1914 from the viewpoint of a typical schoolboy, and to the master-piece of 'Neue Sachlichkeit', *Union der festen Hand* (*Union of the firm hand*, 1931) by 'Erik Reger' (Hermann Dannenberger, 1893–1954). Focusing on the Communist worker Adam Griguszies and his spirited sister Paula, and a group of industrialists identifiable as Krupp, Stinnes and colleagues, Reger gives a lively, factual, and sardonic account of industrial struggles in the Ruhr from the revolutionary upheavals of 1918 to the economic crisis ten years later.

The new sobriety found employment in belated accounts of the First World War. Many war memoirs were chauvinistic, bombastic and clichéd; Zweig's *Grischa* initiated a flood of anti-war books which tried to recap-ture the ordinary soldier's inglorious experience. *Krieg* (*War*, 1928) by 'Ludwig Renn' (Arnold Vieth von Golssenau, 1898–1979) is a stoical, understated book which emphasises war's confusion more than its horror. The blunt truthfulness practised by 'Erich Maria Remarque' (Paul Remark, 1898–1970), in *Im Westen nichts Neues* (1929), which became world-famous as *All quiet on the Western Front*, makes crudity into a virtue: nobody can forget Remarque's description of being under fire. In *Heeresbericht* (*Army report*, 1930), Edlef Köppen (1893–1939) uses montage to juxtapose authentic documents (newspaper extracts, military proclamations) with the disillusioning frontline experiences, recounted in a deflating, factual style, which drive his hero into madness.

Thanks to his refreshingly light and simple style, Joseph Roth (1894–1939) was misleadingly identified with 'Neue Sachlichkeit'. In fact Roth, a Jew born on the eastern edge of the Habsburg Empire who attained fame as a journalist and novelist in 1920s Berlin, cultivates an ironic under-statement which keeps under control a complex of powerful emotions including mockery, nostalgia and near-despair. In *Hotel Savoy* (1924), where the chaos of post-war Eastern Europe finds compelling symbolic expression; in *Hiob* (*Job*, 1930), an acerbic and affectionate portrayal of Russian Jewry in dissolution; and in his masterpiece, *Radetzkymarsch* (1932), the Empire represents a supra-national, quasi-religious ideal which is already being undermined by internal corruption and the 'new religion' of nationalism. Another superb ironist, Siegfried Kracauer (1889–1966), is best known for his epoch-making history of German film, *From Caligari to Hitler* (1948), written in penurious American exile; the critical and sociological essays he wrote as a journalist on the *Frankfurter Zeitung* are still underrated, and his brilliant novels, *Ginster* (1928) and *Georg* (com-pleted 1933, published 1973), are scarcely known. The semi-autobiograph-ical *Ginster*, especially, is saturated in an elusive irony of which the hero, a timid, unassuming architect who, unfit for frontline service, nevertheless has to undergo military training during the war, is less the target than the instrument. The innocent, puzzled honesty of Ginster's responses undercuts the confident clichés of bourgeois convention and jingoistic nationalism more fatally than any polemic.

With Elias Canetti (1905–94), irony hardens into grotesque satire. His novel *Die Blendung* (*The blinding*, 1935), drawing on traditional satire of obsession from Büchner and Gogol to Heinrich Mann and Musil, centres on a harsh, pedantic and sexless scholar, Peter Kien, who falls victim to the manic greed and violence of his servants. Expelled from his arid, book-filled seclusion, Kien roams through an unspecified urban underworld redolent of Vienna, and finally incinerates his library and himself. This bitter and painful comedy unmasks the bankruptcy of academic humanism. As an alternative Canetti proposes the empathy practised (admittedly with imperfect success) by Peter's psychiatrist brother and illustrated by the self-effacing narrator who admits us in turn to the self-enclosed consciousness of each main character. By thus loosening the armour-plating of solipsism, the novel becomes for Canetti the supreme instrument of empathy. Conversely, the ultimate solipsist is the totalitarian ruler who annihilates masses of people to satisfy his power-lust. *Masse und Macht* (*Crowds and power*, 1960), Canetti's contribution to the Central European tradition of polymathy best represented by Spengler, culminates by juxtaposing the paranoid despot Mohammed Tughlak and the solipsistic fantasist Judge Schreber. This impressive study is of course an indirect analysis of the genocidal despot who drove Canetti and many others into exile.

Literature and Nazism

The sympathy of major writers for Fascism is a European phenomenon, illustrated by Pound, Yeats, Céline, Marinetti and Hamsun, which still awaits explanation. In Germany and Austria, two types of right-wing writer welcomed Nazism: the backward-looking and the forward-looking.

Among the backward-looking are most authors of 'Heimatliteratur', the regional literature, praising peasant life and decrying modernity, already illustrated from Polenz and Frenssen. This fiction is hostile to liberal individualism, subordinating its characters to the overriding authority of the narrator and presenting them primarily as links in a chain of generations. 'The peasant is everlasting like the earth itself, for he lives through his race [Geschlecht]', says Karl Heinrich Waggerl (1897–1973) in a typical 'Heimatroman', *Schweres Blut* (*Thick blood*, 1931), which won the Austrian Staatspreis in 1934 because it suited the reactionary politics of the corporate state. The interminable bestseller by Hans Grimm (1875–1959), *Volk ohne Raum* (*Nation without space*, 1926), argues that

Germany's farming class should be preserved by colonial expansion. It illustrates the tendency in extremist literature to discard fiction altogether: the settings are stereotypical, the speeches free from dialect; the protagonist, who emigrates from Lower Saxony to South-West Africa, has no inner life, regarding himself as simply part of his ancestral community, but serves to typify the Germans' misfortunes and voice his creator's geopolitical theses. This documentary tendency is taken further by Artur Dinter (1876–1948) in another bestseller, *Die Sünde wider das Blut* (*The sin against the blood*, 1917), a crazed anti-Semitic diatribe which is often unintentionally funny; it includes ill-integrated discourses on racial science supported by pseudo-factual appendices. These works exemplify a vast body of 'völkisch' writing whose many readers were receptive to Nazism.

While appealing to this constituency by its regressive rhetoric, Nazism also attracted the modern-minded by its rhetoric of crisis and renewal. The important anti-liberal political theorist Carl Schmitt (1888–1985), who joined the Nazi Party in May 1933, argued in *Der Begriff des Politischen* (*The concept of the political*, 1927) that politics depends on crisis and on an existential distinction between friend and foe. A similar awareness of crisis ('Not'), alongside a conception of knowledge as confrontation with existential peril, was urged by Heidegger in his speech of April 1933, 'Die Selbstbehauptung der deutschen Universität' ('The self-assertion of the German university'), marking his installation as Rector of Freiburg University. Whether Nazi leanings are already discernible in the reflections on death, fate and authenticity of Heidegger's *Sein und Zeit* (*Being and time*, 1927) is still under debate. The reality of Nazism soon disillusioned both men, but while Schmitt made ever shabbier concessions to his masters, Heidegger made an arguably escapist turn to contemplating humankind's timeless situation as 'shepherd of Being' and the revelatory power of art.

After the Nazi takeover, Goebbels established the Reichskulturkammer (Reich Chamber of Culture) which, through its subdivisions, energetically organised the arts for propaganda, but showed little interest in modernism. The Reichsschrifttumskammer (Reich Chamber of Literature) favoured the already existing literature of 'blood and soil', but initiated no new developments. Expressionist and Cubist painting was condemned as 'degenerate', confiscated and sometimes destroyed. However, Goebbels did promote the cinema, often for such propagandist films as Hans Steinhoff's celebration of a heroic Nazi martyr, *Hitlerjunge Quex* (1933), and Veit Harlan's *Jud Süß* (1940), an anti-Semitic travesty of Feuchtwanger's novel.

Analogous attempts were made to create cultic, celebratory forms of theatre. Instead of dramatic conflict, we have theatrical unanimity modelling national unity. Thus Hanns Johst's showpiece Nazi play *Schlageter* (1933) is pseudo-dramatic, because the speakers never really disagree. It culminates in the apotheosis of its hero, the Freikorps fighter Albert Leo Schlageter, who was shot in 1923 for terrorism in the French-occupied Ruhr. Among earlier cultic forms, the medieval mystery-play (already adapted for an anti-capitalist critique by Hofmannsthal in *Jedermann*) was revived by Richard Euringer (1891–1953) in *Deutsche Passion 1933* (1933), where Christ's death and resurrection are re-enacted by the nameless German soldier who promises the German people redemption through work. Originally a radio play, this soon joined the repertoire of the 'Thingspiel' movement, which presented dramas in open-air amphitheatres with large-scale audience participation. Though the term comes from the ancient Germanic word for an assembly, the 'Thingspiel' had antecedents in the mass spectacles staged by Socialist workers and scripted by Toller, among others, in the Weimar Republic. Eberhard Wolfgang Möller (1906–72), a close colleague of Goebbels, created its outstanding example, *Das Frankenburger Würfelspiel* (*The Frankenburg game of dice*, 1936), which inaugurated the 1936 Olympic Games. Amid echoes of Aeschylus' *Oresteia* and Kaiser's *Die Bürger von Calais*, authorities from the Emperor downwards are tried before a divine court for a massacre of Protestant peasants in 1625. In dignified verse (unlike Euringer's doggerel), and without overt Nazism, the play forcefully arraigns cynical oppressors. Contemporary parallels, though inadvertent, seem obvious, yet the play was performed repeatedly and criticised only for its religious atmosphere. By 1937, however, the 'Thingspiel' movement had petered out. The only viable forms of Nazi theatre were Hitler's Nuremberg rallies and their filming by Leni Riefenstahl (*Triumph des Willens* (*Triumph of the will*, 1934)).

Forward-looking authors of the right welcomed the supersession of the despised bourgeois era by the Nazi revolution. Yet they also saw history in Nietzschean terms as an eternal recurrence of the same and hence as an aesthetic spectacle. Like Schmitt and Heidegger, they were to find Nazi reality more sordid than their fantasies.

The foremost German representative of fascist modernism is Ernst Jünger (b. 1895). In his war memoir, *In Stahlgewittern* (*In storms of steel*, 1920), he gives a fascinating account of his war service (he was repeatedly wounded and decorated) on the Western Front. The book convinces by its circumstantial detail and by acknowledging, besides the boredom and discomfort of warfare, a range of emotions from compassion to blood-lust. But it entirely ignores the purpose or politics of the War, and it begins to chill when Jünger tells us that the intensity of battle introduced him to 'the depth of trans-personal regions' and initiated him into terror and beyond. *Der Kampf als inneres Erlebnis* (*Combat as inner experience*, 1922) celebrates the primitive thinking of the blood, the ecstasy of destruction, the solidarity of battle-hardened warriors. *Der Arbeiter* (*The worker*, 1932) builds these values into a conception of the imminent future: rejoicing in the downfall of the pampered bourgeoisie and the dissolution of the individual, Jünger prophesies a state composed of dehumanised workers and ruled by an elite of hard men who have regained contact with elemental realities. Meanwhile, Jünger was studying botany and marine biology and cultivating the technique of precise, passionless description that he called 'magic realism', best illustrated in the sketches of *Das abenteuerliche Herz* (*The adventurous heart*, 1929). He remained in Germany after 1933, though he never joined the National Socialist Party and was increasingly repelled by the Nazis' mindless thuggery. In the Second World War he served in the German army, though mostly in occupied Paris.

Jünger expressed his reservations about Nazism in the gripping fantasy-novel *Auf den Marmorklippen* (*On the marble cliffs*, 1939). It recounts, from the viewpoint of a recluse whose devotion to botany represents the life of the spirit, how a highly civilised society is gradually undermined by the machinations of the barbarian Head Forester. The book's allegorical message soon led the authorities to ban it. Yet it shows no conversion to humanism. The narrator displays minimal concern for others; his exact yet loveless botanical studies are disturbingly similar to the cold, god-like detachment with which the barbarians look down on peaceful civilisation. At the very heart of darkness, when the narrator happens on a forest clearing where a dwarf is flaying corpses, he comments that 'life's melody played its deepest, its darkest string', and the final burning of the cities has the 'beauty of destruction'. The narrator watches unperturbed as his life's work goes up in flames; after all, he says repeatedly, destruction and renewal form a natural process. All this implies an alliance between aestheticism and vitalism.

A similar alliance exists in the work of Gottfried Benn. Too much of Benn's poetry disguises paucity of content behind an affected array of neologisms, foreign phrases, and scientific terms. His best work, however, conveys a deep cultural despair. The aggressive, anti-bourgeois ugliness of his Expressionist poems is counterbalanced by a yearning to escape from consciousness altogether into the condition of primeval slime or primitive animality ('Gesänge' ('Songs', 1913)), and from cerebral activity into 'the sea's deep, redeeming blue' ('Untergrundbahn' ('Subway', 1913)). Influenced by Nietzsche and Spengler, Benn takes a melancholy view of history as a perpetual cycle sustained by myths. The myth of Dionysus, he asserts, is still dormant in the Occidental brain ('Orphische Zellen' ('Orphic cells', 1927)). As Germany's crisis deepened, he expressed this view in haunting, cryptic, musical poems such as 'Sieh die Sterne, die Fänge' ('See the stars, the fangs', 1927) and 'Dennoch die Schwerter halten' ('Yet hold the swords', 1933). 'Am Brückenwehr' ('At the Weir', 1934) welcomes the 'new power' as yet more water rushing over the underlying granite.

Benn welcomed Germany's new power with the radio broadcast 'Der neue Staat und die Intellektuellen' ('The new state and the intellectuals', April 1933), which denounced the liberal intelligentsia as unprepared for 'sacrifice and self-surrender to the totality, the state, the race, the immanent'. The essay 'Dorische Kunst' ('Doric art', 1934), another document of Germany's long love-affair with Greece, sets out an amoral, pseudo-scientific conception of power and a modernist conception of art as pure form, ignoring all of human life that lies between. Meanwhile Benn accepted the vice-presidency of the National Writers' Union, and in March 1934 welcomed the Futurist poet Marinetti, president of the corresponding body in Fascist Italy. Disillusioned, however, by Hitler's massacre of Röhm's SA, Benn withdrew into service as an army doctor, which he called 'the aristocratic form of emigration'. His privately circulated poem 'Monolog' ('Monologue', 1943) uses tortuous, often cloacal imagery to denounce the Nazis principally for their vulgarity: as a recantation, it is no more convincing than *Auf den Marmorklippen*. After the war Benn regained fame with his volume *Statische Gedichte* (*Static poems*, 1948). These poems, written in the previous ten years, can be movingly elegiac when personal, but are less convincing when they attempt cosmic despair (as in the pretentious 'Verlorenes Ich' ('Lost I')). Nevertheless, they appealed to a largely conservative post-war audience anxious to catch up with modernism. Benn's lecture 'Probleme der Lyrik' ('Problems of lyric poetry', 1951) describes the poetic word as 'the phallus of the spirit', and poetry as the product of narrowly intellectual activity but without intellectual content. His insistence on a cold, cerebral art, besides recalling the aesthetic views of Tonio Kröger, surely helps to explain the pervasive melancholy of his poetry. More generally, his example shows that a fascist modernism must finally reduce art to a vacuous aestheticism.

Similar but sadder is the case of the Austrian poet Josef Weinheber (1892–1945). The cultural pessimism of his *Adel und Untergang* (*Nobility and decline*, 1934) accompanies a linguistic purism derived from Kraus and a cult of the pure, 'timeless' poem which should be 'rigid' (see 'Zeitloses Lied' ('Timeless song'), with its compelling Benn-like rhythms, and 'Pro domo'). His poems in classical metres now seem less rewarding than the collection, partly in Viennese dialect, *Wien wörtlich* (*Vienna word for word*, 1935). Here Weinheber rejoins a tradition of topographical poetry represented especially by Ferdinand von Saar's *Wiener Elegien* (*Viennese elegies*, 1893). Beneath the charm of Weinheber's poems runs an undercurrent of bitterness and loneliness, often poignant (as in 'Ballade vom kleinen Mann' ('Ballad of the little man')); and his Vienna, even more than Doderer's, is a fragile attempt to construct a 'German-Austrian' identity that obscures the Jewish presence. This becomes uncomfortably clear when the dialect persona in 'Wienerisch' complains that the Jews, having bought out the old nobility, are now corrupting the language, and 'language is blood' ('Sprach, des is Bluat'). Weinheber joined the Nazi Party in 1931, and received high honours from the Nazi authorities. He partially repented of his political actions in the fine poem 'Mit fünfzig Jahren' ('At the age of fifty'; written 1942, posthumously published in *Hier ist das Wort* (*Here is the word*, 1947)), but by then it was too late. As the Russians approached Vienna, Weinheber committed suicide.

Exile and inner emigration

Hitler's accession to power sent many writers into exile. Initially, the more prosperous settled especially on the Riviera, the poorer in Paris, London or Prague. Some reached the USA, where they hugely enriched cultural and intellectual life but often suffered terrible insecurity and loneliness. Communists seeking refuge in the USSR met frosty treatment: even Becher and Lukács narrowly escaped the gulag. As Germany conquered Europe, many writers killed themselves in despair: Tucholsky, Toller, Benjamin, Hasenclever, Carl Einstein, Ernst Weiss . . . Even in remote Brazil, Stefan Zweig (1882–1942), the prolific author of 'Novellen' and biographies, now best remembered for his autobiography *Die Welt von gestern* (*The world of yesterday*, 1942), felt driven to suicide.

In such dark times, novelists and critics found special value in the realist tradition. For Lukács, only realism could present a total picture of society and thus reveal the dialectical conflict between progressive and reactionary forces. But the criticism Lukács wrote in Soviet exile, notably *The historical novel* (first published in Russian, 1938) and the essays later collected in *German Realists of the nineteenth century* (1952), reveals a narrowly conservative taste which provoked the utopian Marxist philosopher Ernst Bloch (1885–1977) to champion the emancipatory potential of Expressionism. Their debate, conducted in 1938 in the Moscow exile journal *Das Wort* (*The word*), was also a struggle for power, as Brecht's comments in his *Arbeitsjournal* (*Work journal*) make clear. Benjamin's undogmatic, modernist sensibility now makes him seem a more sympathetic Marxist critic; but though his famous essay 'Das Kunstwerk im Zeitalter seiner mechanischen Reproduzierbarkeit' ('The work of art in the age of mechanical reproduction', 1936) maintains that modern art has lost its sacral aura and should be politicised, other essays of the thirties, notably that on Kafka (1934), show him returning to his earlier messianism.

A defence of realism more convincing than Lukács's, and a religious outlook less eccentric than Benjamin's, appear in one of the supreme exile masterpieces, *Mimesis: Dargestellte Wirklichkeit in der abendländischen Literatur* (*Mimesis: the representation of reality in Western literature*, 1946), written in Istanbul by the philologist and critic Erich Auerbach (1892–1957). Through a series of stylistic analyses, Auerbach composed an elegy for a cultural tradition, running from Homer and the Bible to Proust and Woolf, that had terminated in barbarism. His conception of tragic realism, derived from his Christian humanism and best exemplified from the New Testament, suggests the deficiencies of secular liberalism when confronted with catastrophe.

Novelists likewise returned to the past in order to defend humanism. Thomas Mann's biblical tetralogy *Joseph und seine Brüder* (*Joseph and his brothers*, 1933–43) attempts to reappropriate myth from its fascist abusers. It presents the story of Jacob and Joseph as a humanist comedy, ending in reunion and reconciliation and ascribed to a playful God who is clearly conceived in the image of the omniscient narrator. The ancient Near East is entrancingly evoked, but violence and grief are kept at an ironic distance that gives humanism too easy a triumph. Heinrich Mann's ambitious novels about the 'people's king' Henri IV of France, *Die Jugend des Königs Henri Quatre* and *Die Vollendung des Königs Henri Quatre* (*The youth* and *The perfecting of King Henri IV*, 1935 and 1938), are thoroughly researched but thinly imagined: though fitfully interesting as cloak-and-dagger romance, their dull style and cardboard characterisation prevent their hero from convincingly foreshadowing democratic humanism. The account of the St Bartholomew's Night massacre, though, has a sombre immediacy absent from Thomas Mann's leisurely epic.

Life in exile, with its squabbles, poverty and political temptations, was most vividly, though somewhat rosily, portrayed by Feuchtwanger in *Exil* (*Exile*, 1940). War soon provided a new subject, best exploited by the Soviet exile Theodor Plievier (1892–1955) in *Stalingrad* (1945), where some epic moments relieve the grim portrayal of the German army being ground down by cold, disease and despair.

Exiles' understanding of contemporary Germany was clouded by distance, wishful thinking, and the underestimation of Hitler that we have seen in Brecht's exile plays. Typically, Feuchtwanger's entertaining novel *Der falsche Nero* (*The false Nero*, 1936) represents him as a plebeian impostor. An exception is *Der Augenzeuge* (*The eyewitness*; written 1938, first published as *Ich – der Augenzeuge* in 1963), by the Prague novelist Ernst Weiss (1882–1940): the narrator encounters 'A. H.' in a military hospital in 1918, and shows remarkable insight into his charisma and its sources. Thomas Mann's essay 'Bruder Hitler' ('Brother Hitler', 1939) perceptively explores Hitler's perverted artistic temperament. The Communist 'Anna Seghers' (Nelly Reiling, 1900–83), in *Das siebte Kreuz* (*The seventh cross*, 1942), stirringly describes an escape from the brutalities of a concentration camp; she does not really need the laboured symbolism announced in the title. *Mephisto* (1936), a chatty *roman à clef* by Klaus Mann (1906–49), centres on an actor whose inner hollowness enables him to excel in the role of Mephisto, and whose opportunism brings him to precarious fame under the patronage of Hermann Goering. Mann provides a bitterly satirical picture of the German cultural élite adjusting to Nazism; but, despite his title, he does not rise from satire to myth. The atmosphere of creeping totalitarianism is more finely caught in Horváth's *Jugend ohne Gott* (*Young people without God*, 1938), a simply written school story depicting the moral pressures placed by Nazism on a teacher, who senses the onset of cold inhumanity, 'the age of the fish'.

'Inner emigration', within Germany but detached from Nazism, seemed possible for many decent writers, despite the moral problem of trying to live under a tyranny without active or at least passive complicity. Such writers were virtually obliged to retreat from the present, either in space or time. Ernst Wiechert (1887–1950), an opponent of Nazism who spent several months in a concentration camp, on his release wrote *Das einfache Leben* (*The simple life*, 1939), in which an ex-navy officer retires from post-war modernity into the pastoral seclusion of East Prussia. Yet a Stifterian idyll hardly seems adequate to the 1930s, while the Goethean humanism of Hans Carossa (1878–1956), whose pleasant *Eine Kindheit* (*A childhood*, 1922) was thought a masterpiece two generations ago, now looks tarnished by his brief co-operation with Nazism. Novels by Christian humanists interrogate power in remote historical settings. Reinhold Schneider (1903–58) tried in *Las Casas vor Karl V.* (1938) to show the power of penitence in protesting against the atrocities committed by the Spaniards in the New World; but his story's impact owes more to its sources than to its artistry. In his far superior, because dramatically constructed novel *Der Großtyrann und das Gericht* (*The despot and the court*, 1935), Werner Bergengruen (1892–1962) resorts to medieval Italy. A mysterious murder occasions an inquiry into the relations of power and justice that demands comparison with Shakespeare's *Measure for Measure*. The novel's cerebral quality is justified by the great concluding trial scene, in which moral revelations come as devastating *coups de théâtre*.

Many writers in 'inner emigration' expressed themselves in relatively innocuous lyric poetry or in secret diaries. Nazism did not hamper the nature poetry of Wilhelm Lehmann (1882–1968; see especially *Der grüne Gott* (*The green god*, 1942)), though disgust with the regime seems to have stifled the greater talent that his older colleague Oskar Loerke

(1884–1941) had shown best in *Pansmusik* (*Pan's music*, 1929). A more varied poet is 'Gertrud Kolmar' (Gertrud Chodziesner, 1894–1943), who died in Auschwitz. Besides the animal poetry of 'Tierträume' ('Animal dreams'), she dramatises various women's voices in the cycle 'Weibliches Bildnis' ('Female portrait') and the French Revolution in 'Robespierre'. Much of her poetry first appeared posthumously as *Das lyrische Werk* (*The lyrical work*, 1955). The outstanding diarist is Theodor Haecker (1879–1945), a literary disciple of Kraus and Kierkegaard, who belonged to the Munich circle of Catholic intellectuals that inspired the anti-Nazi leafleting campaign of the 'White Rose'. Haecker's *Tag- und Nachtbücher* (*Day and night books*), kept from 1939 till shortly before his death, consist of profound theological meditations, especially concerning the evil that he saw temporarily triumphant in Nazi Germany.

The pre-eminent exile novel, and the most searching retrospect on the period leading to Hitler, is Thomas Mann's *Doktor Faustus* (written 1943–5, published 1947). It centres on the biography of the composer Adrian Leverkühn, who typifies the Nietzschean and, according to Mann, quintessentially German urge to transgress conventional norms, to explore frightening and exhilarating regions of experience, and to despise ordinary people. For Mann, the German catastrophe requires a theological perspective: Leverkühn's breakthrough into twelve-tone composition is attributed to his Faustian pact with the Devil, who promises him unrivalled creative powers on condition that he shall not love anyone. His isolation is symbolised by his syphilitic infection which (as with Nietzsche) produces spells of manic energy followed ultimately by madness. He also recalls Nietzsche when he cynically questions the value of humanist culture. Although Leverkühn is remote from politics, his Nietzschean scepticism and the magnificent inhumanity of his music raise the problem of fascist modernism. Mann juxtaposes a description of Leverkühn's grandiose compositions with reports of discussions among Munich intellectuals (all based on actual neo-conservatives) who regard the impending barbarism as an aesthetic thrill.

Leverkühn's biography, however, is recounted by his friend, the decent but plodding schoolmaster Serenus Zeitblom, who represents a rather impoverished humanism. This narrative device not only juxtaposes two aspects of Germany but ensures continual dramatic tension while keeping Leverkühn partly mysterious. As Leverkühn was supposedly born in 1885 and Zeitblom begins his narrative in 1943, we move between the German past and its present consequences: the bombing of German cities, the Normandy landings, and the liberation of concentration camps. In contrast to Leverkühn's uncompromising modernism, Zeitblom's is a realist narrative densely populated by often vivid characters. Thus Mann acknowledges both the technical accomplishments of modernism and its ready alliance with the inhuman, while demonstrating his commitment to the humane values implicit in realist fiction. He also uses the myth of Faust to explore the paradox with which this chapter began: that the intellectual daring and moral strenuousness, the propensity for crisis, peril and self-sacrifice, which are illustrated in some of Germany's highest achievements, could also be degraded into corrupt rhetoric and criminal actions that led to barbarism and disaster.

8

The literature of the German Democratic Republic (1945–1990)

Helen Fehervary

The return of the exiles (1945–1949)

East German literature was born out of the grief and desperate hopes of a generation of writers for whom modernism and politics were intertwined. Some of them – Anna Seghers, Bertolt Brecht, Arnold Zweig, Friedrich Wolf, Johannes R. Becher – were children of the Wilhelmine bourgeoisie who had become internationally renowned during the Weimar Republic. Others – Eduard Claudius, Hans Marchwitza, Willi Bredel, Adam Scharrer – had come from the working class and began writing about production within the worker correspondent movements of the twenties. Still others – the poets Erich Arendt, Stephan Hermlin, Peter Huchel; the novelists Erwin Strittmatter and Stefan Heym; the playwright Alfred Matusche – first established themselves after World War II. They all devoted themselves after Hitler's downfall to the creation of a humanistic, anti-fascist literature which would prevail in the German Democratic Republic for forty years from its official foundation in 1949.

History was not to be on their side. Their childhood years had coincided with the height of German military expansionism. With the suffering and chaos caused by World War I, which these writers experienced as young adults, many of them as soldiers, they willingly surrendered their nationalistic inheritance and became cosmopolitans. In the aftermath of the revolutions in Russia, as well as the failed German revolutions in which a number of them participated, they became committed socialists and communists. They identified with the European avant-garde movements of the time and participated in some of the most fascinating artistic and intellectual projects of the 1920s. In 1933 most of these writers were blacklisted by the National Socialists. Some were arrested and imprisoned. Others were able to escape, often to Paris, which was the centre of the popular front coalition of leftist parties struggling against the spread of fascism across Europe. Many worked with the underground resistance in Germany and fought for the Republic in the Spanish Civil War. In this spirit they created the great literary testimonies of anti-fascist resistance: Friedrich Wolf, *Professor Mamlock* (1934) and *Floridsdorf* (1935);

Seghers, *Der Weg durch den Februar* (*The way through February*, 1935), *Die Rettung* (The rescue, 1937), *Das siebte Kreuz* (*The seventh cross*, 1942); Brecht, *Die Rundköpfe und die Spitzköpfe* (*The roundheads and the pointed heads*, 1933), *Die Gewehre der Frau Carrar* (*Señora Carrar's rifles*, 1937), *Furcht und Elend des Dritten Reichs* (*Terror and misery in the Third Reich*, 1938), and the Svendborg poems (1938).

No one foresaw that the Nazi revolution from the right would prove more appealing to masses of Germans than the left-wing politics of internationalism. The crushing of the Social Democratic Party (SPD) and Communist Party (KPD) resistance during the early years of the Third Reich was equally unexpected. The late thirties brought a nadir of progressive hopes: the defeat of the Spanish Republic, the failure of the popular front, the outbreak of World War II, the German invasion of France, and the loss of Paris as a centre of anti-fascist activity. The news of purges against Bolsheviks and 'fellow travellers' in the Soviet Union, followed by the Stalin–Hitler Pact, shattered the faith of many in the Stalinist version of socialism. Increasingly fearful, isolated, and narrowly escaping death during their flight from Nazi-dominated Europe at the outbreak of the war, German writers fled to such remote and never entirely secure corners of the world as Moscow, New York, Los Angeles, Palestine and Mexico City. At the same time, they became objects of suspicion and surveillance as the early signs of Cold War tensions between the Allies intensified.

By the end of the war a number of prominent writers from the Expressionist and Weimar generation had died. Those who survived had lost not only these contemporaries, but friends and relatives in Gestapo prisons and concentration camps, in Soviet purges, and in the war. To name only a few: Stefan Heym's father was killed by the Gestapo; Brecht's son Frank died on the Russian front; Seghers's aged mother and aunt were deported by the Germans and perished; Stephan Hermlin's father died in the concentration camp at Sachsenhausen, his wife in Auschwitz. If Thomas Mann's *Doktor Faustus* mourned the passing of an era of bourgeois culture, the literary texts produced by these exiles were equally eloquent lamentations on the human suffering inflicted by political events: Arnold Zweig's *Das Beil von Wandsbek* (*The axe of Wandsbek*, 1943); Seghers's *Transit* (1944), *Der Ausflug der toten Mädchen* (*The excursion of the dead girls*, 1945), *Die Toten bleiben jung* (*The dead stay young*, 1949); Brecht's *Mutter Courage* (*Mother Courage*, 1939), *Das Leben des Galilei* (*The life of Galileo*, 1944/47), *Antigone-Modell* (1948). With mixed anticipation and apprehension, and via different routes, passports and visas, these writers gradually returned to Germany after the Allied victory. Now well into middle age and weathered by decades of personal and political turmoil, they devoted the remainder of their lives to what would become a remarkable experiment in twentieth-century letters: the attempt to create a literature and culture of humanity out of the moral devastation bequeathed to our century by Hitler.

Becher and the cultural politics of anti-facism (1945–1958)

As President of the Cultural Union and as GDR Minister of Culture from 1954 to 1958, the poet Johannes R. Becher (1891–1958) had enormous influence on the formation of literary life. A Bavarian Catholic and son of a high-ranking jurist, Becher began his literary career as an Expressionist and worked with the pacifist journals *Die Aktion* and *Die weißen Blätter* (*The white pages*) during World War I. Writing Whitman-like hymns to Rosa Luxemburg and Lenin, he joined the Independent Socialist Party in 1917, the Spartacus League in 1918, the KPD (German Communist Party) in 1919. As a leading KPD figure, he became a deputy to the Reichstag in 1925 and presided over the League of Proletarian-Revolutionary Writers (BPRS) from 1928 to 1933. During exile he was influential in forming the League of Anti-Fascist Writers as well as anti-fascist journals in Prague and Paris. In Moscow he worked closely with KPD-leaders and wrote elegiac sonnets on the German homeland inspired by the poetry of Andreas Gryphius and Friedrich Hölderlin. He also completed an auto-biographical novel *Abschied* (*Farewell*) in the style of the *Bildungsroman*, and the Schillerian play *Winterschlacht* (*Winter battle*) about a young soldier whose conversion from Nazi idealism to pacifism ends in his martyrdom on the Russian front. Generations of East German school-children would later read (and in part memorise) these works, along with those of Brecht, Seghers and the German classics. Becher's late poetry con-tinued to revolve around the tension between tragedy and redemption, not least his 'Auferstanden aus Ruinen' ('Risen from the ruins'), which served as the text for the GDR national anthem.

Becher was a strong supporter of Brecht and other modernists, but his own more conservative aesthetic tastes coincided with the type of socialist realism which had been canonised in the Soviet Union since 1934 and dominated GDR cultural policies during the fifties. Both Soviet and GDR policy favoured bourgeois realism as the forerunner of socialist literature, and rejected modernism as the distorted expression of alienation under late capitalism. The stylistic abstraction of Joyce, Kafka and Proust was characterised as western 'decadence', while the novels of late bourgeois humanists such as Thomas and Heinrich Mann provided the link between the European realists of the nineteenth century and socialist art of the present and future. As the alternative to Nazi barbarism, the emphasis on the German cultural heritage as a 'renaissance of humanism' assumed

critical importance. Hence the appeal of Goethe, Schiller and the philosophers of German idealism – as the German *cultural* alternative to the
political ideas of the French Revolution. This conservative heritage – the
outcome of the Enlightenment not as political public sphere but as
culture–provided the model for the official GDR definition of socialist
realism. Accordingly, socialist art in the GDR was not to be the 'political
weapon' it had been for the avant-gardists of the twenties. Rather, in the
spirit of Goethe's repentent Faust or the call to brotherhood at the end of
Beethoven's Ninth Symphony, it would be the agent of affirmative,
national culture.

As indicated by the realism debates of the 1930s, there were, and continued to be, artistic and political differences between the political exiles in
Moscow and the more heterogeneous group of exiles in Paris (later in
Switzerland, Palestine, the United States and Latin America), who tended
to be modernists. Nevertheless, for most political exiles there were clear
advantages in returning to the eastern zone after 1945. The western Allies,
especially the Americans, were opposed to the idea of a cultural policy
that put on the table a political discussion of fascism and anti-fascism,
hence were hostile to the participation of political exiles – most of them
leftists – in post-war cultural life. By contrast, the Soviet military government and its cultural affairs officer, Colonel Alexander Dymshiz, encouraged German anti-fascists to participate in cultural reconstruction and
devise a largely German-controlled strategy for the arts. The Soviets had
lost twenty million people during the war, and their countryside and
economy had been ravaged. Dismantling the remains of German factories
and military complexes, they hurried to rebuild their own infrastructure,
while tabling the German question from year to year.

Arriving on the heels of the Red Army in the summer of 1945, the
Moscow exiles were the first to return to Berlin. They immediately established the Cultural Union for Democratic Renewal and promoted the
broad-based anti-fascist agenda which had been outlined by the KPD-
controlled and humanistically oriented 'Free Germany Committees'
during exile. With Becher as its president, and the active participation of
liberal and other non-communist writers, the Cultural Union soon represented bourgeois humanist as well as leftist interests and had enormous
impact on post-war cultural life. The Union founded new literary journals
and publishing houses; organised readings, theatre productions, congresses and exhibitions; and brought together writers and artists throughout Germany for discussions and proposals for the implementation of
anti-fascist post-war culture. With chapters in all four occupation zones,
the Cultural Union spanned the political spectrum from bourgeois liberals
and humanists to radical democrats and communists. By late 1947 it had
120,000 members.

Post-war literature in the eastern zone can be divided into two phases: the first a radical-democratic phase from the summer of 1945 to November of 1947, characterised by a broad concept of anti-fascism and the hope for a unified Germany; the second an increasingly restrictive period in the wake of Cold War politics from the end of 1947 to the official German division in 1949. During the first two years, cultural life was characterised by pluralism. Kafka, the French surrealists, contemporary British and American fiction, as well as Soviet writers were discussed alongside the classics and contemporary German texts. The crucial question was not the distinction between modernism and realism, which had so dominated the exile discussions of the thirties, but the autonomy and political responsibility of art. As exemplified by the heated exchange of letters between Thomas Mann and the 'inner emigration' writers Frank Thiess and Walter von Molo, many, if not all, writers who had survived the Third Reich inside Germany saw literature as a private matter of conscience, while exiles believed that unless literature takes public political stands, it loses its autonomy and becomes the tool of politics.

It was in the spirit of autonomy and political responsibility that Becher, as President of the Cultural Union, established ties with the bourgeois or radical humanist writers Ricarda Huch, Gerhart Hauptmann, Nelly Sachs, Lion Feuchtwanger and Thomas Mann, as well as luring permanently to Berlin the distinguished exiles Arnold Zweig, Anna Seghers, Bertolt Brecht and Heinrich Mann (who died in California before he could assume his post as President of the German Academy of the Arts in East Berlin). Aufbau Verlag, which Becher established in August 1945, eventually published the collected works of almost all these writers, as well as the classics. Aufbau had quickly acquired the licences of the largest exile presses (Querido in Amsterdam, El Libro Libre in Mexico, Aurora in New York, Malik in London) and became the main German publisher of the great exile works. Thanks to Becher's efforts, the 'literature society' he envisioned was to some extent realised. After the Soviet Union and Japan, the GDR became the largest international producer of books in proportion to its population. An impressive percentage of this output was literary, and a highly literate readership developed over the years. As in the Soviet Union, it was not the official news media, but contemporary literature which served as the agent of significant public information and opinion, whether in books and journals, at public or private readings, or circulated in manuscript form.

The concept of cultural pluralism guided by a radically democratic mandate was the Cultural Union's expression of the hope held by many for a third alternative to the Cold War: the possibility of a demilitarised, neutral and, for the first time in history, an economically and politically democratic Germany. It was the dream of attempting nationhood once more by means of the liberal ideas of the bourgeois revolution which had failed in 1848. The dream ended with the First Congress of German Writers in Berlin in October 1947. The Cultural Union convened this Congress, where the International PEN was represented by its general secretary Herman Ould, to prevent what Becher feared as politics again 'devouring' literature. In fact, exiled and inner emigration writers at the Congress overwhelmingly supported the concept of an autonomous literature of political responsibility. However, it was the American cultural representative Melvin Lasky who had the last word, his dramatically staged Cold War speech questioning the credibility of any literary initiatives coming from the Soviet-occupied zone. A month later the Cultural Union was banned in the West, and writers in the East were left to fend for themselves in an increasingly restrictive political atmosphere.

The Cold War reached a critical point with the currency reform in the West and the Soviets' response with the blockade of Berlin. A third world war seemed imminent. In August 1948 German writers – this time none of them from the western zones – took part in an international congress for peace in Wrocław. It was attended by five hundred international participants including Paul Eluard, Martin Andersen Nexö, Natalia Ginzburg, Max Frisch, Ivo Andric, Salvatore Quasimodo, Max Pechstein, Paul Hogarth, Fernand Léger and Pablo Picasso (whose *Guernica* of 1937 exemplified the concept that united the artists and writers attending the conference: autonomy as well as the political responsibility of art). Yet this cultural conference, too, fell victim to the Cold War. As if in direct response to Lasky's earlier attack on the Soviets, Alexander Fadeyev, the Secretary General of the Union of Soviet Writers, lashed out against 'western decadence' by targeting Jean-Paul Sartre and other critical Marxists in the West. By the end of the Wrocław conference the cultural parameters of the Cold War had become fixed. Writers and artists from around the world, who theretofore had been involved in a common struggle against fascism, were suddenly faced with a realignment along Cold War lines. Germany continued to be an example to the world – no longer of its own militarism, but of the might of the new superpowers.

During the Cold War Becher – who became Minister of Culture in 1954 – continued to stress co-operation among artists and intellectuals on both sides of what became an intra-German border. His failures exceeded his successes, especially after the workers' uprising in 1953 and the 1956 Hungarian Revolution which coincided with the height of anti-communism in the West. In the GDR, Becher did his best to protect the careers of those who fell into disfavour in ever greater numbers. After the events of 1956 he himself was severely reprimanded by the Party. Despite his last published work – a hastily written biography of Walter Ulbricht, his defender and promoter during their Moscow years – Becher had lost much of his political power by the time he died in 1958.

Stalin's anti-Semitic campaign against 'cosmopolitans' and Zhdanov's hardline cultural policy in the Soviet Union hastened the implementation of a rigid GDR cultural policy. By 1951 the ruling Socialist Unity Party (SED) announced its anti-formalism campaign. Meanwhile, the literary climate in the Federal Republic of Germany was more hostile than ever to exile writers and anti-fascist traditions. As a result, East German writers became increasingly defensive as Cold War tensions took on extreme proportions and created ever more strain between East and West. Anna Seghers's famous remark that she moved to the East because there she could write most freely about the subject matter to which she was committed was echoed by writers in a variety of ways. When asked by a West German reporter why he co-operated with the SED leadership, Bertolt Brecht tactfully expressed his doubts that the Adenauer regime would be interested in discussing his works with him as the GDR leaders did. No matter how uncomfortable the first generation of writers became in the GDR, to most of them life across the border still offered no viable alternative. Indeed, by the mid fifties the anti-fascist West German SPD had been substantially weakened, the KPD outlawed, the arms industry reinstated; and a general amnesty re-established high-level Nazis throughout the institutional fabric of the FRG.

The German revolution which would be both humanistic and political had failed repeatedly over the centuries since the upheavals of the Reformation. In the twentieth century, history proved for a second time that the movement towards progressive, democratic reforms would not come from within the German social fabric, but would be imposed from outside by military defeat. In the hope of an anti-fascist socialist alternative in the East, the former exiles found themselves caught between their traditionally critical positions as autonomous artists and their new role in supporting and legitimating a system of socialism instituted from above. This problem was only exacerbated by the anti-communist Cold War posture of the West. In the East, the problem was compounded by a Stalinist leadership which was hostile to internationalism, threatened by pluralism, and insistent on political and cultural unity. Thus the returning exiles began to struggle with a complex dialectic of critique and legitimation which they and subsequent generations of writers would resolve in various ways.

Poetry after the war

There was no identifiable 'school' of East German poets until the 1960s. Expressionism, Germany's only major poetic movement in the first half of the century, had been decimated by politics and two world wars. Only nature poetry in the style of the inner emigration writer Wilhelm Lehmann survived the Nazi period. The immortal lines of Bertolt Brecht's (1898–1956) exile poem 'An die Nachgeborenen' ('To posterity') precluded an incautious return to this tradition by recalling times in which a conversation about trees was almost a crime as it implied one's silence about so many misdeeds. Brecht's epic style of poetry had the greatest impact on younger poets in both East and West. His most memorable poems from the post-war period are his *Buckower Elegien* (1955). 'Der Radwechsel' ('Changing the wheel'), in the form of a tanka, elegantly demonstrates the ever-present dialectical sensibility in his work:

> Ich sitze am Straßenrand
> Der Fahrer wechselt das Rad.
> Ich bin nicht gern, wo ich herkomme.
> Ich bin nicht gern, wo ich hinfahre.
> Warum sehe ich den Radwechsel
> Mit Ungeduld?

[I sit at the roadside / The driver changes the wheel. / I do not like the place I have come from / I do not like the place I am going to. / Why with impatience do I / Watch him changing the wheel?]

During exile Brecht distinguished between the 'pontifical' and 'profane' traditions. To the first he ascribed an hermetic, metaphoric style from Hölderlin to Hofmannsthal; to the second a poetic integration of art and life from Heine to the cabaret style of Ringelnatz and Tucholsky. Brecht advocated the 'profane' tradition as an antidote to romanticism (and socialist realism). Its radical 'plebeian' origins were the early Renaissance ballad, 'Bänkelsang', Reformation hymns and folk-song, as well as the Japanese *tanka* and *haiku* and Chinese *shih* verse which influenced his entire oeuvre. Although Brecht always strove for 'Volkstümlichkeit', or poetry in a popular vein, like Heine he was critical of agit-prop or purely tendentious verse. Brecht's integration of poetry and politics in the avant-garde tradition compares internationally with that of the Chilean national poet Pablo Neruda.

Like Anna Seghers's collection of *Friedensgeschichten* (*Peace stories*, 1952), Brecht's GDR ballads and songs were pedagogical in an anti-fascist vein and meant to be read by young workers and in schools. (Seghers's and Brecht's work, and the latter's collaboration with the composer Hanns Eisler, can be likened to Zoltán Kodály's pedagogical–musicological efforts in Hungary during that time.) In 1950 Aufbau Verlag published *Hundert Gedichte*, a collection of one hundred of Brecht's poems since 1918 divided into 'Songs', 'Musings', 'Songs for children', 'Ballads', 'Chronicles', 'War primer', 'Songs of praise', 'Marches' and 'Exile poems'. Brecht insisted that the volume be small enough to fit in one's pocket, like the writings of Mao Tse-tung whom he admired as a poet and philosopher. Brecht offered one of his *Kinderlieder* (*Children's songs*, 1950) as the text for the new GDR national anthem. It was his 'Kinderhymne' to internationalism and peace, four rhyming quatrains in the simple style of the sixteenth-century Protestant hymn, but rejected by the Party in favour of Johannes R. Becher's more sombre and patriotic 'Auferstanden aus Ruinen' ('Risen from the ruins').

Louis Fürnberg (1909–57) and Erich Weinert (1890–1953) represented the tradition of political poetry associated with the KPD since the 1920s. Fürnberg was a gifted writer whose versatility in several genres complemented his active political life. His poetry features elements of the ballad, folk-song, agit-prop and the German lyric. Weinert's tendentious style in the tradition of the 1848 'Vormärz' and the Soviet RAPP poets made him the foremost agit-prop poet of the Weimar Republic. During the war Weinert was in the Russian trenches on the Volga front reciting his poetry through a loudspeaker and calling to German soldiers to surrender. With the erosion of a mass-based public sphere in the GDR, his oratorical style lost its impact.

Peter Huchel (1903–81) came from the tradition of German nature poetry. Inspired by the topography of his native Mark Brandenburg, his poetic images evoke landscapes ravaged by history. After serving in the German army and as a Russian prisoner of war, he became artistic director of Berlin Radio, then editor of *Sinn und Form* (*Meaning and form*). The journal was founded by Becher and published such notables as Paul Celan, Neruda, Aragon, Thomas Mann, Brecht, Hans Magnus Enzensberger, Nathalie Sarraute, Ernst Bloch, Ernst Fischer and Jean-Paul Sartre. *Sinn und Form* made possible an international discussion among avant-gardists for thirteen years. For this, Huchel was often under severe attack by Party hardliners, and in 1962 was forced to resign his post. Thereafter he lived in seclusion and emigrated to the West in 1971.

With close ties to the European and Latin American surrealists, Erich Arendt (1903–84) was the GDR's outstanding avant-garde poet. The complex imagery of his work was inspired by his exposure to Mediterranean culture during the Spanish Civil War and later travels to Greece, as well as by indigenous cultures during ten years of exile in Columbia via the Caribbean. His method of free poetic adaptation – above all his much-lauded rendering in German of Neruda's work, also of Whitman, Guillén, Vallejo, Cassou, Alberti, Zalamea, Aleixandre, Hernández, Góngora, Mistral, Asturias – had enormous import for translation and poetic adaption, and for the work of younger poets.

Stephan Hermlin (b. 1915), whose father was a German-Jewish nationalist with a love for the arts and whose mother was English, was raised in a cultured atmosphere of wealth and privilege in Berlin and Swiss boarding schools. In 1931, at the age of sixteen, he became active in the KPD. During French and Swiss exile he became acquainted with the surrealists who decisively influenced him. Together with Arendt, he became a prolific translator and adapter of modern poetry – French, American, Spanish, Hungarian, Russian, Turkish. Hermlin is also a masterful prose writer, essayist and translator. His commitment to internationalism and pacifism led him to take many courageous stands. During a career that spanned over forty years of GDR literature, he intervened tirelessly on behalf of younger writers and became an active mediator between East and West German literary life.

Anna Seghers and narrative prose

Anna Seghers's (1900–83) narrative style set the tone for GDR literature. Through her writing and her personal involvement in GDR literary life as President of the Writers' Union for twenty-five years, she had a crucial impact on subsequent generations of writers, many of whom were women. In contrast to the elegiac quality of Becher's verse, Seghers's work centred on the interplay between historical consciousness and personal activism. Her narrative style displays an amalgam of biblical story-telling and modernist abstraction. She preferred Dostoyevsky's character studies to the naive heroes of the *Bildungsroman*, the expansive landscapes of the Dutch painters to the inwardness of the German novella, and Joseph Conrad's yarn-spinning to Thomas Mann's psychological musings on art and culture. In her open letters to her lifelong friend Georg Lukács during the realism debates of the 1930s, she defended the significance of the writer's subjective experience and the fragmentary, utopian qualities of art.

Born Netty Reiling and from a prominent Jewish family in Mainz, Seghers was exposed early in her life to the emancipatory ideas of the Renaissance and Enlightenment. Her father was a renowned art dealer, her mother a founding member of the Mainz Jewish Women's League. Seghers earned her doctorate at the University of Heidelberg with a dissertation on the image of Jews and Jewishness in Rembrandt. Taking her *nom de plume* from Rembrandt's contemporary Hercules Seghers, she wrote her first major narrative, *Der Aufstand der Fischer von Santa Barbara* (*The revolt of the fishermen*, 1928), in the realistic style of the Dutch painters. The subtle interplay between story-telling and the world of colour and light became the hallmark of her entire oeuvre.

A member of the KPD and Union of Proletarian–Revolutionary Writers since 1928, she fled to Paris in 1933 and became active in the international anti-fascist community. With the invasion of France, she and her family escaped with great difficulty before being granted asylum by the Mexican government under President Cardeñas. In 1947 she returned to Europe as the Cold War threatened hopes for a unified democratic Germany. Berlin was 'a witches' sabbath, even without broomsticks', she remarked to Brecht, whom she met in Paris (Brecht, *Arbeitsjournal* II, p.791). Seghers was internationally acclaimed for her exile novels which first appeared in English: *The seventh cross* (1942), a multi-perspective account of a political prisoner's successful escape from a concentration camp against the background of everyday life in the surroundings of Seghers's native Mainz; and *Transit* (1944), a Kafkaesque, thinly veiled autobiographical depiction of the desperate flight into the diaspora before the Holocaust. Seghers relinquished the montage style of her early works in her post-war novels: *Die Toten bleiben jung* (*The dead remain young*, 1949), *Die Entscheidung* (*The decision*, 1959), *Das Vertrauen* (*Trust*, 1968). Informed by the novels of the European realists, this trilogy traces the history of the German working class from World War I to the consequences of the post-war division. These novels (of which the first is by far the best) reveal how difficult it was for Seghers during the Cold War period to reconcile her affinity for subjective narration with her loyalty to the socialist experiment in post-war Germany, and to socialism *per se*.

Noteworthy is Seghers's short prose, a series of stories and novellas which she began during exile and often described with reference to Boccaccio's *Decamerone*. The allusion to this early example of European prose in the vernacular of the oral tradition was hardly coincidental. As a Marxist and modernist, Seghers believed that the progressive forms and working conditions of early bourgeois art, which was not dominated by the commodity character of capitalism, could serve as models for socialist culture. Accordingly, the artist would no longer legitimate the dominant culture from an individualistic, élitist point of view, but would be a craftsperson working in the interests of the majority – a story-teller in the case of the narrative artist Seghers, an artisan of the theatre in the case of Brecht.

Mixing the familiar and the extraordinary, many of Seghers's novellas, like Boccaccio's, are written in the style of the frame narrative, peopled by a variety of individuals who have had singular experiences yet share a common plight – which is survived in everyday life by the testimony of language. Only now the crises that both disperse and convene these individuals are the 'plagues' of modern times: Indians robbed of their lands and living in the poorest *barrios* of Mexico City; Jewish families fleeing pogroms in Eastern Europe; German women enduring the difficulties of working-class life, or of manning farms during the war; resistance fighters, former Nazis and landless peasants rebuilding an economically and spiritually broken society. As the playwright Carl Zuckmayer once noted, Seghers's German landscapes peopled by working people appear as if drawn by Dürer. Equally familiar with the Mexican muralists' modernist concept of folk art, Seghers saw her own work in terms of a literacy programme to re-educate the German working class.

Seghers's interest in the short forms of what both she and Brecht called 'popular' or 'folk' art also bears on the often debated question of the literary heritage. Ever since Goethe's exemplary *Novelle* (1828), nationalists interpreted the novella as an inherently German form. Official GDR policy also claimed it as part of its classical heritage. Yet Seghers's forebear in this regard was not the conservative Goethe, but the heretical romantic writer Heinrich von Kleist, whose brilliantly crafted novellas defied literary convention as well as bourgeois notions of race, class, sexuality and cultural identity. In dialogic relationship to Kleist, Seghers' *Karibische Geschichten* (*Caribbean stories*, 1962) portray anti-colonial uprisings in the Caribbean in the wake of the French Revolution, drawing implicit parallels between European reaction during the Napoleonic age and the stalemate of Soviet-style socialism following the defeat of the Hungarian Revolution. At the same time, they place European history within an international, multi-cultural context, turning attention to liberation movements which were then exploding around the world.

Seghers never veered from her 'faith in the terrestrial', a phrase she borrowed from Pablo Neruda, or in 'the power of the weak', the biblical title of a late prose collection. In many respects her GDR oeuvre can be compared to the late writings of Tolstoy, to whom she dedicated several essays and whose multiple literary conversions she re-enacted within the parameters of her own time. Like Tolstoy's life's work, which Soviet writers emulated, her texts became the narrative ground upon which later GDR writers – not the least of them Heiner Müller and Christa Wolf – constructed their literary edifices and against whose grain they developed their own styles. Like no other author of her time, Seghers recorded the history of the German working class before the panorama of the twentieth century. Telling stories about people's everyday lives, she avoided historicism and created historical narrative. In this spirit of *mimesis*, she paid homage to the realism of Tolstoy and the Renaissance masters.

The anti-fascist novel

While some novelists of the first generation grappled with socialist realism and contemporary themes, most continued to write in the diverse narrative styles they had developed before 1945. The overriding subject of the post-war novel was the struggle against fascism and the legacy of two world wars.

Arnold Zweig (1887–1968) was a socialist, Zionist and admirer of Sigmund Freud, with whom he maintained a lengthy correspondence. He wrote masterful novels that centred on the human condition while examining the social and psychological complexity of twentieth-century Central Europe. Zweig's most memorable works belong to his World War I cycle, *Der große Krieg der weißen Männer* (*The Great War of the white men*), of which the first novel, *Der Streit um den Sergeanten Grischa* (*The case of Sergeant Grischa*, 1927), made him world-famous. He spent most of his exile years in Palestine where his anti-fascist novel *Das Beil von Wandsbek* (*The axe of Wandsbek*), about a Hamburg butcher's work as a Nazi executioner, first appeared in Hebrew in 1943. Zweig returned to Germany in 1948 and became President of the Academy of the Arts upon Heinrich Mann's death. There he wrote stories, essays and the last three novels of his World War I cycle: *Die Feuerpause* (*The ceasefire*, 1954), *Die Zeit ist reif* (*The time is ripe*, 1957), *Träumen ist teuer* (*Dreaming is dear*, 1962). Combining narrative sophistication with psychological complexity, Zweig's novels belong to a European tradition of realism which GDR writers emulated but few were able to achieve.

Younger than Zweig by a quarter of a century, Stefan Heym (b. 1913) became the *grand seigneur* of GDR dissident writers. The son of a Jewish merchant in Chemnitz who was killed by the Gestapo, Heym emigrated to Prague in 1933. Thereafter he studied in the United States and became editor-in-chief of the German-language anti-fascist weekly *Deutsches Volksecho* (*The German People's Echo*). In 1943 he became a US Army officer engaged in psychological warfare, participated in the invasion of Normandy, and worked as an army journalist in Munich during the occupation. Like Hemingway, Heym recast his colourful life in his fiction. His first two novels – *Hostages* (1942) set in Prague, *Crusaders* (1948) about the war – were American bestsellers. *The eyes of reason* (1951) was a critique of American Cold War policy and met with condemnation. McCarthyism and the changing cultural climate during the Korean War caused Heym to leave the United States in protest, renounce his US citizenship, and seek asylum in East Berlin. Writing in English and publishing simultaneously in German and English, Heym brought to the GDR a fresh, loose journalistic style influenced by the American popular novel. Prohibited by the SED from publishing his manuscript about the 1953 workers' uprising, *Five days in June* (published in West Germany, 1974), as well as others of his novels, Heym satirised political conditions under the guise of history and myth: *The Lenz papers* (1963), *Uncertain friend* (about Ferdinand Lassalle; 1968), *The Queen against Defoe* (1970), *The King David report* (1973), *Collin* (1979), *Ahasver* (1981), *Schwarzenberg* (1984).

Ludwig Renn (1889–1979), born into the Saxon nobility as Arnold

Friedrich Vieth von Golssenau, was a battalion commander in World War I and commanded Dresden security troops against revolutionaries in 1919. Thereafter he travelled widely, studied art history, archaeology, Middle-Eastern and East Asian cultures, and joined the KPD in 1928. Renn's *Krieg* (*War*, 1928), published one year after Zweig's *Grischa* and one year before Remarque's *All quiet on the Western Front*, was the most significant German reportage novel to come out of World War I. Its terse, graphic style became the trademark of all his further writing. Renn spent several years in prison under the Nazis, became Commander of the Thälmann Battalion and Chief of Staff of the Eleventh International Brigade during the Spanish Civil War, and was interned by the Vichy government in 1939. Thereafter he fled to Mexico where he taught at the University of Morelia. He returned to Germany to assume several cultural posts and a chair in anthropology in his native Dresden. Renn exemplified many of his generation whose literary beginnings and extraordinary lives overshadowed their later (largely autobiographical) literary oeuvre. With his stories about Indian and African-American children in Latin America, Renn also contributed to the development of a significant body of children's and youth literature with an internationalist and multi-cultural emphasis. The high quality of this literature was due not only to children's authors like Auguste Lazar (1887–1970) and Alex Wedding (1905–66), but also to Renn, Seghers, Brecht and younger authors like Franz Fühmann and Erwin Strittmatter.

Most writers contributing to the working-class tradition of GDR literature came out of the worker correspondent movement of the twenties, modelled on Fyodor Gladkov and Soviet proletarian literature. Miners, turners, dock workers and masons by trade, these writers were activists from a young age and joined the KPD as early as 1919. The finest writer among them was Eduard Claudius (1911–76). In the thirties Claudius was active in the underground resistance, fought in the Spanish Civil War, was twice wounded, and fled to Switzerland where without a visa he spent six years in prison and labour camps. In early 1945 he fought in the partisan brigade 'Garibaldi' in Italy, became press chief in Munich for the Bavarian Ministry for Denazification in July of 1945, and moved to Potsdam in 1948. His greatest literary achievement was his Spanish Civil War novel *Grüne Oliven und nackte Berge* (*Green olives and naked hills*, 1945), which in its brutal realism can be likened to Hemingway's prose. *Menschen an unsrer Seite* (*People at our side*, 1951), the first and arguably the best of the post-war industrial novels, treats politically complex subject matter later taken up by Brecht and Heiner Müller: the story of the Stakhanovite mason Hans Garbe whose innovations both accelerated production at the Berlin Siemens-Plania plant and alienated him from his fellow workers in the crucial years following the war. Between 1956 and

1961 Claudius was first General Consul of the GDR in Syria, then GDR Ambassador to Vietnam. His stories set in the Middle East and South-east Asia and his autobiography, *Ruhelose Jahre* (*Restless years*, 1968), return to the powerful images and prose style of his first work.

Influenced by Maxim Gorki and Fydor Gladkov, Hans Marchwitza (1890–1965) wrote the trilogy *Die Kumiaks* (1934/52/59) about the life of a miner, and *Roheisen* (*Raw iron*, 1955) about the construction of an iron works plant in the GDR. Willi Bredel (1901–64), who authored several proletarian novels before the war, wrote industrial reportage in the GDR and completed his trilogy about working-class life in Hamburg since the beginning of the century: *Die Väter* (*The fathers*, 1943), *Die Söhne* (*The sons*, 1949), *Die Enkel* (*The grandsons*, 1953). While Adam Scharrer (1889–1948) wrote *Dorfgeschichten einmal anders* (*Village stories told differently for a change*, 1948) in a factual style directly opposed to the 'blood and soil' sentimentality of the Nazi *Heimat* novel, Otto Gotsche's (1904–85) *Tiefe Furchen* (*Deep furrows*, 1949), the first GDR 'peasant novel' about the land reform, demonstrates that socialist realism did not always move beyond the literary predecessors it sought to overcome. Bruno Apitz's (1900–79) *Nackt unter Wölfen* (*Naked among wolves*, 1958), an autobiographical novel about Buchenwald whose subjective style of story-telling contrasts with socialist realism's formal expectations, was the most successful of the early GDR novels on an international scale, and a bestseller in the GDR vying only with Seghers's *Das siebte Kreuz* in nearing one million copies sold.

The work of Erwin Strittmatter (1912–94), who experienced everyday life within Germany under the Nazis, can be seen as a bridge from the first generation to the second. Coming from the landless rural proletariat, Strittmatter learned the baker's trade and worked at odd jobs during the depression. He began writing in the thirties, was incarcerated by the Nazis for insubordination, then drafted into the Wehrmacht, from which he deserted shortly before the end of the war. In 1945 he was awarded a small plot after the land reform in the East and was appointed administrator of several villages where he gathered experience for his later works. A protégé of Brecht, for whom this working-class writer incorporated the 'plebeian' language and humour of the German folk tradition, Strittmatter brought to the GDR – as Günter Grass later brought to the FRG – an earthy style of realism in the tradition of Cervantes and Grimmelshausen. Written from a naive, childlike, at times grotesque perspective, Strittmatter's first two autobiographical novels – *Ochsenkutscher* (*Ox cart driver*, 1951) and *Der Wundertäter* (*The worker of miracles*, 1957; part II in 1973; III in 1980) – trace the perilous course of German history in the first half of our century. His most successful novel was *Ole Bienkopp* (1963), about a renegade farmer in an agrarian collective who carries out utopian dreams of socialism against the wishes of a Party bureacracy unprepared for such active idealism; and more recently *Der Laden* (*The shop*: I, 1983; II, 1987). Also the author of plays, several collections of stories, and children's books, Strittmatter's writing exhibits a 'plebeian consciousness', which in the words of the literary historian Hans Mayer 'developed in the GDR over the years despite the existence of a Party dictatorship and a secret police' (Hans Mayer, *Ein Deutscher auf Widerruf*, 1984).

Bertolt Brecht, Friedrich Wolf and political theatre

Following the war many theatres were in ruins. They had housed the celebrated productions of the Weimar Republic, as well as such Third Reich spectacles as the production of Goethe's *Götz von Berlichingen* in which medieval riders bounded on horseback across the stage of the Berlin Staatstheater, where Hermann Göring had his private box. That theatre stood in ruins for almost four decades, with grass sprouting from its once glorious turrets. Other famous Berlin houses – the Volksbühne, Theater am Schiffbauerdamm, Deutsches Theater – became the sites of the outstanding GDR productions by Wolfgang Langhoff, Wolfgang Heinz, Brecht, Erich Engel, Benno Besson, Fritz Marquardt, Heiner Müller and Ruth Berghaus. Contemporary plays by Eliot, Coward, Odets, Miller, Wilder, Williams, O'Neill, Giraudoux and Anouilh were among the first to be staged after the war. As Germany's humanistic response to Nazi barbarism, the German classics formed the basis of the repertoire. Lessing's appeal for enlightenment and tolerance in the figure of a Jew in Lessing's *Nathan der Weise* (*Nathan the wise*) headed the list, performed 245 times in Berlin between 1945 and 1950, followed by Schiller's plea for freedom from tyranny in *Kabale und Liebe* (*Intrigue and love*) and Goethe's accolade to humanism in *Iphigenie*. In the final scene of *Hamlet*, which premiered in December 1945 in Berlin, the heroic appearance of Fortinbras evoked the victorious Red Army and the transition from an oppressive past to an enlightened future. The newly named Maxim Gorki Theater staged Soviet plays in the Stanislavsky style, which prevailed in provincial and most Berlin theatres.

In contrast to the anti-fascist novel, there was only a small repertoire of anti-fascist plays. The 1946 Berlin production of Günther Weisenborn's *Die Illegalen* (*The illegals*) was considered exemplary. Whereas western productions of Carl Zuckmayer's *Des Teufels General* (*The devil's general*) foregrounded the military and political leadership of the Third Reich, the production of *Illegalen* focused on the history of underground resistance. Most of the anti-fascist plays were by Brecht and Friedrich

Wolf, who along with Erwin Piscator had revolutionised political theatre during the Weimar Republic.

Brecht's (1898–1956) early theatre experiments and the epic plays of his exile period are legend. In 1947 he returned to Europe to re-establish ties which had been broken by the events of 1933. During a first year in Zurich he worked on his 'model' productions of Sophocles' *Antigone* (with a prologue set in the ruins of Berlin) and his *Mutter Courage und ihre Kinder* set during the Thirty Years War – with his wife Helene Weigel in the title roles. Both productions addressed the devastation wrought by Germany on its own people and on Europe. Arriving in East Berlin in late 1948, Brecht was given free rein to establish his own company and henceforth devote himself to staging his own plays: *Mutter Courage* (1949), *Herr Puntila und sein Knecht Matti* (1949), *Die Mutter* (1951), *Der kaukasische Kreidekreis* (*The Caucasian chalk circle*, 1954), *Leben des Galilei* (1956); adaptations of Lenz's *Der Hofmeister* (*The private tutor*, 1950), Molière's *Don Juan* (1953), Shakespeare's *Coriolanus* (1953), Farquhar's *The recruiting officer* (1955); and productions of Seghers's *Der Prozess der Jeanne d'Arc zu Rouen* (*The trial of Joan of Arc at Rouen*, 1952), Erwin Strittmatter's *Katzgraben* (1953), and Becher's *Winterschlacht* (*Winter battle*, 1954).

Under Brecht's artistic direction and Weigel's management (as director of the theatre as well as leading actor and interpreter of epic theatre), the Berliner Ensemble (BE) became a world-renowned company with the participation of some of the finest theatre practitioners from the Weimar era (Caspar Neher, Therese Giehse, Herbert Ihering, Paul Dessau, Hanns Eisler, Ernst Busch, Erich Engel), as well as younger talents from Germany and abroad. The directors, actors, set designers and dramaturges who learned their craft at the BE in the fifties later became the main proponents of epic theatre in East and West: Benno Besson, Egon Monk, Manfred Wekwerth, Peter Palitsch, Uta Birnbaum, Karl von Appen, Angelika Hurwitz, Käthe Reichel, Felicitas Ritsch, Hilmar Thate, Ekkehard Schall, Heinar Kipphardt, Wolf Biermann, Peter Hacks.

Friedrich Wolf (1888–1953) represented the Aristotelian and agit-prop traditions of German political theatre. A physician by profession, he became a pacifist during service in World War I, worked in clinics treating war veterans and the working-class poor, and joined the KPD in 1928. Writing plays under the slogan 'art is a weapon', he is best remembered for *Der arme Konrad* (*Poor Konrad*, 1924) about the German peasant wars, *Cyankali* (1929) about illegal abortion, *Die Matrosen von Cattaro* (*The sailors of Cattaro*, 1930), *Floridsdorf* (1936) about the Vienna workers' uprising, and *Professor Mamlock* (1935) about the Nazi persecution of a middle-class Jewish doctor – which Wolf himself was. During exile Wolf was imprisoned by the Vichy regime in Le Vernet, and spent the war years in the Soviet Union. Thereafter he wrote several more plays and became the first East German ambassador to Poland. His son Konrad Wolf became the leading GDR film-maker and worked in a similar aesthetic vein.

Most of Wolf's plays dramatise failed revolutions, yet project a future symbolised by the final lines 'We'll do it better next time!' from *Die Matrosen von Cattaro*. Revolutionary optimism conveyed by characters with whom his working-class audiences could identify made Wolf's plays enormously successful. His Aristotelian dramaturgy easily accommodated post-war subject matter, as in *Bürgermeister Anna* (*Mayor Anna*, 1950), a play about the land reform and one of the first of innumerable GDR plays whose central character is a woman. The plot revolves around the landless peasant Anna, who unlike the men in her village is open to cooperative farming and becomes aware of her rights as a woman. Appointed mayor by the Party, she succeeds against great odds in raising consciousness among the villagers and effecting change. Wolf's largely working- and lower middle-class audiences had been exposed for twelve years to the mass propaganda of a fascist regime, and in his view needed an empathetic relationship to the new socialist subject matter made possible by positive heroes and closed forms.

Wolf's and Brecht's differences over the 1949 BE production of *Mutter Courage* revealed opposing views of socialist drama. Whereas Wolf's Aristotelian concept focused on a Schillerian conflict of ideas – or, in Marxist terms, individual 'consciousness' – Brecht's epic approach situated dramatic contradiction within the historical circumstances themselves. With the production of *Mutter Courage*, Brecht realised that 'model' which laid the foundation for the subsequent development of epic theatre in the GDR: critical distance instead of identification between actor and character, between the audience and the stage; focus on action, not emotion; open ending, not resolution. The debate with Wolf revolved around the last scene. Having lost all three of her children due to the 'business' of war, Mother Courage continues like a 'hyena of the battlefield' to pull her wagon behind the army, still believing her fortune lies with the war. She is the prototype of the 'negative' character who refuses to learn. Advocates of Aristotelian drama called for a 'positive' ending to demonstrate that human beings – and here importantly: Germans – can change and learn. Brecht nevertheless insisted that only the 'negative' and dialectically open ending could elicit from the audience the kind of productive response which would lead to real change. 'For new content we need new forms' – had long been Brecht's slogan. Like Beckett's *Waiting for Godot* – which Brecht admired and considered staging shortly before his death – *Mutter Courage* suggested that after World War II and Auschwitz, a radical modernism offered the most viable alternative to the idealistic traditions of bourgeois theatre. Nonetheless, Aristotelian drama, not Brechtian epic-dialectical theatre (which Wolf called theatre for the intellectual élite, not for the masses), became the widespread GDR theatre form. Yet Brecht's experiments had the larger impact on younger theatre practitioners, and by the 1960s epic theatre would revolutionise the German stage as well as theatres in Europe and the Third World.

Brecht drafted but did not complete any plays with 'positive' characters and 'non-antagonistic' conflicts. He had grappled with the problem in 1945 with the frame play of *Der kaukasische Kreidekreis*, set in an agricultural co-operative in the Soviet Union. With the 1953 BE production of Erwin Strittmatter's first play about the land reform, Brecht turned to Shakespeare's history plays for help. *Katzgraben* dramatises the fate of a village whose 'old' and 'new' farmers fight things out with each other after the Junker has fled to the West. Its first scene opens on the kitchen-living room of the former manor house, furnished with an overstuffed sofa and an elaborately decorated armoire with the customary rifles and coat of arms. Its current inhabitant, a newly landed farmer who has just returned from the fields in his work clothes, declaims in blank verse about modernisation and the prospect of a paved road that will connect the village to the next town. It is a scene befitting Shakespeare, with the new 'lord of the manor' and his family undergoing the monumental changes (including the restriction of patriarchal authority and the emancipation of women) implied by an historical transfer of power – and with a comic ending. Emphasising techniques of distantiation, Brecht had the original prose recast in blank verse so that, in his words, working people could speak in the language of kings and queens, and thus gain full access to the stage. By having the farmers speak in an elevated style, albeit retaining their 'plebeian' vocabulary and wit, Brecht accomplished for a post-bourgeois audience what Lessing had done for bourgeois theatre by 'mixing' characters from the nobility and the middle class, and having them defy the conventions by speaking in prose. Two hundred years after Lessing, Brecht initiated a 'plebeian' appropriation of the Elizabethan bard which would have enormous consequences for GDR theatre.

One of the best, yet rarely acknowledged, GDR playwrights was Alfred Matusche (1909–73), whose epic plays have more in common with Expressionist drama than with Brechtian theatre. The son of a Leipzig mechanic, Matusche wrote for the Leipzig radio until 1933, after which he worked with the underground resistance. A volume of his poetry was published in Danish translation in 1936; all his manuscripts (poetry, plays, essays, novellas) were destroyed by the Gestapo during a house raid. After 1945 he began to write film-scripts and his balladesque theatre plays about individual encounters with recent German history. *Welche, von den Frauen?* (*Which of the women?*, 1952 but first published posthumously in 1979) rivals Wolfgang Borchert's *Draußen vor der Tür* (*The man outside,* 1947) in its haunting evocation of personal agony and war's destruction, yet also comes to grips with political realities. In *Die Dorfstraße* (*The village street,* 1955), which takes place in the spring of 1945 on the Oder–Neisse border, the historical debt owed by Germans to the Poles is symbolised by a 'pair of eyes' forcefully removed by the Germans from a Polish girl, and surgically transferred to an injured German lieutenant who had 'lost his sight'. Unaware of the source of his 'new sight', the lieutenant surrenders to Polish partisans and henceforth devotes himself to making peace among peoples living at the intersections of old 'village roads' and newly drawn post-war borders. Like many of Matusche's plays, *Nacktes Gras* (*Naked grass,* 1957) presents a strong female protagonist, here one who is active in the anti-fascist resistance, though she is married to a Nazi officer (whom she finally kills for his crimes). *Der Regenwettermann* (*The rainy weather man,* 1963) portrays a magical if doomed relationship between a Jewish boy and a German soldier who refuses to participate in an army massacre of Jewish villagers in Poland. Melding Aeschylean tragedy with epic theatre, Matusche's plays favour psychological and ethical motivation over the rigorous dialectical materialism which characterised the Brecht school. Lyricism and pathos co-exist with understatement, abbreviated dialogue, and dramaturgically 'rough edges', lending these plays an authentic 'plebeian' quality which is often consciously stylised in Brecht. Matusche's unique dramaturgy decisively influenced the next generation's most important playwright Heiner Müller, whose more famous theatrical predecessor was Brecht.

Socialism and utopian thinking (1959–1976)

GDR intellectuals had their great chance for reform during the unrest that followed Krushchev's promise of an anti-Stalinist course in February of 1956. The Party leadership, however, assumed a defensive position and arrested several leading GDR Party reformers, notably Walter Janka, editor-in-chief of Aufbau Verlag, and Wolfgang Harich from the philosophical faculty of the Humboldt University. Both were followers of Georg Lukács, who had joined the Petőfi Circle in Budapest and became Hungarian Minister of Education under Imre Nagy's short-lived revolutionary government in the autumn of 1956. A climate of anti-intellectualism ensued. Although Lukács's theories of realism were still expounded in defence of socialist realism, his name was erased from official history. Modernism was under renewed attack. The philosopher Ernst Bloch and the literary historian Hans Mayer, who had created a progressive atmosphere at the University of Leipzig conducive to critical Marxism and modernism in the arts, were the objects of vicious media campaigns until they moved to the FRG.

The absence of GDR reforms following the revolutionary turmoil of 1956 marked the end of the exile generation's creative period. Brecht died in 1956, shortly before the outbreak of the Hungarian Revolution. Becher, stripped of most of his powers because of his ties to Lukács and other reformers, died in 1958. Seghers, who was implicated along with Janka in an effort to help Lukács escape arrest, became increasingly reclusive. Other writers of this first generation gradually disappeared from the literary scene, accepting bureaucratic or diplomatic posts, writing their memoirs, or simply dying of a hard life and advanced age.

The advent of cultural renewal was marked by the 'Bitterfeld Way', which the SED announced in 1959 as a new programme of cultural exchange between workers and intellectuals. This programme sought to overcome the distinction between bourgeois and working-class literature which had characterised the literature of anti-fascism. Inspired by the worker correspondent movements of the twenties, 'circles of writing workers' were formed (as a few years later in the FRG), while novelists, playwrights and poets spent time in residence at industrial and agricultural sites. Like the West German novel at the end of the 1950s, the literature of Bitterfeld brought to the fore the writers of the younger generation who had known the Nazi years as children (many of them also as Wehrmacht soldiers).

The construction of the Berlin Wall in August 1961 cut off direct access to West Berlin and the FRG, and ended the ever fainter hope of a unified democratic and economically egalitarian Germany. The Wall brought clear economic and political benefits to the GDR. It stopped the exodus of GDR-trained professionals seeking greater prosperity in the FRG's 'economic miracle', and alleviated the GDR's historically defensive posture towards the West. In the cultural sphere the new insularity created a process of self-definition vis-à-vis the FRG, as well as greater freedom for subjective reflection and self-criticism. Nowhere was this process of personal and social identity formation expressed more formidably than in Christa Wolf's novels *Der geteilte Himmel* (*The divided heaven*, 1963) and *Nachdenken über Christa T.* (*The quest for Christa T.*, 1968). If writers like Brecht and Seghers had called for anti-fascism, socialism and humanism in an appeal to a European, and implicitly unified German, sensibility, the second generation wrote in the context of what the Party now defined as a specifically GDR 'socialist national literature'.

More important still was the new climate of public debate and reform in Eastern Europe, coupled with the left, student and Eurocommunist movements in the West. The radical movements in both East and West challenged the Cold War map of Europe (and a nearly post-colonial world) drawn twenty years earlier. Discussions among writers and intellectuals reflected this realignment. The 1963 Kafka conference in Czechoslovakia, for example, was attended by East European intellectuals as well as western Eurocommunists such as Roger Garaudy and Ernst Fischer. Their arguments in favour of recognising the existence of alienation within socialist cultures, hence for the legitimacy of modernist abstraction, were attempts to revitalise Marxism itself and thereby reclaim it from the Party bosses. Added to this was the challenge to the theoretical and political Marxist hegemony of the Soviet Union coming from liberation movements in Asia, Africa and Latin America. This challenge was reflected in GDR writers' and intellectuals' interest in such figures as Nelson Mandela, Patrice Lumumba, Franz Fanon, Aimée Cesaire and Che Guevara, as well as in uncanonical European communists like Rosa Luxemburg, Alexandra Kollontai or Leon Trotzky.

As to literature and the 'German question', a younger, politicised generation of West German writers had emerged since the late fifties. The connections between German history, subjective complicity and morality were as politically charged in the works of Heinrich Böll, Günter Grass, Rolf Hochhuth and Peter Weiss as they were for the young GDR authors. The 1970s saw greater openness and cultural exchange between GDR and FRG writers, and less rigorous distinctions between the two post-war literatures. Nevertheless, the modernist experimentation of Czech, Hungarian, Polish and other East European writers had far greater significance for the GDR than did West German literature, which itself underwent significant changes during this time. Interestingly, while the 1960s and 1970s marked the decline of modernism in the West, in the GDR it reasserted itself and achieved international acclaim.

After only a few years of liberalisation in the early sixties, the GDR leadership retaliated against 'nihilistic' and 'anarchic' tendencies among writers and intellectuals. At the December 1965 plenary session of the Party's Central Committee, some of the most talented of the young writers were censured, among them Günter Kunert, Wolf Biermann, Peter Hacks, Heiner Müller, as well as the older Stefan Heym and the scientist and philosopher Robert Havemann. This cultural freeze worsened following political demonstrations in 1968 against the Soviet (and GDR) military invasion of Czechoslovakia. The year 1968 created a political and cultural caesura, the beginning of a period in which the macrocosmic dream of a perfect social order gave way to more subjective, though still utopian, concern for the relationship between history and everyday life.

Changes within the SED Party structure became increasingly visible in the early sixties when the New Economic System signalled a power shift from the old-style political Party bosses, who had endured street fights and imprisonment by the Nazis, to the younger managers and technocrats. By 1968 Ulbricht had relinquished virtually all of his power, and in 1971 Erich Honecker officially assumed Party leadership with the promise of economic prosperity, a higher standard of living, and 'no more taboos' in the cultural sphere. During the seventies the GDR gained official international recognition and became the greatest producer and consumer within the Soviet bloc. Reflecting this shift in priorities as well as a new professional class of readers, the literature of the seventies displayed a wealth of texts about interpersonal relationships, marriage, career and the politics of everyday life. Whereas the idealistic, radically Marxist sixties had been the great decade of stylistic abstraction in poetry and drama, the seventies were the decade of greater naturalism and prose, much of it by women. This was also the decade in which theories promoted in the West – by neo-Freudians, post-structuralists and feminist theoreticians – combined in the GDR with Marxist traditions of critical theory. During this era western literary criticism first took serious note of GDR literature, hence the greater western attention to its last two decades than to its first no less remarkable twenty-five years.

Johannes Bobrowski and the young lyric poets

A socialist, humanist and devout Christian, Bobrowski (1917–65) belonged to the Christian Democratic Union Party, and both published and worked as literary editor in its Union-Verlag. He was the GDR's greatest poet after the first generation, equally lauded in both Germanies, recipient of the Prize of the Gruppe 47 and the GDR's Heinrich Mann Prize. Like his contemporaries Paul Celan and Nelly Sachs, who lived in Paris and Stockholm respectively, Bobrowski was a poet writing in German whom German history had displaced. Unlike Sachs and Celan, he came from a long line of German Protestants who lived around the Memel River in the Polish, Baltic and north-west Russian regions alongside other peoples – Poles, Lithuanians, Russians and Jews. This ancient landscape, which Germans had devastated over the centuries, became the inspiration for his entire work. He began to write about 'Sarmatien' in 1941 while there as a Wehrmacht soldier on the Russian front, or as he wrote in 1961 in a note for Hans Bender's anthology of German poetry since 1945:

als Fremder, als Deutscher. Daraus ist ein Thema geworden, ungefähr: Die Deutschen und der europäische Osten . . . Eine lange Geschichte aus Unglück und Verschuldung, seit den Tagen des deutschen Ordens, die meinem Volk zu Buch steht. Wohl nicht zu tilgen und zu sühnen, aber eine Hoffnung wert und einen redlichen Versuch in deutschen Gedichten.

[as a foreigner, a German. A theme emerged, something along these lines: the Germans and the European East . . . It is a long history of misfortune and culpability, dating from the days of the Teutonic Order, and my people are accountable for it. Not that this can cancel or atone for that debt, but it may be worth some hope and a sincere effort with some German poems.]

For Bobrowski, as for most GDR writers of the second generation, the Second World War was the pivotal life experience which brought both great suffering and personal transformation. An active member of the Confessional Church with a passion for music, art and writing odes, the young Bobrowski was drafted into the *Wehrmacht* in 1937, then participated in the offensive against Poland, the invasion of France, and the invasion of the Soviet Union. After four years on the eastern front, he spent another five years as prisoner of war in the Soviet Union. There he worked as a coal miner and construction labourer, participated in camp cultural activities as a theatre director, and spent a total of twelve months at 'Antifa'-reorientation schools in Rostov and Gorky. In December 1949 he returned to East Germany and gradually transformed his classically trained poetic style into a morally responsible contemporary form.

In Bobrowski's lyrics, many of them variations on the German ode form, the poet neither comments from afar nor is silent before a ravaged nature. Bobrowski's grieving poetic voice is irreversibly present and responsible for itself, hence capable of memory and love. His lyrics recall the pietist spirit of Klopstock and Hölderlin, who loved the German landscape and language, yet mourned the nation's injustices and the follies of its people. In a burst of creativity during the first half of the 1960s, Bobrowski came on the literary scene with three volumes of poetry – *Sarmatische Zeit* (*Sarmatian time*, 1960), *Schattenland Ströme* (*Shadowland streams*, 1962), *Wetterzeichen* (*Weather signs*, 1966) – as well as some short prose and two novels. These years were marked by the Eichmann trial in Jerusalem and the Auschwitz trials in Frankfurt. Bobrowski's at heart lyrical oeuvre offered post-war literature an eloquent language of mourning with a subjective voice that was admittedly 'German'. Unlike some of his contemporaries, he never surrendered his belief in the ability of (the German) language to guide memory and be morally responsible for the truth. To younger writers he bequeathed the legacy of the carefully weighed word, suggesting that after the Holocaust, a literature of contemplation and sorrow was not only possible, but utopian and humane. In the haunting syntax and tentative cadences of his poetry, the door is left open for a utopian moment which only an unbridled humanism can fill. With an approach to modernism that was both radical and confessional, Bobrowski made possible an entirely new literary sensibility in the GDR.

This sensibility informed the work of the young lyric poets of the 1960s who radically transformed the theory and practice of socialist art. If Bobrowski redefined subjectivity in confessional terms, these poets also celebrated it. Fifteen to twenty years younger than their mentor, they remembered the war years as the chaotic termination of childhood, while socialism became the passage to adulthood and enlightenment. In poetry debates, new anthologies, and public readings before young workers and intellectuals who shared their youthful hopes and historical experience, these poets aggressively redefined socialism in utopian terms and became ever more critical of the existing political structures. Many of them merged the 'pontifical' and 'profane' traditions by melding a terse epic style with the idealistic images and cadences inherited from Klopstock, the young Goethe and Hölderlin. Like the 'Göttinger Hain' and 'Storm and Stress' poets, whose hymns to nature rejected courtly conventions by celebrating the free bourgeois individual, the young GDR poets rebelled against the instrumental rationality of state socialism and announced a new era of individuality and freedom. If the nature imagery of the 'Storm and Stress' expressed Promethean creativity and genius, the GDR poets' metaphoric landscapes linked nature to political activism and the realm of production. Here their inspiration came from the twentieth century – Mayakovsky, Carl Sandburg and the German Expressionists. In Hermlin's and Arendt's poetic translations and adaptations, they became acquainted with modern poetry from Mandelstamm and Endre Ady to William Carlos Williams and Ezra Pound. Many of these young GDR poets were graduates of the Johannes R. Becher Literatur-Institut in Leipzig, where the poet and teacher Georg Maurer (1907–71) took them beyond the official heritage of realism to the European canon of poetry since the Greeks. Many of these poets came from the province of Saxony, whose unique cultural and linguistic history made a distinctive mark on GDR poetry. At a time when West German public life saw a waning of regionalisms and the streamlining of language, GDR poetry (and the verse forms of GDR drama) manifested an extraordinary range of rhythm, colour and imagery. This fecundity was not lastly due to the integration of working-class and peasant idiom into the literary language.

Influenced by the formalism of Alexander Blok and Anna Akhmatova as well as by epic traditions, Sarah Kirsch's (b. 1935) GDR poetry – *Landaufenthalt* (*A stay in the country*, 1967), *Zaubersprüche* (*Conjurations*, 1973), *Rückenwind* (*Tailwind*, 1976) – reveals a detailed, sensuous interconnectedness between human subjectivity and physical nature. For Kirsch, the concept of production derived from the young Marx encompassed the labours of love as well as the workings of the social and natural world. Claiming both public and private realms, her nature imagery bridges the traditional genre gap between love poetry and the poetry of social production. Nowhere is this intertwining more evident than in the early work of Volker Braun (b. 1939) – *Provokation für mich* (*Provocation for myself*, 1965), *Wir und nicht sie* (*We and not they*, 1970), *Gegen die symmetrische Welt* (*Against the symmetrical world*, 1974) – which merges the idealism of Hölderlin's odes with the young Marx's (and Mayakovsky's) dialectical concept of interpersonal and social production.

Internationally known as one of the outstanding poet-singers of this century, Wolf Biermann (b. 1936) came from a communist working-class family in Hamburg. He moved to the GDR in 1953 to become the most radical of the young poets with his satirical ballads and songs written in the decidedly 'profane' tradition of Villon, Heine, Wedekind and Brecht. Biermann was apprenticed at the BE, as well as with the Arnold Schönberg student and Brecht collaborator Hanns Eisler. Strumming his guitar and singing saucy political ballads before young workers and students, he soon provoked GDR authorities with his rebellious stance. By 1965 he had been expelled from the Party and prohibited from publishing or appearing publicly. Thereafter his poems and records circulated privately in the East, while in the West he became the poet laureate of the student movement. His memorable collections – *Die Drahtharfe* (*The wire harp*, 1965), *Mit Marx- und Engelszungen* (*With the tongues of Marx and of angels/Engels*, 1968), *Für meine Genossen* (*For my comrades*, 1973) – combine the romance tradition of the ballad with aspects of the folk-song and German political song.

Other major poets, most of them, like Braun and Sarah Kirsch, of the 'Sächsische Dichterschule' ('Saxon school of poets'), are Hanns Cibulka (b. 1920), Adolf Endler (b. 1930), Uwe Gressmann (1933–69), Reiner Kunze (b. 1933), Rainer Kirsch (b. 1934), Karl Mickel (b. 1935), Heinz Czechowski (b. 1935), B. K. Tragelehn (b. 1936), Kurt Bartsch (b. 1937), Elke Erb (b. 1938) and Bernd Jentzsch (b. 1940). The poems of Günter Kunert (b. 1929) and Inge Müller (1925–66) are distinctively shaped by post-war existentialism and thus differ in tone from the utopian impulse of most second generation poets. The high-pitched tone and terse poetic style of Müller's poetry evoke the vulnerability as well as the political determination of her generation, and the influence of Ringelnatz, Brecht, Akhmatova, Mayakovsky and Attila József. Kunert, an important voice in post-war German poetry as a whole, stands firmly in the epic tradition of Heine, Carl Sandburg, Edgar Lee Masters, Ringelnatz, Tucholsky and Brecht. Akin to the anti-idealistic impulse in Hans Magnus Enzensberger's development, Kunert's laconic, satirical verse exposes vestiges of fascism as well as the contradictions of state socialism.

The re-emergence of modernism in prose

The transition to contemporary themes was made by the members of the second generation. Like many of their predecessors, they began their literary careers after the trauma of war. Yet this parallelism was undercut by acute differences. Whereas the broad scope of the Weimar novel was framed by the political activism which swept Europe following the Russian Revolution, GDR prose originated within a vulnerable, increasingly defensive socialist state. This thematic narrowing of historical alternatives can be seen in the tendency towards short prose, especially the *Erzählung*, which can be either a long short story or a short novel. The utopian promise of socialism was not held out to GDR authors by proletarian class struggle, but by a Stalinist state socialism legitimated by ideology and coercion rather than by the mass of its people. If the social reality of revolution informed the works of Seghers and her contemporaries, the prose of the second generation was characterised by the greater abstraction of remorse for the past and psychological introspection.

The war narratives of the fifties show a variety of Weimar influences as well as the American style of Mailer and Hemingway. The best of these are Erich Loest's (b.1926) *Jungen, die übrig blieben (Boys who survived,* 1950), Franz Fühmann's (1922–84) *Kameraden (Comrades,* 1955), Karl Mundstock's (b. 1915) *Bis zum letzten Mann (To the last man,* 1956), Harry Thürk's (b. 1927) *Die Stunde der toten Augen (The hour of dead eyes,* 1957). Contemporary topics focus on the individual's relationship to industrial, and to a lesser extent agricultural, production. These are found in novels modelled on the *Bildungsroman* – Dieter Noll's (b. 1927) *Die Abenteuer des Werner Holt (The adventures of Werner Holt,* 1960/3), Max Walter Schulz's (b. 1921) *Wir sind nicht Staub im Wind (We're not dust in the wind,* 1962) – as well as in the narratively more challenging *Ole Bienkopp* (1963) by Erwin Strittmatter and *Spur der Steine (Trace of the stones,* 1964) by Erik Neutsch (b. 1931). With his facile, derivative novels – *Die Aula (The auditorium,* 1965), *Das Impressum (The imprint,* 1972) and *Der Aufenthalt (The sojourn,* 1977) – Hermann Kant (b. 1926) made a career for himself as the author of functionary literature.

The post-Stalinist *Erzählung* expresses resistance to the canonical works of nineteenth-century realism and greater flexibility in the depiction of contemporary life, as in Brigitte Reimann's (1933–73) *Ankunft im Alltag (Arrival in everyday life,* 1961), Karl-Heinz Jakobs's (b. 1929) *Beschreibung eines Sommers (Description of a summer,* 1961), Fühmann's *Kabelkran und Blauer Peter (Cable Crane and Blue Peter,* 1961) and Christa Wolf's (b. 1929) *Der geteilte Himmel (The divided heaven,* 1963). Stretching Aristotelian *mimesis* and socialist consciousness to their respective limits, the subjective narrator of this last work is a committed young socialist, whose difficulties in the workplace together with the loss of her lover to the West cause a nervous collapse. Published in the year of the Kafka conference, *Der geteilte Himmel* embodies the transition of GDR literature from an insistence on the imitation of life to subjective narration.

The most compelling prose writer to emerge from the fifties was Uwe Johnson (1934–84), whose *Ingrid Babendererde* (written 1953–6, published posthumously in 1985) and *Mutmassungen über Jakob* (*Speculations about Jacob*, 1959) portray with greater accuracy than any other East or West German writer of his generation the consequences of the German division. Johnson's first novel was rejected by four GDR publishing houses, as well as by Suhrkamp in Frankfurt. When Suhrkamp accepted the second novel in 1959, Johnson moved to West Berlin where he continued to write about his subject matter in *Das dritte Buch über Achim* (*The third book about Achim*, 1961), *Karsch* (1964), *Zwei Ansichten* (*Two views*, 1965), and the voluminous *Jahrestage* (*Anniversaries*, 1970–83). Johnson finally lived in exile from both Germanies – in New York in the 1960s and from 1974 until his death in Sheerness-on-Sea, Kent in England. His highly complex yet sparse, concrete, at times dialect-laden prose is akin to that of William Faulkner and Samuel Beckett, yet also reveals his indebtedness to the works of Brecht and Walter Benjamin. Johnson was exposed to the traditions of critical Marxism and the European avant-garde at the University of Leipzig where he studied with Ernst Bloch and Hans Mayer. His texts are like fields of history 'mined' with the explosive matter of memory and past actions which 'erupt' at unexpected moments and intersect peoples' lives. Reading Johnson, like reading Kafka, is reading modern history from the bottom of the heap, from the perspective of the underground mole. Exacting but never didactic, his narrator is an obstinate dialectical materialist who marks the indelible interconnections between historical events and human lives.

The radical materialism of Johnson's prose was matched only in drama (also informed by Brecht, Benjamin and Beckett). New aesthetic impulses in prose came from an entirely different direction, namely from the Christian Johannes Bobrowski, who espoused the confessional heritage of pietism and the Enlightenment. Like his poetry discussed above, Bobrowski's prose – the novels *Levin's Mühle* (*Levin's mill*, 1964) and *Litauische Claviere* (*Lithuanian pianos*, 1966), the stories in *Böhlendorff und Mäusefest* (*Böhlendorff and feast of mice*, 1965) and *Der Mahner* (*I taste bitterness*, 1967) – bears witness to past German crimes towards the peoples of eastern Europe. Presenting microscopically observed human encounters which suggest a much larger history, Bobrowski's skilful narration ferrets out the motivation behind injustices carried out by groups of 'masters' against those deemed as 'other'. This is notably the case in *Levins Mühle*, the story of a successful scheme organised by the narrator's grandfather in the nineteenth century to destroy a nearby mill and its owner, the Jew Levin. With the complicity of his fellow Baptists and the aid of the German bureaucracy, the grandfather manages to ruin Levin and to run him and his gypsy common-law wife out of the area. The narrative subtly distinguishes between the grandfather's ostensibly God-fearing, church-going friends (where differences between Baptist sects disappear when it comes to helping a brother's cause), and a handful of Levin's supporters – gypsies, Poles, a feisty 'Tante Huse' who defects from the Baptist camp, and a wandering musician whose songs record Levin's story. Bobrowski's narrator is not simply 'unreliable' in the conventional modern sense. The burden of history has in effect split his identity, creating an ongoing tension between his 'natural' inheritance and his 'learned' critical-political sensibilities. The East German prose landscape was suddenly transformed by Bobrowski's profoundly artistic use of language, his dense yet never opaque dialogue and description, and his introduction of a beleaguered yet engaged, investigative narrator who unearths the past with an obsession for factual detail.

The tension created by a doubling of narrative identity was most productive in Christa Wolf's work, which took a radical turn towards modernism during the open literary discussions of the sixties. Like Bobrowski, Wolf was born in the East (in her case claimed after 1945 by Poland) where Germans lived side-by-side with and dominated other peoples. As indicated in her autobiographical novel *Kindheitsmuster* (*Patterns of childhood*, 1976), she experienced a comparatively 'normal' childhood under the Nazi regime within a middle-class family of shopkeepers whose upward mobility during the Third Reich supported schoolgirl ambitions for assimilation and success. Not until the collapse of this world in the spring of 1945 did she begin to suspect the horrific events behind the facade of her life. As a survivor of a concentration camp asks a group of German refugees in the novel: 'Wo habt ihr bloß alle gelebt?' ('Where on earth have you all been living?') Like many of her peers, Wolf underwent a personal conversion after the war and joined the SED in the year of the German division. She advanced within the Party hierarchy as a journalist and literary editor to become a candidate for membership of the Party's Central Committee by the early 1960s. This development was reversed after the Party scorned her defence of young writers at the Central Committee plenary session in 1965, and she, like others of her generation, lost faith in the Party's promises of reform.

Wolf's writing inscribed into the nexus of the present the very estrangement between historical inheritance and utopian desire which Bobrowski had unearthed through the past. In her short novel *Nachdenken über*

Christa T. (*The quest for Christa T.*, 1968), a narrator's fragile relationship to the narrated subject again informs the probing quality of the narrative topography (in Bobrowski, the German Baptist's grandson and the historically elusive Jew Levin; in Wolf, a socially assimilated narrator and the unconventional Christa T.) Christa T. is a girl with independent (and antifascist) views when the narrator first meets her classmate during the war. She is still the irreverent yet vulnerable rebel when they become reacquainted during post-war reconstruction. Whereas the narrator speaks from the vantage point of integration, Christa T.'s desire for authenticity casts her as an outsider within the GDR state (as she was before 1945). She gradually disappears from the mainstream of the 'hop-hop people' and lives in the country with her veterinarian husband and two children, writing letters, journal entries, and fragments of longer works, which the narrator attempts to form into a meaningful whole after Christa T.'s premature death from leukaemia.

Closer to Kafka than to socialist realism, *Nachdenken über Christa T.* signalled a watershed in GDR prose. After Bobrowski's death, Wolf became the post-war generation's foremost prose writer. Her essay *Lesen und Schreiben* (*Reading and writing*, 1968) put forth a utopian concept of narrative that claimed modernism for socialist literature in the context of Auschwitz and the nuclear age:

Prosa kann die Grenzen unseres Wissens über uns selbst weiter hinausschieben. Sie hält die Erinnerung an eine Zukunft in uns wach, von der wir uns bei Strafe unseres Untergangs nicht lossagen dürfen. Sie unterstützt das Subjektwerden des Menschen. Sie ist revolutionär und realistisch; sie verführt und ermutigt zum Unmöglichen.

[Prose can expand the limits of what we know about ourselves. It keeps alive in us the memory of a future which we cannot disown, on pain of destruction. It supports the process by which man becomes a free individual. It is revolutionary and realistic: it seduces and encourages us to do the impossible.]

Wolf, *Dimension des Autors*, 1986, p.332.

The utopian dimension of Wolf's prose is drawn from the late Enlightenment: Klopstock, Lenz, Hölderlin, Böhlendorff, Rahel Varnhagen, Kleist, Karoline von Günderrode, Georg Büchner. These writers, who were precursors of German modernism, were caught up in the contradictions of their times while Goethe and Schiller remained in privileged seclusion at the Court of Weimar. With the failed political revolution in Germany, coupled with the Napoleonic wars, these writers were forced by historical circumstances (which those of GDR socialism seem to have paralleled) to turn their social utopias inward and pursue them in the sphere of interpersonal, everyday life. Both literary sensibility and social experiment, this attitude of radical subjectivity was first evident in Bobrowski's *Böhlendorff* (1965), a narrative reminiscent of Büchner's *Lenz* a century earlier. Bobrowski's narrative initiated what after 1968 became a reassessment of the cultural heritage in subjectively narrated biographical works: Gerhard Wolf's (b. 1929) memorial to Bobrowski in *Beschreibung eines Zimmers* (*Description of a room*, 1968) and his *Der arme Hölderlin* (*Poor Hölderlin*, 1972); Günter de Bruyn's (b.1926) biography of Jean Paul Richter (1975); Volker Braun's *Büchners Briefe* (*Büchner's letters*, 1978); Fühmann's essay on E. T. A. Hoffmann (1979); Christa Wolf's essays on Günderrode (1978), Bettine von Arnim (1979), Büchner (1980), Kleist (1982); and Sigrid Damm's (b. 1940) life of Lenz (1985). In works of fiction the late Enlightenment and early Romanticism provided radical perspectives from which to portray contemporary life in the GDR: Christa Wolf, *Neue Lebensansichten eines Katers* (*A tomcat's new philosophy of life* (1970) after E. T. A. Hoffmann), Ulrich Plenzdorf (b.1934), *Die neuen Leiden des jungen W.* (*The new sufferings of young W.*, 1972), Günter de Bruyn, *Märkische Forschungen* (*Studies of the Mark Brandenburg*, 1978), Christa Wolf, *Kein Ort. Nirgends* (*No place on earth*, 1979). The lyric poetry of the sixties and Stephan Hermlin's *Scardanelli* (1970), a radio play about Hölderlin, were early examples of this sensibility.

With the threat of atomic war, the Eichmann and Auschwitz trials, and the genocide in Vietnam, a focus on the interconnectedness between everyday life and history occasioned a number of largely autobiographical prose works portraying the 'ordinary' aspects of fascism which had shaped these writers' childhood years. The earliest examples were Fühmann's *Erzählungen* in *Stürzende Schatten* (*Tumbling shadows*, 1958), which includes variations on themes from Ambrose Bierce), *Das Judenauto* (*The Jew's motorcar*, 1962), *König Ödipus* (*King Oedipus*, 1966) and *Der Jongleur im Kino* (*The juggler in the movies*, 1970). Set in the area of her native Dresden, Helga Schütz's (b. 1937) prose also reflects on the meaning of a life formed by the early context of fascist history: *Vorgeschichten oder Schöne Gegend Probstein* (*Prehistories or lovely area Probstein*, 1970), *Das Erdbeben bei Sangershausen* (*The earthquake at Sangershausen*, 1972), *Festbeleuchtung* (*Festive illumination*, 1974), *Jette in Dresden* (1977), *Julia oder Erziehung zum Chorgesang* (*Julia or training in choral singing*, 1980). Christa Wolf's *Kindheitsmuster* (*Patterns of childhood*, 1976) is informed by Thomas Mann's *Doktor Faustus* as well as Proust's *A la recherche du temps perdu*. The simultaneously personal, moral and political urgency of Wolf's novel had enormous impact on readers not only in the GDR, but in the West, where it also hastened public discussion about the Holocaust and myriad autobiographical writings in the confessional vein.

Jurek Becker's (b. 1937) *Jakob der Lügner* (*Jacob the liar*, 1968) about life in a Polish ghetto and Fred Wander's (b. 1917) *Der siebente Brunnen* (*The seventh well*, 1970) about Buchenwald were among the first GDR works to portray the subjective experience of the Holocaust solely from the perspective of the Jewish victims. Becker's stylistic virtuosity, akin to the prose of both Heinrich Heine and Günter Grass, is further revealed in *Irreführung der Behörden* (*Confounding the authorities*, 1973), *Der Boxer* (1976, about the question of assimilation for a Jewish concentration camp survivor), *Schlaflose Tage* (*Sleepless days*, 1978), and *Bronsteins Kinder* (*Bronstein's children*, 1986). Informed by the young Marx, Volker Braun wrote in an idealistic yet differentiated vein about individual desire and the realities of GDR socialism, in *Das ungezwungene Leben Kasts* (*Kast's casual life*, 1972) and *Unvollendete Geschichte* (*Unfinished story*, 1975). The same can be said of Sarah Kirsch's stories in *Die ungeheuren bergehohen Wellen auf See* (*Enormous mountainous waves at sea*, 1973), written in her characteristically arabesque style. Günter de Bruyn's novels *Buridans Esel* (*Buridan's ass*, 1968) and *Preisverleihung* (*The award ceremony*, 1972) treat the same topic with ironic detachment and a humorous sense for the banalities of everyday life, while Günter Kunert's indebtedness to Tucholsky is evident in his sardonic prose: *Im Namen der Hüte* (*In the name of hats*, 1967), *Die Beerdigung findet in aller Stille statt* (*The funeral will be private*, 1968), *Kramen in Fächern* (*Rummaging through pigeonholes*, 1969), *Tagträume in Berlin und andernorts* (*Daydreams in Berlin and elsewhere*, 1972), *Gast aus England* (*Guest from England*, 1973).

The emancipation of women and the transformation of gender roles played a significant part in GDR literature from its very beginnings. This topical interest can be attributed to familiarity with Enlightenment ideas about women's emancipation, as well as to the history of socialist feminism in Germany and the classical writings of Engels, Bebel, Zetkin and Alexandra Kollontai. Accordingly, Seghers, Brecht, Friedrich Wolf, Strittmatter and others translated the idealisation of femininity by bourgeois humanism since Lessing and Goethe into a decided preference for strong and subjectively complex working-class women. Politically, the constitutional reality of women's emancipation after 1949 brought GDR women substantial gains while 'raising consciousness' in the work force and larger social infrastructure. The state encouraged women to work, and writers were among the millions of women who entered the work force in larger numbers than ever before. Being a writer in the GDR had little to do with the extremes of romantic poverty versus fame. It was a relatively stable lifestyle in which one belonged to the Writers' Union and was generally guaranteed a job and benefits while writing for a journal or newspaper, working as dramaturge for a theatre, or as an editor in a publishing house. Consequently, the status of women writers was much like that of women employees in other sectors of labour who had equal rights yet struggled with 'subjective' aspects of the 'woman question'. These struggles became the crucial theoretical and political discussions of the seventies. They were played out on the pages of contemporary literary texts, which more than ever before served as the forum for intellectual debate. As regards the quality and importance of women writers, one need only note the pre-eminence of Seghers and Wolf among their respective peers, and their extraordinary impact on GDR literature and abroad. When this is compared with the almost exclusively male network of publishers, editors and critics surrounding the male-dominated Gruppe 47 and its later manifestations in the FRG, one realises how great and how unique were the significance of women and their literary visions in GDR literature and cultural life.

If early GDR (and previously Weimar and exile) literature linked the emancipation of women to social production, GDR prose written by women in the wake of Wolf's *Nachdenken über Christa T.* probed the link between emancipation and 'subjective authenticity', or the 'difficulty of saying "I"' within the larger project of history. This utopian, modernist dimension was built on decades of socialist literature which foregrounded women. In this respect women's writing in the GDR differed fundamentally from that in the West, where most texts sought to deconstruct the paradigms of the male modernists. Following the aforementioned works by Seghers, Wolf, Kirsch, Reimann and Schütz, the most remarkable new novels by women appeared in 1974. Gerti Tetzner's (b. 1936) fledgling *Karen W.*, sensitively though not slavishly modelled on Wolf's narrative style, portrays the difficulties of a woman's self-realisation in both public and private life. Brigitte Reimann's posthumously published *Franziska Linkerhand* (*Franziska lefthand*) achieves the grand scale of the post-Stalinist Soviet production novel (notably Galina Nikolayeva's *The running battle*, 1963), and for the first time in GDR literature presents an intellectually and emotionally complex, professionally competent woman (in this case an architect) at the centre of a construction site whose social design is the future. *Leben und Abenteuer der Trobadora Beatriz nach Zeugnissen ihrer Spielfrau Laura* (*Life and adventures of Trobadora Beatriz as chronicled by her minstrel Laura*) by Irmtraud Morgner (1933–90), who like Reimann had been publishing fiction since the late fifties, attracted greater western attention for its playful depiction of GDR life. A loose, 700–page compilation of tales, legends, stories, songs, dreams and documentation, this novel portrays the 'fantastic' relationship between a female troubadour who challenges chronological time by re-entering the world in 1968, and a Berlin Germanist, mother, streetcar driver and the various and sundry friends with whom she shares life under socialism. The sequel *Amanda* (1983) conjures up witches plagued by devils and other Blocksberg creatures in contemporary Berlin. With

Morgner's death in 1990, the third part of the trilogy, *Die cherubinischen Wandersfrauen* (*Cherubinic pilgrim women*, a reference to the seventeenth-century collection of mystical epigrams by Johannes Scheffler), in which a woman turns into a bird, remained unfinished.

Narratively no less remarkable in their respective genres were the sensitively documented interviews with GDR working women, notably Sarah Kirsch's *Die Pantherfrau* (*The panther woman*, 1973) and Maxie Wander's (1933–77) *Guten Morgen, du Schöne!* (*Good morning, my lovely!*, 1977). The same applies to Wander's posthumously published diaries and letters (1979), reminiscent of Rahel Varnhagen's emotionally articulate prose style. In 1975 the American-born Edith Anderson (b. 1915) edited *Blitz aus heiterm Himmel* (*Bolt out of the blue*), a widely read anthology of commissioned stories about gender changes and androgyny (citing John Stuart Mill, but not Virginia Woolf who became influential only a few years later). The stories by Wolf, Kirsch, Morgner and the male writers Günter de Bruyn, Karl-Heinz Jakobs and Rolf Schneider (b.1932) skilfully juxtapose the range of the possible and the impossible in the context of everyday life and what it means to be 'fully human'. Further examples of prose by women during this time include Helga Schubert (b. 1940), *Lauter Leben* (*Pure life*, 1975); Charlotte Worgitzky, *Die Unschuldigen* (*The innocents*, 1975); Angela Stachowa (b. 1938), *Stunde zwischen Katz und Hund* (*Hour between cat and dog*, 1976); Christine Wolter (b. 1939), *Wie ich meine Unschuld verlor* (*How I lost my innocence*, 1976) and *Die Hintergrundsperson* (*The one in the background*, 1979); Helga Königsdorf (b. 1938), *Meine ungehörigen Träume* (*My impertinent dreams*, 1978), *Der Lauf der Dinge* (*The way things go*, 1982), *Respektloser Umgang* (*Disrespectful company*, 1986); Christa Müller (b. 1936), *Vertreibung aus dem Paradies* (*Expulsion from Paradise*, 1979). The resurgence of women's literature also recalled older women writers: Elfriede Brüning (b. 1910) whose *Partnerinnen* (1978) was the most recent example of prose works devoted to women's lives, of which earlier examples are most notably *Ein Kind für mich allein* (*A child all to myself*, 1950) and *Regine Haberkorn* (1955); and Margarete Neumann (b. 1917), whose narrative technique in the epic style of Brecht and Seghers is exemplified in *Der Weg über den Acker* (*Across the fields*, 1955), *Lene Bastians Geschichte* (*Lene Bastian's story*, 1956) and later works.

GDR women writers of the first and second generation largely rejected feminism as a western concept. Yet their – particularly Christa Wolf's – radical constructions of gender and culture offered international feminists narrative access to the kinds of feminist sensibility which Anglo-American and French feminist theory began to develop in the late 1970s in the relationship between feminism and critical theory. In her 1983 novel

Kassandra Wolf went beyond the question of a socialist utopia to the origins of violence and misogyny in western culture. Written at a critical point of nuclear proliferation, *Kassandra* distinguishes between the repressive complacency of the court at Troy (Soviet bloc socialism) and the violent company of 'Achilles the Beast' (western imperialism). The novel dialectically overturns both these alternatives for the 'concrete utopia' of a textual/historical interlude: a communal way of life among people whom Greek aggression and the defensive rigidity of Troy have turned into social outcasts. The disaster which the Trojan princess Cassandra prophesies to deaf ears ultimately comes about, and she, too, becomes its victim. Yet the testimony of her voice survives in literature, which in Wolf's view should be taken literally so that the earth endures.

GDR prose of the 1960s and 1970s exhibited a feeling of emancipation and community which harked back to the German Romantics (and to the early moderns, not least London's Bloomsbury Group). This hope (and the impossibility of its realisation in the German present) is the subject of Christa Wolf's *Kein Ort. Nirgends* (*No place on earth*, 1979). The novella depicts an imagined meeting in 1804 between the ill-fated writers Heinrich von Kleist and Karoline von Günderrode, whose ideals of friendship and androgyny invited both social stigmatisation and human completion. The narrative was written in the wake of the GDR Politburo's 1976 decision to discontinue liberalisation. The decision quickly led to an exodus of writers and to the collapse of the fragile yet democratically organised literary associations and communities which had unofficially formed themselves since the early sixties. A haunting elegy to a generation and its intellectual heritage, *Kein Ort. Nirgends* evokes with piercing clarity the historical threat to the Enlightenment – and its modern variant of democratic socialism – in the nuclear age.

A fitting conclusion to the modernist design in GDR prose by an author of the first generation was Stephan Hermlin's *Abendlicht* (*Evening light*, 1979), a lyrical montage of faintly Proustian reminiscences about the author's coming of age during the historical watershed of the 1930s. Unlike earlier heroic memoirs by members of Hermlin's generation, *Abendlicht* is a modest elegy to the profundity of an era, and evokes an aura of fragmentation where hesitant words and fleeting images inhabit a fragile historical landscape portending extraordinary change.

Post-Brechtian drama and theatre

While the German and European classics continued to play a central role in GDR theatrical life, new plays with contemporary subject matter assumed greater importance in a society where working-class and student, as well as traditionally middle-class theatre-goers formed the new audiences. Heavily subsidised by the state, the new productions had at their disposal months of rehearsal time and some of the best-trained actors and directors in Europe. Whereas the outstanding productions were inspired by Brecht and European avant-garde theatre, Aristotelian drama prevailed. Memorable examples of the latter, after Friedrich Wolf's plays, are Hedda Zinner's (b. 1907) anti-fascist *Der Teufelskreis* (*The vicious circle*, 1953) and *Ravensbrücker Ballade* (1961), Harald Hauser's (b. 1912) *Am Ende der Nacht* (*At night's end*, 1955) about industrial production, Helmut Sakowski's (b. 1924) *Die Entscheidung der Lene Mattke* (*Lene Mattke's decision*, 1959) about women's emancipation and *Steine im Weg* (*Stones in the way*, 1961) about agricultural production, Claus Hammel's (b. 1932) *Um neun an der Achterbahn* (*At the roller coaster at nine*, 1964) about working-class youth.

Following Brecht's emphasis on comedy in the GDR, some of his students took up this genre to legitimise official policy. Helmut Baierl's (b. 1926) *Die Feststellung* (*Stating the truth*, 1958), for example, used the form of the didactic play ('Lehrstück') to provide pat solutions to the issue of collectivisation on the land, while the title character of his *Frau Flinz* (1961) was a feisty Mother Courage turned GDR patriot. Heinar Kipphardt (1922–82), by training a neurologist and psychiatrist, was chief dramaturge at the Deutsches Theater in the fifties and a far more independent proponent of epic theatre. He took a satirical approach to comedy in *Shakespeare dringend gesucht* (*Desperately seeking Shakespeare*, 1953), a biting attack on mainstream tendencies in GDR theatre, as well as in *Der staunenswerte Aufstieg des Alois Piontek* (*The astonishing rise of Alois Piontek*, 1956) and *Die Stühle des Herrn Szmil* (*Mr Szmil's chairs*, 1958). After this last play was removed from the repertoire, Kipphardt moved to the FRG where he received international acclaim for his documentary plays *In der Sache J. Robert Oppenheimer* (*The case of J. Robert Oppenheimer*, 1964) and *Joel Brand* (1965).

Peter Hacks (b. 1928) moved from Munich to East Berlin in 1955 to study at the BE, and became for a time the best-known and most widely performed representative of post-Brechtian theatre on both sides of the German border. Hacks wrote stylistically polished plays, of which several were memorably staged by the Swiss director Benno Besson, who had also come to Berlin to work with Brecht. *Die Schlacht bei Lobositz* (*The battle at Lobositz*, 1956), *Der Müller von Sanssouci* (*The miller of Sanssouci*, 1958), *Die Kindermörderin* (*The child murderess*, 1958) are historical plays inspired by Brecht's own adapations, such as his *Pauken und Trompeten* (*Trumpets and drums*, 1954) after Farquhar's *The recruiting officer*. With *Die Sorgen und die Macht* (*Troubles and power*, 1958/65) and *Moritz Tassow* (1961/65), Hacks turned to contemporary matters of production. *Moritz Tassow* in particular – about an anarchic poet-swineherd who articulates his dreams of communism in poetically elegant and simultaneously bawdy verse – earned him Party censorship and caused the 1965 production by Besson to be cancelled even though Hacks had rewritten the text several times. With *Der Frieden* (*Peace*, 1962, after Aristophanes' play of that name) Hacks set off on a new direction of classical adaptations, farces and mythological plays where dramatic conflict is neutralised by fantasy and comic delight: *Die schöne Helena* (*Beautiful Helena*, 1964, after Meilhac and Halévy), *Polly* (1965, after John Gay), *Amphitryon* (1967), *Margarete in Aix* (1969), *Omphale* (1970), *Adam und Eva* (1973), *Ein Gespräch im Hause Stein über den abwesenden Herrn von Goethe* (*Charlotte*, 1976), *Rosie träumt* (*Rosie dreams*, 1976), *Senecas Tod* (*Seneca's death*, 1980), *Pandora* (1982), *Fredegunde* (1984), *Die Binsen* (*The rushes*, 1985), *Jona* (1988).

Whereas the comic element of Hacks's later plays renders politics harmless, Hartmut Lange (b.1936), who first worked as an opencast miner and studied at the film academy in Babelsberg, wrote epic plays which went to the heart of Marxist dialectics. *Senftenberger Erzählungen* (*Senftenberg tales*, 1960) exposes the *petit-bourgeois* mentality among GDR workers in the post-war years who vacillate between Party promises of socialism and black marketeering. In *Marski* (1962/63) Lange addressed the debate about the kulaks between Stalin and Bucharin, electing as his central character not a 'new' socialist but an 'old' wealthy farmer with a ravenous ego reminiscent of Brecht's Puntila. *Der Hundsprozeß* (*The dog trial*, 1964), like *Marski* a stylised verse play replete with grotesque imagery and acerbic puns, mocks the 1930s show trials and ends with a picture of Stalin illuminating the stage. With their radical Marxist critique, Lange's plays were neither printed nor performed in the GDR, and in 1965 Lange moved to the Schaubühne am Halleschen Ufer in West Berlin.

Volker Braun (b. 1939), the most idealistic of the young GDR playwrights, strove to merge the materialism of Brechtian dialectics with Schiller's drama of ideas. His talent as a poet reveals itself in the expressionist imagery and sententious dialogue which characterise his plays. Like Lange, Braun worked in opencast mining and studied Marxist philosophy. Like Hacks, he was trained at the BE. As a GDR dramatist Braun stands between these two playwrights, tackling contemporary problems from a radical Marxist perspective, yet allowing theory to be tempered by what was officially known as 'real existing socialism'. Like Hacks's *Moritz Tassow* and Lange's *Marski*, Braun's first play *Kipper Paul Bauch* (*Dumper Paul Bauch*, 1966) portrays the new worker-activist whose creative anarchism comes up against an instrumentally rationalised system of technocrats. Not staged until the early seventies, the play was rewritten three times. Under the new title *Die Kipper* (*The dumpers*, 1972), dramatic interest shifted from the lone idealistic individual to the pragmatic interests of the working collective. Similarly, *Hans Faust* (1968) became *Hinze und Kunze* (1973), and a feminist defence of the rights of a woman worker in *Schmitten* (1969) metamorphosed into a Schillerian, if working-class, domestic tragedy called *Tinka* (1976). Walking a fine line between the comic resolutions offered by Hacks, the grotesque ones by Lange, and the tragic one by Heiner Müller, Braun expanded his subject matter to include the dialectical contradictions of history in *Lenins Tod* (*Lenin's death*, 1971, not staged in the GDR until 1988), *Guevara* (1975, not staged till 1984), *Der Große Frieden* (*The great peace*, 1979, modelled on Brecht's *Turandot*). *Dimitri* (1983) demythologises Schiller's *Demetrius*, while *Simplex Deutsch* (1980) offers a grotesque view of German history via Brecht's *Trommeln in der Nacht* (*Drums in the night*). Like Müller's earlier *Germania* (1971), *Siegfried* (1986) returns to the violent myth of the Nibelungen.

Like Braun, Heiner Müller (1929–1995) grew up in the province of Saxony which produced some of the finest GDR writers. His poetically stunning texts prove him heir to such diverse masters of German drama as Kleist, Hölderlin, Büchner, Grabbe, Hebbel, Hans Henny Jahnn and Brecht. Müller's concept of history was primarily influenced by Marx, Walter Benjamin and Michel Foucault. He transformed Benjamin's 'Angelus Novus' into a 'Hapless Angel' immobilised by the rubble of history and blinded by the future. Heirs to the Holocaust, the Gulag and the nuclear age, Müller's late plays extend the 'fear and terror' of modern theatre since Artaud, Beckett and Genet. Müller's oeuvre falls into four overlapping stages: the early production plays, *Der Lohndrücker* (*The wage shark*, 1956), *Die Umsiedlerin* (*The resettler*, 1961; revised 1964 as *Die Bauern* (*The peasants*)), *Der Bau* (*Construction*, 1964), *Zement* (1972); learning plays, e.g. *Philoktet* (1964, after Sophocles), *Der Horatier* (*The Horatian*, 1968, after Brecht's *Die Horatier und die Kuriatier* (*Horatians and Curiatians*)), *Mauser* (1970, after Brecht's *Die Maßnahme* (*The measures taken*)), *Hamletmaschine* (1977), *Der Auftrag* (*The mission*, 1979), *Wolokolamsker Chaussee* (*Volokolamsk highway*, 1985–7); the later 'Germany' or mythical plays, e.g. *Germania* (1971), *Die Schlacht* (*The slaughter*, 1974), *Leben Gundlings Friedrich von Preussen Lessings Schlaf Traum Schrei* (*Life of Gundling Frederick of Prussia Lessing's sleep dream scream*, 1976), *Quartett* (1980), *Verkommenes Ufer Medeamaterial Landschaft mit Argonauten* (*Despoiled shore Medeamaterial landscape with Argonauts*, 1982), *Anatomie Titus Fall of Rome* (1984).

Like Brecht's, Müller's plays reveal an assemblage of classical theatre history and political texts – from Aeschylus and Shakespeare to Rosa Luxemburg and Ulrike Meinhof – reconsidered in a radically anti-

Aristotelian mode. Whereas Brecht focused on class struggle within bourgeois society, Müller's theme is the history of communism since 1917. In this respect his plays bring to the stage a poetic record of socialist revolution – as Aeschylus dramatised the transition from myth to the polis, or as Shakespeare recorded the emergence of the nation state in his history plays. If the Greeks used the tradition of myth for their theatre, Müller built his drama on the written foundation of (hi)stories by communist authors, from the Soviets Gladkov, Sholokhov and Alexander Bek to the Germans Brecht, Erik Neutsch and Seghers. Taking to heart Brecht's reference to the struggles of the plains that follow the crossing of the mountains, Müller's drama centres on the ever more visible 'subjective' contradictions of socialist revolution in the form of family, sexuality and identity. Formally, too, his plays gradually surrender the plot structure of the societal 'basis' in favour of floating images – a metaphorical landscape of dissociative 'bodies' and 'texts' which randomly 'bombard' rather than strategically 'educate' the audience.

These and other departures from Brecht enabled Müller to transfer epic conflict from the historically significant *situation* to the historically significant *character*. Thus dramatic tension focuses on the extended moment in which the individual is presented with existential choices. In this respect Müller's epic theatre is closer to Shakespeare than was Brecht's. His first play *Der Lohndrücker*, written in the year of the Hungarian Revolution, deals with the subject matter of activism within the industrial workplace which Brecht's *Fatzer*-inspired *Garbe* project left unfinished after 1953. Establishing a tragic prototype of socialist revolution after the Hungarian experience of 1956, Müller's play focuses on the Janus-head of reaction and progress *within* the character. This character-centred dialectic is further embodied by the Party Secretary Flint in *Die Bauern*, by a Leninist Odysseus in *Philoktet*, the failed intellectual, lover and revolutionary in *Hamletmaschine*, a betrayed, emancipated and violent Medea in *Verkommenes Ufer*, and the Soviet commander and the GDR activist-turned-functionary in *Wolokolamsker Chaussee*.

Following his final reckoning with the Soviet Union in *Zement* (1973) and with the European avant-garde in *Hamletmaschine* (1977), Müller's *Der Auftrag* (1979, after an Anna Seghers novella and dedicated to Nelson Mandela) was his first overt gesture to the post-colonial world. Whereas *Quartett* (1980, after Laclos's *Les liaisons dangereuses* and influenced by Foucault) painfully erodes bourgeois conventions of sexuality and gender, *Wolokolamsker Chaussee* (1985–7, informed by the era of *glasnost*) is a mournful tribute to German communism since World War II. Müller's work has had decisive influence on international postmodernist trends in theatre. As he characterised his complex relationship to postmodernism in 1978:

Solange Freiheit auf Gewalt gegründet ist, die Ausübung von Kunst auf
Privilegien, werden die Kunstwerke die Tendenz haben, Gefängnisse zu sein, die
Meisterwerke Komplicen der Macht. Die großen Texte des Jahrhunderts arbeiten
an der Liquidation ihrer Autonomie, Produkt ihrer Unzucht mit dem
Privateigentum, an der Enteignung, zuletzt am Verschwinden des Autors. Das
Bleibende ist das Flüchtige. Was auf der Flucht ist bleibt.

[As long as freedom is based on violence and the practice of art on privileges,
works of art will tend to be prisons; the great works, accomplices of power. The
outstanding literary products of the century work towards the liquidation of
their autonomy (autonomy = product of incest with private property), towards
the expropriation and finally the disappearance of the author. That which is
lasting is fleeting. Whatever is in flight remains.]

Heiner Müller material, 1989, p.23.

Inner emigration, exile, 'glasnost', 'Wende' (1976–1990)

The unravelling of GDR literature *per se* began in 1976. East European
intellectuals and western Eurocommunists renewed their calls for reform
at the Berlin conference of Communist parties in the summer of 1976, and
GDR cultural life became more open that autumn. Nevertheless, on 17
November the SED Politburo – whose members had long differed on the
issue of reform – put a halt to such liberalisation and announced the
expatriation of the poet/singer Wolf Biermann, who had been a thorn in
their side for many years. The Politburo's announcement was made during
Biermann's long-awaited western tour and followed his performance in
Cologne, which was unabashedly critical of the SED and broadcast by
West German television to millions of East as well as West German
viewers. Public outcry in the GDR at the Politburo's action took the form
of spontaneous demonstrations by young people and official statements
of protest by hundreds of artists and intellectuals. The twelve writers who
drafted and first signed the official statement of protest included the vanguard of GDR literary life: Stephan Hermlin, Stefan Heym, Erich Arendt,
Franz Fühmann, Günter Kunert, Heiner Müller, Volker Braun, Christa
and Gerhard Wolf, Sarah Kirsch, Jurek Becker and Rolf Schneider. As a
panic reaction to this first public protest led by convinced socialists and
members of the cultural élite, the Party leadership issued orders for
arrests, expulsions from the Party and the Writers' Union, prohibitions
against publication, and many more reprisals.

These events finally undermined what Johannes R. Becher had envisioned as the GDR 'literature society'. Writers who protested had virtually no chance of furthering their careers unless they recanted (which
some of them did). Of those who were systematically silenced, many
opted to publish in, indeed move to, the West. Thus commenced a major

exodus, and within only a few years some of the GDR's finest artists would reside permanently, or on extended visas, in the West: among them the writers Günter Kunert, Sarah Kirsch, Jurek Becker; the directors Benno Besson and Adolf Dresen; the actors Armin Müller-Stahl, Hilmar Thate, Angelika Domröse and Manfred Krug. Writers with international reputations as well as socialist credentials – notably Hermlin, Müller and Christa Wolf – were able to remain in the GDR while retaining certain privileges. Nevertheless, these authors, too, experienced extreme isolation and disillusionment, as indicated by the elegiac tones of Müller's *Hamletmaschine* (1977) and *Der Auftrag* (1979), Hermlin's *Abendlicht* (1979), Wolf's *Kein Ort. Nirgends* (1979) and *Kassandra* (1983). Indeed, with the rupture between the Party leadership and the GDR's most distinguished artists and intellectuals came an almost complete break between modernism and its utopian mission passed on by Seghers, Brecht and others. Politically weakened and without the grand historical design which had previously defined their work, the GDR's avant-garde writers narrowed the scope of their writing during the eighties. Heiner Müller, for example, turned to directing in East and West his ever more cryptic, deconstructive plays, while Wolf's increasingly monologic autobiographical texts – *Störfall* (*Accident: a day's news*, 1987), *Sommerstück* (*Summer piece*, 1989), *Was bleibt* (*What remains*, 1990) – showed signs of postmodernist minimalism while simultaneously struggling against it.

Most authors who moved to the West continued to write about themes derived from their GDR experience, if at times from an abstract, even opaque perspective. Most vulnerable were those intensely involved with issues of GDR socialism, yet unable to publish there and establish literary credentials before moving to the West. As Heiner Müller observed in 1977:

Die Generation der heute Dreißigjährigen in der DDR hat den Sozialismus nicht als Hoffnung auf das *Andere* erfahren, sondern als deformierte Realität. Nicht das Drama des Zweiten Weltkriegs, sondern die Farce der *Stellvertreterkriege* (gegen Jazz und Lyrik, Haare und Bärte, Jeans und Beat, Ringelsocken und Guevara-Poster, Brecht und Dialektik). Nicht die wirklichen Klassenkämpfe, sondern ihr Pathos, durch die Zwänge der Leistungsgesellschaft zunehmend ausgehöhlt. Nicht die große Literatur des Sozialismus, sondern die Grimasse seiner Kulturpolitik.

[The generation of today's thirty year-olds in the GDR did not experience socialism as hope for the *Other*, but as deformed reality. Instead of the drama of the Second World War, the farce of the *Proxy Wars* (against jazz and poetry, long hair and beards, jeans and rock, bobby socks and Che posters, Brecht and dialectics). Instead of the real class struggles, their pathos – increasingly made hollow by the constraints of an achievement-oriented society. Instead of the great literature of socialism, the grimace of its cultural policies.]

Arbeitsbuch Thomas Brasch, p.128.

Thus Stefan Schütz's (b. 1944) plays, modelled on those of Müller, as well as his novels written in the West beginning with *Medusa* (1986), exhibit immense suffering couched in fantasies of violence, while Monika Maron's (b. 1941) compelling account of stymied bureaucracy and ecological disaster in *Flugasche* (*Flight of ashes*, 1981) was followed by novels replete with rage and disgust at the GDR state. Among these writers, Thomas Brasch (b. 1945) – whose father, like Maron's, was a high-ranking GDR functionary – is perhaps most persuasive as an artist. A dialectical materialist in the school of Brecht and Müller, Brasch became disillusioned with 'real socialism' at an early age. He was arrested and censured after protesting in 1968 against the Warsaw Pact invasion of Czechoslovakia, and with no prospects for publication was among the first to leave the GDR after November 1976. Beginning with *Vor den Vätern sterben die Söhne* (*The sons die before the fathers*, 1977), his sparingly crafted work records his generation's betrayal by the discourses of power, whether past or present, East or West. Echoing Kafka and the authors of 'minor literature', he writes his profoundly anti-ideological plays, prose, poetry and films as existential vehicles for survival within the institutions of ever more anonymously administered mass societies.

Other prose writers who portrayed the fluctuations of GDR life during this time include Erich Köhler (b. 1928), Karl-Heinz Jakobs (b. 1929), Erich Loest (b. 1926), Fritz-Rudolf Fries (b. 1935), Hans-Joachim Schädlich (b. 1935), Kurt Bartsch (b. 1937), Jurek Becker (b. 1937), Helga Königsdorf (b. 1938), Irina Liebmann (b. 1943), Harald Gerlach (b. 1940), Barbara Honigmann (b. 1949) and Angela Krauss (b. 1950). Christoph Hein (b. 1944), a modernist who continued to write and publish in the GDR, excelled in both drama and fiction, and was the only writer to emerge as a major new literary figure. Hein's plays address what Ernst Bloch called the 'uneven' or 'non-synchronous' behaviour of the engaged intellectual during times of crisis: *Lassalle* (1977), *Cromwell* (1978), *Die wahre Geschichte des Ah Q* (*The true story of Ah Q*, 1983, after Lu Hsun), *Passage* (1987, based on the circumstances of Walter Benjamin's suicide in 1940 in Port-Bou), and *Die Ritter der Tafelrunde* (*The Knights of the Round Table*, 1989, about the last days of Camelot during the last days of the GDR). Hein is less interested in the historic world spirits of Hegelian dialectics than in details of the barely remembered lives of ordinary women and men. His meticulous prose (like that of his predecessor Bobrowski) resembles the 'archaeological' work of the West German Alexander Kluge. The title character of *The distant lover* (1982) is an inconspicuous middle-aged man who one day is beaten to death without explanation, while his lover, a physician whose uneventful life revolves around the anonymity of her high-rise apartment and the antiseptic order of her clinic, survives by repressing the past and insisting on her present success and well-being. Employing multiple narrators, *Horn's end* (1985) probes the tragic consequences of Stalinism in the story of a professor of history at the University of Leipzig whom the Party punishes after 1956 by transferring him to a remote provincial post. There he works as an archivist and one day is found in the woods hanging from a tree. In *The tango player* (1989) a young academic – imprisoned on charges that he participated in anti-state activities in 1968 – is set free to become assimilated into the very labyrinthine system that previously expelled him. Hein's riveting narrative style, which strips socialism of its ideology and reduces it to its concrete essentials, belongs to a post-Stalinist, Marxist trend in East European writing since the Hungarian György Konrád's *The case worker* (1969).

Many as yet unpublished writers became active in artistic communities which defied the official mainstream, as in Dresden and the Prenzlauer Berg area of Berlin. Creative work in these communities combined experimental poetry and prose with graphic art, contemporary music and other media, circumventing the official institutions and accessible through privately circulated collections, little magazines, local exhibitions, rock concerts, happenings and performance art. Poetry constituted the most striking new literary movement of this period. Radically opposed to the idealism of the 1960s, young poets rebelled against the politicisation of language in daily life by turning back to the linguistic experiments of futurism, dadaism and surrealism, as well as to concrete poetry, the Vienna School and post-structuralist theory. Most of the new poets were born after 1950. They knew the GDR not as the 'other' or 'better' Germany, but as an authoritarian system of oppression and ecological decline in which discourse, not essence, defined the parameters of reality. If some of this poetry was stylistically more derivative than avant-garde, it nevertheless reflected the sentiments of large numbers of young people during the turbulent eighties. Unlike the best-known writers of the first and second generation, a significant number of the finest poets after 1976 had working-class backgrounds, among them the extraordinary Saxon poet Wolfgang Hilbig (b. 1941), the experimental poet Bert Papenfuss-Gorek (b. 1956), and the lyric poet Uwe Kolbe (b. 1957).

The years 1986–90 were dominated by the idea of *glasnost*, despite the GDR Party leadership's recalcitrant behaviour vis-à-vis Mikhail Gorbachev and the Soviet politics of reform. During this time new cultural agreements were put in place between the GDR and the FRG; Christa Wolf, Volker Braun and Heiner Müller were rehabilitated and awarded the coveted National Prize; Beckett's *Waiting for Godot* was premiered in Dresden; Nietzsche's works were openly debated; Günter Grass was invited for a reading tour; the publication of Uwe Johnson's work was announced; Hans Mayer was feted by the Academy of Arts for the first time since his departure in 1963; and the proceedings of the definitive Tenth Writers' Congress were published while censorship was openly discussed and gradually removed. Nowhere was the atmosphere of *glasnost* more visible than on the GDR stage, which had languished for a decade while its best playwrights, actors, directors and set designers dazzled western audiences with the latest in exiled avant-garde theatre. In 1986, for example, B. K. Tragelehn returned from Bochum to Dresden to stage Heiner Müller's *Die Umsiedlerin*, a production for which he had been arrested in 1961. In 1987 the Volksbühne staged Lothar Trolle's (b. 1944) *Weltuntergang Berlin* (*Decline of the world in Berlin*), while Hein's *Passage* at the Schauspielhaus probed the relationship between communists and politically unaffiliated Jews during the Holocaust. 1988 saw the production of Irina Liebmann's *Berlin Kindl* (*Berlin kid*), which addresses anti-Semitic traces of the past in the present, as well as Volker Braun's *Transit Europa* (after Seghers's exile work), a play which complicates the official GDR interpretation of anti-fascist exile by raising the issue of the Stalin–Hitler pact. In 1988 Heiner Müller directed a new production of his 1956 play *Der Lohndrücker* from the perspective of events leading to the workers' uprising of June 1953. And in 1989 productions of Hein's *Ritter der Tafelrunde* foretold the final crisis of SED leadership later that year. A *Lehrstück* in classical five-part dramatic form, Müller's frequently staged *Wolokolamsker Chaussee* (*Volokolamsk highway*, 1985–8) provided an epic review of GDR history from the 1941 siege of Moscow where Ulbricht and KPD leaders called from Russian trenches to German soldiers to surrender, to these leaders' 'betrayal' of the working class in 1953, and of the next generation in 1968. Müller employed the classic epics of socialist literature as the Greek dramatists had used their myths: the first two acts are based on Alexander Bek's World War II novel *Volokolamsk highway* about the German encirclement of Moscow, while its third act, about GDR Party leaders' denial of the 1953 workers' uprising, builds on and beyond Seghers's 'The duel'.

The actual drama of GDR history intensified during this period as the arena of conflict shifted from the theatres into the streets. While thousands of citizens fled to the West in the summer of 1989 after Hungary opened its borders, thousands of others participated in open meetings and calls for democratic reforms. Church groups and citizens' initiatives soon merged with unions, students and SED members to form a broad-based coalition of opposition groups such as New Forum, Unified Left, Democratic Start and Democracy Now. By early October thousands more citizens travelled by train from Prague to the West, while thousands of others demonstrated in cities throughout the GDR, demanding the government's official recognition of the opposition groups and open elections monitored by the UN. On 9 October, 70,000 people marched peacefully through Leipzig, and by 30 October, the number of demonstrators in that city had grown to half a million.

Artists and intellectuals joined with the various opposition groups and participated actively in what by the autumn had become the first peaceful, democratic German revolution in history. On 28 October the management of the Deutsches Theater confronted the GDR's Stalinist past by honouring Walter Janka (the former director of the Aufbau Verlag, imprisoned after a show trial in 1957) before a packed house. That same day the writers Stephan Hermlin, Stefan Heym, Christa Wolf, Heiner Müller, Christoph Hein, Helga Königsdorf and Günter de Bruyn spoke out against the government and Party leadership in Berlin's Church of Our Saviour before 3,000 people (who had long put far more trust in their writers than in their political leaders). This extraordinary event was followed on 4 November by a televised demonstration of half a million people on Berlin's Alexanderplatz, with speeches by opposition leaders together with the writers Heym, Wolf, Hein and Müller. 'Socialism is inconceivable without democracy', Heym declared in his speech, while Wolf ended hers with 'We are the People!', the words chanted by thousands of GDR citizens in demonstrations that autumn. That weekend alone 15,000 more people left the GDR for the West. On 9 November, after the SED leadership announced the opening of the Berlin Wall, East and West Berliners climbed to its top in celebration, and in the weeks that followed masses of GDR citizens crossed to the West for sightseeing and shopping. On 10 November Wolf read a statement on GDR television – signed by opposition leaders, the writers Heym, Hein, Volker Braun, Ulrich Plenzdorf, the theatre and opera director Ruth Berghaus, and the Dresden Symphony conductor Kurt Masur – asking citizens to 'remain in our homeland': 'What can we promise you? Not an easy life, but a useful one. No swift prosperity, but participation in great changes . . . Help us to build a truly democratic society which also preserves the idea of a democratic socialism.'

Reacting to the GDR's ailing economy, West German Chancellor Kohl proposed a widely broadcast ten-point plan for economic aid in exchange for the introduction of a market economy and German unification. In the daily mass demonstrations that continued throughout the GDR, ever more shouts of 'Greater Germany!' and 'Reunification!' could be heard amidst the usual demands for democratic reforms. On 26 November a large number of artists and intellectuals – among them Heym, Braun and Wolf – circulated a petition against unification and called on the GDR to realise its potential as a socialist alternative to the FRG. In an open letter to Chancellor Kohl on 30 November, the management and ensemble of the Deutsches Theater criticised his plans to have the D-Mark 'purchase free elections in the GDR'. On 1 December Wolf Biermann returned to sing before an enthusiastic crowd in Leipzig, his first such concert since 1965. On 3 December Erich Honecker and the members of the Politburo were expelled from the SED and forced to resign from office along with the entire Central Committee. On 12 December, 2,700 SED delegates elected the 41–year old lawyer and intellectual Gregor Gysi as SED Party Chairman for his promise to steer a 'third course' beyond the FRG's 'economic miracle' and the GDR's Stalinist past. More accurately portending the future was FRG Chancellor Kohl's 19 December speech before jubilant crowds in Dresden about German 'reunification', while the first of many smaller anti-unification demonstrations was held in Berlin.

If 1989 marked the great 'change' or 'turn' called the 'Wende', 1990 turned the 'Wende' on its head. In March 1990, GDR citizens voted overwhelmingly in favour of the economic benefits brought by unification. By the end of that year, both the GDR and FRG had ceased to exist, no longer blunt reminders to the world of the genocidal 'Thousand Year Reich' which had lasted thirteen years. As bitter commentary on the repeated failure of progressive movements in Germany, Heiner Müller directed *Hamlet* at the Deutsches Theater, a lavish eight-hour production whose opening coincided with the March elections. In Müller's interpretation, the tragedy of the melancholy prince still best expressed the German political dilemma (just as the Berlin *Hamlet* production forty-five years earlier had followed the débâcle of 1945). Only, in Müller's production, no Fortinbras appeared, thus leaving the future both open to and void of hope. In Müller's words, 'We've not come very far as long as Shakespeare has to write our plays for us.'

And what of literature itself? Many of its institutions (journals, publishing houses, theatres, schools, universities) were subject to the same fate that befell businesses and factories. They were gradually dismantled or taken over by West German conglomerates whose boards of directors made final decisions as to the future lives and careers of employees. The Writers' Union was disbanded. The Academy of Arts, under its new president Heiner Müller, was able to retain its separate historical identity and status until 1993. While GDR literature ceased to exist, East German literature and its authors quickly came under attack by the West German press. The woman and avowed socialist Christa Wolf was the primary target of scrutiny (all the more curious since the West German media had celebrated her for twenty years as the GDR's foremost 'dissident' writer). From revised assessments of her person and work, to slanderous headlines and elaborate speculation about secret police collaboration, the new *ad hominem* strategy against one of Europe's most distinguished writers was essentially an effort to undermine the very legitimacy of East German literature and to discredit its socialist traditions.

The controversies around Wolf (and other eminent East German authors such as Müller, Hermlin, Seghers and Heym) were in effect a sequel to the notorious historians' debates of the 1980s in West Germany. In these debates, neo-conservative historians challenged the legitimacy of liberal historiography, which had made Germany politically and morally accountable for the Holocaust and two world wars. At stake in both the historians' debates and the debates about East German literature was the Enlightenment and its intellectual heritage. Also at issue were the credibility and the very existence of the critical intellectual who had played such a decisive role throughout modern German history. Indeed, Germany's progressive writers and intellectuals have traditionally been of greater significance to the world than Germany's often reactionary political leaders. From the age of Danton, Robespierre and Napoleon no German political leader is better remembered than are Goethe, Kant, Schiller and Hegel. No German liberals are as beloved as Heine. There were no German Churchills or De Gaulles. Instead, Germany's most renowned anti-fascist fighters were its artists and intellectuals, from Albert Einstein and Hannah Arendt to Heinrich and Thomas Mann, Alfred Döblin, Ernst Toller, Arnold Zweig, Anna Seghers and Bertolt Brecht. Surely the question of East German literature will not be decided in the long run by its current adversaries or their predecessors from the Cold War era. Like the once embattled legacies of Heine, Kafka and Thomas Mann, its legacy, too, will be judged by the test of time, considered reflection by historians and literary critics, and finally, by the endurance of the works themselves in the minds and hearts of their national and international readers.

9

German writing in the West (1945–1990)

MORAY MCGOWAN

Introduction

The forty-five years from the collapse of National Socialist Germany in 1945 to the unification of the two German states in 1990 might seem to be an era with a self-evident beginning and end, for how could events of such magnitude and with such profound social and cultural consequences fail to exert epochal influences on literature? This led, after 1945, to the wide-spread expectation and assertion of a new beginning, a 'Stunde Null' or 'Zero Hour'. Equally, the end of the era was announced as early as 2 October 1990, one day before unification, in the critic Frank Schirrmacher's essay 'Abschied von der Literatur der Bundesrepublik' ('Farewell to the literature of the Federal Republic') in the *Frankfurter Allgemeine Zeitung*.

But the continuities of German literature across the supposed divide of 1945 are as numerous as the discontinuities; and the apparent end of duality in 1990 made manifest continued divergencies, unsurprising after forty years of ideological division and cultural separation. Literature is not immune to social and political processes; but the rethinking provoked by major upheavals in society may take many years to be reflected in the themes and forms of literature. In this sense, the literature 'of' the Federal Republic is still to be written.

Schirrmacher's purpose was in any case not a balanced retrospective but a new campaign in a controversy which had accompanied West German literature through most of its history as part of the perennial German question of the relationship of 'Geist' and 'Macht' ('spirit' and 'power'): is literature's importance to be measured by its role as a socially and morally responsible force within a society, whether affirmative or critical of that society? Or is it an autonomous activity to be evaluated, if at all, in terms of its aesthetic achievement? And ought it, in the Enlightenment tradition, to be an explicatory, educative force for historical progress? Or to seek to disrupt an Enlightenment discourse which has decayed into a hollow or repressive rhetoric? Or to turn away from rationality altogether in order to invoke and celebrate the immaterial and ineffable? In fact, liter-ature's capacity to resist any such categorisations is its lasting fascination.

Schirrmacher argued that unification meant the end not only of GDR literature, fatally wedded as it was, even at its most dissident, to the now defunct socialist state, but of West German literature too. For this had come to be represented by a relatively small group of writers who had established themselves around 1960: especially Heinrich Böll, Günter Grass, Ingeborg Bachmann, Hans Magnus Enzensberger, Uwe Johnson, Martin Walser, Peter Weiss. In the next thirty years, he claimed, West German literary culture was dominated by their fixation on the legacy of the National Socialist past in post-war Germany, by the resulting, historically static image of West German society, and by the humanist ethics that underlay their writing, fulfilling the demands of a guilty society that they educate, enlighten, and parade a critical democratic consciousness. As a result, he argued, these writers retained a representative status long after their writing had ceased to justify it. But now unification would consign them finally and incontrovertibly to the past.

'Die deutsche Gesinnungsästhetik', as fellow critic Ulrich Greiner (*Die Zeit*, 8 October 1990) called judgement of a work's aesthetic worth according to its moral or political stance, had distorted the production and reception of literature in the West as well as in the GDR; it was now time to reinstate an autonomous aesthetics of form. This would end the epoch which had begun in the post-war ruins when, in August 1946, the first number of *Der Ruf* (*The call*), edited by Alfred Andersch and Hans Werner Richter, called for 'a new humanism'. From *Der Ruf* grew *Gruppe 47*, the association of writers and critics (including all the above) whom Schirrmacher and Greiner considered to have exercised the baleful influence of 'Gesinnungsästhetik' on West German literature.

Such views are not wholly invalid: the tendency to define the literature of the 'old' Federal Republic in terms of the work and the values of a small number of writers of a particular generation, born between 1908 (Richter) and 1929 (Enzensberger), was widespread in Germany, perhaps even more so abroad. This focus on a group of writers decisively shaped by their experience of National Socialism as young adults, often as soldiers, obscured or over-simplified highly complex generational patterns: first, the fact that for at least the first two decades, German literature after 1945 was still shaped by an earlier generation whose upbringing had taken place before the First World War in Wilhelmine Germany, for whom therefore the nascent Federal Republic was the fourth political and social system they had experienced. Second, it obscured the emergence in the 1970s and the 1980s of generations of writers for whom the National Socialist past was outside direct experience altogether: it was their parents' or grandparents' trauma, and thus, frequently, a source of resentment, irritation or indifference.

Moreover, Schirrmacher's inclusion of Bachmann, Johnson and Weiss, an Austrian, an ex-GDR writer and an emigré living in Sweden respectively, though it indicates a certain wilful over-simplification of what were far from identical aesthetic or political positions, does not invalidate his list. There are characteristic traits to be identified in modern Austrian, as indeed Swiss-German, literature. But the dominance of the West German literary market meant that most writers from Austria and German Switzerland were drawn into Western German literary culture as a whole. Ex-GDR writers like Johnson, though not considered in this chapter, have also played a prominent and sometimes influential role. The uneasy relationship of Western German literary culture after 1945 to once-exiled writers like Weiss, and vice versa, is a key factor in this culture, as are the lingering effects of the intellectual and cultural diaspora during the Nazi period.

It is also true that the lasting currency of the term 'post-war literature' tends to confirm this literature's thematic and formal self-entrapment in the historical phase from which it emerged. As Botho Strauß wrote in 1989 in a special issue of *Der Spiegel* on Adolf Hitler's one hundredth birthday, all writing and any serious reflection in and on Germany since 1945 are haunted by 'the ugliest German'.

Given the tragic and bloody development of modern German history, one might find it unsurprising, even justified, that a critical realism, informed by a politically committed humanist ethics and ever-conscious of this history, should indeed be profoundly formative of West German literature after 1945. But at no time did it constitute the unique voice of this literature and was often far from the dominant one. *Gruppe 47* was founded in 1947 precisely because *Der Ruf* was banned by the American occupying powers who, in the developing Cold War, had no place for its advocacy of democratic socialism. The group did become a widely influential voice at the end of the 1950s with the success of Böll's *Billard um halb zehn* (*Billiards at half past nine*) and Grass's *Die Blechtrommel* (*The tin drum*) in 1959. But even this success was accompanied by intense controversy; and from the late 1960s *Gruppe 47* was challenged again, both by those who wished once more to separate literature from politics, and by those who believed it was not political enough. It was in disarray from 1967 and was dissolved in 1977. The representative status of the above-mentioned group of socially critical writers as the conscience of the nation grew ever more tenuous, and their humanist optimism ever more eroded: 'Does humanism protect us from nothing?', Andersch asked in his last novel *Der Vater eines Mörders* (*The father of a murderer*, 1980). In *Mittelmaß und Wahn* (*Mediocrity and delusion*, 1988), Enzensberger saw the death of Böll in 1985 as ending an era in which Böll had played a representative role emanating from his origins as a political and moral counter-authority to Konrad Adenauer. By 1990, therefore, Schirrmacher and Greiner were kicking in an open door.

However, there are many possible histories of writing since 1945; the axis between committed ethical-critical realism and aesthetic autonomy offers only one of many possible matrices of literary value. Even though the following survey concentrates on literature in the narrow sense of the printed and spoken word – fiction, drama, poetry, essays – the era 1945–90 was one in which the boundaries of literature were substantially blurred by the development of other media: 'Reading is no longer the central cultural practice', as Hubert Winkels pessimistically put it in *Einschnitte* (*Incisions*, 1988). An exhaustive study would, for example, address the overlaps with film and television in the work of Alexander Kluge, Herbert Achternbusch, Edgar Reitz or Peter Turrini, or with popular song in the often highly literate texts of 'Liedermacher' (singer-songwriters) like Franz Josef Degenhardt or Konstantin Wecker. Moreover, literary history, no less than any other history, is written by the victors; the struggle for West German literature 1945–90 is still underway.

1945–1949

This struggle began in 1945, in the controversy over exile versus 'inner emigration' as the legitimate conservator of German culture against barbarism, and therefore the basis for literary renewal. Thomas Mann's broadcast from exile, 'Deutsche Hörer!' ('German listeners!') of 10 May 1945, two days after the surrender, had been conciliatory, mingling national shame with hopes for future freedom. Frank Thiess (1890–1977) responded that only writers who had stayed in Nazi Germany and experienced oppression, destruction and capitulation at first hand, could speak about and for Germany; indeed, inner emigration was morally finer than having observed the German tragedy from the 'Logen und Parterreplätze' ('the best seats') of exile. Mann, stung by this, responded that all works published in Germany between 1933 and 1945 stank of 'blood and shame' and should be pulped. This controversy's focus on the political morality of authors, rather than the politics, let alone the aesthetics, of their texts lastingly polarised the reception of German literature into moral categories.

However, it was even then a controversy tangential to the realities of literary production in the immediate post-war period: ruins, a collapsed cultural infrastructure, complete dependence on the occupying Allies. Ostensibly, the latter sought to revive the spiritual health of the German people via regeneration of liberal, humanistic culture. In Berlin the first theatre reopened on 18 May 1945, followed the next day by thirty cinemas: cinema played a key communicative role in the ruined infrastructure. Newspapers and magazines rapidly followed. Cultural hunger was considerable; publishers could usually sell every book paper shortages permitted them to print. Short forms – poetry, stories, travelogues, essays, cabaret – rather than longer works characterised the first phase of post-war culture, reflecting the moral and psychological as well as physical chaos which militated against extended creative reflection. Initially, all the occupation authorities tolerated a wide range of views except those demonstrably tainted by Nazism. Thus, one of the first post-war antholo-gies, *De Profundis* (edited by Gunter Groll, 1946) included poets from the murdered socialist Erich Mühsam (1878–1934) through the resistance activist Günther Weisenborn (1902–69) and the 'inner emigré' Hans Carossa (1878–1956) to the Christian conservative Gertrud von le Fort (1876–1971). On 10 May 1946, the anniversary of the Nazi book-burnings of 1933, the 'Day of the Book' was celebrated in all four zones as a common act of memory and cultural regeneration.

But with the onset of the Cold War the Western occupying powers began the reconstruction of western Europe, including the western zones of Germany, as an anti-communist bulwark. Denazification was toned down, halted or reversed. The socialist humanism embraced briefly even by the CDU in its Ahlener Programm of 1946 was ousted by a range of traditional values appropriate to a restoration of German capitalism. Symptomatically, *Der Ruf*, founded by Andersch (1914–80) and Richter (1908–1993) while in a POW camp in the USA as a forum of cultural renewal on the basis of democratic socialism, and encouraged by the US authorities when refounded in Germany in 1946, was banned as subversive by the same authorities in 1947.

The polarisation of the Cold War led rapidly to a divided reception of both pre-1945 and post-1945 German literature. In 1947, the first (and for four decades, the last) Pan-German Writers' Congress ended in disarray. Exile writers were treated with suspicion in a Western Germany uneasy about its own unreconstructed relationship to the Nazi past and resentful of the allegiance many former exiles gave to the socialist East. The recep-tion of Bertolt Brecht and Heinrich Mann was significantly hindered; despite the impact in the immediate post-war years of Friedrich Wolf's exile drama of a Jewish doctor, *Professor Mamlock* (1935, German pre-miere 1946), and Anna Seghers's novel *Das siebte Kreuz* (*The seventh cross*, 1942, German edition 1946), one of the great mid-century articula-tions of humanist resistance, soon Wolf and even Seghers were virtually forgotten in the West. Thus Nazism's far-reaching, though not total, insulation of German culture from its own recent achievement was only partially overcome. Until the 1960s, French existentialism and American realism were better known than the politically committed modernism of the Weimar Republic.

Other traditions survived 1945 almost uninterrupted. The intense expectations of a 'zero hour' allowed many writers to associate themselves with a break with the past which they were not actually making. At the same time, traumatic loss of stable values encouraged the reassurance of familiar forms and ethical positions. One example is the nature poetry of Wilhelm Lehmann (1882–1968), which shows little formal or thematic change after 1945. Lehmann's essay 'Die Entstehung eines Gedichts' ('How a poem takes shape'), much discussed in the latter 1940s, first appeared in *Das Reich* in 1943. In his pre-modern poetry, language is still trusted to mediate reality; thus word and thing are still identical (for example *Abschiedslust* (*The pleasure of leavetaking*, 1962)). His poetological essays like *Dichtung als Dasein* (*Poetry as existence*, 1956)) remained influential into the 1950s.

The neo-classical sonnet prominent since the early 1930s remained so: strict form as a counter to moral disorientation, with conscious echoes of Hölderlin, George and Rilke. It is typically associated with apolitical idealism and Christian conservatism, as in the sequence *Venezianisches Credo* (*Venetian creed*, 1946) by Rudolf Hagelstange (1912–84). The *Moabiter Sonette* (1946) of Albrecht Haushofer (1903–45), testament of an anti-Nazi who died in Moabit prison, is a notable exception. In works like the novel *Das unauslöschliche Siegel* (*The indelible seal*, 1946) by Elisabeth Langgässer (1889–1950) or the poems in *Dies Irae* (1946) by Werner Bergengruen (1892–1964), which stylises the war as divine punishment, Hitler as 'Widergott' or antichrist, the ethos of spiritual nobility in the face of daemonic evil offered an attractive, because socio-politically unspecific and indirect, way of coming to terms with the recent Nazi past, and one which retrospectively legitimated inner emigration: many of these authors, like Bergengruen, Carossa, Albrecht Goes (b. 1908) or Stefan Andres (1906–70), actually enjoyed an enhanced reputation after 1945 and right through the 1950s, as is evident from anthologies and readers of the time. Rudolf Alexander Schroeder (1878–1962) published some forty works in the Nazi period, and continued now to turn out his neo-classical odes and Christian rhetoric (e.g. *Die geistlichen Gedichte* (*Religious poems*, 1949)). He was even considered by Konrad Adenauer a possible author for the national hymn of the new Federal Republic. Schroeder's lecture 'Dichten und Trachten' ('Poetry and striving', 1946; much reprinted), like Langgässer's 'Von der Redlichkeit des Schriftstellers' ('The writer's integrity') continued to celebrate the 'Dichter' as spiritually and morally privileged visionary, as though this attitude had no case to answer regarding its underpinning of the Nazi ideology of the 'Führer'. The case of Reinhold Schneider (1903–58) though, who retained his Christian idealism and campaigned against West German rearmament in the 1950s, suffering denunciation as a communist despite his strict Catholicism, is a reminder of the many differences of degree within this group of religiously orientated authors.

Gestures of common suffering permitted side-stepping of collective responsibility: a widespread defensive response to the international humiliation of the Nuremberg trials and, more individually, of the denazification procedures. The success of Ernst von Salomon's satire on the latter, *Der Fragebogen* (*The questionnaire*, 1951), is symptomatic. A related phenomenon was the large number of utopian and dystopian novels of the late 1940s offering flights from the historical specificity of Nazism and the post-war social order into catastrophes universalised as an existential verity or set in a high-technological future, full of horror or disdain for modern mass society: Franz Werfel (1890–1945), *Der Stern der Ungeborenen* (*Star of the unborn*, 1946); Heinz Risse (1898–1989), *Wenn die Erde bebt* (*When the earth shakes*, 1950); Paul Ettighofer (b. 1896), *Atomstadt* (*Nuclear city*, 1949), Andres's trilogy *Die Sintflut* (*The flood*, 1949–59); *Heliopolis* (1949) by Ernst Jünger (b. 1895), a plea for aristocratic élitism as an antidote to modernity. Hermann Kasack (1896–1966), in his apocalyptic novel *Die Stadt hinter dem Strom* (*The city beyond the river*, 1947; begun 1942), set in a vast city of rubble in the grip of an impenetrable bureaucracy, does not confront the German readership with the real origins of their contemporary misery, but converts the realities into a Kafkaesque nightmare: the world in ruins not as a consequence of fascism, but as an existential verity. The novel *Nekiya. Bericht eines Überlebenden* (*Nekiya – a survivor's report*, 1947) by Hans Erich Nossack (1901–77) draws on the use of Greek myth by the French existentialists (e.g. Sartre's *Les Mouches*), blended with elements of a bleak, sober *Reportage* of a city left deserted by catastrophe. Like Langgässer and Kasack, Nossack presents historical reality as manifestation of a higher, metaphysical meaning.

Ernst Wiechert (1887–1960) had been relatively outspoken for a figure of the 'innere Emigration', which had cost him a spell in a concentration camp. But his account of this, *Der Totenwald* (*Forest of the dead*, 1946), deploys a conventional poetic vocabulary at odds with the realities of incarceration and torture, in strong contrast to the laconic directness of Eugen Kogon's *Der SS-Staat* (*The SS-state*, 1946). Works like *Die Gesellschaft vom Dachboden* (*Attic pretenders*, 1946) by Ernst Kreuder (1903–1972) or the war diaries of Emil Barth (1900–58), *Lemuria* (1946), explicitly reject realism in favour of the imagination as the proper realm of literature. In a society where rational discourse is the property of the powerful, the imagination can be a means to subvert it; but *Die Gesellschaft vom Dachboden*, like Kreuder's second novel, *Die Unauffindbaren* (*The untraceable*, 1948), and *Die größere Hoffnung* (*Herod's children*, 1948) by Ilse Aichinger (b. 1921), is really a continuation of inner emigration, oddly aloof from the reconstitution of cultural consciousness in the aftermath of National Socialism.

In 1948 Barth was the first recipient of the revived Immermann Prize, which from 1933 to 1943 had been one of the principal Nazi literary prizes. Prizes were a telling reflection of continuities. In 1946 the Büchner Prize went to Fritz Usinger (1895–1982), in 1947 the Lessing Prize to R. A. Schroeder, in 1949 the Raabe Prize to Ina Seidel (1885–1974); all had published extensively in Nazi Germany.

There were, though, very different trends in the literature of the latter 1940s, emanating primarily from a generation of writers too young to have made formative political or aesthetic choices during the Weimar period, but old enough to have been soldiers, and to have experienced the contradiction between war and rubble on the one hand and the idealistic values of their 'Gymnasium' education and its articulation in the privileged language of the 'Dichter' on the other, both of which they equated with a morally discredited older generation (though degrees of political commitment and aesthetic innovation cut across generational boundaries). More typical initially than major works were passionate essays calling for a new beginning on the basis of democratic socialism, published in journals like *Der Ruf*, *Die Sammlung* (*The gathering*) or *Die Wandlung* (*The transformation*). The ban on *Der Ruf* and the effort to create an alternative mouthpiece for the views of this generation led to the formation of *Gruppe 47*, aimed, said Richter retrospectively, to promote a new realistic literature devoted to 'political commitment and truth'.

Gruppe 47 had its origins in a cultural climate in which, for many Germans, the experience of hustling for everyday necessities combined with the discrediting of Nazi rhetoric to produce a 'radical suspicion of all ideologies' (Hans Mayer, *Die umerzogene Literatur*, 1991). Scepticism was directed at the language itself, vehicle not only of Goebbels's propaganda but also of wider traditions of anti-democratic thought and inflated idealism within which Nazism had flourished. As Wolfdietrich Schnurre (1920–89) wrote: 'We saw every "And" as a possible Judas. Threw out more words than we took in. Checked if they were hollow. Performed acid tests. Bit into every word before using it.' Wolfgang Weyrauch (1907–80) spoke of the need for a 'Kahlschlag', that is, a stripping away of the forest of corrupt ideas, ideals and language in favour of an 'unmediated realism'. Unintentionally, terms like 'Kahlschlag' echoed the violence of the Nazi rhetoric they were supposed to supplant, and in certain ways 'unmediated realism' endorsed a goal-oriented pragmatism which had little time for mourning or self-critical reflection on the past.

The idea of a 'Kahlschlag' was not only linguistically problematic: many writers who claimed to belong to the 'Zero Hour' had been active in Nazi Germany: Richter and Andersch had published ideologically conformist stories, Weyrauch edited *1940 – junge deutsche Prosa* (*1940 – Young German prose*), Günter Eich (1907–72) written twenty radio plays and published one-third of the poems that later appeared in *Abgelegene Gehöfte* (*Remote farmsteads*, 1948). When this information re-emerged in the 1980s, it severely undermined the moral stance adopted for example by Richter.

'Unmediated realism', addressing the material facts of the latter 1940s, hunger, cold, homelessness, disease, war injuries, was most often found in newspaper and magazine 'Reportagen': factual snapshots of life in the ruined cities, on the black market, in railway waiting rooms and on 'Hamsterfahrten' to trade family heirlooms with farmers for food. In their immediacy and articulation of the common, even if extraordinary experience of millions of ordinary Germans, these 'Reportagen' were a genuinely popular literature whose importance for the constitution of post-war German identity is often overlooked.

This unmediated realism, influenced by American short story writers like Hemingway widely disseminated in late 1940s Germany as part of the Western allies' 're-education' campaign (though, ironically, Hemingway was also published in Nazi Germany), characterises too the (often very) short stories of Schnurre (for example, 'Die Begräbnis Gottes' ('The burial of God', 1947)) or Walter Kolbenhoff (1908–1993). The impact of the latter's 'Die Hände' ('The hands', *Der Ruf*, 1946) depends on the entirely matter-of-fact narration of the difficulties a double amputee with two crude wooden arms has lighting and smoking a cigarette.

The stories of Wolfgang Borchert (1921–47) share similar themes and locations: ruined cities, ruined lives, obsessive hunger, trauma. Many, like 'Das Brot' ('Bread'), achieve the laconic precision of 'Kahlschlag'. In others, like 'Die Elbe', liturgical repetitions and expressionistic stylisation transform the real horrors of the post-war ruins into metaphysical images of alienation.

Heinrich Böll (1917–85), whose work spans and in some ways charts the progress of West Germany from the latter 1940s to the 1980s, began with short stories and novels set amongst ordinary soldiers bewildered and bored by the senselessness of war (*Der Zug war pünktlich* (*The train was on time*, 1949); *Wo warst du, Adam?* (*Adam, where art thou*, 1951)), or in the physical and moral rubble of the post-war German cities. That his 'Bekenntnis zur Trümmerliteratur' ('Commitment to rubble literature'), stressing this work's sympathy for the deprived, appeared in 1952 is a reminder that 'Trümmerliteratur', like 'Kahlschlag', was less an immediate post-war literary trend than a subsequent reaction to the aesthetic and ideological continuities manifest in much literature of the latter 1940s.

Böll's war stories, like Kolbenhoff's *Von unserem Fleisch und Blut* (*Our flesh and blood*, 1947) or Richter's *Die Geschlagenen* (*Beyond defeat*, 1949), show critical solidarity with the ordinary people their figures represent. But these people's very powerlessness and insignificance absolves them of moral responsibility for events. This is the philosophy of the *Landser* or squaddie in all ages, nations and armies, a surprising dehistoricisation given Böll's critical intentions and later work (in the 1980s it emerged that other works, more critical of the ordinary soldier, had been rejected by publishers in the late 1940s). *Stalingrad* (begun 1943/4 in Soviet exile, published 1946) by Theodor Plievier (1892–1955), is very different: a multi-voiced montage of semi-documentary experiences reworked from the accounts of German POWs, which seeks through its form of unvarnished realism (like all such realisms, actually a highly artistic construction) to unmask the propaganda myth of the glory of the *Wehrmacht* even in defeat.

In poetry, the most-cited example of 'Kahlschlag' is Günter Eich's 'Inventur' ('Inventory', written 1946 in a POW camp). In a syntax whose repetitive simplicity records the reduction of physical and spiritual life to its minimum, a prisoner of war itemises his few belongings, the repeated possessive pronoun a defensive gesture indicating that even these pitiful objects are by no means safe. The emotional charge of this and similar poetry rests in the palpable exclusion of emotion. Weyrauch aimed for a similar tone which he called 'Bestandsaufnahme' or stocktaking.

This was one possible response to T. W. Adorno's 1949 indictment of the escapist potential of poetry: 'to write poetry after Auschwitz is barbaric'. But Adorno was also indicating the dilemma of poetic responses to genocide itself. Even when, perhaps precisely when, a poem confronts horror, it may, by giving it poetic form, legitimate it aesthetically as 'cultural property'. The Romanian-German Paul Celan (1920–70), his Jewish identity profoundly traumatised by anti-Semitism and the Holocaust, published 'Todesfuge' ('Death fugue') in 1945, the insistent repetitions of whose fugue form give a nagging power to the haunting images of 'schwarze Milch' ('black milk'), ashes and human hair. The poem is one of the best known in the whole of post-war German literature, partly for problematic reasons: in many anthologies (for example, for schools) it had a token function as virtually the only Holocaust poem (the interaction of horror and mystical hope in Nelly Sachs's *In den Wohnungen des Todes* (*In the habitations of death*, 1947), or *Sternverdunkelung* (*Eclipse of a star*, 1949), for example, receiving far less attention). Eventually Celan came to omit the poem from public readings (while for his part Adorno came to qualify his critique). Celan moved to Paris in 1948; for many surviving German-Jewish writers, exile did not end with the defeat of Nazism, and the virtual absence of German-Jewish voices from post-war literature compounded the effect of genocide itself.

The theatres, closed by Goebbels in 1944, were among the first cultural institutions reopened by the occupation authorities, often in temporary auditoria, for seventy-seven per cent of German theatres were destroyed in the war. Characteristically, the Deutsches Theater in Berlin reopened on 7 September 1945 with a classic disfavoured by the Nazis for its championing of humanistic values in a Jewish protaganist, Lessing's *Nathan der Weise* (*Nathan the Wise*). Both practitioners and audiences looked to theatre to offer spiritual and aesthetic regeneration in materially straitened times. Yet from the start the theatres reflected the hardening fronts of the Cold War: *Nathan* was a substitute for Thornton Wilder's *Our town*, banned by the Soviet authorities as anti-democratic, while in the West, Brecht's work was rarely played. Productions of the classics from the Nazi period were often recycled unchanged, and there were many continuities of personnel, typified by the uninterrupted career of the director Gustav Gründgens from the 1930s to the 1960s. The work of modern American and French playwrights was widely performed (Wilder, Miller, Williams, Anouilh, Sartre, Giraudoux), at the expense of the almost complete exclusion of the drama of the Weimar Republic and of exile writers.

The two best-known German plays of the period address the theme of responsibility in very different ways; neither is unproblematic. The haunting, expressionistically heightened tones of despair and accusation in Borchert's *Draußen vor der Tür* (*The man outside*, 1947) make it one of the most powerful 'Heimkehrer' ('returning soldier') dramas. But its intense focalisation through the protagonist Beckmann encouraged audiences' identification with the victim, rather than confrontation with responsibility for the positions they actually may have adopted in the Nazi period.

Des Teufels General (*The devil's general*: premiered in Zurich 1946; more than 3,200 performances in Germany between 1947 and 1950) by Carl Zuckmayer (1896–1970) also supported the collective repression of responsibility, by presenting complicity with the Nazi state as a Faustian pact, offering the German people a welcome national mythology. The flamboyant flying ace Harras (based on Nazi pilot Ernst Udet) is not a career opportunist, but a noble figure in a tragic conflict (an image of the German officer caste which made the US authorities suppress the play for a time), his Nazi antagonists easy scapegoats in their vulgarity and self-evident evil. As the anti-communist crusade began to legitimate the idea of the 'decent' German soldier, the play was doubly welcome. Zuckmayer himself was no apologist for Nazi Germany – he had been in exile in the USA – and in 1963 he eventually withdrew the play.

The Zurich Schauspielhaus, the sole major German-speaking theatre in mainland Europe to remain outside Nazi control, continued after 1945 to play an important role by mediating the work of contemporary American and European dramatists, including German exiles like Brecht, Brückner, Hasenclever, Kaiser, Wolf, Werfel. It also premiered the first plays by two Swiss writers whose work brought post-war German theatre into contact with the theatrical principles of Brecht and the European drama of the absurd. The requiem form of *Nun singen sie wieder* (*They're singing again*, 1945) by Max Frisch (1911–91) transcends reality in order to present a complex dramatisation of the problem of guilt: a soldier ordered to shoot twenty-one hostages is subsequently haunted by their singing. Its message of personal responsibility is unequivocal: 'es gibt keine Ausflucht in den Gehorsam' ('there is no escape into obedience'). His *Die chinesische Mauer* (*The Great Wall of China*, 1947) dramatises the impotence of the intellectual in the face of totalitarian power. Friedrich Dürrenmatt (1921–90) began with plays addressing the ethical conflict between religion and revolution, *Es steht geschrieben* (*It is written*, 1947) and *Der Blinde* (*The blind man*, 1947).

Otherwise, Franz Werfel's *Jakobowski und der Oberst* (*Jakobowski and the Colonel*, 1947), a comedy of prejudice and survival in which a Jew and an anti-Semitic Polish army officer make common cause to evade the invading German army in 1939, is one of the few plays to have survived in today's repertoire. The oblique moral statements of the historical dramas of Austrian Fritz Hochwälder (1911–86), *Das heilige Experiment* (*The strong are lonely*, 1943; German premiere 1947) and *Der öffentliche Ankläger* (*The public prosecutor*, 1948), were left behind by the more aggressively political and formally innovative drama of the 1960s. *Die Illegalen* (1946), a moving, if sentimentalised account of resistance by Günther Weisenborn, has not survived its brief popularity in the late 1940s, when it played in some 350 theatres. Weisenborn and his reception were typical victims of the Cold War: distrusted as left-wing in the West, and as a Westerner in the East.

The 1950s

In 1949, the foundation of the Federal Republic (and then of the GDR) confirmed the division of Germany for the foreseeable future and the form of the West German state as that of a capitalist liberal democracy. The CDU and its conservative values dominated, as the economic boom of the 1950s generated so much wealth that criticism of its unequal distribution fell largely on deaf ears. The integrative force of prosperity subsumed the extremist and special interest parties that had existed at the outset into the party landscape of CDU/CSU, FDP and SPD which remained essentially unchanged until the rise of the Green Party around 1980. Erich Kästner called the 1950s 'motorisiertes Biedermeier' (roughly, 'bourgeois values on wheels'): the chaos of the late 1940s and its associated sense of openness was replaced by order and unwillingness to risk the stability on which prosperity rested, expressed in Adenauer's slogan 'No experiments' and attacked in Harald Duwe's paintings of stultifying *petit-bourgeois* tedium (e.g. 'Sonntagnachmittag', 1956–60).

Returning stability could be charted in the revived dominance of the novel over the short prose forms of the late 1940s. The novel's criticism of contemporary social experience was, typically, non-conformist ('outsider' narrators were common) rather than specifically political. Amongst the most regarded German-language novels of the period were those of Frisch. Though *Stiller* (1954) may be read as a critique of Swiss society, its real impact was as a work of existential modernism unrelated to a particular social-historical moment, a fictional protocol of a narrator's crisis of identity and the illusion of individual freedom. This theme and its formal realisation was continued in *Homo Faber* (1957), Frisch's indictment of the hubris of technocratic rationality, and reached an extreme of self-referential fictionality in *Mein Name sei Gantenbein* (*A wilderness of mirrors*, 1964). In poetry, alongside the continuity of traditional forms and themes, an international, or at least western-oriented modernism emerged, exploring existential themes rather than ones specific to German historical experience; the drama demonstrated comparable tendencies. Yet artistic and political frustration was mounting, and around 1960 a phase of West German literature began whose impact on public consciousness has rarely been exceeded.

The currency reform of 1948 was a key watershed for culture as for the economy generally, pragmatism replacing speculative idealism. It seemed as though the cultural renewal of the late 1940s had been only a compensation for the lack of material goods. By 1949, the book market too was energetically re-establishing itself; but the already only partial strivings for a new beginning in post-war literature were receding in favour of the conservative tradition and the re-enthronement of a culture that eschewed politics, reflected in Gottfried Benn's *Statische Gedichte* (*Static poems*, 1948) and his novella 'Der Ptolomäer' (1949), with their stress on rigorous form and the expunging of quotidian concerns from literature.

Benn had been compromised by his initial endorsement of Nazism. His reappearance on the literary market in 1948 was characteristic of Cold War reorientation and rapid rehabilitation. By 1950, while exile authors remained largely neglected, openly Nazi writers (to which Benn should not be assigned) like Hans Friedrich Blunck (1888–1961) were publishing freely again, though their work was often too historically specific to be welcomed by a public seeking textual confirmation of its successful metamorphosis into a liberal consumer culture.

This confirmation was offered in superficially critical novels like *Die Autostadt* (*Motorcar city*, 1951) by Horst Mönnich (b. 1918). After the currency reform ends what Mönnich portrays as a chaotic interregnum, the regeneration of Volkswagen production at Wolfsburg is celebrated as the triumph of German know-how, order and discipline. A *Heimkehrer*'s determination to make good exactly mirrors the success ethic of the Federal Republic: 'There is only hard work and the goal one is aiming for, and not weakening'. Similarly, in *Besser zu zweit als allein* (*Better a twosome than alone*, 1950) by Walter Bauer (1904–76), the currency reform (not 1933 or 1945) is the 'flood', the protagonist 'a new Adam', the future a 'private matter'.

Meanwhile, the romantic anti-capitalism and conservative values of Gerd Gaiser (1908–76) ensured both popular success and the praise of conservative critics for his novels: the 'Heimkehrerroman' *Eine Stimme hebt an* (*A voice rings out*, 1950); *Die sterbende Jagd* (*The falling leaf*, 1953; begun 1942!), celebrating comradeship and manly heroism. *Schlußball* (*The final ball*, 1958) is set in a town whose name – Neu-Spuhl (New-rinse) – typifies Gaiser's simplistic allegorising and scorn for plebeian consumerism, shared by Hugo Hartung's *Wir Wunderkinder* (*Children of the miracle*, 1957) or Erich Kuby's *Rosemarie – des deutschen Wunders liebstes Kind* (*Rosemarie, the favourite child of the German miracle*, 1961).

One of the few writers in the early 1950s to combine striking formal innovation with aggressive criticism of the political restoration in nascent West Germany and the impotence of its intellectuals was Wolfgang Koeppen (1909–96). He too had published in the early years of Nazi Germany: a reminder of the dangers of simplistic categories. *Tauben im Gras* (*Doves in the grass*, 1951), influenced by *Reportage* writing and by Joyce's *Ulysses*, takes place during one day in the rubble of post-war Munich. *Das Treibhaus* (*The hothouse*, 1953) is a satire on the political climate of the early phase of the economic boom and shows the Bonn élites as a self-serving, corrupt clique. *Der Tod in Rom* (*Death in Rome*, 1954) portrays a group of ex-Nazis who have gone to ground. These novels emphasise the survival in German society of attitudes and values that had supported Nazism, since they were in fact fundamental to the pride and prestige of modern (post-1871) Germany as a whole. Through their narrative technique (stream-of-consciousness, interior monologue), the world of the novels is experienced as a patchwork of voices, perspectives and temporal planes in which past and present, German history and German mythology, commingle: post-war Germany, later the early Federal Republic, is an unsettling montage of the old and the new, an unnaturally luxuriant hothouse. (In Weisenborn's *Auf Sand gebaut* (*Built on sand*, 1956), the image is of the house of a demi-mondaine built on top of an unexploded bomb.) These works were out of place in the climate of the early 1950s and were unsuccessful, but remain Koeppen's principal achievement.

Arno Schmidt (1914–79) also deployed montages of contradictory discourses in response to a fragmentary and disharmonious reality. In *Leviathan* (1949), natural science is the only reliable counterweight to a pitiless world of tyrannies. Novels like *Brands Heide* (*Brand's heath*, 1951) trace the complex and ironical historical associations of a small, apparently insignificant North German village community. *Das steinerne Herz* (*Heart of stone*, 1956) is one of the first West German treatments of the theme of the divided Germany. In *Die Gelehrtenrepublik* (*The egg-head republic*, 1957), a version of the Cold War is fought out by half-human, half-animal mutants on a floating island in the Sargasso Sea. Schmidt's neglect of linear narrative in favour of Joycean mosaics of puns, allusions, interior monologue and language games reaches its extreme form in *Zettels Traum* (*Zettel's dream*, 1970).

Where Koeppen fatalistically lards the past into his fiction's present, Alfred Andersch (1914–82) seeks to break through the deterministic factuality of the past by transforming 'the historic indicative into the subjunctive' (Klaus Scherpe, *Die rekonstruierte Moderne*, 1992), focusing on an existentialist 'possibility of absolute freedom': moments of individual decision which are the sole roots of authentic social action. In the autobiographical *Die Kirschen der Freiheit* (*Cherries of freedom*, 1952) one such moment is the narrator's desertion in 1944, a theme revived in *Die Rote* (*The redhead*, 1960); another the lost historical chance when, with crowds of other socialists, he watched passively as the SA occupied the trades union buildings in March 1933. The smallest act of protest might have changed history. *Winterspelt* (1974), set during the Ardennes campaign of 1944, explores a similar moment. In *Sansibar oder der letzte Grund* (*Flight to afar*, 1957) the interwoven fates of a Protestant clergyman, a German Jewess, two KPD members and a fifteen–year-old boy combine with an attempt to save a banned work of art into an intense moment of existential choice; the historical specificity of Nazi oppression remains shadowy, invoked only as 'the others': in the Cold War, it could be read, at least unconsciously, as an anti-GDR text.

Heinrich Böll's prose sought an 'aesthetic of the humane' to restore dignity, indeed sublimity, to people marginalised by the success-oriented society. His work offers a worm's-eye view of West Germany, specifically the Catholic Rhineland, as a society which corrupts spontaneous human values like love or faith into institutionally endorsed hypocrisies and which has failed to address the trauma of its Nazi past. The ethical commitment which fired his many essays led in his work to an uneasy mixture of realistic milieus with allegorical tendentiousness, as in the division of the figures in *Billard um halb zehn* (*Billiards at half past nine*, 1959) into 'lambs and buffalo'. The conservative religious values and attacks on consumer materialism that mark his early 1950s novels – *Und sagte kein einziges Wort* (*Acquainted with the night*, 1953), *Haus ohne*

Hüter (*Tomorrow and yesterday*, 1954) and *Das Brot der frühen Jahre* (*The bread of our early years*, 1955) – and his often masterly radio plays and short prose, have certain parallels with Gaiser. However, Böll rejects the division (implicit in Gaiser) between culture and the vulgarity of business and politics. The romanticised falsity of Böll's image of Ireland in *Irisches Tagebuch* (*Irish journal*, 1957) too makes sense as a counter-model to the blend of materialism and cultural snobbery he detested in the German bourgeoisie. Moreover, his 1950s novels also typically invoke an anarchistic energy in the eucharistic symbol of 'Brot': love and sharing are offered as the means to break out of profit-seeking consumer society, themes that recur in later works like *Gruppenbild mit Dame* (*Group portrait with lady*, 1971) with greater political sharpness.

Böll's other key theme is memory: success in post-war society is linked with ability to repress the past. *Billard um halb zehn* treats German history from the *Kaiserreich* to the 1950s through the monologues and flashbacks prompted by the eightieth birthday of the Rhineland architect Hinrich Fähmel. Despite its simplistic elements, it was, both in the heightened bitterness and specificity of its critique of the German failure to address the issue of Nazism and in its cautious ventures into self-reflexive modernist narrative, part of the new impulse in post-war German literature at the end of the 1950s.

Ansichten eines Clowns (*The clown*, 1963) attacks the alignment of the Catholic Church after 1945 with restoration, opportunism and the CDU state. The extreme subjectivity of the narrator Hans Schnier stresses his isolation amidst a self-satisfied 'Wirtschaftswunder' consensus which exemplifies what Alexander and Margarete Mitscherlich were to call *Die Unfähigkeit zu trauern* (*The inability to mourn*, 1967), the inability to address in any real sense one's own historical guilt. The closing image, Schnier in clown garb and make-up on the steps of Bonn railway station, epitomises the role of the literary opposition in Adenauer's Germany: determined, courageous, yet powerless and part-institutionalised. Rage at this powerlessness contributed to the radicalisation of literary culture in the 1960s.

'Whatever may happen to us was decided in the fifties', Martin Walser (b. 1927) remarked in 1960, and his novel *Halbzeit* (*Half-time*, 1960) is a critical stocktaking of the first decade of the economic miracle. Though the narrative is focalised through Kristlein, its language is a de-individualised patchwork, shaped by the internalised clichés and jargons of a society dominated by conformism, capital and the worship of market values, to succeed in which the *petit-bourgeois* intellectual has sacrificed his identity and the humanist values of which this identity is partly constructed. As often in Walser's work (e.g. *Seelenarbeit* (*Soulwork*, 1979)), death and sickness motifs abound. In the latter 1960s, Walser too sought a way out of the fatalism that might logically have followed, via a politicisation of literature and of the writer's role.

Günter Grass (b. 1927), after experimental poetry and forays into absurd drama (*e.g. Onkel, Onkel*, 1958), also moved to a more specifically political literature in *Örtlich betäubt* (*Local anaesthetic*, 1969) and *Aus dem Tagebuch einer Schnecke* (*From the diary of a snail*, 1972), and to an active engagement for the SPD in the 1960s and 1970s. But first he produced his 'Danzig trilogy' *Die Blechtrommmel* (*The tin drum*, 1959), *Katz und Maus* (*Cat and mouse*, 1961) and *Hundejahre* (*Dog years*, 1963). *Katz und Maus*, in which Grass's aim to speak for those many Germans of his generation who did not survive is most evident, is a short novel whose dense patterns of leitmotifs underscore the fate of its anti-hero Mahlke and its narrator Pilenz, whose lives are ruined one way or the other by the collision of puberty with the humanist values of the *Gymnasium*, betrayed by their teachers and perverted by militarism.

Die Blechtrommel, with its unreliable, grotesquely ambiguous narrator, the dwarf Oskar Matzerath, mocked the 1950s novel for the feebleness of its imagination and the pathos of its protagonists' pretensions as moral arbiters and preachers, and became the first West German novel to attract world attention. Oskar has the child's-eye view of the truth; but he is also a monstrous dwarf, and as such represents the perverted viciousness of Nazism. Yet he is also haunted by his guilt for the death of both his putative fathers. *Die Blechtrommel* stresses the role of *petit-bourgeois* values and attitudes in the German catastrophe, which can no longer be shrugged off as blind fate or the machinations of powerful others. The novel's ceaseless traverse of the boundaries between truth and fantasy, the realistic and the grotesque, ensures that the narrated world is always both familiar and estranged, and thus keeps historical experience alive, unsanitised and painful.

In some poetry of the 1950s, nature was now seen not as an idyll but a site of unsettling confrontation with the human condition. Eich's *Botschaft des Regens* (*Message of the rain*, 1955) has a calligraphic terseness that results from suspicion both of ideological language and of stereotyped everyday speech. This poetry deliberately frustrates ready understanding and seeks to offer realities different from those of public language. In this it was influenced by two very different poets, Benn and Celan.

Benn's first post-war volumes like *Statische Gedichte* (1948) and *Trunkene Flut* (*The drunken tide*, 1949) continued his project of resisting political ideology by 'coldness of thought, sobriety, acerbically sharp concepts' and of writing disciplined verse apparently immune from emotional contamination. His concept of 'the absolute poem', a self-enclosed hermetic poetry, and his rejection of participation in the everyday world, expressed in his lecture 'Probleme der Lyrik' ('Problems of poetry', 1951), with its stress on form and 'Artistik' as a corrective for the blandishments of mass society, whether fascist or democratic, had a programmatic status. He was the first recipient of the new Büchner Prize in 1951. In volumes like *Fragmente* (1951) or *Destillationen* (1953), the widespread sensation, in the West Germany of the 1950s, of living in an epoch and a society divorced from its own history, is translated into a nihilistic expression of the overall demise of Western culture.

Public interest in the 1950s in this kind of apolitical modernism was considerable: Hugo Friedrich's *Die Struktur der modernen Lyrik* (*The structure of modern poetry*, 1956), which traced modernist poetry as an international style to its origins in Baudelaire, Rimbaud and Mallarmé, sold 70,000 paperback copies in four years. One could argue, with Hermann Glaser, that the standard lamps and kidney-shaped coffee tables indelibly associated with the 1950s had their literary parallels in lyric poetry which tastefully, but reassuringly unspecifically, displayed its modernist credentials. On the other hand, Adorno, in a 1957 speech on 'Lyrik und Gesellschaft' ('Poetry and society') regarded hermetic poetry as a unique cultural space where freedom from social and political compulsions could be defended and articulated.

This would apply, certainly, to the poetic language of Celan, which after *Mohn und Gedächtnis* (*Poppy and memory*, 1952) increasingly resists discursive interpretation, and seeks the German language's 'musicality' without the false 'euphony' which had accommodated itself even to genocide. The title poem of *Sprachgitter* (*Speech-grille*, 1959) evokes the possibility but also the failure of human communication in the failed gaze of lovers. (Nelly Sachs, in contrast, turns increasingly to Judaic mysticism, transforming oppressive, incomprehensible memory into metaphysical images in *Und niemand weiß weiter* (*And no one knows what to do*, 1957), or *Die Suchende* (*The seeker*, 1966)). Celan committed suicide in 1970. His 'dunkle Lyrik' requires patient attention, but in doing so turns hermetic poetry into a medium for reflection on historical suffering.

Ingeborg Bachmann (1926–73) drew on the hermetic tradition of Celan and the formal rigour of Benn. Though her poetry does indict 'yesterday's executioners', its political quality lies primarily in the longing it provokes for rebellion against an undefined sense of menace and a blank, inhospitable reality, very palpable in the title poem of *Die gestundete Zeit* (*A respite for time*, 1953), where nature offers neither meaning nor transcendence, merely bleakness. The title poem of *Anrufung des großen Bären* (*The invocation of the great bear*, 1956) evokes an indeterminable apocalypse: the nightmares of the post-war, Cold War, atomic age. 'The relationship of trust between self and language and thing is deeply unsettled', she declared: not only the ideologically distorted language of politics, but the unsettling relativities of modern science and the experience of failure in everyday communication contribute to the all-pervading sense of menace.

Karl Krolow (b. 1915), influenced initially by the nature poetry of Loerke and Lehmann (*Die Zeichen der Welt* (*The signs of the world*, 1952)); *Wind und Zeit* (*Wind and time*, 1954)), offered laconic, melancholy responses to the pain of human fallibility and isolation, the continual, fruitless challenge to articulate existential reality in poetry. In the 1960s, he began to use images and concepts from mathematics in conscious tension with the expectations of lyric poetry: *Unsichtbare Hände* (*Invisible hands*, 1962).

Hermetic poetry's focus on form has links to the 'concrete poetry' of the 1950s and 1960s, where, analogously to abstract art, the linguistic material is deployed for its optical and acoustic effects: the visual layout of words on the page, the use of dialect or of conscious phonetic distortion. In forcing one to read old words in new ways (reflecting the insights of linguistic philosophers like Wittgenstein, Whorf and Sapir), it can acquire social meaning by subverting habits of unreflective reading: Franz Mon (b. 1926): *artikulationen* (1959); Helmut Heißenbüttel (b. 1921): *Textbuch* 1–4 (1960–64). The Swiss Eugen Gomringer (b. 1925), in *konstellationen* (1951–69), sought poetic forms to express the modern technological environment in terms of information theory; in contrast, the Austrian 'Wiener Gruppe' of Friedrich Achleitner (b. 1930), H. C. Artmann (b. 1921), Ernst Jandl (b. 1925), Gerhard Rühm (b. 1930) and Oswald Wiener (b. 1935) drew on the Dadaist tradition to disrupt audience expectations in the sleepy provincialism of 1950s Austria.

Concrete poetry's apparently apolitical focus on the shape of language led, via Heißenbüttel's 'Politische Grammatik' of 1959, to a politicised poetry which drew on awareness of how language works, first, to criticise its development as a tool of manipulation, second, to develop politically operative texts that could intervene in public processes (for example, Claus Bremer: *engagierende texte* (*committed texts*, 1966); *Texte und Kommentare* 1968; the epigrammatic work of Arnfried Astel or Erich Fried).

In the early work of H. M. Enzensberger (b. 1929), the sense of menace articulated by Bachmann becomes a more specific critique of false consciousness and consumerism. Enzensberger, like Peter Rühmkorf (b. 1929) in *Heiße Lyrik* (*Fiery lyrics*, 1956) or *Kunststücke* (*Clever tricks*, 1962), revived Brecht's project of a 'Gebrauchslyrik' ('useful poetry'), also adopted by poets like Fried, Volker von Törne or F. C. Delius. Enzensberger's 'Ins Lesebuch für die Oberstufe' ('Into the sixth-form reader') in *Verteidigung der Wölfe* (*In defence of wolves*, 1957), urges: 'Don't read odes, son, read timetables – they're more precise.' Though this

is still as much a style as a political position, works like the title poem of
Landessprache (*Vernacular*, 1960) challenged 'Wirtschaftswunder'
society and its relationship to its recent past as vehemently as the contemporary works of Böll or Grass, and set the stage for Enzensberger's
project, in the 1960s, of the political 'Alphabetisierung' of West German
society.

The *Hörspiel* or radio play reached its artistic peak in the 1950s; radio,
which like cinema played an important role in the rebuilding of the cultural infrastructure after 1945, was a vital source of income for many
writers, and long remained so, though after the introduction of regular
television broadcasts from 1954, the *Hörspiel* gradually lost its public. It
bred specialists like Richard Hey or Fred von Hoerschelmann; in addition,
many well-known writers of the 1950s wrote *Hörspiele*: Aichinger,
Andersch, Bachmann, Böll, Dürrenmatt, Eich, Frisch, Hildesheimer, Jens,
Kaschnitz, Lenz, Walser, Wellershoff, Weyrauch, for example. Often, a
radio version preceded a stage play or prose work; but radio demanded an
aesthetic of its own. The limits of the medium were also its potential: its
complete dependence on sound and silence permitted explorations of the
fluid relationship between the real and the unreal, reality and dream, the
outer and the inner world. In Eich's *Träume* (*Dreams*, 1950), five voices,
each from a different place and a different age, dream threatening dreams;
the epilogue calls for resistance: 'Be sand, not oil, in the cogs of the world':
a characteristically vague non-conformism against a characteristically
vague threat.

As civic wealth revived in the 1950s, so too did the German tradition of
representative theatre buildings (often rebuilt more quickly than schools)
and of theatre-going as a mark of status and civic identity. By 1960 there
were again 300 theatres with their own ensembles. The repertoire
remained conservative: in 1956/57 for example, of about 2,500 productions in German-speaking theatres 150 were of the work of living German
authors, and half of these of 4 authors only. Amongst the few contemporary authors, Frisch and Dürrenmatt continued to dominate: almost all
the plays that have made them lastingly successful are from this period.
Both authors remained under the influence of Brecht's theatrical technique, but questioned his view of the comprehensibility of the world and
the educability of people.

Frisch's 'Morality play without a moral' *Biedermann und die
Brandstifter* (*The fire-raisers*, 1958) focuses on the way fascism feeds off an
apathetic, cowardly or self-deceiving middle class. His *Andorra* (1961) is a
parable on prejudice and the inability to live without 'images'. These plays
offer reassuringly simple models of the moral universe, while refusing to
insist on political consequences. *Andorra* in particular mystifies history:
anti-Semitism is too real to stand as an abstract model for the tragedy to

which prejudice, hypocrisy and bad faith may lead. The three versions of Frisch's existentialist parable of the public prosecutor turned terrorist, *Graf Öderland* (*Count Oederland*, 1951, 1956, 1961) illustrate increasingly acquiescent responses to dilemmas of power, freedom and revolt.

In his 1954 lecture 'Theaterprobleme', Dürrenmatt argues that there are no Schillerean tragic heroes any more, only tragedies, 'directed by world butchers and performed by mincing machines': contemporary power is invisible or opaque, and brutal without grandeur. *Die Ehe des Herrn Mississippi* (*The marriage of Mr Mississippi*, 1952) is a black comedy of empty Cold War rhetoric. *Der Besuch der alten Dame* (*The visit*, 1956) is a grotesque tragicomedy on the abandonment of humanist values for material gain, set in the greedy, hypocritical city of Güllen. *Die Physiker* (*The physicists*, 1962) can be seen as Dürrenmatt's sceptical response to Brecht's *Leben des Galilei*: Möbius has himself certified in order to prevent his invention from becoming known, but in keeping with Dürrenmatt's pessimism, Möbius fails: the clinic's director is herself mad, power-crazed and fully informed of his secret. Thus the scientist's moral agonising is rendered absurd and irrelevant.

The huge and lasting success of these plays, it could be argued, resulted from the fact that they could be as historically specific (or not) as one wished, and offered the uncomplicated cleverness of Brechtian dialectic without the discomfort of political action (the same is often true of productions of Brecht).

The European theatre of the absurd had a strong appeal in Germany: Auschwitz was more palatable if presented as contrary to reason, part of a universal collapse of human meaning. But German dramatists came to the absurd late and largely imitatively: by the time of Hildesheimer's *Die Verspätung* (*The delay*, 1961) and *Nachtstück* (*Nightpiece*, 1963), abstract games were seeming less and less adequate to address specific historical realities of the kind epitomised by the trial of Adolf Eichmann.

The 1960s and 1970s

From the early 1960s CDU hegemony crumbled. The building of the Berlin Wall in 1961 initially intensified Cold War attitudes, but also discredited the CDU's stubborn non-recognition of the GDR. The trial of Eichmann in Jerusalem in 1960 and the Auschwitz trials in Frankfurt in 1963–5 reopened repressed issues of responsibility and guilt. Spectres of continuity with Nazi Germany were raised by high-handed government attempts to gag the magazine *Der Spiegel* in 1962, and by the Emergency Laws eventually passed in 1968. In 1966 the SPD joined the CDU/CSU in the 'Grand Coalition', whose chancellor, Kiesinger, was a known ex-Nazi;

only the tiny FDP remained as a parliamentary opposition. Meanwhile, the recession of 1965/66 brought the first check to sustained prosperity, and the neo-Nazi NPD enjoyed brief electoral success. These developments united disparate energies of protest in an 'extra-parliamentary opposition'. Both the resulting student movement of the late 1960s and the accession of Willy Brandt's SPD/FDP government in 1969 fired hopes (and fears) of radical change. But the student movement rapidly fragmented, and Brandt's replacement by the *Realpolitiker* Helmut Schmidt in 1974 was widely seen as a 'Tendenzwende' or swing back to the right, leading eventually to the CDU's return to power under Helmut Kohl in 1983.

The protest movement is often said to have failed. Certainly its wilder rhetoric remained unfulfilled, and government reaction to the brief upsurge of Marxist parties and of urban terrorism, namely the 'Radikalenerlaß' (Decree against the employment of radicals in public service) of 1972 and the expansion of the surveillance state, raised fears about West Germany's commitment to liberal democracy. Yet the protest movement not only stimulated specific reforms (for example, in education and social welfare), but also fostered widespread socio-political and ecological awareness and a growth of participant democracy, typified by the peace and ecology movements, and grass-roots citizens' initiatives of all kinds. The Federal Republic of the early 1980s was very different to that of the late 1950s.

The literature of the 1960s and 1970s not only reflected these developments but contributed to the flux of political, social and cultural opinion within which they occurred. Literary histories conventionally see in the late 1960s the crisis of literature under the influence of the protest movement and in the early to mid 1970s a return to inward-looking subjectivity in the context of disillusionment with politics and political literature. These marker posts are both helpful and misleading; in fact, literature from around 1960 to around 1980 needs to be seen as a complex continuum.

The broad sweep of cultural change can be traced in the fluctuating role of key journals. *Akzente. Zeitschrift für Dichtung* (*Accents – magazine for poesy*), founded by Hans Bender and Walter Höllerer in 1954, had been a shaping force in the 1950s and early 1960s with its view that art should resist ideological contamination. In 1967 Höllerer left; Bender changed the subtitle to *Zeitschrift für Literatur* and widened the output to include essays and other texts with political and social themes and intentions. But the trends were now being set elsewhere, notably in *Kursbuch*.

Critical intellectuals had been active in the anti-rearmament and other protest movements of the 1950s, and had supported the SPD in the 1961 and especially 1965 elections. Government reaction (characterised by Chancellor Erhard's attack on Rolf Hochhuth as a 'Pinscher' ('terrier') in

1965), the Nazi inheritance, supine state support for the Vietnam war, and the Emergency Laws further moved some writers to associate with radical groups for whom reform was no longer enough. Sometimes, this led to attempts to write political literature, sometimes to a declared eschewal of literature for politics. *Kursbuch*, originally founded by Enzensberger in 1965 as a literary magazine, became the leading forum for politicised intellectuals in the latter 1960s, analysing German issues from a Marxist viewpoint and in the context of multinational capitalism. Its title, borrowed tongue-in-cheek from the sovereign positivism of the German railway timetable, encapsulated its self-confident rationality. This related to a pragmatic modernist tendency in the 1960s and 1970s for writers, recognising that their dependency on powerful media conglomerates had made them into 'media employees' (Enzensberger) rather than poets, to demystify their role and that of literature. Walter Benjamin's 'Das Kunstwerk im Zeitalter seiner technischen Reproduzierbarkeit' ('The work of art in the age of mechanical reproduction') was an important influence. The forming of the 'Verband deutscher Schriftsteller' (German Writers' Association) in 1969 and its affiliation to the printing union in 1973 were a logical consequence, though writers' tendency to resist homogeneity kept the 'Verband' chronically strife-riven.

In 1968 *Kursbuch* 15 appeared, whose critique by Enzensberger, Karl Markus Michel and Walter Boehlich of literature's political impotence has been misrepresented as a clamorous declaration of the 'Death of Literature'. Certainly *Kursbuch* subsequently published largely non-literary issues on political, social and economic themes. But Enzensberger's 'Gemeinplätze, die neueste Literatur betreffend' ('Commonplaces about contemporary literature') insists that literature, political or not, remains literature and is not a substitute for political action. Even while he is urging writers to practise political journalism instead, this also holds open the door for the legitimation of literature *per se*.

By the early 1970s, neither rational analysis nor revolutionary rhetoric seemed any less impotent than apolitical literature, and *Kursbuch* in turn lost its dominant role. *Tintenfisch* (*Octopus*), founded in 1968 by Michael Krüger and Klaus Wagenbach, always stressed the importance of literature in the cultural processes within which political ones take place. It neither rejected subjectivity, nor turned its back on politics, but sought 'to participate through language in the construction of a utopia'. *Literaturmagazin* (1973–) similarly saw literature as 'an important productive force in society for the liberation of the emancipatory imagination', setting the tone for the 1970s symbiosis of the subjective and the political.

The inherent optimism, couched in Marxist jargon, of seeing literature as a 'productive force in society' still underlay much literary discussion throughout the 1970s; yet the fading of the reforming impulses with which the SPD had entered office, the economic stagnation of the mid 1970s, and the growing sense of environmental and nuclear threat, brought disillusion, and a crisis of Enlightenment optimism. In 1978, for example, Enzensberger published both the symptomatically titled long poem *Der Untergang der Titanic* (*The sinking of the Titanic*) and 'Zwei Randbemerkungen zum Untergang' ('Two marginal notes on decline'), in which, in *Kursbuch* itself, he noted the 'crisis of all positive utopias' and stated that 'we do not know the laws of history'.

For Enzensberger, this crisis of historical meaning could and should be met by sustained critical rationalism. For others it was a crisis of reason itself. A new spirit was exemplified, in the 1980s, by the debates on this crisis in *Merkur* (founded in 1947, and, edited in the 1980s by Karl Heinz Bohrer, regaining its influence in a new conservative climate), and by the 'Konkursbuchverlag' ('Bankruptcy publishers'; founded in 1978 by Claudia Gehrke), whose very name asserted the intellectual bankruptcy of *Kursbuch* and the materialist, progressive era it stood for. They did so, though, not as a single, dominant cultural voice but as part of a postmodern plurality of responses, defensive and offensive, celebratory and mourning, to a crisis of monadic models of the individual, society and history.

The distinct form that this crisis took in the particular historical context of West German culture provides further qualification of the neat models of literary historiography. In *Auf dem Weg zur vaterlosen Gesellschaft* (*Society without the father*, 1963) Alexander Mitscherlich describes the replacement of the essentially linear, order-enhancing, identity-affirming Oedipal conflict (The King must die! Long live the King!) by a fatherless society characterised by sibling rivalry manifested in social isolation and consumerist envy of one's neighbour. This provides a psychoanalytical model for the late twentieth-century experience of post- or hypermodernity, with its attendant crisis of fundamental Enlightenment beliefs in individual identity and collective progress.

Its German form, though, was decisively modified by recent history. 'Hitler is my father', declared Rolf Hochhuth in 1976; this unquestionably traumatic encumbrance also offered identity, moral focus and political purpose in the struggle against it, and against a contemporary society morally compromised by its ambivalence towards, and continuities with, Nazi Germany. Moreover, the division of Germany under Cold War conditions meant socialism could be idealised in Oedipal provocation to Western society. The resulting consensus of left-wing critical humanism largely drowned out counter-voices before the latter 1970s.

Around 1960 the father theme can be seen in the disputed paternity of Oskar and his offspring in *Die Blechtrommel*, Hochhuth's assault on the Holy Father in *Der Stellvertreter* (*The representative*, 1962), or Martin

Walser's Hamlet drama *Der schwarze Schwan* (*The black swan*, 1964) and his essay 'Hamlet als Autor' (1964). Around 1980 the theme reappears in autobiographical 'Vater-Bücher' like Siegfried Gauch: *Vaterspuren* (*Traces of the father*, 1979), Ruth Rehmann: *Der Mann auf der Kanzel* (*The man in the pulpit*, 1979) or Christoph Meckel: *Suchbild. Über meinen Vater* (*Wanted poster. About my father*, 1980), and in the revolt of the young knights against the self-satisfaction of Arthur's generation in Tankred Dorst and Ursula Ehler's *Merlin* (1981). Obsessive dependence on a real or surrogate father figure is also central to Botho Strauß's *Rumor* (*Tumult*, 1980) and F. C. Delius's *Ein Held der inneren Sicherheit* (*A hero of internal security*, 1981), where (as in Bernward Vesper's *Die Reise* (*The journey*, 1971), published 1977), the thematic triangle of generation conflict, Nazism and terrorism is especially evident: Delius draws on the fate of Hanns Martin Schleyer, president of the 'Bundesverband der Deutschen Industrie', whose kidnap and murder in 1977 led to the anti-liberal sentiment and resulting left-wing melancholy of the 'German autumn'.

Psychoanalytical and post-structuralist insights were important in identifying the dependency-in-revolt typified by 'Vater-Literatur' but which also underpinned much of the socially critical literature of the 1960s and 1970s. These insights were decisively furthered by the feminist criticism which developed in the 1980s alongside women's writing itself; both grew out of the protest movement and in revolt against its originally patriarchal tendencies. In the 1980s, entrapment in the discourse of patriarchy joined entrapment in the discourse of Enlightenment as interconnected objects of criticism in literature and in literary theory.

However, if by the early 1980s the representative status as the critical consciousness of the nation which had attached to *Gruppe* 47 authors like Böll, Grass, Walser or Enzensberger around 1960 had largely gone, this was a result not only of attacks from the radical left in the late 1960s or from feminists a decade or so later, but also of the critical processes their own work had stimulated. Their unpicking of the legitimacy of Adenauer's paternalism and the culture it embodied and sustained, contributed to a widespread questioning of hierarchies and figureheads, including, of course, alternative figureheads, anti-Adenauers like themselves.

In literary as in political terms, '1968' began well before 1968, as did the counter-currents. The crisis of literature manifested itself not only in calls for literature's abolition or functionalisation, but also in its opposite: texts of self-reflexive fictionality, such as the early work of Peter Handke. The two attacks which impelled the collapse of *Gruppe* 47, after two decades as an important literary forum, reversed the order which a conventional chronology would suggest. Handke's rejection of descriptive realism and political literature as empty rhetoric in 1966 actually *preceded* the disruption of the 1967 meeting by students demanding that the *Gruppe* take a more overtly political stance. On the other hand, while the protest movement left the hazy non-conformism of much post-war literature looking feeble, well before '1968' other literature was developing precisely the materially specific criticism which nurtured and articulated the energies of protest; and, indeed, many of the forms of political protest were anticipated by artistic forms like the 'happenings' of Bazon Brock and Wolf Vostell from the early 1960s.

Moreover, subjectivity and imagination are fundamental to literature; they were not banished from it in the late 1960s and so did not 'return' in the 1970s. Subjectivity was central to the protest movement, attacked only by an undialectically dogmatic minority. A key argument of *Eros and civilisation* (1955) and *An essay on liberation* (1969) by Herbert Marcuse, influential guru of the protest movement, is that identification and mobilisation of the real subjective needs of the individual are inherently subversive of the false needs generated by capitalism: the private is, in some senses, the political. The 'hunger for experience' which Michael Rutschky sees as characterising the 1970s (*Erfahrungshunger*, 1980) is already strongly present in the experiments (communal living, drugs, sexual liberation, the hippie trail to the East) of the 1960s. This is the context for the relegitimation of desire in, for example, the work of Rolf Dieter Brinkmann (see below) or Nicolas Born (*Wo mir der Kopf steht* (*Where my head is*, 1970); *Das Auge des Entdeckers* (*The eye of the discoverer*, 1972)). And the subjectivity to be found in texts of the 1970s ranges from self-fixated 'inwardness' through a characteristically modern sense of the self's radical inauthenticity and dissolution, to synthesis – product in part of the literary debate the protest movement had provoked – of artistic subjectivity, socio-political awareness and literature's formal and imaginative potential.

Meanwhile Peter Handke and, with increasing insistence as the 1970s progressed, Botho Strauß, rejected social criticism and humanist declarations as hollow rhetoric out of place in literature, though their work – after Handke's brief experiments with pop culture – remains within, and consciously seeks to revive, the literary tradition. Their success was accompanied by a decline in the status of authenticity, which had underpinned both the documentary literature of the 1960s and texts of autobiographically subjective experience in the 1970s, in favour of a relegitimation of fictional invention. Handke and Strauß revive too the aloof stance of the 'poet' as privileged visionary, reacting against the concept of the writer as 'media employee', and returning to authorial positions of the 1950s and earlier to serve notice on the materialism of the critical humanist era.

At the beginning of this era, though, in the early 1960s, the West German theatre nurtured a new, political drama which attracted world attention. The physical infrastructure was back in place; prosperity and generous funding meant budgets, ensembles, technical installations and rehearsal times were available for ambitious projects; an old guard of directors (e.g. Gründgens), autocratic, aesthetically conservative and less than eager to investigate issues of complicity, was being replaced by a new generation (Peter Palitsch, Claus Peymann, Peter Stein, Peter Zadek), schooled in Brechtian aesthetics and material analysis and therefore rejecting the absurd theatre of the 1950s, but impatient too with the oblique Brechtian parable (an impatience encapsulated in Günter Grass's play *Die Plebejer proben den Aufstand* (*The plebeians rehearse the uprising*, 1966)). This led to revived interest in the directly political, especially documentary theatre of the 1920s, and it was its leading director, Erwin Piscator, whose productions of Rolf Hochhuth's *Der Stellvertreter*, Heinar Kipphardt's *In der Sache J. Robert Oppenheimer* (*In the matter of J. Robert Oppenheimer*, 1964) and Peter Weiss's *Die Ermittlung* (*The investigation*, 1964) ensured the new theatre its impact and the stage its revived role as political and moral tribunal.

However, one important strand of drama in the early 1960s bypasses documentary methods, though it addresses the same historical traumas. *Stienz* (1963), *Lappschieß* (1964) and *Helm* (1965) by Hans Günter Michelsen (1920–94) have elements of the absurd drama of the 1950s and the physical and moral ruin-landscapes of Borchert. But the plays' focus on post-war Germans' psychopathological entrapment in their own repressed memories resembles the perspective on fascism offered by the Mitscherlichs' *Unfähigkeit zu Trauern* and the analyses of the Frankfurt School. Martin Walser locates the same processes still more firmly in the moral lethargy, opportunism and hypocrisy of *Wirtschaftswunder* society and the German family: *Eiche und Angora* (*The rabbit race*, 1961), *Überlebensgroß Herr Krott* (*Herr Krott, larger than life*, 1963). His essay, 'Hamlet als Autor' (1964) underlines the sense of moral paralysis in these plays, exemplified in *Der schwarze Schwan* (1964) where the son of a concentration camp doctor is driven first mad and then to suicide by indecision and surrogate guilt. Though written in the shadow of the Eichmann and Auschwitz trials, their focus is the less obvious fascism of everyday life. In 1967, Walser, criticising the illusionistic realism of documentary theatre, called his plays 'theatre of consciousness', anticipating 1970s and 1980s theatre's focus on fragments of behaviour rather than on political or psychological wholeness.

Der Stellvertreter is much more overtly political, but though it created an international sensation by indicting a real historical figure, Pope Pius XII, for his failure to condemn Nazi atrocities, it is not documentary as such. In all his plays Hochhuth (b. 1931) draws on historical persons, events and documents to create a conventional Schillerean drama which insists 'that the human being is a moral being' and whose characters wear their author's verdict like the arrows on a convict suit: *Soldaten, Nekrolog auf Genf (Soldiers – an obituary for Geneva*, 1967), attacking Churchill's support for the bombing of civilians; the anti-imperialist *Guerrillas* (1970); *Lysistrata und die NATO* (1972), reworking Aristophanes into an anti-Western tract; *Unbefleckte Empfängnis (Immaculate conception,* 1988), attacking church, state and feminism for their exploitation of the surrogate motherhood issue. *Juristen (Lawyers*, 1979), which, at a time when the war-crimes issue had been reactivated by the American television series *Holocaust*, reopened questions about the post-war careers of the Nazi judiciary, and led to the resignation of the previously popular President of Baden-Württemberg, Hans Filbinger, exemplifies how the sometimes comic-book crudity of Hochhuth's technique unleashes real extra-literary effects: angry rejection of his work, accusing it either of aesthetic inadequacy or factual inaccuracy, stimulates controversy which exposes strata of repressed history beyond those in the plays themselves; at the same time, the latter's simplistic analysis and conventional dramaturgy allow audiences to approach charged and complex themes.

In der Sache J. Robert Oppenheimer by Heinar Kipphardt (1922–82) is more directly documentary, based on the actual hearing in 1954 at which the nuclear scientist Oppenheimer answered charges of being a communist sympathiser. The single set and interrogatory structure heighten the sense of an authentic tribunal. Yet documentary literature is in fact always tendentious, and this necessitates aesthetic intervention. Kipphardt not only condensed the 3,000–page transcript, but rearranged it; his Oppenheimer undergoes a conversion to the idea of the scientist's moral responsibility. *Sedanfeier* (1970), a *Montage aus Materialien des 70er-Krieges*, by letting documents from the Franco-German War of 1870 speak for themselves, transforms them aesthetically into a grotesque parody of militarism. In the 1970s Kipphardt, a qualified psychiatrist, explored the artistic psyche in a mosaic of texts and genres: the television play *Leben des schizophrenen Dichters Alexander März (Life of the schizophrenic poet Alexander März*, 1975), the novel *März* (1976), *März-Gedichte* (1977) and the stage play *März, ein Künstlerleben (März – an artist's life*, 1980). *Bruder Eichmann* (1983) returns to the document-based investigation of historical reality; but as the title suggests, the focus is not comfortable moral indictment of an incomprehensible monster, but the 'banality of evil' (Hannah Arendt, *Eichmann in Jerusalem*, 1963), the psychological dynamic which makes an essentially ordinary man capable of administering genocide. The productive synthesis of the documentary and the subjective perspective reflects the more sophisticated understanding of the relationship of the political and the personal which developed during the 1970s.

The work of Peter Weiss (1916–82) amalgamates formal experiment, political commitment and personal trauma. The son of a Jewish manufacturer, he emigrated in 1934 and lived in Sweden from 1939 until his death. After early experiments in surrealism, the autobiographically based *Abschied von den Eltern (Leavetaking*, 1961) and *Fluchtpunkt (Vanishing point*, 1962) expose the reader, through the absence of textual signposts, to the linguistic and existential disorientation of the emigrant, but also express the optimistic dialectics of struggle.

Die Verfolgung und Ermordung Jean Paul Marats, dargestellt durch die Schauspielgruppe des Hospizes zu Charenton unter Anleitung des Herrn de Sade (usually shortened to *Marat/Sade*, 1964) sets the (fictive) debate between the extreme individualist de Sade and the self-sacrificing revolutionary Marat in an asylum, where rational discourse is repeatedly threatened and finally disrupted by the anarchic energies of the patients. Weiss called it a Marxist piece, but its rhyming of 'revolution' and 'copulation' is closer to Marcuse (or even Wilhelm Reich) and its analysis of repressive tolerance in the hospital's regime – acting revolution is permitted, revolutionary action is stifled by cudgel-wielding orderlies dressed as nurses – is the ironic self-commentary of a political artist. As such, the play remarkably anticipates later debates about politics, art and subjectivity.

Die Ermittlung (1965) in contrast is a documentary work: statements by accused and victims from the Auschwitz trials, selected and ordered but otherwise unchanged, and declaimed in a distanced style on an austere stage. But documentary theatre is never neutral (as Weiss's anti-imperialist *Viet Nam Diskurs*, 1968, confirms); *Die Ermittlung*'s political stance is manifest in its focus on industry's interest in the camps as sources of cheap labour and its thesis of the continuity between Nazism and post-war Germany. In contrast, *Trotzki im Exil* (1970), focusing on contradictions within Marxism, and *Hölderlin* (1971), where poetic vision, born of profound personal engagement, is given equal legitimacy to the quest for political change, both reflect Weiss's continued interest in individual and psychological as well as political and economic liberation.

Around 1970, the tendentious documentary play reached its high point: the critique of capitalism via selective use of documents from the Reformation and the peasant wars in *Martin Luther & Thomas Müntzer oder Die Einführung der Buchhaltung (Martin Luther and Thomas Müntzer or the introduction of bookkeeping*, 1970) by Dieter Forte (b. 1935) reads like a parody today; though writers like Yaak Karsunke (b. 1934) persisted with the form in *Die Bauernoper (The peasant's opera*, 1973) and *Ruhrkampfrevue (Ruhr struggle revue*, 1975), Martin Walser's treatment of comparable historical material already belongs to a new era:

Das Sauspiel (*The swine play*, 1975), set in Nuremberg in 1525/6 and focusing on the betrayal by bourgeois writers and artists of the revolutionary impulses of the *Bauernkrieg* and the Anabaptist revolt, is a sarcastic valediction to protest literature.

But the crisis of documentary drama was as much one of form as of content. In the late 1960s, Tankred Dorst (b. 1925) already argues that the very idea is an oxymoron: 'There's the document. And then there's the play.' Though he preceded his drama of the political playwright and revolutionary *Toller* (1968) by editing a collection of documents, *Die Münchner Räterepublik* (*The Munich Soviet*, 1966), and drew on it extensively for his play, Dorst's purpose is not authentic reconstruction, but a revue-like mosaic of historically significant moments, behaviours, attitudes: 'particles of reality'. In the 1970s and early 1980s, Dorst's *Deutsche Stücke* (co-author: Ursula Ehler) chronicle a family of entrepreneurs between the 1920s and 1950s. Dorst and Ehler's *Merlin* (1979; premiered 1981), with its 40 main characters and 97 scenes over more than 300 pages of text, applies the collage techniques of documentary theatre to the myths of Arthur, the Round Table, Merlin and the Grail, in order to explore the contemporary crisis of reason and the dialectics of history, of light and darkness, progress and conservatism, youth and experience.

Impulses within the protest movement towards political agitation and democratisation of culture encouraged a wide variety of theatrical forms at the end of the 1960s. Street theatre, performances in factories and meeting halls, politicised childrens' theatre, multi-media events and happenings all explored alternatives to bourgeois theatre. These initiatives were mostly short-lived; their influence survived in the youth theatre *Grips-Theater*, or sporadic projects like *Theaterwehr Brandheide*, part of the anti-nuclear protest at Gorleben in the 1980s.

Street or youth theatre may be alternative forms, yet they remain posited on the assumption that political or moral messages can be discursively transmitted. Peter Handke's 'Sprechstücke' ('Speech plays'), though part of the same anti-authoritarian revolt, reject this. Handke (b. 1942) belongs in the Austrian tradition of linguistic criticism, which led him to prefer Ödön von Horváth to what he saw as Brecht's simplistic optimism and mechanistic social analysis; his essay 'Straßentheater und Theatertheater' ('Street theatre and theatre theatre', 1968) rejects politically engaged theatre altogether. He views language as a system of social manipulation which neither conventional realism nor political rhetoric (as text) can escape. Thus artificiality must be shattered by being directly emphasised, as in *Publikumsbeschimpfung* (*Offending the audience*) or *Weissagung* (*Prophecy;* both 1966). *Kaspar* (1968) questions the fundamental Enlightenment assumption that the acquisition of language is the royal road to self-determination, by showing how an 'individual' is created out of deterministic building-blocks of language provided by social rule systems. In a compressed reversal of the 'Bildungsroman', socialisation is shown to be the end of individuality, language acquisition to be acquiescence in self-oppression.

Many radio plays of the time treated similar themes: *Fünf Mann Menschen* (*Five man people*, 1968) by Ernst Jandl (b. 1925) and Friederike Mayröcker (b. 1924), a fifteen-minute parable of the circularity of manipulated existence, typified the new radio plays of the 1960s in breaking with atmospheric illusion to focus on a critique of everyday language; see also Handke's *Hörspiel Nr. 2* (1969) or Wolf Wondratschek's *Paul oder die Zerstörung eines Hörbeispiels* (*Paul or the destruction of an audio-example*, 1969). Other radio plays, including so-called *O-Ton-Hörspiele*, montages of found or collected material, usually with a specific social theme, reflected the trend towards documentary literature. *Ein Blumenstück* (*Flower play*, 1968) by Ludwig Harig (b. 1927) intercuts statements by Rudolf Höß, commandant of Auschwitz, with children's stories and poems from *Des Knaben Wunderhorn*, forcing reflection on the relationship of barbarism and sentimentality. His *Staatsbegräbnis* (*State funeral*, 1969) uses extracts from speeches at Adenauer's funeral to expose the pomp of official language.

The *Neues Volksstück* ('new popular dialect play') which emerged in the late 1960s echoed the consciousness of the inauthenticity of ordinary language which underlay the *Sprechstücke*. It also shared documentary theatre's distrust of the Brechtian parable, but replaced broad historical brush-strokes with the microcosm of social interaction. However, its linguistic and dramaturgical models came from a literary tradition rather than the empirical social reality of the 1960s and 1970s. *Jagdszenen aus Niederbayern* (*Hunting scenes from Lower Bavaria*, 1966) by Martin Sperr (b. 1944) and *Katzelmacher* (*Eyeties*, 1969) by Rainer Werner Fassbinder (1945–82) explore how groups define outsiders in order to persecute them, demonstrating the fascism inherent in the enshrinement of 'peace and order' as civic virtues, and drawing on the dynamics of provincial mentality in the work of Fleißer and on Horváth's exposure of false consciousness in the inauthentic language of his stage figures. The revival of these authors reflects perceived parallels between the Bonn Republic and that of Weimar, the growing interest in everyday as well as high culture, and a desire – influenced indirectly by the social theorists of the Frankfurt School – to explore the social-psychological as well as economic and political roots of fascism.

Sperr's attempts to widen his social reference in a *Bayrische Trilogie* from the village setting of *Jagdszenen* to the small town (*Landshuter Erzählungen* (*Tales from Landshut*, 1967)) and the metropolis (*Münchner Freiheit*, 1971) met with diminishing success. Fassbinder, it became clear, was not really a *Volksstück* author, despite the terse Bavarian-nuanced sociolect of *Katzelmacher*, but rather an explorer of human cruelty and culpability in an 'antiteater' [*sic*]of dark images of the authoritarian personality: for example, *Pre-paradise sorry now* (1969), *Blut am Hals der Katze* (*Blood on the neck of the cat*, 1971) or the nightmarish urban argot of his attack on property speculation in *Der Müll, die Stadt und der Tod* (*Garbage, the city and death*, 1975; not premiered till 1985 because of accusations of anti-Semitism). Another author misleadingly assigned to the *Volksstück* genre because of his use of dialect is Wolfgang Bauer (b. 1941). His iconoclastic, anti-bourgeois texts link pop art and an Austrian tradition of linguistically aware social satire; their blend of morbidity, subcultural jargon and mockery of Austrian provinciality, and critique both of the *Leistungsgesellschaft* ('rat-race society') and the vacuity of much rebellion against it, gave them a considerable originality and impact in the late 1960s: *Magic afternoon* (1968); *Change* (1969). In Bauer's later work, for example *Memory hotel* (1980), surreal elements increasingly dominate.

The most prolific, successful author of the *Neues Volksstück* was Franz Xaver Kroetz (b. 1946), who by 1990 had had some forty plays performed in countless productions worldwide, belying the image of the *Volksstück* as narrowly provincial. Sperr or Fassbinder, or Harald Mueller (b. 1934) in *Großer Wolf* (*Big wolf*, 1968) and *Halbdeutsch* (*Half German*, 1969: a remarkably prophetic portrait of xenophobic violence in an immigrant hostel) focus on group aggression towards outsiders. Most of Kroetz's plays, in contrast, are domestic dramas, and in the early ones the figures direct the aggressions their social deprivation has generated – but which their impoverished language cannot articulate – towards themselves, their families or their unborn children. Thus suicides, domestic murders and attempted or successful abortions are central motifs: *Wunschkonzert* (*Request concert*, 1971); *Wildwechsel* (*Game crossing*, 1971); *Heimarbeit* (*Homeworker*, 1971). Stark, shocking stage images abound, such as the knitting-needle abortion scene in *Heimarbeit* or the masturbation and defloration scenes in *Stallerhof* (1972). But precisely the latter asserts the human right to joy in the most bleak environment. Kroetz is a trained actor and director; the rhythmic pattern of the scenes is carefully crafted and the dialogue, though based on a Bavarian lower-class sociolect, highly artistic: points obscured by his initial insistence on the role of his plays as social documents. Kroetz's commitment to the German Communist Party from 1972 to 1980 led him to reject his own early work as fatalistic, its *dramatis personae* as uncharacteristic of the West German masses, their language insufficiently reflective of working-class resilience. In *Oberösterreich* (*Upper Austria*, 1972), *Das Nest* (1974), *Mensch Meier* (1977) and *Der stramme Max* (*Big Max*, 1978) he portrays more typical members of the German working class. Play by play the characters' socio-economic situation and articulacy improve, so that when now faced by moments of crisis (typically, unemployment or pregnancy as threats to consumer prosperity), they are able to realise the other-determined nature of their lives. The resulting enlightenment is as much moral as political (e.g. *Das Nest*). These plays were among the most performed of the mid 1970s.

In the 1980s, while still seeking to address key social issues such as technology and identity in *Nicht Fisch, nicht Fleisch* (*Neither fish nor flesh*, 1980), unemployment in *Furcht und Hoffnung in der BRD* (*Fear and hope in the FRG*, 1983), the crisis of peasant identity in the face of agricultural modernisation in *Bauern sterben* (*Dead soil*, 1984) and nuclear or environmental apocalypse in his adaptation of Toller's *Hinkemann, Der Nusser* (*The gelding*, 1985), he sought to rediscover the archaic power of his early work: subjectively felt, aesthetically shaped images of social and psychological despair, quickened by moments of tenderness and self-assertion. The pre-modern aesthetic this implies is linked to a range of conservative social attitudes which appear to contradict his social criticism, though they may have aided its reception in the established theatre. Certainly, when Kroetz grants working-class characters the identity crisis customarily reserved for the sensitive intellectual, this archetypal bourgeois theme in a socially critical guise exemplifies the role of the *Neues Volksstück* in the transition, broadly, from a theatre of political morality to one of individual behaviours.

Few other authors of regional, dialect or working-class drama who appeared alongside Kroetz or in his wake have had lasting impact. The fashion for workplace plays like *Eisenwichser* (*The painters,* 1970) by Heinrich Henkel (b. 1937) was short lived. Fitzgerald Kusz (b. 1944), with *Schweig, Bub* (*Quiet, boy!* 1976) or *Stinkwut* (*Filthy stink,* 1979) and Wolfgang Deichsel (b. 1939) with *Bleiwe Losse* (*Leave it be,* 1971) court regional popularity more directly than Kroetz by their use of Franconian and Hessian dialect respectively (the latter through numerous adaptations of Molière). Peter Greiner (b. 1939) enjoyed a brief vogue around 1980 with dramas set typically amongst the spivs, pimps and tarts of the red-light district of Hamburg, celebrating the vitality of the language of the socially marginalised rather than bemoaning its impoverishment: *Kiez* (*The scene,* 1974); *Fast ein Prolet* (*Almost a proletarian,* 1978); *Roll over Beethoven* (1978). In contrast, Felix Mitterer (b. 1948), thirteenth child of a poor peasant woman, offers a pity-based drama in which the handicapped, criminalised and persecuted are championed more intensely even than in the early Kroetz; his work, though, lacks Kroetz's dramatic power and can remain trapped in identificatory pathos: *Kein Platz für Idioten* (*No place for idiots,* 1977), with many parallels in its portrayal of village persecution to Sperr's *Jagdszenen; Stigma* (1983); *Besuchszeit* (*Visiting time*, 1985).

Peter Turrini (b. 1944) grotesquely parodies the *Volksstück* motif of the fascistoid collective which persecutes an outsider in *sauschlachten* (*pig-killing*, 1972). Eschewing the naturalistic realism of the conventional 'Neues Volksstück', it cites, exaggerates and inverts stereotypes of the peasant play and the Viennese 'Volkstheater' to create consciously artificial effects. Turrini sees himself as a subjectively motivated, but politically committed regional writer. These facets remain present throughout his work from *rozznjogd* (*rathunt*, 1971) to *Die Minderleister* (*Lower achievers*, 1988), which like Kroetz's *Nicht Fisch, nicht Fleisch*, focuses on the social fact of technological change: in this case modernisation and mass redundancy in the steel industry. Its pathos and political commitment link it to 'Arbeiterliteratur', its liturgical structures and motifs to the rural *Volksstück* tradition.

The small casts and modest sets of the *Neues Volksstück* both facilitated its production and encouraged its marginalisation to the studio stage of the big state theatres. In the main houses, as the sources of new documentary and political drama dried up, from the late 1960s ambitious directors turned ever more to 'Regietheater', radical adaptations of the classics; and from the late 1970s the anti-dramatic performance art of American Robert Wilson, and GDR dramatist Heiner Müller's dismemberings of German history began to be widely admired.

In her essay 'Kann das Theater aus der Rolle fallen?' ('Can the theatre forget its part?', 1972) Gerlind Reinshagen (b. 1926) rejects directors' theatre and its then still prevalent rhetoric of large-scale social transformation, in favour of accessible small-scale insights into structures and processes of human interaction, including the continuities from fascist to post-fascist society. Her focus is the everyday, her preferred form often a party or gathering, a moment of stocktaking in the flow of normality, her style atmospheric rather than analytical. *Sonntagskinder* (*Sunday's children*, 1976) views everyday life in Nazi Germany through the eyes of the child Elsie, and reveals the horror of normality and the disastrous results of opportunism and political naivety. *Frühlingsfest* (*Spring festival*, 1980) focuses on corrupt business deals in the reconstruction years of the 1950s; Elsa's protest, like Elsie's, is smothered by a society blind to its own deformations. Reinshagen's work is characterised by its respect for the ordinary and the quiet insistence of its poetic imagination.

The plays of Thomas Bernhard (1931–89) in contrast are aggressively nihilistic, portraying life as a sickness for which the only cure is death, and humanity as fundamentally mendacious, a cruel joke, as in the visual metaphor of the thirteen wheelchair-bound cripples at the banquet in *Ein Fest für Boris* (*A party for Boris*, 1970). *Die Macht der Gewohnheit* (*The force of habit*, 1974) is a grotesque comedy of obsessive perfectionism, whose fugue-like circularity exemplifies the musical construction of Bernhard's plays. *Vor dem Ruhestand* (*Before retirement*, 1979), is his most political play, an elegantly constructed triangle of dependencies, hatreds and fears. With these plays, Bernhard established the themes and the aesthetic techniques which his prolific later work essentially revamped.

As early as 1966, Handke's *Selbstbezichtigung* (*Self-accusation*) showed that saying 'Ich' is no guarantee of authentic identity; in 1968, Frisch's *Biografie* played self-reflexively with identity's shifting ambiguities. As Ernst Jandl says, the condition of his protagonist in *Aus der Fremde* (*From far away,* 1980) is reflected in a language in which there is 'no I, no You and no fixed manner of expressing yourself, just, exclusively, the third person and the subjunctive mood'. Such uncertainties are a central motif in the work of Botho Strauß (b. 1944), who emerged in the 1970s as the leading playwright alongside Kroetz. *Die Hypochonder* (*The hypochon-driacs*, 1972) bewildered critics and audiences still struggling to adjust their focus from the broad sweep of documentary theatre to the micro-cosmic social realism of the *Neues Volksstück*, by deliberately frustrating audience expectations of a coherently plotted crime mystery. *Bekannte Gesichter, gemischte Gefühle* (*Familiar faces, mixed feelings*, 1975) uses ballroom dancing as a metaphor for empty relationships and failed communication; the surrealism and dream psychology of *Die Hypochonder* intermingle now with a recognizable German reality. *Trilogie des Widersehens* (*Trilogy of reunion*, 1977) is a tapestry of the fluctuating, unstable relationships of seventeen visitors to the art exhibi-tion 'Kapitalistischer Realismus'. The play is additive rather than dynamic, and portrays the surface of a society, not its roots. Yet it began a fashion of seeing Strauß as the seismographic chronicler of his society. Lotte, the central figure of his next work, *Groß und klein* (*Big and small*, 1978), in her torment at the indifference of her fellow human beings and the silence of God, and her eventual madness, half Joan of Arc, half shuf-fling bag-lady, signals the impending end of the rationalistic, secular humanism that characterised much literature in the 1960s and 1970s.

In poetry, the fluctuations between the political and the subjective took a slightly different course. In the 1960s, the hermetic poetry of Benn or Celan, which each in their different ways had reacted both against the ideological hijacking of language in the Nazi period, and against the con-solatory rhythms of religious and nature poetry, now in turn lost their appeal. Walter Höllerer's call in his 'Thesen zum langen Gedicht' ('Theses on the long poem', 1965) for a poetry closer to spoken language, was directed at the 'laboured preciousness' of Benn as much as the 'solemnity' of Lehmann or Schröder. Peter Rühmkorf too argued for more of the material reality of the everyday. The poetry of the 1960s includes not only specifically political, even agitational work, but also poems of personal experience and a strongly identificatory poetic subject more commonly associated with the 'new subjectivity' of the 1970s, and both trends continue in the latter decade. The communicative impulse they share manifests itself in prose-based rhythms, simple structure and everyday language which avoids hermetic metaphor.

Enzensberger, whose *Museum der modernen Poesie* (1960) urged German poetry to move beyond the European modernism to which it had only belatedly begun to respond, himself uses modernist techniques like dissonance, montage and contrasting registers, but for communicative effects such as surprise, unmasking and insight, not for hermeticism. After Enzensberger's brief advocacy of political journalism and documentary literature in the late 1960s, he offered wry valedictions to the Enlightenment in the 'thirty-seven ballads from the history of progress' in *Mausoleum* (1975), and in *Der Untergang der Titanic* (1978). But amongst the latter's symptomatically complex perspectives there is a key image: an engineer who argues that catastrophes provoke innovations, and as such are part of the dialectic of progress. *Der Untergang der Titanic* draws on, yet stands outside trends in 1970s poetry: while vocabulary, syntax and narrative persona are communicatively accessible, and the autobiographical reminiscences of the euphoria of protest echo those in much post-1968 literature, the poem is self-consciously artistic in its chronological, thematic and metaphoric structures and patterns of allusion, in particular to Dante's *Inferno*. As such it heralds the revival of form in the poetry of the 1980s.

Erich Fried (1921–88), an emigré in London from 1938 till his death, wrote both tender, simple love poetry and uncompromising indictments of imperialism, state-sanctioned violence and the lies of public discourse, using the latter, like Karl Kraus, to reveal the mentalities, values and structures it seeks to hide: *Warngedichte* (*Warning poems*, 1964); *Die Freiheit, den Mund aufzumachen* (*The freedom to open your mouth*, 1972); *Um Klarheit. Gedichte gegen das Vergessen* (*For clarity's sake – poems against forgetting*, 1985). Fried's sometimes over-impassioned didacticism gave his work a notoriety in contrast to the equally committed yet quieter, and much less well-known poetry of Volker von Törne (1934–80): *Wolfspelz* (*Wolf's clothing*, 1968); *Der Affe will nicht die Freiheit* (*The monkey doesn't want freedom*, 1971); *Im Lande vogelfrei* (*Outlawed*, 1981). Like Christoph Meckel (b. 1935), with whom he collaborated on *Die Dummheit liefert uns ans Messer* (*Stupidity will lead us to slaughter*, 1967), von Törne deploys traditional forms such as ballad, folk-song and nature poetry to indict both 'Wirtschaftswunder' society and the injustice and barbarism of human history. Both had active Nazi fathers, and issues of memory, repression and collective responsibility are everpresent in their work, though both avoid simplistic moralising.

Fried's fellow Austrian Ernst Jandl (b. 1925) is equally alert to language: volumes like *sprechblasen* (*speech bubbles,* 1968) or *dingfest* (*held fast,* 1973) reveal the dialectic of playfulness and critical seriousness in his work. In *wischen möchten* (*like to know/wipe,* 1974) he turns abstract slogans into fresh insights into the realities they seek to hide; *der gelbe hund* (*yellow dog,* 1980) explores psychopathological language.

The work of Friederike Mayröcker (b. 1924) stands largely outside the trends sketched in this section. It explores the human desire, epitomised by the poetic imagination, to escape one's self and yet be oneself, to transcend, and come into the inheritance of, human experience. *Ausgewählte Gedichte 1944–1978* (*Selected poems,* 1979) shows how in the 1950s her combination of spoken language and folk-tale motifs contrasts markedly with Bachmann's portentousness; in the 1960s, drawing on the English Metaphysicals and on Novalis, she investigates the flux, transitions and contrasts, which rather than fixed interpretative models, characterise contemporary experience and consciousness. She draws on an eclectic, encyclopaedic range of vocabularies, registers and discourses, which, in the 1970s, gives way to a more introspective approach. Mayröcker's work avoids linear causalities and hierarchical aesthetic valuations; adjacent poems may exhibit strict form and anarchic formlessness, as in *Winterglück* (*Winter happiness,* 1986).

Franz Josef Degenhardt (b. 1931) – with Hanns-Dieter Hüsch, Peter Schütt and Dieter Süverkrüp the leading representative of the political song movement that developed in the 1960s from anti-nuclear and peace protest activities, with links to cabaret and the political satire of the 1920s – wrote lyrics aggressively critical of the restoration of old Nazis and the socio-economic inequalities of post-war Germany: *Spiel nicht mit den Schmuddelkindern* (*Don't play with the urchins,* 1967); *Kommt an den Tisch unter Pflaumenbäumen* (*Come to the table under the plum trees,* 1979). His novels take a similar social-critical line, from *Die Zundschnüre* (*The fuse,* 1973) to his novel of the political music scene, *Der Liedermacher* (*The song-maker,* 1982). By the late 1970s, his work had sold in six figures, a reminder that political literature continued to be written, published and bought in the 1970s.

However, the dogmatism which suppressed the self-reflective poetic 'Ich' was short-lived and far from universal. Michael Rutschky argues in *Erfahrungshunger* that the protest movement's seductively simple 'utopia of general concepts' gave way to a fog of uncertainty: 'Try finding your way about in the seventies', as a figure says in Strauß's *Groß und klein*. Consequently, reassurance was sought in tangible subjective experience. But already in the late 1960s 'Alltagslyrik ('the poetry of the everyday') began to resist the separation between the private and the public sphere. Its free verse and colloquial syntax and vocabulary aim to bridge the gap to everyday communication. Nicolas Born (1937–79) in *Marktlage* (*State of the market*, 1967) calls programmatically for a move away from the old poetics, which just encouraged 'poeticising'. Rejecting symbol and metaphor, his aim was simple, direct formulations and a rejection of poetic intensification in favour of a naive reflection of experienced reality, an aim which ignores how much language is manipulable in a world of mediated concepts.

Jürgen Theobaldy (b. 1944), in his analysis of German poetry since 1965, *Veränderung der Lyrik* (*Changes in poetry*, 1976; with Gustav Zürcher), and the accompanying anthology *Und ich bewege mich doch. Gedichte vor und nach 1968* (*And I'm still moving. Poems before and after 1968*, 1977), emphasises the idea that the everyday language of 'Alltagslyrik' resists the synthetic, distorted language of powerful political and economic interests. But his critique of the arid conceptualisations of public discourse, including implicitly that of political theorising, is as dependent as Born's on the naive assumption of subjective authenticity. Theobaldy's poetry (*Blaue Flecken* (*Bruises*, 1974); *Zweite Klasse* (*Second class*, 1976)) is autobiographical, but also, typically by focalising its perspective through the 'Du'-form, articulates commonplace experiences of average educated but not privileged citizens of post-68 Germany, a world defined physically by the everyday and metaphorically by the space between politicisation and apathy, optimism and cynicism. The same is true of his novels *Sonntags Kino* (*Sunday flicks*, 1978) and *Spanische Wände* (*Spanish walls*, 1981).

The themes of 'Alltagslyrik' – eating, shopping, work, relationships – and the settings – household, bed, cinema, pub, workplace – suggest, and sometimes produce, banality (e.g. Christoph Derschau (1944–1995), *Den Kopf voll Suff und Kino* (*A head full of booze and flicks*, 1976)). But they may also awaken respect for the unobserved, chart changing (particularly gender) roles or indicate the fragility or limitations of everyday experiences in the face of environmental change or social norms: Günter Herburger (b. 1932): *Ziele* (*Goals*, 1977); Karin Kiwus (b. 1942): *Von beiden Seiten der Gegenwart* (*From both sides of the present*, 1976); Ralf Thenior (b. 1945): *Traurige Hurras* (*Sad Hurrahs*, 1977). In *Nach Mainz!* (*To Mainz!* 1977), Ursula Krechel (b. 1947) blends reminiscences of postwar youth, retrospectives on the protest movement, and critique of gender roles with a feminist perspective on the everyday. Her *Verwundbar wie in den besten Zeiten* (*Vulnerable like in the good old days*, 1979) reflects the pessimism of the late 1970s: 'Aufbruch, Bruch, Abbruch. / Das Wir ist verstört/ das Ich längst begraben' ('Breaking out, breaking, breaking off / The We is destroyed / The I long buried').

Everyday themes and communicative goals also characterise a revival of dialect poetry in the 1970s, such as the numerous volumes of *Bamberger Mund(un)-artiges* by Gerhard C. Krischker (b. 1947), collected as *fai obbachd* (1986); Kurt Sigel (b. 1931): *Uff Deiwelkommraus* (1975); Manfred Bosch (b. 1947): *Uf den Dag warti* (1976); Oswald Andrae (b. 1926): *Hollt doch die Duums für den Sittich* (1983). Conservative nostalgia is less apparent here than growing ecological and regional consciousness, a critical defence of 'Heimat' against capitalist encroachment, a similar awareness of linguistic marginalisation to that which informs the *Neues Volksstück*, and a political concept of 'dialect as weapon' (the Alsatian poet André Weckmann, b. 1924, writing in 1978) against the hollow smoothness of public rhetoric in the *Hochsprache*. This echoes the subversive and self-reflexive use of dialect by the concrete poets and the 'Wiener Gruppe' in the 1950s; another important forerunner is H. C. Artmann (b. 1921) and his *med ana schwoazzn dintn* (*with black ink*, 1958).

In his lifetime, the work of Rolf Dieter Brinkmann (1940–75) was damned both by high culture as pornographic and facile, and by a dogmatic left as laying the ground for a new fascism. In the 1980s, though, Brinkmann was recognised as a precursor of postmodernism with considerable influence on West German and later on GDR poetry. In volumes like *Ohne Neger* (*No blacks*, 1965) *Die Piloten* (1968); *Standfotos* (*Stills*, 1968) and *Gras* (1970), Brinkmann attacked the privileged role both of the poet and of the poetic image as a metaconstruct imbued with higher reality: 'There is no other material than what is accessible to all and which everyone has to do with every day': Brinkmann). His prose too, like the novel *Keiner weiß mehr* (*No one knows any more*, 1968), anticipates the 'Neue Subjektivität' of the 1970s. Brinkmann was influenced by American beat and underground poetry and by Leslie Fiedler's promulgation of a postmodern aesthetic subverting artistic norms by drawing on the images, texts and products of popular culture. He translated Frank O'Hara's *Lunch poems* (1969) and edited the anthologies *Silver screen* (1969) and, with Ralf-Rainer Rygulla, *ACID* (1969). *Westwärts 1 & 2* (1975), where Brinkmann counters the destructive sloppiness of media culture with a new attention to form, illustrates the strengths of his associative poetic method of 'Collages of everyday madness' in articulating the consciousness of his generation and its epoch. Browsing through American poetry (O'Hara, William Carlos Williams) in a cheap Bayswater hotel after watching Stanley Kubrick's *2001* in a Soho cinema, the poet's mind is filled with fragmentary images: a magazine photo of Eva Braun, charred corpses, the computer/bone/tool sequence from Kubrick's film, snatches of music, childhood memories of the BBC wartime call-sign and of chocolate from occupation soldiers. Behind the seeming casualness and apparently random layout of the texts, Brinkmann's alert observation of his own subjective sensations vividly expresses the postmodern experience of the world *through* and *as* mediated images, simultaneity and multiple voices in the fragmented self, while also historically locating his generation's ambiguous fascination with American culture.

Jürgen Becker (b. 1932) whose roots lie in experimental art and concrete poetry (with performance artist Wolf Vostell, he published *Phasen*, 1960, and *Happenings*, 1965), also deploys fragmentary syntax and line breaks, as well as the montages, wipes, overlays and flashbacks of film. 'Fragment aus Rom' (*Schnee* (*Snow*, 1971)) intercuts everyday reality and snatches of popular culture and pop art (the Beatles' *Good day sunshine,* Andy Warhol) with politics (Italian elections, NATO, the US 6th Fleet), celebrating pop culture's greater energy, but also noting echoes of Nazi rallies in a Rolling Stones concert. There are parallels to the sense of menace in Bachmann, and to the multiple voices of Koeppen's associative narrative. *In der verbleibenden Zeit* (*In the time remaining*, 1979) reflects the pessimism of the late 1970s, but also a return to form and a leavening of everyday realism with a rediscovered poetic imagination. Contemporary life is always lived 'in the echo of the shots and shouts': obsessive recall is unleashed by seeing bread queues, or men with dogs and sticks on the edge of the woods. Everyday sensations are triggers of a silenced history where the poet seeks 'the remains of my voice still hanging on the wires', tries to reintegrate historical experience before and after 'the tear went right through the letters': this, implicitly, remains the task of German poetry at least in those generations traumatised, whether as perpetrators, bystanders or victims, by mid-twentieth-century German history.

West German prose writing of the 1960s and 1970s embraces texts of great formal and thematic variety: conventionally narrated novels and stories of the everyday; novels which formally and thematically seek to explore the relationship of the past and the present in German culture within a narrative mode which remains part of the bourgeois realist tradition; documentary texts of various kinds; the revival of a literature of working-class experience; radical formal and linguistic experiment within the traditional modernist avant-garde; and texts, often anthologies, which challenge genre boundaries and literary convention by importing elements from trivial and popular culture.

Gabriele Wohmann (b. 1932) characterises the novel and short story of everyday experience, with a domestic, though not necessarily autobiographically subjective, focus. From *Sieg über die Dämmerung* (*Victory over the dusk*, 1960), she has portrayed average members of the prosperous middle classes, focusing on human relationships and communication problems in family contexts. The observations are sharp, the style cool and distant. The novel *Ernste Absicht* (*Serious intent*, 1970), for example, treats a familiar theme of the period, the individual's loss of self in the

face of social pressures, through a conventional topos: the inner monologue of a woman awaiting an operation whose illness is the sickness of
the whole society.

The strongly ideological tenor of Martin Walser's critique of prosperity and the empty rituals of bourgeois life, for example in *Das Einhorn*
(*The unicorn*, 1966), expressed often through images of psychosomatic
illness, or by Kristlein's Oblomov-like bedridden state in *Der Sturz* (*The
fall*, 1973), made him particularly susceptible to the argument for politicisation or abandonment of literature. The resulting crisis of self-legitima-
tion is noticeable in the uneasy narrative style of *Fiktion* (1970). In the late
1970s, with the revived status of the literary imagination, *Ein fliehendes
Pferd* (*Runaway horse*, 1978) narrates, with limpid and poetic brevity, the
explosion of aggression that overcomes Halm, a schoolteacher whose life-
strategy of emotional hermithood is challenged by an ebullient former
schoolfriend. In *Brandung* (*Breakers*, 1985) Halm, now fifty and on a guest
professorship in the USA, is invigorated by the combination of climate,
lifestyle, ocean, youthful students and the sense of California as the fron-
tier to the future. The title is a crucial image: chaos, uncertainty, latent yet
manifest energy. The novel finely balances the romantic, tragic and inherently ridiculous in the theme of middle-aged rejuvenation. *Dorle und Wolf*
(*No man's land*, 1987) reflects on German division, deploying, like Böll in
Frauen vor Flußlandschaft (*Women in a river landscape*, 1985), the
conventions of the spy story.

The 'Cologne realism' exemplified by Dieter Wellershoff (b. 1925), and
in which, too, Brinkmann, Born and Herburger have their roots, uses precisely described everyday events in the manner of the *nouveau roman* to
illuminate contemporary reality (for example, the anthology *Ein Tag in
der Stadt* (*A day in the city*, 1962)). Wellershoff's *Ein schöner Tag* (*A beautiful day*, 1966) and *Die Schattengrenze* (*The shadow boundary*, 1969) are
phenomenological studies of the hollow inauthenticity and ritualised
behaviour of the *petit-bourgeoisie*: Wellershoff portrays family domesticity as neurotic and inescapable repetition. Meanwhile, close attention to
the minutiae of everyday experience had led, in the work of other
'Cologne realists' like Born or Brinkmann, to the experience of the dissolution and fragmentation of the self, as can be traced in Born's development from *Der zweite Tag* (*The second day*, 1965) to *Die erdabgewandte
Seite der Geschichte* (*The hidden side of the story*, 1976). The awareness
of self-dissolution characteristic of the 'new subjectivity' of the 1970s and
anticipated by Born and Brinkmann can in fact be found much earlier, in
the constitution of the self as a multi-voiced, other-determined product of
a media society and its insistent consumerist exhortations (the
'Radiokopf' or 'radio-head', as Jürgen Becker's *Felder*, 1964, calls it) in
Heißenbüttel's *Textbücher* (1960–67), Barbara König's *Die Personen-*

person (The person person, 1965), or, in more socially specific form, in Walser's *Das Einhorn* or Wellershoff's urban novels. Rural isolation, though, could also be an image of the fragmentation, indeed pathological implosion of the self, as in Thomas Bernhard's novels, *Frost* (1963), *Verstörung (Gargoyles,* 1967) and *Das Kalkwerk (The lime works,* 1970).

Siegfried Lenz (b. 1926) established himself in the 1950s with novels and short stories which echo the techniques of Hemingway and the ideas of Sartre and Camus: for example, *Der Mann im Strom (The man in the current,* 1957). *Deutschstunde (The German lesson,* 1968) confirmed him as one of West Germany's most popular writers. Its earnest didacticism almost a decade after the anarchic verve with which Grass had raised similar themes in *Die Blechtrommel* is symptomatic of the conventional limitations of Lenz's intensely well-meaning prose. Lenz's conventional realism requires laborious justification for each piece of Siggi's privileged knowledge, limiting the reader's perception of history to that of a provincial sideshow. *Das Vorbild (An exemplary life,* 1973), *Heimatmuseum (Folk museum,* 1978), *Der Verlust (The loss,* 1981) and *Exerzierplatz (Parade ground,* 1985) continue the uneasy fluctuation between his fascination for realistic details and his tendency to didactic parable.

Though the main significance of Böll's work remains the passionate insistence of his humanist critique, his work is not unchangingly traditional in form. He introduces a strongly self-ironic narrative tone in *Entfernung von der Truppe (Absent without leave,* 1964), and moves away from first-person protagonist to the 'report' form in *Ende einer Dienstfahrt (End of a mission,* 1966), while retaining the clownesque perspective of amused but despairing distance from the absurdity of conventional society, to the damaging social consequences of which, though, Böll never becomes apathetically resigned. In *Gruppenbild mit Dame* (1971) he ironises the conventions of documentary literature, letting his wholly fictional story be narrated and annotated by a pseudo-objective 'Verfasser' ('Compiler'), often abbreviated 'Verf.', devoted to dismantling the prejudices against Leni Gruyten and her social and sexual norm-transgressions. In *Die verlorene Ehre der Katharina Blum (The lost honour of Katharina Blum,* 1974), Böll's response to the character assassination techniques of the tabloid press, especially *Bild,* the narrator's claimed objectivity is again ironised by his troubadour-like idealisation of the aloof Katharina. This sentimentalising, by comparison with Dieter Wellerhoff's near-contemporaneous *Einladung an alle (Invitation to all,* 1972), the fictionalised biography of a petty criminal which also attacks the media-driven hysteria of public opinion, obscures the other key theme of Böll's novel, the manipulation of the constitutional state by a powerful triangle of big business, media and the CDU.

Fürsorgliche Belagerung (The safety net, 1979) portrays the paradox of the anti-liberal measures used to protect liberty. It can be argued that the novel's pessimistic view of liberal democracy is reflected in its form: a reversion from the 'overt extra-diegetic narrator' of his 1960s and 1970s fiction to the 'indirect interior monologue' of his 1950s novels (J. H. Reid), though, like *Ende einer Dienstfahrt* and Böll's last novel *Frauen vor Flußlandschaft,* it plays in postmodern fashion with expectations of the thriller or detective genre. The latter responds to the flurry of corruption scandals among the West German élite in the mid-1980s with a series of unresolved puzzles – dumped documents, people whose names must not be uttered, unexplained imprisonment, an anonymous burglar who, instead of stealing, meticulously dismantles the grand pianos of the wealthy – seen through multiple and sometimes unidentifiable focalisers.

Hermann Lenz (b. 1915), in a series of autobiographical novels from *Verlassene Zimmer* (*Abandoned rooms,* 1966) to *Der Wanderer* (*The wanderer,* 1986), creates a world which unites the real and the potential, the experienced, the dreamed and the feared, and through a 'dissolution of the narrative present' (Lenz) illustrates the ever-presence of the past. The attitude of Edgar Hilsenrath (b. 1926) to the past, at least in his best-known novel *Der Nazi und der Friseur* (*The Nazi and the hairdresser,* 1977) is to turn his trauma of Jewish experience into a gruesome fable of human prejudice and blind stereotyping. Max Schulz, who looks Jewish but is a ruthless Nazi, returns from the war with a sack of gold teeth and adopts the identity of his friend Finkelstein, whose Aryan appearance did not save him from extermination. Schulz's post-war career as a persecuted Jew, playing on German guilt, ends as an honoured citizen of the new state of Israel. *Das Märchen vom letzten Gedanken* (*The fable of the last thought,* 1989) narrates the early twentieth century genocide of the Armenians by the Turks as an archaic folk-tale. For Hilsenrath, human brutality cannot be approached by direct realistic narrative.

A rejection of realistic narrative from a completely different standpoint, yet which draws together many strands of the time and anticipates important trends of the 1970s and 1980s, is *die verbesserung von mitteleuropa. roman* (*the improvement of central europe. a novel,* 1969), by Oswald Wiener (b. 1935). Active in the 'Wiener Gruppe' in the 1950s, he was then influenced by Wittgenstein and Fritz Mauthner and developed a more rigorous linguistic criticism, whilst experimenting with the consciousness-expanding effects of drugs and sickness; trained in cybernetics, he also developed Olivetti's data-processing systems from 1959–67. His monstrous text combines these influences in a vast file-cabinet of fragments of European culture, whose form mocks the conventions of both the novel and the scholarly treatise. But more is at stake here than anti-bourgeois formalist games. The rejection of coherent narrative reveals, but also encourages, the fragmentation of the self, as an act of resistance

against the tyranny of predetermined concepts, and exposes the alienation produced by the congruence of linguistic and social conventions;
these, rather than reality, set the limits of our social experience. The
novel's central thesis of an 'Ich' rendered spuriously autonomous by the
use of cybernetic technologies which allow it to create realities at will,
anticipate both Virtual Reality and its false promises of ultimate self-
realisation and the postmodernist conception of the world as 'simulation'
and as a jungle of signs to which the reader alone can attach significations.

Significantly, Wiener's novel was greatly admired by Peter Handke,
always a vituperative critic of social relaism. Handke's essays and short
prose (e.g. *Die Innenwelt der Außenwelt der Innenwelt* (*The inner world
of the outer world of the inner world*, 1969)) linked him initially to the
formal experimentation of the 'Wiener Gruppe', and to documentary
writing in the Dadaist and pop art rather than political sense. Accusing
Gruppe 47 of 'descriptive impotence', but also rejecting the apparent
alternative of political literature almost before it had appeared, ensured
him relative isolation but also excellent publicity, and he remained a
leading literary figure throughout the 1970s and 1980s. Like his early
plays, his first prose texts, for example, *Die Hornissen* (*The hornets*,
1966), undermine the concept of a self-determining subject by extreme
self-referentiality. In *Die Angst des Tormanns beim Elfmeter* (*The goalie's
fear of the penalty kick*, 1970), states of mind, rather than causal rationality, determine the perception of reality in a manner which, lacking the
reassuring familiarity of the Romantic uncanny, is bizarrely disturbing.
His subsequent prose, while retaining a fastidious narrative sensitivity,
links his initially iconoclastic work more and more to the German literary
tradition. In *Das Gewicht der Welt* (*The weight of the world*, 1977)
Handke, returning to one of Wiener's themes, rejects all the 'Universal-
Pictures', the social, political, psychological, ontological constructs that
preform perception. He seeks to empty himself of this other-determined
subjectivity by an 'unmediated, simultaneously recorded reporting' to
replace meaning, the rationalistic construction that robs the individual of
the immediacy of experience.

An extreme of disenchantment with imaginative fiction and the privileged position of the bourgeois writer led to a 'literature of non-authors' –
volumes of taped interviews like *Bottroper Protokolle* (1968), edited by
Erika Runge (b. 1939) or subjective autobiographies whose apparent art-
lessness means they rely largely on traditional patterns of popular fiction:
Rosalie Rother's *Rosalka oder wie es eben so ist* (*Rosalka or that's just
how it is*, 1969); Wolfgang Werner's *Vom Waisenhaus ins Zuchthaus*
(*From orphanage to prison*, 1969). This brief fashion remains important
in that its quasi-documentary, autobiographical articulation of subjective
experience was a route by which excluded groups could enter literary

discourse; from it emerged both the new women's writing of the 1970s and 1980s, and the 'Gastarbeiterliteratur' which was the forerunner of an increasingly sophisticated and differentiated literature of migrant authors in the 1980s.

Nazi idealisations of the worker, the gravitation of writers like Willi Bredel and Ludwig Turek to the GDR, and indeed the integrative effects of prosperity led to the neglect of the world of work in West German literature. So the foundation of *Gruppe 61* by Fritz Hüser in 1961 with miners' union funding and the goal of reflecting both the specifics of working-class life and the wider material and political issues of industrial society, was genuinely innovative, another example of the fundamental reorientation of German literature around 1960.

Max von der Grün (b. 1928), himself a miner and the *Gruppe*'s most famous member, actually rejected the concept of working-class literature for its ghettoising effect. His novels, for example, *Männer in zweifacher Nacht* (*Men in double darkness*, 1962) or *Stellenweise Glatteis* (*Icy patches*, 1973), are most vivid when they describe work conditions, especially underground, though von der Grün, drawing on a tradition extending back to Romanticism, tends to demonise the machine and the mine. His domestic dialogue and portrayals of relationships rely formally and linguistically on conventional devices. But his work, like that of Kroetz, is important for showing that working-class figures too may have identity crises, and that these crises have specific material causes in the dehumanisation of work and the threat or reality of unemployment.

The work of Günter Wallraff (b. 1942), initially associated like von der Grün's with *Gruppe 61*, was in fact very different: subjective reportage, in the tradition of Egon Erwin Kisch or Upton Sinclair, on the alienation and exploitation in industrial and lower-level white-collar work: *Wir brauchen Dich. Als Arbeiter in deutschen Industriebetrieben* (*We need you. As a worker in German factories*, 1966); *13 unerwünschte Reportagen* (*13 unwelcome reports*, 1969); *Neue Reportagen* (1972). Wallraff's investigative method, using a false identity to get behind the public relations mask of capitalist organisations, earned him fame, huge sales and bitter attacks when he turned it on the *Bild-Zeitung*, in *Der Aufmacher. Der Mann, der bei "Bild" Hans Esser war* (*The Man who was Hans Esser at the Bild-Zeitung*, 1977); two further volumes followed. His reportage on his experiences in the role of the Turk Ali Levant, *Ganz Unten* (*The lowest of the low*, 1985), in which he exposed the racism and discrimination ever-present under the surface of West German liberal democracy, sold 1.8 million copies in four months, but also raised doubts about the probity of his techniques when it became apparent that not all the experiences and not all their textual formulations were those of Wallraff himself. Wallraff's work in any case calls the polarity of document versus subjectivity into question: one has only to note that the most famous Turk in German literature, Ali Levant, is a fiction, to recognise the complex ironies of his work.

Documentary literature was already being questioned by the protest movement itself, which was concerned not only with political change, but with a release and legitimation of imagination and desire. As the established critical literature of an older generation politicised itself in the course of the 1960s, the younger protesting generation took provocative, subversive recourse to popular and trivial forms, disrespect being fundamental to rebellion. The anthology *März Texte 1* (1969), published by the März-Verlag, was dedicated to 'an expanded subjectivity and spontaneity' and a 'new sensibility' and offered a huge variety of texts: political articles, agit-prop pamphlets, travel writing, poems, comic strips, pin-ups and pornography, accounts of drug trips, films, music, consumer goods. This open eclecticism was only later driven out by dogmatic theorising and a more passive, navel-gazing subjectivity: *both* were in a sense parallel retreats from the actionism that lay at the heart of the protest movement.

'New subjectivity' was not wholly new in the 1970s. But it found willing readers as the euphoria of protest ebbed: *Lenz* (1973) by Peter Schneider (b. 1940) *Klassenliebe* (*Class love*, 1973) by Karin Struck (b. 1947), Handke's *Die Stunde der wahren Empfindung* (*A moment of true feeling*, 1975) and *Die linkshändige Frau* (*The left-handed woman*, 1975) and even Strauß's ironic *envoi* to the trend almost before it had begun, *Die Widmung* (*The dedication*, 1976), were all widely read. Subjective themes and forms can be seen in autobiographical writing of all kinds, in the biographies of parents, from Handke's *Wunschloses Unglück* (*A sorrow beyond dreams*, 1972) via Struck's *Die Mutter* (1975) to the 'Vater-Bücher' at the end of the decade, in sensitive, inward-looking novels with telling titles, like Hans Jürgen Fröhlich (b. 1932), *Im Garten der Gefühle* (*In the garden of feelings*, 1975) or Nicolas Born, *Die erdabgewandte Seite der Geschichte* (1976). Self-destructive subjectivity, expressed in madness, sickness, alcohol and drug abuse, was a common theme: Maria Erlenberger (pseudonym: date of birth unknown), *Der Hunger nach Wahnsinn* (*The hunger for madness*, 1977); Ernst Herhaus (b. 1932), *Kapitulation. Aufgang einer Krankheit* (*Capitulation. The emergence of an illness*, 1977). What one could call 'lumpen subjectivity', exploration, without any tendency to idealise working-class life, of the introspections, self-hatreds and raging self-assertions of a working class robbed of proletarian self-respect is the distinctive aspect of the novels *Die Sünden der Armut* (*The sins of poverty*, 1975) and *Ein Unding der Liebe* (*A monstrosity of love*, 1981) by Ludwig Fels (b. 1948).

One text draws many of these themes together into a remarkable, if fragmentary and wayward, document of its time: Bernward Vesper's

(1938–71): *Die Reise* (*The journey*, published posthumously 1977). When his one-time partner (in real life, Gudrun Ensslin) turns to active terrorism with the dissipation of the student movement, the autobiographical narrator, occupied by a complex love–hate relationship to his father, the Nazi poet Will Vesper, turns to hallucinogenic drugs. *Die Reise* was originally to be called *Der Trip* or *Der Haß* (*Hatred*); it is a massive, unfinished monument to a generation caught between a love their parents could not give and which the children yearned for but would not accept, a materially saturated society, a protest movement tearing itself apart, and part-understood and indiscriminately used forms of rebellion via drugs, sexual and social experiment.

Die Reise is not another *Blechtrommel*; it remains a ruin. But Grass too has never been able to match his first extraordinary novel. *Der Butt* (*The flounder*, 1977) traces women's contribution to human culture from pre-history to the present in a multi-dimensional narrative, mingling myth and realism, abstraction and earthiness. While Grass succeeds in mocking male pretensions and indicting their culmination in technocratic destructiveness, his idealisation of matriarchy also depends on male stereotypes. *Die Rättin* (*The rat*, 1986), a rat's retrospective history of humanity after the latter's self-immolation in a neutron explosion, exemplifies Grass's aesthetic goal of 'Vergegenkunft', a simultaneity of history, memory, present, and utopian and dystopian future. Like *Die Blechtrommel*, *Der Butt* and *Die Rättin* have narrators who move ambiguously between omniscient objectivity and subjective involvement and between abstraction and sensual participation. But while the unreliable Oskar is real enough to confront the reader with his or her own ambivalence, both the flounder and the rat combine over-demonstrative inventiveness with a lack of this constructively irritant connection to the reader.

The complex dialectic of aesthetics and politics is the theme of Peter Weiss's final and greatest work, *Ästhetik des Widerstands* (*Aesthetics of resistance*, begun 1971, completed 1980, and published in three parts in 1975, 1978 and 1981). From the opening pages, the reflections of three young working-class men studying the Pergamon altar, whose power stems from the tension between the dynamic physicality of the depicted events and the change-resistant medium of the stone, a tension which itself reflects the contradiction between the longings of the dispossessed for change and empowerment and the factors resisting this change, this dialectic is fundamental to the novel. In giving a version of his earlier self a working-class rather than bourgeois background, and allowing him to participate alongside authentic historical figures in the struggles of the German workers' movement in Nazi Germany and in the Spanish Civil War, Weiss not only creates the autobiography he would have liked to have had but also seeks to reappropriate Western art, from the Pergamon altar to Picasso's *Guernica*, for the classes excluded from participating in it, and so to mobilise the achievements of Western culture for the struggle against barbarism. The novel restates Keats in the sense that for it beauty is the empowerment to resist, and those aesthetic experiences (whereby activity is important) which contribute to this empowerment are beautiful. A long section describes Brecht's intensive study of Brueghel's apocalyptic paintings in the search for an aesthetic to engage with the horrors of the contemporary world. Others are literally a working-class *Bildungsroman*, portraying detailed critical engagement by the young working-class narrator and his friends with an improbable range of works of art and literature. It challenges, moreover, Communist orthodoxy: Weiss's project is aimed at overcoming the undialectic rejection of the modernism of Joyce, Kafka, Schönberg, Stravinsky, Klee and Picasso. This too is wish-projection rather than realism.

The third volume is a melancholy reflection on the failure of left-wing art, even at its high point in the Weimar Republic, to influence political events. Moreover, from a perspective beyond the revelations accompanying the collapse of communism in Eastern Europe, the confrontation, in the reading process, with the idealistic, almost wilful blindness of the narrator towards the realities of censorship, betrayal and internecine brutality in the International Brigades seems to prefigure the end of the blind faith of the Western left. Like *Die Blechtrommel* two decades earlier, *Ästhetik des Widerstands* expresses in its form the tortuous contradictions of its age. But in its extensive use of a range of cultural knowledge most middle-class, let alone possible working-class readers, no longer possess, it is also itself an elitist work, indeed a doomed project in an age dominated by other media than the book and other values than those of the humanist *Gymnasium*. In that sense, it indeed marks the end of an era.

The 1980s

Well before the election of Helmut Kohl's CDU government in 1983, conservative retrenchment was underway. In the 1980s, mass unemployment, high labour and social costs, demographic imbalance, environmental strains, budget cuts and political interference in the arts heightened the sense of stagnation and reversal. Controversies over the stationing of missiles and the building of nuclear power stations briefly revived the representative oppositional status of writers like Böll. Economic and political pressures abroad kept up the rate of migration to Germany despite the slackening of labour demand; as a result, the national question gained an extra dimension in historically charged issues of asylum, exile and ethnic identity. In the 'historians' dispute' of the mid-1980s, conservative historians sought to relativise German war guilt and the Holocaust within a broader pattern of anti-humanist brutality and genocide in the modern world.

The resulting 'new lack of coherence' (Habermas) of the 1980s is more than the confusion in which an age close to the present manifests itself to an observer. It is compounded by the widespread influence of postmodernism and related feminist and post-structuralist theories and their desire to deconstruct and decentre the values and vocabularies of Western rationalism, historical coherence and linear narrative, perceived to have underpinned patriarchy and oppression. Thus, alongside somewhat beleaguered adherents to the Enlightenment faith in progress, we find a bewildering plurality of theories and fashions, drawing on multivalent or amorphous, irrational and pre-rational modes of thought, on myth, anthropology and psychoanalysis. The last named, together with feminist culture's theorising of physicality, and the post-colonial critique of Western rationality, brought a renewed interest in primal scenes, holy rituals, the body and death. Klaus Theweleit's psychoanalytical study of Freikorps literature, *Männerphantasien* (*Male fantasies*, 1977/78) became a key text. Walter Benjamin was re-read, but the focus now was the fragmentary, associative *Das Passagenwerk* (*Passages*, written in the 1930s, published 1983).

The consequences for writing in the 1980s were fluidity between genres and media; a loss of historicity; a perception of literature's self-referentiality or intertextuality, the idea that texts engage with other texts rather than an empirical world, and that realistic literature is therefore a contradiction; dissolution of the discrete, self-determining subject; non-hierarchical alternatives to linear narrative, be it fragmentation and discontinuity, the amorphous 'rhizome' advocated by Deleuze and Guattari or the lateral instantaneity of a networked, digitised world. However, the plurality of styles, techniques and themes included both continuities from the critical realism of much 1970s literature, and attempts to restore the gnostic, ineffable status of literature and with it the privileged status of the *Dichter* and his initiates, to counter the concept of the writer as a dethroned figure in a cultural arena in which literature was no longer central.

It would thus be wrong to see West German literature of the 1980s as characterised only by anti-realism, apolitical mystification or conceptual games. There has been a revival of regionalism, ranging across the spectrum of political positions from eco-radicalism to conservative nostalgia, and from experimental dialect poetry to traditional descriptive realism. The German question remained persistent. Examples from Grass's *Kopfgeburten* (*Headbirths*, 1980) through Peter Schneider's *Der*

Mauerspringer (1982), Walser's *Dorle und Wolf* (*No man's land*, 1985) and *Die Bürgschaft* (*The bond*, 1985) by Thorsten Becker (b. 1958) to Schneider's essays *Deutsche Ängste* (*German anxieties*, 1988) with their dreams of a pluralist, post-Wall fusion of the two socio-economic systems show both literature's anticipatory qualities and its tangential relationship to historical processes. The 'Berlin encounters', East–West meetings of writers as part of a peace initiative in 1981 and 1983, were important signals for a closer interchange of German literature in the 1980s.

Böll, Grass, Walser continued to publish realistic novels. The *Jahrestage* (*Anniversaries*) of Uwe Johnson (1934–84), begun in 1968 and completed in 1983, have a complex narrative structure and strongly subjective perspective, but the realistic intention of this major post-war novel, set between August 1967 and August 1968, with many flashbacks to the Nazi and early GDR past, is unquestionable. Traditional realistic narrative, with a clear concept of historical and material causation, a concern for readability, but also a sensitivity to many of the issues raised in the new cultural theories of the 1980s, is exemplified by the work of Uwe Timm (1940–). *Kerbels Flucht* (*Kerbel's flight*, 1980) develops the themes of disillusion from *Heißer Sommer* (*The hot summer*, 1974), his novel of the protest movement, into a persuasive analysis of affluent alienation. *Morenga* (1978) explores a forgotten chapter of German colonial history to show how Eurocentric arrogance and colonial greed mendaciously ideologise genocide as a civilising mission. *Der Schlangenbaum* (*The snake tree*, 1986) confronts the rationalistic confidence of a German engineer with the elemental forces of the jungle. For Timm not nature but the alliance of technocratic hubris with rapacious European capitalism and corrupt Third World dictatorship are the sources of disorder, arbitrary violence and irrational destruction in the attempt to impose an inappropriate order. *Kopfjäger* (*Headhunter*, 1991) is noteworthy both as a fable about the greed and materialism of the old Federal Republic's last phase, and as a plea for narrative story-telling, making sense, as a preserve of humanist values.

Much cited as a postmodern novel (and certainly one of the most successful German novels of the century – six million copies in twenty-eight languages by 1988) was *Das Parfum* (*Perfume*, 1985) by Patrick Süskind (b. 1949). It plays with the forms of the gothic novel and the detective thriller, with pastiches and borrowings, from Kleist, Grass, Lovecraft, Nietzsche and Bataille. Moreover, in centring the novel on perfume, a synthetic stimulant of the senses, Süskind has provided an extended exploration of Baudrillard's idea of 'Simulation'.

Christoph Ransmayr (b. 1954) also achieved bestseller status with *Die letzte Welt* (*The last world*, 1988), though like Peter Sloterdijk's *Der Zauberbaum* (*The enchanted tree*, 1985), which investigates the roots of psychoanalysis in eighteenth-century occultism, it lacks Süskind's bodice-ripping appeal. *Die letzte Welt*'s quest for Ovid and the manuscript of his *Metamorphoses* dissolves the boundaries between reality and fiction in a maze of allusions and inversions; its undertone is conservative reassurance, since we always know that the *Metamorphoses* will survive the dictatorship that threatens them.

Like Ransmayr's *Die Schrecken des Eises und der Finsternis* (*The terrors of ice and darkness*, 1984), Sten Nadolny (b. 1942), in *Die Entdeckung der Langsamkeit* (*The discovery of slowness*, 1983), uses the reconstruction of a polar expedition to reflect on the contemporary world. This is a typical 1980s theme from the poem *Nordwestpassage* by Guntram Vesper (b. 1941) to the 'Elementargedicht' *Nach der Natur* (*After nature*, 1988) by W. G. Sebald (b. 1944). Nadolny's novel invokes the virtues of slowness and duration in direct opposition to a contemporary world of acceleration, and of information and sensation overload, themes developed in *Selim oder die Gabe der Rede* (*Selim or the gift of speaking*, 1990) which interweaves two traditions of narration, and two contrasting focalisations (the German Alexander and the Turkish Selim), in a panoramic novel of the Federal Republic. 'Simulation', the overriding sense of artificiality, is explicitly invoked by Bodo Morshäuser (b. 1953) in *Die Berliner Simulation* (1983). Asked who in Berlin actually works, the narrator answers: 'I think we're all in films'. Persons, events and emotions coalesce indistinguishably with their historical or fictional antecedents (Isherwood, André Breton).

The fiction of Hanns-Josef Ortheil (b. 1951) retains more narrative coherence than his cultural essays, laced with American and French postmodernism, might lead one to expect. *Schwerenöter* (*Philanderers*, 1987) uses the contrasting lives of twin brothers from the 1940s to the 1980s for a panorama of the Federal Republic; not, though, a linear 'Bildungsroman' in which individual and social histories harmonise, but a picture of fragmentary heterogeneity. In *Agenten* (1989), a career-oriented generation pursues social and material success with uninhibited pragmatism.

As an aesthetics of social intervention was replaced by one of art as liberation from political, religious or other ideologies of salvation, the 1980s brought many echoes of early Romanticism's critique of reason and its association of beauty and truth. In the case of Peter Handke, a longing to escape conceptual pre-programming develops from the linguistic scepticism of his early work, through *Die Stunde der wahren Empfindung* (*The moment of true feeling*, 1975) to a series of semi-fictional, semi-essayistic texts in the 1980s, where the poetic imagination becomes the means of reconnecting the individual to self and cosmos. In *Phantasien der Wiederholung* (*Repetition*, 1983), the poet is a visionary messenger, and socially critical writers, blinded by a neurotic and repressive desire for rational explanation, are anathema. In *Nachmittag eines Schriftstellers* (*Afternoon of a writer*, 1987), the writer's task is to voice the 'Urtext', the primeval text within himself. While Handke's insistence that 'das Gefüge', the structure, remains of prime importance, still privileges the artist's shaping intelligence (essentially a bourgeois idea), his prose in the 1980s successfully engenders 'slowness' and 'duration' against the destructive accelerations of the contemporary world.

Brigitte Kronauer's narrative project resembles Handke's. Kronauer (b. 1940) sets out to challenge the compulsion to force experience through the 'Geschichtswolf', the mincer of narrative causality. The 'Gehäus' of her first novel, *Frau Mühlenbach im Gehäus* (1980) is the dwelling and also the prison Frau Mühlenbach erects with her unbroken, unreflecting conversion of experience into narrative. In *Rita Münster* (1983) the title figure undergoes an experimental dissolution of the boundaries of the self, and gains the energy from a moment of epiphany to re-imagine her past life, and in *Berittener Bogenschütze* (*Mounted archer*, 1986) Roth is shaken out of his inauthentic life of surrogate experience by a moment of *kairos* (a key term in the new gnosticism), the moment when even mundane things radiate their meaning. Kronauer's affinity to *fin-de-siècle* symbolism is underlined by the narrative situation of *Die Frau in den Kissen* (*The woman in the cushions*, 1990): a trance-like state, cut loose from the control mechanisms of rational consciousness, enables her narrator to mediate an oceanically non-linear perception of reality.

In the 1970s, Botho Strauß had explored the self- dissolution that results from the discovery of the multiple voices in the self: *Marlenes Schwester* and *Theorie der Drohung* (*Marlene's sister, Theory of menace*, 1974), *Die Widmung* (*The dedication*, 1976), *Rumor* (*Tumult*, 1980). *Paare, Passanten* (*Couples, passers-by*, 1981) had contained a much-cited valediction to the critical dialectics of Adorno; the loose, associative, semi-fictional form of its sketches and reflections on the 'Zeitgeist' was exemplary for much 1980s writing. The novel *Der junge Mann* (*The young man*, 1984), in its vast, open-ended form, multiple levels, time planes, focalisations, intertextual borrowings, interpolated Romantic novellas, allegories and set-pieces of social satire and cultural-philosophical dispute, make it a representative postmodern novel. In its self-stylisation as a 'RomantischerReflexionsRoman' it invokes Schlegel's call for the novel to be an 'encyclopaedia' of the whole spiritual life of an individual of genius, only to undercut the pathos of this project with repeated ironies. The middle three books of the novel have the irrational dream-logic of *Alice in Wonderland*, and reflect the revival of myth and fairy-tale in the postmodern crisis of Enlightenment. Without myth and metaphor, says one figure, we are simply not linked to 'die Ordnung des Lebendigen' ('the vital order'), to 'ether and earth, animal and plant'. The novel hovers between myth as reactionary transformation of history into labyrinthine nature and myth as reason's necessary companion. Indeed, virtually every idea in this cornucopia of themes, forms, motifs and discourses is ironically relativised by its own opposite, so that an ideological reading necessarily founders.

Paare, Passanten had already mocked 'the pea-brained circularity' of a long-since ossified, self-satisfied social criticism. *Niemand Anderes* (*No one else*, 1987) called explicitly for a 'a neo-gnostic link to orders beyond sociocentric thought', a project his later prose, like the *Fragmente der Undeutlichkeit* (*Fragments of obscurity*, 1989), seeks to realise. Here, the writer's task is to create non-understanding, a mystical 'Cloud of Unknowing' in which gnostic revelation is possible.

Hubert Fichte (1935–86), in his planned nineteen-volume, unfinished *Geschichte der Empfindlichkeit* (*History of sensitivity*, 1987ff.) pursues an 'Ethnopoesie', in which his sensitivity to human difference is widened into a deconstruction of Eurocentrism via an exploration of non-Western, non-rationalistic, cultural practices, especially in the Caribbean. Drawing on multi-voiced narrative techniques first practised in his novel of Hamburg subculture *Die Palette* (*The palette*, 1968), *Hotel Garni* (1987) plays with multiple constructions of position – age, biography, class, gender, sexual orientation; it invokes but resists the reification both pornography and rational science practise on the human body. Fichte equates pornography with colonialism: both share the master–slave paradigm. He also criticises Lévi-Strauss's anthropology as itself an exploitative form of colonialism. Fichte's complex work, interweaving his own life history, his society, the lives and societies of very different others, exploring the relationship of texts to spoken language and to photography, practises radical intertextuality and intermediality.

In the 1960s and early 1970s Ingeborg Bachmann, Marlen Haushofer (1920–70) and Unica Zürn (1916–70) had published texts engaging with women's damaged lives and their enmeshment in the patterns and myths of femininity and female sexuality, breaking with descriptive realism in order to demonstrate, in the language and structure of the text, the cultural construction of gender relationships. *Malina* (1971) for example, part of Bachmann's unfinished *Todesarten* trilogy, is a dialogue between reason (Malina) and its Other (the female narrator): in an Enlightenment discourse where the female is relegated to largely passive 'nature', the narrator has neither name nor clear identity.

However, at the time, the emerging women's movement took little notice of these texts. The anthologies edited by Erika Runge: *Frauen. Versuch einer Emanzipation* (*Women – an attempt at emancipation*, 1969), and Alice Schwarzer: *Der kleine Unterschied und seine großen Folgen* (*The small difference and its big consequences*, 1975) mark off a phase where women's writing was characterised by autobiographical narration of implicitly typical female experience. Most texts of the 1970s still depended on a conception of female subjectivty to attain which it was enough to assert it: Karin Struck (b. 1937), *Klassenliebe* (*Love and class*, 1973), Margot Schröder (b. 1937), *Ich stehe meine Frau* (*I can take it like a woman*, 1975). The most radical in terms of discursive content was Verena Stefan's *Häutungen* (*Shedding*, 1975): disillusioned by her loss of self in heterosexual relationships, the narrator returns from the Other to the One, to lesbian relationships as a return to a lost childhood harmony and holism. Subsequently much decried for essentialism and ideologisation of the natural, *Häutungen* was doubtless important in its time, since it also directed attention to women's entrapment in patriarchal language.

Autobiographical modes and realistic narrative flourished on into the 1980s: Angelika Mechtel (b. 1943), *Wir sind arm, wir sind reich* (*We're poor, we're rich*, 1977); Karin Reschke (b. 1940), *Memoiren eines Kindes* (*A child's memoirs*, 1981). Ingeborg Drewitz (1923–1986), in *Gestern war heute. Hundert Jahre Gegenwart* (*Yesterday was today. A hundred years of the present*, 1978), shows the changes and the constants of women's experience through five generations.

From the latter 1970s though, the interpenetration of primary literary texts and secondary aesthetic and philosophical reflections that characterises postmodernism became an important factor in women's writing with the reception of Cixous and Irigaray. Influenced by Julia Kristeva's *The revolution in poetic language* (German 1978) and a dissatisfaction with simplistic autobiographical realism, feminist readers returned to Bachmann, Zürn and Haushofer with altered attention.

Christa Wolf's scepticism about the integrity of the self and of narrative authenticity in *Kindheitsmuster* (1977) was another key influence. Linear narrative is replaced by self-reflexive explorations of and experiments with the textual constitution of women's reality. This may be topographical, as in *Das Bildnis der Jakobina Völker* (*The portrait of Jakobina Völker*, 1980) by Birgit Pausch (b. 1942) or mythical, as in *Michel, sag ich* (*Michael, I say*, 1984) by Ulla Berkéwicz (b. 1951), or Mechtel's *Gott und die Liedermacherin* (*God and the singer*, 1983). In *Meine Schwester Antigone* (*My sister Antigone*, 1984) by Grete Weil (b. 1906), the narrator's painful engagement with the Antigone myth (a motif in all Weil's novels) becomes a means to unlock the truths of her memory and her Jewish identity she has been using myth to escape.

Christa Reinig's *Entmannung* (*Emasculation*, 1977), an early example of the move away from autobiographical narration, is a sarcastic fantasy arguing for the dismantling of myths of maleness in the female as well as the male consciousness. With *Der Wolf und die Witwen* (*The wolf and the widows*, 1980) and *Die ewige Schuld* (*Eternal guilt*, 1982), it established her as a brilliant writer of satire and grotesque comedy. Reinig inverts the pattern of male perpetrator and female victim, mocking the women who prove themselves inadequate in their new role. Her narrative technique is a furious and irreverent montage of incompatible registers and breaks in causal logic.

Disenfranchised within patriarchal language, women experience the body highly ambiguously, as the site where sickness, including mental illness, can function both as symptom of the malaise and possibility to escape the social order. While in the texts of Anne Duden (b. 1942): *Übergang* (*The opening of the mouth*, 1982); *Das Judasschaf* (*The Judas sheep*, 1985) the body functions as semiotic marker both of lived aggression and of nightmare images from the unconscious, in Ulrike Kolb's (b. 1942) *Idas Idee* (*Ida's idea*, 1985), the heroine intentionally becomes so fat that her body breaks free, unleashing the libidinous energies normally corseted by the social order. The body is the place, moreover, where the triangle of sexuality, violence and social power is experienced: Karin Reschke (b. 1940), *Dieser Tage über Nacht* (*Overnight in these days*, 1984). In *Verfolgte des Glücks* (*Hunted by happiness*, 1982), Reschke explores a more subtle form of power, reconstructing a life of Henriette Vogel, whose suicide alongside Heinrich von Kleist in 1811 has been virtually erased within a patriarchally oriented history. In *Valerie oder Das unerzogene Auge* (*Valerie or: the untrained eye*, 1986) by Erica Pedretti (b. 1930), the gradual dissolution of the model's identity as the artist's picture takes shape provides a telling image of one of the concerns of 1980s feminist aesthetics: the way in which under the male gaze woman becomes image and vanishes from history as an active subject.

Theatre by women (including the dance pieces of Pina Bausch) was a major cultural force in 1980s Germany. Gisela von Wysocki (b. 1940), in much-cited volumes of essays *Fröste der Freiheit* (*Freedom's chills*, 1981) and *Weiblichkeit und Modernität* (*Femininity and modernity*, 1982), explores women's attempts to escape from the spaces male projections assign them. *Auf Schwarzmärkten* (*At black markets*, 1983) declares: 'Die alte Welt kotzt Vatersprache aus' ('The old world spews out father-language'). Her plays pursue these ideas: *Abendlandleben oder Apollinaires Gedächtnis* (*Old World life, or Apollinaire's memory*, 1987) literally stages the mind of the surrealist poet as an intersection point for the discourses of European culture. *Schauspieler, Tänzer, Sängerin* (*Actor, dancer, chanteuse*, 1988) dramatises the fact that woman's role in cultural history has been to *play* the role of woman. Wysocki's concern is to show the apparently natural as accreted and constructed 'Geschichtete', both layered ('geschichtet') and turned into history ('Geschichte').

Friederike Roth (b. 1948) repeatedly explores the discrepancy between dreams and reality, whether in the dialogic realism of *Ritt auf die*

Wartburg (*A ride up the Wartburg*, 1981), where four ordinary West German women on a brief excursion to the GDR experience the grotesque gap between reality and their expectations and projections, or the elegiac interplay of fantasy and reality, and the destruction of love through objectification, in *Die Klavierspielerin* (*The woman pianist*, 1981) or *Die einzige Geschichte* (*The only story*, 1985). This sensitivity contrasts with the shock tactics and mordant intellectuality of Elfriede Jelinek (b. 1946), whose garish figures are constructs of the clichéd language they speak. *Clara S.* (1982) portrays woman as victim, man as beast. *Krankheit oder Moderne Frauen* (*Sickness or: modern women*, 1987) explodes conventional realism, pitting women slaughtered by patriarchy but returned as vampires against male fantasies and practices of power over women and nature.

Two plays by Bodo Kirchhoff (b. 1948), *Das Kind oder die Vernichtung von Neuseeland* (*The child or the destruction of New Zealand*, 1979) and *Body building* (1979) typify postmodernist drama, reflecting the theories of Jacques Lacan (subject of Kirchhoff's Ph.D. thesis). As in Handke's *Kaspar*, the figures are mouthpieces for a linguistically structured and mediated order. Rainald Goetz (b. 1954), with doctorates in both medicine and history, and experience in psychiatric medicine, addresses similar themes in texts of immense density and complexity, but above all angry energy: the multi-layered prose *Irre* (*Crazy*, 1983), *Hirn* (*Brain*, 1985) and *Kontrolliert* (*Controlled*, 1988), which explore psychiatric illness and terrorism as symptoms of a sick normality (to which the left-liberal culture of 'Be.' and 'Ge.' – Böll and Grass – belongs), and as routes to its subversion. The dramatic trilogy *Krieg* (*War*, 1988) rages across great swathes of German psycho-history in a tight quasi-mathematical structure from 'Welt, Revolution, Bier' (*Heiliger Krieg* (*Holy war*)) through 'Familie, Kunst, Haß' (*Schlachten* (*Battles*)) to 'Ich, Wort, Tod' (*Kolik* (*Rage*)).

For Botho Strauß, a 'play' is exactly that: the crisis of humanism is a matter for knowingly self-conscious comedy. So a play in which a man is dismembered is called *Kalldewey, Farce* (1981). Typically, Strauß's plays explore a conjuncture of the mundane and the mythical. *Der Park* (1984) asks what if the magical spirit of *A Midsummer Night's Dream* were to infiltrate the contemporary world? But Oberon and Titania awaken only cynicism, confusion and aggression. Their project was always doomed, for Shakespeare's magical forest is now a filthy urban park, and the supposedly rational mortals are gripped by new myths, ideologies and prejudices. *Die Zeit und das Zimmer* (*Time and the room*, 1988) epitomises the tension in Strauß's work between (a somewhat mannered) playfulness and intellectuality: it calls for witty, cabarettistic production, yet it posits a grasp of Heidegger's dense treatise *Sein und Zeit* (*Being and time*).

Peter Handke's later plays take portentous stands against nihilism; *Das Spiel vom Fragen* (*The game/play of questions*, 1990) calls for a 'Psalmenton' in its long, patient, wordless search for meaning. 'Eternal peace is possible', declares *Über die Dörfer* (*Across the villages*, 1982); 'Be heavenwards. See the dancing pulse of the sun and trust your simmering hearts.' Much distinguishes Handke and Strauß; they share, though, a reassertion of gnostic meaning beyond the postmodernist demolition of historical meaning.

Political theatre, in the broadest sense of plays that seek to instruct, enlighten or stimulate reflection or outrage at contemporary or historical reality, was the exception in the 1980s, though not wholly absent. Besides Hochhuth, Kroetz, Kipphardt's *Bruder Eichmann* and Peter Weiss's tendentiously anti-capitalist reworking of Kafka, *Der neue Prozeß* (*The new trial*, 1983), a new, popular 'Zeitstück' emerged with Klaus Pohl (b. 1952). *Das Alte Land* (*The old country*, 1984) portrays a German village in the continuities and contradictions of the early post-war years: profiteering, opportunism, anti-communism, antipathy towards refugees. *Heißes Geld* (*Hot money*, 1988), a farce based on the corruption scandals that became commonplace in 1980s West Germany, typifies the element of opportunism in Pohl's choice of themes. Harald Mueller's *Totenfloß* (*The death raft*, 1984, revised 1986), a dystopian nightmare of Germany's environmental future, was given sensational urgency by Chernobyl.

Georg Tabori (b. 1914), a Hungarian Jew who has worked in German and Austrian theatres since the early 1970s, is paradoxically free to transgress taboos on comic treatment of the horrors of history. Avoiding moralising pathos, his grisly, yet witty and sensual comedies are peopled by the grotesques of a raging, traumatised imagination. In *Jubiläum* (1983), the ghost of a father murdered, like Tabori's own, in Auschwitz, offers his son, who has been asking whether it was bread or bodies that were baked in the ovens there, his 'Laib'(= loaf; 'Leib' = body): a bewildering collage of communion, cannibalism (cf. *Die Kannibalen*, 1969), parricide, the Oedipus and Hamlet themes of post-war German culture. In the farce *Mein Kampf* (1987), the hapless Hitler is advised by the Jewish hawker Schlomo Herzl to go into politics, then spared by Death, a female tramp, who recognizes his talents as her future assistant. Tabori's gradual recognition as a force in German theatre, even though he writes in English, is characteristic of the dissolution of cultural homogeneity in the 1980s.

In German poetry in the 1980s the exercise of poetic form within the free space of the imaginative text is once again recognised both as inherently pleasurable and as a potential resistance against other-determined forms of social discourse, which reach deep into the supposed authenticity of the individual subject. Even for those writers for whom traditional forms remain suspect, the alternative is not a consistent conversational tone, but an aggressive multiple conjunction of registers, vocabularies and syntactic patterns.

The shift from 'Alltagslyrik' to poetologically scrupulous reflections of damaged life gained important impulses from ex-GDR poets: Sarah Kirsch, whose nature poetry, even in idyllic moments, is shot through, often satirically, with images of social deformation: for example, *Erdreich* (*Earthly kingdom*, 1982); and Günter Kunert, the sheer negativity of whose apocalyptic pessimism urges another, better reality: *Abtötungs-verfahren* (*Mortification procedures*, 1980); *Stilleben* (*Still life*, 1982).

In the work of F. C. Delius (b. 1943), traditional forms are still some-times harnessed to political intent. His 'Ode an die Flugzeugträger' ('Ode to aircraft carriers') in *Die unsichtbaren Blitze* (*The invisible flashes*, 1981) evokes the monumentality of the ships, only to sink them. But, of course, only on paper: the irony (reflected in the poem itself) which perpetually calls political literature into question.

The elegy re-emerged, expressing millenarial pessimism and seeking the dignity of form for the damaged self: Michael Krüger (b. 1943): *Aus der Ebene* (*From the plain*, 1982); Ursula Krechel: *Vom Feuer lernen* (*Learning from the fire*, 1985). The mood is melancholy, the style laconic and elliptical; the titles of *Die verschwindende Welt* (*The vanishing world*, 1985) by Peter Hamm (b. 1937), and *Juniabschied* (*June leave-taking*, 1984) by Rolf Haufs (b. 1935) are symptomatic.

Characteristically, Enzensberger is already invoking the elegy for ironic purposes in *Die Furie des Verschwindens* (*The fury of disappearance*, 1980), in marked contrast to Handke's *Gedicht auf die Dauer* (*Poem to permanence*, 1986), where he takes up his search for, and affirmation of, moments of meaning and harmony in a world of fractured, hollow dis-courses. The poem may be meant as a reprise to Strauß's *Diese Erinnerung an einen, der nur einen Tag zu Gast war* (*This memory of a guest who only stayed one day*, 1985). Strauß's own model is Rilke's *Duino Elegies*, his intention twofold: to appeal for intensity, devotion and form in a super-ficial age, and to legitimate eroded or historically burdened values like 'Liebe', 'Heimat' and 'Vaterland'.

Writers previously associated with 'Alltagslyrik' like Theobaldy (*Die Sommertour*, 1983, with allusions to Georg Heym) and *Midlands* (1984), or Michael Buselmeier (*Auf, auf, Lenau!* (*Rise up, Lenau!*, 1986)) re-engage, though not uncritically, with poetic tradition. Though this canon-ical tradition, be it 'Minnesang' or Goethe, Mörike or George, might now be quarried rather than re-enthroned, it was no longer decried as a bour-geois fetish, but valued as a locus of resistance to cultural destruction.

The spirit of the age is expressed in Ulla Hahn's turning from studies of politically interventionist 'operative literature' to elegantly crafted (and best-selling) love poetry. From *Herz über Kopf* (*Heart over head*, 1982) to *Unerhörte Nähe* (*Unheard-of intimacy*, 1988) Hahn (b. 1948) draws unashamedly on traditional verse forms and motifs. Though not without irony or elements of 1980s feminst consciousness, her work wraps the irritations of experience in the comfort of artistry, creating a 'postrevolutionary rococo' (Ralf Schnell, *Geschichte der deutschsprachigen Literatur seit 1945*, 1993).

Wolf Wondratschek's almost equally successful *Die Einsamkeit der Männer* (*The loneliness of men*, 1983), reworks Malcolm Lowry's *Under the volcano*, mixing colloquialism and literary borrowings in an elaborate intertextuality which stresses the openness and indeterminacy of all perspectives and positions.

The poetic project of the Romanian German Oskar Pastior (b. 1927), most obvious at his hugely popular readings, is to direct attention back to the sound and form of words, by playing with language in the free zone between sense and nonsense; meaning is never eradicable, but is whisked past the listener by Pastior's verbal pyrotechnics like scraps of landscape past the window of a speeding train: *Lesungen mit Tinnitus. Gedichte 1980–1985* (*Readings with tinnitus. Poems 1980–1985*, 1986).

A postmodern poetry which builds on modernist doubts about mimetic realism to question representation in all its forms, including the poetic subject's legitimacy and ability to create metaphoric meaning, necessarily takes recourse to the word, as opposed to the image (since the latter is the word 'meaning' something else). Thus Pastior, the 'Wiener Gruppe' and their Dadaist antecedents have influenced younger poets like Gerhard Falkner (b. 1951), whose *der atem unter der erde* (*the breath below the earth*, 1984) or the cycle 'gebrochenes deutsch' ('broken German') in *wemut* [*sic*] (*melancholy*, 1989), practise a disorienting dissection of syntax. The poems in *geschmacksverstärker* (*flavour enhancer*, 1989) by Thomas Kling (b. 1957) are sound sculptures; with extreme elision, jargon, colloqualism and associative leaps, they seek to capture the speed and energy of the high-tech, short-wave, no-time culture. Felix Philipp Ingold (b. 1942), too, in the title poem of *Echtzeit* (*Realtime*, 1989), demonstrates how in the computer age, every sentence, every idea, is endlessly, effortlessly and instantly variable and recombinable.

In complete contrast, for Rose Ausländer (1907–88), representative of a traumatised and decimated generation of German Jews, whose poems in *Und preise die kühlende Liebe der Luft* (*And praise the air's cooling love*, 1988) still echo the horrors of Nazi persecution, language is a refuge and a means to piece together 'the dismembered song' and 'the shattered pane of time'. The horrors of history make language too important to be dissipated in postmodern games.

In the 1980s, as West Germany painfully became aware of its transition into a multi-cultural society (with 4.9 million foreign residents by 1989), literature that addresses migrant experience developed, including but never co-terminous with the naively autobiographical 'Gastarbeiterliteratur' of the anthologies through which it first became widely known, like *In zwei Sprachen leben* (*Living in two languages*, 1983); *Zwischen Fabrik und Bahnhof* (*Between factory and railway station*, 1981) or *Sehnsucht im Koffer* (*Longing in a suitcase*, 1981). Some writers insisted on the term 'Gastarbeiterliteratur' precisely because it named an exploitation process and an outsider status experienced by all migrant workers. The story 'Die Rückkehr von Passavanti' ('Passavanti's return', 1976) by Franco Biondi (b. 1947) has become a classic of *Gastarbeiter* experience, showing the migrant labourer with his cardboard suitcase as disoriented, embittered, rootless, his dreams of return doomed to disillusion.

But many writers, like the Iranian Cyrus Atabay (1926–96), whose antecedents range from classical Persian literature to Gottfried Benn, do not fit the stereotype. A Turkish writer like Yüksel Pazarkaya (b. 1940) is equally at home in the Islamic and the European canon. Some younger writers have biographies that defy national pigeonholing, and this is reflected in their writing: Nevfel Cumart (b. 1964), born in Germany of Turkish parents, brought up by a German foster family, calls Turkey 'my homeland', but first visited it at the age of nine. He writes formally and linguistically confident, economical lyric poetry in his *German* 'mother tongue', which reveals a poetic subject troubled but enriched by its complex identity, for example, *Das ewige Wasser* (*The eternal water*, 1990).

Güney Dal's novel *Wenn Ali die Glocken läuten hört* (*When Ali hears the bells ringing*, 1979) has many typical themes and milieus of 'Gastarbeiterliteratur'. But the intercut scenes and multiple focalisers permit a complex and differentiated portrayal of how experiences before as well as after migration condition the very disparate attitudes and deep divisions of Turks in contemporary Germany. Dal's *Europastraße 5* (German 1981) displays in its narrative form the multiple voices in the individual Turkish experience: the consciousness of the central character, Salim, becomes the arena in which conflicting cultural forces fight their battles, and migrant experience is expressed not in autobiographical complaint, but in the broken consciousness mediated by the narrative structure.

The work of Turkish women writers manifests in most concentrated and dynamic form the multiple tensions of ethnic and sexual discrimination. The recurrence of daughter figures stresses the dialectic of linkage to, and liberation from, a tradition of female Muslim identity, and there is a common experience of confrontation with Western images of the Muslim woman in which these authors do not recognise themselves. However, this literature too is stylistically and thematically very differentiated: Saliha Scheinhardt (b. 1950), e.g. *Frauen, die sterben, ohne daß sie gelebt haben* (*Women who die before they have lived*, 1983), whose protagonists come from the underdeveloped regions of Turkey, from Anatolian villages and the slums of the big cities, and whose work has emancipatory goals; Aysel Özakin (b. 1942), e.g. *Die Leidenschaft der Anderen* (*The passions of others*, 1983), whose autobiographical texts reflect the profound unsettlement of their sense of self which educated, big-city bred Turkish women experience at the German equation of Turkish with Anatolian peasant, and the resulting bitterness of a writer established as an avant-garde feminist before emigrating from Turkey for political reasons.

In contemporary migrant literature in German, the common, migration-related socio-economic and cultural experiences of exclusion and discrimination combine both with specific factors of ethnic and cultural background, class, generation and gender, and the shaping force of the individual literary imagination, to produce a highly diverse literature. It should be seen not as a ghettoised 'minority literature' but as what Deleuze and Guattari have called a 'minor literature', one written from outside the sites of power in a given language culture (their example is the Prague Jewish identity of Kafka's literature in German) which therefore 'deterritorialises' literature and liberates it from the sterile affirmation of national culture. Aras Ören (b. 1939), the Berlin Turkish writer whose twenty-plus volumes of poetry and stories since the early 1970s have brought him international recognition for their interweaving of Turkish and German lives, perspectives and literary forms, insists on the achievement and cultural-historical importance of migrant culture: 'One will no longer be able to speak of a new Europe without taking account of our part in it.'

Austrian and Swiss literature: A brief sideways glance

Throughout most of our period, both Austrian and German-Swiss literature have remained orientated towards the dominant literary market of the Federal Republic; German-Swiss writers and readers know German literature much better than that of their French, Italian or Romansch compatriots, and, like their Austrian counterparts, regard publication in German imprints like Suhrkamp as the real accolade. Stressing archetypal Austrianness or Swissness risks marginalising these literatures as regional phenomena, and thus many of the most distinctive works have already been discussed; yet their contextual, thematic and aesthetic specificities merit brief consideration.

Post-war Austria was permitted by the occupying Allies to see itself as liberated rather than compromised, an attitude encouraged by the 'Habsburg myth' (Claudio Magris, *Der Habsburgische Mythos in der österreichischen Literatur*, 1966), which, celebrating a nostalgically defined distinctiveness, glossed over Austria's role in National Socialism. As late as 1986, most voters shared Kurt Waldheim's view that his Nazi past did not debar him from the Presidency. Hence the anti-Austrian tirades of Bernhard or Jelinek. Bernhard's *Heldenplatz* (*The heroes' square*, 1988) brought the repressed past onto the stage of the 'Burgtheater', Austria's national theatre, provoking the Viennese public, before they had even seen it, to behave exactly as his play shows them doing. But Jelinek's thematically similar *Burgtheater* (1984) could not be produced there, female defilers being doubly anathema to Austrian conservatism.

From 1945 until the early 1960s, the novel above all reflected conservative continuity in ambitiously sweeping works, often begun in the 1930s, by Heimito von Doderer (1896–1956): *Die Dämonen* (*The demons*, 1956); Albert Paris Gütersloh (1887–1973): *Sonne und Mond* (*Sun and moon*, 1962); and Georg Saiko (1892–1962): *Der Mann im Schilf* (*The man in the reeds*, 1955). This conservative tradition continues in *Moos auf den Steinen* (*Moss on the stones*, 1956) by Gerhard Fritsch (1924–69), personifying the clash of tradition and modernity in the choice between suitors faced by an Imperial officer's daughter in a decaying Baroque castle, and the invocation of wholeness in the novels of Matthias Mander (b. 1933), like *Der Kasuar* (*The cassowary*, 1979) and *Der Sog* (*The slipstream*, 1989).

The same values celebrated in *Moos auf den Steinen* are satirised in Fritsch's later novel *Fasching* (*Carnival*, 1967) as provincial hypocrisy. In the 1970s, complacency was assaulted by stark novels like *Schöne Tage* (*Beautiful days*, 1974) by Franz Innerhofer (b. 1944), which develops a remarkable narrative style to evoke the near speechless, brutalised world of the child, Holl, behind the rural idyll. The trilogy *Das wilde Kärnten* (*Wild Carinthia*, 1979–82) by Josef Winkler (b. 1953) also goes beyond rural realism to eruptive, metaphor-laden explorations of homosexuality and death. Similarly, the working-class experience in the novels of Michael Scharang (b. 1941) like *Charly Traktor* (1973) or *Der Sohn eines Landarbeiters* (*The son of a farm labourer*, 1974) takes forms closer to the poetic lumpen subjectivity of Ludwig Fels than to a well-meaning 'literature of the world of work'.

New perspectives on language are, moreover, central to the major innovatory contribution modern Austrian writing has made to German literature as a whole: the experimental work of the 'Wiener Gruppe' and the 'Forum Stadtpark' in Graz. These authors seek to shatter the illusion of reality created by the language we use to represent it. The 'Wiener Gruppe' re-excavated surrealism and Dada, reviled by National Socialism and subsequently kept at bay by post-war Austrian conservatism. They turned readings into performances and took performances onto the streets, anticipating developments conventionally associated with the late 1960s. Wiener's *die verbesserung von mitteleuropa* (*the improvement of central europe*) or the *Lexikon-Roman* (1970) of Andreas Okopenko (b. 1930), challenge narrative linearity and the causal determinisms that underlie it. Against the then current trend in West German literature towards social realism, Konrad Bayer (b. 1932) with *der kopf des vitus bering* (*the head of vitus bering*, 1965), a hallucinatory montage of documents related to the seventeenth-century explorer, erodes comfortable assumptions about scientific rationalism and its rejection of the occult.

'Forum Stadtpark' grew up round the journal *Manuskripte*, edited and published in Graz by Alfred Kolleritsch (b. 1931) from 1960; Peter Handke has been its most prominent member. The critique of narrative conventions by the 'Wiener Gruppe' cleared the ground for the 'Stadtpark' authors to return to forms which made their work generally more accessible and successful, while resisting the politicised social realism then current in West Germany. Besides Wittgenstein, whose ideas were ever-present in intellectual circles in 1960s Austria, influences were the French *nouveau roman*, Russian formalism, or the Austrian psychiatrist Leo Navratil's *Schizophrenie und Sprache* (*Schizophrenia and language*, 1966). In *Geometrischer Heimatroman* (*Geometric local novel*, 1969) Gerd Jonke (b. 1946) describes the village in terms of sterile convention and dehumanised spatial relationships. In the novels of Barbara Frischmuth (b. 1941), such as *Die Klosterschule* (*The convent school*, 1968), with its montages of the rules and the realities of Catholic boarding school life, the shaping force and means of implementation of this oppression is language itself. Gerhard Roth (b. 1932), in *die autobiographie des albert einstein* (1972), echoes Konrad Bayer's critique of the hubris of scientific rationality, deconstructing positivistic logic in favour of the surreal imagination; his novel *Landläufiger Tod* (*A typical death*, 1984) is a bricolage of fragmentary discourses.

In the 1980s, Austrian women's writing exhumed its buried tradition by re-reading Bachmann, Aichinger and Haushofer. The 'Vater-Literatur' of the late 1970s was followed by (often bitterly) critical re-examinations of the mother-daughter relationship, in *Die Züchtigung* (*The chastisement*, 1985) by Waltraud Anna Mitgutsch (b. 1948) and Jelinek's *Die Klavierspielerin* (*The woman pianist*, 1983). Jelinek's scurrilous, eclectic poetry, her plays, which lurch between the impenetrably erudite and the language and motifs of popular pornography, and her prose – from the pop art *wir sind lockvögel, baby!* (*we're decoys, baby!* 1970) through *Die Ausgesperrten* (*The locked out*, 1980), which roots terrorist violence in the alienations of family life in the prosperous, stuffy 1950s, to the controversial psycho-sexual explorations of *Lust* (*Desire,* 1989) – exemplify Austrian writing's experimental orientation.

In post-war Switzerland, 'spiritual national defence', the necessary response to the Nazi threat, developed seamlessly into anti-communism. To criticise this consensus by questioning economic links with Nazi Germany or the treatment of refugees was to threaten Swiss 'liberty'. Conservative affirmation, for example, the four-volume novel *Alles in Allem* (*All in all,* 1952–5) by Kurt Guggenheim (1896–1983), or *Der Schweizerspiegel* (*The mirror of the Swiss,* 1938; revised 1955) by Meinrad Inglin (1893–1971), held sway. Though not restricted to Frisch and Dürrenmatt, critical voices were isolated: the poetry of Alexander Xaver Gwerder (1923–52); Hans Albrecht Moser's (1882–1978) dystopian novel *Vineta* (1955); the *Notizen* (1944–81) of Ludwig Hohl (1904–80).

However, from the 1960s on, there emerged an ever-wider variety of literary responses to the contradiction between, on the one hand, the images of upstanding Alpine yeomanry and of stability, solidity and neutrality in the national mythology, and, on the other, the reality of a dynamic industrial and service economy, multinationally interdependent and environmentally unstable.

The universal application of the plays of Frisch and Dürrenmatt should not obscure the function of Andorra or Güllen as comments on 'spiritual national defence' and its mythologisations of history (for example, in the plays of Cäsar von Arx). Subsequent Swiss drama has ranged widely: historical, documentary forms in the 1970s like Hans-Jörg Schneider (b. 1938): *Der Erfinder* (*The inventor,* 1973); Thomas Hürlimann (b. 1951): *Großvater und Halbbruder* (*Grandfather and half-brother,* 1981); Schneider's dialect drama of atavistic terror *Sennentunschi* (1972); the nightmare comedies of Urs Widmer (b. 1938), *Nepal* (1977) or *Stan und Ollie in Deutschland* (1979), or the minimalist plays of Jörg Laederach (b. 1945), like *Körper Brennen* (*Body burn,* 1986). But no dramatist has filled the gap left by the relative failure of the later plays of Frisch (*Triptychon,* 1979; *Jonas und sein Veteran,* 1989) and Dürrenmatt (*Achterloo,* 1983).

Stiller's indictment of complacent inertia influenced much subsequent German-Swiss fiction, notably *Der Stumme* (*The mute,* 1959) by Otto F. Walter (1927–94), *Die Hinterlassenschaft* (*The inheritance,* 1965) by Walter Matthias Diggelmann (1927–79), *Albissers Grund* (*Albisser's reason,* 1974) by Adolf Muschg (b. 1934) and *Die Rückfahrt* (*The return journey,* 1977) by E. Y. Meyer (b. 1946). Similarly, Dürrenmatt's black-comic pessimism and his obsessive return to subterranean labyrinths in the themes and structure of his prose, from *Die Stadt* (*The city,* 1952) to *Minotaurus* (1983), as a counter-model to the Swiss idyll, influenced *Abwässer* (*Drainwater,* 1963) by Hugo Loetscher (b. 1929) and *Die künstliche Mutter* (*The artificial mother*, 1982) by Hermann Bürger (1942–89). The scale of this inheritance in prose has overshadowed the achievement of modern German-Swiss poets like Erika Burkart (b. 1921), who from *Der dunkle Vogel* (*The dark bird*, 1953) to *Schweigeminute* (*One minute's silence*, 1988) seeks to heal the 'Schöpfungsriß' ('the tear across creation') between humanity and nature.

Der Stumme typifies the second generation of post-war German-Swiss literature; the existential 'problem of Switzerland' is replaced by focus on the socio-economic problems of a specific area or a social group. Peter Bichsel (b. 1935) endorses the Swiss identity for his work that Walter underplays; but his use of popular idiom, critically reflected, as a weapon against alienation and manipulation, has many affinities to Walter. The success of *Kindergeschichten* (*Children's stories*, 1969) revived the creative use of Helveticisms. *Rosa Loui* (1967) by Kurt Marti (b. 1921) meanwhile began a trend for critical poetry in dialect which mined the oppositional potential in the lack of written norms for 'Schweizerdeutsch'.

West German political literature is paralleled in *Die Hinterlassenschaft*, which investigates official Swiss attitudes during the Nazi period and their anti-communist continuities, in the critique of consumerism in Loetscher's *Noah. Roman einer Konjunktur* (*Noah – novel of a boom*, 1967), in the 'Arbeitswelt' texts of Silvio Blatter (b. 1946), like *Genormte Tage, verschüttete Zeit* (*Standardised days, squandered time*, 1976), and in the Wallraff-like *Reportagen aus der Schweiz* (*Reportages from Switzerland*, 1974) of Nikolaus Meienberg (b. 1940). Walter's *Die Verwilderung* (*Reverted to the wild*, 1977) explores the rise and fall of a rural commune in a multi-voiced collage of fictional narratives, documentary and pseudo-documentary material. Franz Böni (b. 1952) portrays Switzerland from below, through the fates of dropouts, immigrants and the underprivileged: *Der Knochensammler* (*The rag-and-bone merchant*, 1981); *Die Wanderarbeiter* (*The migrant workers*, 1981).

Paul Nizon (b. 1929) is a staunch opponent of this socially critical literature. Together with extreme subjectivity, linguistic sensitivity and recourse to metaphyical mysticism in novels from *Canto* (1963) to *Im Bauch des Wals* (*In the stomach of the whale*, 1989), this gives him a role in contemporary German-Swiss literature comparable in some ways to that of Handke or Strauß.

Within German-Swiss women's writing, the work of Gertrud Leutenegger (b. 1948) is particularly striking: *Vorabend* (*The evening before*, 1975) subverts patriarchally determined descriptive realism and causality through exuberant non-linearity. *Kontinent* (1985), an associative interweaving of narrative strands, confronting the rural and the industrial, Switzerland and the wider world, conservation and progress, also exemplifies the heightened environmental consciousness of contemporary Swiss writing, a response to the threats posed by advanced industrialisation in a small crowded country. Her essay 'Das verlorene Moment' ('The lost moment', 1979) argues that the replacement of 'spiritual national defence' by the scepticism of Frisch, Walter or Diggelmann, while necessary, has severed a vital emotional link to the past which reinstating myth and the irrational (as in her *Ninive*, 1977, and *Meduse*, 1988) will restore.

Imaginative exuberance also characterises the cornucopian novels of Gerold Späth (b. 1939), even the vision of contemporary Switzerland as a repressive, life-denying society in *Commedia* (1980). Urs Widmer rejects the strait-jacket of realism in favour of black comic inventiveness and celebration of the imagination against a grey reality in *Die Forschungsreise* (*The research expedition*, 1974) and *Die gestohlene Schöpfung* (*The stolen creation*, 1984). Jörg Laederach's *Flugelmeyers Wahn* (*Flugelmeyer's madness*, 1986) reflects contemporary experience in breathlessly energetic, fragmentary forms.

Just as 'constriction' provokes 'flight' in Swiss culture (Paul Nizon), solid well-being generates madness and morbidity as psychosomatic symptoms of social deformation: a theme in Muschg's *Albissers Grund*, in the tortuously macabre narratives of Burger, like *Schilten* (1976), and in *Mars* (1977) by Fritz Zorn (pseudonym for Fritz Angst, 1944–76), which links its narrator's fatal cancer to the crippling effects of his Swiss bourgeois upbringing.

In the novel *Blösch* (1983) by Beat Sterchi (b. 1949) the Italian migrant labourer Ambrosio, dismissed from the farm when his employer mechanises, works in a slaughterhouse, where years later he faces Blösch, his favourite cow, as, ruined by the milking machine, she awaits her death with innate dignity. Despite the anthropomorphic pathos, this is a moving metaphor of Swiss society's estranged relationship to the nature that is part of its Alpine mythology.

Unification and Germany's revived geopolitical as well as economic hegemony in Europe are already, as we saw at the outset of this chapter, leading to re-readings of German literature before 1990. Their effect on the future of German literature, whether seen as a whole or as a plurality of literatures in German, is uncertain. The GDR, as a closed historical epoch, is beginning to engender literary retrospectives; the Federal Republic and the culture it nurtured in the decades before 1990 still await their *War and Peace*. In the rapid social and political transformations of the twentieth century, writers' formative experience often lies one or more historical epochs earlier than the one in which it finds expression in their writing. We have seen that 'post-war' German writers include some who grew up in Wilhelmine Germany and many whose formative years were spent in the

Weimar Republic or in Nazi Germany. Only in the 1970s did writers appear in any numbers who could be said to be children of the post-war world itself. The moral and political values and the aesthetic possibilities manifested in the culture of the 1970s and 1980s to those growing up in these decades will bear their fruit well into the next century.

Select bibliography

This bibliography is divided into nine sections, each corresponding to one of the chapters of the book and compiled by the author of that chapter. It aims to provide a starting point for the advanced undergraduate and the intelligent layperson rather than a complete listing for the specialist, and has no ambition to provide a substitute for the many specialised bibliographies in existence. It is intended as an acknowledgment of those scholarly works the author has found useful in writing the relevant chapter, as well as indicating the way in which the author thinks the period may most usefully be approached.

For reasons of space, primary material has only been listed for the period before 1450, when knowing what edition to use is a vital first step. In addition, each section of the bibliography has been arranged according to the needs of the relevant literary period. Individual works are highlighted in the Old High German period and authors in the High Middle Ages, for instance, genres come to prominence in the early modern period, while there is more focus on literary movements in the nineteenth century and so on. We have nonetheless tried to make the arrangement within each section as clear as possible.

Abbreviations

ABäG   *Amsterdamer Beiträge zur älteren Germanistik*
GLL   *German Life and Letters*
JEGPh   *Journal of English and German Philology*
PBB   *Beiträge zur Geschichte der deutschen Sprache und Literatur*
    The suffix H indicates those numbers of the journal published in Halle (GDR) between 1955 and 1980.
    The suffix T indicates those numbers of the journal published in Tübingen (FRG) between 1955 and 1980.
PMLA   *Proceedings of the Modern Languages Association*
SPIGS   Scottish Publications in Germanic Studies

1 The Carolingian period and the early Middle Ages (750–1100)

Primary literature

German anthologies

Braune, Wilhelm, *Althochdeutsches Lesebuch*, ed. by Ernst Ebbinghaus, 16th edn, Tübingen: Niemeyer, 1979.

Diemer, Joseph, *Deutsche Gedichte des XI. und XII. Jahrhunderts*, Vienna: Braumüller, 1849.

  Genesis und Exodus nach der Millstätter Handschrift, 1862; repr. Wiesbaden: Sändig, 1971.

Heyne, Moritz, *Kleinere altniederdeutsche Denkmäler*, Paderborn: Schöningh, 2nd edn, 1877; repr. Amsterdam: Rodopi, 1970.

Köbler, G., *Sammlung kleinerer althochdeutschen Sprachdenkmäler*, Gießen: Arbeiten zur Rechts- und Sprachwissenschaft, 1986.

Maurer, Friedrich, *Die religiösen Dichtungen des 11. und 12. Jahrhunderts*, Tübingen: Niemeyer, 1964–70.

Mettke, Heinz, *Altdeutsche Texte*, Leipzig: Bibl. Institut, 1970.

  Älteste deutsche Dichtung und Prosa, Leipzig: Reclam, 1976.

Miller, Carol L., 'The Old High German and Old Saxon charms', Unpublished Ph.D. thesis, Washington University, St Louis, 1963.

Müllenhoff, Karl, and Scherer, Wilhelm, *Deutsche Poesie und Prosa aus dem VIII-XII Jahrhundert*, 3rd edn by Elias v. Steinmayer, Berlin: Weidmann, 1892, repr. 1964.

Papp, Edgar, *Codex Vindobonensis 2721*, Göppingen: Kümmerle, 1980.

Schlosser, Horst Dieter, *Althochdeutsche Literatur*, 2nd edn, Frankfurt a. M.: Fischer, 1989.

Steinmeyer, Elias von, *Die kleineren althochdeutschen Sprachdenkmäler*, 1916; repr. as 2nd edn, Berlin and Zurich: Weidmann, 1963.

Steinmeyer, Elias von, and Sievers, Eduard, *Die althochdeutschen Glossen*, Berlin: Weidmann, 1879–1922.

Waag, Albert, *Kleinere deutsche Gedichte des 11. und 12. Jahrhunderts*, new edn by Werner Schröder, Tübingen: Niemeyer, 1972.

Wilhelm, Friedrich, *Denkmäler deutscher Prosa des 11. und 12. Jahrhunderts*, Munich: Hueber, 1916; repr. 1960.

Wipf, Karl A., *Althochdeutsche poetische Texte*, Stuttgart: Reclam, 1992.

German works

Abrogans, Der deutsche, ed. by G. Baesecke, Tübingen: Niemeyer, 1931.

Annolied, Das, ed. and trans. by Eberhard Nellmann, Stuttgart: Reclam, 1975.

Exodus, Die altdeutsche, ed. by Edgar Papp, Munich: Fink, 1968.

Genesis, Die altdeutsche, ed. by Viktor Dollmayr, Halle: Niemeyer, 1932.

Genesis, Die frühmittelhochdeutsche Wiener, ed. by Kathryn Smits, Berlin: Schmidt, 1972.

Glossen zum Alten Testament, Althochdeutsche, ed. by Herbert Thoma, Tübingen: Niemeyer, 1975.

Heliand, Der. Ausgewählte Abbildungen zur Überlieferung, ed. by Burkhard Taeger, Göppingen: Kümmerle, 1985.

Heliand und Genesis, ed. by Otto Behaghel, 9th edn by Burkhard Taeger, Tübingen: Niemeyer, 1984; trans. (German) Felix Genzmer, *Heliand* (Stuttgart: Reclam, n.d.); trans. (English) Mariana Scott, (Chapel Hill: University of North Carolina Press, 1966).

Isidor, Der althochdeutsche, ed. by Hans Eggers, Tübingen: Niemeyer, 1964.

'Die "Klosterneuburger Bußpredigten": Untersuchung und Edition', by N. F.

Palmer, in *Überlieferungsgeschichtliche Editionen und Studien zur Deutschen Literatur des Mittelalters*, ed. by K. Kunze et al., Tübingen: Niemeyer, 1989, pp. 210–44.

Monsee fragments, The, ed. by George A. Hench, Strasbourg: Trübner, 1890.

Notkers des Deutschen Werke, ed. by E. H. Sehrt and Taylor Starck, Halle/Saale: Niemeyer, 1933–5, edn cont. by James C. King and Petrus Tax, Tübingen: Niemeyer, 1972f.

Otfrid von Weißenburg, *Evangelienharmonie*, facs. of Vienna MS. ed. by Hans Butzmann, Graz: Akademische Druck- und Verlagsanstalt, 1972.

Otfrids Evangelienbuch, ed. by Paul Piper, 2nd edn, Freiburg/Tübingen, 1882–7, repr. Hildesheim: Olms, 1982; ed. by Oskar Erdmann, Halle: Waisenhaus, 1882; *Altdeutsche Textbibliothek* edition, 7th edn by Ludwig Wolff, Tübingen: Niemeyer, 1973. Partial German trans. by Gisela Vollmann-Profe, Stuttgart: Reclam, 1987.

(*Paris conversation-book*): Wolfgang Haubrichs and Max Pfister, *In Francia fui*, Stuttgart: Steiner, 1989.

Speculum Ecclesiae, ed. by Gerd Mellbourn, Lund and Copenhagen: Gleerup and Munksgaard, 1944.

(*Strasbourg oaths*): Florus van der Rhee, 'Die Strassburger Eide, altfranzösisch und althochdeutsch', *ABäG* 20 (1983), 7–25.

Tatian, ed. by Eduard Sievers, Paderborn: Schöningh, 1892; repr. 1966.

Williram, *The Expositio in Cantica Canticorum*, ed. by Erminnie H. Bartlemez, Philadelphia: American Philosophical Society, 1967.

Latin anthologies

Brittain, Frederick (ed.), *The Penguin book of Latin verse*, Harmondsworth: Penguin, 1960.

Dreves, G. M., and Blume, C., *Analecta Hymnica Medii Aevi*, Leipzig: Altenburg, 1886–1922.

Freiherr vom Stein Gedächtnis-Ausgabe, ed. by Reinhold Rau, (Quellen zur karolingischen Reichsgeschichte) Darmstadt: Wiss. Buchgesellschaft, 1968–.

Godman, Peter, *Poetry of the Carolingian renaissance*, London: Duckworth, 1985.

Kaiser, Andreas, *Lateinische Dichtungen zur deutschen Geschichte des Mittelalters*, Munich and Berlin: Oldenbourg, 1927.

Langosch, Karl, *Lyrische Anthologie des lateinischen Mittelalters*, Darmstadt: Wiss. Buchgesellschaft, 1968.

Loyn, Henry R., and Percival, John, *The reign of Charlemagne: documents on Carolingian government and administration*, London: St Martin's Press, 1975.

MGH = *Monumenta Germaniae Historica*, Hanover etc., 1826f.: *Poetae Latini aevi Carolini*, (four volumes plus supplements, ed. by Ernst Dümmler, Ludwig Traube, Paul von Winterfeld and Karl Strecker, 1881–1923; *Poetae Latini* v is on *Die Ottonenzeit*, ed. by Karl Strecker and Norbert Fickermann, 1937–9, and vi/i contains *Waltharius*, ed. by Karl Strecker, 1951. Laws are in the section *Leges*, annals in the *Scriptores*. The sub-series *Scriptores rerum Germanicum in usum scholarum separatim editi* contains Adam of Bremen, ed. by Bernhard Schmeidler, 1917; the *Hildesheim Annals*, ed. by Georg Waitz, 1878; the *Cambridge songs*, ed. by Karl Strecker,1926, 2nd edn 1955; the *Ecbasis cuiusdam captivi*, ed. by K. Strecker, 1935; Einhard, ed. by Oswald Holder-Egger, 1911; Liutprand of Cremona, ed. by Josef Becker, 1915; Widukind of Corvey, ed. by Paul Hirsch and Hans-Eberhard Lohmann, 1935 and Wipo, ed. by Harry Bresslau, 1915. The separate editions of the *Epistolae* include Froumund, ed. by Karl Strecker, 1925.

PL = Migne, J. P., *Patrologia Latina*, Paris, 1844–64: vols. 100–1: Alcuin; 107–12: Hrabanus; 119: Lupus; 142: Bruno of Würzburg; 89 and 146: Otloh; 143: Hermann the Lame; 167–70: Rupert of Deutz; 146: Adam of Bremen; 171: Embricho.

Raby, F. J. E., *The Oxford book of medieval Latin verse*, Oxford: Clarendon, 1959.

Waddell, Helen, *Medieval Latin lyrics*, [1929] Harmondsworth: Penguin, 1952.
More Latin lyrics, London: Gollancz, 1980.

Latin works

(Amarcius): *Sexti Amarcii Galli Piosistrati sermonum libri 4*, ed. by Karl Manitius, Weimar: Monumenta Germaniae Historica, 1969.

The annals of Fulda, trans. by Timothy Reuter, Manchester and New York: Manchester University Press, 1992.

The annals of St-Bertin, trans. by Janet L. Nelson, Manchester and New York: Manchester University Press, 1991.

Ecbasis cuiusdam captivi, ed. and trans. by Edwin H. Zeydel, Chapel Hill: University of North Carolina Press, 1963.

Einhard, *Life of Charlemagne*, ed. by H. W. Garrod and R. B. Mowat, Oxford: Clarendon, 1915; trans. (with *De Carolo Magno*) by Lewis Thorpe, *Two lives of Charlemagne*, Harmondsworth: Penguin, 1969.

Eupolemius, *Das Bibelgedicht*, ed. by Karl Manitius, Weimar: Monumenta Germaniae Historica, 1973.

Hrotsvitha of Gandersheim: Karl Strecker, *Hrotsvithae Opera*, 2nd edn, Leipzig: Teubner, 1930. Hrotsvitha, *Dulcitius* and *Abraham*, German trans. by Karl Langosch, Stuttgart: Reclam, 1975.

The law of the Salian Franks, trans. by Katherine F. Drew, Phildalephia: University of Pennsylvania Press, 1991.

Notker Balbulus: Wolfram von den Steinen, *Notker der Dichter und seine geistige Welt*, Berne: Francke, 1948.

(Ratpert): Peter Osterwalder, *Das althochdeutsche Galluslied Ratperts und seine lateinischen Übersetzungen durch Ekkehart IV*, Berlin and New York: de Gruyter, 1982.

Ruodlieb, ed. by Gordon B. Ford, Leiden: Brill, 1966; ed. and German trans. by Fritz Peter Knapp, Stuttgart: Reclam, 1977; English trans. by Edwin H. Zeydel, Chapel Hill: University of North Carolina Press, 1959.

(*Waltharius*): ed. with analogues by Marion Dexter Learned, *The saga of Walther of Aquitaine*, 1892, repr. Westport, CT: Greenwood, 1970; German trans. by Karl Langosch, *Waltharius. Ruodlieb. Märchenepen*, Basle and Stuttgart: Schwabe, 1956; English trans. by Dennis M. Kratz, *Waltharius and Ruodlieb*, New York, Garland, 1984, and Brian Murdoch, *Walthari*, Glasgow: SPIGS, 1989.

Secondary literature

Background and general works

Berschin, Walter, *Eremus und Insula. St Gallen und die Reichenau im Mittelalter*, Wiesbaden: Reichert, 1987.

Beyerle, K. (ed.), *Die Kultur der Abtei Reichenau*, Munich: Münchener Drucke, 1924f.

Bischoff, Bernhard, *Mittelalterliche Studien*, Stuttgart: Hiersemann, 1966–81.
   Paläographie des römischen Altertums und des abendländischen Mittelalters, 2nd edn, Berlin: Schmidt, 1987; trans. Dáibhí Ó Cróinín and David Ganz, *Latin Palaeography*, Cambridge: Cambridge University Press, 1990.

Bolgar, R. R., *The classical heritage and its beneficiaries*, Cambridge: Cambridge University Press, 1963.

Bolgar, R. R. (ed.), *Classical influences on European culture* AD 500–1500, Cambridge: Cambridge University Press, 1971.

Bullough, Donald A., *Carolingian renewal: sources and heritage*, Manchester: Manchester University Press, 1991.

Clark, J. M., *The Abbey of St Gall*, Cambridge: Cambridge University Press, 1926.

Copeland, Rita, *Rhetoric, hermeneutics and translation in the Middle Ages*, Cambridge: Cambridge University Press, 1991.

Curtius, Ernst Robert, *Europäische Literatur und lateinisches Mittelalter*, Berne: Francke, 1948; 11th edn, Tübingen and Basle, 1993; trans. by Willard R. Trask as *European literature and the Latin Middle Ages*, London: Routledge and Kegan Paul, 1953.

Dronke, Peter, *The medieval lyric*, London: Hutchinson, 1968.

Dutton, Paul Edward, *Carolingian civilisation. A reader*, Peterborough, Ontario: Broadview, 1993.

Ernst, Ulrich, and Neuser, Peter-Erich (eds.), *Die Genese der europäischen Endreimdichtung (Wege der Forschung)*, Darmstadt: Wiss. Buchgesellschaft, 1978.

Geith, Karl-Ernst, *Carolus Magnus*, Berne and Munich: Francke, 1977.

Godman, Peter, *Poets and emperors. Frankish politics and Carolingian poetry*, Oxford: Clarendon, 1987.

Green, D. H., *The Carolingian lord*, Cambridge: Cambridge University Press, 1965.

Hardison, O. B., *Christian rite and Christian drama in the Middle Ages*, Baltimore: Johns Hopkins Press, 1965.

Haubrichs, Wolfgang, *Die Kultur der Abtei Prüm zur Karolingerzeit*, Bonn: Röhrscheid, 1979.

Henkel, Nikolaus, and Palmer, Nigel F. (eds.), *Latein und Volkssprache im deutschen Mittelalter*, Tübingen: Niemeyer, 1992.

Henzen, Walter, *Schriftsprache und Mundarten*, 2nd edn, Berne: Francke, 1954.

Hildebrandt, M. M., *The external school in Carolingian society*, Leiden: Brill, 1992.

Karl der Große. Lebenswerk und Nachleben, ed. by Wolfgang Braunfels,

Düsseldorf: Schwann, 1965; esp. 11. *Das geistige Leben*, ed. by Bernard Bischoff.

Kettler, Winfried, *Das Jüngste Gericht*, Berlin: de Gruyter, 1977.

Kieckhefer, Richard, *Magic in the Middle Ages*, Cambridge: Cambridge University Press, 1989.

King, K. C., 'The earliest German monasteries', in *Selected essays on medieval German literature*, ed. by John L. Flood and A. T. Hatto, London: Institute of Germanic Studies, 1975, pp. 98–124.

Knapp, Peter Fritz, *Die Literatur des Früh- und Hochmittelalters*, Geschichte der Literatur in Österreich, ed. by Herbert Zeman, vol. 1, Graz: Akademische Druck- und Verlagsanstalt, 1994.

Kolb, Herbert, 'Himmlisches und irdisches Gericht in karolingischer Theologie', *Frühmittelalterliche Studien* 5 (1971), 284–308.

Laistner, M. L. W., *Thought and letters in Western Europe, AD 500–900*, 2nd edn, London: Methuen, 1957.

Lammers, Walther, *Geschichtsdenken und Geschichtsbild im Mittelalter (Wege der Forschung)*, Darmstadt: Wiss. Buchgesellschaft, 1965.

McKitterick, Rosamond, *The Frankish church and the Carolingian reforms*, Cambridge: Cambridge University Press, 1977.

    The Frankish kingdoms under the Carolingians 751–987, London and New York: Longman, 1983.

    The Carolingians and the written word, Cambridge: Cambridge University Press, 1989.

McKitterick, Rosamond (ed.), *Carolinigian culture; emulation and innovation*, Cambridge: Cambridge University Press, 1993.

Milde, Wolfgang, *Der Bibliothekskatalog des Klosters Murbach aus dem 9. Jahrhundert*, Heidelberg: Winter, 1968.

Neuendorff, Dagmar, *Studie zur Entwicklung der Herrscherdarstellung in der deutschsprachigen Literatur des 9.–12. Jahrhunderts*, Stockholm: Almqvist and Wiksell, 1982.

Ohly, Friedrich, *Vom geistigen Sinn des Wortes im Mittelalter*, Darmstadt: Wiss. Buchgesellschaft, 1966.

Prinz, Friedrich, 'Monastische Zentren im Frankenreich', *Studi Medievali* Ser. 3/19 (1978), 571–90.

Renoir, Alain, *A Key to old poems*, University Park and London: Pennsylvania State University Press, 1988.

Schwarz, Werner, *Schriften zur Bibelübersetzung und mittelalterlicher Übersetzungstheorie*, London: Institute of Germanic Studies, 1985.

Singer, Samuel, 'Karolingische Renaissance', *Germ. Rom. Monatsschrift* 13 (1925), 187–201 and 243–58.

Smalley, Beryl, *The study of the Bible in the Middle Ages*, 3rd edn, Oxford: Blackwell, 1983.

Sullivan, Richard E., 'The Carolingian age: reflections on its place in the history of the Middle Ages', *Speculum* 64 (1989), 267–306.

Wallace-Hadrill, J. M., *The long-haired kings*, London: Methuen, 1962.

    The barbarian West 400–1000, 3rd edn, London: Hutchinson, 1967.

German literature

General works and collections of essays

Althochdeutsch (*Festschrift Rudolf Schützeichel*), ed. by Rolf Bergmann, Heinrich Tiefenbach and Lothar Voetz, Heidelberg: Winter, 1982.

Baesecke, Georg, *Kleinere Schriften zu althochdeutscher Sprache und Literatur*, ed. by Werner Schröder, Berne and Munich: Francke, 1966.

Bertau, Karl, *Deutsche Literatur im europäischen Mittelalter* Munich: Beck, 1972f.

De Boor, Helmut, *Die deutsche Literatur von Karl dem Großen bis zum Beginn der höfischen Dichtung 770–1170*, 7th edn, Munich: Beck, 1966.

Bostock, J. Knight, *A handbook on Old High German literature*, 2nd edn by K. C. King and D. R. McLintock, Oxford: Clarendon, 1976.

Buttell, Marie Pierre, *Religious ideology and Christian humanism in German Cluniac verse*, Washington DC: Catholic University of America Press, 1948.

Ehrismann, Gustav, *Geschichte der deutschen Literatur bis zum Ausgang des Mittelalters* I. *Die althochdeutsche Literatur*, Munich: Beck, 1932, repr. as 2nd edn, 1954.

Eis, Gerhard, *Altdeutsche Handschriften*, Munich: Beck, 1949.

Vom Werden altdeutscher Dichtung, Berlin: Schmidt, 1962.

Fischer, Hanns, *Schrifttafeln zum althochdeutschen Lesebuch*, Tübingen: Niemeyer, 1966.

'Deutsche Literatur und lateinisches Mittelalter', in *Werk-Typ-Situation*, ed. by Ingeborg Glier et al., Stuttgart: Metzler, 1969, pp. 1–19.

Flood, John L., and Yeandle, David N. (eds.), *mit regulu bithuungan. Neue Arbeiten zur althochdeutschen Poesie und Sprache*, Göppingen: Kümmerle, 1989.

Gentry, Francis G., *Bibliographie zur frühmittelhochdeutschen geistlichen Dichtung*, Berlin: Schmidt, 1992.

Groseclose, J. Sidney, and Murdoch, Brian O., *Die althochdeutschen poetischen Denkmäler*, Stuttgart: Metzler, 1976.

Harms, Wolfgang, *Der Kampf mit dem Freund oder Verwandten*, Munich: Fink, 1963.

Haubrichs, Wolfgang: see Heinzle, Joachim

Hauck, Karl (ed.), *Zur germanisch-deutschen Heldensage* (*Wege der Forschung*), Darmstadt: Wiss. Buchgesellschaft, 1965.

Heinzle, Joachim (ed.), *Geschichte der deutschen Literatur von den Anfängen bis zum Beginn der Neuzeit*: I/i: Wolfgang Haubrichs, *Die Anfänge* (Frankfurt a. M.: Athenäum, 1988) and I/ii: Gisela Vollmann-Profe, *Von den Anfängen bis zum hohen Mittelalter*, Frankfurt a. M.: Athenäum, 1986.

Hoffmann, Werner, *Altdeutsche Metrik*, Stuttgart: Metzler, 1967.

Hoffmann von Fallersleben, A., *Geschichte des deutschen Kirchenliedes bis auf Luthers Zeit*, 1854, 3rd edn 1861; repr. Hildesheim: Olms, 1965.

Johnson, L. P., Steinhoff, H.-H., and Wisbey, R.A. (eds.), *Studien zur frühmittelhochdeutschen Literatur*, Berlin: Schmidt, 1971.

Kartschoke, Dieter, *Altdeutsche Bibeldichtung*, Stuttgart: Metzler, 1975.

Bibeldichtung, Munich: Fink, 1975.

Masser, Achim, *Bibel- und Legendenepik des deutschen Mittelalters*, Berlin: Erich Schmidt, 1976.

Maurer, Friedrich, 'Salische Geistlichendichtung', *Der Deutschunterricht* 5 (1953), ii, 5–10.

Meissburger, Gerhard, *Grundlagen zum Verständnis der deutschen Mönchsdichtung im 11. und 12. Jahrhundert*, Munich: Fink, 1970.

Murdoch, Brian O., *Old High German literature*, Boston: Twayne, 1983.

Peters, Elisabeth, *Quellen und Charakter der Paradiesesvorstellungen in der deutschen Dichtung des 9. bis 12. Jahrhunderts*, Breslau: Marcus, 1915.

Rupp, Heinz, 'Über das Verhältnis von deutscher und lateinischer Literatur im 9.-12. Jahrhundert', *Germ. Rom. Monatsschrift* 39 (1958), 19–34.

Forschung zur althochdeutschen Literatur 1945–1962, Stuttgart: Metzler, 1965.

Deutsche religiöse Dichtungen des 11. und 12. Jahrhunderts, 2nd edn, Berne and Munich: Francke, 1971.

Schlosser, Horst Dieter, *Die literarischen Anfänge der deutschen Sprache*, Berlin: Schmidt, 1977.

Schreyer-Mühlpfordt, Brigitta, 'Sprachliche Einigungstendenzen im deutschen Schrifttum des Frühmittelalters', *Wissenschaftliche Annalen* 5 (1956), 295–304.

Schröbler, Ingeborg, 'Fulda und die althochdeutsche Literatur', *Literaturwissenschaftliches Jahrbuch der Görres-Gesellschaft* 1 (1960), 1–26.

Schröder, Werner, 'Der Geist von Cluny und die Anfänge des frühmittelhochdeutschen Schrifttums', *PBB* 72 (1950), 343–71.

Schröder, Werner, *Grenzen und Möglichkeiten einer althochdeutschen Literaturgeschichte*, Leipzig: Sächsische Akademie, 1959 = Berichte 105/ii.

Schützeichel, Rudolf, *Codex Pal. Lat. 52*, Göttingen: Vandenhoek and Ruprecht, 1982.

Schwab, Ute, *Einige Beziehungen zwischen altsächsischer und angelsächsischer Dichtung*, Spoleto: CISAM, 1988.

See, Klaus von, *Germanische Verskunst*, Stuttgart: Metzler, 1967.

Soeteman, C., *Deutsche geistliche Dichtung des 11. und 12. Jahrhunderts*, 2nd edn, Stuttgart: Metzler, 1971.

Sonderegger, Stefan, 'Frühe Übersetzungsschichten im Althochdeutschen', *Festschrift für Walter Henzen*, ed. by W. Kohlschmidt and P. Zinsli, Berne: Francke, 1965, pp. 101–14.

'Frühe Erscheinungsformen dichterischer Sprache im Althochdeutschen', *Festschrift für Max Wehrli*, ed. by S. Sonderegger et al., Zurich and Freiburg i. Br.: Atlantis, 1969, pp. 53–81.

Althochdeutsch in St Gallen. Ergebnisse und Probleme der althochdeutschen Sprachüberlieferung in St Gallen vom 8. bis zum 12. Jahrhundert, St Gallen: Ostschweiz, 1970.

Althochdeutsche Sprache und Literatur, Berlin: de Gruyter, 1974.

Sonderegger, Stefan (ed.), *Das Althochdeutsche von St Gallen: Texte und Untersuchungen zur sprachlichen Überlieferung St Gallens vom 8. bis zum 12. Jahrhundert*, Berlin: de Gruyter, 1970.

Sowinski, Bernhard, *Lehrhafte Dichtung des Mittelalters*, Stuttgart: Metzler, 1971.

Stammler, Wolfgang, *Deutsche Literatur des Mittelalters. Verfasserlexikon*, Berlin and Leipzig: de Gruyter, 1933–55; 2nd edn by Kurt Ruh, Berlin: de Gruyter, 1978–.

Uecker, Heiko, *Germanische Heldensage*, Stuttgart: Metzler, 1972.

Vollmann-Profe, Gisela: see Heinzle, Joachim

Glosses and translations

Baesecke, Georg, *Der deutsche Abrogans und die Herkunft des deutschen Schrifttums*, Halle: Niemeyer, 1930.

Die Überlieferung des althochdeutschen Tatian, Halle: Niemeyer, 1948.

Bergmann, Rolf, *Verzeichnis der ahd. und alts. Glossenhandschriften*, Berlin and New York: de Gruyter, 1973.

Betz, Werner, 'Zum St. Galler Paternoster', *PBB/H* 82 (1961 = *Festschrift für Elisabeth Karg-Gasterstädt*), 153–6.

Eggers, Hans, 'Die altdeutschen Beichten', *PBB/H* 77 (1955), 89–123; 80 (1958), 372–403; 81 (1959), 78–122.

Haubrichs, Wolfgang, 'Zum Stand der Isidor-Forschung', *Zeitschrift für deutsche Philologie* 94 (1975), 1–15.

Huisman, Johannes A., 'Die Pariser Gespräche', *Rheinische Vierteljahresblätter* 33 (1969), 272–96.

Masser, Achim, 'Die althochdeutschen Übersetzungen des Vaterunsers', *PBB/T* 85 (1963), 35–45.

Matzel, Klaus, *Untersuchung zur Verfasserschaft, Sprache und Herkunft der althochdeutschen Übersetzungen der Isidor-Sippe*, Bonn: Röhrscheid, 1970.

Mayer, H., *Althochdeutsche Glossen: Nachtrag*, Toronto and Buffalo: University of Toronto Press, 1974.

Must, G., 'Das St. Galler Paternoster', *Akten des V. Congresses des IVG*, Berne and Frankfurt a. M.: Peter Lang, 1976, II, 396–403.

Nordmeyer, George, 'On the Old High German Isidor and its significance for early German prose writings', *PMLA* 73 (1958), 23–35.

Ostberg, Kurt, *The Old High German Isidor*, Göppingen: Kümmerle, 1979.

Penzl, Herbert, 'Stulti sunt Romani', *Wirkendes Wort* 35 (1985), 240–8.

Schwarz, Alexander, 'Glossen als Texte', *PBB/T* 99 (1977), 25–36.

Splett, Jochen, *Abrogans-Studien*, Wiesbaden: Steiner, 1976.

Wieland, Gernot R., 'The glossed manuscript: classbook or library book', *Anglo-Saxon England* 14 (1986), 153–73.

Prayers and charms

Bacon, I., 'Versuch einer Klassifizierung altdeutscher Zaubersprüche und Segen', *Modern Language Notes* 67 (1952), 224–32.

Edwards, Cyril, 'Tohuwabohu: the *Wessobrunner Gebet* and its analogues', *Medium Aevum* 53 (1984), 263–81.

Eis, Gerhard, *Altdeutsche Zaubersprüche*, Berlin: de Gruyter, 1964.

Ganz, Peter F., 'Die Zeilenaufteilung im *Wessobrunner Gebet*', *PBB/T* 95 (1973 = *Festschrift I. Schröbler*), 39–51.

Geier, Manfred, 'Die magische Kraft der Poesie', *Deutsche Vierteljahrsschrift* 56 (1982), 359–85.

Hampp, I., 'Vom Wesen des Zaubers im Zauberspruch', *Der Deutschunterricht* 13/1 (1961), 58–76.

Ködderitzsch, Rolf, 'Der 2. Merseburger Spruch und seine Parallele', *Zeitschrift für celtische Philologie* 33 (1974), 45–57.

Murdoch, Brian, 'But did they work?', *Neuph. Mitteilungen* 89 (1988), 358–69.

'*Drohtin, uuerthe so!*', *Literaturwissenschaftliches Jahrbuch der Görres-Gesellschaft* 32 (1991), 11–37.

Pörnbacher, Hans, 'Der eino almahtico cot', in *Festschrift für Werner Hoffmann*, ed. by W. Fritsch-Rößler et al., Göppingen: Kümmerle, 1991, pp. 18–29.

Schwab, Ute, *Die Sternrune im Wessobrunner Gebet*, Amsterdam: Rodopi, 1973.

Seiffert, L., 'The metrical form and composition of the *Wessobrunner Gebet*', *Medium Aevum* 31 (1962), 1–13.

Voorwinden, Norbert, 'Das *Wessobrunner Gebet*', *Neophilologus* 59 (1975), 390–404.

Heliand and Old Saxon Genesis

Eichhoff, Jürgen, and Rauch, Irmengard (eds.), *Der Heliand* (*Wege der Forschung*), Darmstadt: Wiss. Buchgesellschaft, 1973.

Hagenlocher, Albrecht, *Schicksal im Heliand*, Cologne and Vienna, Böhlau, 1975.

Murphy, G. Ronald, *The Saxon savior*, New York and Oxford: Oxford University Press, 1989.

Rathofer, J., *Der Heliand. Theologischer Sinn als tektonische Form*, Cologne and Graz: Böhlau, 1962.

Schwab, Ute, 'Ansätze zu einer Interpretation des Altsächsischen Genesisdichtung', *Annali dell'Istituto Orientale di Napoli*, FG 17 (1974), 111–86; 18 (1975), 7–88; 19 (1976), 7–52; 20 (1977), 7–79.

Zwei Frauen vor dem Tode, Brussels: Belgian Academy of Sciences, 1989.

Weringha, Juw fon, *Heliand und Diatessaron*, Assen: van Gorcum, 1965.

Zanni, Roland, *Heliand, Genesis und das Altenglische*, Berlin and New York: de Gruyter, 1980.

Otfrid

Archibald, Linda, 'Cur scriptor theotisce dictaverit', Unpublished Ph.D. thesis, Stirling University, 1988.

Belkin, Johanna, and Meier, Jürgen, *Bibliographie zu Otfrid von Weißenburg und zur altsächsischen Bibeldichtung*, Berlin: Schmidt, 1975.

Ernst, Ulrich, 'Die Magiergeschichte in Otfrids *Liber Evangeliorum*', *Annali dell'Istituto Orientale di Napoli*, FG 15 (1972), 81–138.

Der Liber Evangeliorum Otfrids von Weißenburg, Cologne and Vienna: Böhlau, 1975.

Freytag, Wiebke, 'Otfrids Briefvorrede *ad Liutbertum*', *Zeitschrift für deutsches Altertum* 111 (1982), 168–93.

Gasser, Raphaela, '*Propter lamentabilem vocem hominis*', *Freiburger Zeitschrift für Philologie und Theologie* 17 (1970), 3–83.

Greiner, Susanne, *Das Marienbild Otfrids von Weißenburg*, Cologne and Vienna: Böhlau, 1987.

Hartmann, Reinildis, *Allegorisches Wörterbuch zu Otfrieds von Weißenburg Evangeliendichtung*, Munich: Fink, 1971.

Haubrichs, Wolfgang, *Ordo als Form*, Tübingen: Niemeyer, 1969.

Hellgardt, Ernst, *Die exegetischen Quellen von Otfrids Evangelienbuch*, Tübingen: Niemeyer, 1981.

Kleiber, Wolfgang, *Otfrid von Weißenburg*, Berne and Munich: Francke, 1971.

Kleiber, Wolfgang (ed.), *Otfrid von Weißenburg* (*Wege der Forschung*), Darmstadt: Wiss. Buchgesellschaft, 1978.

Krogmann, Willy, 'Otfrid und der Heliand', *Niederdeutsches Jahrbuch* 82 (1959), 39–55.

McKenzie, Donald A., *Otfrid von Weißenburg: narrator or commentator*, Stanford and London: Stanford University Press, 1946. See review by J. K. Bostock, *Medium Aevum* 16 (1947), 53–7.

Michel, Paul, and Schwarz, Alexander, *unz in obanentig. Aus der Werkstatt der karolingischen Exegeten Alcuin, Erkanbert und Otfrid von Weißenburg*, Bonn: Bouvier, 1978.

Patzlaff, Rainer, *Otfrid von Weißenburg und die mittelalterliche versus-Tradition*, Tübingen: Niemeyer, 1975.

Schulz, K., *Studien zu Art und Herkunft des variierenden Stils in Otfrids Evangeliendichtung*, Munich: Fink, 1967.

Shimbo, Masahiro, *Wortindex zu Otfrids Evangelienbuch*, Tübingen: Niemeyer, 1990.

Vollmann-Profe, Gisela, *Kommentar zu Otfrids Evangelienbuch I*, Bonn: Habelt, 1976.

Smaller rhymed poems

Beck, Heinrich, 'Zur literaturgeschichtliche Stellung des ahd. *Ludwigsliedes*', *Zeitschrift für deutsches Altertum* 103 (1974), 37–51.

Berg, Elisabeth, 'Das *Ludwigslied* und die Schlacht bei Saucourt', *Rheinische Vierteljahresblätter* 29 (1964), 175–99.

Bergmann, Rolf, 'Zu der althochdeutschen Inschrift aus Köln', *Rheinische Vierteljahresblätter* 30 (1965), 66–9.

Dittrich, M.-L., '*De Heinrico*', *Zeitschrift für deutsches Altertum* 84 (1952/3), 264–308.

Fouracre, P. 'The context of the Old High German *Ludwigslied*', *Medium Aevum* 54 (1985), 87–103.

Harvey, Ruth, 'The provenance of the Old High German *Ludwigslied*', *Medium Aevum* 14 (1945), 1–20.

Haubrichs, Wolfgang, *Georgslied und Georgslegende im frühen Mittelalter*, Königsstein i. T.: Scriptor, 1979.

Helm, Karl, 'Zur altdeutschen Hausbesegnung', *PBB* 69 (1947), 358–60.

Kemper, Raimund, 'Das *Ludwigslied* im Kontext zeitgenössischer Rechtsvorgänge', *Deutsche Vierteljahrsschrift* 56 (1982), 161–73.

'Das *Ludwigslied* – eine politische Lektion', *Leuvense Bijdragen* 72 (1983), 59–77.

Lefranq, P., *Rithmus teutonicus ou Ludwigslied?*, Paris: Droz, 1945.

Ludwig, Otto, 'Der althochdeutsche und der biblische Psalm 138', *Euphorion* 56 (1962), 402–9.

Menhardt, Hermann, 'Die Überlieferung des althochdeutschen 138. Psalms', *Zeitschrift für deutsches Altertum* 77 (1940), 76–84.

Moser, Hugo, 'Vom Weingartner Reisesegen zu Walthers Ausfahrtsegen', *PBB*/H 82 (1961 = *Festschrift für Elisabeth Karg-Gasterstädt*), 69–89.

Müller, Robert, 'Das *Ludwigslied* – eine Dichtung im Dienste monarchischer Propaganda für den Kampf gegen die Normannen', in *Sprache-Text-Geschichte*, ed. by P. K. Stein et al., Göppingen: Kümmerle, 1980, pp. 441–77.

Murdoch, Brian, 'Saucourt and the *Ludwigslied*', *Revue belge de philologie et d'histoire* 55 (1977), 841–67.

Naumann, H., *Das Ludwigslied und die verwandten lateinischen Gedichte*, Halle: Klinz, 1932.

Pezzo, Rafaella del, 'Cristo e la Samaritana', *Annali dell'Istituto Orientale di Napoli* FG 14 (1971), 105–116.

Schwarz, Werner, 'The *Ludwigslied* – a ninth-century poem', *Modern Language Review* 42 (1947), 467–73.

Stavenhagen, Lee, 'Das *Petruslied*', *Wirkendes Wort* 17 (1967), 21–8.

Strasser, Ingrid, 'Zum St Galler Spruch im Cod. 105, Seite 1', *Zeitschrift für deutsches Altertum* 110 (1981), 243–53.

Uhlirz, Mathilde, 'Der Modus *de Heinrico* und sein geschichtlicher Inhalt', *Deutsche Vierteljahrsschrift* 26 (1952), 153–61.

Urmoneit, Erika, *Der Wortschatz des Ludwigsliedes*, Munich: Fink, 1973.

Ursprung, Otto, 'Das Freisinger Petrus-Lied', *Die Musikforschung* 5 (1952), 17–21.

Wehrli, Max, 'Gattungsgeschichtliche Betrachtungen zum *Ludwigslied*', in *Philologia Deutsch. Festschrift zum 70. Geburtstag von Walther Henzen*, ed. by Werner Kohlschmidt et al., Berne: Francke, 1965, pp. 9–20.

Willems, Franz, 'Psalm 138 und althochdeutscher Stil', *Deutsche Vierteljahrsschrift* 29 (1955), 429–46.

Muspilli

Finger, Heinz, *Untersuchungen zum Muspilli*, Göppingen: Kümmerle, 1977.

Minis, Cola, *Handschrift, Form und Sprache des Muspilli*, Berlin: Schmidt, 1966.

Mohr, Wolfgang, and Walter Haug, *Zweimal Muspilli*, Tübingen: Niemeyer, 1977.

Hildebrandslied

Baesecke, Georg, *Das Hildebrandlied*, Halle: Niemeyer, 1945.

Gutenbrunner, Siegfried, *Von Hildebrand und Hadubrand*, Heidelberg: Winter, 1976.

Hatto, A. T., 'On the Excellence of the *Hildebrandslied*', *Modern Language Review* 68 (1973), 820–38.

Hoffmann, Werner, 'Das *Hildebrandslied* und die indo-germanische Vater-Sohn-Kampf-Dichtung', *PBB*/T 92 (1970), 26–42.

Kolb, Herbert, 'Hildebrands Sohn', in *Studien zur deutschen Literatur des Mittelalters*, ed. by R. Schützeichel and U. Fellmann, Bonn: Bouvier, 1979, pp. 51–75.

Kolk, H. van der, *Das Hildebrandslied. Eine forschungsgeschichtliche Darstellung*, Amsterdam: Scheltema and Holkema, 1967.

Krogmann, Willy, *Das Hildebrandslied in der langobardischen Urfassung hergestellt*, Berlin: Schmidt, 1959.

Lawson, Richard, 'The *Hildebrandslied* originally Gothic?' *Neuph. Mitteilungen*

74 (1973), 333–9.

Lühr, Rosemarie, *Studien zur Sprache des Hildebrandsliedes*, Frankfurt a. M. and Berne: Peter Lang, 1982.

McDonald, William C., 'Too softly a gift of treasure: a re-reading of the Old High German *Hildebrandslied*', *Euphorion* 78 (1984), 1–16.

Meier, H. H., 'Die Schlacht im *Hildebrandslied*', *Zeitschrift für deutsches Altertum* 119 (1990), 127–38.

Norman, Frederick, *Three essays on the Hildebrandslied*, ed. by A. T. Hatto, London: Institute of German Studies 1973.

Renoir, Alain, 'The armor of the *Hildebrandslied*', *Neuph. Mitteilungen* 78 (1977), 389–95.

Schröder, Werner, 'Hildebrands tragische Blindheit und der Schluß des *Hildebrandsliedes*', *Deutsche Vierteljahrsschrift* 37 (1963), 481–97.

Twaddell, W. F., 'The *Hildebrandlied* manuscript in the USA', *JEGPh* 73 (1974), 157–68.

Wagner, Norbert, '*Cheiseringu getan*', *Zeitschrift für deutsches Altertum* 104 (1975), 179–88.

Wisniewski, Roswitha, 'Hadubrands Rache', *ABäG* 9 (1975), 1–12.

Notker, Williram and late prose

Cruel, Rudolf, *Geschichte der deutschen Predigt im Mittelalter* 1879; repr. Darmstadt: Wiss. Buchgesellschaft, 1966.

Dittrich, M.-L., 'Willirams von Ebersberg Bearbeitung der *Cantica Canticorum*', *Zeitschrift für deutsches Altertum* 82 (1948/50), 47–64.

'Die literarische Form von Willirams *Expositio in Cantica Canticorum*', *Zeitschrift für deutsches Altertum* 84 (1952/3), 179–97.

Henkel, Nikolaus, *Studien zum Physiologus im Mittelalter*, Tübingen: Niemeyer, 1976.

Lloyd, Albert J., *The manuscripts and fragments of Notker's psalter*, Giessen: Schmitz, 1958.

Luginbühl, Emil, *Studien zu Notkers Übersetzungskunst*, 1933; repr. Berlin: de Gruyter, 1970.

Morvay, Karin, and Grube, Dagmar, *Bibliographie der deutschen Predigt des Mittelalters*, Munich: Beck, 1974.

Schmid, Hans-Ulrich, *Althochdeutsche und frühmittelhochdeutsche Bearbeitung lateinischer Predigten*, Frankfurt a. M., Berne, New York: Peter Lang, 1986.

Schröbler, Ingeborg, *Notker III von St Gallen als Übersetzer und Kommentator von Boethius*, Tübingen: Niemeyer, 1953.

Schupp, Volker, *Studien zu Williram von Ebersberg*, Berne and Munich: Francke, 1978.

Schwab, Ute, 'Eber, Aper und Porcus', *Annali dell'Istituto Orientale di Napoli* FG 8 (1967), 1–137.

Steinen, W. von den, *Notker der Dichter und seine geistige Welt*, Berne: Francke, 1948.

Early Middle High German poems

Beyschlag, Siegfried, *Die Wiener Genesis. Idee, Stoff und Form*, Vienna and Leipzig: Hölder-Pichler-Tempsky, 1942.

Eßer, Josef, *Die Schöpfungsgeschichte in der altdeutschen Genesis*, Göppingen: Kümmerle, 1987.

Green, Denis H., *The Millstätter Exodus. A crusading epic*, Cambridge: Cambridge University Press, 1966.

Knab, Doris, *Das Annolied. Probleme seiner literarischen Einordnung*, Tübingen: Niemeyer, 1962.

Murdoch, Brian, *The fall of man in the early MHG biblical epic*, Göppingen: Kümmerle, 1972.

'Treasures stored in heaven', *ABäG* 33 (1991), 89–115.

Voorwinden. N. Th. J., *Merigarto*, Leiden: Universitaire Pers, 1973.

Voss, Hella, *Studien zur illustrierten Millstätter Genesis*, Munich, Beck, 1962.

Wells, David A., *The Vorauer Moses and Balaam*, Cambridge: Modern Humanities Research Association, 1970.

Latin literature

Bolton, W. F., *Alcuin and 'Beowulf'. An eighth-century view*, New Brunswick, NJ: Rutgers University Press, 1978.

Borck, Karl-Heinz, 'Der Tanz von Kölbigk', *PBB* 76 (1954), 241–320.

Contreni, John L., 'Carolingian Biblical Studies', in *Carolingian essays*, ed. by Uta-Renate Blumenthal, Washington DC: Catholic University of America Press, 1983, pp. 71–98.

Dronke, Peter, *Medieval Latin and the rise of European love-lyric*, 2nd edn, Oxford: Clarendon Press, 1968.

Dronke, Peter, and Dronke, Ursula, (eds.) *Barbara et antiquissima carmina*, Barcelona: Seminario de lit. medieval, 1977.

Ebenbauer, Alfred, *Carmen Historicum. Untersuchungen zur historischen Dichtung im karolingischen Europa*, Vienna: Braumüller, 1978–.

Fichte, Joerg O. 'Der Einfluß der Kirche auf die mittelalterliche Literaturästhetik', *Studia Neophilologica* 48 (1976), 3–20.

Georgi, Annette, *Das lateinische und deutsche Preisgedicht des Mittelalters*, Berlin: Erich Schmidt, 1969.

Godman, Peter, 'Louis "the Pious" and his poets', *Frühmittelalterliche Studien* 19 (1985), 240–89.

Godman, Peter, and Collins, Roger (eds.), *Charlemagne's heir. New perspectives on the reign of Louis the Pious*, Oxford: Clarendon Press, 1990.

Herding, Otto, 'Zum Problem des karolingischen "Humanismus" mit besonderer Rücksicht auf Walafrid Strabo', *Studium Generale* 7 (1948), 389–97.

Klopsch, Paul, 'Prosa und Vers in der mittellateinischen Literatur', *Mittellateinisches Jahrbuch* 3 (1966), 9–24.

Klopsch, Paul, *Einführung in die mittellateinische Verslehre*, Darmstadt: Wiss. Buchgesellschaft, 1972.

Kottje, Raymund, and Zimmermann, Harald, *Hrabanus Maurus*, Wiesbaden: Steiner, 1982.

Laistner, M. L. W., 'A ninth-century commentary on the Gospel According to Matthew', *Harvard Theological Review* 20 (1927), 129–49.

Langosch, Karl, *Die deutsche Literatur des lateinischen Mittelalters*, Berlin: de Gruyter, 1964.

Profile des lateinischen Mittelalters, Darmstadt: Wiss. Buchgesellschaft, 1967.

Waltharius. Die Dichtung und die Forschung, Darmstadt: Wiss. Buchgesellschaft, 1973.

Lateinisches Mittelalter, 4th edn Darmstadt: Wiss. Buchgesellschaft, 1983.

Langosch, Karl (ed.), *Mittellateinische Dichtung (Wege der Forschung)*, Darmstadt: Wiss. Buchgesellschaft, 1969.

Leclerq, Jean, 'Ecrits monastiques sur la Bible aux IXe-XIIe siècle', *Medieval Studies* 15 (1953), 95–106.

Löwe, Heinz, 'Regino von Prüm und das historische Weltbild der Karolingerzeit', *Rheinische Vierteljahrsblätter* 17 (1952), 151–79.

McClure, Judith, 'The biblical epic and its audience in late antiquity', in *Papers of the Liverpool Latin Seminar III (1981)*, ed. by Francis Cairns (Liverpool: Cairns, 1981), 305–21.

McGee, Timothy J., 'The role of the *Quem Quaeritis* dialogue in the history of western drama', *Renaissance Drama* NS 7 (1976), 177–91.

Manitius, Max, *Geschichte der lateinischen Literatur des Mittelalters*, Munich: Beck, 1911–31; repr. 1964–5.

Ploss, Emil, *Waltharius und Walthersage*, Hildesheim: Olms, 1969.

Raby, Frederic J., *A history of Christian-Latin poetry from the beginnings to the close of the Middle Ages*, 2nd edn, Oxford: Clarendon Press, 1953.

A history of secular Latin poetry in the Middle Ages, 2nd edn, Oxford: Clarendon Press, 1957.

Reudenbach, Bruno, 'Das Verhältnis von Text und Bild in "De laudibus sanctae crucis" des Hrabanus Maurus', in *Geistliche Denkformen in der Literatur des Mittelalters*, ed. by Klaus Grubmüller et al., Munich: Fink, 1984, pp. 282–320.

Schaller, Dieter, 'Vortrags- und Zirkulardichtung am Hofe Karls des Großen', *Mittellateinisches Jahrbuch* 6 (1969), 14–36.

Schröbler, Ingeborg, 'Glossen eines Germanisten zu Gottschalk von Orbais', *PBB/T* 77 (1955), 89–111.

Suchomski, Joachim, *'Delectatio' und 'Utilitas'*, Berne and Munich: Francke, 1975.

Taeger, Burkhard, *Zahlensymbolik bei Hraban, bei Hincmar und im Heliand*, Munich: Beck, 1970.

Wallach, Liutpold, *Alcuin and Charlemagne. Studies in Carolingian history and literature*, Ithaca, NY: Cornell University Press, 1959.

2 The high and later Middle Ages (1100–1450)

Primary literature

Anthologies

Bartsch, Karl (ed.), *Die Schweizer Minnesänger*, revised edn by Max Schiendorfer, Tübingen: Niemeyer, 1990.

Cramer, Thomas (ed.), *Die kleineren Liederdichter des 14. und 15. Jahrhunderts*, 4 vols., Munich: Fink, 1977–85.

von der Hagen, Friedrich Heinrich (ed.), *Gesammtabenteuer. Hundert alt-deutsche Erzählungen*, 3 vols., Stuttgart and Tübingen: Cotta, 1850; repr. Darmstadt: Wiss. Buchgesellschaft, 1961.

von Kraus, Karl, *Liederdichter des 13. Jahrhunderts*, 2nd edn, rev. by Gisela Kornrumpf, 2 vols., Tübingen: Niemeyer, 1978.

Lachmann, Karl (ed.), *Des Minnesangs Frühling. I: Texte*, 37th edn, rev. by Hugo Moser and Helmut Tervooren, Stuttgart: Hirzel, 1982.

Maurer, Friedrich (ed.), *Die religiösen Dichtungen des 11. und 12. Jahrhunderts*, 3 vols., Tübingen: Niemeyer, 1964–70.

Schönbach, Anton E. (ed.), *Altdeutsche Predigten*, 3 vols., Graz, 1886–91; Darmstadt 1964.

Schröder, Werner (ed.), *Kleinere deutsche Gedichte des 11. und 12. Jahrhunderts. Nach der Auswahl von Albert Waag*, 2 vols., Altdeutsche Textbibliothek 71–2, Tübingen: Niemeyer, 1972.

Individual editions

Priester Adelbrecht
Johannes Baptista, in Maurer, *Die religiösen Dichtungen*, II, pp. 328–41.

Albert von Augsburg
Geith, Karl-Ernst (ed.), *Albert von Augsburg: Das Leben des Heiligen Ulrich*, Quellen und Forschungen NF 39, Berlin, New York: de Gruyter, 1971.

Albrecht
Wolf, Werner, and Nyholm, Kurt (eds.), *Albrechts [von Scharfenberg] Jüngerer Titurel*, 3 vols., Deutsche Texte des Mittelalters 45, 55, 61, 73 and 77, Berlin: Akademie-Verlag, 1955–92.

Albrecht von Halberstadt
Last, Martin, 'Neue Oldenburger Fragmente der Metamorphosen-Übertragung des Albrecht von Halberstadt', *Oldenburger Jahrbuch* 65 (1966), 41–60.

Leverkus, Wilhelm, 'Aus Albrechts von Halberstadt Übersetzung der Metamorphosen Ovids', *Zeitschrift für deutsches Altertum* 11 (1859), 358–74.

Lübben, August, 'Neues Bruchstück von Albrecht von Halberstadt', *Germania: Vierteljahrsschrift für deutsche Alterthumskunde* 10 (1865), 237–45.

Das Anegenge
Neuschäfer, Dietrich (ed.), *Das Anegenge. Textkritische Studien, diplomatischer Abdruck, kritische Ausgabe, Anmerkungen zum Text, Medium aevum* 8, Munich: Fink, 1968.

Annolied
Nellmann, Eberhard (ed.), *Das Annolied. Mittelhochdeutsch und neuhochdeutsch*, 3rd revised edn, Stuttgart: Reclam, 1986.

Priester Arnolt
Geith, Karl-Ernst, *Priester Arnolts Legende von der Heiligen Juliana: Untersuchungen zur lateinischen Juliana-Legende und zum Text des deutschen Gedichtes*, Ph.D. thesis, Freiburg/Br., 1965.

Arnsteiner Marienlied
In Maurer, *Die religiösen Dichtungen*, I, pp. 432–452.

Frau Ava
Schacks, Kurt (ed.), *Die Dichtungen der Frau Ava*, Wiener Neudrucke 8, Graz: Akademische Druck- und Verlagsanstalt, 1986.

Baumgartenberger Johannes Baptista
In Maurer, *Die religiösen Dichtungen*, II, pp. 134–139.

Berthold von Regensburg
Pfeiffer, Franz, and Strobl, Joseph (eds.), *Berthold von Regensburg: Vollständige Ausgabe seiner deutschen Predigten*, 2 vols., Vienna: Braumüller, 1862–80; repr., with a preface by Kurt Ruh, Berlin: de Gruyter, 1965.

Boner, Ulrich
Pfeiffer, Franz (ed.), *Ulrich Boner: Der Edelstein*, Dichtungen des deutschen Mittelalters 4, Leipzig: Göschen, 1844.

Carmina Burana
Vollmann, Benedikt Konrad (ed.), *Carmina Burana. Texte und Übersetzungen*, Bibliothek des Mittelalters 13, Frankfurt a. M.: Deutscher Klassiker Verlag, 1987.

Deutschenspiegel
Eckhardt, Karl August, and Hübner, Alfred (eds.), *Deutschenspiegel und Augsburger Sachsenspiegel*, Monumenta Germaniae historica: Fontes iuris germanici antiqui NS III, 2nd edn., Hanover: Hahn, 1933.

Dukus Horant
Ganz, Peter F., Norman, Frederick, and Schwarz, Werner, *Dukus Horant*, Altdeutsche Textbibliothek: Ergänzungsreihe 2, Tübingen: Niemeyer, 1964.

Ebner, Christine
Peters, Ursula, and Bürkle, Susanne (eds.), *Christine Ebner: Leben und Offenbarungen*, forthcoming.
Schröder, Karl (ed.), *Der Nonne von Engelthal Büchlein von der genaden uberlast*, Bibliothek des litterarischen Vereins zu Stuttgart 108, Tübingen: Litterarischer Verein, 1871.

Meister Eckhart
Largier, Niklaus (ed.), *Meister Eckhart: Werke. Texte und Übersetzungen*, 2 vols., Bibliothek des Mittelalters 20–21, Frankfurt a. M.: Deutscher Klassiker Verlag, 1993.

Eike von Repgow
Eckhardt, Karl August (ed.), *Sachsenspiegel. I: Landrecht. II. Lehnrecht*, 2 vols., Monumenta Germaniae Historica: Fontes iuris germanici antiqui NS I/1–2, 3rd edn, Göttingen: Musterschmidt-Verlag, 1973.

Eilhart von Oberg
Buschinger, Danielle (ed.), *Eilhart von Oberg: Tristrant. Edition diplomatique des manuscrits et traduction en français moderne avec introduction, notes et*

index, Göppinger Arbeiten zur Germanistik 202, Göppingen: Kümmerle, 1976.

Bußmann, Hadumod (ed.), *Eilhart von Oberg: Tristrant. Synoptischer Druck der ergänzten Fragmente mit der gesamten Parallelüberlieferung*, Altdeutsche Textbibliothek 70, Tübingen: Niemeyer, 1969.

Elsbeth von Oye

Schneider-Lastin, Wolfram, *Elsbeth von Oye: Offenbarungen*, Studia germanica, Basle: Francke, at press.

Frauenlob

Stackmann, Karl, and Bertau, Karl (eds.), *Frauenlob (Heinrich von Meissen): Leichs, Sangsprüche, Lieder. 1. Teil: Einleitungen, Texte. 2. Teil: Apparate, Erläuterungen*, 2 vols., Abhandlungen der Akademie der Wissenschaften in Göttingen, philologisch-historische Klasse, 3. Folge, Nr. 120, Göttingen: Vandenhoeck and Ruprecht, 1981.

Gottfried von Straßburg

Bechstein, Reinhold (ed.), *Gottfried von Straßburg: Tristan*, rev. edn by Peter Ganz, Deutsche Klassiker des Mittelalters NF 4, Wiesbaden: Brockhaus, 1978.

Graf Rudolf

Ganz, Peter F. (ed.), *Graf Rudolf*, Philologische Studien und Quellen 19, Berlin: Erich Schmidt, 1964.

Die gute Frau

Sommer, Emil, 'Die gute Frau. Gedicht des dreizehnten Jahrhunderts', *Zeitschrift für deutsches Altertum* 2 (1842), 385–481.

Hartmann von Aue

Paul, Hermann, and Wolff, Ludwig (eds.), *Hartmann von Aue: Der arme Heinrich*, 15th edn, rev. by Gesa Bonath, Altdeutsche Textbibliothek 3, Tübingen: Niemeyer, 1984.

Leitzmann, Albert, and Wolff, Ludwig (eds.), *Hartmann von Aue: Erec*, 6th edn, rev. by Christoph Cormeau and Kurt Gärtner, Altdeutsche Textbibliothek 39, Tübingen: Niemeyer, 1985.

Paul, Hermann, and Wolff, Ludwig (eds.), *Hartmann von Aue: Gregorius*, 14th edn, rev. by Burghart Wachinger, Altdeutsche Textbibliothek 2, Tübingen: Niemeyer, 1992.

Benecke, Georg Friedrich, Lachmann, Karl, and Wolff, Ludwig (eds.), *Hartmann von Aue: Iwein*, trans. and notes by Thomas Cramer, 3rd rev. edn, Berlin and New York: de Gruyter, 1981.

Heinrich, Reinhart Fuchs

Düwel, Klaus et al. (eds.), *Der Reinhart Fuchs des Elsässers Heinrich*, Altdeutsche Textbibliothek 96, Tübingen: Niemeyer, 1984.

Heinrich von dem Türlin

Scholl, Gottlob Heinrich Friedrich (ed.), *Heinrich von dem Türlin: Diu Crône*, Bibliothek des litterarischen Vereins in Stuttgart 27, Tübingen: Litterarischer Verein, 1966; repr. Amsterdam: Rodopi, 1966.

Heinrich von Mügeln

Jahr, Willy (ed.), *Heinrich von Mügeln: Der meide kranz*, Ph.D thesis, Leipzig, Borna-Leipzig: Noske, 1908.

Stackmann, Karl (ed.), *Die kleineren Dichtungen Heinrichs von Mügeln*, 3 vols., Deutsche Texte des Mittelalters 50–2, Berlin: Akademie-Verlag, 1959.

Heinrich von Veldeke

Kartschoke, Dieter (ed.), *Heinrich von Veldeke: Eneasroman. Mittelhochdeutsch/Neuhochdeutsch*, Stuttgart: Reclam, 1986.

Frings, Theodor, and Schieb, Gabriele (eds.), *Die epischen Werke des Henric van Veldeken. I: Sente Servas – Sanctus Servatius*, Halle a. S.: Niemeyer, 1956.

Herbort von Fritzlar

Frommann, Georg Karl (ed.), *Herbort's von Fritslâr liet von Troye*, Bibliothek der gesammten deutschen National-Literatur 5, Quedlinburg and Leipzig: Basse, 1837; repr. Amsterdam: Rodopi, 1966.

Herzog Ernst

Pörnbacher, Hans, and Pörnbacher, Irmtraud (eds.), *Spielmannsepen I: König Rother, Herzog Ernst. Texte, Nacherzählungen, Anmerkungen und Worterklärungen*, Darmstadt: Wiss. Buchgesellschaft, 1984.

Sowinski, Bernhard (ed.), *Herzog Ernst. Ein mittelalterliches Abenteuerbuch*, Stuttgart: Reclam, 1970.

Hugo von Trimberg

Ehrismann, Gustav (ed.), *Der Renner von Hugo von Trimberg*, 4 vols., Bibliothek des litterarischen Vereins in Stuttgart 247–8, 252, 256, Tübingen: Litterarischer Verein, 1908–11; repr., with an appendix by Günther Schweikle, Berlin: de Gruyter, 1970.

Innsbrucker Osterspiel

Meier, Rudolf (ed.), *Das Innsbrucker Osterspiel. Das Osterspiel von Muri*, Stuttgart: Reclam, 1962.

Johann von Würzburg

Regel, Ernst (ed.), *Johann von Würzburg: Wilhelm von Österreich. Aus der Gothaer Handschrift*, Deutsche Texte des Mittelalters 3, Berlin: Weidmann, 1906.

Johannes von Tepl

Hüber, Arthur (ed.), *Der Ackermann aus Böhmen*, Altdeutsche Quellen 1, 3rd edn, Leipzig: Hirzel, 1965.

Bertau, Karl (ed.), *Johannes de Tepla Civis Zacensis: Epistola cum Libello ackerman und Das büchlein ackermen. Nach der Freiburger Hs. 163 und nach der Stuttgarter Hs. HB X 23*, 2 vols., Berlin and New York: de Gruyter, 1994.

Kaiserchronik

Schröder, Edward (ed.), *Deutsche Kaiserchronik*, Monumenta Germaniae Historica: Deutsche Chroniken 1, Hanover: Hahn, 1884; repr. Berlin: Weidmann, 1964.

Kaufringer, Heinrich
Sappler, Paul (ed.), *Heinrich Kaufringer: Werke*, Tübingen: Niemeyer, 1972.

Kirchberger Schwesternbuch
Birlinger, Anton, 'Die Nonnen von Kirchberg bei Haigerloch', *Alemannia* 11 (1883), 1–20.
Roth, F. W. E., 'Aufzeichnungen über das mystische Leben der Nonnen von Kirchberg bei Sulz während des 14. und 15. Jahrhunderts', *Alemannia* 21 (1893), 103–48.

Klage
Bartsch, Karl (ed.), *Diu Klage mit den Lesarten sämmtlicher Handschriften*, Leipzig: publisher, 1875; repr. Darmstadt: Wiss. Buchgesellschaft, 1964.

Kolmarer Liederhandschrift
Müller, Ulrich, Spechtler, Franz Viktor, and Brunner, Horst (eds.), *Die Kolmarer Liederhandschrift der Bayerischen Staatsbibliothek München (Cgm 4997)*, facsimile edition, 2 vols., Litterae 35, Göppingen: Kümmerle, 1976.

König Rother
See under *Herzog Ernst.*

Pfaffe Konrad
Kartschoke, Dieter (ed.), *Das Rolandslied des Pfaffen Konrad. Mittelhochdeutsch/Neuhochdeutsch*, Stuttgart: Reclam, 1993.

Konrad von Fußesbrunnen
Fromm, Hans, and Grubmüller, Klaus (eds.), *Konrad von Fußesbrunnen: Die Kindheit Jesu. Kritische Ausgabe*, Berlin, New York: de Gruyter, 1973.

Konrad von Würzburg
Schröder, Edward (ed.), *Kleinere Dichtungen Konrads von Würzburg*, 3 vols., Berlin: Weidmann, 1924–6.
Gereke, Paul (ed.), *Konrad von Würzburg: Die Legenden*, 3 vols., Altdeutsche Textbibliothek 19–21, Tübingen: Niemeyer, 1925–7; rev. edn of vol. 3, ed. by Winfried Woesler, 1974.
  Konrad von Würzburg: Engelhard, 3rd edn, rev. by Ingo Reiffenstein, Altdeutsche Textbibliothek 17, Tübingen: Niemeyer, 1982.
Bartsch, Karl (ed.), *Konrads von Würzburg Partonopier und Meliur, Turnei von Nantheiz, Sant Nicolaus, Lieder und Sprüche*, Vienna: Braumüller, 1871; repr., with an appendix by Rainer Gruenter, Berlin: de Gruyter, 1970.
von Keller, Adelbert (ed.), *Der trojanische Krieg von Konrad von Würzburg*, Bibliothek des litterarischen Vereins in Stuttgart 44, Tübingen: Litterarischer Verein, 1858; repr. Amsterdam: Rodopi, 1965.

Kudrun
Bartsch, Karl (ed.), *Kudrun*, 5th edn, rev. by Karl Stackmann, Wiesbaden: Brockhaus, 1980.

Pfaffe Lambrecht
Kinzel, Karl (ed.), *Lamprechts Alexander nach den drei Texten mit dem Fragment*

des Alberic von Besançon und den lateinischen Quellen, Germanistische Handbibliothek 6, Halle a. S.: Buchhandlung des Waisenhauses, 1884.

Lucidarius
Gottschall, Dagmar, and Steer, Georg (eds.), *Der deutsche 'Lucidarius'. Bd. 1: Kritischer Text nach den Handschriften*, Texte und Textgeschichte 35, Tübingen: Niemeyer, 1994.

'Marienklagen'
Schönbach, Anton (ed.), *Über die Marienklagen. Ein Beitrag zur Geschichte der geistlichen Dichtung in Deutschland*, Graz: Leuschner und Lubensky, 1874.

Marienleich aus Muri
In Maurer, *Die religiösen Dichtungen*, 1, pp. 453–61.

Mariensequenz aus St. Lambrecht
In Maurer, *Die religiösen Dichtungen*, 1, pp. 464–6.

Mechthild von Magdeburg
Neumann, Hans (ed.), *Mechthild von Magdeburg: 'Das fließende Licht der Gottheit'. Nach der Einsiedler Handschrift in kritischem Vergleich mit der gesamten Überlieferung*, rev. by Gisela Vollmann-Profe, 2 vols., Münchener Texte und Untersuchungen 100–1, Munich: Artemis, 1990–3.

Medingen songs
Lipphardt, Walther, 'Niederdeutsche Reimgedichte und Lieder des 14. Jahrhunderts in den mittelalterlichen Orationalien der Zisterzienserinnen von Medingen', *Niederdeutsches Jahrbuch* 95 (1972), 66–131.

Mittelfränkische Reimbibel
Kraus, Carl (ed.), *Mittelhochdeutsches Übungsbuch*, 2nd, rev. edn, Heidelberg: Winter, 1926; pp. 1–17, pp. 239–40.

Der Mönch von Salzburg
Spechtler, Franz Viktor (ed.), *Die geistlichen Lieder des Mönchs von Salzburg*, Quellen und Forschungen NF 51, Berlin: de Gruyter, 1972.

Moriz von Craûn
Pretzel, Ulrich (ed.), *Moriz von Craûn*, Altdeutsche Textbibliothek 45, 4th, rev. edn, Tübingen: Niemeyer, 1973.

Neidhart
Bennewitz-Behr, Ingrid (ed.), *Die Berliner Neidhart-Handschrift c (mgf 779). Transkription der Texte und Melodien*, Göppinger Arbeiten zur Germanistik 356, Göppingen: Kümmerle, 1981.
Wießner, Edmund, and Fischer, Hanns (eds.), *Die Lieder Neidharts*, 4th edn, rev. by Paul Sappler, melodies ed. by Helmut Lomnitzer, Altdeutsche Textbibliothek 44, Tübingen: Niemeyer, 1984.

Nibelungenlied
Bartsch, Karl, and de Boor, Helmut (eds.), *Das Nibelungenlied*, 22nd edn, rev. by Roswitha Wisniewski, Mannheim: Brockhaus, 1988.

Orendel

Schröder, Walter Johannes (ed.), *Spielmannsepen* II: *Sankt Oswald, Orendel, Salman und Morolf. Texte, Nacherzählungen, Anmerkungen und Worterklärungen*, Darmstadt: Wiss. Buchgesellschaft, 1976.

Osterspiel von Muri

See under *Innsbrucker Osterspiel*.

Oswald

See under *Orendel*.

Oswald von Wolkenstein

Klein, Karl Kurt et al. (eds.), *Die Lieder Oswalds von Wolkenstein*, 3rd edn, rev. by Hans Moser, Norbert Richard Wolf and Notburga Wolf, Altdeutsche Textbibliothek 55, Tübingen: Niemeyer, 1987.

Hofmeister, Wernfried, *Oswald von Wolkenstein: Sämtliche Lieder und Gedichte. Ins Neuhochdeutsche übersetzt*, Göppinger Arbeiten zur Germanistik 511, Göppingen: Kümmerle, 1989.

Pilatus

Weinhold, Karl, 'Zu dem Pilatusgedicht. Text, Sprache und Heimat', *Zeitschrift für deutsche Philologie* 8 (1877), 253–88.

Der Pleier

Bartsch, Karl (ed.), *Der Pleier: Meleranz*, Bibliothek des litterarischen Vereins in Stuttgart 60, Tübingen: Litterarischer Verein, 1861; repr., with an appendix by Alexander Hildebrand, Hildesheim and New York: Olms, 1974.

Prosa-Lancelot

Kluge, Reinhold (ed.), *Lancelot. Nach der Heidelberger Pergamenthandschrift Pal. Germ. 147*, 3 vols., Deutsche Texte des Mittelalters 42, 47 and 63, Berlin: Akademie-Verlag, 1948–74.

Rudolf von Ems

Junk, Victor (ed.), *Rudolf von Ems: Alexander. Ein höfischer Roman des 13. Jahrhunderts*, 2 vols., Bibliothek des litterarischen Vereins in Stuttgart 272 and 274, Leipzig: Hiersemann, 1928–9; repr. Darmstadt: Wiss. Buchgesellschaft, 1970.

Pfeiffer, Franz (ed.), *Rudolf von Ems: Barlaam und Josaphat*, Dichtungen des deutschen Mittelalters 38, Leipzig:, 1843; repr. Berlin: de Gruyter, 1965.

Asher, John A. (ed.), *Der guote Gêrhart von Rudolf von Ems*, Altdeutsche Textbibliothek 56, 3rd rev. edn, Tübingen: Niemeyer, 1989.

Ehrismann, Gustav (ed.), *Rudolfs von Ems Weltchronik. Aus der Wernigeroder Handschrift*, Deutsche Texte des Mittelalters 20, Berlin: Weidmann, 1915; repr. Dublin and Zurich: Weidmann, 1967.

Junk, Victor (ed.), *Rudolfs von Ems Willehalm von Orlens. Aus dem Wasserburger Codex der fürstlich Fürstenbergischen Hofbibliothek in Donaueschingen*, Deutsche Texte des Mittelalters 2, Berlin: Weidmann, 1905; repr. Dublin and Zurich: Weidmann, 1967.

Salman und Morolf

See under *Orendel*.

Karnein, Alfred (ed.), *Salman und Morolf*, Altdeutsche Textbibliothek 85, Tübingen: Niemeyer, 1979.

St. Georgener Predigten

Rieder, Karl (ed.), *Der sogenannte St. Georgener Prediger aus der Freiburger und der Karlsruher Handschrift*, Deutsche Texte des Mittelalters 10, Berlin: Weidmann, 1908.

St. Katharinentaler Schwesternbuch

Meyer, Ruth (ed.), *Das 'St. Katharinentaler Schwesternbuch'. Untersuchung – Edition – Kommentar*, Münchener Texte und Untersuchungen 104, Tübingen: Niemeyer, 1994.

St. Trudperter Hohes Lied

Ohly, Friedrich (ed.), *Das St. Trudperter Hohe Lied. Kritische Ausgabe*, Bibliothek des Mittelalters, Frankfurt a. M.: Deutscher Klassikerverlag, forthcoming.

Schwabenspiegel

Eckhardt, Karl August (ed.), *Schwabenspiegel. Kurzform*, 4 vols., Monumenta Germaniae Historica: Fontes iuris germanici antiqui NS iv/1–3 and v, Hanover: Hahn, 1960–4.

Schweizer Anonymus

Fischer, Hanns (ed.), *Eine Schweizer Kleinepiksammlung des 15. Jahrhunderts*, Altdeutsche Textbibliothek 65, Tübingen: Niemeyer, 1965.

Seuse, Heinrich

Bihlmeyer, Karl (ed.), *Heinrich Seuse: Deutsche Schriften*, Stuttgart: Kohlhammer, 1907; repr. Frankfurt a. M.: Minerva, 1961.

Speculum ecclesie

Mellbourn, Gert (ed.), *Speculum ecclesie. Eine frühmittelhochdeutsche Predigtsammlung (Cgm. 39)*, Lunder germanistische Forschungen 12, Lund and Copenhagen: Gleerup and Munksgaard, 1944.

Straßburger Alexander

See under Pfaffe Lambrecht.

Der Stricker

Moelleken, Wolfgang Wilfried, Agler-Beck, Gayle, and Lewis, Robert E. (eds.), *Die Kleindichtung des Strickers*, 5 vols., Göppinger Arbeiten zur Germanistik 107/1–5, Göppingen: Kümmerle, 1973–8.

Schwab, Ute (ed.), *Der Stricker: Tierbispel*, Altdeutsche Textbibliothek 54, Tübingen: Niemeyer, 1960.

Fischer, Hanns (ed.), *Der Stricker: Verserzählungen*, 2 vols., Altdeutsche Textbibliothek 53 [2nd edn] and 68, Tübingen: Niemeyer, 1967.

Resler, Michael (ed.), *Der Stricker: Daniel von dem Blühenden Tal*, Altdeutsche Textbibliothek 92, 2nd rev. edn, Tübingen: Niemeyer, 1995.

Bartsch, Karl (ed.), *Karl der Große von dem Stricker*, Bibliothek der gesammten deutschen National-Literatur 35, Quedlinburg and Leipzig: Basse, 1857; repr., with an appendix by Dieter Kartschoke, Berlin: de Gruyter, 1965.

Sunder, Friedrich

Ringler, Siegfried, *Viten- und Offenbarungsliteratur in Frauenklöstern des Mittelalters. Quellen und Studien*, Münchener Texte und Untersuchungen 72, Zurich and Munich: Artemis, 1980.

Tannhäuser

Siebert, Johannes (ed.), *Der Dichter Tannhäuser. Leben – Gedichte – Sage*, Halle a. S.: Niemeyer, 1934.

Tauler, Johannes

Vetter, Ferdinand (ed.), *Die Predigten Taulers aus der Engelberger und der Freiburger Handschrift sowie aus Schmidts Abschriften der ehemaligen Straßburger Handschriften*, Deutsche Texte des Mittelalters 11, Berlin: Weidmann, 1910; repr. Dublin and Zurich: Weidmann, 1968.

Thomasin von Zerklaere

Rückert, Heinrich (ed.), *Der wälsche Gast des Thomasin von Zirclaria*, Bibliothek der gesammten deutschen National-Literatur 30, Quedlinburg and Leipzig: Basse, 1852; repr., with an introduction by Friedrich Neumann, Berlin: de Gruyter, 1965.

Trierer Floyris

De Smet, Gilbert, and Gysseling, Maurits, 'Die Trierer Floyris-Bruchstücke', *Studia Germanica Gandensia* 9 (1967), 157–83.

Ulrich von dem Türlin

Schröder, Werner (ed.), *'Arabel'-Studien* i–v, Akademie der Wissenschaften und der Literatur (Mainz): Abhandlungen der geistes- und sozialwissenschaftlichen Klasse 1982,6; 1983,4; 1984,9; 1988,6–7 and 1993,4, Wiesbaden: Steiner, 1982–93.

Ulrich von Etzenbach

Rosenfeld, Hans-Friedrich (ed.), *Ulrich von Etzenbach: Wilhelm von Wenden*, Deutsche Texte des Mittelalters 49, Berlin: Akademie-Verlag, 1957.

Ulrich von Liechtenstein

Spechtler, Franz Viktor (ed.), *Ulrich von Liechtenstein: Frauendienst*, Göppinger Arbeiten zur Germanistik 485, Göppingen: Kümmerle, 1987.

Ulrich von Türheim

Gröchenig, Hans, and Pascher, Peter Hans (eds.), *Ulrich von Türheim: Cligès. Ausgabe der bisher bekannten Fragmente vermehrt um den Neufund aus St. Paul im Lavanttal, Einleitung und buchkundliche Beschreibung*, Armarium 2, Klagenfurt, 1984.

Kerth, Thomas (ed.), *Ulrich von Türheim: Tristan*, Altdeutsche Textbibliothek 89, Tübingen: Niemeyer, 1979.

Hübner, Artur (ed.), *Ulrich von Türheim: Rennewart. Aus der Berliner und Heidelberger Handschrift*, Deutsche Texte des Mittelalters 39, Berlin: Weidmann, 1938.

Ulrich von Zatzikhoven

Hahn, Karl August (ed.), *Ulrich von Zatzikhoven: Lanzelet. Eine Erzählung*,

Frankfurt a. M.: Brönner, 1845; repr., with an appendix by Frederick Norman, Berlin: de Gruyter, 1965.

Vorauer Bücher Moses

Diemer, Joseph, 'Geschichte Joseph's in Aegypten nach der Vorauer Handschrift', *Sitzungsberichte der kaiserlichen Akademie der Wissenschaften in Wien*, phil.-hist. Kl. 47 (1864), 636–87; 48 (1864), 339–423.

Wallersteiner Margaretalegende

Bartsch, Karl, 'Wetzels heilige Margareta', *Germanistische Studien: Supplement zur Germania* 1 (1872), 1–30.

Walther von der Vogelweide

Cormeau, Christoph (ed.), *Walther von der Vogelweide Leich, Lieder, Sangsprüche*, 14th, completely rev. edn of the text established by Karl Lachmann, with contributions by Thomas Bein and Horst Brunner, Berlin: de Gruyter, 1996.

Wernher der Gärtner

Panzer, Friedrich, and Ruh, Kurt (eds.), *Wernher der Gartenaere: Helmbrecht*, 10th edn, rev. by Hans-Joachim Ziegeler, Altdeutsche Textbibliothek 11, Tübingen: Niemeyer, 1993.

Wirnt von Grafenberg

Kapteyn, J. M. N. (ed.), *Wigalois der Ritter mit dem Rade von Wirnt von Grafenberg*, Rheinische Beiträge und Hülfsbücher zur germanischen Philologie 9, Bonn: Klopp, 1926.

Wittenwiler, Heinrich

Brunner, Horst (ed.), *Heinrich Wittenwiler: Der Ring. Frühneuhochdeutsch/Neuhochdeutsch*, Stuttgart: Reclam, 1991.

Wolfram von Eschenbach

Lachmann, Karl (ed.), *Wolfram von Eschenbach*, 6th edn, Berlin and Leipzig: de Gruyter, 1926; repr. Berlin 1965.

Wapnewski, Peter (ed.), *Die Lyrik Wolframs von Eschenbach. Edition, Kommentar, Interpretation*, Munich: Beck, 1972.

Mohr, Wolfgang (ed.), *Wolfram von Eschenbach: Titurel, Lieder. Mittelhochdeutscher Text und Übersetzung*, Göppinger Arbeiten zur Germanistik 250, Göppingen: Kümmerle, 1978.

Heinzle, Joachim (ed.), *Wolfram von Eschenbach: Willehalm nach der Handschrift 857 der Stiftsbibliothek St. Gallen*, Altdeutsche Textbibliothek 108, Tübingen: Niemeyer, 1994.

Secondary literature

Selected literary histories

Bertau, Karl, *Deutsche Literatur im europäischen Mittelalter*, 2 vols., Munich: Beck, 1972.

De Boor, Helmut, *Die höfische Literatur. Vorbereitung, Blüte, Ausklang, 1170–1250*, Geschichte der deutschen Literatur von den Anfängen bis zur Gegenwart 2, 11th edn, rev. by Ursula Hennig, Munich: Beck, 1991.

Die deutsche Literatur im späten Mittelalter. Zerfall und Neubeginn. Teil 1: 1250–1350, Geschichte der deutschen Literatur von den Anfängen bis zur Gegenwart 3/1, Munich: Beck, 1962.

Bumke, Joachim, *Geschichte der deutschen Literatur im hohen Mittelalter*, Deutsche Literatur im Mittelalter 2, Munich: Deutscher Taschenbuch Verlag, 1990.

Cramer, Thomas, *Geschichte der deutschen Literatur im späten Mittelalter*, Deutsche Literatur im Mittelalter 3, Munich: Deutscher Taschenbuch Verlag, 1990.

Ehrismann, Gustav, *Geschichte der deutschen Literatur bis zum Ausgang des Mittelalters*, 4 vols., Munich: Beck, 1900; 2nd edn of vol. 1, 1932; repr. 1959.

Glier, Ingeborg, *Die deutsche Literatur im späten Mittelalter, 1250–1350. Teil 2: Reimpaargedichte, Drama, Prosa*, Geschichte der deutschen Literatur von den Anfängen bis zur Gegenwart 3/2, Munich: Beck, 1987.

Heinzle, Joachim, *Vom hohen zum späten Mittelalter. Teil 2: Wandlungen und Neuansätze im 13. Jahrhundert (1220/30–1280/90)*, Geschichte der deutschen Literatur von den Anfängen bis zum Beginn der Neuzeit 2/2, 2nd edn, Tübingen: Niemeyer, 1994.

Kartschoke, Dieter, *Geschichte der deutschen Literatur im frühen Mittelalter*, Deutsche Literatur im Mittelalter 1, Munich: Deutscher Taschenbuch Verlag, 1990.

Knapp, Fritz Peter, *Die Literatur des Früh- und Hochmittelalters in den Bistümern Passau, Salzburg, Brixen und Trient von den Anfängen bis zum Jahre 1273*, Geschichte der Literatur in Österreich von den Anfängen bis zur Gegenwart 1, Graz: Akademische Druck- und Verlagsanstalt, 1994.

Ruh, Kurt et al. (eds.), *Die deutsche Literatur des Mittelalters. Verfasserlexikon*, 2nd, completely rev. edn, 9 vols. to date, Berlin and New York: de Gruyter, 1978–95.

Rupprich, Hans, *Die deutsche Literatur vom späten Mittelalter bis zum Barock. Teil 1: Das ausgehende Mittelalter, Humanismus und Renaissance, 1370–1520*, Geschichte der deutschen Literatur von den Anfängen bis zur Gegenwart 4, Munich: Beck, 1970.

Salmon, Paul B., *Literature in medieval Germany*, London: The Cresset Press, 1967.

Vollmann-Profe, Gisela, *Von den Anfängen zum hohen Mittelalter. Teil 2: Wiederbeginn volkssprachiger Schriftlichkeit im frühen Mittelalter*, Geschichte der deutschen Literatur von den Anfängen bis zum Beginn der Neuzeit 1/2, 2nd edn, Tübingen: Niemeyer, 1994.

Wehrli, Max, *Geschichte der deutschen Literatur vom frühen Mittelalter bis zum Ende des 16. Jahrhunderts*, 2nd edn, Stuttgart: Reclam, 1984.

Selected monographs

Blank, Walter, *Die deutsche Minneallegorie. Gestaltung und Funktion einer spät-mittelalterlichen Dichtungsform*, Germanistische Abhandlungen 34, Stuttgart: Metzler, 1970.

Brunner, Horst (ed.), *Die deutsche Trojaliteratur des Mittelalters und der frühen Neuzeit. Materialien und Untersuchungen*, Wissensliteratur im Mittelalter 3, Wiesbaden: Reichert, 1990.

Brunner, Horst, and Wachinger, Burghart (eds.), *Repertorium der Sangsprüche und Meisterlieder des 12. bis 18. Jahrhunderts*, 12 vols. to date, Tübingen: Niemeyer, 1986–94.

Bumke, Joachim, *Studien zum Ritterbegriff im 12. und 13. Jahrhundert*, Beihefte zum Euphorion 1, 2nd edn, Heidelberg: Winter, 1977; English translation by W. T. H. Jackson and Erika Jackson, New York: AMS Press, 1982.

  Mäzene im Mittelalter. Die Gönner und Auftraggeber der höfischen Literatur in Deutschland 1150–1300, Munich: Beck, 1979.

  Höfische Kultur. Literatur und Gesellschaft im hohen Mittelalter, 2 vols., 4th edn, Munich: Deutscher Taschenbuch Verlag, 1987; English trans. by Thomas Dunlap, Berkeley, CA, and London: University of California Press, 1991.

Fischer, Hanns, *Studien zur deutschen Märendichtung*, 2nd edn, revised Johannes Janota, Tübingen: Niemeyer, 1983.

Flasch, Kurt, *Einführung in die Philosophie des Mittelalters*, 2nd edn, Darmstadt: Wiss. Buchgesellschaft, 1989.

Freytag, Hartmut, *Die Theorie der allegorischen Schriftdeutung und die Allegorie in deutschen Texten besonders des 11. und 12. Jahrhunderts*, Bibliotheca Germanica 24, Berne and Munich: Francke, 1982.

Geith, Karl-Ernst, *Carolus Magnus. Studien zur Darstellung Karls des Großen in der deutschen Literatur des 12. und 13. Jahrhunderts*, Berne and Munich: Francke, 1977.

Gillespie, George T., *A catalogue of persons named in German heroic literature (700–1600) including named animals and objects and ethnic names*, Oxford: Clarendon Press, 1973.

Glier, Ingeborg, *Artes amandi. Untersuchung zu Geschichte, Überlieferung und Typologie der deutschen Minnereden*, Münchener Texte und Untersuchungen 34, Munich: Artemis, 1971.

Green, Dennis H., *Irony in medieval romance*, Cambridge: Cambridge University Press, 1979.

  Medieval listening and reading: the primary reception of German literature 800–1300, Cambridge: Cambridge University Press, 1994.

Grubmüller, Klaus, *Meister Esopus. Untersuchungen zu Geschichte und Funktion der Fabel im Mittelalter*, Münchener Texte und Untersuchungen 56, Zurich and Munich: Artemis, 1977.

Haas, Alois Maria, *Sermo mysticus. Studien zu Theologie und Sprache der deutschen Mystik*, Dokimion 4, Freiburg i. Ue.: Universitätsverlag, 1979.

Haug, Walter, 'Die Symbolstruktur des höfischen Epos und ihre Auflösung bei Wolfram von Eschenbach', *Deutsche Vierteljahrsschrift für Literaturwissenschaft und Geistesgeschichte* 45 (1971), 668–705.

  Literaturtheorie im deutschen Mittelalter. Von den Anfängen bis zum Ende des 13. Jahrhunderts, 2nd, rev. edn, Darmstadt: Wiss. Buchgesellschaft, 1992.

Haug, Walter, and Wachinger, Burghart, *Positionen des Romans im Spätmittelalter*, Fortuna vitrea 1, Tübingen: Niemeyer, 1991.

Heinzle, Joachim, *Mittelhochdeutsche Dietrichepik. Untersuchungen zur Tradierungsweise, Überlieferungskritik und Gattungsgeschichte später Heldendichtung*, Münchener Texte und Untersuchungen 62, Munich and Zurich: Artemis, 1978.

Heinzle, Joachim (ed.), *Modernes Mittelalter. Neue Bilder einer populären Epoche*, Frankfurt a. M. and Leipzig: Insel, 1994.

Henkel, Nikolaus, and Palmer, Nigel F. (eds.), *Latein und Volkssprache im deutschen Mittelalter 1100–1500. Regensburger Colloquium 1988*, Tübingen: Niemeyer, 1992.

Honemann, Volker, and Palmer, Nigel F. (eds.), *Deutsche Handschriften 1100–1400. Oxforder Kolloquium 1985*, Tübingen: Niemeyer, 1988.

Jones, Martin H., and Wisbey, Roy (eds.), *Chrétien de Troyes and the German Middle Ages: papers from an international symposium*, Arthurian Studies 26, Cambridge: Brewer, 1993.

Kasten, Ingrid, *Frauendienst bei Trobadors und Minnesängern im 12. Jahrundert. Zur Entwicklung und Adaptation eines literarischen Konzepts*, Germ.-Rom. Monatsschrift: Beiheft 5, Heidelberg: Winter, 1986.

Kern, Peter, *Trinität, Maria, Inkarnation. Studien zur Thematik der deutschen Dichtung des späteren Mittelalters*, Philologische Studien und Quellen 55, Berlin: Erich Schmidt, 1971.

Küsters, Urban, *Der verschlossene Garten. Volkssprachliche Hohelied-Auslegung und monastische Lebensform im 12. Jahrhundert*, Studia humaniora 2, Düsseldorf: Droste, 1985.

Linke, Hansjürgen, 'Germany and German-speaking central Europe', in *The theatre of medieval Europe: new research in early drama*, ed. by Eckehard Simon, Cambridge: Cambridge University Press, 1991, pp. 207–24.

Masser, Achim, *Bibel- und Legendenepik des deutschen Mittelalters*, Grundlagen der Germanistik 19, Berlin: Erich Schmidt Verlag, 1976.

McMahon, James, *The music of early Minnesang*, Columbia, SC: Camden House, 1990.

Mittler, Elmar, and Werner, Wilfried (eds.), *Codex Manesse. Katalog der Ausstellung vom 12. Juni bis 2. Oktober 1988, Universitätsbibliothek Heidelberg*, Heidelberger Bibliotheksschriften 30, 2nd edn, Heidelberg: Braus, 1988.

Morvay, Karin, and Grube, Dagmar, *Bibliographie der deutschen Predigt des Mittelalters. Veröffentlichte Predigten*, Münchener Texte und Untersuchungen 47, Munich: Beck, 1974.

Ohly, Friedrich, *Der Verfluchte und der Erwählte. Vom Leben mit der Schuld*, Rheinisch-Westfälische Akademie der Wissenschaften: Vorträge G207, Opladen: Westdeutscher Verlag, 1976; English trans. by Linda Archibald, Cambridge: Cambridge University Press, 1992.

'Vom geistigen Sinn des Wortes im Mittelalter (1958/59)', in *Schriften zur mittelalterlichen Bedeutungsforschung*, ed. by Friedrich Ohly, 2nd edn, Darmstadt: Wiss. Buchgesellschaft, 1983, 1–31.

Palmer, Nigel F., *German literary culture in the twelfth and thirteenth centuries. An inaugural lecture delivered before the University of Oxford on 4 March 1993*, Oxford: Clarendon Press, 1993.

Pérennec, René, *Recherches sur le roman arthurien en vers en Allemagne aux XIIe et XIIIe siècles*, 2 vols., Göppinger Arbeiten zur Germanistik 393/1–2, Göppingen: Kümmerle, 1984.

Peters, Ursula, *Literatur in der Stadt. Studien zu den sozialen Voraussetzungen und kulturellen Organisationsformen städtischer Literatur im 13. und 14. Jahrhundert*, Studien und Texte zur Sozialgeschichte der Literatur 7, Tübingen: Niemeyer, 1983.

Religiöse Erfahrung als literarisches Faktum. Zur Vorgeschichte und Genese frauenmystischer Texte des 13. und 14. Jahrhunderts, Hermaea NF 56, Tübingen: Niemeyer, 1988.

Pörksen, Uwe, *Der Erzähler im mittelhochdeutschen Epos. Formen seines Hervortretens bei Lamprecht, Konrad, Hartmann, in Wolframs Willehalm und in den 'Spielmannsepen'*, Philologische Studien und Quellen 58, Berlin: Erich Schmidt, 1971.

Ruh, Kurt, *Höfische Epik des deutschen Mittelalters. I: Von den Anfängen bis zu Hartmann von Aue. II: 'Reinhart Fuchs', 'Lanzelet', Wolfram von Eschenbach, Gottfried von Straßburg*, 2 vols., Grundlagen der Germanistik 7 and 25, Berlin: Erich Schmidt, 1972–80; 2nd edn of vol. 1, 1977.

'Epische Literatur des deutschen Spätmittelalters', in *Europäisches Spätmittelalter*, ed. by Willi Erzgräber, Neues Handbuch der Literaturwissenschaft 8, Wiesbaden: Athenaion, 1978, pp. 117–88.

'Geistliche Prosa', in *Europäisches Spätmittelalter*, ed. by Willi Erzgräber, Neues Handbuch der Literaturwissenschaft 8, Wiesbaden: Athenaion, 1978, pp. 565–605.

Geschichte der abendländischen Mystik. Bd. I: Die Grundlegung durch die Kirchenväter und Mönchstheologie des 12. Jahrhunderts. Bd. II: Frauenmystik und Franziskanische Mystik der Frühzeit, Munich: Beck, 1990–3.

Sayce, Olive, *The medieval German lyric, 1150–1300: the development of its themes and forms in their European context*, Oxford: Oxford University Press, 1982.

Schneider, Karin, *Gotische Schriften in deutscher Sprache. Bd. I: Vom späten 12. Jahrhundert bis um 1300*, 2 vols., Wiesbaden: Reichert, 1987.

Schnell, Rüdiger, *Causa amoris. Liebeskonzeption und Liebesdarstellung in der mittelalterlichen Literatur*, Bibliotheca Germanica 27, Berne: Francke, 1985.

Scholz, Manfred Günter, *Hören und Lesen. Studien zur primären Rezeption der Literatur im 12. und 13. Jahrhundert*, Wiesbaden: Steiner, 1980.

Schweikle, Günther, *Minnesang*, Slg Metzler 244, Stuttgart: Metzler, 1989.

Simon, Eckehard (ed.), *The theatre of medieval Europe: new research in early drama*, Cambridge: Cambridge University Press, 1991.

Sturlese, Loris, *Die deutsche Philosophie im Mittelalter. Von Bonifatius bis zu Albert dem Großen (748–1280)*, trans. from the Italian by Johanna Baumann, Munich: Beck, 1993.

Suchomski, Joachim, *'Delectatio' und 'Utilitas'. Ein Beitrag zum Verständnis mittelalterlicher komischer Literatur*, Bibliotheca Germanica 18, Berne and Munich, 1975.

Wehrli, Max, *Literatur im deutschen Mittelalter. Eine poetologische Einführung*, Stuttgart: Reclam, 1984.

Wolf, Alois, *Variation und Integration: Beobachtungen zu hochmittelalterlichen Tageliedern*, Impulse der Forschung 29, Darmstadt: Wiss. Buchgesellschaft, 1979.

Literature on individual authors and texts
Meister Eckhart
Davies, Oliver, *Meister Eckhart: mystical theologian*, London: SPCK, 1991.
Ruh, Kurt, *Meister Eckhart. Theologe, Prediger, Mystiker*, 2nd, revised edn, Munich: Beck, 1989.

Frauenlob
Schröder, Werner (ed.), *Cambridger 'Frauenlob'-Kolloquium 1986*, Wolfram-Studien 10, Berlin: Erich Schmidt, 1988.

Gottfried von Strassburg
Huber, Christoph, *'Tristan und Isolde'. Eine Einführung*, Artemis Einführungen 24, Munich: Artemis, 1986.
Jaeger, C. Stephen, *Medieval humanism in Gottfried von Strassburg's Tristan und Isolde*, Heidelberg: Winter, 1972.

Hartmann von Aue
Cormeau, Christoph, and Störmer, Wilhelm, *Hartmann von Aue. Epoche – Werk – Wirkung*, 2nd rev. edn, Munich: Beck, 1993.
Jackson, W. H., *Chivalry in twelfth-century Germany: the works of Hartmann von Aue*, Arthurian studies 34, Cambridge: Brewer, 1994.
McFarland, Timothy, and Ranawake, Silvia (eds.), *Hartmann von Aue: changing perspectives*. London Hartmann Symposium 1985, Göppinger Arbeiten zur Germanistik 486, Göppingen: Kümmerle, 1988.

Johannes von Tepl
Hahn, Gerhard, *Der Ackermann aus Böhmen des Johannes von Tepl*, Erträge der Forschung 215, Darmstadt: Wiss. Buchgesellschaft, 1984.

Kaiserchronik
Ohly, Friedrich, *Sage und Legende in der Kaiserchronik. Untersuchungen über Quellen und Aufbau der Dichtung*, Forschungen zur deutschen Sprache und Dichtung 10, Münster, 1940; repr. Darmstadt: Wiss. Buchgesellschaft, 1968.

Konrad von Würzburg
Brandt, Rüdiger, *Konrad von Würzburg*, Erträge der Forschung 249, Darmstadt: Wiss. Buchgesellschaft, 1987.

Neidhart
Schweikle, Günther, *Neidhart*, Slg Metzler 253, Stuttgart: Metzler, 1990.
Simon, Eckehard, *Neidhart von Reuental*, Twayne World Authors' Series 364, Boston: Twayne, 1975.

Nibelungenlied
Ehrismann, Otfrid, *Nibelungenlied: Epoche – Werk – Wirkung*, Munich: Fink, 1987.
Haymes, Edward R., *The Nibelungen: history and interpretation*, Illinois medieval monographs 2, Urbana and Chicago: University of Illinois Press, 1986.
Heinzle, Joachim, *Das Nibelungenlied*, Artemis Einführungen 35, Munich: Artemis, 1987.

Oswald von Walkenstein

Schwob, Anton, *Oswald von Wolkenstein. Eine Biographie*, Schriftenreihe des Südtiroler Kulturinstitutes 4, 3rd edn, Bozen, 1982.

Prosa-Lancelot

Schröder, Werner (ed.), *Schweinfurter 'Lancelot'-Kolloquium 1984*, Wolfram-Studien 9, Berlin: Erich Schmidt, 1986.

Der Stricker

Ragotzky, Hedda, *Gattungserneuerung und Laienunterweisung in Texten des Strickers*, Studien und Texte zur Sozialgeschichte der Literatur 1, Tübingen: Niemeyer, 1981.

Ulrich von Liechtenstein

Peters, Ursula, *Frauendienst. Untersuchungen zu Ulrich von Liechtenstein und zum Wirklichkeitsgehalt der Minnedichtung*, Göppinger Arbeiten zur Germanistik 46, Göppingen: Kümmerle, 1971.

Walther von der Vogelweide

Hahn, Gerhard, *Walther von der Vogelweide. Eine Einführung*, Artemis Einführungen 22, Munich: Artemis, 1986.

McFarland, Timothy, and Ranawake, Silvia (eds.), *Walther von der Vogelweide: twelve studies*, Oxford German Studies 13, Oxford: Meeuws, 1982.

Wittenwiler, Heinrich

Lutz, Eckhart Conrad, *Spiritualis fornicatio. Heinrich Wittenwiler, seine Welt und sein 'Ring'*, Konstanzer Geschichts- und Rechtsquellen 32, Sigmaringen: Thorbecke, 1990.

Wolfram von Eschenbach

Bumke, Joachim, *Wolfram von Eschenbach*, Slg Metzler 36, 6th, revised edn., Stuttgart: Metzler, 1990.

Green, Dennis H., and Johnson, Peter L., *Approaches to Wolfram von Eschenbach: five essays*, Mikrokomos 5, Berne: Peter Lang, 1978.

Kiening, Christian, *Reflexion-Narration. Wege zum 'Willehalm' Wolframs von Eschenbach*, Hermaea NF 63, Tübingen: Niemeyer, 1991.

Kratz, Henry, *Wolfram von Eschenbach's Parzival: an attempt at a total evaluation*, Bibliotheca Germanica 15, Berne: Francke, 1973.

3 The early modern period (1450–1720)

Histories of literature and general works

Becker-Cantarino, Barbara, *Der lange Weg zur Mündigkeit. Frau und Literatur 1500–1800*, Stuttgart: Metzler, 1987.

Breuer, Dieter, *Oberdeutsche Literatur 1565–1650. Deutsche Literaturgeschichte und Territorialgeschichte in frühabsolutistischer Zeit*, Munich: Beck, 1979.

Brinker-Gabler, Gisela (ed.), *Deutsche Literatur von Frauen*, vol. 1: *Vom Mittelalter bis zum Ende des 18. Jahrhunderts*, Munich: Beck, 1988.

Burger, Heinz Otto, *Renaissance, Humanismus, Reformation. Deutsche Literatur im europäischen Kontext*, Bad Homburg, Berlin, Zurich: Gehlen, 1969.

Cameron, Ewan, *The European Reformation*, Oxford: Clarendon Press, 1991.

Casey, Paul F., *The Susanna theme in German literature*, Bonn: Bouvier, 1976.

De Boor, Helmut, and Newald, Richard, *Geschichte der deutschen Literatur von den Anfängen bis zur Gegenwart*. vol.4: Rupprich, Hans, *Die deutsche Literatur vom späten Mittelalter bis zum Barock. Das ausgehende Mittelalter, Humanismus und Renaissance 1370–1520*, Munich: Beck 1970; vol.5: Newald, Richard et al., *Die deutsche Literatur vom Späthumanismus zur Empfindsamkeit 1570–1750*, Munich: Beck, 1967.

Elton, Geoffrey, *Reformation Europe 1517–1559*, London: Collins, 1963.

Engelsing, Rolf, *Analphabetentum und Lektüre. Zur Sozialgeschichte des Lesens in Deutschland zwischen feudaler und industrieller Gesellschaft*, Stuttgart: Metzler, 1974.

Forster, L.W., *The icy fire. Five studies in European Petrarchism*, Cambridge: Cambridge University Press, 1969.

The poet's tongues: multilingualism in literature, Cambridge: Cambridge University Press, 1970.

Garber, Klaus (ed.), *Nation und Literatur im Europa der Frühen Neuzeit. Akten des Ersten Internationalen Osnabrücker Kongresses zur Kulturgeschichte der Frühen Neuzeit*, Tübingen: Metzler, 1989.

Glaser, Horst Albert (ed.), *Deutsche Literatur. Eine Sozialgeschichte*, vol. 2: *Von der Handschrift zum Buchdruck. Spätmittelalter-Reformation-Humanismus 1320–1572*, ed. by Ingrid Bennewitz and Ulrich Müller, Reinbek: Rowohlt, 1991; vol. 3: *Zwischen Gegenreformation und Frühaufklärung. Späthumanismus, Barock 1572–1740.*, ed. by Harald Steinhagen, Reinbek: Rowohlt, 1985.

Grenzmann, Ludger, and Stackmann, Karl (eds.), *Literatur und Laienbildung im Spätmittelalter und in der Reformationszeit*, Stuttgart: Metzler, 1984.

Grimm, Günter E., and Max, Frank Rainer, *Deutsche Dichter*. Bd.2, *Reformation, Renaissance und Barock*, Stuttgart: Reclam, 1988.

Hoffmeister, Gerhart, *German Baroque literature. The European perspective*, New York: Ungar, 1982.

Deutsche und europäische Barockliteratur, Slg Metzler 234, Stuttgart: Metzler, 1987.

Israel, Jonathan, *European Jewry in the age of mercantilism 1550–1750*, Oxford: Clarendon Press, 1985.

Kleinschmidt, Erich, *Stadt und Literatur in der frühen Neuzeit. Voraussetzungen und Entfaltung im südwestdeutschen, elsässischen und schweizerischen Städteraum*, Cologne, Vienna: Böhlau, 1982.

Könnecker, Barbara, *Die deutsche Literatur der Reformationszeit*, Munich: Beck, 1975.

Koselleck, Reinhart, *Critique and crisis: enlightenment and the pathenogenesis of modern society*, Oxford: Berg, 1988.

Krailsheimer, A.J. (ed.), *The continental Renaissance*, Harmondsworth: Penguin, 1971.

Limon, Jerzy, *Gentlemen of a company. English players in central and eastern*

Europe 1590–1660, Cambridge: Cambridge University Press, 1985.

Noe, Alfred, *Der Einfluß des italienischen Humanismus auf die deutsche Literatur vor 1600*, Tübingen: Niemeyer, 1993.

Parker, Geoffrey, *The Thirty Years War*, London, New York: Routledge, 1984.

Scribner, R.W., *For the sake of simple folk. Popular propaganda for the German Reformation*, Cambridge: Cambridge University Press, 1981.

The German Reformation, London: Macmillan, 1986.

Skrine, Peter, *The Baroque: literature and culture in seventeenth century Europe*, London: Methuen, 1978.

Steinhagen, Harald, and von Wiese , Benno (eds.), *Deutsche Dichter des 17. Jahrhunderts. Ihr Leben und Werk*, Berlin: Erich Schmidt, 1984.

Szyrocki, Marian, *Die deutsche Literatur des Barock*, Stuttgart: Reclam, 1979.

Tatlock, Lynne (ed.), *The graph of sex and the German text: gendered culture in early modern Germany 1500–1700*, Chloe 19, Amsterdam: Rodopi, 1994.

Valentin, Jean-Marie, *Le théâtre des jésuites dans les pays de langue allemande (1554–1680). Salut des âmes et ordre des cités*, 3 vols., Berne: Peter Lang, 1978.

Valentin, Jean-Marie (ed.), *Gegenreformation und Literatur. Beiträge zur interdisziplinären Erforschung der katholischen Reformbewegung*, Beihefte zum *Daphnis* 3, Amsterdam: Rodopi, 1979.

Walz, Herbert, *Deutsche Literatur der Reformationszeit: eine Einführung*, Darmstadt: Wiss. Buchgesellschaft, 1988.

Wells, C. J., *German. A linguistic history to 1945*, Oxford: Clarendon Press, 1985.

Wunder, Heide, *'Er ist die Sonn', sie ist der Mond. Frauen in der frühen Neuzeit*, Munich: Beck, 1992.

Genres

Aikin, Judith P., *German Baroque drama*, Boston: Twayne, 1982.

'Happily ever after: an alternative affective theory of comedy and some plays by Birken, Gryphius and Weise', *Daphnis* 17 (1988), 55–76.

Daphnis : Special comedy number, 17 (1988), Heft 1.

Alexander, Robert J., *Das deutsche Barockdrama*, Slg Metzler 209, Stuttgart: Metzler, 1984.

Bircher, Martin, and Haas, Alois M. (eds.), *Gedichtinterpretationen von Spee bis Haller*, Berne: Francke, 1973.

Herzog, Urs, *Der deutsche Roman des 17. Jahrhunderts*, Stuttgart: Kohlhammer, 1976.

Hoffmeister, Gerhart, *Der Schelmenroman im europäischen Kontext*, Amsterdam: Rodopi, 1986.

Kemper, Hans-Georg, *Deutsche Lyrik der frühen Neuzeit*, vol.1: Epochen- und Gattungsprobleme. Reformationszeit; vol.2: Konfessionalismus; vol.3: Barock-Mystik, Tübingen: Niemeyer, 1986–7.

Könnecker, Barbara, *Satire im 16. Jahrhundert. Epoche – Werk – Wirkung*, Munich: Beck, 1991.

Meid, Volker, *Der deutsche Barockroman*, Slg Metzler 128, Stuttgart: Metzler, 1974.

Barocklyrik, Slg Metzler 227, Stuttgart: Metzler, 1986.

Meid, Volker (ed.), *Gedichte und Interpretationen*, Bd. 1 Renaissance und Barock, Stuttgart: Reclam, 1982.

Michael, Wolfgang F., *Das deutsche Drama der Reformationszeit*, Berne: Peter Lang, 1984.

Newman, Jane, *Pastoral conventions: poetry, language and thought in seventeenth-century Nuremberg*, Baltimore and London: Johns Hopkins University Press, 1990.

Rötzer, Hans Gerd, *Der Roman des Barock 1600–1700. Kommentar zu einer Epoche*, Munich: Winkler, 1972.

Schade, Richard E., *Studies in early German comedy*, Columbia, SC: Camden House, 1988.

Schings, Hans-Jürgen, 'Gryphius, Lohenstein und das Trauerspiel des 17. Jahrhunderts', in *Handbuch des deutschen Dramas*, ed. by Walter Hinck, Düsseldorf: Bagel, 1980.

Schöne, Albrecht, *Emblematik und Drama im Zeitalter des Barock*, Munich: Beck, 1968.

Segebrecht, Wulf, *Das Gelegenheitsgedicht. Ein Beitrag zur Geschichte und Poetik der deutschen Lyrik*, Stuttgart: Metzler, 1977.

Szarota, Elida Maria, *Künstler, Grübler und Rebellen. Studien zum europäischen Märtyrerdrama des 17. Jahrhunderts*, Berne: Francke, 1967.

Geschichte, Politik und Gesellschaft im Drama des 17. Jahrhunderts, Berne, Francke, 1976.

Voßkamp, Wilhelm, *Utopieforschung: interdisziplinäre Studien zur neuzeitlichen Utopie*, Stuttgart: Metzler, 1982.

Voßkamp, Wilhelm (ed.), *Schäferdichtung*, Hamburg: Hauswedell, 1977.

Individual authors

Abraham à Sancta Clara

Eybl, Franz M., *Abraham à Sancta Clara: vom Prediger zum Schriftsteller*, Tübingen: Niemeyer, 1992.

Angelus Silesius

See Scheffler, Johannes

Balde, Jacob

Jacob Balde und seine Zeit: Akten des Ensisheimer Kolloquiums 15–16 Okt. 1982, Berne: Peter Lang, 1986.

Beer, Johann

Krämer, Jörg, *Johann Beers Romane, Poetologie, Poetik und Rezeption niederer Texte im späten 17. Jahrhundert*, Berne: Peter Lang, 1991.

Bidermann, Jakob

Best, Thomas W., *Jakob Bidermann*, Boston: Twayne, 1975.

Böhme, Jakob

Weeks, Andrew, *Jakob Böhme. An intellectual biography of the 17th century philosopher and mystic*, Albany: State University of New York Press, 1991.

Brant, Sebastian

Zeydel, Edwin H., *Sebastian Brant*, New York: Twayne, 1967.

Celtis, Konrad

Wuttke, Dieter, and Zinn, Ernst, *Humanismus als integrative Kraft: die philosophia des deutschen Erzhumanisten Conrad Celtis: eine ikonologische Studie zu programmatischer Graphik Dürers und Burgkmairs*, Nuremberg: H. Carl, 1985.

Erasmus

McConica, James, *Erasmus*, Past Masters, Oxford: Oxford University Press, 1991.

Fischart, Johann

Ertz, Stefan, *Fischart und die Schiltburgerchronik: Untersuchungen zum Lale- und Schildbürgerbuch*, Cologne: Gabel, 1989.

Honegger, Peter, *Die Schiltburgerchronik und ihr Verfasser Johann Fischart*, Hamburg: Hauswedell, 1982.

Fleming, Paul

Sperberg-McQueen, Marian, *The German poetry of Paul Fleming: studies in genre and history*, Chapel Hill: University of North Carolina Press, 1990.

Frischlin, Nikodemus

Price, David, *The political dramaturgy of Nikodemus Frischlin. Essays on humanist drama in Germany*, Chapel Hill and London: University of North Carolina Press, 1990.

Röckelein, Hedwig, *Casimir Bumiller, . . . ein unruhig Poet. Nikodemus Frischlin 1547–1590*, Ballingen: Veröffentlichungen des Staatsarchives, 1990.

Grimmelshausen

Berns, Jörg Jochen, 'Die Zusammenfügung der Simplicianischen Schriften. Bemerkungen zum Zyklus-Problem', *Simpliciana. Jahrbuch der Grimmels-hausen-Gesellschaft* x (1988), 301–325.

'Libuschka und Courasche. Bemerkungen zu Grimmelshausens Frauenbild', Teil i: Dokumentation, *Simpliciana* xi (1989) 215–60 and Teil ii: Darlegungen, *Simpliciana* xii (1990), 417–42.

Feldges, Mathias, *Grimmelshausen 'Landstörtzerin Courasche'. Eine Interpretation nach der Methode des vierfachen Schriftsinnes*, Berne: Francke, 1969.

Feldman, Linda Ellen, 'The rape of Frau Welt. Transgression, allegory and the grotesque body in Grimmelshausen's *Courasche*', *Daphnis* 20 (1991), 61–80.

Heßelmann, Peter, *Simplicissimus Redivivus. Eine kommentierte Dokumentation der Rezeptionsgeschichte Grimmelshausens im 17. und 18. Jahrhundert (1667–1800)*, Frankfurt a. M: Klostermann, 1992.

Mannack, Eberhard, 'Hans Jakob Christoffel von Grimmelshausen', in *Deutsche Dichter des 17. Jahrhunderts. Ihr Leben und Werk*. Ed. by Benno von Wiese and Harald Steinhagen, Berlin: Erich Schmidt, 1984, pp. 517–552.

Meid, Volker, *Grimmelshausen: Epoche – Werk – Wirkung*, Munich: Beck, 1984.

Negus, Kenneth, *Grimmelshausen*, New York: Twayne, 1974.

Solbach, Andreas, 'Erzählskepsis bei Grimmelshausen im *Seltzamen Springinsfeld*', *Simpliciana* xii (1990), 323–340.

Weydt, Günther, *Nachahmung und Schöpfung im Barock. Studien um Grimmelshausen*, Berne: Francke, 1968.

Hans Jakob Christoffel von Grimmelshausen, Slg Metzler 99, Stuttgart: Metzler, 1971.

Weber, Alexander, 'Über Naturerfahrung und Landschaft in Grimmelshausens *Simplicissimus*', *Daphnis* 23 (1994), 61–84.

Greiffenberg, Catharina Regina von

Daly, Peter M., *Dichtung und Emblematik bei Catharina Regina von Greiffenberg*, Bonn: Bouvier, 1976.

Gryphius, Andreas

Berghaus, Günther, *Die Quellen zu Andreas Gryphius' Trauerspiel 'Carolus Stuardus'. Studien zur Entstehung eines historisch-politischen Märtyrerdramas der Barockzeit*, Tübingen: Niemeyer, 1984.

Kaiser, Gerhard (ed.), *Die Dramen des Andreas Gryphius. Eine Sammlung von Einzelinterpretationen*, Stuttgart: Metzler, 1968.

Kaminski, Nicola, *Der liebe Eisen-harte Noth. "Cardenio und Celinde" im Kontext von Gryphius' Märtyrerdramen*, Tübingen: Niemeyer, 1992.

Mannack, Eberhard, *Andreas Gryphius*, 2nd edn, Slg Metzler 76, Stuttgart: 1986.

Mauser, Wolfram, *Dichtung, Religion und Gesellschaft im 17. Jahrhundert. Die "Sonnete" des Andreas Gryphius*, Munich: Fink, 1976.

Steinhagen, Harald, *Wirklichkeit und Handeln im barocken Drama. Historisch-ästhetische Studien zum Trauerspiel des Andreas Gryphius*, Tübingen: Niemeyer, 1977.

Günther, Johann Christian

Bütler-Schön, Helga, *Dichtungsverständnis und Selbstdarstellung bei Johann Christian Günther. Studien zu seinen Auftraggedichten, Satiren und Klageliedern*, Bonn: Bouvier, 1981.

Pott, Hans-Georg (ed.), *Johann Christian Günther*, Paderborn, Munich, Vienna: Schöningh, 1988.

Lohenstein, Daniel Casper von

Aikin, Judith P., *The mission of Rome in the dramas of D.C. von Lohenstein. History as prophecy and polemic*, Stuttgart: Akademischer Verlag, 1976.

Béhar, Pierre, *Silesia Tragica. Epanouissement et fin de l'école dramatique silésienne dans l'oeuvre tragique de Daniel Casper von Lohenstein (1635–1683)* Wiesbaden: Harrassowitz, 1988.

Lotichius Secundus, Petrus

Zon, Stephen, *Petrus Lotichius Secundus, Neo-Latin Poet*, Berne: Peter Lang, 1983.

Luther, Martin

Arnold, Heinz Ludwig (ed.) *Martin Luther*, Munich: text + kritik, 1983.

Bluhm, Heinz, *Martin Luther. Creative translator*, St Louis: Concordia, 1965.

Junghans, Helmar (ed.), *Leben und Werk Martin Luthers von 1526 bis 1546. Festgabe zu seinem 500. Geburtstag*, 2 vols., Göttingen: Vandenhoeck and Ruprecht, 1983.

Lohse, Bernhard, *Martin Luther. Eine Einführung in sein Leben und sein Werk*, Munich: Beck 1983.

Maximilian I

Müller, Jan-Dirk, *Gedechtnus. Literatur und Hofgesellschaft um Maximilian I*, Munich: Fink, 1982.

Mitternacht, Johann Sebastian

Sorg, Norbert, *Restauration und Rebellion – die deutschen Dramen Johann Sebastian Mitternachts. Ein Beitrag zur Geschichte des protestantischen Schuldramas im 17. Jahrhunderts*, Freiburg: Hochschulverlag, 1980.

Opitz, Martin

Becker-Cantarino, Barbara (ed), *Martin Opitz. Studien zu Leben und Werk*, *Daphnis* 11 (1982).

Garber, Klaus, *Martin Opitz, 'der Vater der deutschen Dichtung'. Eine kritische Studie zur Wissenschaftsgeschichte der Germanistik*, Stuttgart: Metzler, 1976.

Rebhun, Paul

Casey, Paul F., *Paul Rebhun. A biographical study*, Stuttgart: F. Steiner Verlag, 1986.

Sachs, Hans

Bumke, Joachim, Cramer, Thomas, Kaiser, Gerhard, and Wenzel H. (eds.), *Hans Sachs – Studien zur frühbürgerlichen Literatur im 16. Jahrhundert*, Berne: Peter Lang, 1978.

Klein, Dorothea, *Bildung und Belehrung. Untersuchungen zum Dramenwerk des Hans Sachs*, Stuttgart: Heinz, 1988.

Könnecker, Barbara, *Hans Sachs*, Slg Metzler 94, Stuttgart: Metzler, 1971.

Scheffler, Johannes

Sammons, Jeffrey L., *Angelus Silesius*, New York: Twayne, 1967.

Schirmer, David

Harper, A.J., *David Schirmer. A poet of the German Baroque*, Stuttgart 1977.

Johannes Secundus

Endres, Clifford, *Joannes Secundus. The Latin love elegy in the Renaissance*, Hamden, CT.: Anchor Books, 1981.

Spee, Friedrich von

Battafarano, Italo Michele (ed.), *Friedrich von Spee. Dichter, Theologe und Bekämpfer der Hexenprozesse*, Trento: Luigi Reverdito Editore, 1988.

Stieler, Caspar

Aikin, Judith P., *Scaramutza in Germany. The dramatic works of Caspar Stieler*, Pennsylvania State University Press: Pennsylvania, 1989.

Weise, Christian

Barner, Wilfried, *Barockrhetorik. Untersuchungen zu ihren geschichtlichen Grundlagen*, Tübingen: Niemeyer, 1970.

Mannack, Eberhard, 'Geschichtsverständnis und Drama. Zu Weises *Masaniello*', *Daphnis*, 12 (1983), 247–266.

Zesen, Philipp von

Ingen, Ferdinand van, *Philipp von Zesen*, Slg Metzler 96, Stuttgart: Metzler, 1970.

4 The German Enlightenment (1720–1790)

Histories of literature

Becker-Cantarino, Barbara, *Der lange Weg zur Mündigkeit: Frau und Literatur (1500–1800)*, Stuttgart: Metzler, 1987.

Beutin, Wolfgang et al., *Deutsche Literaturgeschichte von den Anfängen bis zur Gegenwart*, Stuttgart: Metzler, 1979.

Bürger, Christa, Bürger, Peter, Schulte-Sasse, Jochen (eds.), *Aufklärung und literarische Öffentlichkeit*, Frankfurt a. M.: Suhrkamp, 1980.

Grimminger, Rolf (ed.), *Deutsche Aufklärung bis zur Französischen Revolution 1680–1789*, vol. 3 of *Hansers Sozialgeschichte der deutschen Literatur vom 16. Jahrhundert bis zur Gegenwart*, Munich: Deutscher Taschenbuch Verlag, 1980.

Hinck, Walter (ed.), *Europäische Aufklärung* I , vol. 11 of *Neues Handbuch der Literaturwissenschaft*, ed. by Klaus von See, Frankfurt a. M.: Akad. Verlagsgesellschaft Athenaion, 1974.

Kiesel, Helmuth, and Münch, Paul, *Gesellschaft und Literatur im 18. Jahrhundert: Voraussetzungen und Entstehung des literarischen Markts in Deutschland*, Munich: Beck, 1977.

Kohlschmidt, Werner, *Geschichte der deutschen Literatur vom Barock bis zur Klassik*, Stuttgart: Reclam, 1965.

Newald, Richard, *Ende der Aufklärung und Vorbereitung der Klassik*, 6th edn, vol. 6 part 1 of De Boor/Newald, *Geschichte der deutschen Literatur von den Anfängen bis zur Gegenwart*, Munich: Beck, 1973.

Genres

Becker-Cantarino, Barbara, 'Leben als Text: Briefe als Ausdrucks- und Verständigungsmittel in der Briefkultur und Literatur des 18. Jahrhunderts', in *Frauen Literatur Geschichte: Schreibende Frauen vom Mittelalter bis zur Gegenwart*, ed. by Hiltrud Gnüg and Renate Möhrmann, Stuttgart: Metzler, 1985, pp. 83–103.

Ebrecht, Angelika, Nörtemann, Regina, and Schwarz, Herta (eds.), *Brieftheorie des 18. Jahrhunderts: Texte, Kommentare, Essays*, Stuttgart: Metzler, 1990.

Gallas, Helga, and Heuser, Magdalene (eds.), *Untersuchungen zum Roman von Frauen um 1800*, Tübingen: Niemeyer, 1990.

Huyssen, Andreas, *Drama des Sturm und Drang: Kommentar zu einer Epoche*, Munich: Winkler, 1980.

Martens, Wolfgang, *Die Botschaft der Tugend: Die Aufklärung im Spiegel der deutschen moralischen Wochenschriften*, Stuttgart: Metzler, 1968.

Meise, Helga, *Die Unschuld und die Schrift: Deutsche Frauenromane im 18. Jahrhundert*, Berlin, Marburg: Guttandin und Hoppe, 1983.

Runge, Anita, and Steinbrügge, Lieselotte (eds.), *Die Frau im Dialog: Studien zu Theorie und Geschichte des Briefes*, Stuttgart: Metzler, 1991.

Schieth, Lydia, *Die Entwicklung des deutschen Frauenromans im ausgehenden 18. Jahrhundert: Ein Beitrag zur Gattungsgeschichte*, Berne: Peter Lang, 1987.

Sørensen, Bengt Algot, *Herrschaft und Zärtlichkeit: Der Patriarchalismus und das Drama im 18. Jahrhundert*, Munich: Beck, 1984.

Szondi, Peter, *Die Theorie des bürgerlichen Trauerspiels im 18. Jahrhundert: Der Kaufmann, der Hausvater und der Hofmeister*, ed. by Gert Mattenklott, Frankfurt a. M.: Suhrkamp, 1973.

Touaillon, Christine, *Der deutsche Frauenroman des 18. Jahrhunderts*, 1919, repr. Berne: Peter Lang, 1979.

Vosskamp, Wilhelm, 'Dialogische Vergegenwärtigung beim Schreiben und Lesen: Zur Poetik des Briefromans im 18. Jahrhundert', *Deutsche Vierteljahrsschrift* 45 (1971), 80–116.

Other selected aspects

Adler, Hans, 'Fundus Animae – der Grund der Seele: Zur Gnoseologie des Dunklen in der Aufklärung', *Deutsche Vierteljahrsschrift*, 62, 2 (Juni 1988), 197–220.

Bahr, Ehrhard (ed.), *Was ist Aufklärung? Thesen und Definitionen*, Stuttgart: Reclam, 1974.

Barnard, F. M., *Herder's social and political thought: from enlightenment to nationalism*, Oxford: Clarendon Press, 1965.

Batscha, Zwi, and Garber, Jörn (eds.), *Von der ständischen zur bürgerlichen Gesellschaft: Politisch-soziale Theorien im Deutschland der zweiten Hälfte des 18. Jahrhunderts*, Frankfurt a. M.: Suhrkamp, 1981.

Bayer, Oswald, 'Selbstverschuldete Vormundschaft: Hamanns Kontroverse mit Kant um *wahre* Aufklärung', in *Der Wirklichkeitsanspruch von Theologie und Religion: Die sozialethische Herausforderung, Ernst Steinbuch zum 70. Geburtstag*, ed. by Dieter Henke, Günther Kehrer and Gunda Schneider-Flume, Tübingen: J. C. B. Mohr, 1976, pp. 3–34.

Beaujean, Marion, 'Das Bild des Frauenzimmers im Roman des 18. Jahrhunderts', *Wolfenbüttler Studien zur Aufklärung*, III (1976), 9–28.

Bloch, Ruth H. 'Untangling the roots of modern sex roles: a survey of four centuries of change', *Signs* 4, 2 (Winter 1978), 237–52.

Blochmann, Elisabeth, *Das 'Frauenzimmer' und die 'Gelehrsamkeit': Eine Studie über die Anfänge des Mädchenschulwesens in Deutschland*, Heidelberg: Quelle und Meyer, 1966.

Bovenschen, Sylvia, *Die imaginierte Weiblichkeit: Exemplarische Untersuchungen zu kulturgeschichtlichen und literarischen Präsentationsformen des Weiblichen*, Frankfurt a. M.: Suhrkamp, 1979.

Boyle, Nicolas, *Goethe: the poet and the age*. Vol. 1: *The poetry of desire (1749–1790)*, Oxford: Clarendon Press, 1991.

Brummack, Jürgen, '"Herders Polemik gegen die '"Aufklärung"''', in *Aufklärung und Gegenaufklärung in der europäischen Philosophie und Politik von der Antike bis zur Gegenwart*, ed. by Jochen Schmidt, Darmstadt: Wiss. Buchgesellschaft, 1989, pp. 277–93.

Bürger, Christa, *Tradition und Subjektivität*, Frankfurt a. M.: Suhrkamp, 1980.

Clery, E.J., 'Women, publicity and the coffee-house myth', *Women: a cultural review* 2, 2 (Summer 1991), 168–77.

Conrady, Karl Otto, 'Über "Sturm und Drang"-Gedichte Goethes. Anmerkung zu ihrem historischen Ort und zu ihrer heutigen Bedeutung', in his *Literatur und Germanistik als Herausforderung: Skizzen und Stellungnahmen*, Frankfurt a. M.: Suhrkamp, 1974, pp. 125–53.

Conrady, Karl Otto (ed.), *Lyrik des 18. Jahrhunderts*, Reinbek: Rowohlt, 1968.

Dawson, Ruth, '"And this shield is called – self-reliance": emerging feminist consciousness in the late eighteenth century', in *German women in the eighteenth and nineteenth centuries: a social and literary history*, ed. by Ruth-Ellen B. Joeres and Mary Jo Maynes, Bloomington, IN: Indiana University Press, 1986, pp. 157–74.

Duden, Barbara, 'Das schöne Eigentum. Zur Herausbildung des bürgerlichen Frauenbildes an der Wende vom 18. zum 19. Jahrhundert', *Kursbuch* 47 (März 1977), 125–42.

Elias, Norbert, *The civilizing process: the history of manners*, trans. by Edmund Jephcott, New York: Urizen, 1978.

Power and civility: The civilizing process, volume II, trans. Edmund Jephcott, New York: Pantheon, 1982.

Flax, Jane, 'Postmodernism and gender relations in feminist theory', *Signs* 12, 4 (Summer 1987), esp. 624–5.

'Is Enlightenment emancipatory?', in Flax, *Disputed subjects: essays on psychoanalysis, politics and philosophy*, New York: London: Routledge, 1993, pp. 75–91.

Foucault, Michel, 'What is Enlightenment? (Was ist Aufklärung?)', in *The Foucault reader*, ed. by Paul Rabinow, New York: Pantheon, 1984, pp. 32–50.

Friedrichsmeyer, Sara, and Becker-Cantarino, Barbara (eds.), *The Enlightenment and its legacy: studies in German literature in honor of Helga Slessarev*, Bonn: Bouvier, 1991.

Friess, Ursula, *Buhlerin und Zauberin: Eine Untersuchung zur deutschen Literatur des 18. Jahrhunderts*, Munich: Fink, 1970.

Gaier, Ulrich, 'Gegenaufklärung im Namen des Logos: Hamann und Herder', in *Aufklärung und Gegenaufklärung in der europäischen Philosophie und Politik von der Antike bis zur Gegenwart*, ed. by Jochen Schmidt, Darmstadt: Wiss. Buchgesellschaft, 1989, pp. 261–76.

Gilman, Sander L. *Jewish self-hatred: anti-Semitism and the hidden language of Jews*, Baltimore, London: Johns Hopkins University Press, 1986 [on Moses Mendelssohn, esp. pp. 87–98].

'The image of the black in the aesthetic theory of the eighteenth century', in Gilman, *On blackness without blacks: essays on the image of the black in Germany*, Boston: Hall, 1982, pp. 19–34.

Goodman, Katherine R. and Waldstein, Edith (eds.), *In the shadow of Olympus: German women writers around 1800*, Albany, NY: State University of New York Press, 1992.

Gustafson, Susan E., 'Beautiful statues, beautiful men: the abjection of feminine imagination in Lessing's *Laokoon*', *PMLA* 108 5 (October 1993), 1083–97.

Habermas, Jürgen, *Strukturwandel der Öffentlichkeit: Untersuchungen zu einer*

Kategorie der bürgerlichen Gesellschaft, Darmstadt, Neuwied: Luchterhand, 1962.

Harpham, Geoffrey Galt, 'So . . . What *is* Enlightenment? An inquisition into modernity', *Critical Inquiry* 20 (Spring 1994), 524–56.

Hausen, Karin, 'Die Polarisierung der 'Geschlechtscharaktere' – Eine Spiegelung der Dissoziation von Erwerbs- und Familienleben', in *Sozialgeschichte der Familie in der Neuzeit Europas. Neue Forschungen*, ed. by Werner Conze, Stuttgart: Klett, 1976, pp. 363–93.

Herrmann, Ulrich, 'Erziehung und Schulunterricht für Mädchen im 18. Jahrhundert', *Wolfenbütteler Studien zur Aufklärung*, III (1976), 101–27.

Hinck, Walter (ed.), *Sturm und Drang: Ein literaturwissenschaftliches Studienbuch*, Königstein/Ts.: Athenäum, 1978.

Hinske, Norbert (ed.), *Ich handle mit Vernunft: Moses Mendelssohn und die europäische Aufklärung*, Hamburg: Felix Meiner, 1981.

Horkheimer, Max, and Adorno, Theodor W., *Dialectic of Enlightenment*, trans. by John Cumming, New York: Continuum, 1972.

Huyssen, Andreas, 'Das leidende Weib in der dramatischen Literatur von Empfindsamkeit und Sturm und Drang: Eine Studie zur bürgerlichen Emanzipation in Deutschland', *Monatshefte* 69, 2 (Summer 1977), 159–73.

Joeres, Ruth-Ellen B. '"That girl is an entirely different character!" Yes, but is she a feminist? Observations on Sophie von La Roche's *Geschichte des Fräuleins von Sternheim*', in *German women in the eighteenth and nineteenth centuries: a social and literary history*, ed. by Ruth-Ellen B. Joeres and Mary Jo Maynes, Bloomington, IN: Indiana University Press, 1986, pp. 137–56.

Martens, Wolfgang, 'Leserezepte fürs Frauenzimmer: Die Frauenzimmerbibliotheken der deutschen Moralischen Wochenschriften', *Archiv für Geschichte des Buchwesens*, XV (1975), columns 1143–1200.

Mattenklott, Gert, and Scherpe, Klaus R. (eds.), *Westberliner Projekt: Grundkurs 18. Jahrhundert: Die Funktion der Literatur bei der Formierung der bürgerlichen Klasse Deutschlands im 18. Jahrhundert (Materialien)*, Kronberg/Ts.: Scriptor, 1974.

Westberliner Projekt: Grundkurs 18. Jahrhundert (Analysen), Kronberg/Ts.: Scriptor, 1976.

Mauser, Wolfram, and Becker-Cantarino, Barbara (eds.), *Frauenfreundschaft – Männerfreundschaft: Literarische Diskurse im 18. Jahrhundert*, Tübingen: Niemeyer, 1991.

Mendus, Susan, 'Kant: "an honest but narrow-minded bourgeois"?', in *Women in Western political philosophy: Kant to Nietzsche*, ed. by Ellen Kennedy and Susan Mendus, New York: St Martin's Press, 1987, pp. 21–43.

Nörtemann, Regina, 'Die Begeisterung eines Poeten in den Briefen eines Frauenzimmers. Zur Korrespondenz der Caroline Christiane Lucius mit Christian Fürchtegott Gellert', in *Die Frau im Dialog: Studien zur Theorie und Geschichte des Briefes*, ed. by Anita Runge and Lieselotte Steinbrügge, Stuttgart: Metzler, 1991, pp. 13–32.

Prokop, Ulrike, 'Die Einsamkeit der Imagination. Geschlechterkonflikt und literarische Produktion um 1770', in *Deutsche Literatur von Frauen*, vol. 1, ed. by Gisela Brinker-Gabler, Munich: Beck, 1988, pp. 325–65.

Rasch, William, '*Mensch, Bürger, Weib*: Gender and the limitations of late 18th-century neohumanist discourse', *The German Quarterly* 66, 1 (Winter 1993), 20–33.

Rüsen, Jörn, Lämmert, Eberhard, and Glotz, Peter (eds.), *Die Zukunft der Aufklärung*, Frankfurt a. M.: Suhrkamp, 1988.

Sauder, Gerhard, 'Aufklärung des Vorurteils – Vorurteile der Aufklärung', *Deutsche Vierteljahrsschrift* LVII, 2 (1983), 259–77.

Schenda, Rudolf, *Volk ohne Buch: Studien zur Sozialgeschichte der populären Lesestoffe 1770–1910*, Munich: Deutscher Taschenbuch Verlag, 1970.

Schiebinger, Londa, 'Skeletons in the closet: the first illustrations of the female skeleton in eighteenth-century anatomy', in *The making of the modern body. Sexuality and society in the nineteenth century*, ed. by Catherine Gallagher, and Thomas Laqueur, Berkeley, CA: University of California Press, 1987, pp. 42–82.

Schott, Robin May, *Cognition and eros: a critique of the Kantian paradigm*, University Park, PA: Pennsylvania State University Press, 1993.

Stolpe, Heinz, *Aufklärung, Fortschritt, Humanität: Studien und Kritiken*, Berlin, Weimar: Aufbau, 1989.

Der Traum der Vernunft: Vom Elend der Aufklärung: eine Veranstaltungsreihe der Akademie der Künste, Berlin. 1. Folge, Darmstadt, Neuwied: Luchterhand, 1985.

Wessels, Hans-Friedrich (ed.), *Aufklärung: Ein literaturwissenschaftliches Studienbuch*, Königstein/Ts.: Athenäum, 1984.

5 Aesthetic humanism (1790–1830)

Literary and intellectual history

Behler, Ernst, *German Romantic literary theory*, Cambridge: Cambridge University Press, 1993.

Brinkmann, Richard (ed.), *Romantik in Deutschland. Ein interdisziplinäres Symposion*, Stuttgart: Metzler, 1978.

Conrady, Karl Otto (ed.), *Deutsche Literatur zur Zeit der Klassik*, Stuttgart: Reclam, 1977.

Eichner, Hans (ed.), '*Romantic' and its cognates. The European history of a word*, Manchester: Manchester University Press, 1972.

Frank, Manfred, *Einführung in die frühromantische Ästhetik. Vorlesungen*, Frankfurt a. M.: Suhrkamp, 1989.

Glaser, Horst Albert (ed.), *Deutsche Literatur. Eine Sozialgeschichte*, 10 vols., Reinbek: Rowohlt, 1980–1.

Koselleck, Reinhard, *Kritik und Krise. Eine Studie zur Pathogenese der bürgerlichen Welt*, 2nd edn, Frankfurt a. M.: Suhrkamp, 1976 [1st edn, Freiburg i. Br., Munich, 1959].

Mandelkow, Karl-Robert, *Goethe in Deutschland. Rezeptionsgeschichte eines Klassikers*, 2 vols., Munich: Beck, 1980–9.

Pikulik, Lothar, *Frühromantik. Epoche – Werk – Wirkung*, Munich: Beck, 1992.

Reed, T. J., *The classical centre. Goethe and Weimar 1775–1832*, London: Croom Helm, 1980.

Schulz, Gerhard, *Die deutsche Literatur zwischen Französischer Revolution und Restauration*, vol. 7, parts 1 and 2 of *Geschichte der deutschen Literatur von den Anfängen bis zur Gegenwart*, ed. by Helmut de Boor and Richard Newald, Munich: Beck, 1983–9.

Sengle, Friedrich, *Biedermeierzeit. Deutsche Literatur im Spannungsfeld zwischen Restauration und Revolution 1815–1848*, 3 vols., Stuttgart: Metzler, 1971–80.

Stopp, Elisabeth C., *German Romantics in context. Selected essays 1971–86*, collected by Peter Hutchinson, Roger Paulin, and Judith Purver, London: Bristol Classical Press, 1992.

Ueding, Gerd, *Klassik und Romantik. Deutsche Literatur im Zeitalter der Französischen Revolution 1789–1815*, vol. IV of *Hansers Sozialgeschichte der deutschen Literatur vom 16. Jahrhundert bis zur Gegenwart*, ed. by Rolf Grimminger, Munich: Hanser, 1988.

Wittkowski, Wolfgang (ed.), *Verlorene Klassik? Ein Symposium*, Tübingen: Niemeyer, 1985.

Revolution und Autonomie. Deutsche Autonomieästhetik im Zeitalter der Französischen Revolution, Tübingen: Niemeyer, 1990.

History and social history

Baker, Keith Michael, Furet, François, Lucas, Colin, and Ozouf, Mona (eds.), *The French Revolution and the creation of modern political culture*, 3 vols., Oxford: Pergamon Press, 1989.

Bruford, W. H., *Germany in the eighteenth century: the social background of the literary revival*, Cambridge: Cambridge University Press, 1935.

Ellwein, Thomas, *Die deutsche Universität. Vom Mittelalter bis zur Gegenwart*, Königstein/Ts.: Athenäum, 1985.

Habermas, Jürgen, *Strukturwandel der Öffentlichkeit. Untersuchungen zu einer Kategorie der bürgerlichen Gesellschaft*, Frankfurt a. M.: Suhrkamp, 1991 [1st edn 1962].

Hertz, Deborah, *Jewish high society in old regime Berlin*, New Haven, London: Yale University Press, 1988.

Sagarra, Eda, *A social history of Germany 1648–1914*, London: Methuen 1977.

Schnabel, Franz, *Deutsche Geschichte im 19. Jahrhundert*, 4 vols, Freiburg i. Br.: Herder, 1929–37.

Wehler, H.-U, *Deutsche Gesellschaftsgeschichte*, 4 vols., Munich: Beck, 1987f.

Themes

Aurnhammer, Achim, *Androgynie. Studien zu einem Motiv in der europäischen Literatur*, Cologne, Vienna: Böhlau, 1986.

Barkhoff, Jürgen, and Sagarra, Eda (eds.), *Anthropologie um 1800*, Munich: Iudicium, 1992.

Barkhoff, Jürgen, *Magnetische Fiktionen. Literarisierung des Mesmerismus in der Romantik*, Stuttgart, Weimar: Metzler, 1995.

Barner, Wilfried, Lämmert, Eberhard, and Oellers, Norbert (eds.), *Unser Commercium. Goethes und Schillers Literaturpolitik*, Stuttgart: Cotta, 1984.

Becker-Cantarino, Barbara, *Der lange Weg zur Mündigkeit. Frau und Literatur (1500–1800)*, Stuttgart: Metzler, 1987.

Behler, Ernst, *Unendliche Perfektibilität. Europäische Romantik und Französische Revolution*, Paderborn, Munich, Vienna: Schöningh, 1990.

Behler, Ernst, and Hörisch, Jochen (eds.), *Die Aktualität der Frühromantik*, Paderborn, Munich, Vienna: Schöningh, 1987.

Beiser, Frederick C., *Enlightenment, revolution, and Romanticism. The genesis of modern German political thought, 1790–1800*, Cambridge, MA, London: Harvard University Press, 1992.

Blamberger, Günter, *Das Geheimnis des Schöpferischen oder:* Ingenium est ineffabile? *Studien zur Literaturgeschichte der Kreativität zwischen Goethezeit und Moderne*, Stuttgart: Metzler, 1991.

Böhme, Hartmut, *Natur und Subjekt*, Frankfurt a. M.: Suhrkamp 1988.

Bovenschen, Silvia, *Die imaginierte Weiblichkeit. Exemplarische Untersuchungen zu kulturgeschichtlichen und literarischen Präsentationsformen des Weiblichen*, Frankfurt a. M.: Suhrkamp, 1979.

Brinkmann, Richard (ed.), *Deutsche Literatur und Französische Revolution. Sieben Studien*, Göttingen: Vandenhoeck and Ruprecht, 1974.

Bürger, Christa, *Leben Schreiben. Die Klassik, die Romantik und der Ort der Frauen*, Stuttgart: Metzler, 1990.

Cook, Roger F., *The demise of the author. Autonomy and the German writer, 1770–1848*, New York, Berne: Peter Lang, 1993.

Cunningham, Andrew, and Jardine, Nicholas (eds.): *Romanticism and the sciences,* Cambridge: Cambridge University Press, 1990.

Davies, Martin L., *Identity or history? Marcus Herz and the end of Enlightenment*, Detroit: Wayne State Universtiy Press, 1995.

Engelsing, Rolf, *Der Bürger als Leser. Lesergeschichte in Deutschland 1500–1800*, Stuttgart: Metzler, 1974.

Frank, Manfred, *Der kommende Gott. Vorlesungen über die neue Mythologie*, Frankfurt a. M.: Suhrkamp, 1982.

Gallas, Helga, and Heuser, Magdalene (eds.), *Untersuchungen zum Roman von Frauen um 1800*, Tübingen: Niemeyer, 1990.

Haferkorn, Hans Jürgen, 'Der freie Schriftsteller. Eine literarisch-soziologische Studie über seine Entstehung und Lage in Deutschland zwischen 1750 und 1800', *Archiv für die Geschichte des Buchwesens* 5 (1964), 523–712.

Hertz, Deborah, *The literary salon in Berlin 1790–1806. The social history of an intellectual institution*, Minneapolis: University of Minnesota Press, 1979.

Izenberg, Gerald N., *Impossible individuality. Romanticism, revolution, and the origins of modern selfhood*, Princeton, NJ: Princeton University Press, 1992.

Kord, Susanne, *Ein Blick hinter die Kulissen. Deutschsprachige Dramatikerinnen im 18. und 19. Jahrhundert*, Stuttgart: Metzler, 1992.

Martino, Alberto, *Die deutsche Leihbibliothek. Geschichte einer literarischen Institution*, Wiesbaden: Harrassowitz, 1990.

Müller, Klaus-Detlef, *Autobiographie und Roman. Studien zur literarischen Autobiographie der Goethezeit*, Tübingen: Niemeyer, 1976.

Och, Gunnar, 'Alte Märchen von der Grausamkeit der Juden. Zur Rezeption judenfeindlicher Blutschuld-Mythen durch die Romantiker', *Aurora* 51 (1991), 81–94.

Imago judaica. Juden und Judentum im Spiegel der deutschen Literatur 1750–1812, Würzburg: Königshausen and Neumann, 1995.

Paulsen, Wolfgang, *Die Frau als Heldin und Autorin. Neue kritische Ansätze zur deutschen Literatur*, Berne, Munich: Francke, 1979.

Pfotenhauer, Helmut, *Literarische Anthropologie. Selbstbiographien und ihre Geschichte – am Leitfaden des Leibes*, Stuttgart: Metzler, 1987.

Polheim, Karl Konrad, *Die Arabeske. Ansichten und Ideen aus Friedrich Schlegels Poetik*, Munich, Paderborn, Vienna: Schöningh, 1966.

Reuchlein, Georg, *Bürgerliche Gesellschaft, Psychiatrie und Literatur. Zur Entwicklung der Wahnsinnsthematik in der deutschen Literatur des späten 18. und frühen 19. Jahrhunderts*, Munich: Fink, 1986.

Saul, Nicholas (ed.), *Die deutsche literarische Romantik und die Wissenschaften*, Munich: Iudicium, 1991.

Schenda, Rudolf, *Volk ohne Buch. Studien zur Sozialgeschichte der populären Lesestoffe 1770–1910*, Frankfurt a. M.: Klostermann, 1970.

Schmidt, Jochen, *Die Geschichte des Genie-Gedankens in der deutschen Literatur, Philosophie und Politik 1750–1945*, 2 vols., Darmstadt: Wiss. Buchgesellschaft, 1985.

Schöne, Albrecht, *Säkularisation als sprachbildende Kraft. Studien zur Dichtung deutscher Pfarrerssöhne*, second edition, Göttingen: Vandenhoeck and Ruprecht, 1968 [first edn, 1958].

Schott, Heinz (ed.), *Franz Anton Mesmer und die Geschichte des Mesmerismus*, Stuttgart: Steiner, 1985.

Stephan, Inge, *Literarischer Jakobinismus in Deutschland (1789–1806)*, Stuttgart: Metzler, 1976.

Strohschneider-Kohrs, Ingrid, *Die romantische Ironie in Theorie und Gestaltung*, 1960; 2nd edn, Tübingen: Niemeyer, 1977.

Thalmann, Marianne, *Romantiker entdecken die Stadt*, Munich: Nymphenburger, 1965.

Ward, Albert, *Book-production, fiction and the German reading public 1740–1800*, Oxford: Clarendon Press, 1974.

Weber, Ernst, *Lyrik der Befreiungskriege (1812–1815). Gesellschaftspoetische Meinungs- und Willensbildung durch Literatur*, Stuttgart: Metzler, 1991.

Ziolkowski, Theodor, *German Romanticism and its institutions*, Princeton, NJ: Princeton University Press, 1990.

Genres

Aust, Hugo, *Novelle*, Slg Metzler 256, Stuttgart: Metzler, 1990.

Behler, Ernst, *Die Zeitschriften der Brüder Schlegel. Ein Beitrag zur Geschichte der deutschen Romantik*, Darmstadt: Wiss. Buchgesellschaft, 1983.

Böschenstein-Schäfer, Renate, *Idylle*, Slg Metzler 63, Stuttgart: Metzler, 1967.

Bohrer, Karl-Heinz, *Der romantische Brief. Die Entstehung ästhetischer Subjektivität*, Munich: Suhrkamp, 1987.

Ellis, John M., *Narration in the German Novelle. Theory and interpretation*, Cambridge: Cambridge University Press, 1974.

Hadley, Michael, *The German novel in 1790. A descriptive account and critical bibliography*, Berne: Peter Lang, 1973.

Hinck, Walter, *Die deutsche Ballade von Bürger bis Brecht*, Göttingen: Vandenhoeck and Ruprecht, 1978.

Jacobs, Jürgen, *Wilhelm Meister und seine Brüder. Untersuchungen zum deutschen Bildungsroman*, Munich: Fink, 1972.

Killy, Walter, *Wandlungen des lyrischen Bildes*, Göttingen: Vandenhoeck and Ruprecht, 1956.

Kindermann, Heinz, *Theatergeschichte der Goethezeit*, Vienna: H. Bauer, 1949.

Lamport, Frank J., *German classical drama. Theatre, humanity and nation 1750–1850*, Cambridge: Cambridge University Press, 1990.

Mahoney, David F., *Der Roman der Goethezeit*, Stuttgart: Metzler, 1988.

Neumann, Gerhard, *Ideenparadiese. Untersuchungen zur Aphoristik von Lichtenberg, Novalis, Friedrich Schlegel und Goethe*, Munich: Fink, 1976.

Ostermann, Eberhard, *Das Fragment. Geschichte einer ästhetischen Idee*, Munich: Fink, 1991.

Paulin, Roger, *The brief compass. The nineteenth-century German Novelle*. Oxford: Clarendon Press, 1985.

Rohner, Ludwig, *Kalendergeschichte und Kalender*, Wiesbaden: Athenäum, 1978.

Schieth, Lydia, *Die Entwicklung des deutschen Frauenromans im ausgehenden 18. Jahrhundert. Ein Beitrag zur Gattungsgeschichte*, Frankfurt a. M., Berne, New York, Paris: Peter Lang 1987.

Segebrecht, Wulf, *Das Gelegenheitsgedicht. Ein Beitrag zur Geschichte und Poetik der deutschen Lyrik*, Stuttgart: Metzler, 1977.

Sengle, Friedrich, *Das historische Drama in Deutschland. Geschichte eines Mythos*, 1952; 3rd edn, Darmstadt: Wiss. Buchgesellschaft, 1974.

Suppan, Wolfgang, *Volkslied*, Slg Metzler 52, Stuttgart: Metzler, 1978.

Swales, Martin, *The German Novelle*. Princeton, NJ: Princeton University Press, 1977.

Tismar, Jens, *Kunstmärchen*, Slg Metzler 155, Stuttgart: Metzler, 1977.

Wührl, P.-W., *Das deutsche Kunstmärchen. Geschichte, Botschaft und Erzählstrukturen*, Heidelberg: Quelle and Meyer, 1984.

Yates, W. E., *Tradition in the German sonnet*, Berne, Frankfurt a. M.: Peter Lang, 1981.

Individual authors

Arnim, Achim von

Knaack, Jürgen, *Achim von Arnim, nicht nur Poet. Die politischen Anschauungen Arnims in ihrer Entwicklung. Mit ungedruckten Texten und einem Verzeichnis sämtlicher Briefe*, Darmstadt: Thesen Verlag, 1976.

Wingertszahn, Christof, *Ambiguität und Ambivalenz im erzählerischen Werk Achim von Arnims. Mit einem Anhang unbekannter Texte aus Arnims Nachlaß*, Frankfurt a. M.: R. G. Fischer, 1990.

Arnim, Bettina von

Bäumer, Konstanze, *'Bettine, Psyche, Mignon'. Bettina von Arnim und Goethe*, Stuttgart: Verlag Hans Dieter Heinz/Akademischer Verlag, 1986.

Bonaventura

Sammons, Jeffrey L., *The 'Nachtwachen von Bonaventura'. A structural interpretation*, London, The Hague, Paris: Mouton, 1965

Brentano, Clemens

Brandstetter, Gabriele, *Erotik und Religiosität. Eine Studie zur Lyrik Clemens Brentanos*, Munich: Fink, 1986.

Fetzer, John, *Romantic Orpheus. Profiles of Clemens Brentano*, Berkeley: University of California Press, 1974.

Frühwald, Wolfgang, *Das Spätwerk Clemens Brentanos (1815–1842). Romantik im Zeitalter Metternich'scher Restauration*, Tübingen: Niemeyer, 1977.

Kastinger-Riley, Helene M., *Clemens Brentano*, Stuttgart: Metzler, 1985.

Eichendorff, Joseph von

Bormann, Alexander von, *Natura loquitur. Naturpoesie und emblematische Formel bei Joseph von Eichendorff*, Tübingen: Niemeyer, 1968.

Pott, Hans-Georg (ed.), *Eichendorff und die Spätromantik*, Paderborn: Schöningh, 1985.

Fichte, Johann Gottlieb

Rohs, Peter, *Johann Gottlieb Fichte*, Munich: Beck, 1991.

Goethe, Johann Wolfgang von

Bahr, Erhard, *Die Ironie im Spätwerk Goethes: 'diese sehr ernsten Scherze'. Studien zum 'West-östlichen Divan', zu den 'Wanderjahren' und zu 'Faust II'*, Berlin: Erich Schmidt, 1972.

Boyle, Nicholas, *Goethe. The poet and the age*, Vol. I: *The poetry of desire (1749–1790)*, Oxford: Clarendon Press, 1991.

Chiarini, Paolo (ed.), *Bausteine zu einem neuen Goethe*, Frankfurt a. M.: Athenäum, 1987.

Reed, T.J., *Goethe*, Oxford: Clarendon Press, 1984.

Schöne, Albrecht, *Goethes Farbentheologie*, Munich: Beck, 1987.

Wittkowski, Wolfgang (ed.), *Goethe im Kontext. Kunst und Humanität, Naturwissenschaft und Politik von der Aufkärung bis zur Restauration. Ein Symposium*, Tübingen: Niemeyer, 1984.

Grimm, Jacob and Wilhelm

Kamenetsky, Christa, *The Brothers Grimm and their critics. Folktales and the quest for meaning*, Athens: Ohio University Press, 1992.

Wyss, Ulrich, *Die wilde Philologie. Jacob Grimm und der Historismus*, Munich: Beck, 1979.

Günderrode, Karoline von

Goozé, Marjanne E. 'The seduction of Don Juan: Karoline von Günderrode's romantic rendering of a classic story', in *The Enlightenment and its legacy. Studies in German literature in honor of Helga Slessarev*, ed. by Sara Friedrichsmeyer and Barbara Becker-Cantarino, Bonn: Bouvier, 1992, pp. 117–29.

Hölderlin, Friedrich

Constantine, David, *Friedrich Hölderlin*, Munich: Beck, 1992.

Doering, Sabine, *Aber was ist diß? Form und Funktion der Frage in Hölderlins dichterischem Werk*, Göttingen: Vandenhoeck and Ruprecht, 1992.

Ryan, Lawrence, *Hölderlins 'Hyperion'. Exzentrische Bahn und Dichterberuf*, Stuttgart: Metzler, 1965.

Hoffmann, E. T. A.

Auhuber, Friedhelm, *'In einem fernen dunklen Spiegel'. E. T. A. Hoffmanns Poetisierung der Medizin*, Opladen: Westdeutscher Verlag, 1986.

Feldges, Brigitte, and Stadler, Ulrich, *E. T. A. Hoffmann. Epoche – Werk – Wirkung*, Munich: Beck, 1986.

Matt, Peter von, *Die Augen der Automaten. E. T. A. Hoffmanns Imaginationslehre als Prinzip seiner Erzählkunst*, Tübingen: Niemeyer, 1971.

Jean Paul

Harich, Wolfgang, *Jean Pauls Revolutionsdichtung. Versuch einer neuen Deutung seiner heroischen Romane*, Reinbek: Rowohlt, 1974.

Wiethölter, Waltraud, *Witzige Illuminationen: Studien zur Ästhetik Jean Pauls*, Tübingen: Niemeyer, 1979.

Kleist, Heinrich von

Fischer, Bernd, *Ironische Metaphysik. Die Erzählungen Heinrich von Kleists*, Munich: Fink, 1988.

Schmidt, Jochen, *Heinrich von Kleist. Studien zu seiner poetischen Verfahrensweise*, Tübingen: Niemeyer, 1974.

Wellbery, David E. (ed.), *Positionen der Literaturwissenschaft. Acht Modellanalysen am Beispiel von Kleists 'Das Erdbeben in Chili'*, Munich: Beck, 1985.

Kotzebue, August von

Maurer, Doris, *August von Kotzebue. Ursachen seines Erfolges. Konstante Elemente der unterhaltenden Dramatik*, Bonn: Bouvier, 1979.

Lessing, Gotthold Ephraim

Boyle, Nicholas, 'Lessing, biblical criticism and the origins of German classical culture', *GLL* N.S. 34 (1981), 196–213.

Levin Varnhagen, Rachel

Hahn, Barbara, and Isselstein, Ursula (eds.), *Rahel Levin Varnhagen. Die Wiederentdeckung einer Schriftstellerin*, Göttingen: Vandenhoeck and Ruprecht, 1987.

Novalis

Kurzke, Hermann, *Romantik und Konservatismus. Das 'politische' Werk Friedrich von Hardenbergs (Novalis) im Horizont seiner Wirkungsgeschichte*, Munich: Fink, 1983.

Mähl, Hans-Joachim, *Die Idee des goldenen Zeitalters im Werk des Novalis. Studien zur Wesensbestimmung der frühromantischen Utopie und zu ihren ideengeschichtlichen Voraussetzungen*, Heidelberg: Winter, 1965.

Schanze, Helmut, *Aufklärung und Romantik. Untersuchungen zu Friedrich Schlegel und Novalis*, 1966; 2nd edn, Nuremberg: H. Carl, 1976.

Schiller, Friedrich

Aurnhammer, Achim, Manger, Klaus, and Strack, Friedrich (eds.), *Schiller und die höfische Welt*, Tübingen: Niemeyer, 1990.

Riedel, Wolfgang, *Der Spaziergang. Ästhetik der Landschaft und Geschichtsphilosophie der Natur bei Schiller*, Würzburg: Königshausen and Neumann, 1989.

Sharpe, Lesley, *Friedrich Schiller. Poetry and politics*, Cambridge: Cambridge University Press, 1991.

Wittkowski, Wolfgang (ed.), *Friedrich Schiller. Kunst, Humanität und Politik in der späten Aufklärung*, Tübingen: Niemeyer, 1982.

Schlegel, August Wilhelm

Schenk-Lenzen, Ulrike, *Das ungleiche Verhältnis von Kunst und Kritik. Zur Literaturkritik August Wilhelm Schlegels*, Würzburg: Königshausen and Neumann, 1991.

Schlegel, Dorothea

Schmitz, Walter, '"...nur eine Skizze, aber durchaus in einem großen Stil": Dorothea Schlegel', in Gerhard P. Knapp (ed.), *Autoren damals und heute. Literaturgeschichtliche Beispiele veränderter Wirkungshorizonte*, Amsterdam: Rodopi, 1991, pp. 91–131.

Schlegel, Friedrich

Hudgins, Esther, *Nicht-epische Strukturen des romantischen Romans*, The Hague, Paris: Mouton, 1975.

Zovko, Jure , *Verstehen und Nichtverstehen bei Friedrich Schlegel. Zur Entstehung und Bedeutung seiner hermeneutischen Kritik*, Stuttgart, Bad Cannstatt: Frommann-Holzboog, 1990.

Schleiermacher

Nowak, Kurt, *Schleiermacher und die Frühromantik. Eine literaturgeschichtliche Studie zum romantischen Religionsverständnis und Menschenbild am Ende des 18. Jahrhunderts in Deutschland*, Göttingen: Vandenhoeck and Ruprecht, 1986.

Tieck, Ludwig

Frank, Manfred, *Das Problem 'Zeit' in der deutschen Romantik. Zeitbewußtsein und Bewußtsein von Zeitlichkeit in der frühromantischen Philosophie und in Tiecks Dichtung*, 2nd edn, Paderborn: Schöningh, 1990.

Paulin, Roger, *Ludwig Tieck. A literary biography*, Oxford: Oxford University Press, 1985.

Wackenroder, Wilhelm Heinrich

Kemper, Dirk, *Sprache der Dichtung. Wilhelm Heinrich Wackenroder im Kontext der Spätaufklärung*, Stuttgart, Weimar: Metzler, 1993.

Werner, Zacharias

Kozielek, Gerard, *Das dramatische Werk Zacharias Werners*. Wrocław: Zakład Narodowy im. Ossolińskich, 1967.

6 Revolution, resignation, realism (1830–1890)

General works and histories of literature

Anderle, Martin, *Deutsche Lyrik des 19. Jahrhunderts. Ihre Bildlichkeit: Metapher – Symbol – Evokation*, Bonn: Bouvier, 1979.

Finney, Gail, *The counterfeit idyll: the garden ideal and social reality in nineteenth-century fiction*, Tübingen: Niemeyer, 1984.

Hohendahl, Peter Uwe, *Literarische Kultur im Zeitalter des Liberalismus 1830–1870*, Munich: Beck, 1985.

McInnes, Edward, *Das deutsche Drama des 19. Jahrhunderts*, Berlin: Schmidt, 1983.

Ward, Mark (ed.), *From Vormärz to fin de siècle: essays in nineteenth-century Austrian literature*, Blairgowrie, Scotland: Lochee publications, 1986.

Wiese, Benno von (ed.), *Deutsche Dichter des 19. Jahrhunderts: ihr Leben und Werk*, 2nd edn, Berlin: Schmidt, 1979.

Novel, novella and Bildungsroman

Aust, Hugo, *Novelle*, Slg Metzler 256, Stuttgart: Metzler, 1990.

Berman, Russell A., *The rise of the modern German novel: crisis and charisma*, Cambridge, MA: Harvard University Press, 1986.

Bruford, Walter H., *The German tradition of self-cultivation: 'Bildung' from Humboldt to Thomas Mann*, Cambridge: Cambridge University Press, 1975.

Clements, Robert J., and Gibaldi, Joseph, *Anatomy of the novella: the European tale collection from Boccaccio and Chaucer to Cervantes*, New York: New York University Press, 1977.

Jacobs, Jürgen, and Krause, Markus, *Der deutsche Bildungsroman: Gattungsgeschichte vom 18. bis zum 20. Jahrhundert*, Munich: Beck, 1989.

Mayer, Gerhart, *Der deutsche Bildungsroman: von der Aufklärung bis zur Gegenwart*, Stuttgart: Metzler, 1992.

Paine, J. H. E., *Theory and criticism of the Novelle*, Bonn: Bouvier, 1979.

Paulin, Roger, *The brief compass: the nineteenth-century German Novelle*, Oxford: Clarendon Press, 1985.

Pötters, Wilhelm, *Begriff und Struktur der Novelle: linguistische Betrachtungen zu Boccaccios 'Falken'*, Tübingen: Niemeyer, 1991.

Polheim, Karl K. (ed.), *Theorie und Kritik der deutschen Novelle von Wieland bis Musil*, Tübingen: Niemeyer, 1970.

Selbmann, Rolf, *Der deutsche Bildungsroman*, Slg Metzler 214, 2nd edn, Stuttgart: Metzler, 1994.

Springer, Mary Doyle, *Forms of the modern novella*, Chicago: University of Chicago Press, 1975.

Swales, Martin, *The German Novelle*, Princeton, NJ: Princeton University Press, 1977.

The German Bildungsroman from Wieland to Hesse, Princeton, NJ: Princeton University Press, 1978.

Wiese, Benno von, *Novelle*, 6th edn, Slg Metzler 27, Stuttgart: Metzler, 1975.

Women writers

Belemann, Claudia, and Niethammer, Ortrun (eds.), *Ein Gitter aus Musik und Sprache: feministische Analysen zu Annette von Droste-Hülshoff*, Paderborn: Schöningh, 1993.

Bramkamp, Agatha C., *Marie von Ebner-Eschenbach: the author, her time, and her critics*, Bonn: Bouvier, 1990.

Cocalis, Susan (ed.), *The defiant muse: German feminist poems from the middle ages to the present*, New York: The Feminist Press/City University of New York, 1986.

Fout, John C. (ed.), *German women in the nineteenth century: a social history*, New York: Holmes and Meier, 1984.

Fox, Thomas C., 'Louise von François: A feminist reintroduction', *Women in German Yearbook*, III, ed. by Marianne Burkhard and Edith Waldstein, Lanham, MD: University Press of America, 1986.

Gaier, Ulrich, *Annette und das Geld: die Droste, die Schriftstellerei, das Fürstenhäuschen*, Konstanz: Stadler, 1993.

Herminghouse, Patricia, 'Seeing double: Ida Hahn-Hahn (1805–1880) and her challenge to feminist criticism', in *Out of line/ 'Ausgefallen'* (see below), pp. 255–78.

Klausmann, Christina, 'Louise Dittmar (1807–1884): Ergebnisse einer biographischen Spurensuche', in *Out of line/'Ausgefallen'* (see below), pp. 17–39.

Joeres, Ruth-Ellen, and Burkhard, Marianne (eds.), *Out of line/'Ausgefallen': the paradox of marginality in the writings of nineteenth-century German women*, Amsterdam: Rodopi, 1989.

Lipp, Carola, and Bechtold-Comforty, Beate (eds.), *Schimpfende Weiber and patriotische Jungfrauen: Frauen im Vormärz und in der Revolution von 1848/49*, Moos: Elster, 1986.

Möhrmann, Renate, *Die andere Frau: Emanzipationsansätze deutscher Schriftstellerinnen im Vorfeld der Achtundvierziger Revolution*, Stuttgart: Metzler, 1977.

Möhrmann, Renate (ed.) *Frauenemanzipation im deutschen Vormärz: Texte und Dokumente*, Stuttgart: Reclam, 1978.

Rose, Ferrel, *The guises of comedy: Marie von Ebner-Eschenbach's female artists*, Columbia: Camden House, 1994.

Steiner, Carl, *Of reason and love: the life and works of Marie von Ebner-Eschenbach (1830–1916)*, Riverside, CA: Ariadne Press, 1994.

Worley, Linda Kraus, 'The "odd" woman as heroine in the fiction of Louise von François', *Women in German Yearbook*, IV, ed. by Marianne Burkhard and Jeanette Clausen, Lanham, MD: University Press of America, 1988, 155–65.

'Louise von François (1817–1893): Scripting a life', in *Out of Line/'Ausgefallen'*, see above pp. 161–86.

Junges Deutschland and Vormärz

Baur, Uwe, *Dorfgeschichte: zur Entstehung und gesellschaftlichen Funktion einer literarischen Gattung im Vormärz*, Munich: Fink, 1978.

Cortesi, Antonio, *Die Logik von Zerstörung und Größenphantasie in den Dramen Christian Dietrich Grabbes*, Berne: Peter Lang, 1986.

Dedner, Burghard, and Hofstaetter, Ulla (eds.), *Romantik im Vormärz*, Marburg: Hitzeroth, 1992.

Freund, Winfried (ed.), *Grabbes Gegenentwürfe. Neue Deutungen seiner Dramen: zum 150. Todesjahr Christian Dietrich Grabbes*, Munich: Fink, 1986.

Grimm, Reinhold, *Love, lust and rebellion: new approaches to Georg Büchner*, Madison: University of Wisconsin Press, 1985.

Hauschild, Jan-Christoph and Vahl, Heidemarie (eds.), *Verboten! Das junge Deutschland 1835: Literatur und Zensur im Vormärz*, Düsseldorf: Droste, 1985.

Hermand, Jost (ed.), *Das junge Deutschland. Texte und Dokumente*, Stuttgart: Reclam, 1966.

Der deutsche Vormärz: Texte und Dokumente, Stuttgart: Reclam, 1967.

Hinck, Walter, *Von Heine zu Brecht: Lyrik im Geschichtsprozeß*, Frankfurt a. M.: Suhrkamp, 1978.

Hosfeld, Rolf, *Die Welt als Füllhorn. Heine: das neunzehnte Jahrhundert zwischen Romantik und Moderne*, Berlin: Oberbaum, 1984.

Kaiser, Herbert, *Studien zum deutschen Roman nach 1848: Karl Gutzkow: Die Ritter vom Geiste, Gustav Freytag: Soll und Haben, Adalbert Stifter: Der Nachsommer*, Duisburg: Braun, 1977.

May, Erich J., *Wiener Volkskomödie und Vormärz*, Berlin: Henschel, 1975.

Reddick, John, *Georg Büchner, the shattered whole*, Oxford: Clarendon Press, 1995.

Richards, David G., *Georg Büchner and the birth of modern drama*, Albany: State University of New York Press, 1977.

Sammons, Jeffrey L., *Six essays on the young German novel*, 2nd edn, Chapel Hill: University of North Carolina Press, 1975.

Seidler, Herbert, *Österreichischer Vormärz und Goethezeit: Geschichte einer literarischen Auseinandersetzung*, Vienna: Verlag der österreichischen Akademie der Wissenschaften, 1982.

Vaßen, Florian (ed.), *Restauration. Vormärz und 48er Revolution*, Stuttgart: Reclam, 1975.

Wabnegger, Erwin, *Literaturskandal: Studien zur Reaktion des öffentlichen Systems auf Karl Gutzkows Roman 'Wally, die Zweiflerin' (1835–1848)*, Würzburg: Königshausen and Neumann, 1987.

Witte, Bernd (ed.), *Vormärz: Biedermeier, Junges Deutschland, Demokraten 1815–1848*, Reinbek: Rowohlt, 1980.

Biedermeier

Bernd, Clifford (ed.), *Der arme Spielmann: new directions in criticism*, Columbia, SC: Camden House, 1988.

Budde, Bernhard, and Schmidt, Ulrich (eds.), *Gerettete Ordnung: Grillparzers Dramen*, New York: Peter Lang, 1987.

Fehr, Karl, *Jeremias Gotthelf. Poet und Prophet, Erzähler und Erzieher: zu Sprache, dichterischer Kunst und Gehalt seiner Schriften*, Berne: Francke, 1986.

Fliegner, Susanne, *Der Dichter und die Dilettanten: Eduard Mörike und die bürgerliche Geselligkeitskultur des 19. Jahrhunderts*, Stuttgart: Metzler 1991.

Godwin-Jones, Robert, *Narrative strategies in the novels of Jeremias Gotthelf*, Frankfurt a. M., Berne, New York: Peter Lang, 1986.

Graevenitz, Gerhard von, *Eduard Mörike, die Kunst der Sünde: zur Geschichte des literarischen Individuums*, Tübingen: Niemeyer, 1978.

Hannemann, Bruno, *Johann Nestroy, nihilistisches Welttheater und verflixter Kerl: zum Ende der Wiener Kömodie*, Bonn: Bouvier, 1977.

Hein, Jürgen, *Das Wiener Volkstheater: Raimund und Nestroy*, Darmstadt: Wiss. Buchgesellschaft, 1978.

Holst, Günther, *Das Bild des Menschen in den Romanen Karl Immermanns*, Meisenheim am Glan: Hain, 1976.

Kamann, Matthias, *Epigonalität als ästhetisches Vermögen: Untersuchungen zu Texten Grabbes und Immermanns, Platens und Raabes, zur Literaturkritik des 19. Jahrhunderts und zum Werk Adalbert Stifters*, Stuttgart: M and P, 1994.

Keller, Thomas, *Die Schrift in Stifters 'Nachsommer': Buchstäblichkeit und Bildlichkeit des Romantextes*, Cologne: Böhlau, 1982.

Lorenz, Dagmar, *Franz Grillparzer: Dichter des sozialen Konflikts*, Vienna: Böhlau, 1986.

Nemoianu, Virgil, *The taming of romanticism: European Literature and the age of Biedermeier*, Cambridge, MA: Harvard University Press, 1984.

Ottomeyer, Hans and Laufer, Ulrike (eds.), *Biedermeiers Glück und Ende: die gestörte Idylle 1815–48*, Munich: Hugendubel, 1987.

Schmidt-Bergmann, Hansgeorg, *Ästhetizismus und Negativität: Studien zum Werk Nikolaus Lenaus*, Heidelberg: Winter, 1984.

Sengle, Friedrich, *Biedermeierzeit: Deutsche Literatur im Spannungsfeld zwischen Restauration und Revolution, 1815–1848*, 3 vols., Stuttgart: Metzler, 1971–80.

Swales, Martin, and Swales, Erika, *Adalbert Stifter: a critical study*, Cambridge, Cambridge University Press, 1984.

Yates, W. E., and McKenzie, John R. P. (eds.), *Viennese popular theatre: a symposium*, Exeter: University of Exeter Press, 1985.

Realism

Artiss, David, *Theodor Storm: studies in ambivalence, symbol and myth in his narrative fiction*, Amsterdam: Benjamins, 1978.

Auerbach, Erich, *Mimesis: the representation of reality in western literature*, trans. by Willard R. Trask, Princeton, NJ: Princeton University Press, 1953.

Aust, Hugo, *Literatur des Realismus*, 2nd edn, Slg Metzler 157, Stuttgart: Metzler, 1981.

Bance, Alan, *Theodor Fontane, the major novels*, Cambridge: Cambridge University Press, 1982.

Bernd, Clifford A., *German poetic realism*, Boston: Twayne, 1981.

Brinkmann, Richard, *Wirklichkeit und Illusion: Studien über Gehalt und Grenzen des Begriffs Realismus für die erzählende Dichtung des neunzehnten Jahrhunderts*, 3rd edn, Tübingen: Niemeyer, 1977.

Brown, Marshall, 'The logic of realism: a Hegelian approach', *PMLA* 96 (1981), 224–41.

Bucher, Max, et al. (eds.), *Realismus und Gründerzeit: Manifeste und Dokumente zur deutschen Literatur 1848–1880*, 2 vols., Stuttgart: Metzler, 1975–81.

Cowen, Roy, *Der poetische Realismus: Kommentar zu einer Epoche*, Munich: Winkler, 1985.

Denkler, Horst (ed.), *Romane und Erzählungen des bürgerlichen Realismus: neue Interpretationen*, Stuttgart: Reclam, 1980.

Evans, Tamara S., *Formen der Ironie in Conrad Ferdinand Meyers Novellen*, Berne: Francke, 1980.

Fenner, Birgit, *Friedrich Hebbel zwischen Hegel und Freud*, Stuttgart: Klett-Cotta, 1979.

Fetzer, John F., Hoermann, Roland and McConnell, Winder (eds.), *In search of the poetic real: essays in honor of Clifford Albrecht Bernd on the occasion of his sixtieth birthday*, Stuttgart: Heinz, 1989.

Finney, Gail, 'Poetic realism: Theodor Storm, Gottfried Keller, Conrad Ferdinand Meyer', in *European writers: the romantic century*, ed. by Jacques Barzun, vol.6, New York: Schribner's, 1985, 913–42.

Furst, Lilian R. (ed.), *Realism*, London: Longman, 1992.

Furst, Lilian, *All is true: the claims and strategies of realist fiction*, Durham: Duke University Press, 1995.

Garland, Henry B., *The Berlin novels of Theodor Fontane*, New York: Oxford University Press, 1980.

Glaser, Horst A. (ed.), *Vom Nachmärz zur Gründerzeit: Realismus 1848–1880*, Reinbek: Rowohlt, 1982.

Hart, Gail, *Readers and their fictions in the novels and novellas of Gottfried Keller*, Chapel Hill: University of North Carolina Press, 1989.

Hermand, Jost, and Grimm, Reinhold (eds.), *Realismustheorien in Literatur, Malerei, Musik und Politik*, Stuttgart: Kohlhammer, 1975.

Holub, Robert C., *Reflections of realism: paradox, norm, and ideology in nineteenth-century German prose*, Detroit: Wayne State University Press, 1991.

Huyssen, Andreas (ed.), *Bürgerlicher Realismus*, Stuttgart: Reclam, 1988.

Jackson, David A., *Theodor Storm: the life and works of a democratic humanitarian*, New York: St Martin's Press, 1992.

Joeres, Ruth-Ellen B., 'Introduction', *Wally the Skeptic*, trans. by Joeres, Berne: Herbert Lang, 1974.

Kaiser, Nancy A., *Social integration and narrative structure: pattern of realism in Auerbach, Freytag, Fontane, and Raabe*, New York: Peter Lang, 1986.

Kittler, Friedrich, *Der Traum und die Rede: eine Analyse der Kommunikationssituation Conrad Ferdinand Meyers*, Berne: Francke 1977.

Kohl, Stephan, *Realismus: Theorie und Geschichte*, Munich: Fink, 1977.

Kreuzer, Helmut, and Koch, Roland (eds.), *Friedrich Hebbel*, Darmstadt: Wiss. Buchgesellschaft, 1989.

Lukács, Georg, *Realism in our time: literature and the class struggle*, trans. by John and Necke Mander, New York: Harper and Row, 1964.

Studies in European realism, New York: Grosset and Dunlap, 1964.

Essays on realism, ed. by Rodney Livingstone. trans. by David Fernback, Cambridge: MIT Press, 1980.

Martini, Fritz, *Deutsche Literatur im bürgerlichen Realismus 1848–1898*, 4th edn, Stuttgart: Metzler, 1981.

Menninghaus, Winfried, *Artistische Schrift: Studien zur Kompositionskunst Gottfried Kellers*, Frankfurt a. M.: Suhrkamp, 1982.

Müller, Klaus-Detlef (ed.), *Bürgerlicher Realismus: Grundlagen und Interpretationen*, Königstein/Ts.: Athenäum. 1981.

Preisendanz, Wolfgang, *Humor als dichterische Einbildungskraft: Studien zur Erzählkunst des poetischen Realismus*, 2nd edn, Munich: Eidos, 1976.

Wege des Realismus: zur Poetik und Erzählkunst im 19. Jahrhundert, Munich: Fink, 1977.

Richter, Claus, *Leiden an der Gesellschaft: vom literarischen Liberalismus zum poetischen Realismus*, Königstein/Ts.: Athenäum, 1978.

Schneider, Michael, *Geschichte als Gestalt: Formen der Wirklichkeit und Wirklichkeit der Form in Gustav Freytags Roman 'Soll und Haben'*, Stuttgart: Heinz, 1980.

Thomas, Lionel, *Otto Ludwig's Zwischen Himmel und Erde*, Leeds: Maney, 1975.

Thunecke, Jörg (ed.), *Formen realistischer Erzählkunst: Festschrift für Charlotte Jolles*, Nottingham: Sherwood Press, 1979.

Turner, David, *Roles and relationships in Otto Ludwig's narrative fiction*, Hull: University of Hull Press, 1975.

Ward, Mark G. (ed.), *Perspectives on German realist writing: eight essays*, Lewiston, NY: Mellen Press, 1994.

Widhammer, Helmuth, *Die Literaturtheorie des deutschen Realismus (1848–1860)*, Slg Metzler 152, Stuttgart: Metzler, 1977.

7 From Naturalism to National Socialism 1890–1945

General accounts

Berman, Russell A., *The rise of the modern German novel: crisis and charisma*, Cambridge, MA: Harvard University Press, 1986.

Furness, Raymond, *The twentieth century 1890–1945*, The literary history of Germany, vol. 8, London: Croom Helm, 1978.

Hermand, Jost, and Trommler, Frank, *Die Kultur der Weimarer Republik*, Munich: Nymphenburger Verlagshandlung, 1978.

Midgley, David (ed.), *The German novel in the twentieth century: beyond realism*, Edinburgh: Edinburgh University Press, 1993.

Pascal, Roy, *From naturalism to expressionism: German literature and society 1880–1918*, London: Weidenfeld and Nicolson, 1973.

Rasch, Wolfdietrich, *Zur deutschen Literatur seit der Jahrhundertwende*, Stuttgart: Metzler, 1967.

Taylor, Ronald, *Literature and society in Germany*, 1918–1945, Brighton: Harvester, 1980.

Movements and periods

Dada

Sheppard, Richard W., 'What is Dada?', *Orbis Litterarum* 34 (1979), 175–207.

Exile literature

Pike, David, *German writers in Soviet exile, 1933–1945*, Chapel Hill: University of North Carolina Press, 1982.

Stephan, Alexander, *Die deutsche Exilliteratur. Eine Einführung*, Munich: Beck, 1979.

Walter, Hans-Albert, *Deutsche Exilliteratur 1933–1950*, 4 vols., Stuttgart: Metzler, 1978–88.

Expressionism

Allen, Roy F., *Literary life in German Expressionism and the Berlin circles*, Göppinger Arbeiten zur Germanistik 129, Göppingen: Kümmerle, 1974.

Anz, Thomas, *Literatur der Existenz: literarische Psychopathographie und ihre soziale Bedeutung im Frühexpressionismus*, Germanistische Abhandlungen 46, Stuttgart: Metzler, 1977.

Denkler, Horst, *Drama des Expressionismus: Programm, Spieltext, Theater*, Munich: Fink, 1967.

Dierick, Augustinus P., *German Expressionist prose: theory and practice*, Toronto, Buffalo, London: University of Toronto Press, 1987.

Knapp, Gerhard P., *Die Literatur des deutschen Expressionismus*, Munich: Beck, 1979.

Krull, Wilhelm, *Prosa des Expressionismus*, Slg Metzler 210, Stuttgart: Metzler, 1984.

Lämmert, Eberhard, 'Das expressionistische Verkündigungsdrama', in Hans Steffen (ed.), *Der deutsche Expressionismus: Formen und Gestalten*, Göttingen: Vandenhoeck and Ruprecht, 1965, pp. 138–56.

Martens, Gunter, *Vitalismus und Expressionismus: ein Beitrag zur Genese und Deutung expressionistischer Stilstrukturen und Motive*, Studien zur Poetik und Geschichte der Literatur 22, Stuttgart: Kohlhammer, 1971.

Ritchie, J. M., *German expressionist drama*, Twayne's World Authors Series 421, Boston: G. K. Hall, 1976.

Rötzer, Hans Gerd (ed.), *Begriffsbestimmung des literarischen Expressionismus*, Wege der Forschung 380, Darmstadt: Wiss. Buchgesellschaft, 1976.

Thomke, Hellmut, *Hymnische Dichtung im Expressionismus*, Berne and Munich: Francke, 1972.

Viviani, Annalisa, *Das Drama des Expressionismus: Kommentar zu einer Epoche*, Munich: Winkler, 1970.

Fin de siècle

Fischer, Jens Malte, *Fin de siècle: Kommentar zu einer Epoche*, Munich: Winkler, 1978.

Le Rider, Jacques, *Modernity and crises of identity: culture and society in fin-de-siècle Vienna*, trans. by Rosemary Morris, Cambridge: Polity, 1993.

Schorske, Carl E., *Fin-de-siècle Vienna: politics and culture*, New York: Knopf, 1979.

Worbs, Michael, *Nervenkunst: Literatur und Psychoanalyse im Wien der Jahrhundertwende*, Frankfurt a. M.: Europäische Verlagsanstalt, 1983.

Inner emigration

Klieneberger, H. R., *The Christian writers of the inner emigration*, The Hague: Mouton, 1968.

Schnell, Ralf, *Literarische Innere Emigration 1933–1945*, Stuttgart: Metzler, 1976.

National Socialism

Amann, Klaus, *Der Anschluß österreichischer Schriftsteller an das dritte Reich*, Literatur in der Geschichte, Geschichte in der Literatur 16, Frankfurt a. M.: Athenäum, 1988.

Herf, Jeffrey, *Reactionary modernism: technology, culture and politics in Weimar and the Third Reich*, Cambridge: Cambridge University Press, 1984.

Ketelsen, Uwe-K., *Völkisch-nationale und nationalsozialistische Literatur in Deutschland 1890–1945*, Slg Metzler 142, Stuttgart: Metzler, 1976.

Ritchie, J. M., *German literature under National Socialism*, London: Croom Helm, 1983.

Naturalism

Cowen, Roy C., *Der Naturalismus: Kommentar zu einer Epoche*, Munich: Winkler, 1973.

Kayser, Wolfgang, 'Zur Dramaturgie des naturalistischen Dramas', in his *Die Vortragsreise*, Berne: Francke, 1958, pp. 214–31.

Osborne, John, *The naturalist drama in Germany*, Manchester: Manchester University Press, 1971.

Neue Sachlichkeit

Denkler, Horst, 'Sache und Stil: die Theorie der "Neuen Sachlichkeit" und ihre Auswirkungen auf Kunst und Dichtung', *Wirkendes Wort* 18 (1968), 167–85.

Themes

Aschheim, Steven E., *The Nietzsche legacy in Germany 1890–1990*, Berkeley: University of California Press, 1992.

Bridgwater, Patrick, *The German poets of the First World War*, London: Croom Helm, 1985.

Brinker-Gabler, Gisela (ed.), *Deutsche Literatur von Frauen*, 2 vols., Munich: Beck, 1988.

Frederiksen, Elke (ed.), *Die Frauenfrage in Deutschland 1865–1915: Texte und Dokumente*, Stuttgart: Reclam, 1981.

Grimm, Günter E., and Bayerdörfer, Hans-Peter (eds.), *Im Zeichen Hiobs: jüdische Schriftsteller und deutsche Literatur im 20. Jahrhundert*, Königstein/Ts.: Athenäum, 1985.

Jelavich, Peter, *Munich and theatrical modernism: politics, playwriting and performance*, Cambridge, MA: Harvard University Press, 1986.

Keith-Smith, Brian (ed.), *German women writers 1900–1933: twelve essays*, Lewiston, NY, and Lampeter: Mellen, 1993.

McKenzie, John R. P., *Social comedy in Austria and Germany 1890–1933*, British and Irish Studies in German Language and Literature 8, Berne: Peter Lang, 1992.

Michaels, Jennifer E., *Anarchy and Eros: Otto Gross' impact on German Expressionist writers*, Utah Studies in Literature and Linguistics 24, New York, Berne, Frankfurt: Peter Lang, 1983.

Mitchell, Breon, *James Joyce and the German novel 1922–1933*, Athens, OH: Ohio University Press, 1976.

Richards, Donald R., *The German bestseller in the 20th century: a complete bibliography and analysis 1915–1940*, Berne: Herbert Lang, 1968.

Rohrwasser, Michael, *Der Stalinismus und die Renegaten: die Literatur der Exkommunisten*, Stuttgart: Metzler, 1991.

Rossbacher, Karlheinz, *Heimatkunstbewegung und Heimatroman: Zu einer Literatursoziologie der Jahrhundertwende*, Stuttgart: Klett, 1975.

Serke, Jürgen, *Böhmische Dörfer: Wanderungen durch eine verlassene literarische Landschaft*, Vienna and Hamburg: Zsolnay, 1987.

Steinberg, Michael P., *The meaning of the Salzburg Festival: Austria as theater and ideology, 1890–1938*, Ithaca: Cornell University Press, 1990.

Stern, J. P., *The dear purchase: a theme in German modernism*, Cambridge: Cambridge University Press, 1995.

Travers, Martin, *German novels on the First World War and their ideological implications, 1918–1933*, Stuttgarter Arbeiten zur Germanistik 102, Stuttgart: Heinz, 1982.

Individual authors

Andreas-Salomé, Lou
Livingstone, Angela, *Lou Andreas-Salomé: her life and writings*, London: Gordon Fraser, 1984.

Arp, Hans
Döhl, Reinhard, *Das literarische Werk Hans Arps 1903–1930: zur poetischen Vorstellungswelt des Dadaismus*, Germanistische Abhandlungen 18, Stuttgart: Metzler, 1967.

Bahr, Hermann
Daviau, Donald G., *Der Mann von Übermorgen: Hermann Bahr 1863–1934*, Vienna: Österreichischer Bundesverlag, 1984.

Ball, Hugo
Mann, Philip, *Hugo Ball: an intellectual biography*, Bithell Series of Dissertations 13, London: Institute of Germanic Studies, 1987.

Barlach, Ernst
Kaiser, Herbert, *Der Dramatiker Ernst Barlach: Analysen und Gesamtdeutung*, Munich: Fink, 1972.

Beer-Hofmann, Richard
Elstun, Esther N., *Richard Beer-Hofmann: his life and work*, University Park, PA, and London: Pennsylvania State University Press, 1983.

Benjamin, Walter

Wolin, Richard, *Walter Benjamin: an aesthetic of redemption*, New York: Columbia University Press, 1982.

Benn, Gottfried

Ridley, Hugh, *Gottfried Benn: ein Schriftsteller zwischen Erneuerung und Reaktion*, Opladen: Westdeutscher Verlag, 1990.

Brecht, Bertolt

Benjamin, Walter, *Understanding Brecht*, London: New Left Books, 1973.

Dickson, Keith, *Towards Utopia: a study of Brecht*, Oxford: Clarendon Press, 1978.

Klotz, Volker, *Bertolt Brecht: Versuch über das Werk*, 4th edn, Bad Homburg v.d.H.: Athenäum, 1971.

Mittenzwei, Werner, *Das Leben des Bertolt Brecht*, 2 vols., Berlin: Aufbau, 1986.

Sokel, Walter H., 'Brecht und der Expressionismus', in Grimm, Reinhold, and Hermand, Jost (eds.), *Die sogenannten Zwanziger Jahre*, Schriften zur Literatur 13, Bad Homburg v.d.H., Berlin, Zurich: Gehlen, 1970, pp. 47–74.

Whitaker, Peter, *Brecht's poetry: a critical study*, Oxford: Clarendon Press, 1985.

Willett, John, *The theatre of Bertolt Brecht*, 3rd edn, London: Methuen, 1977.

Broch, Hermann

Ritzer, Monika, *Hermann Broch und die Kulturkrise im Frühen 20. Jahrhundert*, Stuttgart: Metzler, 1988.

Schlant, Ernestine, *Hermann Broch*, New York: Twayne, 1978.

Canetti, Elias

Roberts, David, *Kopf und Welt: Elias Canettis Roman 'Die Blendung'*, Munich: Hanser, 1975.

Döblin, Alfred

Dollenmayer, David B., *The Berlin Novels of Alfred Döblin*, Berkeley: University of California Press, 1988.

Müller-Salget, Klaus, *Alfred Döblin: Werk und Entwicklung*, Bonner Arbeiten zur deutschen Literatur 22, Bonn: Bouvier, 1972.

Doderer, Heimito von

Hesson, Elizabeth C., *Twentieth century Odyssey: a study of Heimito von Doderer's 'Die Dämonen'*, Studies in German Literature, Linguistics, and Culture 9, Columbia, SC: Camden House, 1982.

Weber, Dietrich, *Heimito von Doderer: Studien zu seinem Romanwerk*, Munich: Beck, 1963.

Einstein, Carl

Ihekweazu, Edith, 'Immer ist der Wahnsinn das einzig vermutbare Resultat. Ein Thema des Expressionismus in Carl Einsteins *Bebuquin*', *Euphorion* 76 (1982), 180–97.

Penkert, Sibylle, *Carl Einstein: Beiträge zu einer Monographie*, Palaestra 255, Göttingen: Vandenhoeck and Ruprecht, 1969.

Feuchtwanger, Lion

Kahn, Lothar, *Insight and action: the life and work of Lion Feuchtwanger*, Rutherford, NJ, and London: Associated University Presses, 1975.

Kröhnke, Karl, *Lion Feuchtwanger – der Ästhet in der Sowjetunion*, Stuttgart: Metzler, 1991.

Fleisser, Marieluise

McGowan, Moray, *Marieluise Fleisser*, Munich: Beck, 1987.

George, Stefan

Landfried, Klaus, *Stefan George – Politik des Unpolitischen*, Literatur und Geschichte 8, Heidelberg: Stiehm 1975.

Morwitz, Ernst, *Kommentar zu dem Werk Stefan Georges*, Munich and Düsseldorf: Küpper, 1960.

Goebbels, Joseph

Bonwit, Marianne, '*Michael*, ein Roman von Joseph Goebbels, im Licht der deutschen literarischen Tradition', *Monatshefte* 49 (1957), 193–200.

Goering, Reinhard

Davis, Robert Chapin, *Final mutiny: Reinhard Goering, his life and art*, Stanford German Studies 21, New York, Berne, Frankfurt a. M., Paris: Peter Lang, 1987.

Mayer, Sigrid, 'Reinhard Goerings *Seeschlacht*: "klassisches" Drama des Expressionismus', *Seminar* 14 (1978), 45–62.

Hauptmann, Elisabeth

Horst, Astrid, *Prima inter pares. Elisabeth Hauptmann, die Mitarbeiterin Bertolt Brechts*, Würzburg: Königshausen and Neumann, 1992.

Hauptmann, Gerhart

Guthke, Karl S., *Gerhart Hauptmann: Weltbild im Werk*, 2nd edn, Munich: Francke, 1980.

Sprengel, Peter, *Gerhart Hauptmann: Epoche – Werk – Wirkung*, Munich: Beck, 1984.

Heidegger, Martin

Ott, Hugo, *Martin Heidegger: a political life*, trans. by Allan Blunden, London: Harper Collins, 1993.

Hesse, Hermann

Boulby, Mark, *Hermann Hesse: his mind and his art*, Ithaca: Cornell University Press, 1967.

Timms, Edward, 'Hesse's therapeutic fiction', in Peter Collier and Judy Davies (eds.), *Modernism and the European Unconscious*, Cambridge: Polity, 1990, pp. 165–81.

Heym, Georg

Bridgwater, Patrick, *Poet of Expressionist Berlin: the life and work of Georg Heym*, London: Libris, 1991.

Eykman, Christoph, *Die Funktion des Häßlichen in der Lyrik Georg Heyms, Georg Trakls und Gottfried Benns*, Bonner Arbeiten zur deutschen Literatur 11, Bonn: Bouvier, 1965.

Schneider, Karl Ludwig, *Der bildhafte Ausdruck in den Dichtungen Georg*

Heyms, Georg Trakls und Ernst Stadlers, Probleme der Dichtung 2, Heidelberg: Winter, 1954.

Hofmannsthal, Hugo von

Alewyn, Richard, *Über Hugo von Hofmannsthal*, 4th edn, Göttingen: Vandenhoeck and Ruprecht, 1967.

Daviau, Donald G., 'Hugo von Hofmannsthal and the Chandos letter', *Modern Austrian Literature* 4 (1971), i. 28–44.

Mayer, Mathias, *Hugo von Hofmannsthal*, Slg Metzler 273, Stuttgart and Weimar: Metzler, 1993.

Miles, David H., *Hofmannsthal's novel 'Andreas': memory and self*, Princeton, NJ: Princeton University Press, 1972.

Horváth, Ödön von

Balme, Christopher B., *The reformation of comedy: genre critique in the comedies of Ödön von Horváth*, Otago German Studies 3, Dunedin: University of Otago, 1985.

Jahnn, Hans Henny

Freeman, Thomas, *Hans Henry Jahnn. Eine Biographie*, Hamburg: Hoffmann and Campe, 1986.

Wohlleben, Joachim, *Versuch über 'Perrudja'. Literarhistorische Betrachtungen über Hans Henny Jahnns Beitrag zum modernen Roman*, Tübingen: Niemeyer, 1985.

Johst, Hanns

Pfanner, Helmut F., *Hanns Johst: vom Expressionismus zum Nationalsozialismus*, The Hague and Paris: Mouton, 1970.

Jünger, Ernst

Meyer, Martin, *Ernst Jünger*, Munich: Hanser, 1990.

Stern, J. P., *Ernst Jünger: a writer of our time*, Cambridge: Bowes and Bowes, 1952.

Kafka, Franz

Anderson, Mark, *Kafka's clothes: ornament and aestheticism in the Habsburg fin de siècle*, Oxford: Clarendon Press, 1992.

Politzer, Heinz, *Franz Kafka: parable and paradox*, Ithaca: Cornell University Press, 1962.

Robertson, Ritchie, *Kafka: Judaism, politics, and literature*, Oxford: Clarendon Press, 1985.

Kaiser, Georg

Kenworthy, B. J., *Georg Kaiser*, Oxford: Blackwell, 1957.

Williams, Rhys W., 'Culture and anarchy in Georg Kaiser's *Von morgens bis mitternachts*', *Modern Language Review* 83 (1988), 364–74.

Kracauer, Siegfried

Mülder, Inge, *Siegfried Kracauer – Grenzgänger zwischen Theorie und Literatur: seine frühen Schriften 1913–1933*, Stuttgart: Metzler, 1985.

Kraus, Karl

Fischer, Jens Malte, *Karl Kraus: Studien zum 'Theater der Dichtung' und Kulturkonservatismus*, Kronberg: Scriptor, 1973.

Timms, Edward, *Karl Kraus, apocalyptic satirist: culture and catastrophe in Habsburg Vienna*, New Haven and London: Yale University Press, 1986.

Wagner, Nike, *Karl Kraus und die Erotik der Wiener Moderne*, Frankfurt a. M.: Suhrkamp, 1982.

Kubin, Alfred

Lippuner, Heinz, *Alfred Kubins Roman 'Die andere Seite'*, Berne and Munich: Francke, 1977.

Rhein, Phillip H., *The verbal and visual art of Alfred Kubin*, Riverside, CA: Ariadne Press, 1989.

Lasker-Schüler, Else

Bauschinger, Sigrid, *Else Lasker-Schüler: ihr Werk und ihre Zeit*, Poesie und Wissenschaft 7, Heidelberg: Stiehm, 1980.

Cohn, Hans W., *Else Lasker-Schüler: the broken world*, Anglica Germanica, series 2, Cambridge: Cambridge University Press, 1974.

Lukács, Georg

Löwy, Michael, *Georg Lukács: from Romanticism to Bolshevism*, London: New Left Books, 1979.

The Brothers Mann

Hamilton, Nigel, *The Brothers Mann*, London: Secker and Warburg, 1978.

Mann, Heinrich

Roberts, David, *Artistic consciousness and political conscience: the novels of Heinrich Mann 1900–1938*, Australian and New Zealand Studies in German Language and Literature 2, Berne and Frankfurt a. M.: Herbert Lang, 1971.

Mann, Thomas

Bergsten, Gunilla, *Thomas Manns 'Doktor Faustus': Untersuchungen zu den Quellen und zur Struktur des Romans*, 2nd edn, Tübingen: Niemeyer, 1974.

Böhm, Karl Werner, *Zwischen Selbstzucht und Verlangen: Thomas Mann und das Stigma Homosexualität*, Würzburg: Königshausen and Neumann, 1991.

Koopmann, Helmut (ed.), *Thomas-Mann-Handbuch*, Stuttgart: Kröner, 1990.

Reed, T. J., *Thomas Mann: the uses of tradition*, Oxford: Clarendon Press, 1974.

Ridley, Hugh, *Mann: 'Buddenbrooks'*, Landmarks of World Literature, Cambridge: Cambridge University Press, 1987.

Sheppard, Richard, '*Tonio Kröger* and *Der Tod in Venedig*: from bourgeois realism to visionary modernism', *Oxford German Studies* 18/19 (1989–90), 92–108.

Musil, Robert

Luft, David S., *Robert Musil and the crisis of European culture 1880–1942*, Berkeley, Los Angeles, London: University of California Press, 1980.

Payne, Philip, *Robert Musil's 'The man without qualities': a critical study*, Cambridge Studies in German, Cambridge: Cambridge University Press, 1988.

Stopp, Elisabeth, 'Musil's "Törleß" – content and form', *Modern Language Review* 63 (1968), 94–118.

Panizza, Oskar

Brown, Peter D. G., *Oskar Panizza: his life and works*, New York, Frankfurt a. M., Berne: Peter Lang, 1983.

Piscator, Erwin

Innes, C. D., *Erwin Piscator's political theatre*, Cambridge: Cambridge University Press, 1972.

Reger, Erik

Hermand, Jost, 'Erik Reger: *Union der festen Hand* (1931)' in *Unbequeme Literatur. Eine Beispielreihe*, Heidelberg: Stiehm, 1971, pp. 150–75.

Rilke, Rainer Maria

Batterby, K. A. J., *Rilke and France: a study in poetic development*, Oxford Language and Literature Monographs, Oxford: Oxford University Press, 1966.

Belmore, H. W., *Rilke's craftsmanship: an analysis of his poetic style*, Oxford: Blackwell, 1954.

Engel, Manfred, *Rilkes 'Duineser Elegien' und die moderne deutsche Lyrik*, Germanistische Abhandlungen 58, Stuttgart: Metzler, 1986.

Mason, Eudo C., *Lebenshaltung und Symbolik bei Rainer Maria Rilke*, 2nd edn, Oxford: The Marston Press, 1964.

Schwarz, Egon, *Das verschluckte Schluchzen: Poesie und Politik bei Rainer Maria Rilke*, Frankfurt a. M.: Athenäum, 1972.

Stephens, Anthony R., *Rilkes 'Malte Laurids Brigge': Strukturanalyse des erzählerischen Bewußtseins*, Australian and New Zealand Studies in German Language and Literature 3, Berne and Frankfurt a. M.: Herbert Lang, 1974.

Roth, Joseph

Bronsen, David, *Joseph Roth: eine Biographie*, Cologne: Kiepenheuer and Witsch, 1974.

Hackert, Fritz, *Kulturpessimismus und Erzählform: Studien zu Joseph Roths Leben und Werk*, Berne: Peter Lang, 1967.

Sack, Gustav

Eibl, Karl, *Die Sprachskepsis im Werk Gustav Sacks*, Munich: Fink, 1970.

Schmitt, Carl

Bendersky, Joseph W., *Carl Schmitt: theorist for the Reich*, Princeton, NJ: Princeton University Press, 1983.

Schnitzler, Arthur

Swales, Martin, *Arthur Schnitzler: a critical study*, Oxford: Clarendon Press, 1971.

Thompson, Bruce, *Schnitzler's Vienna: image of a society*, London: Routledge, 1990.

Yates, W. E., *Schnitzler, Hofmannsthal, and the Austrian theatre*, New Haven and London: Yale University Press, 1992.

Sternheim, Carl

Wendler, Wolfgang, *Carl Sternheim: Weltvorstellung und Kunstprinzipien*, Frankfurt a. M.: Athenäum, 1966.

Williams, Rhys W., *Carl Sternheim: a critical study*, Berne and Frankfurt a. M.: Peter Lang, 1982.

Toller, Ernst

Dove, Richard, *He was a German: a biography of Ernst Toller*, London: Libris, 1990.

Trakl, Georg

Casey, T. J., *Manshape that shone: an interpretation of Trakl*, Oxford: Blackwell, 1964.

Killy, Walther, *Über Georg Trakl*, 3rd edn, Göttingen: Vandenhoeck and Ruprecht, 1967.

Wedekind, Frank

Boa, Elizabeth, *The sexual circus: Wedekind's theatre of subversion*, Oxford: Blackwell, 1987.

Hibberd, J. L., 'The spirit of the flesh: Wedekind's Lulu', *Modern Language Review* 79 (1984), 336–55.

Midgley, David, 'Wedekind's Lulu: from "Schauertragödie" to social comedy', *German Life and Letters* 38 (1984–5), 205–32.

Rothe, Friedrich, *Frank Wedekinds Dramen: Jugendstil und Lebensphilosophie*, Germanistische Abhandlungen 23, Stuttgart: Metzler, 1968.

Weinheber, Josef

Nadler, Josef, *Josef Weinheber: die Geschichte seines Lebens und seiner Dichtung*, Salzburg: Müller, 1952.

Yates, W. E., 'Architectonic form in Weinheber's lyric poetry: the sonnet "Blick vom oberen Belvedere"', *Modern Language Review* 71 (1976), 73–81.

Weininger, Otto

Le Rider, Jacques, *Der Fall Otto Weininger: Wurzeln des Antifeminismus und Antisemitismus*, trans. by Dieter Hornig, Vienna: Löcker, 1985.

Werfel, Franz

Jungk, Peter Stephan, *Franz Werfel: eine Lebensgeschichte*, Frankfurt a. M.: Fischer, 1987.

Yates, W. E., 'Franz Werfel and Austrian poetry of the First World War', in Lothar Huber (ed.), *Franz Werfel: an Austrian writer reassessed*, Oxford, New York, Munich: Berg, 1989, pp. 15–36.

Zweig, Arnold

Midgley, David R., *Arnold Zweig: eine Einführung in Leben und Werk*, Frankfurt a. M.: Athenäum, 1987.

8 The literature of the German Democratic Republic

Arnold, Heinz Ludwig (ed.), *Bestandsaufnahme Gegenwartsliteratur*, Munich: edition text + kritik, 1988.

Arnold, Heinz Ludwig, and Meyer-Gosau, Frauke (eds.), *Literatur in der DDR: Rückblicke*, Munich: edition text + kritik, 1991.

Arnold, Heinz Ludwig, and Wolf, Gerhard (eds.), *Die andere Sprache: Neue DDR-Literatur der 80er Jahre*, Munich: edition text + kritik, 1990.

Bathrick, David, *The powers of speech: the politics of culture in the GDR*, Lincoln: University of Nebraska Press, 1995.

Brockmann, Stephen, and Rabinbach, Anson (eds.), *New German Critique: special issue on German unification* 52 (Winter 1991).

Breuer, Dieter (ed.), *Deutsche Lyrik nach 1945*, Frankfurt a. M.: Suhrkamp, 1987.

Chiarloni, Anna, Sartori, Gemma, and Cambi, Fabrizio (eds.), *Die Literatur der DDR 1976–1986: Akten der Internationalen Konferenz, Pisa, Mai 1987*, Pisa 1988.

Deiritz, Karl and Krauss, Hannes, (eds.), *Der deutsch-deutsche Literaturstreit oder 'Freunde, es spricht sich schlecht mit gebundener Zunge': Analysen und Materialien*, Hamburg, Zürich: Luchterhand Literaturverlag, 1991.

Verrat an der Kunst? Rückblick auf die DDR-Literatur, Berlin: Aufbau, 1993.

Emmerich, Wolfgang, *Kleine Literaturgeschichte der DDR: 1945–1988*, Frankfurt a. M.: Luchterhand, 1989.

Flores, John, *Poetry in East Germany*, New Haven: Yale, 1971.

Fox, Thomas, *Border crossings: an introduction to East German prose*, Ann Arbor: University of Michigan Press, 1993.

Franke, Konrad, *Die Literatur der DDR*, 3rd edn, Frankfurt a. M. Fischer, 1980.

Geerdts, Hans Jürgen, et al., *Literatur der Deutschen Demokratischen Republik: Einzeldarstellungen*, 3 vols., Berlin: Volkund Wissen, 1974, 1979, 1987.

Haase, Horst, et al., *Geschichte der Literatur der DDR*, Berlin: Volk und Wissen, 1976.

Hasche, Christa, Schölling, Traute, and Fiebach, Joachim, *Theater in der DDR: Chronik und Positionen*, Berlin: Henschel, 1994.

Hässel, Margarete, and Weber, Richard, *Arbeitsbuch Thomas Brasch*, Frankfurt a. M.: Suhrkamp, 1987.

Herminghouse, Patricia, and Hohendahl, Peter (eds.), *Literatur der DDR in den 70er Jahren*, Frankfurt a. M.: Suhrkamp, 1983.

Literatur und Literaturtheorie in der DDR, Frankfurt a. M.: Suhrkamp, 1976.

Heym, Stefan, and Heiduczek, Werner (eds.), *Die sanfte Revolution*, Leipzig/Weimar: Gustav Kiepenheuer, 1990.

Hilzinger, Sonja, *'Als ganzer Mensch zu leben ...': Emanzipatorische Tendenzen in der neueren Frauen-Literatur der DDR*, Frankfurt a. M., Berne, New York: Peter Lang, 1985.

Kane, Martin (ed.), *Socialism and the literary imagination: essays on East German writers*, New York, Oxford: Berg, 1991.

Koebner, Thomas (ed.), *Tendenzen der deutschen Gegenwartsliteratur*, 2nd edn, Stuttgart: Kröner, 1984.

Mayer, Hans, *Ein Deutscher auf Widerruf: Erinnerungen*, 2 vols., Frankfurt a. M.: Suhrkamp, 1984.

Die umerzogene Literatur: Deutsche Schriftsteller und Bücher 1945–1967, Berlin: Siedler, 1988.

Der Turm von Babel: Erinnerung an eine Deutsche Demokratische Republik, Frankfurt a. M.: Suhrkamp, 1991.

Mittenzwei, Werner (ed.), *Theater in der Zeitenwende: Zur Geschichte des Dramas und des Schauspieltheaters in der DDR 1945–1968*, 2 vols., Berlin: Henschel, 1975.

Profitlich, Ulrich, (ed.), *Dramatik der DDR*, Frankfurt a. M.: Suhrkamp, 1987.

Reid, J.H., *Writing without taboos: the new East German literature*, New York, Oxford, Munich: Berg, 1990.

Robinson, David W. (ed.), *No man's land: East German drama after the wall, contemporary theatre review*, vol. 4, part 2 (1995)

Scherpe, Klaus, and Winckler, Lutz (eds.), *Frühe DDR-Literatur, Traditionen, Institutionen, Tendenzen*, Berlin: Argument, 1987.

Schivelbusch, Wolfgang, *Sozialistisches Drama nach Brecht: Drei Modelle: Peter Hacks – Heiner Müller – Hartmut Lange*, Darmstadt/Neuwied: Luchterhand, 1974.

Schmitt, Hans-Jürgen (ed.), *Die Literatur der DDR*, Munich, Vienna: Hanser, 1983.

Staritz, Dietrich, *Geschichte der DDR, 1949–85*, Frankfurt a. M.: Suhrkamp, 1985.

Tate, Dennis, *The East German novel: identity, community, continuity*, New York: St Martin's Press, 1984.

Trommler, Frank, *Sozialistische Literatur in Deutschland: Ein historischer Überblick*, Stuttgart: Kröner, 1976.

Williams, Rhys W., Parker, Stephen, and Riordan, Colin, *German writers and the Cold War, 1945–61*, Manchester, New York: Manchester University Press, 1992.

Wolf, Gerhard, *Wortlaut Wortbruch Wortlust: Dialog mit Dichtung: Aufsätze und Vorträge*, Leipzig: Reclam, 1988.

The interested reader may also wish to consult the following German and English language periodicals which contain valuable articles, essays and other materials pertaining to GDR literature and culture as well as to discussions among critics and scholars since 1989.

Alternative, Berlin-West, 1958–82.

Basis, USA/FRG, 1971–80.

Deutschland Archiv, Cologne, 1968–.

Freitag, Berlin, 1990–.

GDR Bulletin, St Louis, MO, 1975.

GDR Monitor, Dundee/Amsterdam, 1979–91.

German Monitor, Amsterdam, 1992–.

Neue Deutsche Literatur, Berlin, 1953–.

New German Critique, Milwaukee, WI/Ithaca, NY, 1973–.

Sinn und Form, Berlin, 1949–.

Sonntag, Berlin, 1946–90.

Studies in GDR Culture and Society, Washington, DC, 1979–.

Theater der Zeit, Berlin, 1946–.

Weimarer Beiträge, Berlin and Weimar, 1955–.

9 German writing in the West

Reference works

Arnold, Heinz Ludwig (ed.), *Kritisches Lexikon zur deutschsprachigen Gegenwartsliteratur*, Munich: edition text + kritik, 1978f.

Moser, Dietz-Rüdiger et al. (eds.), *Neues Handbuch der deutschsprachigen Gegenwartsliteratur seit 1945*, rev. edn, Munich: Deutscher Taschenbuch Verlag, 1993.

Schlosser, Horst Dieter, *dtv-Atlas zur deutschen Literatur*, 5th edn, Munich: Deutscher Taschenbuch Verlag, 1992.

Cultural history and background studies

Arendt, Hannah, *Eichmann in Jerusalem. A report on the banality of evil*, New York: Viking, 1963.

Arnold, Heinz Ludwig (ed.), *Literaturbetrieb in der Bundesrepublik Deutschland*, Munich: edition text + kritik, 1981.

Barner, Wilfried (ed.), *Literaturkritik – Anspruch und Wirklichkeit*, Stuttgart: Metzler, 1990.

Benz, Wolfgang (ed.), *Die Bundesrepublik Deutschland. Geschichte in drei Bänden*. Band 3: *Kultur*, Frankfurt a. M.: Fischer, 1983.

Burns, R. A., and van der Will, Wilfried, *Protest and democracy in West Germany*, Basingstoke: Macmillan, 1988.

Diner, Dan (ed.), *Zivilisationsbruch. Denken nach Auschwitz*, Frankfurt a. M.: Fischer, 1988.

Fohrbeck, Karla, and Wiesand, Andreas Johannes, *Von der Industriegesellschaft zur Kulturgesellschaft? Kulturpolitische Entwicklungen in der Bundesrepublik Deutschland*, Munich: Beck, 1989.

Glaser, Hermann, *Bundesrepublikanisches Lesebuch. Drei Jahrzehnte geistiger Auseinandersetzung*, Munich, Vienna: Hanser, 1978.
  Kulturgeschichte der Bundesrepublik Deutschland, 3 vols., Munich: Hanser 1985, 1986, 1989.

Habermas, Jürgen, *Die neue Unübersichtlichkeit*, Frankfurt a. M.: Suhrkamp, 1985.

Habermas, Jürgen (ed.), *Stichworte zur geistigen Situation der Zeit*, 2 vols., Frankfurt a. M.: Suhrkamp, 1979.

Hermand, Jost, *Kultur im Wiederaufbau. Die Bundesrepublik Deutschland 1945–1965*, Frankfurt a. M.: Ullstein, 1989.

Horkheimer, Max, and Adorno, T. W., *Dialektik der Aufklärung*, 1944, repr. Frankfurt a. M.: Fischer 1971.

Horx, M., *Das Ende der Alternativen*, Munich, Vienna: Hanser, 1985.
  Die wilden Achtziger, Munich, Vienna: Hanser, 1987.

Huyssen, Andreas, and Scherpe, Klaus (eds.), *Postmoderne. Zeichen eines kulturellen Wandels*, Reinbek: Rowohlt, 1986.

King, Janet K., *Literarische Zeitschriften 1945–1970*, Stuttgart: Metzler, 1974.

Kreuzer, Helmut, *Veränderungen des Literaturbegriffs*, Göttingen: Vandenhoeck and Ruprecht, 1975.

Mitscherlich, Alexander, *Auf dem Weg zur vaterlosen Gesellschaft. Ideen zur Sozialpsychologie*, Munich: Piper, 1963.

Mitscherlich, Alexander and Margarete, *Die Unfähigkeit zu trauern. Grundlagen kollektiven Verhaltens*, Munich: Piper, 1967.

Müller, Helmut L., *Die literarische Republik. Westdeutsche Schriftsteller und die Politik*, Weinheim, Basle: Beltz, 1982.

Parkes, K. Stuart, *Writers and politics in West Germany*, London: Croom Helm, 1986.

Podewils, C. Graf (ed.), *Tendenzwende? Zur geistigen Situation in der Bundesrepublik*, Stuttgart: Klett, 1975.

Roth, Ralf, and Rucht, Dieter (eds.), *Neue soziale Bewegungen in der Bundesrepublik Deutschland*, Frankfurt a. M., New York: Campus, 1987.

Rühle, Günther, *Die Büchermacher. Von Autoren, Verlegern, Buchhändlern, Messen und Konzernen*, Frankfurt a. M.: Suhrkamp, 1985.

Rüsen, Jörn, Lämmert, Eberhard, and Glotz, Peter (eds.), *Die Zukunft der Aufklärung*, Frankfurt a. M.: Suhrkamp, 1988.

Rutschky, Michael, *Erfahrungshunger. Ein Essay über die siebziger Jahre*, Cologne: Kiepenheuer und Witsch, 1980.

Schneider, Michael, *Den Kopf verkehrt aufgesetzt oder Die melancholische Linke. Aspekte des Kulturzerfalls in den siebziger Jahren*, Darmstadt, Neuwied: Luchterhand, 1981.

Sontheimer, Karl, *Zeitenwende*, Hamburg: Hoffmann und Campe, 1983.

Vormweg, Heinrich, *Das Elend der Aufklärung. Über ein Dilemma in Deutschland*, Darmstadt, Neuwied: Luchterhand, 1984.

Wiesand, Andreas, and Fohrbeck, Karla, *Literatur und Öffentlichkeit in der Bundesrepublik Deutschland*, Munich, Vienna: Hanser, 1976.

General literary histories, overviews, thematic studies

[* indicates extensive bibliography]

Adelson, Leslie, *Making bodies, making history. Feminism and German identity*, Lincoln, London: University of Nebraska Press, 1993.

Arnold, Heinz Ludwig (ed.), *Handbuch zur deutschen Arbeiterliteratur*, 2 vols., Munich: edition text + kritik, 1977.

Die Gruppe 47. Ein kritischer Grundriß, rev. edn, Munich: edition text + kritik, 1987.

Bestandsaufnahme Gegenwartsliteratur, Munich: edition text + kritik, 1988.

Die drei Sprünge der westdeutschen Literatur, Göttingen: Wallstein, 1993.

Die westdeutsche Literatur 1945 bis 1990: Ein kritischer Überblick, 2nd edn, Munich: Deutscher Taschenbuch Verlag, 1995.

Arnold, Heinz Ludwig, and Reinhardt, Stephan (eds.), *Dokumentarliteratur*, Munich: edition text + kritik, 1973.

Balzer, Berndt et al., *Die deutschsprachige Literatur in der Bundesrepublik Deutschland*, Munich: Iudicium, 1988.

Barner, Wilfried (ed.), *Geschichte der deutschen Literatur von 1945 bis zur Gegenwart (= Geschichte der deutschen Literatur von den Anfängen bis zur Gegenwart, Bd. XII)*, Munich: Beck, 1994.*

Batt, Kurt, *Revolte intern. Betrachtungen zur Literatur in der Bundesrepublik*, Munich: Beck, 1975.

Baumgart, Reinhart, *Deutsche Literatur der Gegenwart*, Munich: Hanser, 1994.

Berg, J. et al., *Sozialgeschichte der deutschen Literatur von 1918 bis zur Gegenwart*, Frankfurt a. M.: Fischer, 1981.*

Bohn, Volker, *Deutsche Literatur seit 1945*, Frankfurt a. M.: Suhrkamp, 1995.

Brettschneider, Werner, *Zorn und Trauer. Aspekte deutscher Gegenwartsliteratur*, Berlin: Erich Schmidt, 1979.

Briegleb, Klaus, 1968. *Literatur in der antiautoritären Bewegung*, Frankfurt a. M.: Suhrkamp, 1992.*

Briegleb, Klaus, and Weigel, Sigrid (eds.), *Gegenwartsliteratur seit 1968*, vol. 12 of *Hansers Sozialgeschichte der deutschen Literatur vom 16. Jahrhundert bis zur Gegenwart*, Munich: Hanser, 1992.*

Bullivant, Keith, *The future of German literature*, Oxford, Providence, RI: Berg, 1994.

Demetz, Peter, *Postwar German literature*, New York: Harcourt, Brace, Jovanovich, 1970.

After the fires. Writing in the Germanies, Austria and Switzerland, New York: Harcourt, Brace, Jovanovich, 1986.

Drews, Jörg et al., *Kultur und Macht. Deutsche Literatur 1949–1989*, Bielefeld: Aisthesis, 1992.

Durzak, Manfred (ed.), *Deutsche Gegenwartsliteratur. Ausgangspositionen und aktuelle Entwicklungen*, Stuttgart: Reclam, 1981.

Eggert, Hartmut, Profitlich, Ulrich, and Scherpe, Klaus R. (eds.), *Geschichte als Literatur. Formen und Grenzen der Repräsentation von Vergangenheit*, Stuttgart: Metzler, 1990.

Fetscher, Justus et al. (eds.), *Die Gruppe 47 in der Geschichte der Bundesrepublik*, Würzburg: Königshausen and Neumann, 1991.

Fischbach, Peter, Hensel, Horst, and Naumann, Uwe (eds.), *Zehn Jahre Werkkreis Literatur der Arbeitswelt. Dokumente, Analysen, Hintergründe*, Frankfurt a. M.: Fischer, 1979.

Fischer, Ludwig (ed.), *Literatur in der Bundesrepublik Deutschland bis 1967*, vol. 10 of *Hansers Sozialgeschichte der deutschen Literatur vom 16. Jahrhundert bis zur Gegenwart*, Munich: Hanser, 1986.*

Fischer, Sabine, and McGowan, Moray, 'From Pappkoffer to pluralism: migrant writing in the German Federal Republic', in R. King, J. Connell, P. White (eds.), *Writing across worlds: literature and migration*, London: Routledge, 1995, pp.39–56.

Franke, Hans-Peter et al., *Geschichte der deutschen Literatur 6: Von 1945 bis zur Gegenwart*, Stuttgart: Klett, 1983.

Gilman, Sandor L., 'Jewish writers in contemporary Germany', in Gilman, *Inscribing the other*, Lincoln, London: University of Nebraska Press, 1991, pp.249–78.

Hahn, Ulla, *Literatur in der Aktion. Zur Entwicklung operativer Literaturformen in der Bundesrepublik*, Wiesbaden: Athenaion, 1978.

Hinderer, Walter, *Arbeit an der Gegenwart. Zur deutschen Literatur seit 1945*, Würzburg: Königshausen and Neumann, 1994.

Humble, Malcolm, and Furness, Ray, *Introduction to German literature 1871–1990*, London: Macmillan, 1994.

Kaiser, Gerhard R. (ed.), *Gegenwart*, volume 16 of Best, Otto F., Schmitt, and Hans-Jürgen (eds.), *Die deutsche Literatur. Ein Abriß in Text und Darstellung*, Stuttgart: Reclam, 1984.

Koebner, Thomas, *Unbehauste. Zur deutschen Literatur in der Weimarer Republik, im Exil und in der Nachkriegszeit*, Munich: edition text + kritik, 1992.

Koebner, Thomas (ed.), *Tendenzen der deutschen Gegenwartsliteratur*, 3rd edn, Stuttgart: Kröner, 1984.

Lüdke, Werner Martin (ed.), *Literatur und Studentenbewegung. Eine Zwischenbilanz*, Opladen: Westdeutscher Verlag, 1977.

Ludwig, Michael, *Arbeiterliteratur in Deutschland*, Stuttgart: Metzler, 1976.

Lützeler, Paul M., and Schwarz, Egon (eds.), *Deutsche Literatur in der Bundesrepublik seit 1965*, Königstein/Ts.: Athenäum, 1980.

Mayer, Hans, *Die umerzogene Literatur. Deutsche Schriftsteller und Bücher 1945–1967*, Frankfurt a. M.: Suhrkamp, 1991.

  Die unerwünschte Literatur. Deutsche Schriftsteller und Bücher 1968–1985, Frankfurt a. M.: Suhrkamp, 1992.

McCormick, Richard W., *Politics of the self. Feminism and the postmodern in West German literature and film*, Princeton, NJ: Princeton University Press, 1991.

Müller, Heidy M., *Die Judendarstellung in deutschsprachiger Erzählprosa (1945–1981)*, Königstein/Ts.: Athenäum, 1984.

New German Critique 46 (1989): thematic issue on migrant identity and culture.

Pelzer, J. (ed.), *Literatur in der Bundesrepublik Deutschland. Phasen und Aspekte*, Stuttgart: Klett, 1990.

Pestalozzi, Karl, von Bormann, Alexander, and Koebner, Thomas (eds.), *Vier deutsche Literaturen? – Literatur seit 1945 – nur die alten Modelle? – Medium Film – das Ende der Literatur?* Akten des VII. Internationalen Germanisten-Kongresses, Göttingen 1985, Band 10, Tübingen: Niemeyer, 1986.

Raddatz, Fritz J., *Die Nachgeborenen. Leseerfahrungen mit zeitgenössischer Literatur*, Frankfurt a. M.: Fischer, 1983.

Reeg, Ulrike, *Schreiben in der Fremde. Literatur nationaler Minderheiten in der Bundesrepublik Deutschland*, Essen: Klartext, 1988.

Rothmann, Kurt, *Deutschsprachige Schriftsteller seit 1945 in Einzeldarstellungen*, Stuttgart: Reclam, 1985.

Scherpe, Klaus R., *Die rekonstruierte Moderne. Studien zur deutschen Literatur nach 1945*, Cologne, Weimar, Vienna: Böhlau, 1992.

Schlant, Ernestine, and Rimer, J. Thomas (eds.), *Legacies and ambiguities. Postwar fiction and culture in West Germany and Japan*, Baltimore, London: Johns Hopkins University Press, 1991.

Schmidt, Ricarda, *Westdeutsche Frauenliteratur der siebziger Jahre*, 2nd edn, Frankfurt a. M.: R. G. Fischer, 1990.

Schnell, Ralf, *Geschichte der deutschsprachigen Literatur seit 1945*, Stuttgart, Weimar: Metzler, 1993.

Schutte, Jürgen (ed.), *Dichter und Richter. Die Gruppe 47 und die deutsche Nachkriegsliteratur*, Berlin: Akademie der Künste Westberlin, 1988.

Schütz, Erhard, and Vogt, Jochen, *Einführung in die deutsche Literatur des 20. Jahrhunderts*. Band 3: *Bundesrepublik und DDR*, Opladen: Westdeutscher Verlag, 1980.

Sölçün, Sargut, *Sein und Nichtsein. Zur Literatur in der multikulturellen Gesellschaft*, Bielefeld: Aisthesis, 1992.

Stephan, Inge, Venske, Regula, and Weigel, Sigrid, *Frauenliteratur ohne Tradition? Neun Autorinnenporträts*, Frankfurt a. M.: Fischer, 1987.

Trommler, Frank, 'Der "Nullpunkt 1945" und seine Verbindlichkeit für die Literaturgeschichte', *Basis. Jahrbuch für deutsche Gegenwartsliteratur* 1 (1970), 9–25.

Vogt, Jochen, '*Erinnerung ist unsere Aufgabe*'. Über Literatur, Moral und Politik 1945–1990, Opladen: Westdeutscher Verlag, 1991.

Vogt, Jochen (ed.), '*Das Vergangene ist nicht tot, es ist nicht einmal vergangen.*' *Der Nationalsozialismus im Spiegel der Nachkriegsliteratur*, Essen: Klartext, 1984.

Wagener, Hans (ed.), *Gegenwartsliteratur und Drittes Reich. Deutsche Autoren in der Auseinandersetzung mit der Vergangenheit*, Stuttgart: Reclam, 1977.

Weigel, Sigrid, *Die Stimme der Medusa. Schreibweisen in der Gegenwartsliteratur von Frauen*, Dülmen-Hiddingsel: tende, 1987.

'Literatur der Fremde – Literatur in der Fremde', in Klaus Briegleb, and Sigrid Weigel (eds.), *Gegenwartsliteratur seit 1968*, Munich: Hanser, 1992, pp. 182–229.

Bilder des kulturellen Gedächtnisses. Beiträge zur Gegenwartsliteratur, Dülmen-Hiddingsel: tende, 1993

Wilke, Sabine, *Poetische Strukturen der Moderne. Zeitgenössische Literatur zwischen alter und neuer Mythologie*, Stuttgart: Metzler, 1992.

Žmegač, Viktor (ed.), *Geschichte der deutschen Literatur vom 18. Jahrhundert bis zur Gegenwart*, Band III/2: 1945–80, Königstein/Ts.: Athenäum, 1984.

Genres

Poetry

Arnold, Heinz Ludwig (ed.), *Politische Lyrik*, 3rd edn, Munich: edition text + kritik, 1984.

Bender, Hans (ed.), *Mein Gedicht ist mein Messer. Lyriker zu ihren Gedichten*, 2nd edn, Munich: List, 1961.

Bender, Hans, and Krüger, Michael (eds.), *Was alles hat Platz in einem Gedicht? Aufsätze zur deutschen Lyrik seit 1965*, Munich: Beck, 1977.

Breuer, Dieter (ed.), *Deutsche Lyrik nach 1945*, Frankfurt a. M.: Suhrkamp, 1988.

Domin, Hilde, *Wozu Lyrik heute?* Frankfurt a. M.: Fischer, 1993.

Friedrich, Hugo, *Die Struktur der modernen Lyrik*, 2nd edn, Reinbek: Rowohlt, 1967.

Gnüg, Hiltrud, *Entstehung und Krise literarischer Subjektivität*, Stuttgart: Metzler, 1983.

Hartung, Harald, *Deutsche Lyrik seit 1965. Tendenzen, Beispiele, Porträts*, Munich: Piper, 1985.
Kaiser, Gerhard, *Geschichte der deutschen Lyrik*. Band 2: *Von Heine bis zur Gegenwart*, Frankfurt a. M.: Suhrkamp, 1991.
Korte, Hermann, *Geschichte der deutschen Lyrik seit 1945*, Stuttgart: Metzler, 1989.
Schäfer, Hans Dieter, 'Zusammenhänge der deutschen Gegenwartslyrik', in Manfred Durzak (ed.), *Deutsche Gegenwartsliteratur*, Stuttgart: Reclam, 1981, pp.166–203.
Theobaldy, Jürgen, and Zürcher, Gustav, *Veränderung durch Lyrik. Westdeutsche Gedichte seit 1965*, Munich: edition text + kritik, 1976.
Zürcher, Gustav, *'Trümmerlyrik'. Politische Lyrik 1945–1950*, Kronberg: Scriptor, 1977.

Prose

Bance, Alan, *The German novel 1945–1980*, Stuttgart: Heinz, 1980.
Bullivant, Keith, *Realism today. Aspects of the West German novel*, Leamington Spa, New York: Berg, 1987.
Bullivant, Keith (ed.), *The modern German novel*, Leamington Spa, New York: Berg, 1987.
Durzak, Manfred (ed.), *Der deutsche Roman der Gegenwart*, 3rd edn, Stuttgart: Kohlhammer, 1979.
(ed.), *Die deutsche Kurzgeschichte der Gegenwart*, Stuttgart: Reclam, 1980.
Lützeler, Paul M. (ed.), *Deutsche Romane des 20. Jahrhunderts. Neue Interpretationen*, Königstein/Ts.: Athenäum, 1983.
Roberts, David, and Thomson, Philip J. (eds.), *The modern German historical novel: paradigms, problems, perspectives*, Oxford: Berg, 1990.
Ryan, Judith, *The uncompleted past: postwar German novels and the Third Reich*, Detroit: Wayne State University Press, 1983.
Scholl, Joachim, *In der Gemeinschaft des Erzählers. Studien zur Restitution des Epischen im deutschen Gegenwartsroman*, Heidelberg: Winter, 1990.
Schwan, Werner, *Ich bin doch kein Unmensch. Kriegs- und Nachkriegszeit im deutschen Roman*, Freiburg: Rombach, 1990.
Thomas, R.H., and van der Will, Wilfried, *The German novel and the affluent society*, Manchester: Manchester University Press, 1968.
Williams, Arthur, Parkes, Stuart, and Smith, Roland (eds.), *Literature on the threshold. The German novel in the 1980s*, Oxford, New York: Berg, 1990.

Drama (including radio drama) and theatre

Aust, Hugo, Haida, Peter, and Hein, Jürgen (eds.), *Volksstück. Vom Hanswurstspiel zum sozialen Drama der Gegenwart*, Munich: Beck, 1989.
Blumer, A., *Das dokumentarische Drama der sechziger Jahre in der Bundesrepublik Deutschland*, Meisenheim: Hain, 1977.
Brauneck, Manfred, *Theater im 20. Jahrhundert*, 2nd edn, Reinbek: Rowohlt, 1986.
Buddecke, Wolfram, and Fuhrmann, Heinz, *Das deutschsprachige Drama seit 1945*, Munich: Winkler, 1981.

Calandra, Denis, *New German dramatists*, London: Macmillan, 1983.
Döhl, Reinhard, *Das neue Hörspiel*, 2nd edn, Darmstadt: Wiss. Buchgesellschaft, 1992.
Fischer-Lichte, Erika, *Kurze Geschichte des deutschen Theaters*, Tübingen, Basle: Francke, 1993.
Hensel, Georg, *Das Theater der siebziger Jahre*, Stuttgart: Deutsche Verlagsanstalt, 1980.
    Spiel's noch einmal. Das Theater der achtziger Jahre, Frankfurt a. M.: Suhrkamp, 1990.
Innes, C. D., *Modern German drama*, Cambridge: Cambridge University Press, 1979.
Ismayr, Wolfgang, *Das politische Theater in Westdeutschland*, 2nd edn, Königstein/Ts.: Hain, 1985.
Kienzle, Siegfried, *Schauspielführer der Gegenwart*, 5th edn, Stuttgart: Reclam, 1990.
Kluge, Gerhard (ed.), *Studien zur Dramatik in der Bundesrepublik Deutschland*, Amsterdam: Rodopi, 1983.
Mennemeier, Franz Norbert, *Modernes deutsches Drama*, Band 2: *1933 bis zur Gegenwart*, Munich: Fink, 1975.
Neumann, R., and Nowoselsky, S. (eds.), *Fürs Theater schreiben. Über zeitgenössische Theaterautorinnen*, Bremen: Zeichen und Spuren, 1986.
Pikulik, Lothar, Kurzenberger Hajo, and Guntermann, Georg (eds.), *Deutsche Gegenwartsdramatik*, 2 vols., Göttingen: Vandenhoeck and Ruprecht, 1987.
Rühle, Günther, *Theater in unserer Zeit*, Frankfurt a. M.: Suhrkamp, 1976.
    Anarchie in der Regie? Theater in unserer Zeit 2, Frankfurt a. M.: Suhrkamp, 1983.
Sebald, W.G. (ed.), *A radical stage. Theatre in Germany in the 1970s and 1980s*, Oxford, New York, Hamburg: Berg, 1988.
Weber, R. (ed.), *Deutsches Drama der achtziger Jahre*, Frankfurt a. M.: Suhrkamp, 1992.
Würffel, Stefan Bodo, *Das deutsche Hörspiel*, Stuttgart: Metzler 1978.

Periods

The 1940s and 1950s

Bänsch, Dieter (ed.), *Die fünfziger Jahre. Beiträge zu Politik und Kultur*, Tübingen: Narr, 1985.
Drews, Jörg (ed.), *Vom 'Kahlschlag' zu 'Movens'. Über das langsame Auftauchen experimenteller Schreibweisen in der westdeutschen Literatur der fünfziger Jahre*, Munich: edition text + kritik, 1980.
Endres, Elisabeth, *Die Literatur der Adenauerzeit*, Munich: Steinhausen, 1980.
Hermand, Jost, Peitsch, Helmut, and Scherpe, Klaus R. (eds.), *Nachkriegsliteratur in Westdeutschland 1945–1949*. 2 vols., Berlin: Argument, 1982, 1983.
Schneider, Rolf, *Theater in einem besiegten Land. Dramaturgie der deutschen Nachkriegszeit 1945–49*, Frankfurt a. M., Berlin: Ullstein, 1989.

Wehdeking, Volker, and Blamberger, Günther, *Erzählliteratur der frühen Nachkriegszeit (1945–1952)*, Munich: Beck, 1990.

Widmer, Urs, *1945 oder die 'Neue Sprache'*, Düsseldorf: Pädagogischer Verlag Schwann, 1966.

Zürcher, Gustav, *'Trümmerlyrik'. Politische Lyrik 1945–1950*, Kronberg: Scriptor, 1977.

The 1960s and 1970s

Bullivant, Keith (ed.), *After the 'death' of literature. West German writing of the 1970s*, Oxford, New York, Munich: Berg, 1989.

Gerlach, Ingeborg, *Abschied von der Revolte. Studien zur deutschsprachigen Literatur der 70er Jahre*, Würzburg: Königshausen and Neumann, 1994.

Hage, Volker, *Die Wiederkehr des Erzählers. Neue deutsche Literatur der 70er Jahre*, Frankfurt a. M., Berlin: Ullstein, 1982.

Hinton Thomas, R., and Bullivant, Keith, *Literature in upheaval. West German writers and the challenge of the 1960s*, Manchester: Manchester University Press, 1974.

Hörisch, Jochen, and Winkels, Hubert (eds.), *Das schnelle Altern der neuesten Literatur*, Düsseldorf: claassen, 1985.

Kramer Ruoff, K., *The politics of discourse. Third thoughts on 'new subjectivity'*, Berne, New York: Peter Lang, 1993.

Lüdke, Werner Martin (ed.), *Nach dem Protest. Literatur im Umbruch*, Frankfurt a. M.: Fischer, 1979.

Mattenklott, Gerd, and Pickerodt, Gerhart (eds.), *Literatur der siebziger Jahre*, Berlin: Argument, 1985.

Reich-Ranicki, Marcel, *Entgegnung. Zur deutschen Literatur der siebziger Jahre*, Stuttgart: DVA, 1979.

Reinhold, Ursula, *Tendenzen und Autoren. Zur Literatur der 70er Jahre in der BRD*, Berlin: Dietz, 1982.

Roberts, David, 'Tendenzwenden. Die sechziger und siebziger Jahre in literaturhistorischer Perspektive', *Deutsche Vierteljahrsschrift*, 56 (1982), 290–313.

The 1980s

Hage, Volker, *Schriftproben. Zur deutschen Literatur der achtziger Jahre*, Reinbek: Rowohlt, 1990.

Hage, Volker et al. (eds.), *Deutsche Literatur 1981 [and ff.]. Ein Jahresüberblick*, Stuttgart: Reclam, 1982f. [annual survey]

Janetzki, Ulrich, and Rath, W. (eds.), *Tendenz Freisprache. Texte zu einer Poetik der achtziger Jahre*, Frankfurt a. M.: Suhrkamp, 1992.

Kreuzer, Helmut (ed.), *Pluralismus und Postmodernismus. Zur Literatur- und Kulturgeschichte der achtziger Jahre*, 2nd edn, Frankfurt, Berne, New York, Paris: Peter Lang, 1991.

Ortheil, Hanns-Josef, *Schauprozesse. Beiträge zur Kultur der 80er Jahre*, Munich: Piper, 1990.

Raddatz, Fritz J., *Eine dritte deutsche Literatur. Stichworte zu Texten der Gegenwart*, Reinbek: Rowohlt, 1987.

Winkels, Hubert, *Einschnitte. Zur Literatur der 80er Jahre*, Cologne: Kiepenheuer and Witsch, 1988.

Austrian literature

Aspetsberger, Friedbert, and Lengauer, Hubert (eds.), *Zeit ohne Manifeste? Zur Literatur der siebziger Jahre in Österreich*, Vienna: Österreichischer Bundesverlag, 1987.

Aspetsberger, Friedbert, Frei, Norbert, and Lengauer, Hubert (eds.), *Literatur der Nachkriegszeit und der fünfziger Jahre in Österreich*, Vienna: Österreichischer Bundesverlag, 1984.

Best, Alan, and Wolfschütz, Hans (eds.), *Modern Austrian writing. Literature and society after 1945*, London: Wolff, 1980.

Daviau, David G. (ed.), *Major figures of contemporary Austrian literature*, New York: Peter Lang, 1987.

Major figures of modern Austrian literature, Riverside, CA: Ariadne, 1988.

Greiner, Ulrich, *Der Tod des Nachsommers. Aufsätze, Porträts, Kritiken zur österreichischen Gegenwartsliteratur*, Munich, Vienna: Hanser, 1979.

Illusionen – Desillusionen? Zur neueren realistischen Prosa und Dramatik in Österreich, edited by the Walter-Buchebner-Gesellschaft, Vienna, Cologne: Böhlau, 1989.

Jandl, P., and Findeis, M. (eds.), *Landnahme. Der österreichische Roman nach 1980*, Vienna, Cologne: Böhlau, 1989.

Laemmle, Peter, and Drews, Jörg (eds.), *Wie die Grazer auszogen, die Literatur zu erobern*, Munich: edition text + kritik, 1975.

Landa, Jutta, *Bürgerliches Schocktheater. Entwicklungen im österreichischen Drama der sechziger und siebziger Jahre*, Frankfurt a. M.: Athenäum, 1988.

Magris, Claudio, *Der habsburgische Mythos in der österreichischen Literatur*, Salzburg: Müller, 1966.

McVeigh, Joseph, *Kontinuität und Vergangenheitsbewältigung in der österreichischen Literatur seit 1945*, Vienna: Braumüller, 1988.

Menasse, R., *Die sozialpartnerschaftliche Ästhetik: Essays zum österreichischen Geist*, Vienna: Sonderzahl, 1990.

Müller, Karl, *Zäsuren ohne Folgen. Das lange Leben der literarischen Antimoderne Österreichs seit den 30er Jahren*, Salzburg: Otto Müller, 1990.

Rühm, Gerhard (ed.), *Die Wiener Gruppe*, expanded edn, Reinbek: Rowohlt, 1985.

Schmidt, Ricarda, and McGowan, Moray (eds.), *From high priests to desecrators. Contemporary Austrian writers*, Sheffield: Sheffield Academic Press, 1993.

Sebald, W. G., *Die Beschreibung des Unglücks*, Salzburg: Residenz, 1985.

Unheimliche Heimat, Salzburg: Residenz, 1991.

Vansant, Jacqueline, *Against the horizon. Feminism and postwar Austrian women writers*, New York, London: Greenwood, 1988.

Zeman, Herbert (ed.), *Studien zur österreichischen Erzählliteratur der Gegenwart*, Amsterdam: Rodopi, 1992.

Zeyringer, Klaus, *Innerlichkeit und Öffentlichkeit. Österreichische Literatur der achtziger Jahre*, Tübingen, Basle: Francke, 1992.

German-Swiss literature

Acker, Robert, and Burkhard, Marianne (eds.), *Blick auf die Schweiz. Zur Frage der Eigenständigkeit der Schweizer Literatur seit 1970*, Amsterdam: Rodopi, 1987.

Butler, Michael, and Pender, Malcolm (eds.), *Rejection and emancipation: writing in German-speaking Switzerland 1945–1991*, Oxford, Munich, New York: Berg, 1991.

Flood, John L. (ed.), *Modern Swiss literature: unity and diversity*, London: Institute of Germanic Studies, 1985.

Grotzer, Peter (ed.), *Aspekte der Verweigerung in der neueren Literatur aus der Schweiz*, Zurich: Ammann, 1988.

Pezold, Klaus (ed.), *Entwicklungstendenzen der deutschsprachigen Literatur der Schweiz in den sechziger und siebziger Jahren*, Leipzig: Karl Marx Universität, 1984.

Pezold, Klaus et al.: *Geschichte der deutschsprachigen Schweizer Literatur des 20. Jahrhunderts*, Berlin: Volk und Wissen, 1991.

Pulver, E., and Dellach, S. (eds.), *Zwischenzeilen. Schriftstellerinnen der deutschen Schweiz*, 2nd edn, Berne: Zytglogge, 1989.

von Matt, Beatrice (ed.), *Antworten. Die Literatur der deutschsprachigen Schweiz in den achtziger Jahren*, Zurich: Verlag Neue Zürcher Zeitung, 1991.

Walzer, P. (ed.), *Lexikon der Schweizer Literatur*, Basle: Lenos, 1991.

Zeller, Rosmarie, *Der Neue Roman in der Schweiz. Die Unerzählbarkeit der modernen Welt*, Freiburg (CH): Universitäts-Verlag, 1992.

Zeltner-Neukomm, Gerda: *Das Ich ohne Gewähr. Gegenwartsautoren aus der Schweiz*, Zurich/Frankfurt a. M.: Suhrkamp, 1980.

Index